The Masculine Self

Sixth Edition

Andrew P. Smiler
Private Practice

Christopher Kilmartin
University of Mary Washington

2019
Sloan Publishing
220 Maple Road
Cornwall on Hudson, NY 12520

Library of Congress Control Number: 2018952997

Cover photo by Donna Cuic, Dreamstime
Cover design by K&M Design

© 2019 by Sloan Publishing, LLC

Sloan Publishing, LLC
220 Maple Road
Cornwall-on-Hudson, NY 12520

All rights reserved. No portion of this book may be reproduced, in any form or by any means, without permission in writing from the Publisher.

Printed in the United States of America

10 9 8 7 6 5 4 3 2 1

ISBN-13: 978-1-59738-064-5
ISBN-10: 1-59738-064-4

For Jim and Larry, who raised us well.

Contents

Preface xi

1. Introduction
  Gender/Sex 3
  A Singular Definition of Masculinity 4
  The Definition of Masculinity In United States History 7
 What is Men's Studies? 10
  Origins of Men's Studies 14
 Key Debates for Studying Men and Masculinity 15
  Essentialism vs. Social Constructionism 15
  Positive vs. Negative 16
  To Whom Should Men Be Compared? Women or Other Men? 17
  Stereotypes vs Reality 17
  Academics and Activists 17
  Activism 18
  Sexism and Violence Against Women 18
  Men's Health 18
  Men's Rights 19
 Academic Organizations 19
 Summary 20
 Glossary 21

2. Multiple Masculinities 24
  Masculinities and Cultural Power 25
 Masculinities within the United States 26
  African American Men 27
  Asian American Men 31
  Latino Men 33
  Social Class 36
  Sexual Orientation 37
 Masculinity Around the Globe 40

Summary   45
Glossary   47

3. **Masculinity in the Public Sphere   50**
   Power   50
   Power Structures   52
   Power over Women   55
   Sexism   55
   Chivalry   57
   Activism and Challenging Sexism   58
   The Impact on Men   60
   Power over Gay Men   61
   The Early Twentieth Century   61
   1970s: A Period of Change   62
   1980s: A Step Backward   63
   Recent History   64
   The Impact on Heterosexual Men   66
   Losing Male Power? Boys and Men in Crisis   67
   Advocating For Men   69
   Summary   71
   Glossary   72

4. **Models for Understanding and Measuring a Singular Masculinity   75**
   The Gender Binary: Masculinity or Femininity   76
   Male-Female Comparison, also known as "Sex Differences"   77
   The Measurement of Characteristics   77
   Research in Sex Comparison   79
   The Gender Identity Model   81
   Gender Role Identity Measures   82
   Limitations and Criticisms of the Gender Binary   83
   Beyond the Binary: Theories Combining Masculinity and Femininity   84
   The Androgyny Model   84
   Androgyny Measures   85
   Sexism   86
   Limitations and Criticisms of Theories Combining Masculinity and Femininity   87
   Bye, Bye Binary: Masculinity Alone and Complicated   88
   Masculine Roles, Scripts, Norms, and Ideologies   88
   Measuring Masculinity Alone   90
   Strain and Stress Models   91
   Strain and Stress Measures   92
   Limitations and Criticisms of Masculinity-Alone   93

Summary   93
Glossary   95

5. **Biologically Based Theoretical Perspectives on Males and Gender**   96
   Chromosomal and Hormonal Approaches   98
      Criticism of Chromosomal and Hormonal Approaches   100
   Evolutionary Psychology   100
      Sexuality   102
      Violence   102
      General Critique of Evolutionary Psychology   103
      Gender-Based Critique of Evolutionary Claims   106
      Specific Critiques of Evolutionary Claims   108
   The Child Inside the Man: Psychoanalytic Perspectives   109
      The Freudian Legacy   110
      The Oedipus Conflict   113
      Oedipus and Masculinity   114
      Critique of Freud   116
   Identifying with Mom: Ego Psychology and Masculinity   117
   Summary   120
   Glossary   121

6. **"It's the Way I was Raised": Socially-Based Theoretical Perspectives on Males and Gender**   123
   The Gendered Child: Early Experience   124
   Early Experience at School   127
   Situational Influence   128
   Milestones   131
   Theoretical Explanations   132
      Experience: Social Cognitive Theory   132
      Criticism of Social Cognitive Theory   135
      Society: Social Structural Theory (aka Social Role Theory)   135
      Criticism of Social Structural Theory   136
      Experience & Society: Gendered Scripts   137
      Criticism of Gender Schema Theory   139
   Summary   140
   Glossary   141

7. **It Never Lies, and It Never Lies Still: Emotion and Masculinity**   143
   Defining and Studying Emotionality   144
   Male–Female Comparisons in Emotional Expression   145
   The Special Case of Anger   148
   Self-Disclosure   149
   Learning Restrictive Emotionality   150
   Benefits and Costs of Restrictive Emotional Display Rules   152

Benefits 153
Costs 154
Alexithymia 156
Other Costs 156
Expanding Men's Emotional Display Rules 157
Summary 159
Glossary 159

8. **No Man Is An Island: Men in Relationships** 161
   Relationship Basics 162
   The Influence of Maleness and Masculinity 163
   Male Social Development 163
   Masculinity 164
   Context 167
   Friendships 168
   Male-Only Friendship Groups 168
   Male-Male Friendship Dyads. 170
   Male-Female Friendship Dyads 171
   Romantic Relationships 172
   Male-Female Dating Relationships 172
   Male-Male Dating Relationships 173
   Marriage and Long-Term Romantic Relationships 174
   Male-Female Couples 175
   Male-Male Couples 176
   Summary 177
   Glossary 178

9. **Fathers and Fathering** 180
   History of Fathers at Home 181
   Becoming a Father 182
   Who Becomes a Father? 183
   Anticipating Fatherhood 184
   Parenting 185
   Quality of the Child-Parent Relationship 186
   Quality of the Adults' Relationships 186
   Resource Availability 187
   Parenting, Sex, and Gender 188
   Similarities and Differences Between Mothers and Fathers 189
   Divorce and Father Absence 190
   Stay-At-Home-Fathers 193
   Sons' Masculinity 193
   Summary 195
   Glossary 197

10. **Pleasure and Performance: Male Sexuality** 198
    Male-Female Comparisons 199

Sexual Orientation   200
  Origins   200
  Rates   202
  Sex and Masculinity   202
  Risk-Taking   205
  Competition   206
  Intimacy   207
  Sexual Development   208
  Puberty   208
  Adulthood & Older Age   210
  Male Hypoactive Sexual Desire Disorder   211
  Erectile Dysfunction   211
  Ejaculatory Problems   213
Television, Movies, and Pornography   213
  Scope   214
  Attitudes   215
  Men's Sexual Problems   216
Summary   217
Glossary   219

11. **Men at Work: Jobs, Careers, and Masculinity   221**
    A History of Work and the Sexes   222
    Sex and Race in Employment Patterns   226
    Men in Female-Dominated Vocations   228
    Net Worth Equals Self Worth: The Socialization to Work   228
      Positive Aspects of Masculinity and Work   229
      Negative Aspects of Masculinity and Work   230
    Working in the Modern World   235
      Male-Female Relationships in the Workplace   235
      Sexual Harassment   236
    Summary   242
    Glossary   244

12. **Boys Will Be Boys: Men and Violence   245**
    Differences Based on Sex and Race   246
    Masculinity and Violence   249
    Antifemininity   250
    Status and Achievement   251
    Inexpressiveness and Independence   252
    Adventurousness and Aggressiveness   252
    Factors Specific to Rape   253
    Psychosocial Factors Related to Violence   253
    Separation and Connection to Others   254
    Externalizing Style   255
    Attention, Praise, and Status   256
    Drug Use   256

  Access to Weapons   256
  Which Men Are Most Likely to be Violent?   258
 The Biological Perspective   260
  Evolutionary Psychology   260
  Genes   261
  Testosterone   261
  Models and Media   263
  Paternal Modeling   263
  Media Modeling   263
  Interventions   265
  Individual-Level Interventions   266
  Community- and Cultural-Level Interventions   267
 Summary   268
 Glossary   271

13. The Risk of Masculinity   273
 Combat   273
 Contact Sports   275
 Male Victims and Survivors of Sexual Assault and Rape   278
 Aging Men   280
 Summary   282
 Glossary   283

14. Surviving and Thriving: Men and Physical Health   285
 Sex and Racial Differences in Morality and Disease Rates   286
 Sex Differences   286
 Racial and Ethnic Differences   288
 Biogenic Explanations for Group Differences   292
 Genetic Differences   293
 Hormonal Differences   294
 Psychogenic Explanations for Group Differences   294
 Self-Destructive Behaviors   295
 Neglectful Behaviors   298
 Risk Behaviors   299
 Physical Problems with Psychological Inputs   299
 Summary   305
 Glossary   306

15. Coping in a Difficult World: Men and Mental Health   307
 Defining Mental Health   308
  Men, Masculinity and Mental Disorders   310
 Mental Health Issues for Men   312
  Substance Abuse   312
  Personality Disorders   315
  Depression   317

Marriage and Men's Mental Health   318
Counseling and Psychotherapy with Men   319
    Men as a Special Population   320
    Men's Issues in Counseling and Psychotherapy   321
Summary   326
Glossary   327

References   **329**
Name Index   **387**
Subject Index   **405**

Preface

To the Student

You may never have heard of Men's Studies before signing up for this course or picking up this textbook. Perhaps you've asked "We have women's studies, but why don't we have men's studies?" Maybe you've wondered what's the deal with people saying things like "man up," be man," "grow a pair," or "stop being such a sissy." In this book, and the course that goes along with it, we'll take a close and critical look at these kinds of social demands, including where they come from and how they influence the real lives of boys and men. You'll learn about the ways our cultural stereotypes about masculinity have the potential to do real harm to *everyone*. You'll also learn that most boys and men only fit these stereotypes some of the time and in some ways, and that boys and men lead more complicated lives than our culture expects. Men and boys are not simple, even though are culture often assumes they are. Ultimately, we hope this book helps you start to think about the lives of boys and men in ways that are more complicated than you're used to and that this book challenges and changes some of the ways you think about, interact with, and behave around boys and men.

To the Instructor

This sixth edition marks a substantial change in *The Masculine Self*, most notably the retirement of Chris Kilmartin from academia. Chris' name still appears on the book—and you may recognize some of his writing throughout the text—but after about twenty years, he's decided to let someone else take over. That someone else is Andrew P. Smiler, who helped co-author the fifth edition; call that an apprenticeship if you will. For me, it was more like the difference between teaching one day of a class and teaching an entire course.

If you've used a prior edition of *The Masculine Self*, this edition will be notably different from what has come before. Two of the most obvious changes are thematic. For one, the main text is more intersectional than it has been, directly addressing the ways that masculinity interacts with other identities based on race, ethnicity, sexual orientation and socio-economic status. I'll note up front that although attention to these groups of men has improved throughout the text, discussion tends to focus on group differences and is somewhat sporadic, being more consistent in some chapters than others. The limitations here are primarily my own and I intend to improve this in the seventh edition, but at times, the limitations reflect the literature. The literature on gay men, for example, has largely focused on their sexual behaviors and dating habits, with much less attention to other parts of their lives (Parent & Bradstreet, 2017). Accordingly, these variations are prefaced in Chapter 1 and explored in Chapter 2, instead of being located in Chapters 5 and 6, with discussion pulling from both the masculinities and intersectionality literatures.

This emphasis on masculinities and intersectionality contributed to another decision: the book is set explicitly within the context of United States culture. To better contextualize and discuss these differences, I chose to focus more deeply and narrowly on masculinities within the United States. References to masculine norms outside the U.S. are still included in the book, but they are somewhat shorter than in previous editions. However, the greater attention to U.S. culture also allowed me to introduce more topics that are—or could be—relevant to students' daily lives, or that may be points of contention in mainstream U.S. culture. These connections are intended to help students connect the material to their own lives, and also to point out opportunities for activism for those who want to help improve men's lives.

There are also structural and thematic changes. Prior editions of the text began with an introduction (Chapters 1 and 2), continued through a discussion of a variety of theoretical approaches (Chapters 3 through 7), and then explored a variety of topical issues such as work, relationships, and health. This edition has eliminated the theoretical section and expanded the topical content; as noted above, some of the theoretical content has been embedded in other chapters. More specifically, the chapter on phenomenological perspectives (Chapter 7) has been omitted entirely. A new chapter (#3) that addresses some aspects of masculinity within the public sphere of American culture has been added; this chapter contains both new material and older content that has been shifted from other chapters. For a complete list of what has moved, what has been added, and what has been omitted, please visit my webpage and click on "The Masculine Self": http://www.andrewsmiler.com/author.

Many of these changes reflect some of my goals for the book. Consistent with Jim O'Neil and Sara Renzulli's (2013) discussion of the importance of teaching the Psychology of Men, I believe that *The Masculine Self* is a type of intervention into men's lives. To achieve this goal as a textbook author, I've also adopted the recommendation of Michael Addis, Abigail Mansfield, and Matthew Syzdek (2010) that our research and writing needs to be functional and pragmatic. Accordingly, I have made an effort to highlight some topical areas, as well as some interventions and alternatives, that may be more easily adopted and applied by students.

Ultimately, the sixth edition of *The Masculine Self* is another attempt to cover the territory of men's studies as comprehensively as possible, while understanding that it is not possible to cover this territory in full detail in a single textbook. The book summarizes and synthesizes the latest research, while integrating it with classic work that remains relevant to the topics under discussion. At the same time, *The Masculine Self* tells stories about real boys and men, not just abstracted and idealized human beings. As with Dr. Kilmartin's original approach to the text, and my own experience as blogger and public speaker, storytelling remains an important component of the writing. Therefore, I continue to try to give research a human face without sacrificing a full explanation of its complexity.

Dr. Smiler's Thoughts

I'm not really sure when I became a scholar of men's studies or an expert in the field, but it seems to have happened somewhere along the way. Writing a textbook, especially an introductory text, is an act of hubris and humility. It requires knowing something about everything, and not just one or two isolated and interesting facts, but enough to write a meaningful chapter that educates others. This is not what I signed up for when I went to grad school either the first time—to become a therapist—or the second time—to become a professor. Now I've come full circle and inhabit both of those roles and careers. My day job—or morning job, really, because that's when I do my best writing—is as an author who helps bring academic knowledge to a broader audience. My afternoon and evening job is to be a therapist. And yes, I work primarily with teen boys, adult men, and their families.

I hope this book causes you to think differently about boys and men. I hope the book inspires you to see them in a different light, to recognize when our society's expectations of men causes them to stop talking or change the subject. And I hope this book helps you recognize that guys aren't simple Neanderthals who just want to be an Alpha. We're more—much more—complicated than that.

Acknowledgements

No book comes into being on its own, and that's probably more true of a textbook than any other type of book out there. Bill Webber has done an amazing job of overseeing the entire process of editing and production for Sloan Publishers, and has done so for several editions now. From an intellectual standpoint, this book wouldn't be here if it weren't for the men and women who started asking questions about why we teach men to behave this-way-but-not-that-way, as well as how we can change it. Several are named in Chapter 1, but there are many, many more whose names I'll never know.

The biggest thank you of all goes to Christopher Kilmartin, who started writing this textbook 20 years ago and has now entrusted it to me. You were one of the first scholars of men's studies that I ever met and my life would surely be poorer if I'd never met you.

—Andrew P. Smiler
September 2018

Chapter 1

Defining Men's Studies

What does it mean to be a man? Is there a difference between "being a man" and "being a real man" and if so, what? Perhaps you've recently told someone to "man up," "turn in their man card," or get out of the "manbox." What exactly are you trying to say? These statements invoke an ideal—or a stereotype—but what exactly is that ideal and where did it come from?

From a different perspective, we might ask why you need to invoke masculinity at all? Why not say something like "toughen up" or "take charge"? How does that connect to having a penis or a Y chromosome or understanding that you're male? A guy might describe his penis in many ways, but "tough" isn't usually one of them. In Figure 1.1, comedian and author Erin Judge offers her perspective on how to identify a real man.

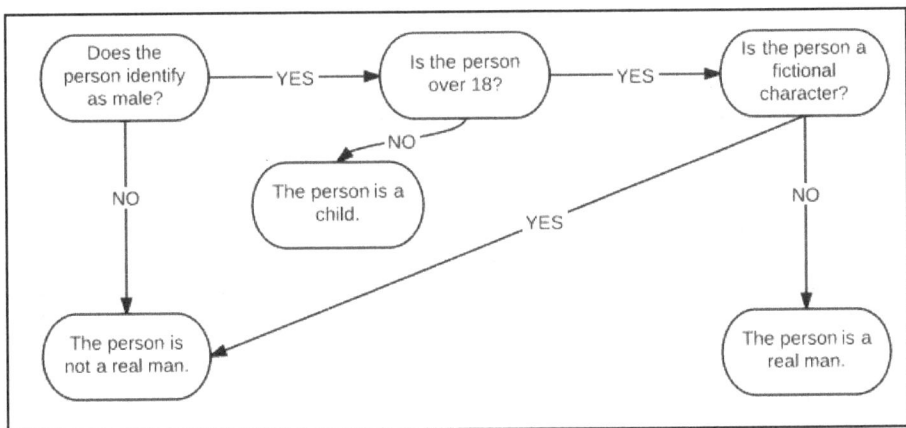

Figure 1.1 Determining Who Is a Real Man

1

When you think about it, what does masculinity mean to you? Perhaps it means "Snips and snails and puppy dog tails," a childhood answer to the question, "What are little boys made of?" And what are little girls made of? "Sugar and spice and everything nice." These sayings purport to describe personality differences between the sexes. It is not too difficult to interpret the statement about girls. Sugar and spice are pleasant and palatable. A "sweet" person is someone who can evoke positive responses from others, someone who cares about people. The statement about boys is a little more cryptic, but it seems to evoke images of being dirty, scattered, and hyperactive (puppy dog tails don't remain still for very long.)

From the earliest days of childhood, cultures bombard children with messages about what it means to be masculine. These messages serve to communicate expectations for their behavior. Some messages, like the ones described above, are verbal. Others are more subtle, such as a parent's communication of silent approval for behaviors like refusing to cry when one is sad or hurt, or selecting toys that they consider appropriate for boys. Because a good deal of behavior is learned through imitation, boys receive many of these messages through merely observing the behaviors of men in their families, neighborhoods, and in the media.

These messages have powerful effects on boys, who often learn to act in culturally-defined "masculine" ways and to avoid behaviors that are considered "feminine." The social settings in which adult men find themselves tend to reinforce these standards. For example, a man who displays aggression at a business meeting might gain the approval of his colleagues, whereas a woman might experience disapproval for exactly the same behavior.

What is masculinity? How does one define it? According to current United States stereotypes, a man can be described as having certain personality traits:

Strong	Tough
Independent	Aggressive
Achieving	Unemotional
Hard-working	Physical
Dominant	Competitive
Heterosexual	Forceful

We could also describe him in terms of activities or behaviors, i.e., what a man *does*:

Earns money	Initiates sex
Solves problems	Gets the job done
Takes control	Plays or watches sports
Takes action	Takes risks
Enjoys hunting & fishing	Is the primary breadwinner/earner
Protects women and children	

We can describe him in terms of proscribed activities, i.e., what a man *does not do* (see Box 1.1 for a definition that seems to come from a different era):

Cry	Back down
Express feelings (except anger, lust)	Perform "women's work"
Connect with others emotionally	Ask for help
Behave in feminine ways	

We can describe him in terms of stereotypical *roles*:

Athlete	Working man
Father/Family man	Husband
Player	Leader
Professional	Buddy

Gender/Sex

The biological categorization of sex is perhaps the most basic division among human beings and often the first characteristic we notice about others. Even very young children are able to make this distinction (Maccoby, 1998), and a profound distinction it is. Throughout the text, we'll make a distinction between **sex**, which refers to an individual's physiological or biological status, and **gender**, which refers to the cultural expectations based on an individual's sex (Lips, 2008; Unger, 1979). Gender is a broader and more inclusive term than *sex*, as it refers to behaviors, personal beliefs, and social processes that are determined by biology and/or social forces (Lips, 2008).

Obviously, reproductive roles (childbirth, impregnation, and lactation) are bound in biology, but the socially perceived division of behavior based on sex goes far beyond reproduction into areas of work, child care, and social convention. Cultures even ascribe personality characteristics such as aggressiveness or nurturance disproportionately to one sex or the other. Many people believe that males and females should wear different colors, drink different drinks, enjoy different activities, and desire different things in relationships.

We use the terms *male* and *female* when referring to sex and the terms *masculine* and *feminine* when referring to gender. Although biological forces may have effects on social behaviors, the use of biological terms (e.g., *male aggression, maternal instinct*) to describe behaviors communicates the assumption that biological forces have been demonstrated to be the singular causes of those behaviors, a discussion we'll address in more detail in Chapter Five. The connection between biology and behavior is an empirical matter, i.e., one that researchers investigate through scientific methods.

Our definitions of sex and gender rely on a binary, either-or conception of these ideas. The presence of individuals with disorders of sexual development, also known as "intersex" or "intersexual" (Villain et al., 2007), reminds us that nature provides more than two options, while the presence of individuals who are transgender or gender non-conforming (GNC), reminds us that many

> **Box 1.1**
> **A Negative Description of Masculinity**
>
> The following is a definition of "gentleman" from an old version of the handbook of the Virginia Military Institute:
>
> > Without a strict observance of the fundamental code of honor, no man, no matter how 'polished' can be considered a gentleman. The honor of a gentleman demands the inviolability of his word and the incorruptibility of his principles. He is the descendant of the knight, the crusader, he is the defender of the defenseless and the champion of justice—or he is not a gentleman.
> >
> > A gentleman *does not* discuss his family affairs in public or with acquaintances.
> >
> > *Does not* speak more than casually about his wife or girlfriend.
> >
> > *Does not* go to a lady's house if he is affected by alcohol. He is temperate in the use of alcohol.
> >
> > *Does not* lose his temper nor exhibit anger, fear, hate, embarrassment, ardor, or hilarity in public.
> >
> > *Does not* hail a lady from a club window.
> >
> > *Never* discusses the merits or demerits of a lady.
> >
> > *Does not* borrow money from a friend, except in dire need. Money borrowed is a debt of honor and must be repaid as promptly as possible. Debts incurred by a deceased parent, brother, sister, or grown child are assumed by honorable men as a debt of honor.
> >
> > *Does not* display his wealth, money, or possessions.
> >
> > *Does not* put his manners on and off, whether in the club or in a ballroom. He treats people with courtesy, no matter what their social positions may be.
> >
> > *Does not* slap strangers on the back nor so much as lay a finger on a lady.
> >
> > *Does not* 'lick the boots of those above him' nor 'kick the face of those below him on the social ladder.'
> >
> > *Does not* take advantage of another's helplessness or ignorance and assumes that no gentleman will take advantage of him.
> >
> > A gentleman respects the reserves of others but demands that others respect those which are his.
> >
> > A gentleman *can* become what he wills to be..."
>
> Notice that the positive parts of the description (what gentlemen are and what they do) are rather vague: defender of the defenseless, champion of justice, etc. These are high ideals that do not necessarily transfer easily into a prescription for any specific behavior. When the description turns to negative guidelines (what gentlemen do not do), however, there are very specific behaviors stated. You might notice the prohibitions against acknowledging a connection to another person ("never speaks more than casually about his wife or girlfriend"), expressing emotion ("does not exhibit fear, hate, ardor..."), and being vulnerable or in need of help ("does not borrow money from a friend..."). The last line reflects the masculine value on self-determination.

individuals do not adhere to the notion of only two sexes or only two genders (American Psychological Association, 2015).

A Singular Definition of Masculinity

In their classic book, Deborah David and Robert Brannon (1976) posited that American masculinity had four primary characteristics. These tenets have been adopted by a broad range of scholars (e.g., O'Neil et al., 1982; Levant et al., 1992) and were subsequently relabeled as the "Boy Code" (Pollack, 1998). Today, you might find the "manbox" defined in these terms.

1. *Antifemininity*: Males are encouraged from an early age to avoid behaviors, interests, and personality traits that are considered "feminine." Accordingly, men are directed to not show emotion, sometimes referred to as "emotional stoicism," because emotion is often considered a central and defining characteristic of femininity (Bem, 1974; Spence & Helmreich, 1978). Feminine professions such as elementary school teacher, nurse, or secretary are also to be avoided. In current day America, this notion also causes us to question men who display substantial concern with their appearance via fashion/clothing, styling, or product. In the beginning of the twenty-first century, these men were dubbed "Metrosexuals" (Coad, 2008). Because gay men are stereotyped as feminine (Kranz, Probstle, & Evidis, 2017; Madon, 1997), this injunction also directs men to avoid behaviors that might be construed as homosexual. We'll discuss male emotionality in depth in Chapter Seven. Brannon and David (1976) originally called this injunction "No Sissy Stuff."

2. *Status and Achievement*: Men gain status by being successful in all that they do, especially in sports, work, and sexual "conquest." Powerful men earn the respect and admiration of others. Or, in the words of UCLA football coach "Red" Sanders, "Winning is not the best thing, it is the only thing." This directive prescribes ambition as a trait that men should have and encourages them to demonstrate and strive for leadership positions. Professional success can validate the masculinity of a man who is respected in a profession that might be considered "feminine," such as cooking or fashion design (David & Brannon, 1976). We'll discuss men's work lives in more detail in Chapter Eleven. David and Brannon originally called this "(Be a) Big Wheel."

    The combination of Antifemininity and Status & Achievement support the notion that men are inherently superior to women, and thus can be seen as justifications for **sexism** which is defiined as prejudicial attitudes and behaviors against women (Schwartz, McDermott, & Martino-Harms, 2016), and **heterosexism**: the preferential treatment of heterosexuals over non-heterosexuals. We'll address sexism in Chapters Three and Four, and heterosexism (and homophobia) in Chapters Two and Four. If one assumes that masculinity is inherently White, then the Big Wheel principle can be used to justify **racism**, a set of behaviors, values, and attitudes that reflect a belief in the innate superiority of one race over another. In the United States, Whites are favored.

3. *Inexpressiveness and Independence*: Men should be strong, sturdy, independent, and in control of themselves, even in the most difficult of situations. Further, they should solve problems without help, keep their

feelings to themselves, and disdain any display of weakness. Strength is often defined in terms of physical strength and possibly physical stamina. However, strength can also be defined in terms of strength of character, which may appear as strength of belief, dedication (to a cause), or stubbornness. The emphasis on independence means that interdependence, also known as **communality**, is to be avoided; communality is often identified as a central component of femininity (Bem, 1974; Parsons & Bales, 1955; Spence & Helmreich, 1978), and thus may be particularly important for demonstrating masculinity. David and Brannon originally called this injunction *"The Sturdy Oak."*

4. *Adventurousness and Aggressiveness*: Masculinity is characterized by a willingness to take (physical) risks and become violent if necessary. Some authors interpret this tenet as authorizing cheating, while discouraging respect for authority and rules. Unlike the other directives, which specify general goals (e.g., don't be feminine, gain power), this tenet tells men how to achieve their goals: take risks. In this way, bravery is prescribed for men while caution and cowardice are proscribed. At the extreme, this masculine tenet contributes to and condones men's violence, a topic we'll discuss in more detail in Chapter Twelve and Thirteen. David and Brannon originally labeled this injunction *"Damn the torpedoes, full speed ahead,"* which is (or was) a traditional expression in the United States Navy that is attributed to Admiral David Farragut during the Civil War's Battle of Mobile Bay. Others call this injunction "Give 'em Hell."

Many theorists (Chodorow, 1978; O'Neil, 1981a; Brannon, 1985; Hartley, 1959) consider *antifemininity* to be the central organizing principle from which all other masculine social demands derive. In other words, social expectations devalue and punish the open display of emotions, vulnerability, orientations toward relationships, and caution because these characteristics are culturally defined as feminine. Being dependent, passive, and having low power (or status) have also typically been associated with femininity (Bem, 1974; Parsons & Bales, 1955; Spence & Helmreich, 1978).

Any system of rules needs an enforcement mechanism. To those who succeed—regularly or only occasionally—go the spoils: fame, success, money, power, and the most attractive sexual partners (or spouses). We might even call them "The Man." But rewards aren't sufficient to make the system work for everyone, because not everyone can or will succeed. This means masculinity must be *policed*, defined as the use of insults and slurs to "encourage" boys and men to behave in ways that are more consistent with the cultural definition of masculinity. Verbal taunts that rely on antifemininity and antihomosexuality such as "sissy," "don't be such a girl," and "fag" are most common (Pascoe, 2007; Plummer, 2001; Reigeluth & Addis, 2017; Rosenberg, Gates, Richmond, & Sinno, 2017). Policing masculinity is common and there is ample evidence that, beginning early in childhood, adults and peers punish males for acting in feminine ways more harshly than they punish females who act in masculine ways (Carver, Egan, & Perry, 2004; Lytton & Romney, 1991; McCreary, 1994). Elementary school-aged boys who act in feminine ways over months and years often find themselves with few or no friends, as the targets of bullies, and feeling more depressed and anxious than other boys (Carver et al., 2004). We'll explore issues of sexism and homophobia in more detail in Chapter Three.

To get a sense of how deeply ingrained masculine injunctions are for male who have grown up in the U.S., ask a close male friend if he would be willing to do any of the activities in Box 1.2: Masculinity Violations. Alternately, you might imagine your own reaction if you saw a man doing one of these things.

The Definition of Masculinity In United States History

Although most people believe that the definition of masculinity has not changed (Steinberg & Biekman, 2016), our definition has evolved in response to changes in the spirits of the times across history. Historian Anthony Rotundo (1993) described three different definitions of masculinity that dominated American culture between the Revolutionary War and the modern era. We also describe some changes during the modern era here and continue some aspects of this discussion in later chapters as it applies to those topics, such as changes in our perception of work (Chapter Eleven), violence (Chapters Twelve and Thirteen), and sexuality (Chapter Ten) in men's lives.

Colonial times promoted a *communal masculinity*. Here, masculinity emphasized a man's usefulness to the community, determined by meeting

---

Box 1.2
Masculine Gender Role Violation Exercises

The behaviors listed below are often difficult for men because they violate one or more tenets of masculinity. Consider what it might take to convince a man to enact one of these behaviors, or your own likely reactions if you saw a man engaging in one of these behaviors.

1. Wear colored nail polish to class or some other public place for several days.
2. If you are in a satisfying romantic relationship, talk at length with some male friends about how much you love that person and how good they make you feel, without talking about sex.
3. Tell a male friend how much you value his friendship, without being drunk.
4. Spend a half hour in a conversation with a group of people without interrupting or telling a story.
5. Walk to class carrying your books at your chest instead of at your side.
6. Share an umbrella with another man.
7. Make a comment about the physical attractiveness of some man.

the needs and expectations of one's family and neighbors. There was a fundamental value of male superiority that was based in the belief of men's supposedly greater ability than women to reason and to control emotions. These beliefs were the bases of laws and other social arrangements that gave men and women unequal status. Men were understood to be virtuous and superior to women, while women were seen as deficient and a source of temptation that could corrupt otherwise virtuous men. One result of these beliefs is that men—at least those successful or lucky enough to own property instead of being property—were allowed to vote but women were not (Rotundo, 1993). Novels and films such as *The Crucible* and *The Scarlet Letter* illustrate this version of masculinity.

After the revolution and through the Victorian Era, from approximately 1780 to 1900, the nation began to emphasize a ***self-made manhood***. Economic success took precedence over community concerns, and was demonstrated through business and professional success and the accumulation of wealth. Competition began to be seen as a legitimate means to an end, with an expectation that the most deserving—and perhaps most righteous?—man would be the most successful. At the same time, competition became ever-present; men competed not only in the marketplace, but also in other "homosocial preserves" (all-male environments) such as men's clubs and sporting events. This shift was accompanied by a greater emphasis on individual strivings that allowed men to channel their "passions" into expressions of dominance and independence. Self-control was also prized, with men expected to "tame" their passions. During this era, men came to be seen as selfish and aggressive while women were seen as virtuous people whose social role was to civilize and control the animal passions of men (Rotundo, 1993; see also Kimmel, 1996). The definition of masculinity provided in Box 1.1 dates from this era. Historical figures and folk heroes such as Lewis and Clark, Paul Bunyan, and Davy Crockett illustrate this version of masculinity.

The self-made manhood era was also characterized by the *doctrine of separate spheres,* a cultural assumption that men and women were fundamentally different and thus functioned best in settings (spheres) that conformed to their supposedly natural proclivities. Women's domain was defined as the home, men's as the world-at-large; note that these domains, and thus men and women, were seen as opposites. People considered the world to be an evil and dangerous place from which "fragile" women must be protected. A man came home from work to renew himself for the next day's battle under women's care. However, too much influence from women's sphere was believed to feminize and thus emasculate men. Spending too much time at home or in the company of women could lead (some) men to feel an increased need to prove themselves to other men in places away from the home—in sports, at clubs, and for children, in an aggressive "boy culture" (Kimmel, 1996; Rotundo, 1993).

The late nineteenth and early twentieth centuries saw the rise of ***passionate manhood,*** which Rotundo describes as, "in some respects an elaboration of self-made manhood, but it stretched those beliefs in directions that would have shocked the old individualists of the early 1800s" (p. 5). Competition and aggression shifted from being a means to an end to being ends in and of themselves. Men's proving ground shifted from the realms of work and all male groups to the individual himself, particularly in comparison to other men. Rotundo describes this social change:

> Where nineteenth-century views had regarded the self and its passions suspiciously as objects of manipulation (self-control, self-denial), twentieth-century opinion exalted them as a source of identity and personal worth (self-expression, self-enjoyment). Play and leisured entertainment—once considered marks of effeminacy—became approved activities for men as the nineteenth century ended.... A man defined his identity not just in the workplace but through modes of enjoyment and self-fulfillment outside of it. In a world where the passions formed a vital part of the self, older forms of virtue—self-restraint, self-denial, became suspect. (p. 6)

Although the era was dominated by unrestrained pursuit of one's passions, there was some cultural pushback. Christian revivalism was strong and contributed to the Temperance movement and Prohibition (1920–1933) movements that encouraged men to control their desire for alcohol, among other passions. Although some homosexual behavior had been tolerated in prior eras as long as it was done discreetly, homophobic injunctions became more common and explicit (Kimmel, 1996). We'll discuss this issue in more detail in Chapter Three.

The early part of the passionate manhood era coincided with other substantial shifts in American society, including large numbers of European immigrants, urbanization, and industrialization (Rotundo, 1993; Smiler, Kay, & Harris, 2008). Mandatory education became the law of the land in the early 1900s. It was common for men to work in factories and stores six days per week (with the seventh reserved for church), often working more than 10 hours per day (Zinn, 2015). Recognizing that boys were now spending most of their time with women—their mothers and their teachers—but not side-by-side with their fathers on the family farm, a group of men created an organization to help get boys back to nature, learn self-reliance, and build good masculine character. That organization still exists: the Boy Scouts of America (Hantover, 1978); their credo, with its emphasis on honesty, loyalty, trustworthiness, and thriftiness, is derived directly from the era's notions of what it means to be a good man.

By the middle of the twentieth century, group needs had come to overshadow individual achievement. Two world wars had ended both American isolationism and large scale voluntary enlistment in the military (Fancher, 1985). Increases in modernization and industrialization contributed to the rise of large corporations that fueled the need for a different model of masculinity. Thus, the *organization man*, with his ability to subsume personal goals for the good of the company, came to prominence. Conformity was favored over individuality, and men understood that they could be replaced at any time by their fellow (male) co-worker. For men who were unable to lead at work, a broad range of community organizations from fraternal lodges through neighborhood associations through youth athletic leagues provided a multitude of opportunities (Baumeister, 2007; Putnam, 2000). Class differentiation, including distinctions between "blue collar" and "white collar" jobs, became more prominent (Coad, 2008); we will address this in more detail in Chapter Three. Ultimately, the ethos of this era may be best represented by the male business uniform of dark suit with white shirt and a tie.

At the same time, masculinity was increasingly associated with an emotionally "cool" style that valued emotional stoicism, defined as not showing one's feelings, a stark contrast with the Victorian Era's passions. Anger, which was seen as healthy for boys and men, was the only exception (Stearns, 1994). This image of masculinity was typically paired with an idealized female partner who would stay at home to care for the house, the children, and her husband after his long day, a continuation/modification of the Victorian doctrine of separate spheres. In current day America, as well as in many research studies, this version of masculinity and male breadwinning is often referred to as "traditional" masculinity (or "traditional" gender roles), although as we'll see in Chapter Eleven, this era is the only time in United States history when this formulation of family was idealized.

The 1950s also featured a boy crisis. Here, concerns focused on boys who were unwilling to conform to the image of the organization man, with its focus on conformity to corporate culture and acceptance of the rules. Adults of the day worried about "juvenile delinquents" and devoted substantial cultural resources to preventing boys from becoming delinquents, asking police, counselors, and social scientists to help fix the problem (Stearns, 1994). Epitomized by actor James Dean and his characters, this version of masculinity would be rehabilitated and reclaimed over the next two decades through sympathetic depictions in *West Side Story*, *The Outsiders*, *Grease*, and *Happy Days*. This is one example of white masculinity managing and reclaiming its undesirable variants, a cultural "option" that is unavailable to other American ethnic groups (Carroll, 2010).

We see common threads of current conceptions of masculinity in all of these historical phases: independence, antifemininity, toughness, competition, homophobia, and aggression. Yet the relative emphases of these attributes changed from era to era.

WHAT IS MEN'S STUDIES?

Men's studies is an academic discipline focused on examining males as beings whose experiences are influenced by their culture's definitions of what it means to be a man. We believe that studying men offers several benefits. Men's studies includes researchers from many fields; this book relies primarily on research from the fields of psychology and sociology, as well as history, anthropology, literature and media studies, linguistics, health science, and philosophy.

Because media is so embedded in today's culture, we provide a number of examples from popular media and periodically turn specifically to research on the effect of media. Research intended to document the effects of mass media dates back to the first half of the twentieth century and gained prominence with the creation of both television and television networks. Research clearly demonstrates that media inputs are connected to people's attitudes (or beliefs) as well as their behaviors. A variety of mechanisms have been proposed and investigated, including total exposure (i.e., time), models, viewers' motivations and purposes, among others (Bandura, Ross, & Ross, 1963a; Gerbner, Gross, Morgan, & Signorielli, 1994; Van Evra, 1998), and each of these approaches has found some level of support (L. M. Brown, Lamb, & Tappan, 2009; J. Brown, Steele, & Walsh-Childers, 2002; Shanahan & Morgan, 1999; Ward, 2015). Theoretical models have become increasingly complex over the last 30 years, coinciding with the shift from over-the-air to cable television and the subsequent expansion of channels, as well as the general public's greater access to the Internet. As such, models of understanding the media's effects have increasingly attempted to differentiate the medium (e.g., television, Internet) and the content (e.g., "Friends," sports websites) as well as the ways in which the individual and the content are mutually influencing (Ward, 2015; Ward, Seabrook, Giaccardi, & Zuo, 2016). For example, a man who identifies as a "jock" might routinely choose media content and associated technologies that feeds his interest in sports, while also being alerted to new content and technologies about sports that might be of interest.

The field of men's studies can be said to address a broad range of questions and topics, including:

- The United States Constitution states that "all men are created equal." We might ask if all men have equal access to the ability to prove their masculinity?
- Emotion is part of our human (and mammalian) heritage, yet men in many cultures are taught to suppress their feelings. We can examine the benefits and costs of suppressing this part of one's self.
- Intimacy is often described as a basic human need (Freud, 1925; Maslow, 1943), yet men in many cultures are encouraged to minimize the importance of interpersonal relationships. What benefits and costs do men experience from de-emphasizing relationships?
- In the United States, men commit the vast majority of acts of violence and are also the majority of victims. For example, they commit 90 percent of homicides and comprise approximately 75 percent of homicide victims (Cooper & Smith, 2011). We can ask why the numbers are so heavily biased toward males?

- The average lifespan of a man is significantly shorter than a woman's (Molla, 2013). We can ask why this is the case?
- Work outside the home has historically been a (mostly) male endeavor. Recent increases in modernization and technology, combined with the shift to the "service" economy, have challenged this dynamic. We can ask how men adjust to the change?

Another way to define Men's Studies is through examination of its products. Here, we turn to a series of **content analyses**, which is research that documents and examines the content of published products to identify specific themes and the frequency with which those themes occur. Analysis of conference presentations at the multidisciplinary American Men's Studies Association conference reveals three particularly common themes: representations of men/masculinity, men and racial issues, and psychological/emotional topics (Cohen & Suen, 2012). Examination of articles published in the journal *Psychology of Men and Masculinity* reveals a different focus that reflects the journal's grounding in psychology. Here, the most common topics have been men's mental health, men's relationships, and violence (Wong, Steinfeldt, Speight, & Hickman, 2010).

Most Men's Studies scholars come from profeminist or mythopoetic frames of reference. The general approach is to take seriously the influence of gender on men and articulate its effects. **Profeminist**-oriented scholars rely on the central tenets of feminism, particularly evidence that cultural ideas about gender influence a broad range of individual-level behaviors and that society is structured to favor men-as-a-group over women-as-a-group (Okun, 2014). **Mythopoetic** scholars tend to draw from and focus on symbolic expressions of masculinity that are found in myths, literature, and religious ideals.

There exists a good deal of confusion about Men's Studies from people of all genders. Given that men do and have held the majority of power in the United States (and elsewhere), it might seem odd to study them. However, there are also many men who feel—or are—quite powerless and have been damaged by harsh masculine socialization. By virtue of their greater social power, men are also in a unique position to help shift this power into better balance. Men need an understanding of the effects of masculine privilege to do so, and only a gender-aware perspective can bring this understanding. (We use the hyphenated construction "men-as-a-group" in several places in this book to emphasize that we are talking about men in the aggregate, as there are great variations among men.)

Some people believe that as women's power and prominence have increased, men have had great difficulty dealing with them, a perception that relies on the notion that power is a **zero sum game** in which gains by one group represent losses by another group. It is true that many men have trouble dealing with strong women, often because they were socialized to believe that men should be powerful and dominant and that they are inherently better than women. As a result, they may experience strong women as threats to masculinity. This is an issue that men must address, because women *are* powerful, and men must learn to accept and deal with them in constructive ways. Men's Studies can enlighten us to various aspects of relationships between the sexes and contribute to agendas for alliances between the sexes. In effect, Men's Studies parallels and complements Women's Studies by showing not only how sexism harms women but also how it harms men (O'Neill & Renzulli, 2013).

Some people assume that Men's Studies is meant to oppose Women's Studies, with the two fields explicitly competing to discredit each other. The purpose of studying men from a gender-aware perspective is not to further oppress women, but to address quality of life issues for men and women. Men's issues are often very compatible with women's issues, and many Men's Studies scholars believe that enhancing women's power will also enhance men's power. In the abstract, empowering women to obtain higher education and work for pay outside the home allows heterosexual couples to choose which parent, or both, can generate the highest income instead of assuming that the man will be responsible for earning most (or all) of their money. Similarly, if we can understand the causes of gender-based violence, most of which is perpetrated by men against women, we can take steps to decrease that violence, which would improve the quality of life for both women and men.

Some people argue that researchers and historians long focused exclusively on men and ignored women. In fact, many research studies in the early days of psychology were undertaken using only male participants, as if male behaviors generalized to the entire human race. Critics observed that in psychological research "even the rat was white and male" (Guthrie, 1976; Mays, 1988). Yet much of this scholarship uses men as idealized or prototypical representatives of humanity and thus is "about men only by virtue of not being about women" (Brod, 1987a, p. 264; see also Kimmel, 1987). That is, male research participants were presented as historical, political, and cultural actors without consideration of their masculinity. Men's Studies moves masculinity and gender from the periphery of inquiry into its center by studying men *as men*.

The research in psychology provides a useful example. An analysis of approximately 100 keywords from the PsycInfo database from 1887 to 1997, combined with the terms "male," "female," "male subjects," and "female subjects," demonstrates the historical imbalance favoring males as research subjects. This can be seen in Figure 1.2. But the pattern was reversed as a result of feminist concerns in the 1970s, with studies that included only girls and women coming to dramatically outnumber studies that included only boys and men (Moon & Hoffman, 2000; Moon, 2016, personal communication). Although many American colleges and universities offer degrees in gender studies, the State University of New York at Stony Brook appears to be the only United States institution offering a Master's degree in Men's Studies (as of the middle of 2017).

Finally, we would also suggest that teaching—and learning about—Men's Studies creates another way to improve men's lives. You, reading this text and taking this course, will have the opportunity to learn about men's lives in ways that few people do. As a result, you'll be better able to identify both healthy and unhealthy behaviors, why men engage in those behaviors, and how to support or change those behaviors. Whether you focus on your own life or the lives of boys and men around you, you'll have plenty of opportunities.

Origins of Men's Studies

In the beginning of the 1960s, a group of thinkers began to make strong critiques of mainstream social science theory and research methods. Known as *feminism,* this school of thought highlights ways in which women's perspectives and lives had been ignored in most (or all) disciplines and that these perspectives were often fundamentally different from the perspectives and lives that were highlighted in textbooks (Rutherford & Granek, 2010; Shields & Dicicco, 2011). Feminist theorists and activists urged people to take seriously the idea that people's sex and gender have important effects on their behavior and on the ways that others react to them. These ideas about female development, functioning, and perspectives gave rise to a new academic field, Women's Studies, which subsequently created a stronger awareness of people as *gendered beings* (Shields & Dicicco, 2011).

During the last 50 years, modern feminist scholars have convincingly demonstrated that gender affects virtually every area of life, including politics, family organization, literature, art, individual psychology, international relations, and views of history (Shields & Dicicco, 2011). Women's Studies has emerged as a legitimate field of multidisciplinary intellectual inquiry. College

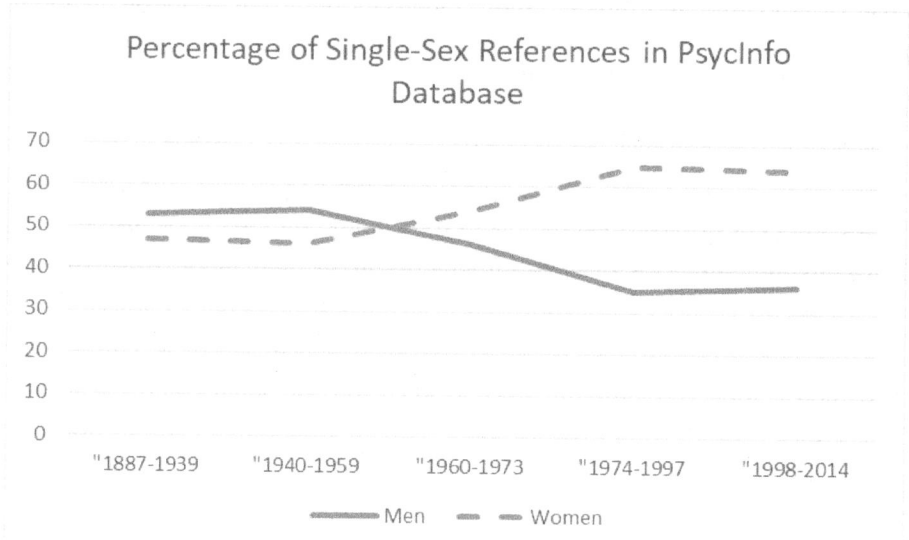

Figure 1.2 References on Male and Female Research Participants in the PsycInfo Database

and university courses, research programs, and even entire academic departments have been developed to place gender and women's perspectives into our culture's body of knowledge.

In the early 1970's, scholars began to expand this awareness into a new area, Men's Studies (Brooks & Levant, 1999; O'Neil & Renzulli, 2013). They began to ask the question, "If the experience of being female has a profound effect on a woman's behavior and on others' reactions to her, does the experience of being male have similarly powerful implications for men?" The answer would seem to be an emphatic "yes."

KEY DEBATES FOR STUDYING MEN AND MASCULINITY

As we discussed earlier, research on men and masculinity draws from a wide range of academic fields. Yet there are a number of debates regarding gender that appear regularly in most, if not all, of those academic fields. Before you read further, answer these questions for yourself. The ways in which you answer these questions will influence your reaction to what you learn in this course. These same assumptions shape the analyses reported in this book.

- Is men's behavior *primarily* the result of men's biological inheritance or the culture they live in?
- Overall, is masculinity *mostly* a positive force that contributes to society or a negative force that drains resources from society?
- Is it *more beneficial* to compare men to women or to compare different sub-groups of men to each other?
- On average, is the behavior of real-life men *mostly similar* to our stereotypes of men, or mostly different from those stereotypes?

Essentialism vs. Social Constructionism

One major debate in gender studies is the distinction between essentialist and social constructionist models. **Essentialists** argue that the collections of attitudes, behaviors, and social conditions that we call masculinity are "hardwired" into males through biology (see Thornhill & Palmer, 2000) and/or the heritability of human psyche (see Jung, 1959/1989; Bly, 1990). They view masculinity as static, non-historical, cross-cultural, cross-situational, and mostly unchanging over time. From this perspective, gender change is either impossible or it involves the use of powerful force to constrain what is seen as "naturally" male. In everyday language, the essential perspective is a "nature" perspective that points to biological or evolutionary causes for male-typical behavior, often the Y chromosome or the hormone testosterone. When a masculine behavior appears to be stable from one generation to the next or appears in country after country (such as the use of all-male militaries), this is often taken as evidence of an essential position. We'll explore perspectives that emphasize evolutionary, biological, and physiological factors in more detail in Chapter Five.

The opposing view of *social constructionists* is summarized by Michael Kimmel (1994), who views masculinity as "a constantly changing collection of meanings that we construct through our relationships with ourselves, with each other, and with our world. Manhood is neither static nor timeless; it is historical. Manhood is not the manifestation of an inner essence; it is socially constructed. Manhood does not bubble up to consciousness from our biological makeup; it is created in culture. Manhood means different things at different times to different people." (p. 120). From this perspective, social definitions of masculinity are quite malleable and thus have the potential to shift in response to changes in ideologies, values, social conditions, economic factors, and historical events. Here, the emphasis is placed on nurture or learning, with behaviors described as the result of social forces. Evidence of substantial differences from one generation to the next, from one country to another, or one racial or ethnic group to another are often taken as support for constructivist arguments. We'll explore differences based on race and ethnicity in Chapter Two and throughout the book, while in Chapter Six we'll review theories that emphasize environmental, social, and cultural factors.

Even the most extreme essentialists do not deny the influence of social forces on behavior, just as even the most extreme social constructionists do not deny the effect of biology. However, scholars show a strong tendency to position themselves within one camp or the other. Essentialist E.O. Wilson (1979) once remarked that biology holds behavior on a "leash," but Steven J. Gould (1987) adds that the important debate is about the length and tightness of that leash. Essentialists like Wilson see it as very short and tight; but Gould (1987) sees the leash as "long and nonconstraining, though well worth our continued examination" (p. 115). Consistent with Darwin's original presentation of evolution and a variety of developmental theories, we view male typical behavior as the result of both nature and nurture, essential and constructivist perspectives.

Positive vs. Negative

The research has tended to focus on men's shortcomings and the problematic aspects of masculinity, such as restricted emotional displays, (hyper-)independence, sexism, and a willingness to use violence to solve problems (Kiselica, Benton-Wright, & Englar-Carlson, 2016; Wetherell & Edley, 2014). We summarize much of this literature throughout the book. However, this need not be the case. Masculine directives to be self-reliant after soliciting input from others, display courage and risk-taking, and serve as a financial provider-worker can all be seen as strengths (Kiselica et al., 2016).

For example, Keith Kline (2016) found that young men whose masculinity was challenged had physiologically *better* responses to the pain-inducing cold pressor task than did men whose masculinity was not challenged. (The *cold pressor task* involves leaving an extremity in an ice bath. Extended exposure to cold causes pain which subsides quickly when the limb is removed from the ice and does not cause any permanent damage.)

To Whom Should Men Be Compared? Women or Other Men?

If we want to better understand boys and men, who do we compare and contrast their behavior with? Some researchers focus on ***between-group differences***, the comparison of two easily identifiable groups, such as men vs. women. Other researchers focus on ***within-group differences***, the comparison of different subgroups within one easily identifiable group. Within-group research compares men who demonstrate a particular behavior or attribute with men who don't demonstrate that characteristic. In practice, more than two sub-groups may be compared in a within–group study (e.g., comparing those with low, moderate, and high scores). We'll discuss some of the political implications of these issues in Chapter Two and some of the technical and statistical implications of these approaches in Chapter Four.

Stereotypes vs Reality

You've already begun to learn about the complexity of masculinity. **Stereotypes** are defined as simplistic and generalized characterizations of a group. They may be held up as an image that people in that group should aspire to, with rewards for those who fit the idealized stereotype and penalties for those who don't. In the United States, the male stereotype tends to be more narrowly defined than the female stereotype, which means men have less "range" available to them. At the same time, people tend to view the male stereotype less positively than the female stereotype (Steinberg & Diekman, 2016). Research demonstrates that the stereotypes are often quite different from the reality of most people's lives (Connell, 1995; Smiler, 2013)

Academics and Activists

There have been a large number of groups that have attempted to help men. Some have offered help via studying men to identify their strengths and weaknesses. Others have provided direct help. Here, help refers to a broad variety of targets that include decreasing violence against women, men's health, and improving father's rights.

Describing her own development as a feminist psychologist, Riger (2016) talks about her burgeoning anger. It began when she worked on a crisis line for women experiencing domestic violence, was heightened when a professor in her doctoral program told her that she was more likely to get pregnant than earn her Ph.D., and has continued to this day when she sees or experiences sexism. She sees a direct connection between the efforts of academics, who help document and define a problem as well as their ability to redefine or reframe a problem), and activists who work to change women's lives (Riger, 2016). Although this anger has contributed to cultural changes that have helped women (Riger, 2016; Shields & Dicicco, 2016; Rutherford & Granek, 2010), connections between men's studies scholars and men's activists have been relatively few and somewhat strained (e.g., Brooks & Levant, 1999; Doyle & Femiano, 1999).

Activism

As feminist thought and feminist activism became more prominent in the 1970s, activists' attention turned toward men. Some groups sought to help men understand and even change in response to feminism's critiques of United States culture. Other groups were formed to oppose those changes, and yet others were less clearly connected to the male-female power dynamics. We list some of the most common points of emphasis here and defer discussion of male-female cultural politics for Chapter Three.

Sexism and Violence Against Women

In some ways, the National Organization of Men Against Sexism (NOMAS), may have had the largest impact of any organization. NOMAS was born when a group of men who'd enrolled in a women's studies course at the University of Tennessee (Knoxville) organized the first conference on Men and Masculinity in 1975. Conferences have been held annually ever since and the National Organization for Changing Men (NOCM) was formed in 1982. In 1990, the NOMAS name was adopted. The organization has always been pro-feminist, gay affirming, and clearly opposed to restrictive gender roles (NOMAS history; n.d.). Their mission and focus has expanded over the years, including explicit stances against racism and human trafficking, among other issues (NOMAS Principles, n.d.).

Over the years, a variety of organizations have followed NOMAS' lead and worked to reduce sexism, especially violence against women (Okun, 2014). We'll focus more directly on the issue that has been known as "domestic violence" and "interpersonal violence" (IPV) in Chapter Twelve. Current organizations include the White Ribbon Campaign, A Call to Men, He for She, Promundo, Men Can Stop Rape, and the Mentors in Violence Prevention (MVP) program, as well as publicaitons such as *XY Magazine* and *VoiceMale*.

Men's Health

In recent years, as men's studies scholars have identified a set of health vulnerabilities specific to males, organizations have begun attempts to address the health needs and problems of this population. In the United States, the most visible group is the Men's Health Network, a nonprofit organization that supports education, research, and political action (such as lobbying Congress to establish an Office of Men's Health) to improve men's wellness. The World Congress on Men's Health has a similar mission in the international context. The Movember Foundation's initial focus was on raising awareness of prostate and testicular cancers, and has since expanded to most facets of men's health, including suicide and mental health. They may be best known for their November mustache campaign.

Men's Rights

Throughout these periods and continuing today, a number of Men's Rights groups have been created; online, these individuals identify themselves as Men's Rights Activists (MRAs). There do not appear to be academic or activist organizations that have developed out of this movement, although there are a number of websites dedicated to this perspective. Published works typically point to an anti-feminist perspective that focuses on combatting feminist political action and the "sissifying" of men (Farrell, 1993; Hoff Sommers, 2000). Similar themes were found among the "father's rights" groups of the 1980s and 1990s. Given the focus on cultural power, we discuss these groups in more detail in Chapter Three.

ACADEMIC ORGANIZATIONS

Research on men, masculinity, and masculinities (the plural, because there's more than one way to be a man; see Chapter Two), has expanded dramatically since the 1970s (Cochran, 2010; Smiler, 2004; Wong & Wester, 2016). Much of this research has been fostered by two academic organizations, through annual conferences, journals devoted to the topic, and mentoring.

The *American Men's Studies Association* (AMSA) was formally created in 1991, but its roots go back another decade (Doyle & Femiano, 1999). The National Organization for Men (NOM), which became the National Organization for Changing Men (NOCM) and eventually the National Organization for Men Against Sexism (NOMAS), included a "task group" that was focused on the academic study of men. By 1989, leaders of the task group decided they wanted to form their own organization. Although some concerns were logistical such as timing and focus of the annual conference, the groups also differed on the role of feminism. At that time, AMSA's leaders supported feminist ideals but wanted to be ideologically pluralistic (Doyle & Femiano, 1999). Debates about the prominence and role of feminism, including the inclusion of feminism in AMSA's mission statement, continue to this day (AMSA, n.d.). For many years, AMSA worked in partnership with *Men's Studies Press* to publish several academic journals, of which the *Journal of Men's Studies* is the oldest, first published in 1992. Key figures include Harry Brod, Clyde Franklin II, Michael Kaufman, James Doyle, and Mike Messner.

The *Society for the Psychological Study of Men and Masculinity (SPSMM)* is also known as Division 51 of the American Psychological Association (APA). Like AMSA, SPSMM developed from other existing organizations; in this case, a combination of subgroups and task forces from other APA divisions, including the Women's Division. Like AMSA, SPSMM's founders recognized the influence of feminist thought as important to the organization's work, but have not enshrined feminism in their mission statement (Brooks & Levant, 1999; Cochran, 2010). Indeed, one of the greatest challenges they faced was ensuring that the new division would not be founded in opposition to feminism, as had occurred shortly after the formation of the women's division (Brooks & Elder, 2016). (APA Policy prohibits its divisions from having mission statements and goals that are in direct opposition to each other.) SPSMM was given tentative status in 1995 and permanent status in 1997, consistent with APA guidelines. SPSMM's journal, *Psychology of Men and Masculinity*, was first published in 2000. Key figures include Ron Levant, Gary Brooks, Mark Kiselica, Joseph Pleck, and James O'Neil.

SUMMARY

We began this chapter by asking about the definition of a real man. We've seen that the current American cultural ideal of how men should act is multifaceted, and that this definition has changed since the birth of the United States. Writing in 1949, Anthropologist Margaret Mead's questions remain relevant today:

> How are men and women to think about their maleness and their femaleness in this twentieth century, in which so many of our old ideas must be made new? Have we over-domesticated men, denied their natural adventurousness, tied them down to machines that are after all only glorified spindles and looms, mortars and pestles and digging sticks, all of which were once women's work? Have we cut women off from their natural closeness to their children, taught them to look for a job instead of the touch of a child's hand, for status in a competitive world rather than a unique place by a glowing hearth? In educating women like men, have we done something disastrous to both men and women alike, or have we only taken one further step in the recurrent task of building more and better on our original human nature?... These are questions which are being asked in a hundred different ways in contemporary America. (Mead, 1949, p. 13)

In many ways, the goal of Men's Studies is to answer these questions (and others). The goals of this discipline are to understand men's experiences and the forces that shape those experiences, at the level of the individual or small group, as well as at the cultural level. Like many fields, some concerns have become central, appearing and re-appearing in a broad range of topics. This includes some topics where activists have differing goals that reflect some of these debates.

Some key points:

1. Masculinity can and has been described in a range of ways, that have included both directions on what to do and what not to do, as well as directions focused on specific attitudes to hold or behaviors to engage in.
2. We distinguish between *sex*, which refers to relatively strict definitions related to biological male-ness and female-ness, and *gender*, which refers to cultural beliefs about the implications of being male or female.
3. We offered a single, multi-faceted definition of masculinity that includes antifemininity, status and achievement, inexpressiveness and independence, and adventurousness and aggressiveness.
4. Within the United States., the definition of masculinity has changed over time, including changes in the central focus of what it means to "be a man."
5. Men's studies is an academic discipline focused on examining males as beings whose experiences are influenced by their culture's definitions of what it means to be a man. Men's studies draws scholars from a broad range of academic disciplines.
6. Men's Studies includes several ongoing debates: essentialism vs. social constructionism, the balance between positive vs. negative aspects of masculinity, questions about which groups men should be compared to, and comparisons between stereotypes and reality.
7. We traced the history of some activist groups, including the National Organization of Men Against Seixsm (NOMAS) and the National Organization for Changing Men (NOCM).
8. We traced the history of some of the largest Men's Studies groups, including the two largest academic organizations: The American Men's Studies Association (AMSA) and the Society for the Psychological Study of Men and Masculinity (SPSMM).

GLOSSARY

Sex: Refers to an individual's physiological or biological status.

Gender: Refers to the cultural expectations based on an individual's sex.

Sexism: Prejudicial attitudes and behaviors against women.

Heterosexism: The preferential treatment of heterosexuals over non-heterosexuals.

Racism: A set of behaviors, values, and attitudes that reflect a belief in the innate superiority of one race over another.

Communality: An emphasis on interdependence.

Communal masculinity: A form of masculinity that emphasized a man's usefulness to the community, determined by meeting the needs and expectations of one's family and neighbors. This was the dominant form in the United States during colonial times.

Self-made manhood: A form of masculinity that emphasized economic success hrough business and professional success and the accumulation of wealth. This was the dominant form of masculinity during the Victorian Era.

The Doctrine of Separate Spheres: A cultural assumption that men and women were fundamentally different and thus functioned best in settings (spheres) that conformed to their supposedly natural proclivities.

Passionate manhood: A form of masculinity focused on the self in comparison to other men via the unrestrained pursuit of one's passions.

Men's studies: An academic discipline focused on examining males as beings whose experiences are influenced by their culture's definitions of what it means to be a man.

Profeminist-oriented scholars: Scholars who rely on the central tenets of Feminism, particularly evidence that cultural ideas about gender influence a broad range of individual-level behaviors and that society is structured to favor men-as-a-group over women-as-a-group.

Mythopoetic scholars: Scholars who tend to draw from and focus on symbolic expressions of masculinity that are found in myths, literature, and religious ideals.

Content analyses: Research that documents and examines the content of published products to identify specific themes and the frequency with which those themes occur.

Zero sum game: The idea that gains in power by one group represent losses by another group.

Feminism: A school of thought that highlights ways in which women?s perspectives and lives have been ignored in most (or all) disciplines and that these perspectives were often fundamentally different from the perspectives and lives that were highlighted in textbooks.

Essentialism: A school of thought that argues that the collections of attitudes, behaviors, and social conditions that we call masculinity are "hard-wired" into males through biology.

Social constructionism: A school of thought that argues that definitions of masculinity are quite malleable and have the potential to shift in response to changes in ideologies, values, social conditions, economic factors, and historical events.

Between-group differences: The comparison of two easily identifiable groups, such as men vs. women.

Within-group differences: The comparison of different subgroups within one easily identifiable group (e.g., two different groups of men).

Cold pressor task: A laboratory procedure in which the research participant places an extremity in an ice bath. Extended exposure to cold causes pain which subsides quickly when the limb is removed from the ice and does not cause any permanent damage.

Stereotypes: Simplistic and generalized characterizations of a group.

Chapter Two

Multiple Masculinities

In Chapter One, we introduced a singular definition of masculinity that consisted of four components. But why is there only one definition? Self-expression and having choices are central components of American culture (and other Western nations), so why does the same culture insist that there's only one "correct" way to be masculine? Researchers and theorists have increasingly explored the idea that there are many *masculinities*, different forms of masculinity that co-exist within a single culture and across different cultures. At the micro-level, we might consider differences between "jocks" and "nerds," for example (Ashmore, Del Boca, & Beebe, 2002; Barber, Eccles, & Stone, 2001; Smiler 2006a). At the macro-level, we might explore differences between African-American, Asian-American, European-American, and Latino definitions of masculinity. Studying these different masculinities helps us explore within-group differences among American men, as well as between-group differences through comparisons between different nations' definitions of masculinity. This research can help clarify the contradiction between the relatively high power of men-as-a-group and the relatively low level of power that many individual men experience, particularly men from groups that are discriminated against.

In this chapter, we detail a range of definitions of masculinity that differ from America's culturally dominant definition. We note that the dominant form is rooted in the history of White Americans, as that segment of the population was and is most numerous and has always dominated the American political, judicial, economic, vocational, and entertainment systems. Based on this dominance, one could easily argue that the masculinity described thus far is better labeled "White Masculinity." We start by considering definitions of masculinity from several non-White American ethnic groups, then turn to distinctions based on social class and sexual orientation. Note that we do not address the experience of transgender individuals in the text because the research database is quite small and because there is no clear consensus on what masculinity might mean within this population (Singh & dickey, 2017). Throughout, we make note of challenges that men face related to directives to achieve financial success, economic power, and status levels that are not equally available to all men. Finally, we briefly look outside the United States at other definitions of masculinity.

Masculinities and Cultural Power

We begin with discussion of power dynamics. *The term "masculinities" was originally coined by sociologist R. W. Connell (1995), who suggested that different forms of masculinity can be indexed, in part, by their similarity to the culture's primary definition as well as the amount of cultural power assigned to that form.* Connell defined **hegemonic masculinity** as a culture's idealized form of masculinity. Individuals who demonstrate the greatest level of conformity to their culture's ideal receive the greatest amount and greatest range of cultural rewards. In current day America, the hegemonic form is the single definition described in Chapter One; the rewards of living out this version of masculinity include money, power, status, and access to the most attractive sexual partners. Although they emphasize different enactments of masculinity, self-identified "jocks" and "tough guys" could be said to represent hegemonic masculinity (Smiler, 2006b).

Connell also describes the existence of **complicit masculinities**, which refers to forms of masculinity that possess many, but not all, attributes of the hegemonic form; these variations help maintain the power structure instead of actively trying to change it. They also receive cultural benefits for their masculine enactments, although not to the same extent as individuals who enact the hegemonic form. Self-identified (and stereotypical) "businessman" and sexually promiscuous "players" fit this category (Smiler, 2006b). There are also **marginalized masculinities**. This term refers to forms of masculinity that possess few or no aspects of hegemonic masculinity while also maintaining the current set of power relations. Marginalized masculinities refers to individuals who subscribe to the hegemonic definition but are mostly or wholly unable to enact that version of masculinity and thus receive few or no cultural benefits from being masculine. Self-identified or stereotypical "nerds" and "family men" both fit this category (Smiler, 2006b).

Connell (1995) also argued that there exists set of **subordinated masculinities**, versions of masculinity that offer a notably different definition of masculinity and challenge the status quo. These versions of masculinity do not receive any cultural benefits for their enactments of masculinity, are suppressed and may be oppressed, and individuals who adhere to them may suffer legal consequences. Connell, writing in 1995, relied on gay male masculinity as an example. Working class masculinity may also be seen as subordinated (Connell, 1995; Lefkowitz, 1997). In current day United States culture, any non-White masculinity can and has been characterized this way, as we'll address throughout the chapter; the notably differential rates of incarceration—1.41 percent of Black men, compared to 0.38 percent of Latinos and 0.28 percent of White men (Nellis, 2016)—can be taken as a sign of just how oppressed these particular non-white masculinities are. Systemic inequalities in education, employment (and thus income), and the enforcement of laws all contribute to these disparities in incarceration. We'll describe some of those factors later in the chapter, as well as later in the text.

In this chapter, we introduce the concept of *intersectionality*, which refers to the ways that different statuses or categorization systems, such as ethnicity and social class, may interact to influence an individual's beliefs about and enactments of gender (Shields, 2008). For example, many people have different conceptions, expectations, and stereotypes of "a man," "a white man," and "a black man" (Ghavami & Peplau, 2013). Although researchers and reviewers continue to debate the best ways to apply the intersectionality approach to understanding people's lives, the existing literature clearly demonstrates that the experience of a Black Man is not simply the "addition" of what it means to be a man "plus" what it means to be Black (Ghavami & Peplau, 2016; Shields, 2008; Wong, Liu, & Klann, 2016).

MASCULINITIES WITHIN THE UNITED STATES

Because racial characteristics such as skin color are visible, race often plays a prominent role in American social relations. The United States is a collection of many peoples, and each group has cultural modes of thought, language, customs, food, religion, and dress that make it distinctive. A *culture* is defined as the "belief systems and value orientations that influence customs, norms, practices, and social institutions, including psychological processes" (APA, 2002). Race is a poorly defined term that refers to a group that individuals are assigned to based on characteristics such as skin color or hair type, while *ethnicity* refers to "the acceptance of the group mores and practices of one's culture of origin and the concomitant sense of belonging" (APA, 2002). Note that neither race nor ethnicity has widely accepted formal definitions (APA, 2002). *Acculturation* refers to the adaptations made to a "new" culture due to prolonged interaction with that culture; thus, it refers to adopting some aspects of a culture although it does not require giving up or abandoning those same aspects of one's original culture (Maffini & Wong, 2012).

In many cases, dominant cultures consider people of minority races to be "different" in important ways. *Racism* is a set of behaviors, values, and attitudes that reflect a belief in the innate superiority of one race over another. **Institutional racism** refers to racist laws, practices, and customs that enforce the superiority of one race over another. Both individual and institutional racism can profoundly influence people's behavior and senses of self, producing predictable psychological responses such as low self-esteem, suspiciousness of people from the dominant culture, stress, and anger (Aronson, 2012; Hammond, Fleming, & Vila-Torres, 2016). Particularly relevant for our discussion are ways in which racism has shaped the ways that minority groups have been allowed to engage with the hegemonic definition of masculinity, as well as how they have developed and practiced their own versions of masculinity.

To illustrate the effects of race and ethnicity on masculinity, we will briefly describe some of the research on the three largest minority groups men in the United States: Latino, African American, and Asian men, all of whom have prominent ethnic identities. A complete understanding of these groups' experiences with masculinity requires a thorough understanding of the systematic inequality that pervades the educational, economic, criminal justice, health care, and other major institutions of mainstream United States society. Such scope is beyond the range of this text, although we briefly address some aspects of inequality here and in later chapters. We continue in alphabetical order, describing the three largest United States ethnic minority groups: African-Americans, Asians, and Latinos.

Table 2.1 provides a brief demographic picture of these three minority groups, along with Non-Hispanic Whites (the majority group; we define the term Hispanic later in the chapter). At times, we refer to groups as either *overrepresented* or *underrepresented* in various statistics. To be over- (or under-) represented on a measure, the group most account for a notably different percentage in that category than they do in the general population. For example, Blacks are overrepresented among those living in poverty because they account for approximately 13 percent of the population but 24 percent of those living below the poverty level. Non-Hispanic Whites are under-represented among those living in poverty, because they account for approximately 62 percent of the general population and 41 percent of those in poverty. Note that this description of Non-Hispanic Whites partly obscures the fact that a greater percentage (and a greater number) of Non-Hispanic Whites live in poverty than any other racial or ethnic group.

African American Men

Black or African American culture has come to define masculinity on its own terms, with some similarities and several differences from the White, hegemonic definition. We remind readers that any given Black man may demonstrate and reflect few, some, or all of the characteristics we list here, in the same way that any White man may do regarding the hegemonic definition. In an interview-based study of more than 150 adult Black men, Hammond and Mattis (2005) identified 15 distinct themes. Most common was the notion of responsibility-accountability, which refers to responsibility toward oneself, one's family, and others, as well as being accountable for one's actions, thoughts, and behaviors; this aspect of masculinity was reported by nearly half of all participants. Other common themes included autonomy, providing and making one's way in the world (i.e., "waymaking"), spirituality-religiosity, and moral rectitude-values (Hammond & Mattis, 2005). Other interviews

Table 2.1
Key Demographic Trends Among the Four Largest U.S. Racial/Ethnic Groups

	Total in 1000s	White, non-Hispanic	Hispanic	Black	Asian
Population 2014	318,748	62.2%	17.4%	12.2%	5.45
Median income 2015	$56,516	$60,109	$45,148	$36,898	$77,166
Uninsured rate	—	6.7%	16.2%	11.1%	7.5%
Incarceration rate	—	0.28%	0.38%	1.4%	n/a
Poverty	-42,100	41.2%	21.4%	24.1%	11.4%
Predicted population 2060	416,795	43.6%	28.6%	14.3%	9.3%
Education (age 25 or older)					
High school diploma or higher	212,312	92.3%	66.7%	87%	89.1%
Bachelor's degree or higher	212,132	36.2%	15.5%	22.5%	53.9%
Advanced degree	212,132	13.5%	4.7%	8.2%	21.4%

Population figures are in thousands. Population figures from Colby & Ortman, 2015. Poverty figures and uninsured rates from Proctor, Semega, & Kollar, 2016. Education figures from Ryan & Bauman, 2016. Incarceration rates from The Sentencing Project, 2016.

based studies have identified similar themes, as well as leadership (particularly role-modeling) and mental toughness (Pompper, 2010; Rogers, Sperry, & Levant, 2015). Undergraduate young men 18 to 25 years old also tend to identify not acting like a girl (i.e., "antifeminity") and being sexually promiscuous as important aspects of masculinity, but their elders rarely do (Pompper, 2010).

In a classic work, Richard Majors and Janet Mancini Billson (1992) described a social style that many African American males adopt to survive psychologically: the *cool pose*. Cool pose involves a set of ritualized behaviors that involve toughness, detachment, control, and a stylish, sometimes flamboyant presentation. Majors and Billson describe it thus:

> The purpose of posing and posturing—being cool—is to enhance social competence, pride, dignity, self-esteem, and respect. Cool enhances masculinity. Being cool also expresses bitterness, anger, and distrust toward the dominant society for many years of hostile mistreatment and discrimination. Cool pose helps keep the dominant society off balance and puzzled and accentuates the expressive self. (p. 105)

This kind of psychological response is a show of pride and strength and a refusal to display vulnerability. Cool pose is also used to teach men to restrain their anger, as expressing it directly to someone more powerful can lead to negative consequences.

Practices that are based in mutual insults are also longstanding. Today, they form a central component of rap music but their historical roots include "playing the dozens"—a ritualized game of insulting one another. An older African American man traced the survival value of being able to do so back to the days of slavery:

> It was a game slaves used to play, only they wasn't just playing for fun. They was playing to teach themselves and their sons how to stay alive. The whole idea was to learn to take whatever the master said to you without answering back or hitting him 'cause that was the way a slave had to be, so's he could go on living. (Guffy, 1971, in Majors and Billson, 1992, p. 101)

As the quote explains, the ability to take an insult and hold one's temper was literally a life-and-death skill.

African American men have struggled for many generations in response to a mainstream culture that has denied them personhood and dignity. Generations of Blacks were brought to the colonies and the (early) United States against their will, as slaves, with no legal rights, protections, or status. Even after the American Civil War, laws were constructed and enforced—or not enforced—in ways that favored Whites and disadvantaged blacks. The 1960s-era Civil Rights movement helped shed light on and end many of these practices. However, this movement did not necessarily change minds, nor did it end all racist practices (Franklin, 1984). Indeed, adult African American men were often referred to as *"boys"* until the late 1960s, and occasionally still today, a label that denies their status as adults (Franklin, 1984). These historical roots, as well as recent and current manifestations, contribute to current day problems such as high rates of unemployment, drug and alcohol abuse, premature death by violence and preventable diseases, crime victimization, and incarceration (Gibbs, 1992; Hammond et al., 2016). The term "Black Lives Matter" emphasizes the ways in which Black people in America continue to struggle for dignity, respect, and equality from Whites (Hall, Hall, & Perry, 2016; Oeur, 2016).

As can be seen in Table 2.1, Blacks continue to suffer lingering effects from these discriminatory practices. Their median household income is approximately one-third less than the national median and they are overrepresented among those living in poverty, with a rate nearly double their presence in the general population. They are also overrepresented among those who are uninsured and dramatically overrepresented among those who are incarcerated (The Sentencing Project, 2016). Although Blacks are outnumbered by Non-Hispanic Whites by approximately 5:1 in the general population, the ratio reverses among the prison population, where Blacks outnumber whites by approximately the same 5:1 ratio (Nellis, 2016). And although Blacks receive high school degrees at rates only slightly lower than Non-Hispanic Whites and Asians, they received Bachelor's and other advanced degrees at much lower rates.

In the United States and many other countries, men are expected to be the primary (or only) wage earner. Although they achieved emancipation from slavery in the nineteenth century, Black men's access to economic opportunities have been limited by laws, customs, discriminatory hiring practices, and lower quality education. In the late 1800s, many Black people found subsistence living in the exploitive system of share cropping. Even these jobs became untenable following the dramatic improvement of farm technology in the 1940s. As a result, many African Americans migrated from the rural south to northern cities to seek work in industry. This was the largest internal migration in United States history, and 81 percent of African Americans continue to live in large urban areas (Hines & Boyd-Franklin, 2005). The availability of industrial work decreased as the United States moved to post-industrial economies, creating high unemployment and underemployment among African Americans (Lemann, 1991; Wilson, 1987). Individualistic explanations of problems in these communities (i.e., that African Americans are not as bright, hard-working, or ambitious as everyone else) are victim-blaming rationalizations that ignore the centuries-long history of racism in the United States (Wilson, 1987). These systemic denials contribute to the Cycle of Poverty described in Box 2.1.

This widespread and persistent lack of access to economic success, and thus an inability to demonstrate masculinity through economic means, stands in dramatic contrast to White masculinity, where boys often grow up with the social message that "power and control are their birthright" (Lee, 1990, p. 126). Given the challenges in establishing themselves via work and career, and thus their difficulty establishing themselves as breadwinners, is it any wonder why many young black men are resentful toward and angry at the broader American culture?

Researcher Wizdom Hammond and her colleagues have argued that the stress of being a Black man in the United States is also a component of Black masculinity. Fear of being accused of a crime and not receiving a fair trial, or being killed by a police officer in the process of being stopped or arrested (Hall et al., 2016), would clearly seem to be a source of perpetual stress. Stress is linked with poorer physical health in a variety of ways, such as hypertension. At the same time, many African Americans mistrust the medical system due to a series of racist events, including allowing Black men to experience the worst effects of syphilis despite knowledge that a cure existed (aka the "Tuskeegee Syphilis study"), and the uncredited and unpaid use of Henrietta Lacks' blood across decades of medical research. Thus, it should be of little surprise that Black men (and women) are less likely than White men (and women) to seek medical help and less likely to follow doctor's orders, and thus die at higher rates of these diseases (Hammond et al., 2016). We return to this issue during our discussion of physical health in Chapter Fourteen.

In the United States, stereotypes of Black men often describe them as athletic, violent, criminals, unintelligent, and lazy. Among the 15 most common characteristics of Black men, "athletic" was the only characteristic that could be described as positive (Ghavami & Peplau, 2013). Black men have often been portrayed as hypersexual and as a threat to White women, a rationale that was

> **Box 2.1**
> **The Cycle of Poverty**
>
> *Poverty* refers to an individual or family with a very low income; in 2015, the United States federal government defined this rate as $24,257 for a family of two adults with two children (Proctor et al., 2016), equivalent to a single individual earning approximately $12/hour, working forty hours per week for fifty weeks out of the year. Imagine two children, one growing up in a family living in poverty and the other growing up in a middle-class family with at the median income of $56,516. Because better schools tend to be found in better neighborhoods, the impoverished child receives an education that isn't quite as good as his middle-class "peer." Further, the impoverished child is much less likely to have parents who have attended (or graduated) from college, or to know anyone who has done so, while the middle class child is much more likely to have at least one adult that he knows well who graduated from college. Between schooling and access to college graduate(s), the average child growing up in poverty is much less likely to enroll in or complete college than the average middle class child. And because income is correlated with education level (Proctor et al., 2016), this means the impoverished child will probably earn less than his middle class peer. Further, because his family has fewer (and possibly no) financial resources, his family can offer much less of a "safety net" than the average middle class child experiences. The result is that the child who grows up in poverty is much more likely to live in poverty as an adult than a child who grows up in the middle class, which means that their children will also experience these kinds of differences. This pattern is referred to as the *cycle of poverty*.
>
> Financial issues aren't the only challenge. Children who grow up in poverty are at greater risk for a broad range of problems, including poorer physical health, poorer mental health, and poorer access to healthcare (Crosby, Ortega, & Stevens, 2013; Gillespie & Hurvitz, 2013; Meyer et al., 2013; Zack, 2013). Thus, the average child who grows up in poverty has to avoid or overcome more obstacles than a child who grows up in a middle class family. In this way, health, healthcare, and criminality exacerbate the cycle of poverty.

used to help rationalize slavery and, later, discriminatory laws (Ghavami & Peplau, 2013; Herbert, 2002).

Asian American Men

Asian-American men hail from a wide range of countries, spanning the Middle East (e.g., Jordan, Iraq) to the Pacific Rim (e.g., China, Japan) and the Indian subcontinent, each with its own unique history and gendered traditions (Liu, 2002). The greatest numbers hail from China, the Philippines, India, Korea, and Vietnam (Perez & Hirshman, 2009), and people who originate from these country have been the primary focus of research. Despite national and cultural differences, many Americans view Asians as indistinguishable from one another (Chan, 2004). In this section, we address the experiences of Asian-Americans; we examine cross-national differences later in the chapter.

In current day America, Asian masculinities bear some similarities to and demonstrate some differences from White masculinity. For example, breadwinning and having (high) social status remain important. However, Asian-American men are less likely to see masculinity as a central part of themselves (or even important), and they don't typically define masculinity and femininity as opposites. They are more likely than White American men to describe being polite and reliable as part of masculinity, and they typically view completing domestic tasks—housekeeping—as a form of caring for their family (Iwamoto & Kaya, 2016).

In one oft-cited study, more than 80 percent of male Asian-American undergraduates described themselves as reliable, polite, having a good sense of humor, considerate, having high income potential, ambitious, and sensitive to (others') feelings. A majority also described themselves as independent, willing to complete domestic tasks, romantic, and valuing equal gender roles (Chua & Fujino, 1999). Asian-American men's descriptions included all characteristics identified by a majority of male Asian-born students studying at the same university, and added several additional characteristics (e.g., sense of humor, romantic). Asian-American students' self-descriptions were more different than similar to the self-descriptions of White men from the same university. Similarities included being reliable, considerate, polite, and having high income potential, but White men differed from Asian-American men because the majority described themselves as physically affectionate, masculine, having a strong personality, and being sexually exciting, among other factors (Chua & Fujino, 1999).

American stereotypes of Asian men tell a different story, describing them as cunning, nasty, and violent (through martial arts for men from Pacific Rim countries and terrorism for men of Middle Eastern descent), often in ways that threaten White Americans. At the same time, they are also often presented as effeminate, submissive, doing "women's work," sexually awkward or asexual, overly competitive, lacking leadership ability, and otherwise inferior to their White counterparts (Iwamoto & Kaya, 2016; Wong, Liu, & Klann, 2016). Actor Jackie Chan's characters provide a useful illustration of racial differences on screen; unlike White "action" stars who routinely have romantic or sexual relations with women on screen, Chan almost never does (Lee, 2009).

Differences among Asian men, particularly those from Pacific nations and those from Middle Eastern nations have rarely been explored in the same study. However, when they were, striking differences were found. American undergraduates' stereotypes of men from Pacific nations—the default group of Asian Americans—were depicted as intelligent, short, nerdy, quiet, good at math, and bad drivers. This is quite different from the stereotype of Middle Eastern men, who were seen as bearded, dark-skinned, terrorists, sexist, and speaking English with an accent (Ghavami & Peplau, 2013).

Asians from Pacific rim nations and India are sometimes described as being *the model minority* because, as a group, they are hard-working, self-reliant and economically successful, as indicated by education, income, and insured rates in Table 2.1. Note that Asians outperform all other ethnic groups, including Whites, on most of these indicators (Proctor et al., 2016). Further, from the perspective of White society, Asians and Asian-Americans have been politically non-resistant, conform to "proper" work and moral values, and typically have father-headed households (Chua & Fujino, 1999). This image is consistent with mid-twentieth century conceptions of the (White) "Family man."

Yen Le Espirtu (2007) notes that there are two "distinct chains of emigration from Asia: one comprising the relatives of working-class Asians and the other of highly trained immigrants. In other words, today's Asian American men both join Whites in the well-paid, educated white collar sector of the workforce *and* join Latino immigrants in lower-paying secondary sector jobs" (p. 37). Immigrants from China, Japan, Korea, and India tend to be in the former group, with relatively high levels of education and income, wheras immigrants from Vietnam, Cambodia, and Laos—countries ravaged but not rebuilt by the United States after the war in Vietnam—tend to have relatively lower levels of education and income and may struggle to earn a living wage. Whites' inability to distinguish Asian peoples may lead to a perception of *all* Asians as relatively privileged.

United States policy has discriminated against Asians and Asian-Americans, although not as extensively as it has toward African-Americans. For example, in the late nineteenth and early twentieth century, federal immigration policy allowed for an influx of Chinese men but very few Chinese women, so many married men left their wives and children behind out of necessity (Chua & Fujino, 1999). As a result, the sex ratio in this ethnic group in 1890 was an astounding 27 males for every woman; there were similar, although not as pronounced, patterns for people from Japan, Korea, and the Philippines. That era's racism prevented Asian men from dating or marrying outside of their race, leaving heterosexual Asian men effectively desexualized; "bachelor societies" developed in a re-definition of the family. Immigration policies became gender egalitarian years later, and many Asian wives and (then adult) children emigrated to join their husbands and fathers after decades apart.

During World War II, the United States government incarcerated ("interned") more than 100,000 Japanese and Japanese Americans, In addition to undermining their dignity, the laws allowed the United States government to seize property (and money) of those interned, which effectively erased the economic gains of a generation and contributed to a pervasive sense of hopelessness. Later, many Asian men served in the war and helped to reduce prejudice against Asian peoples (Espiritu, 2008).

Latino Men

The term *Hispanic* is used by the United States government to refer to all Spanish-speaking ethnic groups, including individuals from Spain, and reflects areas of Spanish conquest and colonization. The terms *Latino, Latina,* and *Latinx* (pronounced La-teen-x, which is used instead of specifying a person's gender) refer to individuals who hail from the region known as Latin America, which extends from Mexico in North America to the southernmost tip of South America (Garcia-Preto, 2005; Perez & Hirschman, 2009). Although the terms refer to people from many of the same countries, there are not identical. People from Spain are Hispanic but not Latinx, while people from Brazil are Latinx but not Hispanic (because they were conquered by the Portuguese). Current United States government practice is to focus on Hispanics, not Latinos, and distinguish between Non-Hispanic Whites and Hispanics. In less formal parts of United States culture, the terms are often used interchangeably. Additionally, some people refer to these individuals as "Brown," providing a parallel term for Black and White. In this section, we address the experience of being Latino in the United States; we address cross-national definitions of masculinity later in the chapter.

As indicated in Table 2.1, Hispanics currently comprise the largest minority group. Federal estimates suggest that by 2060, there will be more children (under age 18) of Hispanic descent than of any other descent (although Non-Hispanic Whites will still be the most numerous group in the general population; Colby & Ortman, 2015). At present, however, Hispanics have reason for concern; they earn approximately 20 percent less than the median household, they are more likely to live in poverty, more likely to be uninsured, and have notably lower levels of educational attainment at all levels than non-White Hispanics and Asians. They are also incarcerated at a higher rate than Non-Hispanic Whites (but less frequently than Blacks).

The histories and ethnic identities of Latinos from different countries are often very different from one another. For example, many immigrants from Central America left due to war, such as the civil wars in El Salvador and Nicaragua during the 1980s, or were forcibly displaced from their homes before coming to the United States (Comas-Díaz, 1993). As a result, these immigrants often came from low socioeconomic backgrounds and had relatively little preparation for moving to the United States. In contrast, many Chilean and Cuban immigrants had made arrangements and established local support before emigrating; they also tend to have more educational advantage and higher socioeconomic status. One recent analysis of United States Census data suggests Mexico, Puerto Rico, and Cuba have produced the greatest numbers of Latinos in the United States population (Perez & Hirshman, 2009); we note that Puerto Rico is a U.S. Protectorate and thus all of its people are United States citizens.

Of particular importance for our discussion of masculinity are notions of family, *familismo, maschismo, cabillerismo, and respeto*; we do not address the female gender role, *marianismo*. For many Latinx Americans, the term family includes grandparents, parents, and their children, as well as their parents' (and possibly grandparents') brothers and sisters and their children. From a child's perspective, "family" includes grandparents, parents, aunts and uncles, and cousins. This is similar to the European-American notion of "extended" family and quite different from the narrower European-American view of family as consisting of parents and children, and possibly the parents' parents (or the child's grandparents). This perspective on family is part of the reason why Latinx-American children often grow up in very close contact with many different members of their family, which may also make it harder to move away from the family when choosing a college or starting a career.

Familismo refers to loyalty, commitment, and dedication to the family, typically manifested by supporting, protecting, and providing for the family. Men who are unable to fulfill this aspect of Latino life often see themselves as unmanly (Ojeda & Organista, 2016). Familismo can also lead men into a behavior that may appear paradoxical: emigrating to another country where employment opportunities are better as a form of providing, although it requires leaving their family.

Personalismo refers to valuing the person-oriented dimensions of a relationship over the task-oriented dimensions of that relationship. This principal prioritizes the interpersonal relationship, thus emphasizing connection between individuals and diminishing the desire for a more distant "buddy" type relationship. *Personalismo* leads Latino men to routinely and automatically ask about their male friends' families because that is a part of their well-being (Ojeda & Organista, 2016).

Simpatía refers to the prescription for pleasant, non-conflictual interactions that include social agreeableness, modesty, and consideration of other people's needs. This involves tolerating and ignoring minor disagreements so they do not to interfere with the overall quality of the relationship or become the focus of extended disagreement (Ojeda & Organista, 2016).

Respeto is defined as demonstrating respect and deference to those of higher status, where higher status is the result of older age, professional role, or being male (vs. female). The male-female dimension reflects a patriarchal history but does not necessarily mean that women have little or no say, with substantial variation from one country to the next and one family to the next (Ojeda & Organista, 2016).

Machismo and caballerismo both contain elements also found in hegemonic White masculinity. In translation to the United States, *machismo* has come to reflect negative aspects of the male role such as sexism, chauvinism, and violence. *Caballerismo* is roughly parallel to the concept of chivalry (which we'll discuss in Chapter Three), with a focus on proper and respectful manners, following an ethical code, humility, and righting wrongs (Arciniega, Anderson, Tovar-Blank, & Tracey, 2008; Ojeda & Organista, 2016.) In one study of Mexican Americans, men provided strong endorsement of *caballerismo* but only moderate support for *machismo* (Arciniega et al., 2008).

The dominant stereotype of Latinos depicts them as macho, poor, dark-skinned, day laborers who may also be promiscuous and short. Of the 15 most common descriptors offered, hard-working was the only positive (Ghavami & Peplau, 2013). This stereotype is clearly different from the principles of Latino life described above, and would seem to reflect an uncritical acceptance of the population statistics provided in Table 2.1 combined with mass media portrayals of Latinos as drug-dealing criminals.

Social Class

We now shift away from race and ethnicity as markers of masculinities and focus on distinctions related to social class. **Social class**, or simply "class," refers to the individual's sense of place on society's social ladder, using terms such as poor, working class, middle class, upper middle class, or rich. The terms refer to sets of beliefs and values related to formal education, materialism-consumption, freedoms-lifestyle, etiquette, and language (Liu, 2016). Social scientists often use the term **socio-economic status (SES)** and measure it by asking about income or education levels, which provide a rough approximation of social class (Liu, 2016).

In the United States, *working class* or *"blue collar" masculinity* is characterized by several components, including physical labor, strength, toughness, working with one's hands, and lower levels of education (i.e., less than a college degree), while also embracing a certain amount of countercultural anti-establishment sentiment that includes violating minor laws (i.e., misdemeanors) and social norms (e.g., bad manners) (Carroll, 2011; Connell, 1995; Lefkowitz, 1997; Liu, 2016). Nationalism, or patriotism, is also a component (Carroll, 2011). This is typically compared to a *professional class* or *"white collar" masculinity* that is part of the hegemonic norm. White collar masculinity is characterized by "brains" (not brawn), good manners, the use of proper grammar, and the completion of a bachelor's degree (or more). White collar employment is associated with professional and managerial positions, sometimes referred to colloquially as "desk jobs." Individuals with higher levels of education typically offer lower levels of endorsement of "traditional" gender roles and greater endorsement of egalitarian gender roles (e.g., Levant & Richmond, 2007). The terms "blue collar" and "white collar" seem to have originated in the mid-twentieth century and were also accompanied by "pink collar" jobs such as receptionist and secretary that were typically held by women. Hamilton Carroll (2011) notes that men may adopt the norms and identity of a social class without necessarily experiencing its wages. He points to a range of professional sports teams, including several iterations of the Super Bowl champion New England Patriots, who presented themselves as having a working class ethos despite that fact that almost all players (and most coaches) earned in excess of one million dollars that season.

Living in poverty is characterized by more than just a very low income. As described earlier, the United States Federal government defined the poverty rate as $24,257 for a family of two adults with two children (in 2015; Proctor et al., 2016). Federal statistics indicate that there were 43.1 million Americans living in poverty in 2015, approximately 13.5 percent of the population, with fewer impoverished men than women. Individuals with lower levels of education, especially those who did not complete high school or obtain a GED, are more likely to be living in poverty (Proctor et al., 2016). The experience of poverty varies depending on where an individual lives. Poor individuals who reside in metropolitan areas often find themselves living in neighborhoods that have high crime rates, which often means relatively fewer businesses (due to fear of theft). These neighborhoods often also include high levels of pollution, a high population density (i.e., mostly apartments) with minimal green space, and relatively poorer schools. Impoverished Blacks and Hispanics are overrepresented as residents of these neighborhoods. By contrast, poor individuals who live in rural areas may also find themselves living in areas with relatively few businesses, but often without the other negatives found in impoverished metropolitan neighborhoods. Impoverished Whites are overrepresented in these areas.

In the United States, masculinity is explicitly and tightly bound to social class via directives to be the primary breadwinner. Reviewing the literature, William Liu (2016) observed that men who struggle to find good-paying full time employment typically report feeling stressed about their difficulty providing financially for their family and may feel unmanly. As we discussed earlier in the chapter, generations of Black men have faced substantial challenges in finding and maintaining employment. This has also been true for other non-White groups, although not as persistently or severely throughout American history. (We review men's experiences and challenge in the workplace in Chapter Eleven.)

Having insufficient finances due to insufficient employment can lead some men to see themselves as powerless, at least in comparison to other men (Connell, 1995). Friends, family members, potential romantic and sexual partners, and others may also view them this way (e.g., Ehrenreich, 1983; Schmitt, 2005). These "underpowered" men may find that one way to "resolve this contradiction is a spectacular display, embracing the marginality and stigma and turning them to account. At the personal level, this translates as a constant concern with front or credibility." (Connell, 1995, p. 116). Physical strength, interpersonal dominance and violence, masculine posturing, misogyny, and even family violence may all be used in the individual's efforts to (re)gain social power (Connell, 1995; Ehrenreich, 1983; Gelles, 1997). In essence, these men rely on the negative aspects of masculinity as a defense against powerlessness. We note that these strategies appear at all class and income levels, but are more common among low income than middle income men. The specific strategies employed—if any—are the result of the ways that economic conditions interact with individual psychology and other social forces.

Sexual Orientation

And finally, we turn to sexual orientation and focus specifically on what it means to be a gay man. In this section, we address gay men's experiences and their definitions of masculinity. Generally speaking, male homosexuality has typically been seen as a violation of masculine directives to not be effeminate; some scholars refer to these anti-homosexuality norms as "anti-femininity's vicious little brother" because of the way they are used to police masculinity and oppress gay men. We describe ways this has been manifest in the United States public sphere in Chapter Three. Before continuing with our discussion of the person-level experience of gay men, it is important to note that research on gay men has focused extensively on HIV and AIDS, sexuality (especially as related to disease prevention), and body image, with notably less attention to other issues (Parent & Broadstreet, 2017; Sanchez, 2016). Because the research on individuals who are bisexual is even smaller than that of gay men, we do not address this population in the text.

What does it mean to be a gay man? Throughout the twentieth century, the dominant stereotype of gay men described them as effeminate, having a thin or slight build (as opposed to being "built" and muscular), enjoying Broadway musicals, interested in fashion and thus well-groomed, and not interested in sports (Madon, 1997). The reality is that gay men's lives and interests vary as widely as do straight men's, with many demonstrating little resemblance to this stereotype. Gay men are also perceived as hypersexual, with a high sex drive. Although gay male culture does include a highly visible sexual component, not all gay men participate in this component of the culture (Savin-Williams, 2005; Shilts, 1987/2007). At the population level, gay men are more likely to report physical and mental health problems than straight men, with the rate of physical problems elevated in part due to relatively higher levels of HIV and AIDS in the gay community, although the disparities have become smaller over the last few decades (Parent & Broadstreet, 2017; Sanchez, 2016). We address HIV and AIDS in more detail in Chapter 13.

It is important to note that identifying as a non-heterosexual man is not wholly dependent on sexual behavior per se. The term **men who have sex with men** (sometimes abbreviated MSM) is being increasingly used to acknowledge that, in addition to gay and bisexual men, some heterosexually identified men engage in homosexual sex and thus must be included in relevant research and outreach programs. In the African-American community, men who do this, usually in secret, are described as being "on the Down Low" (King & Hunter, 2004). We discuss male sexuality in more detail in Chapter 10.

Non-heterosexually identified men are not immune to the social pressures of mainstream cultural masculinity, and they must find solutions to the contradictions of these pressures and their sexualities (Szymanski, Kashubeck-West, & Meyer, 2008). Although some non-heterosexual men have traditionally masculine characteristics, they are more likely than heterosexual men to consider and adopt a broader range of gendered behavior (Heyl, 1996). It is possible that an awareness of being different frees an individual to consider more than the usual options, and to develop a sense of identity by clarifying and affirming what he is not, i.e., a masculine man as defined by the society (Herek, 1985). As heterosexual men may affirm their in-group identities by contrasting themselves with the out-group of men of other sexualities, a parallel process may take place with regard to the gendered behaviors of members of the outgroup. In other words, the statement of what one is may begin with a statement of what one *is not*.

Attitudes and laws regarding homosexuality have shifted dramatically in the United States over the last century, as we'll discuss in Chapter Three, which means that generations of gay men have had different experiences in their formative years. This timespan has also seen an increase in the number and size of gay communities and neighborhoods within some larger cities, providing the gay community with bars and restaurants, as well as service professionals (doctors, lawyers) and retailers who cater to their styles and specific needs. These changes have contributed to very different formative experiences for recent generations of gay men (Levine, 1991). The increasing openness, awareness, and acceptance of gay life has changed gay men's willingness to "come out" as well as their experience of shame regarding their sexual orientation. However, it is important to note that gay men who came of age between 1900 and 1940 (to whom we will refer as the "first cohort") often passed through adulthood without ever *coming out*, defined as informing others of one's sexual orientation. Many remained closeted for their entire lives (Herdt & Boxer, 1991).

Those who came of age between 1940 and 1969 (the "second cohort"), a period marked by the United States' participation in World War II and the Korean War, and ending with the Stonewall Riot, often came to awareness and fulfillment of their same-sex erotic desires while serving in the armed forces. The *Mattachine Society*, an underground network of gay men, was founded in the 1950s and provided a new level of community, as did the emergence of gay bars in the 1960s (Herdt & Boxer, 1991). Still, gay communities largely remained secretive, and partly as a result, many men experienced their sexualities in negative terms (Levine, 1991). The hiding of such an important part of the self is often associated with feelings of shame.

Gay Pride Day marks the June anniversary of the *Stonewall Riot*, which ushered in a new age of coming out and political activism. The riot began when the police entered the Stonewall Inn in the early morning hours of June 28, 1969, to harass those in the bar; unlike prior events, the gay men in the bar resisted arrest and the event started a series of protests over the next several days. Men in the third, post-Stonewall cohort felt more free to express themselves in gay-affirmative ways, and gay neighborhoods like Greenwich Village in New York and The Castro in San Francisco grew in size and visibility. There was mass coming out and an ethic of "free love" and recreational sex (Herdt & Boxer, 1991). This cohort was relatively short, lasting from approximately 1969 to the early days of the 1980s.

The next cohort came of age in the early 1980s during the early days of the AIDS epidemic. The disease was originally named Gay-Related Immune Disorder (GRID) because the vast majority of the early cases were among gay men. By the mid-1980s, the disease was known by its medically accurate name, Acquired Immune Deficiency Syndrome (AIDS), and understood to be the result of harm caused by the Human Immunodeficiency Virus (HIV).

The AIDS epidemic brought radical changes in sexual behaviors and lifestyles. Whereas the gay male community had been known for its promotion of anonymous and non-monogamous sexuality during the prior decade, it began to emphasize long-term couples and monogamy (Levine, 1991; Shilts, 1987/2007). At the same time, gay communities began to make concerted efforts to support young gay men in the process of coming out. The sieges of AIDS and homophobic backlash appear to have brought the gay community together, and gay life was increasingly marked by a service orientation to the rest of the community and a renewed political activism that fought for access to health care, social services, and better access to ill partners who were hospitalized (Pharr, 1997a; Shilts, 1987/2007). Because it was difficult to hide the diseases, or the psychological effects of caring for and burying those suffering from AIDS, it was very difficult for HIV-positive gay men to remain closeted and thus many people learned that friends and family members were gay. Some scholars argue that greater acceptance of homosexuality is at least partly due to the number of people who came out during this era (Pharr, 1997a).

Gay men who have come of age since 2000 have grown up in an era where being gay is accepted by the majority of their peers (and most adults), coming out during adolescence is fairly common, a large number of successful and easily recognizable figures from the entertainment world are openly gay, and media portrayals of gay men have become both more common and less bound by the dominant stereotype (Savin-Williams, 2005). In addition, access to employer-based spousal benefits and legal protections from discrimination are not unusual, although they are not necessarily available in all parts of the United States. This experience is strikingly different than the experience gay men experienced 50 or 100 years earlier.

MASCULINITY AROUND THE GLOBE

Thus far, we have discussed ways that the definition of masculinity changes within United States culture based on ethnicity, social class, and sexual orientation. Next, we consider ways in which cultures define masculinity differently, and thus have different versions of hegemonic masculinity, a concept described as ***cultural relativism***. We will not provide an exhaustive review of all of the ways in which masculinity is defined across time and place—to do so would require several volumes. Keep in mind that these cultural forces exert pressure on men to behave and experience themselves in certain ways, but that the reactions of individual men to this pressure are widely variable. Consider the following:

- Anthropologist Margaret Mead (1935) described three tribes she observed in New Guinea. According to Mead, the Mundugumor tribe was characterized by aggressive behavior in both men and women. The Arapesh tribe valued non-aggression for both sexes. The Tchambuli expected females to be aggressive and males to be passive, the opposite of most Western cultures.

- Tahitian men are no more aggressive than women, do not appear to feel pressured to appear different than women, and have no fear of acting in ways that Westerners would characterize as effeminate. For example, men will dance together in ways that include close bodily contact and rubbing together, without demonstrating any anxiety (Gilmore, 1990).
- In much of the Middle East and South America, men express their emotions as freely as women. There is a great deal of cultural variation in the gendered expression of emotion, with some cultures considering women to be the "emotional sex," some allowing wide latitude for expression in both sexes, and some expecting both men and women to control their emotions (Wade & Tavris, 2008).
- The culture of Truk Island (in the south Pacific) is marked by heavy drinking and brawling among men; the Trukese consider fighting to be sexy (Gilmore, 1990).
- The kinds of employment that are considered "women's work" and "men's work" vary to a significant degree from culture to culture (Wade & Tavris, 2008). For example, in Greek or Indian restaurants, seating customers and waiting on tables are considered men's work. In Polish and Ethiopian eateries, women perform these functions (Rybarczyk, 1994).
- The Samburu (East Africa) stress the element of generosity in masculinity (Gilmore, 1990).

Perhaps the most important and ambitious anthropological work on men and gender is David Gilmore's (1990) *Manhood in the Making*. Gilmore studied many cultures around the world and described important commonalities and differences in social conceptions of masculinity. He found a "family resemblance" in masculinities for most (but not all) of the world. In the majority of the cultures Gilmore studied, masculinity was characterized by strength, risk taking, avoidance of femininity, aggression, and sexual initiative. These findings mirror the hegemonic American definition, as do results from other multi-national studies (Adler, 1993; Williams & Best, 1990a).

Gilmore also noted that, in most of the world, masculinity is regarded as an achievement—something that the culture must build into males through various socialization processes (hence the title of his book). The dominant conception is that men do not become masculine simply by growing into adulthood. Instead, they must endure **a *rite of passage*** defined as some sort of trial by which they prove their adult male status. For boys, these rites typically involve considerable individual effort, considerable physical pain, or both; some examples are provided in Box 2.2. Many rites explicitly focus on separation from mother in particular or women/femininity in general. Observing that rites of passage are fairly common for boys and extremely rare for girls, anthropologist Gilbert Herdt suggested that "Femininity unfolds naturally, whereas masculinity must be achieved, and here is where the male ritual cult

> **Box 2.2**
> **Male Initiation Rituals**
>
> *Following are some rites of passage described by Gilmore (1990):*
>
> Samburu (East Africa): Adolescent boys are subjected to "bloody circumcision rites" to which they "must submit without so much as flinching under the agony of the knife. If a boy cries out while his flesh is being cut, if he so much as blinks an eye or turns his head, he is shamed for life as unworthy of manhood, and his entire lineage is shamed as a nursery of weaklings" (p. 13). The cutting may last four minutes or more.
>
> The New Guinea highlands: Boys must endure "whipping, flailing, beating, and other forms of terrorization by older men" (p. 14).
>
> Tewa (indigenous peoples of New Mexico): Boys are taken away from their homes, undergo ritual purification, and are beaten by Kachina spirits (their fathers in disguise). The stiff yucca whip causes bleeding and leaves permanent scars.
>
> Sambia (New Guinea): In addition to physical beating, boys undergo a blood-letting ritual in which "stiff, sharp grasses are thrust up the nostrils until the blood flows copiously" (p. 156).

steps in." (Herdt, 1982, p. 55). Across most if not all of these rituals, whether physically painful or not, is the idea that childhood is left behind; many rituals involve the symbolic death of the boy as a part of the birth of the man (Gilmore, 1990; Raphael, 1988). Recall that we briefly discussed American men's need to prove their masculinity in Chapter 1.

By focusing on the activities that boys are expected to complete during their rites of passage, researchers draw conclusions about that culture's definition of masculinity, or at least male adulthood. The examples in Box 2.2 suggest that many cultures have evolved social processes that dissuade men from their natural inclinations to avoid pain and express their feelings. Defining adult manhood (or masculinity) in such terms suggests that men fulfill specific functions within social groups and that emotional or physical vulnerability are often viewed as being incompatible with these functions.

Social psychologists often view members' maintenance of initiation rites in the context of *cognitive dissonance*, the tendency to have one's behavior match one's values and attitudes (Aronson, 2012). When a person conforms his or her behavior to extreme demands, he or she is then motivated to endorse the values and attitudes that are connected with these demands. In other words, if I endure a hardship, it is vital to my sense of self to believe that the outcome was worth the pain; otherwise I am a fool. Cognitive dissonance explains the intense loyalty to a group that many people exhibit when they have gone to great lengths to become a part of that group and also the willingness to do harmful acts to justify one's beliefs (Tavris & Aronson, 2008).

The ubiquity of initiation rites also helps understand the experiences of those who don't conform to gender norms. (Recall your experience with Box 1.2: Male Gender Role Violations.) Anthropologist Margaret Mead (1949) noted that these "misfits"—people who do not fit their culture's expectations—were not treated very well by the rest of the society, regardless of that society's definition of masculinity.

Cross-national studies have demonstrated a range of similarities, although sometimes as a matter of degree instead of as a matter of type. For example, one research team asked participants how important each of nine different components of masculinity were. Their sample consisted of between 1,500 and 9,300 men aged 20 to 75 in each of eight countries from the Americas and Western Europe. Their results, listed in Table 2.2, are placed in the order they were ranked by the entire sample of nearly 28,000 men. The table reveals both similarities and differences across these nations. Similarities include the consistently high ratings for "being seen as a man of honor" and "being in control of your own life" as the two highest ranked items (except in Germany), while "being physically attractive" and "having success with women" were consistently the least important factors. We also see differences in rankings. Unfortunately, the use of a survey does not allow us to examine participants' explanations of why they ranked these factors as they did. (Similarities and differences are more evident with the raw scores provided in the original article.)

These findings also reveal a problem we'll discuss in Chapter Four: researchers' definitions of masculinity matter. Here, there are no references to aspects of masculinity such as being a "family man." This list is noteworthy for its inclusion of both positive and negative aspects of masculinity; that is not always the case.

A similar study was conducted in five Asian nations, with four additional components of masculinity. In each country, the research teams surveyed approximately 1,900 to 3,000 men aged 20 to 75. Their results are in Table 2.3, in the order they were ranked by the entire sample of nearly 11,000 men. These results are more variable, especially in the top half of the rankings. Here, no single factor is ranked number one in more than one country.

Note the relatively low ratings for "having a manly image." As we noted earlier, Asian-Americans are less likely than European-Americans to identify masculinity as part of their self image; that cultural characteristic is reflected in this chart as well.

Some scholars have argued that cultural similarities in gender roles are partly due to Western European and American military and economic conquest of other parts of the globe (Connell, 1993). Indeed, the greater level of similarities in Table 2.2 (Europe and the Americas) as compared to Table 2.3 (Asia), as well as the differences between the two tables, lends some credence to this argument. At the same time, being honorable, autonomous ("in control of your own life"), and an earner/provider ("having a good job") point to the centrality of these aspects of masculinity, regardless of where one is on the planet.

The United States and other Western nations have become more aware of and attentive to Transgender and "gender non-conforming" individuals during the 2010s. This has resulted in greater awareness of the binary notions

Table 2.2
Rankings of Aspects of Masculinity Across American and European Nations

	All	Mexico	Brazil	U.K.	Germany	France	Italy	Spain
Being seen as a man of honor	#1	#1	#1	#2	#5	#1	#2	#1
Being in control of your own life	#2	#2	#2	#1	#1	#2	#1	#2
Having the respect of friends	#3	#4	#4	#3	#3	#3	#3	#3
Having a good job	#4	#3	#3	#4	#2	#5	#4	#4
Coping with problems on your own	#5	#5	#7	#6	#4	#4	#5	#6
Having an active sex life	#6	#6	#5	#7	#6	#6	#6	#5
Having financial stability	#7	#7	#7	#6	#5	#7	#7	#7
Being physically attractive	#8	#9	#9	#8	#8	#9	#8	#9

Table 2.3
Rankings of Aspects of Masculinity Across Asian Nations

	China	Japan	Korea	Maylasia	Taiwan
Having a good job	#2	#2	#5	#1	#3
Being seen as a man of honor	#3	#1	#7	#4	#2
Being in control of your own life	#4	#3	#2	#5	#1
Being a family man*	#5	#4	#1	#2	#7
Having lots of money	#1	#6	#4	#3	#4
Coping with problems on your own	#7	#5	#6	#7	#5
Having the respect of friends	#6	#7	#8	#6	#6
Having success with women	#9	#10	#3	#13	#8
Having an outgoing personality*	#8	#8	#11	#8	#9
Having a manly image	#10	#9	#9	#10	#12
Avoiding shameful situations	#11	#11	#12	#9	#10
Having an active sex life	#13	#12	#10	#11	#11
Being physically attractive	#12	#13	#13	#12	#13

of male-or-female, masculine-or-feminine. Although much of Western culture has virtually ignored individuals who don't fit the two-category systems, some other cultures have extensive norms for dealing with them. One frequently cited example is the North American Indian *berdache*, an anatomical male who behaves much like most of the females of the tribe. These people are not considered to be deviant males and they are not scorned or shamed for their behaviors. Thus, we cannot use Mead's term and consider them gender misfits. Instead, *berdache* is a third gender within the tribe (Williams, 1996). Several other cultures also have more than two genders, often called *third genders*. Examples include, the *hijiras* of northern India, the *xaniths* of Oman, and the *nadle, alyha,* and *hwame* of the Mohave Indians, all of whom fulfill culturally approved social and sexual roles apart from the usual masculine and feminine genders (Doyle & Paludi, 1998; Herdt, 1994, 2004). Although only a minority of cultures have more than two genders, they provide an expanded view of the possibilities.

SUMMARY

1. As we can see from these examples, definitions of masculinity vary within American culture based on race/ethnicity, social class, and sexual orientation, and definitions of masculinity also vary from one nation to the next. This indicates that gender roles—or masculinity, at least—is not constant across historical eras, within or across cultures, or even across contexts and situations. Instead, it is influenced by a variety of factors, including ethnic patterns, economic conditions, religion, language, family socialization, cultural expectations, and the spirit of the times. Further, we note that many males who are members of a specific group will not conform to that (sub-)group's norms.

2. Within the context of United States culture, men have always lived in a world where their ways of being are privileged over those of most others, although our discussion revealed that groups of men vary in their access to those privileges. Summarizing issues related to privilege, sociologist Michael Kimmel (1994) observed that "Men's experience of powerlessness is *real*—the men actually feel it and certainly act on it—but it is not *true*, that is, it does not actually describe their condition" (p. 137). Thus, being in the privileged group is no guarantee of individual happiness or fulfillment (Johnson, 2001).

3. In Chapter One, we introduced the essentialism vs. social constructionism debate. Essentialists tend to highlight the similarities found across cultures, such as the prominence of being a breadwinner and the lack of attention to male physical attractiveness, and deduce that such similarities are *primarily* due to biology, possibly as the result of evolutionary pressures (e.g. Barash & Lipton, 1997). Social constructionists tend to highlight the variations, pointing to ways that being honorable or a fam-

ily man vary across cultures, and searching for factors in the local setting that are likely to have produced these different points of emphasis. We note that neither side in this debate believes gender roles are due solely to biological or cultural factors, but rather which "side" has the bigger impact and what the magnitude of that impact is.

4. Large cultures have a range of versions of masculinity that can be ranked by their similarity to the cultural ideal, which is called hegemonic masculinity and receives the greatest level of cultural power.
5. Complicit and marginalized masculinities have some, or none, of the same components, support the status quo, and receive less cultural power. Subordinated masculinities typically challenge the hegemonic definition and are often persecuted.
6. Racial and ethnic minority groups within the United States have experienced discriminatory laws and practices that have largely prevented members of those groups from achieving all aspects of hegemonic masculinity, and thus they have not received the same amount of cultural power as White men.
7. Asian and Hispanic cultures have some expectations of men rooted in their native cultures that are different from the White hegemonic form.
8. "Working class" and "professional" men espouse and enact versions of masculinity that are somewhat different from each other. Some, but not all, of these differences are related to differences in earning power.
9. In the United States, masculinity has long been defined as heterosexual. This has deprived gay men of some aspects of privilege while also serving as a mechanism for persecution.
10. Many cultures require boys to endure a rite of passage to be formally recognized as a man, and thus "earn" the responsibilities and privileges of being recognized as an adult.
11. Members of different cultures may rate a single aspect of masculinity as having a similar level of importance, or they may see that aspect of masculinity quite differently.

GLOSSARY

Masculinities: The idea that different forms of masculinity co-exist within a single culture and across different cultures, and that multiple masculinities within a single culture have different amounts of cultural power. **Acculturation:** the adaptations made to a "new" culture due to prolonged interaction with that culture.

Hegemonic masculinity: A culture's idealized form of masculinity.

Complicit masculinities: Forms of masculinity that possess many, but not all, attributes of the hegemonic form and support the current set of power relations.

Marginalized masculinities: Forms of masculinity that possess few or no aspects of hegemonic masculinity while also maintaining the current set of power relations.

subordinated masculinities: Forms of masculinity that offer a notably different definition of masculinity and challenge the status quo.

Intersectionality: The ways that different statuses or categorization systems, such as ethnicity and social class, may interact to influence an individual's beliefs about and enactments of gender.

Culture: The belief systems and value orientations that influence customs, norms, practices, and social institutions, including psychological processes.

Ethnicity: The acceptance of the group mores and practices of one's culture of origin and the concomitant sense of belonging.

Institutional racism: Racist laws, practices, and customs that enforce the superiority of one race over another.

Acculturation: The adaptations made to a "new" culture due to prolonged interaction with that culture.

Overrepresented: When a group accounts for a notably higher percentage of people in a specific category than they do in the general population.

Underrepresented: When a group accounts for a notably lower percentage of people in a specific category than they do in the general population.

cool pose: A form of Black masculinity defined by a set of ritualized behaviors that involve toughness, detachment, control, and a stylish, sometimes flamboyant presentation.

Poverty: To an individual or family with a very low income.

The model minority: A stereotyping description of Asian-Americans as successful due to hard work and self-reliance.

Familismo: Loyalty, commitment, and dedication to the family, typically manifested by supporting, protecting, and providing for the family.

Personalismo: Valuing the person-oriented dimensions of a relationship over the task-oriented dimensions of that relationship.

Simpatía: The prescription for pleasant, non-conflictual interactions that include social agreeableness, modesty, and consideration of other people's needs.

Respeto: Demonstrating respect and deference to those of higher status, where higher status is the result of older age, professional role, or being male (vs. female).

Social class: The individual's sense of place on society's social ladder, using terms such as poor, working class, middle class, upper middle class, or rich.

Socio-Economic Status (SES): A rough approximation of social class.

Blue collar or **working class masculinity:** A form of masculinity characterized by physical labor, strength, toughness, working with one's hands, and lower levels of education (i.e., less than a college degree), while also embracing a certain amount of countercultural anti-establishment sentiment that includes violating minor laws (i.e., misdemeanors) and social norms (e.g., bad manners).

White collar or professional class masculinity: A form of masculinity characterized by physical labor, strength, toughness, working with one's hands, and lower levels of education (i.e., less than a college degree), while also embracing a certain amount of countercultural anti-establishment sentiment that includes violating minor laws (i.e., misdemeanors) and social norms (e.g., bad manners).

Men who have sex with men (MSM): A term that includes any male who has sex with other males, regardless of their label as gay, straight, bisexual, or another term.

Coming out: Informing others of one's sexual orientation. Use of this term has expanded to include the experience of telling others of any minority status or disease that may not be evident.

Mattachine Society: An underground network of gay men during post-World War II America.

Stonewall Riot: A series of protests in support of (and mostly by) gay men and lesbians in response to police harassment. The initial event occurred at the Stonewall Inn in the early morning hours of June 28, 1969.

cultural relativism: Ways in which cultures define concepts and constructs differently, and thus have different versions of them. Here, we refer to the ways in which definitions of hegemonic masculinity vary across cultures.

A rite of passage: A trial or ritual by which children or teens prove their adult status. Here, we refers to rites that signal the move from "boy" to "man."

Cognitive dissonance: The tendency to have one's behavior match one's values and attitudes.

Berdache: An anatomical male within some North American Indian tribes who behaves much like most of the females of the tribe.

Chapter Three

Masculinity in the Public Sphere

In the United States, people often talk about men and women as "opposite sexes" and sometimes say there's a "battle of the sexes." These notions fit comfortably within masculinity's anti-femininity and power components, which direct men to seek power over others, especially when "others" refers to people understood to be feminine or female. At the same time, there are many people who talk about boys in crisis, with some commentators going so far as to argue that there's a "war against boys" (Hoff-Sommers, 2000).

In this chapter, we address masculinity in the United States' public debates and political sphere. Within this framework, we focus specifically on masculinity's relationships with women and feminism, as well as its relationship with homosexuality, all of which are related to ideas of power. We also summarize several crises of masculinity over the last century. In Chapter Two, we discussed the idea that there are several masculinities, each of which is associated with different amounts of cultural power. Some discussions in this chapter address these differences, but others do not.

POWER

Power, defined as the ability to have the desired effect on an individual or group (Winter, 2016), is a word that occupies a central place in the world of gender studies. As Michael Kaufman (1994) stated, "In a world dominated by men, the world of men is, by definition, a world of power. That power is a structured part of the economies and systems of political and social organization; it forms part of the core of religion, family, forms of play, and intellectual life" (p. 142). Collectively, men have the vast majority of power in the forms of money, social influence, and control of the world. For instance, approximately half of the population is male, yet males are overrepresented in United States national and state level political offices; at the end of 2017, men held approximately 79 percent of the seats in the United States Senate, 80 percent of seats in the United States House of Representatives, 76 percent of state governorships, 78 percent of state senator seats, and 74 percent of state representative seats (Center for American Women in Politics, 2017). The disparity is larger among large corporations; in mid-2017, men served as chief executive officers (CEOs) at 93.6 percent of the Fortune 500 companies (an index of the 500 largest companies, based on their gross receipts and the number of people employed). Although these values demonstrate the ways that women are substantially underrepresented in these positions of power, they also represent significant improvement when compared to the same statistics thirty years ago.

As we attend to power dynamics at the national and cultural level, it is important to consider another question: why compare men and women or why compare one group of men to another? Reviewing the literature in the mid-1990s, feminist psychologist Alice Eagly (1995) suggested three primary purposes in research on *sex differences* between males and females, as this body of research was called. One was to determine whether or not differences "really" exist and how large such differences were, after examining other possible explanations such as poor measurement, consistency of findings across studies, and who serves as research participants. Another closely related goal was to identify (negative) attitudes toward a group that may help explain how such differences are created, which would allow interventions to prevent such differences from being replicated for the next generation and possibly allow remediation among current generations. Finally, researchers could also determine if people's stereotypes accurately reflected reality and if those stereotypical beliefs were amenable to change.

What are the meanings of these similarities and differences? On the one hand, it is clear that predicting an individual's behavior based on his or her biological sex is not a very fruitful enterprise, and that people should only make generalizations about the sexes with extreme caution, if at all. On the other hand, as researcher Kay Deaux (1985) pointed out, a small difference at the *midpoint* of a distribution may be accompanied by a relatively large difference at the *extremes* of the distribution. For example, although there is a very small difference between normal (average) men and women on physical aggression, there are many more highly aggressive men than there are highly aggressive women. In fact, men commit more than eight times more violent crimes than women (U.S. Department of Justice, 2008). Thus, small sex differences can have important implications when extremes of the behavior have major consequences (as is the case with violent behaviors). Clearly, however, saying that all men are aggressive is a gross inaccuracy because most are not. When differences exist, even when they are small, they give us clues to the strengths and weaknesses of each gender role and the characteristic struggles of men and women. These clues contribute to the awareness of the psychological importance of gender.

Researchers have made comparisons between males and females on a variety of dimensions. Historically, this area of research has been referred to as the study of "sex differences" rather than "sex similarities" or "sex comparisons." Research on sex differences is among the older areas of psychological study, with papers on the topic dating back as far as 1908 (Hare-Mustin & Marecek, 1990b). Some researchers define an ***alpha bias*** as the focus on male-female differences, and contrast this with ***beta bias***, the focus on studies examining similarity (Hare-Mustin & Marecek, 1990a). Ultimately, measurement of sex differences relies on a simple question: are you female or male? We'll discuss the research methodology of comparing—and not comparing—men and women in Chapter Four.

Power Structures

In discussions related to male-female differences, and elsewhere throughout the text, we employ the terms ***men-as-a-group*** (and ***women-as-a-group***) to highlight the fact that we are referring to men (and women) at a very general level, and not to specific men or relatively small groups of men (or women; Lerner, 1986). Men-as-a-group are often referred to as ***privileged***, which is defined formally as having greater and relatively easier access to societal benefits than others. In the United States, men, and especially White men, have a variety of experiences that are privileged from women's perspective. For example, men typically believe that people will take them seriously and that they can go out in public with little expectation of being followed or sexually harassed. They see people who look like them widely and positively portrayed in media (although there are exceptions), take college courses that routinely give attention to members of their sex as important historical actors (while rarely mentioning that those actors are male), and see members of their sex disproportionately represented at the highest positions in government, business, education, and other institutional structures. Less noticeable are men's experience of being paid better than women for the same work (in many settings), having their successes and failures attributed to their effort and ability but not their gender, and the "option" of working in a female-dominated profession without expectation of harassment or a lower salary than their co-workers.

One metaphor for the invisibility of privilege is flying first class on an airplane. You have a great deal more room than people in the coach class in the rear of the aircraft and are served better food, but you do not know that others are cramped and hungry unless you turn around and look at them, and then try to imagine how they feel. Privilege, however, is often based on one's relative position. That first class passenger may view individuals with access to private passenger planes as privileged, and thus see themselves as not-privileged. Peggy McIntosh (2009) describes privilege as "an invisible weightless knapsack of special provisions, assurances, tools, maps, guides, codebooks, passports, visas, clothes, compass, emergency gear, and blank checks" (p. 12).

Ted Bunch likened privilege to having an "E-Z Pass" that allows one to bypass lines of cars at toll booths. Bunch, an African American man, said that the first time he used his E-Z Pass, he thought, "this is what it's like to be a White man in America!" (Bunch & Porter, 2003).

In the United States (and some other countries), privilege is granted on the basis of gender (male), as well as race (White), sexual orientation (heterosexual), and social class (professional employment and/or wealth). Some theorists describe these four systems of categorization as *master statuses* (Rosenblum & T. M. Travis, 2003) because they typically take precedence over other systems or statuses, such as age, religious affiliation, marital status, parenthood status, or specific profession. In practice, privilege "allows" the preferred group to expect to be treated in a way that non-privileged groups must strive for, termed *entitlement*, as well as the privilege of being the default version of that category and thus *unmarked* (Rosenblum & T. M. Travis, 2003). Box 3.1 describes some of the implications of marked and unmarked statuses.

Karen Rosenblum and Toni-Michelle Travis note that "those in marked statuses appear to be operating from an 'agenda' or 'special interest,' while those in unmarked statuses can appear to be agenda-free." (2003, p. 182). Criticisms of people in unmarked statuses are more likely to refer to the individual ("He was a lousy mechanic"), conveying the assumption that the rest of the group are competent until proven otherwise. Conversely, criticism of people from marked statuses may include the assumption that the entire group is flawed ("I shouldn't have let a woman mechanic work on my car").

Patriarchy is a system in which a society confers greater levels of economic power, influence, and prestige on males-as-a-group compared to females-as-a-group. Dominance over women has been part of the definition of masculinity throughout American history, as described in Chapter One. According to his-

---

Box 3.1
The Language of "Marking"

With regard to gender, the unmarked status (e.g., "judge") presents men as the taken-for-granted norm and the marked status ("woman judge") presents women as the stigmatized exception. Nancy Bonvillain (2001) notes that many female names are derived from male names by adding endings like -a, -ette, and -ine (e.g., Alexandra, Bernadette, Josephine) as markers, and that the ending -ette is also used as a diminutive, which denotes smallness ("kitchenette," "booklet," "cigarette"). Women who advocated voting rights in the early twentieth century were termed "suffragettes." Modern feminist scholars now refer to them as "suffragists" to erase the diminutive implication.

One can see a good deal of marked and unmarked statuses in academic institutions' athletic teams. For example, the men's team is the (unmarked) "Eagles," and the woman's team is the "Lady Eagles." This naming convention leads to some fascinating biological possibilities such as the "Lady Bulls," "Lady Stallions," and "Lady Stags" because those terms often refer to uncastrated males that are used for breeding purposes. (Stags, a term for deer, also lends its name to all male events such as "stag parties.") These titles convey a secondary status for girls' and women's athletics.

torian Gerda Lerner (1986), patriarchy has existed in most parts of the world for more than 5,000 years. It is expressed in the typical behaviors that people believe are appropriate for males and females, in the dominant values of the culture, in social customs and economic arrangements, and in what Lerner terms "leading metaphors, which become part of the cultural construct and explanatory system." (p. 212). For example, many theologies are constructed around male gods and female subservience, which, by extension, privileges male experience over female experience in the collective consciousness of the culture. In many places (including the United States well into the twentieth century), male-centered ideologies have been used to justify the exclusion of women from educational opportunities, owning property, voting, or having legal recourse if their husbands rape them. Although laws in many parts of the world prohibit discrimination against women, the persistence of patriarchal ideologies and traditions continues to bestow on men a disproportionate amount of social power and privilege.

Many historians and anthropologists believe that patriarchy evolved in reaction to societies' economic needs. In her landmark book, *The Creation of Patriarchy*, Gerda Lerner (1986) argued that male domination of women was largely embedded in the development of agriculture. Prior to the Neolithic period, humans lived in hunter/gatherer societies that were largely nomadic. In these foraging societies, children were not the economic resource that they later became. Their existence meant that there were more mouths to feed on a daily basis, and children only became valuable if they could develop to a point where they could produce more food than they consumed. Because it was difficult for people in these societies to accumulate surpluses of food or to stay in one place, children stretched resources and inhibited mobility. Accordingly, hunter/gatherer societies were relatively gender-egalitarian, as women, who often did more gathering than men, produced more than their share of the wealth (food).

The character of work and survival changed radically with the development of the ability to cultivate crops and maintain food surpluses. At that point, children became a labor resource, and having lots of them meant that a family or social group could till more land and thus have a much better chance of accumulating wealth. The relative burden of moving the children to more plentiful sources of food fell away, as groups could stay in the same places for generations. Land also became a valuable resource to be defended. With the advent of agriculture, women became most valuable for producing children, and similarly to land, they became a resource to acquire. The society then had an interest in controlling women's reproductive capacities, and, by extension, their sexuality. The means of *production* for women became the means of *reproduction*. Relatively recent changes that allow women to control reproduction (e.g., contraceptives), as well as the shift from an industrial workplace to a service and knowledge workplace, have altered these dynamics. We address this topic in more detail when we discuss cultural factors on the development of masculinity in Chapter Six and when we discuss Work in Chapter Eleven.

Power over Women

Being dominant over women has been part of the definition of masculinity throughout American history, as described in Chapter One. At times, the justification relied on beliefs about the "natural order," which suggests a framework rooted in essentialism. Given that many nations, including the United States, have long included and highlighted this power differential, it is hardly surprising that we often and easily think about differences between boys and girls, men and women. Indeed, American children sometimes spontaneously sort themselves into gender-based groups to compete against each other (Hilliard & Liben, 2010; Thorne, 1993). At the cultural level, we often refer to male–female competition as the "battle of the sexes" despite the fact that most people have friends, date, have sex with, and marry people on the other side of the "battle." In this section, we examine some implications of seeing these two groups as being in competition or combat, or viewed as "opposites."

The term "opposite sex" communicates that male and female are not only different, they are contrary and opposites, an idea that has received only partial support (Constantinople, 1973). As discussed in Chapter One, masculinity is defined in part by the antifemininity principle, although femininity does not have a similar anti-masculinity principle (Levant, Richmond, Cook, House, & Aupont, 2007) This view of the sexes is analogous to acids and bases—adding acid to a base makes the substance more acidic, and vice versa. A more modern view would conceptualize the sexes as different but not opposite, like salt and pepper or Android and iOS operating systems. In this view, we would be more accurate to use the term "other sex." Humans have 46 chromosomes; only one is different between the sexes. In fact, males and females share 99.8 percent of their genetic material (Eliot, 2009). Even reproductive roles are not opposite; they are complementary. We would not describe impregnation as the opposite of gestation, or, to use a basic parallel to genitalia, a bolt as the opposite of a nut or an arm the opposite of a sleeve.

SEXISM

Sexism is defined as a form of prejudice that leads to a range of negative outcomes for women and may occur at both the individual and societal levels (Schwartz, McDermott, & Martino-Harms, 2016). In effect, sexism is the mechanism that privileges men-as-a-group in comparison to women-as-a-group. Researchers have identified several different forms of sexism. Systemic sexism describes large-scale policies, customs, and practices that privilege men and disadvantage women. Examples include the legal ability to fire women from their jobs because they became pregnant, the practice of paying people different wages based on their gender, and the refusal to admit female students to many colleges and universities prior to the 1970s. In one of the more dramatic examples, American women were encouraged to seek employment in manufacturing jobs—including the production of military equipment and munitions—while men were overseas fighting World War II, and then expected to leave the workplace when the men came home (French & Poska, 2006). These institutional practices, legal at the time, illustrate ways in which patriarchy may be thought of as large scale or "macro-level" sexism.

Individual people can also hold sexist beliefs and researchers have identified several types of sexism that function at the level of the individual. In an impressive program of research undertaken with more than 15,000 people in 19 countries, Peter Glick and Susan Fiske (2001) demonstrated that an individual's sexism can take two different but related forms. **Hostile Sexism**, the hatred of women, is the kind of sexism that springs to mind when one thinks of prejudicial attitudes toward women. However, overall attitudes toward women within a population are usually quite positive and often highlight women's ability to be nice, caring, and nurturing (Glick, 2005; Steinberg & Dickman, 2016). Glick and Fiske (2001) called this the "women are wonderful" effect, and also noted that it is typically accompanied by beliefs that women need men's protection, help, and financial support; in effect, it assumes women are incompetent to make "serious" or "important" decisions on their own. They called this set of beliefs **Benevolent Sexism** and criticized it for rewarding women's cooperation in a system that denies them significant resources while reducing their resistance to this inequality. Thus, it allows men to "maintain a positive self-image as protectors and providers who are willing to sacrifice their own needs to care for the women in their lives... [and] promises that men's power will be used to women's advantage, if only [women] can secure a high-status male protector" (p. 111).

Other aspects of sexism include *interpersonal sexism*, which refers to sexist behavior in social contexts. Examples include calling an adult women "girl" or "honey" or similar terms because they indicate her status is something other than an adult human. A woman who limits her own potential because she has received repeated messages that she is incompetent and has incorporated these messages into her sense of self is a victim of *internalized sexism*. Although these forms of sexism are presented here as distinct categories, they are interrelated. Sexist culture perpetuates all forms of sexism.

Because we live in a patriarchal society that trains its members to accept male dominance and female submission, and we all witness males' overrepresentation in positions of power, it is reasonable to expect that most people—and especially most men—will have at least a low level of sexist thought unless they have actively worked to eliminate it. Even then, some level of *implicit bias*, defined as the subconscious devaluation of a group, may remain because it is often more difficult to change sexist reactions that may be emotional and unconscious than one's conscious beliefs about women. Research demonstrates that prejudiced and non-prejudiced people do not differ in stereotype activation (Fazio & Olson, 2003). However, the non-prejudiced person has made a commitment to be aware of and resistant to the tendency to stereotype. Over time, the stereotype activation itself decreases (Kawakami, Dovidio, Moll, Hermsen, & Russin, 2000). To reduce sexism, a person must expend efforts to understand socialization and gender role attitudes, recognize when he or she is engaging in stereotypical thinking and resist inclinations to behave in sexist ways. Over time, this "self-training" should lead to nonsexist responses that are somewhat automatic. Making this change takes continued, conscious effort (Schwartz et al., 2016).

Chivalry

Chivalry is a term derived from the French *Chevalier*, a heavily armed horseman in the French military (Keen, 1984). It is a set of attitudes and behaviors directed toward women by men of privilege. (In medieval times, horsemen were knights and/or nobles; most common men could not afford horses.) Chivalry is a form of benevolent sexism that manifests itself in a set of "gentlemanly" helpful behaviors such as holding a door open for a woman, helping her get seated at a dining table, standing when she enters or leaves a room, and filling her wine glass at social occasions. Glick (2005) points out that these are "trivial niceties" that send the message that women are special, but that they are also incompetent and in need of men's assistance (because they are unable to seat themselves or fill their own wine glasses). Chivalry also secures women's cooperation with male dominance by undermining women's resistance to it. Chivalric men believe that they are being helpful to women, but most do not help with things that have a greater impact such as gendered pay inequity, child care, or men's violence against women.

Chivalry is believed to communicate respect for women, but true respect involves listening to the other person's desires and negotiating relationship behaviors. In contrast to true respect, chivalry is a rigid set of rules based on the faulty assumption that all women are alike and all men must treat them the same way. Many of the men whom our students have interviewed express disappointment and anger that many women seem not to appreciate their chivalric behavior, an indication that these gestures are undertaken not for the woman's sake, but to bolster the man's self-image.

The concept of chivalry could potentially be replaced with a system of beliefs that values courtesy, civility, helping those in need, and thoughtfulness. We often tell men that if they are treating women differently than they treat other men, they ought to have a good reason for doing so. For instance, one might help a short woman to put her baggage into an overhead bin on a plane, given men's average advantage in height and upper body strength. On the other hand, should a man help a tall, female bodybuilder to store her luggage? Should an old man in poor health offer his seat to a young, fit woman on a crowded bus? Should a young, fit woman offer her seat to a father carrying a newborn baby? Box 3.2 provides several other belief systems that could be employed instead of relying on gender as an organizing framework.

> **Box 3.2**
> **Reducing Gender Schematic Processing**
>
> Sandra Bem (1998) notes that there are many ways to think about people without reference to their gender. The first three of these are Bem's suggestions, the remainder are ours.
>
> 1. *Individual differences schema*: people vary widely in their habits, attitudes, and temperament. A person may act aggressively, not because he is a man, but because he has an aggressive personality and/or finds himself in a situation in which aggression is adaptive.
> 2. *Cultural relativism schema*: "different people believe different things" (p. 271). Roman Catholics do not allow women to be priests, but some Episcopalians do.
> 3. *Sexism schema*: although beliefs differ, some beliefs about gender are wrong. Women should be allowed to be Roman Catholic priests.
> 4. *Situational pressure schema*: people tend to behave in certain ways when situations exert different pressures. A man may keep his feelings to himself while with his male friends, not because men are unemotional, but because other men might not give him a compassionate response. He may be very emotionally expressive as a client in psychotherapy or when he is in the company of women who are his friends.
> 5. *External variability schema*: people do not always behave in concert with how they feel; two people can vary to a great extent in their external reactions to exactly the same internal thoughts and feelings. Two men may hold equally sexist attitudes, but one decides not to display them because he wants the approval of women.

Activism and Challenging Sexism

Not surprisingly, a variety of individuals and organizations have attempted to challenge sexist behaviors and beliefs. They are usually categorized as *feminists* because their initial efforts focused on increasing equality by changing and eliminating laws and policies that prevented women from gaining power. Feminist victories include changing women's access to all forms of higher education (which had been highly restricted in the 1950s), allowing women to initiate divorce (nationally), preventing employers from firing women who became pregnant, and encouraging companies and women to have female presidents and directors (Davis, 1991). We refer to men who support these ideas as *profeminist* (Okun, 2014).

Language is one area in which sexism has been challenged. Language is important because it can communicate gender expectations in subtle ways, and linguistic distinctions between the sexes have received a good deal of attention in recent years. Sexist terms like chairman, mankind and the use of the generic masculine pronoun "he" (instead of chairperson, humankind, and "they") communicate that males are the standard and females the exceptions. People frequently complain that using newer, non-sexist terms is awkward and overly "P.C." ("politically correct"); we discuss some of these objections in Box 3.3. However, many researchers have discovered that the use of masculine-biased language results in readers and listeners predominantly perceiving

> **Box 3.3**
> **Sexist Language, Non-Sexist Language, and "Political Correctness"**
>
> Consider the many sex-specific terms contained in the English language. Many proponents of gender egalitarianism have leveled strong criticisms against the uses of sexist role terms and the generic masculine. They suggest gender neutral terms like: police officer, humankind, fire fighter, and server, and a change in the linguistic convention of the generic "he" to constructions such as they. Some have even suggested the adoption of a new set of pronouns that are gender neutral such as "hir" or "tir." Several of the arguments against these changers are provided below, along with counter-arguments.
>
> *Challenge*: Everybody is used to the old way of doing things and knows what the communicator is referring to. Therefore, there is no reason to change. To change a pronoun is to change standard English, which nobody should do.
>
> *Reply*: Language is not a static entity. It changes in response to the needs of the culture. If I were to tell you a story, you would naturally envision the events in your mind's eye. There is evidence that, when readers or listeners apprehend the generic masculine, they imagine males (Lips, 2008). Most children are not aware that masculine pronouns can potentially refer to females (Hyde, 1984). Therefore, the use of this construction constitutes poor communication when one is trying to refer to people of either sex.
>
> *Challenge*: Using terms like "they" rather than "he" is bulky and interrupts the flow of writing and speaking.
>
> *Reply*: It is true that these terms are sometimes bulky and awkward, but people should be willing to tolerate this mild discomfort rather than passively communicating that males' experience constitutes a standard and females' experience a variation. As Basow (1992) stated, "Use of the generic 'he' is not just an arbitrary custom, but a continuing statement about the social roles of men and women" (p. 142). They also include individuals who identify themselves as neither male nor female.
>
> *Challenge*: The movement toward non-sexist language is just another example of political correctness ("P.C."), a movement designed to make people feel guilty for not being a member of an oppressed minority group.
>
> *Reply*: "Political correctness" is a pejorative term used by people who seek to maintain the current power structure. Calling someone "P.C." is an attempt to shame them for their sensitivity and respectfulness. The demonization of the term is a political strategy to influence people to refuse adoption of the principle to maintain the status quo of male dominance.

males (Gastil, 1990; Hamilton, 1991). Therefore, the use of generic masculine language is poor communication.

Richardson (2009) describes a variety of ways in which the common use of the English language disparages women. For instance, it is quite common to refer to adult females as girls, implying that, like children, they are immature and relatively powerless. An adult man is rarely referred to as a boy except in a conscious attempt to disparage him. Richardson also notes the variant gender meanings of linguistically equivalent terms such as master (someone with power) and mistress (a sexual partner), governor (official) and governess (nanny), lord and lady. "Sir and mister [are] titles of courtesy, but at some time, madam, miss, and mistress have come to designate, respectively, a brothelkeeper, a prostitute, and an unmarried sexual partner of a male." (p. 120). These biases also appear in scientific writing, as described in Box 3.4.

> **Box 3.4**
> **Sexism in Scientific Language?**
>
> Martin (1991) provides an interesting perspective on the use of language to smuggle gender stereotypes into scientific language. She notes that most human sexuality books describe conception as a set of events that involve active (male) sperm swimming to and penetrating passive (female) eggs. In reality, female reproductive anatomy is anything but passive. Within women's bodies, cilia direct sperm along the path to the egg, and the egg changes chemically to favor some sperm but not others. Zuk (2005) observed that several scholarly articles refer to young birds as "illegitimate" when they had been fathered by males that were not pair-bonded with the mother "as if their parents had tiny avian marriage licenses and chirped their vows" (p. 14). Another paper refers to "wife-sharing" among male birds. Cases in which more than one female are associated with a male are never referred to as "husband sharing." Zuk points out that this language casts the males as the active parties—"they 'share' the female, as if she were a six-pack of beer" (p. 14). The subtext of subjective gender stereotypes finds its way into language even in fields many people consider "objective."

The Impact on Men

Holding sexist beliefs may provide men with a sense of self-esteem because, no matter what else, they may see themselves as superior to women, and thus are better than half the population. Research demonstrates that men who hold sexist beliefs are more likely to endorse other negative aspects of masculinity ideology, such as a drive for power or the belief that violence is acceptable in general (Mahalik et al., 2003; Murnen, Wright, & Kaluzny, 2002; Smiler, 2006a). Literature reviews indicate that these sexist beliefs are consistently related to greater support for rape myths, greater masculine gender role stress, less positive mental health and more negative mental health (separately), and lower likelihood of seeking help for mental health problems (Murnen, Wright, & Kaluzny, 2002; O'Neil, 2008; Wong, Ho, Wang, & Miller, 2017).

Benevolent sexist beliefs contribute to relatively poor perceptions of men-as-a-group. As noted earlier, people see women as wonderful; at the same time, they often view men as arrogant, emotionally cold, aggressive, and exploitive. This belief structure supports the characterization of men as being oriented toward dominance and power (Glick et. al., 2004). In fact, individual men report liking and trusting women more than they do other men, a positive out-group bias that is not seen in other forms of prejudice such as racism (Steinberg & Dickman, 2016). Overall, these attitudes are disrespectful of men and yet, in some ways, minimize men's responsibility for changing men. If "men suck" or "men are simple," one might ask (with exasperation) how men could possibly address their own problems? From a pragmatic perspective, it seems unrealistic to expect that women would change men or that men would allow this to happen (because that would imply men do not have power over women). If change is truly desired, then men and women will need to work together toward a shared purpose.

Power over Gay Men

United States culture also distinguishes between straight and gay men. As we discussed in Chapter One, masculinity is a status that boys and men must achieve and maintain; insults based on sexual orientation such as "fag" are commonly used to police "inappropriate" behavior (Pascoe, 2007; Reigeluth & Addis, 2016; Rosenburg et al. 2017). **Homophobia** refers to the hostility, fear, and intolerance of sexual attraction or behavior between persons of the same sex. It is a widespread phenomenon that manifests itself in a variety of ways, including the avoidance of nonsexual intimate behaviors between men, use of the term "no homo," derogatory terms for and jokes about gays, societal bigotry against homosexuals, and even unprovoked violence against persons perceived as gay. In this section, we focus on how this dynamic has appeared within United States culture and politics for approximately the last century. While recent gains in public acceptance of homosexuality and homosexuals may—or may not—signify losses for straight men, they reflect important advances in gay men's ability to fulfill the breadwinner role and provide for themselves, as well as their partners and any children they might have.

The Early Twentieth Century

The label "homosexual" as a description of a person, and not merely a behavior, emerged in the United States in the 1880s (Rotundo, 1993). This era was also marked by the doctrine of separate spheres, which rigidly defined and separated men's and women's roles. Barbara Sherman Heyl (1996) describes the effect of this new term:

> Until that time the moral and legal debates on homosexual behavior centered on just that—behavior. The shift in focus defined homosexuality as a 'state of being' that could exist prior to and without any overt homosexual act and, from somewhere inside the person, compelled a lifelong habitual preference for same-sex partners. Homosexuals became a highly stigmatized category of persons. (p. 121)

Anthony Rotundo (1993) traces the late eighteenth-century shift from a linguistic tendency of describing the behavior (e.g., "sodomy," "unnatural acts") to the use of a variety of new and pejorative words that label the person—"degenerate," "pervert," "fairy." This depiction of homosexuality was partly backed by religious tracts from early Catholic theologians, including Augustine, who declared that sexual activity was strictly for procreation and not pleasure or self-expression (Nelson, 1997), a position that invalidates non-procreative (gay) sex as well as self-identification based on sexual orientation. As a result of the social polarization of homosexuals and heterosexuals, people whose sexual desires were oriented toward their same sex began to think of themselves as distinct social groups. They formed communities in large cities to find support in a mainstream environment that persecuted them, and to develop relationships with people who would nurture their social and sexual identities.

One lingering outcome of this era is that "homosexual" and "feminine" became parallel and negative concepts in reference to masculine character. Both concepts and their terms have been increasingly used to shape the redefinition of masculinity, with insults used to police masculinity (Rotundo, 1993). Prior to this era, males engaged in romantic nonsexual friendships with one another, writing passionate letters to one another and often sleeping in the same bed. But romantic friendships disappeared with the new homophobia of the late nineteenth century, as it dramatically increased men's motivation to distinguish themselves from the feminine. Close male-male friendships developed into *buddyships* in which men bonded around sports, work, and antifemininity rather than sharing their emotional lives more directly. Thus, homophobia had, and continues to have, negative effects on both gay and heterosexual men.

During this era, many U.S. states passed laws prohibiting the most common same-sex sexual behaviors, even though it was legal for heterosexual couples to engage in these same behaviors. These "sodomy laws" were ruled unconstitutional by the United States Supreme Court in the landmark Lawrence vs. Texas case in 2003 (sodomylaws.org, 2009). When Freud (1925) wote about gender roles and sexuality in the early decades of the twentieth century, he viewed it as part of the range of normal functioning and called gay men as **gender inverted** because their patterns of thought and behavior resembled women's patterns. Freud did not see homosexuality as pathological. The idea that gay men are gender inverted has since been invalidated, because they show as much variation in their enactments of masculinity as do straight men. However, the importance of being either not gay or explicitly heterosexual remains as part of the hegemonic definition of masculinity (David & Bannon, 1976; Levant et al., 2007; Parent & Moradi 2011).

Thus, by the middle of the twentieth century, gay men lived in an American culture that had given local officials the ability to arrest, jail, and seize the property of gay men for acts they performed in private with willing partners. Further, homosexuality was classified as a mental disorder. Because of American's beliefs about the (in)competence of the mentally ill and the emphasis on conformity to majority norms, this was a substantial threat that gave heterosexuals substantial power to control gay men's (and gay women's) behavior by threatening to expose their sexual orientation.

1970s: A Period of Change

The Stonewall Inn was a popular gay bar in the Greenwich Village area of New York City. On June 28, 1969, police cleared the bar of patrons and shut it down, ostensibly for liquor law violations. As the police emerged from the bar, a crowd of angry gay men threw objects at them and a riot ensued. Herdt and Boxer (1991) describe Stonewall as a watershed historical event in gay political activism, one that crystallized a gay liberation movement that had begun quietly in the 1950s. In other words, it was the gay community's coming out (see Chapter Two), and it moved the focus of the gay world "from the secretive bar to the far more elaborate gay and lesbian communities of major cities around the world" (p.1). Herdt and Boxer describe individual coming out and community pride as emblematic of the transition from *homosexual* (secret) to *gay* (public and affirmative). Gay Pride Day marks the June anniversary of the Stonewall riot, which ushered in a new age of coming out and political activism.

A few years later, in 1973, the American Psychiatric Association removed homosexuality from its official list of mental disorders. The World Health Organization (WHO) followed suit twenty years later, in 1993 (van Hertum, 1992). Harvey Milk, an openly gay man, was elected to San Francisco's Board of Supervisors (i.e., city council) in 1978 and assassinated 11 months later. During this decade, support for gay legal rights increased, partly as a function of more generally liberal political and sexual attitudes.

1980s: A Step Backward

Today, we know and understand that the blood-borne Human Immunodeficiency Virus (HIV) can wreak havoc on the immune system, weakening it to the point where an individual develops Acquired Immuno-Deficiency Syndrome (AIDS). People with AIDS often die from a variety of diseases that are otherwise unusual in Western nations. In 1980, we did not know any of this, nor did medical researchers or doctors understand that there were such things as blood-born viruses (Shilts, 1987/2007). When gay young men who were otherwise healthy started dying at unusually high rates from these atypical causes, they received little sympathy from the public or the Reagan administration (Shilts, 1987/2007). To the extent that Gay Related Immune Disorder (GRID)—the disease's name in the early 1980s—and its victims were discussed in public, it was often as the result of unacceptable and deviant behavior whose victims were at fault. This belief was reinforced when the disease spread to drug users; hemophiliacs, who began succumbing to the disease as a result of blood transfusions, were seen as unfortunate but innocent victims. (The gay community had reliably participated in blood drives as a part of public service in the late 1970s and early 1980s; Shilts, 1987/2007.)

Despite thousands of dying and dead Americans, the Reagan administration did not allocate additional money to the Centers for Disease Control (CDC) or National Institutes of Health (NIH), instead directing the political appointees who headed those agencies to say they had sufficient funds. President Ronald Reagan did not mention AIDS at any time during his presidency, even when family friend and movie star Rock Hudson died of AIDS-related causes in 1987.

Local governments varied in their responses. In New York City, Mayor Ed Koch's administration followed the Reagan administration's lead and provided little to no official help. Efforts in New York were primarily led and coordinated by Gay Men's Health Crisis (GMHC), which performed a broad range of services such as identifying and educating medical professionals willing to work with HIV-infected individuals, facilitating transportation for infected individuals, providing basic legal advice, providing companions/assistants known *AIDS Buddies* who would perform "simple" tasks such as grocery shopping and keeping people company; in essence, they replicated many services that could have been provided by the city's Department of Human Services (Shilts, 1987/2007).

Things were different in the cities of San Francisco and Los Angeles, where gay men were much more likely to be out of the closet and had some measure of political organization and power. The San Francisco Department of Public Health, San Francisco General Hospital, and, to a lesser extent, the Los Angeles County Department of Public Health, would all play prominent roles in supporting AIDS patients and fighting against the epidemic (Shilts, 1987/2007).

Some prominent fundamentalist Christian leaders publicly stated that AIDS was a punishment from God for homosexuals' sins, expanding on the Religious Right's characterization of homosexuality as immoral and a sin against God (Rosin & Edsall, 1998). Because many people believe in a *just world*—the idea that bad things happen to bad people (Aronson, 2012)—gay men became both the victims of this disease and a public scapegoat for it. The prominence of these positions in the United States, then and now, as well as the lack of federal research funding, contributed to the spread of HIV and AIDS globally, not just in the United States.

Recent History

Over the last thirty years, there has been a continuous and expanding acceptance of homosexuality (McCormack Savin-Williams, 2005). Seminal events include a series of benefits and galas in support of AIDS research by Hollywood's biggest stars following Rock Hudson's death (Shilts, 1987/2007). In 1998, the murder of 21-year-old Matthew Shepard by two straight men who admitted going to a gay bar to find and beat a gay man drew national attention and would ultimately contribute to the creation of the *Matthew Shepard and James Byrd Jr. Hate Crimes Prevention Act* in 2009. By 2013, gay men were no longer seen as deviant and their masculinity was no longer subordinate. When 18-year-old Tyler Clementi committed suicide because he thought his roommate posted video of him having sex with another man, news coverage was consistently sympathetic to the deceased (Cohen & Brooks, 2014). Throughout this time period, many singers and actors have publicly acknowledged their homosexuality, as have an increasing number of athletes (Anderson, Magrath, & Bullingham, 2016). Some of these individuals, such as Rob Halford of the metal band Judas Priest and Welsh National Rugby Team captin Ian Gareth, explicitly counter the stereotype of gay men as effeminate.

Based on the belief that homosexuality is a sign of mental illness or a sign of poor character, some psychologists developed a treatment designed to convert gays to heterosexuality (Edwards, 1996). This treatment is called *reparative therapy* or *conversion therapy*, connoting that homosexuality is a pathological condition in need of repair. By 2017, reparative therapy had been explicitly outlawed by several U.S. states and a number of countries, and defined as unethical by a broad range of professional organizations, including the American College of Physicians, the American Psychological Association, and the American Counseling Association, among others (Daniel & Butkus, 2015; Task Force on Appropriate Therapeutic Responses to Sexual Orientation, 2009; Whitman, Gosoff, Kocet, & Tarvydas, 2013; see review by Drescher et al., 2016).

In 1994, United States President Bill Clinton directed the U.S. Department of Defense (DoD) to refrain from discriminating against closeted members of the armed forces, while allowing the DoD to bar those who were openly gay, lesbian, or bisexual from serving. This directive, known as *"Don't Ask, Don't Tell"* (DADT), reversed much of the policy that had originally been enacted in 1942, when the United States armed forces first specified that homosexual behavior was grounds for a court martial and discharge from the service. DADT was subsequently repealed under the Obama administration in 2011 (defense.gov, 2011), and has been accompanied by very few problems, indicating remarkable progress in the reduction of homophobia (Packard, 2014).

More recently, gay men and lesbians have sought the legal right to get married. From a legal perspective, marital status is important because there are more than 1,000 federal protections and rights for which marital status in part determines eligibility; people who are unable to legal marry are thus excluded from these protections (General Accounting Office, 2004). Specifically, the ability to marry provides legal protections and rights to jointly-owned or "community" property (such as a house), custody and visitation rights for children between (ex-)partners living apart, the right to make health decisions for an incapacitated partner, the right to file a wrongful death suit if a partner dies as the result of negligence or wrongdoing, the ability to refrain from testifying against one's partner in a criminal trial, and automatic ownership of a deceased partner's estate without paying inheritance taxes.

In 2003, Massachusetts became the first U.S. state to allow same sex marriage; by 2014, eighteen other states had joined it. The remaining states had laws and/or constitutional amendments banning same-sex marriage (gaymarriage.procon.org, 2014). In 2013, the United States Supreme Court ruled unconstitutional the 1996 Defense of Marriage Act (DOMA) (freedomtomarry.org, 2013) and the following year it refused to review a case in which Virginia's same-sex marriage ban was overturned, effectively expanding the right to marry from 19 to 30 states. As we write in 2017, same-sex marriage is permitted in all 50 U.S. states and a range of other countries around the globe. A similar and parallel movement has caused corporations and some local municipalities to expand spousal benefits to cohabiting same-sex couples (when and where legal marriage was not an option) and to adopt corporate policies that prevent discrimination based on sexual orientation (Joyce, 2005). Prior to the widespread legalization of marriage in the United States, the federal government began providing some employment benefits such as health care to same-sex partners of domestic federal employees as well as Foreign Service personnel in 2009 (Kessler, 2009; Wilson, 2009).

The Impact on Heterosexual Men

Given this history, we might then consider what impact homophobia and the increasing acceptance of homosexuality have on straight men at the individual level, and not simply the group level that we've described thus far. Throughout the historical time periods described here, legal and cultural sanctions against gay men provided straight men with a group to define themselves against or in opposition to. As such, individual straight men were provided with a (minimal) level of status and self-esteem through beliefs such as "at least I'm not gay." In effect, homophobia functions to trap men into rigid gender roles, including aspects of masculinity that limit their friendships with other men. Endorsement of homophobic beliefs—or the closely related need to demonstrate heterosexuality (Moradi & Parent, 2009)— is strongly related to other aspects of hegemonic masculinity (Korobov, 2004; Levant et al., 2007; Mahalik et al., 2003; Smiler, 2006). Prioritization of heterosexuality is not directly related to either better or worse mental health, although it is related to greater unwillingness to seek therapeutic help for mental health problems (Wong et al., 2017).

At the same time, homophobia helps create anxiety among straight men when asked to consider the possibility of same-sex erotic feelings. One method of dealing with this anxiety is to defend against it by placing very rigid boundaries between the self and other men. The man who claims to have absolutely no clue about male attractiveness or who becomes violent when dealing with gay men wants it to be absolutely clear to everyone (including himself) that he does not have an ounce of homosexuality in his body. We discuss male intimacy in greater detail in Chapter Eight.

Homophobia can also arise, in part, from an unconscious view of the homophobe's feelings about the self that is projected on to gay men. At base, homophobia is about the fear of unwanted sexual attention; one might think that this fear would give men empathy for women, who often get this kind of attention, but that seems not to be the case. Behind this fear may be some assumptions about male sexuality. First is the belief that male sexuality is indiscriminate. Second is the belief that male sexuality is predatory in nature—that males will seek out people on whom to impose their sexual desires without regard for that person's wishes. Why else would, for example, a middle-aged, overweight, balding man who isn't particularly attractive to most women believe that any gay man would be sexual with him? If a straight man can psychologically place these unacceptable feelings outside of the self, then he can hate the feelings without hating himself. This style is fairly common in males, who are usually socialized to deal with conflicts externally rather than to "look inside" and think about how they feel (Lynch & Kilmartin, 2013).

The hypothesis that homophobia is a defense against homoerotic feelings received some support in an important study by Adams, Wright, and Lohr (1996), who measured physiological responses to erotic stimuli. These researchers used the results from a homophobia questionnaire to divide self-reported heterosexual men into two groups: men with high levels of homophobia and men with low levels. Then, they showed these men videotapes of heterosexual, lesbian, and male homosexual sex. Using a device known as a *penile plethysmograph*, which records changes in the circumference of the penis and thus the strength of an erection, they measured research participants' physiological arousal in response to the videotapes. Although both groups of men showed signs of sexual arousal while viewing the heterosexual and lesbian tapes, only the high homophobia group showed arousal in response to the male homosexual tapes. The researchers surmised that homophobic men deny or are unaware of their own homoerotic arousal.

Gay men are not immune to homophobia, and the anxiety created by these feelings sometimes compounds an already difficult process of understanding the sexual self in the context of a heterosexist culture. The gay man who has learned to hate homosexuality in his childhood may find himself dealing with feelings of self-hatred in adulthood. On one level, he knows that these feelings are irrational. On another, they seem quite real and difficult to ignore.

LOSING MALE POWER? BOYS AND MEN IN CRISIS

The late 1990s and early twenty-first century witnessed a good deal of dialogue in the popular culture on the emotional lives of boys. Led by William Pollack's (1998) bestseller, *Real Boys: Rescuing Our Sons from the Myths of Boyhood*, a number of writers began to explore emotional, scholastic, and criminality problems that show a highly imbalanced sex ratio. Laura Bush, wife of the then-President of the United States, spoke publicly about concerns over boys' problems, thus giving the debate a very high profile (NPR, 2005) as Pollack and others offered solutions to difficulties boys encounter in managing their emotional lives in a culture that expects stoicism, violence, and high levels of independence (see also Gurian & Stevens, 2005; Polce-Lynch, 2002).

This era was neither the first nor the last time the American public has (briefly) expressed concern about the "boy crisis" or a "crisis of masculinity." As we described in Chapter One, such a crisis occurred in the 1920s due to cultural shifts related to industrialization, migration to cities from rural areas, and the beginning of mandatory schooling (through grade six), all of which contributed to the perception that boys' decreased time away from their fathers and away from their "natural" access to outdoor spaces were problematic (Hantover, 1978).

The 1950s also featured a boy crisis that directly challenged most components of the then-dominant definition of masculinity. Here, concerns focused on boys who were unwilling to conform to the image of the organization man, with its focus on conformity to corporate culture and acceptance of the rules. The rebels' "uniform" of white t-shirt, blue jeans, and leather jacket with greased, slicked-back hair remains recognizable today (Smiler, 2006b). Adults of the day worried about "juvenile delinquents" and devoted substantial cultural resources to preventing boys from becoming delinquents; police officers, counselors, and social scientists were all asked to help fix the problem (Stearns, 1994). Epitomized by actor James Dean and his characters, this version of masculinity would transform the juvenile delinquents of "West Side Story" and "The Outsiders" into the fun-loving and harmless guys in "Grease." In daily life, divisions among White ethnic groups were lessened, and thus Italians, Greeks, Jews, and other were increasingly accepted and included within the category "White." This transformation is an example of White masculinity's ability to manage and reclaim its undesirable variants, a cultural "option" that is unavailable to other American ethnic groups (Carroll, 2010).

The Great Recession of 2007–2008 contributed to a masculinity crisis. There were substantial job losses in "traditional" male-dominated careers such as manufacturing and construction, with new jobs tending to be concentrated in service fields that emphasized "feminine" skills such as interpersonal interaction and care-taking, as well as high-tech skills for the developing digital economy. In essence, the recession challenged men's ability to function as the primary or sole breadwinner. We address this topic in greater detail in Chapter Eleven.

Education has been a focal point of some of these arguments, with some commentators arguing that boys have been shortchanged by schools relative to girls. One author claimed that feminism is waging a "war" against boys by demanding that boys behave like girls (Sommers, 2001). As evidence, supporters of this position cite statistics indicating that boys achieve lower average grades in school and are a shrinking minority in the college student population (Gurian, 2005). Behind this argument are the assumptions that feminism is males' enemy and that the sexes are adversarial (i.e., attention paid to girls' problems leads boys to be "shortchanged").

The data offer both support and challenges for this claim. As Table 3.1 indicates, females received more associate's degrees than males in 1980–1981, with males receiving more bachelor's and graduate degrees. A decade later, women earned more batchelor's degrees than men and the number of graduate degrees had become nearly equal. For the classes of 2001 and 2011, women outnumbered men at every degree level. Some people interpret these data as evidence that men are in decline and may need specialized programs to enter (and complete) college to achieve parity. Yet the data also show that more men than ever are receiving degrees, a trend that suggests that men are not in decline. Further, males' standardized test scores and working-world achieve-

Table 3.1
Degrees Received for Males and Females

	AA	Males	Graduate	AA	Females	Graduate
1980–81	183,819	469,625	220,455	226,355	465,175	177,907
1990–91	198,634	504,045	225,084	283,086	590,493	223,326
2000–01	231,645	531,840	261,941	347,220	712,331	331,146
2010–11	361,408	734,159	371,352	582,098	981,894	523,397

Note: Data from the National Center of Education Statistics, 2015abcd

ment are as strong as they ever were (Sadker, 2000), demonstrating that, if there is a war, it is clearly not a very successful one.

It is important to note that changes in the male:female ratio are not uniform across racial and ethnic lines. Nationally, the ratio had been skewed in favor of males until approximately 1995, with women dominating since that time. Blacks reached parity in approximately 1985, Latinx reached parity in approximately 1990, non-Hispanic Whites reached parity in approximately 1995, and Asian-Americans reached parity in approximately 2007 (Ryan & Bauman, 2016).

Males-as-a-group earn more than females-as-a-group at every level of education (Proquest, 2016), and so one possibility is that males have more avenues to employment than females without college. However, going to college continues to add significantly to earning potential throughout life. Therefore, choosing not to go to college when one has the resources to do so is not a rational choice for many. One group of scholars notes that labor market considerations do not explain the sex imbalance of the college student population. Rather, males are more likely than females to place a high value on self-sufficiency and earning as opposed to long-term investment and the relatively dependent role of college student (Leicht, et. al., 2007). This gender identity conflict hypothesis and its interaction with race and class awaits further study.

Advocating For Men

As we've seen, the last century has included substantial legal gains for women and homosexuals. Reaction among men—and groups who work with or claim to represent them—can be categorized in two ways. Some adopt what may be called a profeminist approach and are generally supportive of these gains, while others see the gains as a threat to men.

From the latter perspective, policies that attempt to create a gender-balanced workforce are seen as "reverse sexism" or sexist practice against men. In reality, these attitudes have not lead to policies, customs, or widespread practices that disadvantage men by preventing them from gaining or keeping employment, although they have made hiring more competitive by limiting the number of men (or women) who can be hired for a particular type of job at a particular company. We'll address other workplace challenges in Chapter Eleven.

Self-described Men's Rights Advocates (MRAs) and the Men's Rights Movement (MRM) claim to speak for men, and often point to works by authors such as William Farrell (1993) and Susanna Hoff Sommers (2000), which are clearly written as opposition to the Feminist movement. MRAs do not appear to have created any organizations that directly help men or raise consciousness of men's issues, formal fundraising activities, a viable academic journal, annual conferences, or other traditional markers of a social movement (Blake, 2015; Serwer & Baker, 2015). However, they do seem to be effective at mobilizing substantial numbers of "Internet trolls" who argue against feminist positions and harangue prominent women. Their comments, which are often explicitly misogynistic, racist, and include threats of rape and physical harm, have resulted in journalist Jessica Valenti and Ghostbusters star Leslie Jones closing their social media accounts, at least temporarily. One MRM author acknowledged this is "an unusual political strategy" explaining that MRM "is almost exclusively an online movement, and its discussions and literature are generally posted in various online platforms. In terms of political action, many MRMs reject the possibility of engaging constructively with the current 'gynocentric' culture, and thus refuse to work within mainstream society" (Hodapp, 2015, p. viii). One journalist has gone as far as to describe the MRA belief system as a "gateway drug" to White Nationalist beliefs such as those on display in Charlottesville, Virginia during the summer of 2017 (Futrelle, 2017). Given the lack of engagement with or within existing power structures, the MRA claim to represent men seems spurious, at least from an academic perspective.

A favored tactic of MRAs is to argue that #NotAllMen engage in a behavior, and thus calling on "men" to address an issue is inappropriate. This line is often used to stop a conversation instead of directing that conversation toward a solution. As we'll see through this text, the statement that "not all men do X" is often factually correct. At the same time, when the majority of people who do X are men, there is legitimacy in identifying the issue as something that men should address. For example, although only a minority of all men are incarcerated during their lifetimes, nearly 90 percent of those who are incarcerated are male.

At the same time, but from a perspective that is more supportive of the gains described in this chapter, men have become more involved in gender equality movements. Organizations such as Promundo work internationally to promote men's greater involvement during pregnancy and in childrearing, and thus help change the ways that men function as husbands and fathers; changes can be as "simple" as encouraging husbands to drive their wives to pregnancy-related doctors' appointments and providing them access to a health care professional to whom they can ask questions (Peacock & Barker, 2014). Others have focused on efforts to end gender-based violence, especially in the United States (Okun, 2014); we detail some of these approaches in Chapter Twelve. The Movember foundation, with their signature November mustache campaign, encourages men to pay more attention to their health. Organizations such as Oxfam and the World Health Organization have also made efforts to reach out to and support men in various ways (Ferguson, et. al., 2004; Krug, et. al., 2002; Ruxton, 2004; Heilman, Hebert, & Paul-Gera, 2014). Most, if not all, of these organizations may be described as profeminist.

SUMMARY

In this chapter, we've discussed some of the ways that the cultural power of masculinity in the United States has been used against two groups, women and gay men, as well as concerns about the potential loss of male power. The discussion revealed blatant and subtle ways that men's institutional and structural power has been employed to disenfranchise these groups through laws, prejudicial attitudes, and other avenues. Although this use of power is designed to benefit men-as-a-group, we noted ways in which these attitudes and behaviors can and do harm that same group of men. As we discussed in Chapter Two regarding masculinities, the societal benefits of hegemonic masculinity are not equally available to all men, and thus many men experience little to no benefit from the power structures that have harmed women and gay men. We believe that many men are not aware of the cost they pay for the "benefits" they (don't) receive.

The debates about how boys are harmed by various social forces will likely continue, but as many scholars (Sadker, 2000; Kimmel, 1999; Pollack, 2000b), have pointed out, we should be careful not to be lulled into playing a game of "boys against the girls." It is clear that both boys and girls face problems that are somewhat specific to their sexes. Addressing the typical male problems of poor school achievement, criminality, bullying, impoverished emotional lives, and suicide need not come at the expense of a focus on girls' struggles.

Some key points:

- Power is not and has not been equally shared within United States society, and that power has been used in a variety of ways to limit the power of women and gay men.
- Sexism and chivalry are specific manifestations of power structures that are designed to keep women dependent on men.
- A number of authors have proposed methods of challenging and lessening the effects of sexism, and by extension decreasing men's power over women, with varying degrees of success. Challenges have included issues of language, men's participation in parenting, and reduction of legal forms of discrimination against women.
- The hegemonic form of masculinity in the United States prioritized demonstrations of heterosexuality through the twentieth

century and engaged in a range of methods of suppressing male homosexuality.
- The last several decades have seen substantial gains in the public acceptance of homosexuality, with some concurrent legal and political gains. However, those gains have been tenuous at times and remain controversial as we write this text in 2018.
- The spread of HIV and AIDS in the United States was worsened by the ways that homophobia influenced federal policy. (Those decisions also facilitated the spread of HIV and AIDS globally, although we did not describe that impact in the text.)
- Men pay some costs for sexism. At the group level, women are generally viewed more favorably than men. At the individual level, men who are more sexist are likely to support other aspects of masculinity such as dominance and the belief that violence is an acceptable way of solving problems, while also experiencing poorer mental health.
- Men also pay some costs for homophobic beliefs. At the group level, it restricts men's lives by making emotional intimacy more difficult among male-male dyads and in all-male groups. At the individual level, homophobia can make men—regardless of their sexual orientation—unnecessarily fearful of other men.
- Boys, men, and masculinity have experienced a number of crises over time. Just as the definition of masculinity has changed (see Chapter One), so have the specific details of these crises. However, the crises always revolve around challenges and potential changes in the definition of hegemonic masculinity.

GLOSSARY

Power: The ability to have the desired effect on an individual or group.

Sex differences: The reference name for research literature documenting differences between males and females.

Alpha bias: The focus on studies examining differences between males and females.

Beta bias: The focus on studies examining similarities between males and females.

Men-as-a-group (and **women-as-a-group**): A term referring to men (and women) at a very general level, and not to specific men or relatively small groups of men.

Privilege: Having greater and relatively easier access to societal benefits than others.

Master statuses: Systems, categories, or statuses of individuals that typically take precedence over other systems, categories, or statuses.

Entitlement: The experience of privilege by which the preferred group expects to be treated in a way that non-privileged groups must strive for.

Unmarked Status: The privilege of being the default version of that category and thus not having one's status included when that category is described. For example, "professional athlete" instead of "male professional athlete."

Marked Status: The absence of privilege, as manifested having one's status included when that category is described. For example, "female professional athlete" instead of "professional athlete."

Patriarchy: A system in which a society confers greater levels of economic power, influence, and prestige on males-as-a-group compared to females-as-a-group.

Sexism: A form of prejudice that leads to a range of negative outcomes for women and may occur at both the individual and societal levels.

Systemic sexism: Large-scale policies, customs, and practices that privilege men and disadvantage women.

Hostile Sexism: The kind of sexism that springs to mind when one thinks of prejudicial attitudes toward women. Hostile sexism includes the hatred of women.

Benevolent Sexism: Beliefs that women need men's protection, help, and financial support (because they are incompetent to make "serious" or "important" decisions on their own).

Interpersonal sexism: Sexist behavior in social contexts.

Internalized sexism: A girl or woman who limits her own potential because she has received repeated messages that she is incompetent and has incorporated these messages into her sense of self.

Implicit bias: The subconscious devaluation of a group.

Chivalry: A set of attitudes and behaviors centered on social niceties, such as men opening doors for women. The original use of the term focused on behavior toward women by men of privilege.

Homophobia: The hostility, fear, and intolerance of sexual attraction or behavior between persons of the same sex.

Buddyships or buddies: Men's creation of social bonds and friendship around sports, work, and antifemininity rather than sharing their emotional lives more directly.

Gender inverted: The idea that gay men's patterns of thought and behavior resembled women's patterns.

AIDS Buddies: Volunteer companions who would perform simple tasks for those suffering from AIDS, such as providing transportation, signing up for services, grocery shopping and keeping people company.

Belief in a just world: The idea that bad things happen to bad people.

Reparative therapy: A therapeutic "treatment" designed to change sexual orientation from homosexual to heterosexual. It has been identified as unethical by all relevant major professional groups and outlawed in a range of jurisdictions. Also known as conversation therapy.

Don't Ask, Don't Tell (DADT): United States military policy that allowed active duty service members to serve their country as long as they did not reveal having same-sex attractions or behaviors. It also prohibited other service members from asking about sexual orientation. The policy was considered progressive, although it still allowed individuals who were open about having same-sex attractions to be discharged.

(Penile) plethysmograph: A device that records changes in the circumference of the penis and thus the strength of an erection.

Chapter Four

Models for Understanding and Measuring a Singular Masculinity

Masculinity is complicated. Like any complex psychological phenomenon, researchers have developed a variety of ways of studying and measuring it. In this chapter, we examine some big-picture, or meta-theoretical, conceptualizations of masculinity and how each of these affects how masculinity is measured. We address broad conceptions (which we call **models**) and measurement together because the manner in which researchers measure masculinity is determined by how they understand it (Morawski, 1985; Smiler, 2004).

Before we talk about researchers' definitions of masculinity, take a moment to consider your own. You might ask yourself "what does it mean to be a real man?" If you ask the Internet that question, you might learn that "real men do it [move things] in one trip" or "real men don't buy girls/women." You might also remember commercials about Man Laws.

In Chapter One, we discussed the four masculine injunctions described by Deborah David and Robert Brannon (1976). Consider the directive that boys and men should be adventurous. Perhaps you are someone who readily seeks out adventure through your behavior: skateboarding tricks, not studying as much as you should, or being the first person to volunteer for anything. At times, researchers focus on *cognitions*, defined as thoughts or attitudes, such as the belief that it is good or important to be adventurous or take risks. At the *affective* or emotional level, you might see adventurousness as exciting or scary, as something that makes you feel happy, excited, or nervous (in a good way). The ***ABC model*** (Affect, Behavior, and Cognition), describes reactions as not only being what you think (cognition) but also how you feel (affect) and what you do (behavior). The ABC model is important because it helps delineate the ways in which people can have multiple and inconsistent responses to the same event (Myers, 2008).

Imagine, for example, that you arrive in biology and sit next to Dave in your usual spot. The two of you usually talk sports and are lab partners, but you don't "hang out" as close friends do. As you sit down, you realize that Dave is wearing a dress. Your affect may include anxiety because you're not sure how to respond; fear or desire that Dave will hit on you; fear that bigoted people will assault Dave; and pride in Dave for being so courageous to flaunt a powerful social norm. At the behavioral level, you have to decide whether or not you're going to say anything about his fashion choice (because speech is a form of behavior). If you choose to say something, you then have to decide if it will be supportive or not. At the cognitive level, and linked to your behavior, are your thoughts about men wearing dresses. You may find yourself wondering if Dave is sending a message about his gender identity or his sexual orientation, if Dave lost a bet, or if Dave has a nice butt. The ABC model is quite popular in some areas of psychology and some of these distinctions appear in the theories and measures we'll discuss in this chapter.

The conceptualizations, definitions, and measures of masculinity in this chapter are mostly consistent with the notion that there is only one (culturally) preferred way to be masculine. This definition of masculinity may contain multiple components, as we saw in Chapter One, but these different components all add up to a single definition of masculinity. Literature reviews suggest this approach dominates psychologists' approach to assessments of masculinity and represents more than half of the studies published in the academic journal *Psychology of Men and Masculinity* (Wong, Steinfeldt, Speight, & Hickman, 2010; Wong & Horn, 2016).

Researchers' perceptions of masculinity as positive or negative are embedded in the aspects of masculinity they choose to assess and the ways they label those masculine components. There is little difference in the survey questions assessing "emotional control" and "self-reliance" on the Conformity to Male Norms Index (Mahalik et al., 2003) when compared to the "restrictive emotionality" and "extreme self-reliance" of the revised Male Role Norms Index (Levant et al., 2007), but the scale names have different connotations.

The Gender Binary: Masculinity or Femininity

You're undoubtedly familiar with the rather widely-held belief that men and women are opposites with different but complementary strengths, an outgrowth of the Victorian notion of separate spheres described in Chapter One. The areas of difference most often cited include: aggressiveness, nurturance, mathematical ability, verbal ability, visual-spatial ability, achievement motivation, competitiveness, dominance, morality, conformity, and communication styles. Many television programs and popular books have capitalized on people's tendency to think in gender dualisms by displaying "experts" who make sweeping generalizations about sex differences.

This dualistic, either-or notion is called the ***gender binary*** because it is made up of only two options, male and female (or masculine and feminine).

CHAPTER 4   MODELS FOR UNDERSTANDING AND MEASURING • 77

This binary is at the root of common insults against boys and men such as "you throw like a girl" or "don't be such a sissy." The gender binary leads to a simple classification of people: they're either masculine or feminine; there is no in-between.

Male-Female Comparison, also known as "Sex Differences"

Are males and females really different? More accurately, we might ask: *how different* are males and females? Or *how similar* are the sexes? These questions are empirical ones—we cannot know the answers without careful scientific investigations. We addressed the political and cultural implications of comparing men and women in Chapter Three.

The Measurement of Characteristics

If one measures enough people in a population on any psychological characteristic and then graphs the results, the picture that emerges nearly always approximates a normal curve (Figure 4.1). Most people's scores on the dimension of study cluster around the middle (average) of the distribution, and relatively few people's scores are found at the extremes. For example, if we were to give an intelligence test to 10,000 people, most would score around the average of 100 IQ points, approximately 2.5 percent of people would have very high scores that qualify them as gifted, and a similar number of people would have very low scores that might qualify them as developmentally delayed (Fancher, 1985). The majority of people would score somewhere between

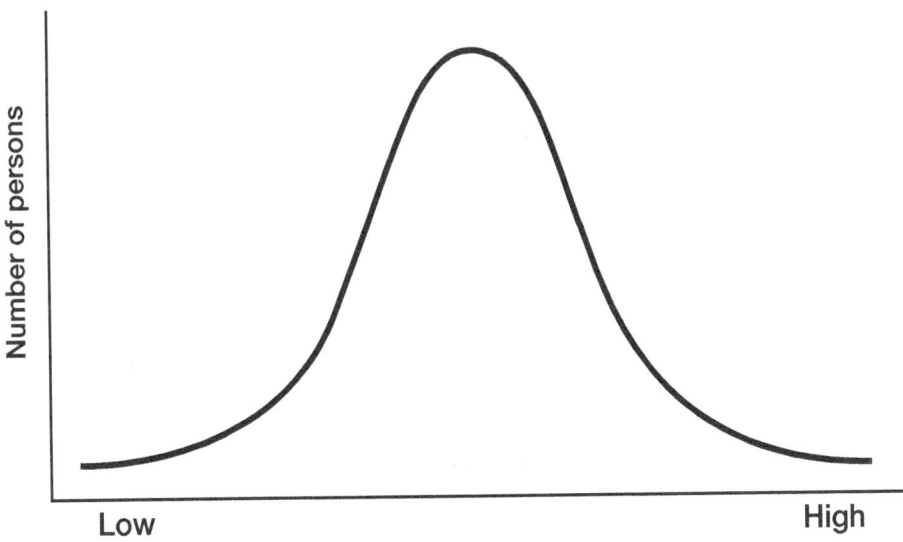

Figure 4.1   The Normal Curve

these two extremes. (Today, a diagnosis of developmentally delayed requires more than just a low IQ.)

Sex comparison research tends to treat males and females as two different populations and describes average differences between the population of females and that of males with reference to the characteristic of interest. Within each group, the distribution of scores usually approximates a normal curve. The sex comparison question is, "to what extent do the curves diverge and overlap?" A large sex difference would look like Figure 4.2. A small difference would look like Figure 4.3.

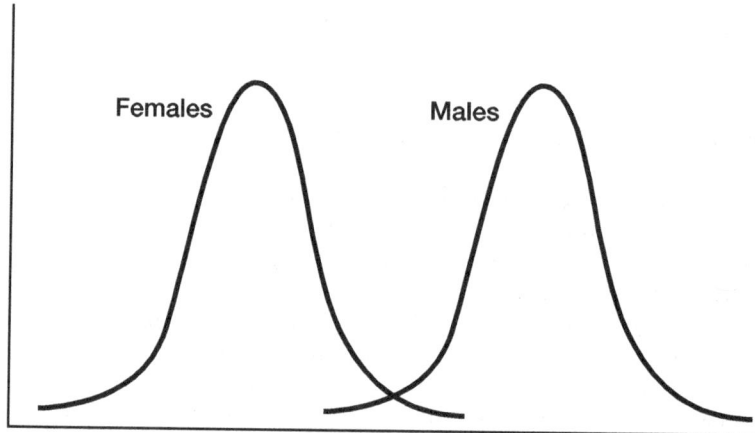

Figure 4.2 A Large Sex Difference

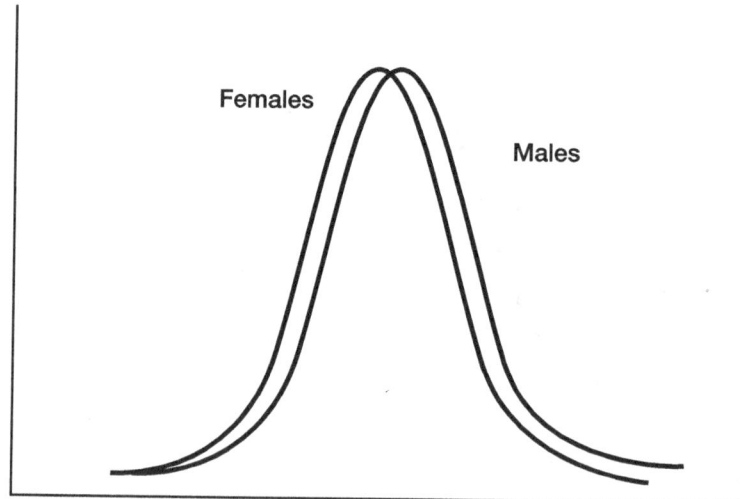

Figure 4.3 A Small Sex Difference

Differences are nearly always a matter of *degree* because there are so few behaviors that are seen exclusively in one sex and not the other. Men may be more aggressive, but obviously women also display aggressive behaviors. Women may be nurturing more often, but men can also nurture. In fact, the only behaviors which are seen exclusively in one sex or the other are those associated with reproductive roles: women can menstruate, give birth, and lactate; men can impregnate (Money, 1987).

Research in Sex Comparison

An in-depth review of the voluminous sex comparison literature is well beyond the scope of this book. What follows is the barest summary of some studies in which scholars have organized large amounts of research. Reviews of the literature come in two forms. A *narrative review* provides a text-based summary of the research, much like this textbook does. A *meta-analysis* provides a mathematic aggregation of the research. In other words, it combines the results of many studies to describe what the body of research, taken together, indicates.

In 1974, Eleanor Maccoby and Carol Jacklin published the first extensive (narrative) review of child sex comparison literature. They concluded that, despite the efforts of researchers to find sex differences in a wide variety of areas, very few true differences were convincingly demonstrated. Maccoby and Jacklin concluded that sex differences were found in four areas: girls had greater verbal ability, boys had greater mathematical and visual-spatial ability, and boys were more aggressive. Note that the existence of a difference does not tell us anything about *why* that difference exists. In Chapter Five we will discuss biologically-based hypotheses for these differences and in Chapter Six we'll talk about socially-based explanations for them.

Although the sex differences found by Maccoby and Jacklin were statistically significant, in every case where they found a difference, the size of the difference *between* the sexes was much smaller than the variability *within* the population of males or the population of females. Graphic displays of differences resembled Figure 4.3, not Figure 4.2. Figure 4.4 illustrates the relative sizes of between-sex and within-sex differences. For instance, although boys-as-a-group outperformed girls-as-a-group in mathematics, girls who did very well still outperformed the vast majority of boys; boys who did very poorly were still outperformed by the vast majority of girls. See Box 4.1 for a discussion of sex comparison in various performances.

These performances tell us that it is possible for the sex of the participant to become a secondary or even irrelevant consideration compared with other dimensions.

As evidence that even these average differences are not necessarily physiologically based, recent studies of mathematics performance on the Scholastic Aptitude Test (SAT) and other one-time tests indicate that girls have virtually caught up with boys in the 20 years following Maccoby and Jacklin's 1974 work

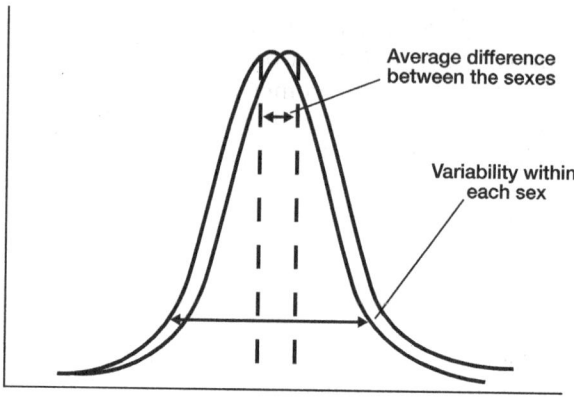

Figure 4.4 Within-Group and Between-Group Variance

Box 4.1
Sex Comparisons in Performance

In 1964, the world record for the women's marathon (a 26.2 mile footrace) was around three hours and 30 minutes. The men's record at that time was around two hours and ten minutes. Most people at the time probably believed that this rather large difference was due to biological differences between the sexes, but if we fast forward to 2009, the women's record had improved by one hour and 15 minutes (2:15:25) and the men's record, around six minutes (2:03:59). What appeared in 1964 to be a robust sex difference turns out to be rather small by comparison, and who is to say that some talented woman might not someday eclipse the men's record?

Small sex differences do not tell us anything about individual men and women. Paula Radcliffe, the women's marathon world record holder as of 2005, can outperform 99 percent of male marathoners. As the only female playing in a 2005 Professional Golf Association (PGA) tournament, a very young Michelle Wie barely missed the cut (qualification for the final two rounds of the tournament, based on performance in the first two rounds). Fifteen years of age at the time, Wie was undoubtedly better than 99 percent of male golfers and probably better than 100 percent of 15-year-old male golfers. In fact, she posted a better score than 48 male professional golfers in that tournament. In response, one sportswriter opined that "gender is becoming irrelevant to golf." (Jenkins, 2005, p. E7).

98-pound Sonya Thomas has won many competitive eating contests, beating some very large men. She has eaten seven 12-ounce hamburgers in 10 minutes, 43 tacos in 11 minutes, 23 barbecue sandwiches in 12 minutes, nearly 5 pounds of fruitcake in 10 minutes, and, in the buffalo chicken wing eating contest, she beat a 415-pound man by eating 167 wings (Carlson, 2004). In 2005, she won bratwurst and grilled cheese sandwich eating contests in addition to consuming 44 lobsters in 12 minutes, easily outdistancing her competition ("Eating Champ Downs 44 Lobsters in Win," 2005).

Women also hold the record for the fastest swimming of the English Channel in both directions, and for the number of times that feat was accomplished (Allison Streeter, 32 times). In 1998, Paula Newby Fraser's Ironman Triathlon time was faster than all but 10 of the male contestants. Ann Trason twice completed the 100-mile Western States Endurance run ahead of all but one male, and Susan Butcher won the Iditarod dog sledding race four times (Lips, 2008). Race car driver Danica Patrick has been a Top 10 finisher in both Nascar and IndyCar Series

> races, outperforming many other drivers who do not qualify for racing's top tiers as well as many who do qualify.
>
> At age 64, Diana Nyad became the first person to swim from Cuba to Florida without the use of a protective shark cage, something no male had done as of 2017 (Sloane, Hanna, & Ford, 2013).

(Hedges & Nowell, 1995; Lindberg, Hyde, Petersen, & Linn, 2010). At the same time, results from a meta-analysis of school grades indicates that females outperform males overall, and in every core subject area (language, math, science, social studies, etc.), from elementary through graduate school, and throughout the twentieth century. The difference in academic grades is small and represents the difference between a B and a B+, as in Figure 4.3. At the same time, this difference is consistent (i.e., few or no exceptions), pervasive, and widespread (Voyer & Voyer, 2014). Regardless of whether the review relies on a narrative or meta-analytic process, researchers often find that the differences are not as widesread as expected. (Deaux, 1985; Hyde, 2005; Hyde & Plant, 1995; Leaper & Tenenbaum, 2002; Lytton & Romney, 1991; Voyer & Voyer, 2014). In her meta-analysis, Janet Hyde (2005) found that 75 percent of psychological gender differences are in either the small or "close to zero" range.

As discussed in Chapter Three, and as illustrated in Figures 4.2 and 4.3, knowing that there is an average difference between men and women tells us little about the magnitude of that difference and nothing about a randomly selected "person on the street." Moreover, knowledge of a difference between the groups "men" and "women" obscures the extent of overlap between the two groups. It also obscures other factors that may cause or contribute to these differences, such as the effects of stereotypes and discriminatory practices.

The Gender Identity Model

The oldest psychological model of gender roles carried with it the assumption that it was important for boys and men to display "appropriately masculine" behavior and for girls and women to be "appropriately feminine." These *Gender Identity Models* included the conceptualization of femininity and masculinity as opposites, relying on the gender binary we described earlier, illustrated in Figure 4.4. Although this model allows the identification of feminine men and masculine women, there are no options for someone being "neither masculine nor feminine" or "both masculine and feminine."

Within the gender identity perspective, sex differences are understood to be based in biology and/or some sort of "natural order." The assumption here is that men are and should be different from women because of differences between the sexes in natural social roles, a position characteristic of the *essentialist* approach to gender. Gender differences were assumed to pervade virtually every aspect of human experience, including affect, behavior, and cognition.

Another assumption of the Gender Identity Model is that the healthiest and most productive men are those who are the most masculine. Thus, a fundamental developmental task for every boy is to establish an appropriate *gender role identity*, or a solid and appropriate sense of himself as masculine. This notion remains with us today and can be heard when people talk about boys' need for a father or "father figure" who will show him how to "be a man."

Because masculinity and femininity were seen as opposites, boys and men who displayed feminine traits were seen as having problems and considered to be unhealthy. To some thinkers, including Freud (1925), gay men were seen as *gender inverted*; they were physiological males but displayed all the characteristics of femininity. For now, it is important to say that Freud did not consider homosexuality an illness. Rather, he viewed it as a variation, much like left-handedness, which is seen in a minority of the population but is not a pathology (Money, 1987b).

Historically, some theorists (Toby, 1966; Adorno, Frenkel-Brunswick, Levinson, & Sanford, 1950) have proposed that insecure masculine gender identity leads men into exaggerated behaviors that are attempts to prove their masculinity to others as well as to the self. These behaviors have been labeled *hypermasculine* and include violence, physical risk taking, and hostility directed toward women and gays. The picture that emerges is of a man who is not really masculine, but is more of a caricature of masculinity used to cover up insecurity.

Gender Role Identity Measures

Terman and Miles (1936) published the first measure of masculinity and femininity in 1936. Called the Attitude Interest Analysis Test to disguise its purpose to test takers, it is often referred to as the MF test today and consisted of approximately 450 multiple choice questions. Each question had four possible responses, including one to three masculine responses, one to three feminine responses, and zero to two neutral responses. (Only one category had two responses for any particular question.). A masculine response received a score of +1, a neutral one a score of 0, and a feminine one a score of –1. The total was then computed; a positive score indicated the person was masculine and a negative score indicated femininity. For example, test takers were asked to read the word on the left (in all capitals) and then read across the line and circle the word that they think is the best match for the word on the left.

POLE:	Barber	Cat	North	Telephone
DATE:	Appointment	Dance	Fruit	History

The masculine answers for Pole are cat and telephone; for Date they are dance, fruit, and history. Feminine answers for Pole are north and for Date are appointment.

In her review of Terman and Miles' MF test, Jill Morawski (1985) described how to get a highly masculine or highly feminine score: "Masculinity scores are gained by replying that you dislike foreigners, religious men, women cleverer than you are, dancing, guessing games, being alone, and thin women. Femininity points are accrued by indicating dislike for sideshow freaks, bashful men, riding bicycles, giving advice, bald-headed men, and very cautious people" (p. 206).

This scale became a prototype for other early attempts at gender measurement. The Minnesota Multiphasic Personality Inventory (MMPI) (Hathaway & McKinley, 1951) and the updated MMPI-2 (Butcher, Dahlstrom, Graham, Tellegen, & Kaemmer, 1989) are used to diagnose a broad variety of mental illnesses including thought, anxiety, and personality disorders. The questionnaires contain more than 500 statements to which the person answers "true" or "false" in relation to the self, such as "I have often wished I were a girl" (or if you are a girl) "I have never been sorry that I am a girl."

The original MMPI contained an "Mf" scale that was originally designed to differentiate male heterosexuals from homosexuals (Groth-Marnat, 2003). The MMPI-2 maintained the Mf scale, which can produce scores indicating how strongly an individual conforms to the dominant male and female stereotypes (Graham, 1992).

A few other scales based on a similar conception of gender roles followed. Among these were the California Psychological Inventory (CPI) "Fe" scale (Gough, 1957), the Strong Vocational Interest Inventory (Strong, 1943), and the Feminine Gender Identity Scale (Freund, Nagger, Langevin, Zajac, & Steiner, 1974).

Limitations and Criticisms of the Gender Binary

The gender binary allows only two options: masculine and feminine. In an extensive narrative review of studies relying on these types of measures, Anne Constantinople (1973) found this generation of measures to rely on questionable assumptions, including the notion that researchers could sum the scores from ~450 test items to produce a single meaningful score or that masculinity and femininity were complete opposites. (Are the responses for the Pole or Date example really opposite?) Constantinople concluded that masculinity and femininity were independent constructs and also that they were partly opposed.

One of the major criticisms of the MMPI and the CPI was that they used relatively insignificant aspects of the personality (e.g., liking mechanics magazines) to make inferences about characteristics of central importance like sexual orientation, level of aggressiveness, and gender identity (Pleck, 1975), and thus confused gender with both sexual orientation and physiological (or "natal") sex. Men who reported traditionally feminine interests such as cooking were described—and occasionally diagnosed—as having poor adjustment and lack of masculinity.

For its original purpose, the MMPI's "Mf" scale was a total failure, probably because of the flaws in theory described above. Currently, this scale is considered to be a measure of breadth and stereotypy of interest. College-educated men tend to score more "feminine" on this scale compared with the general population of men (Groth-Marnat, 2003). Under the original intent of the scale, this finding would mean that college men tend to be disturbed with gender identity problems. The reality is that these men tend to be less stereotypical than the general population of men in their preferences for activities, perhaps as the consequences of higher than average intelligence and socioeconomic level, and more experiences of being exposed to a broad range of ideas.

Today, we know there are more than two gender labels, including transgender, genderqueer, and a-gender (i.e., not gendered). We have also learned that sexual orientation is separate from gender. Football player Michael Sam, Welsh national rugby team captain Gareth Thomas, and heavy metal rocker Rob Halford of Judas Priest have all publicly acknowledged their homosexuality and yet they all seem to fit American cultural conceptions of what it means to be highly masculine.

BEYOND THE BINARY: THEORIES COMBINING MASCULINITY AND FEMININITY

As you already know, gender is about more than your genitalia. Theories of androgyny and sexism came out of the feminist movement of the 1970s. Both approaches address masculinity and femininity together, but instead of positioning them as opposites, they're seen as independent entities—a key assumption differentiating them from gender identity models. They also include the assumption that gender is socially constructed, as described in Chapter One.

The Androgyny Model

Gender theorists and researchers began to question the Gender Identity Model's assumption that masculinity and femininity were opposites, as depicted in Figure 4.4. Theorists like Sandra Bem, Janet Spence, and Robert Helmreich argued that masculinity and femininity are not opposite. For example, traditionally masculine realms like work and reason are not antithetical to traditionally feminine realms like home and emotion, as work and home are not opposites. These theorists believed that it was possible and desirable for people to have *both* masculine and feminine traits. Thus, a person could be effective both at work and at home, and could be both rational and emotional.

They proposed the *androgyny model*, which assumes that femininity and masculinity should be measured separately. Each person displays some

Figure 4.5 A Bipolar View of Gender Role Identity

amount of masculinity and also displays some amount of femininity, as indicated by the axes in Figure 4.5. Simplifying this into low and high scores, each individual can then be categorized in one of four ways:

Androgynous: high in both femininity and masculinity
Masculine: high in masculinity and low in femininity
Feminine: high in femininity and low in masculinity
Undifferentiated: low in both femininity and masculinity

It is important to note that any person, regardless of his or her physiological sex, can be placed in any one of these four categories. When a man is classified as masculine and a woman is classified as feminine, they are considered *gender-typed* or *gender-conforming*. When a man is classified as feminine or a woman is classified as masculine, they are considered to be *cross-gender-typed* (Bem, 1974; Spence & Helmreich, 1978).

Androgyny theorists think of traditional femininity and masculinity as strategies for adaptation (Bem, 1993). Sometimes it is adaptive to express one's feelings (feminine); sometimes it is better to shut down one's emotions and get the job done (masculine). In stereotypical personality development, each sex acquires about half of the attitudes, skills, and behaviors necessary for coping in the world. Theoretically, the person who can incorporate both masculine and feminine characteristics into the personality will have a wide repertoire of coping strategies at his or her disposal, and this gender flexibility renders the person more adaptive than a traditionally gender-typed person. Thus, for some theorists, androgyny is seen as a mental health ideal. We'll review this proposition in Chapter Five.

Androgyny Measures

The most popular of the androgyny measures was the Bem Sex Role Inventory (BSRI) (Bem, 1974), a list of 60 adjectives, 20 of which are descriptive of traditional masculinity (e.g., "self-reliant," "analytical"), 20 of traditional femininity (e.g., "warm," "gentle"), and 20 gender neutral (e.g., "conscientious," "likable"). The person rates themselves on each adjective using a seven-point scale ranging from "never or almost never true" to "always or almost always true." All adjectives reflect the socially desirable aspects of each gender role due to the theory that the combination of positive traits of both roles is the ideal.

The Personality Attributes Questionnaire (PAQ), published by Janet Spence and Robert Helmreich (1978) has also been very popular. It consists of eight masculine- and eight feminine-typed adjectives, most of which describe socially desirable traits. Using a five-point scale from "not at all" to "very," participants indicate how aggressive or emotional they are (e.g., "not at all aggressive" to "very aggressive").

The BSRI and PAQ yield separate scores for masculinity and femininity. To determine what category an individual fits in to, the researcher begins by computing the group averages for masculinity and femininity. Then each individual's masculinity score is compared to the average masculinity score to determine if the person has a low or high score, then the process is repeated with femininity scores. Finally, the person is classified into one of the four groups (androgynous, feminine, masculine, undifferentiated) based on the combination of high or low scores.

Sexism

Psychologists define *sexism* as prejudicial attitudes and behaviors against women. We include it in this section because it requires conceptions of both masculinity and femininity. For example, one might comfort a female friend when she exhibits vulnerability, but avoid a male friend who exhibits the same behavior. Or the assertive behavior of a man might be described as "forceful" while the identical behavior, performed by a woman, might be labeled "bitchy."

Because some beliefs about gender can be subtle, because we have a natural propensity toward categorizing and stereotyping, because there are emotional and unconscious aspects to gender roles, and because we have all been socialized in a gender schematic and sexist society, we are probably all at least a little sexist. Here, we address measurement of sexism because it is an aspect of the anti-femininity component of masculinity; we address the various types of sexism and their cultural implications in more detail in Chapter Three.

Two Forms of Sexism. The initial discussion and measures of sexism focused on beliefs that seem obviously sexist today, such as "swearing is worse for a girl than a guy" (Galambos, Petersen, Richards, & Gitelson, 1985). Not surprisingly, both male and female college students have become less and less likely to agree with statements of this sort since the 1970s (Twenge, 1997a). *Mad Men's* Don Draper may have been typical for his time, but it's hard to imagine that kind of attitude and behavior is typical of most men.

Today, researchers are more likely to focus on constructs such as hostile sexism and benevolent sexism, which we introduced in Chapter Three. Hostile sexism refers to the hatred of women, while benevolent sexism refers to subtler attitudes and behaviors that suggest women are less capable than men.

Across 19 nations, Peter Glick, Susan Fiske, and their colleagues (Glick et al., 2000) found that hostile sexism scores tended to be lower than benevolent sexism scores. They also found remarkably high correlations between hostile and benevolent sexism within all of the cultures they studied. In countries where there was strong endorsement of hostile sexism, people also showed a strong tendency to endorse benevolent sexism. In the opinion of these researchers, these two forms of sexism act in complementary fashion as justifications of gender inequality (Glick & Fiske, 2001). Boxes 4.2 and 4.3 list some ways to reduce sexism against women.

Prejudices also extend toward men, who are often seen as arrogant, emotionally cold, aggressive, and exploitive. In fact, men report liking and trusting women more than they do other men, a positive out-group bias that is not seen in other forms of prejudice such as racism. This attitude is disrespectful of men, at least in some ways, yet it also supports the characterization of men as being oriented toward dominance and power (Glick, et. al., 2004; Steinberg & Diekman, 2016). Prejudices may be assessed directly or indirectly; indirect measures are sometimes called measures of *implicit bias.*

Limitations and Criticisms of Theories Combining Masculinity and Femininity

Results from studies relying on androgyny theory demonstrated that women often benefitted from it, but men did not (Hoffman & Borders, 2001). The BSRI and PAQ have both been criticized for relying strictly on positive characteristics, which lead Spence and Helmreich to develop the Extended PAQ that adds eight negative characteristics of masculinity and eight negative characteristics of femininity (Spence, Helmreich, & Holahan, 1979). The focus on positive traits may be one reason why mean scores for both male and female undergraduates increased for both the femininity and masculinity scales of both measures from the 1970s through the 1990s, although they have plateaued since then (Donnelly & Twenge, 2016; Twenge, 1997b). Between the rising means and the older age of these scales, Andrew Smiler and Marina Epstein (2010) recommended limited use of the PAQ. They further suggested the BSRI only be used for replications of earlier studies because it has poor psychometric properties.

Research on sexism has been affected by a trend toward more egalitarian responses over the years, at least among adolescents and undergraduates (Twenge, 1997a). It has been limited by a focus on attitudes that privilege men over women, with minimal discussion of the reverse: attitudes that privilege women over men. Discussion of, and especially the practice of, benevolent sexism has also met criticism. Young men with whom we have spoken have complained that they were taught to hold the door open for everyone, but they are asked about, and sometimes criticized, when they do this for women.

> **Box 4.2**
> **Reducing Sexism (Against Women)**
>
> Although it may be difficult to change sexist *behaviors*, it is often even more difficult to change sexist *reactions* that may be emotional and unconscious. Prejudiced and non-prejudiced people do not differ in *stereotype activation* (Fazio & Olson, 2003). However, the non-prejudiced person has made a commitment to be aware of and resistant to the tendency to stereotype. Over time, the stereotype activation itself decreases (Kawakami, Dovidio, Moll, Hermsen, & Russin, 2000). To reduce sexism, a person must expend efforts to understand socialization and gender role attitudes, recognize when he or she is engaging in stereotypical thinking, and resist inclinations to behave in sexist ways. Over time, this "self-training" should lead to nonsexist responses that are somewhat automatic.
>
> The concept of chivalry could potentially be replaced with values of courtesy, civility, helping those in need, and thoughtfulness. We often tell men that if they are treating women differently than they treat other men, they ought to have a good reason for doing so. For instance, one might help a short woman to put her baggage into an overhead bin on a plane, given men's average advantage in height and upper body strength. On the other hand, should a man help a tall, female bodybuilder to store her luggage? Should an old man in poor health offer his seat to a young, fit woman on a crowded bus? Should a young, fit woman offer her seat to a father carrying a newborn baby?
>
> Several women have described this same scenario to us. The woman is walking toward a public building with a set of doors that opens into a small foyer, where there is a second set of doors that open into the place of business. A man opens the outer door for her, which is courteous. Because she enters the foyer first, she reaches the inner set of doors and opens it for the man, who then refuses to walk through first. She is being equally courteous, but he does not accept her courtesy because he has learned that men do not accept help from women. Does his behavior reflect a respectful attitude?

BYE, BYE BINARY: MASCULINITY ALONE AND COMPLICATED

The third set of models and measures, focused solely on masculinity, also relied heavily on the feminist critique of psychology in the 1970s. As with other measures of that era, they carry with them the assumptions that masculinity is constructed rather than essential, that masculinity and femininity are separate entities, and that masculinity is multidimensional or multifaceted. This assumption of multidimensionality best incorporates the four facets we have discussed thus far; at eleven distinct facets of masculinity, the Conformity to Male Norms Index (Mahalik et al., 2003) assesses the greatest number of components (per Smiler & Epstein, 2010).

Masculine Roles, Scripts, Norms, and Ideologies

In practice, the following theories all rely on our cognitive abilities. We'll define each of the models briefly, then discuss the gender role approach in more detail to illustrate its strengths and weaknesses.

Role Theory is an appeal to behavior akin to that of an actor on screen or stage. Gender roles, however, are not limited to one particular venue (or television show), but rather extend across all aspects of an individual's life. The focus here is very much on the individual with minimal attention to the context in which they find themselves.

Script Theory appeals to a computer script (or program), where a script is defined as a set of instructions for what to do in a given situation (Bem, 1993). Scripts may be context specific, so there is some balance and interplay between the individual and the context. Schema-based approaches are similar and the two terms (script, schema) are sometimes used interchangeably although they should not be because they are derived from different theoretical approaches with different background assumptions. For our purposes, you might also think of scripts as recipes or formulas.

Norm-based approaches are descriptions of commonly held standards of behavior to which people attempt to adhere (Mahalik et al., 2003). Norms may be broad and cultural, like the expectation that American men rarely (or never) wear skirts in their day-to-day lives (Pleck, 1981a, 1995). Norms can also be much more localized and micro-contextualized. For example, you might have one professor who insists on being called "doctor" or "professor" and another who insists that you use their first name. Like script theory, the focus is on the interplay between the individual and the context.

Ideological approaches position masculinity as a belief system (Levant, 1996). In this way, they are comparable to an individual's system of values, political beliefs, or religious beliefs in that they provide an overarching set of ideals about how people should behave. Similar to role theory, the focus here is on the individual with little attention to the context.

Below, we discuss role theory in detail to provide a sense of how gender roles work and some of the problems of this approach. We focus on role theory because many of the subsequent approaches were developed by adopting the strengths of role theory while attempting to address its weaknesses.

Social roles define a set of expected behaviors for a person in any given social position. For example, the social role of student includes the expectations that one will attend classes, take tests, and complete assignments. Note that the role comprises expectations but not necessarily performance. Some students do not fulfill their assigned role while others vary in how well they fulfill that role (David and Brannon, 1976).

A **gender role** is a generalized social role, one that cuts across many situations and is comprised of a set of expectations for affect, behavior, and cognition that is based on a person's (perceived) physiological sex. If you were to obtain a part in a stage play, you would have a script that told you what to say and how to behave while acting. On occasion, actors will improvise, saying or doing things that are not in the script. If you decided to do so, the director of the play might or might not tolerate it, depending on his or her rigidity and on whether or not your improvisation was consistent with the role. However, if you were to improvise too extensively or in a way that was inconsistent with the role, the director would probably discipline you or throw you out of the play. If you feel strongly enough about changing the role, you might be willing to risk this outcome.

Actors (we use this term to refer to all genders, as is increasingly the convention) know that they have to stick to their roles to keep their jobs. Social roles are a little less well defined than stage roles; nobody gives a boy an explicit script telling him how to act in masculine ways (although beer commercials with descriptions of "man laws" come close). But social roles and gender roles are every bit as powerful. One may incur severe punishment for stepping outside of one's prescribed role and great social approval for staying within it. In the gender role arena, for instance, a boy who cries or plays with girls may be ostracized by his male peers. The power of gender roles is most evident when the prescriptions of the role are violated, as we alluded to when discussing violations of masculinity at the beginning of the chapter (Box 4.1).

Who are the "directors" of the "plays" when it comes to gender roles? They are everyone who can reward the individual for staying within gender role boundaries and everyone who can punish the person for stepping outside of them. They are real-life and media models who display stereotypical behavior or talk in ways that reinforce stereotypical beliefs about men and women. Families, friends, employers, romantic partners, media figures and others all have the power to enforce gender role norms. Sometimes their sanctions are subtle, such as a mildly disapproving look. At other times they are more overt, through insults like "you throw like a girl" or a refusal to befriend a man who is too effeminate.

Because men (and women) are socialized in a gender-typed society, they often internalize gender roles and become their own "directors" to some extent. A great many men incorporate masculine stereotypes and norms into their ideal self-concepts and attempt to live up to these norms. If one accepts such standards uncritically, then the content of masculine gender role norms becomes the yardstick by which the man judges his worth. Pleck (1981b) described such men as "prisoners of manliness" who compulsively conform their behavior to masculine role norms and lose sight of their individuality in the process. Instead of prioritizing gender as a way to organize and understand the people around us, we could adopt a different frame of reference. Box 4.3 lists several alternatives.

MEASURING MASCULINITY ALONE

Regardless of the exact theoretical approach, all measures of this type are often labeled as measures of *Masculinity Ideology* because the focus is on individual beliefs, or ideas, about what masculinity means (Smiler, 2004; Smiler & Epstein, 2010; Thompson & Bennett, 2015a; Thompson & Pleck, 1995). Participants are given a series of questions and asked to use a scale from one to four (or six or seven) to indicate the strength of their agreement

> **Box 2.4**
> **Reducing Gender Schematic Processing**
>
> Sandra Bem (1998) notes that there are many ways to think about people without reference to their gender. The first three of these are Bem's suggestions, the remainder are ours.
>
> *Individual differences schema*: people vary widely in their habits, attitudes, and temperament. A person may act aggressively, not because he is a man, but because he has an aggressive personality and/or finds himself in a situation in which aggression is adaptive.
>
> *Cultural relativism schema*: "different people believe different things" (p. 271). Roman Catholics do not allow women to be priests, but some Episcopalians do.
>
> *Sexism schema*: although beliefs differ, some beliefs about gender are wrong. Women should be allowed to be Roman Catholic priests.
>
> *Situational pressure schema*: people tend to behave in certain ways when situations exert different pressures. A man may keep his feelings to himself while with his male friends, not because men are unemotional, but because other men might not give him a compassionate response. He may be very emotionally expressive as a client in psychotherapy or when he is in the company of women who are his friends.
>
> *External variability schema*: people do not always behave in concert with how they feel; two people can vary to a great extent in their external reactions to exactly the same internal thoughts and feelings. Two men may hold equally sexist attitudes, but one decides not to display them because he wants the approval of women.

(from "completely disagree" to "completely agree") or the extent to which a statement describes them (from "does not describe me at all" to "describes me very much"). For example, the Male Role Attitudes Scale (Pleck, Sonenstein, & Ku, 1993) asks participants to indicate how much they agree or disagree with statements like "It is essential for a guy to get respect from others" using a four-point scale.

Most scales provide separate scores for each component of masculinity, although some of the shortest scales, such as the 8-item Male Role Attitudes Scale (Pleck et al., 1993) provide only a total score. The longest scale published to date is the Conformity to Masculine Norms Inventory (CMNI; Mahalik et al., 2003) which consists of 94 items that assess eleven distinct components of masculinity. The use of subscales allows researchers to pinpoint which aspect(s) of masculinity have the strongest connection to the outcomes (or dependent variables) being examined.

Strain and Stress Models

Other related models include the emphasis that not only is masculinity complex, but also that the effort of living up to its standards of behavior is inherently stressful. In introducing his Gender Role Strain theory, James O'Neil (1981a) pointed out that compulsive dominance, passivity, and emotional constriction are downright maladaptive. He also argued, as did Josph Pleck (O'Neil, 1982; Pleck, 1981a, 1981b), that trying to become androgynous presented a different—but still potentially stressful—set of standards that may be even more challenging to live up to than the expectations of traditional masculinity alone. For men, traditional gender roles include demands for competitiveness, aggression, and task orientation. Androgyny demands emotional expression, relationship orientation, and gentleness *in addition to* the role requirements of traditional masculinity.

The key assumptions of strain and stress models include the hypotheses that (a) trying to be masculine is inherently stressful; (b) masculinity and masculine role stress have several distinct components that can be measured individually; (c) masculinity and femininity are partial opposites; and (d) masculinity is constructed.

Gender Role Strain is a psychological situation in which gender role demands have negative consequences for the individual, or for others, while also limiting the individual's human potential (O'Neil, 1981a; 2008). The negative effects of masculine gender role strain can be described in terms of stress, conflict, physical health, and mental health problems for the individual. Violence and poor relationships are potential negative consequences for others who come into contact with the individual.

A person experiences this strain when gender role demands conflict with his or her *naturally occurring tendencies*. For example, males in most Western cultures are socialized to be unemotional. For a naturally emotional man, the demand created by this socialization may cause him to feel a good deal of pressure to conform his behavior to the cultural norm. As a result, he may experience negative consequences, such as depression or high blood pressure. The net effect of gender role strain is the restriction of the person's ability to reach his or her full human potential (O'Neil, 1981a, 2008). In the above example, the man's depression or high blood pressure may restrict his potential by lowering his functioning in his work, affecting his relationship with his partner, or even shortening his life.

Strain and Stress Measures

There are two measures of strain and stress. James O'Neil's Gender Role Conflict Scale (GRCS) has been much more popular than Richard Eisler and Jay Skidmore's (1987) Masculine Gender Role Stress Scale (MGRSS). These measures were developed for use with only male subjects and are designed to assess the degree to which a man endorses attitudes, behaviors, and values that have been associated with negative psychological effects.

On each scale, participants respond to a set of statements using a scale anchored by "strongly agree" to "strongly disagree." The MGRSS, for example, asks participants to indicate how stressful "having a female boss" is (or would be) using a seven-point scale anchored at the extremes by "not at all stressful" and "very stressful." The GRCS is the most frequently used of any masculinity-only measure (Whorley & Addis, 2006; Wong & Horn, 2016) and we will refer to its findings throughout the latter half of this text. It examines four categories of conflict:

1. *Success, Power, and Competition*: the pressure to gain wealth, obtain authority, and be a winner.
2. *Restrictive Emotionality*: difficulty in expressing one's feelings or allowing others to do so.
3. *Restrictive Affectionate Behavior between Men*: limiting the expression of warm feelings for other men.
4. *Conflict between Work and Family Relations*: difficulty balancing these sometimes conflicting demands.

Limitations and Criticisms of Masculinity-Alone

The approaches described above—roles, scripts, norms, and ideologies—highlight conceptually different aspects of people's beliefs about masculinity, and all focus on the individual's cognitions about masculinity. These scales have been criticized for focusing on the more problematic aspects of masculinity, such as extreme self-reliance and emotional stoicism (Kiselica et al., 2016; Wade, 2015). They have also been criticized for generating relatively low average scores; such scores suggest that men-as-a-group don't particularly believe in or adhere to the descriptions of masculinity being assessed (Smiler, 2013; Thompson & Bennett, 2015; Thompson & Pleck, 1995).

Another criticism is that they often do not reconcile differences but simply provide different points of emphasis. For example, the Conformity to Masculine Norms Inventory emphasizes conformity and thus provides participants with "I" statements such as "In general, I will do anything to win." However, the Male Role Norms Inventory, Revised (MRNI-R, Levant et al. 2007) focuses on participants' normative beliefs and thus asks about "men" with questions such as "A man should always be the boss." Yet researchers have discovered differences between young men's self-descriptions ("I") and their descriptions of "most men" (Street, Kimmel, & Kromrey, 1995). Perhaps this finding is not surprising, as most people see themselves as somewhat gender nonconforming, and most men (and probably most women as well) overestimate the gender conformity of same-sex peers (Kilmartin, Smith, Green, Heinzen, Kuchler, & Kolar, 2008).

SUMMARY

Theorists and researchers have taken a variety of approaches to the data-driven study of masculinity. These definitions matter, because they guide what is assessed and what is ignored, as well as the balance between positive and negative attributes of masculinity. Consider the pair of multi-national studies discussed in Chapter Two (Tables 2.2 and 2.3); one assessed nine aspects of masculinity while the other assessed thirteen. Does this difference, which includes items such as "being a family man" and "having a manly image" seem important?

In this chapter, we reviewed three broad approaches, addressing the ways they describe the relationship between masculinity and femininity, as well as how complexly they define masculinity. Table 4.1 lists several of the key assumptions that delineate psychological approaches. However, it is not clear how important these differences are, and direct comparisons are rare. In one meta-analysis that included both types of measures, as well as the BSRI's masculinity scale, researchers found the same pattern of results for all measures of masculinity reviewed: men with higher masculinity scores were more supportive of attitudes that facilitate sexual assault against women (Murnen, Wright, & Kaluzny, 2002). A separate correlational study that included the different types of measures found that men with higher masculinity scores expressed greater desire for higher numbers of sexual partners (Walker, Tokar, & Fischer, 2000). Measures include and reflect the assumptions of the theory under which they are developed.

1. Measures and approaches to the measurement of gender and masculinity have changed over time.
2. Binary models of gender emphasize male or female, or masculine vs. feminine.
3. Reviews of the research on sex differences indicate that (group) average differences tend to be small.
4. Gender Identity Models rely on the assumption that men need to be masculine to have healthy development.

Table 4.1
Summary of Measurement Approaches

	Essential or Constructed?	Relationship Between Masculinity and Femininity	Number of Scores	Focus
Gender Binary				
Gender Identity	Essential	Opposites	1	
Sex Comparison	Essential	Opposites	1	
Beyond Binary				
Androgeny	Constructed	Separate	2 (Masc., Fem.)	
Sexism	Constructed	Related	1	Cognition
Bye Bye Binary				
Masculinity Alone	Constructed	Partial opposites	Multiple	Cognition
Strain & Stress	Constructed	Partial opposties	Multiple	Cognition

5. In effect, gender identity measures tend to measure conformity to gender stereotypes.
6. Androgyny models position masculinity and femininity as separate constructs.
7. Androgyny models include the assumption that the ability to draw from both masculinity and femininity leads to healthy development.
8. Sexism focuses on power relations between males and females.
9. Sexism takes many forms, including institutional sexism, internalized sexism, benevolent sexism, and hostile sexism.
10. Masculinity Ideology approaches position masculinity as a multifaceted construct that is partially opposed to femininity.
11. Stress and Strain approaches include the assumption that efforts to adhere to cultural expectations of masculinity are inherently problematic.

GLOSSARY

Models: Broad conceptions of masculinity that describe how it works.

ABC model (Affect, Behavior, and Cognition): A model that describes an indivdual's reactions (to a thought, feeling, or event) as not only being what they think (cognition) but also how they feel (affect) and what they do (behavior).

Gender binary: The idea that gender is made up of only two options, male and female (or masculine and feminine), and functions in an either-or fashion.

Narrative review: A text-based summary of the available research. A textbook is an example of a narrative review.

Meta-analysis: A mathematical aggregation of the research that combines the results of many studies to describe what the body of research, taken together, indicates.

Androgyny model: The idea that femininity and masculinity are separate dimensions, not opposites, and thus any given individual can demonstrate both feminine and masculine attributes.

Androgynous: The term for an individual who is relatively high in both femininity and masculinity.

Undifferentiated: The term for an individual who is relatively low in both femininity and masculinity.

Implicit bias: One type of indirect measure of prejudice.

Role theory: A model of gender that positions conformity to a culture's gender norms as similar to the behavior of an actor on screen or stage.

Script theory: A model of gender that positions conformity to a culture's gender norms as similar to a computer script (or program) that provides a set of instructions for what to do in a given situation.

Norm-based theories: Models of gender that position conformity to gender norms as conformity to commonly held standards of behavior.

Ideological theories: Models of gender that position conformity to gender norms as a system of beliefs that provide an overarching set of ideals about how people should behave.

Social roles: A set of expected behaviors for a person in any given social position.

Gender role: A social role that cuts across many situations and is comprised of a set of expectations for affect, behavior, and cognition that is based on a person's gender.

Masculinity ideology: A set of models and measures that focus on individual's beliefs, or ideas, about what masculinity means.

Gender role strain: A psychological situation in which gender role demands have negative consequences for the individual, or others, while also limiting the individual's human potential.

Chapter Five

Biologically-Based Theoretical Perspectives on Males and Gender

One obvious place to begin a study of male behavior and experience is with biological theory. In this chapter, we explore three approaches that take biology as the starting point for explanations of gender. Strictly biological approaches highlight effects based explicitly on genetic allotment, either arising from the so-called "sex hormones" or hormones such as testosterone. Evolutionary Psychology attempts to apply the theory of evolution to social behaviors. Psychoanalysis is a narrative of how basic biological survival mechanisms interact with human relationships to form the personality, part of which is gendered.

Parents of large families often say that their children have differing personalities, and that these differences were evident even in the first few days after they were born. Such differences could be due to misperception or memory distortion on the part of the parents, or from prenatal events such as difficult pregnancies. But it is also possible that what these parents perceive are some real differences that are based in biology.

Developmental psychologists have long known that infants differ in *psychological temperament*. Some babies are relatively quiet and content. Others have higher activity levels or are more disposed toward crankiness. Temperamental differences are thought to be determined largely by infants' genes, hormones, and other biological forces, which may continue to affect their behavior throughout their lives (Thomas & Chess, 1977; Weinberg, Rahdert, Coliver, & Glantz, 1998; Zeenah, Boris, & Larrieu, 1997).

It is clear that males and females have differing biologies in some ways, although we should keep in mind that in *most* ways, they do not. There are differences in genetic and hormonal composition that lead to average male/female differences in height, weight, muscularity, genitalia, and secondary sex characteristics such as breasts and facial hair. There is little dispute that biological sex differences produce these usual physical differences, most of which are *average* differences as discussed in Chapter Four. But, to what extent do they produce *behavioral* sex differences as well? The central question concerns to what extent "boys will be boys" because of their biological compositions, and to what extent "boys will be boys" because we socialize them to act in certain ways. In this chapter, we focus on biological explanations to that question. In the next chapter, we'll address answers focused on the socialization process.

A rather complex sequence of biological events is necessary to ensure that most healthy men and women will have the physiological wherewithal to reproduce (Fausto-Sterling, 2000). Of course, the development of these basic structures is not enough to ensure the survival of the species. Sexual behaviors are also necessary. There is little doubt that hormonal events affect brain structures and pathways, which then have strong influences over these behaviors. But what is the difference in the biological basis of *sexual* behaviors (those necessary for reproduction) on the one hand, and *gender role* behaviors (social behaviors attributed strongly to either males or females) on the other?

CHROMOSOMAL AND HORMONAL APPROACHES

The twenty-third pair of human chromosomes are called the *sex chromosomes*. Individuals who have two X chromosomes, XX, are female and those with an XY combination are male. Many people are unaware that approximately one or two of every 1,000 live births does not follow this pattern (Fausto-Sterling, 2000). Individuals who are neither XX nor XY are often referred to as "intersexual" or "intersexed"; a number of medical groups, as well as advocacy groups, have begun using the these individuals as having a *disorder of sexual development* (DSD; Vilain et al., 2007). Table 5.1 lists several of these disorders and the frequency with which a child is born with that disorder.

This list includes a pair of disorders that focus on the "sex hormones," estrogen and testosterone, and not chromosomal issues per se. When all such disorders—chromosomal, hormonal, and others, are included, we may be talking about as many as one or two of every 100 births (Fausto-Sterling, 2000).

Table 5.1   Frequency of Selected Disorders of Sexual Development

Disorder	Frequency (among live births)
Klinefelter's Syndrome (XXY)	1 in 1,000
Other non-XX or non-XY	1 in 1,666
Androgen Insensitivity Syndrome (complete)	1 in 13,000
Androgen Insensitivity Syndrome (partial)	1 in 130,000
Congenital Adrenal Hyperplasia ("Classic" CAH)	1 in 13,000
Total number of people whose bodies differ from standard male or female	1 in 100

Values from the Intersex Society of North America (ISNA, undated)

Here, we focus on two disorders regarding testosterone. Keep in mind that all humans, regardless of their chromosomal allotment, produce testosterone, and that prior to puberty, boys and girls have similar amounts of testosterone. Testosterone's functions include bone growth (size, density) and muscle mass. There are certain times when testosterone interacts with the Y-chromosome in ways that are particularly male-oriented. One is approximately 8 weeks after conception. If the fetus has a Y-chromosome, it triggers the release of testosterone so that male genitalia, as well as the related musculature and vasculature, are formed. Without testosterone at this point in time, children develop female genitalia. Another is puberty.

Androgen Insensitivity Syndrome (AIS), which can be either complete (CAIS) or partial (PAIS), describes individuals whose bodies are unable to break down and process *androgens*, a class of hormones that includes testosterone and adrenaline, both of which are produced by the adrenal gland. XY Males who have AIS are unable to process testosterone, in much the same way that an individual who is lactose intolerant can't process lactose (and thus becomes ill if he or she ingests milk products). One result is that XY males with AIS do not develop normally-sized male genitalia. At birth, they may have a vagina, a micropenis, or another structure that is neither vagina nor penis. Those who appear to have a vagina at birth are often assumed to be female; their disorder is not typically discovered until puberty. For children whose condition is evident at birth, the parents face a series of difficult decisions described in Box 5.1.

Another disorder is *Congenital Adrenal Hyperplasia* (CAH), in which the developing fetus is exposed to a large dose of androgens in utero at just the right (wrong?) moment and the fetus subsequently becomes "masculinized" and develops a penis. This exposure causes no problems if it's an XY fetus, but it does alter the development of an XX fetus. One such result is a change in genital development that may lead to a penis, a micropenis, or some other structure. Although only a small percentage of the population has CAH, these

---

Box 5.1
Decisions for Parents Whose Children Have Ambiguous Genitalia

The American Association of Pediatrics once described the birth of such child as a "social emergency" (AAP, 2000) but has subsequently changed its stance. Nonetheless, many parents and medical personnel still react to this unexpected phenomenon as though it is a major problem. Parents face a series of difficult questions, including:

What will we tell family and friends?

Do we choose a gender, and possibly plastic surgery, now, or do we wait? If we wait, how long?

What happens if we choose the "wrong" gender?

There are no easy answers to these questions, and professional guidelines continue to be rewritten and evolve as we learn more. Parents who choose plastic surgery for their children aren't choosing a one-time surgery; they are committing themselves and their child to a series of surgeries throughout childhood and adolescence.

individuals often have an ongoing connection to the medical system that has allowed researchers to study them in some detail. Most of the research has relied on children's and parent's reports of their children's behavior, although some observational studies have been conducted.

In general, research tends to show that CAH girls are more masculine and less feminine than non-CAH girls. Similarly, AIS boys tend to be more feminine and less masculine than non-AIS boys. CAH boys and AIS girls do not differ from their same-sex peers (Cohen-Bendahan, van de Beek, & Berenbaum, 2005).

However, findings tend to be specific to some aspects of masculinity (or femininity) and some sex hormones, but not others, and some findings are more consistent than others. Evidence that males have relatively better performance on tasks such as *spatial rotation*, defined as the ability to mentally rotate an object, are linked to androgens is fairly robust, for example, while evidence that women have relatively better performance on verbal fluency tasks are less consistent. One group of reviewers concluded that "it seems likely that androgens are responsible for some of the differences between the sexes in these traits, although it is not as clear how much they contribute to variations within males and within females" (Cohen-Bandahan et al., 2005, p. 377). The picture is further complicated by the fact that testosterone levels vary naturally during the day and that specific situations, such as being challenged or becoming sexually aroused, further increase testosterone (Archer, 2006).

Criticism of Chromosomal and Hormonal Approaches

This approach to the study of gender has received some criticism. One concern is the lack of detail in exactly how a chromosome or a hormone produces a behavior. This is particularly troubling given evidence that hormones contribute to male–female differences but androgens, for example, do not explain differences between males (Cohen-Bandahan et al., 2005). The reliance on a gender binary to measure masculinity and femininity in this area of research is another concern (Smiler & Epstein, 2010).

EVOLUTIONARY PSYCHOLOGY

Evolutionary psychology (EP) is an approach to the study of human behavior that focuses on the adaptive value of behavior. An *adaptive behavior* is one that would have allowed ancestral humans to survive in a life-threatening environment or would have provided individuals with an advantage that would have increased the likelihood that they would produce offspring and thus pass their genes on to the next generation (Tooby & Cosmides, 2005). As you might guess, this work finds its roots in Charles Darwin's (1871) evolutionary theory and the idea of "survival of the fittest."

EP posits that our brain is comprised of different modules, each of which has a particular function. Over time, modules may come to be used in a situation other than the situation which shaped their evolution. When this happens, a behavior is said to have been *exapted* (Tooby & Cosmides, 2005). Aspects of the visual system that help us quickly identify motion, which developed in the wild and allowed proto-humans to recognize prey and other hunters, are currently being exapted to help people obtain high scores in video games like Halo. Whether or not this will ultimately lead to a reproductive advantage for the player is an open question.

At its best, EP draws together knowledge from many segments of study, including emotion, cognition, developmental, and biological psychology. It also draws from other fields such as computer science (because some aspects of cognition are computer-like), history (because biological change is a slow process), sociology and demography (because evolutionary change should be apparent throughout the species), and anthropology (because different types of cultures, such as hunter-gatherer tribes, tell us something about how widespread a phenomenon is and give us models for much earlier forms of civilization). Some of EP's basic tenets were established by an earlier approach known as sociobiology, although EP has attempted to address some of the problems associated with sociobiology (Tooby & Cosmides, 2005).

Evolutionary psychologists conduct work on a broad variety of topics, but we will highlight two areas because they are the root of several important male-female comparisons and align with issues of masculinity: sex and violence. Both of these topics will be the focus of later chapters, but we address them here briefly. Evolutionary psychology positions sex differences in sexual behavior as the result of differences in males' and females' *reproductive investments*, which in turn affect the *reproductive strategies* of each sex. Reproductive investment refers to the amount of time and resources that are expended in producing offspring. Reproductive strategy is the behavioral pattern employed to ensure that one's genes will be passed on to the succeeding generation (Buss & Schmitt, 1993; Schmitt, 2005).

According to EP, reproductive investment differs dramatically for women and men and creates different reproductive strategies. Physiologically, males need only a few seconds to make their genetic contribution to the reproductive process. Millions of sperm can be deposited in this period of time, and a healthy young male can ejaculate several times a day. Males are capable of impregnating females for almost all of their adult lives, making sperm an abundant and renewable resource.

In contrast, females usually only produce one ovum each month and have a more limited number of reproductive years. Therefore, females have a greater investment in the reproductive process than males. In humans, females carry and nourish the fetus for nine months, during which time they cannot begin another pregnancy. Following birth, they must feed and protect children during the period of helpless infancy if the young are to survive. Whereas sperm are an abundant resource, eggs are a relatively scarce one.

Sexuality

These differences in reproductive investment have led to sex-differentiated reproductive strategies, according to EP theorists. The female must be selective in her choice of sexual partner and should choose a high-status male who can provide for and protect her and the child. The male, on the other hand, has two options. He might adopt a short-term mating strategy in which he tries to impregnate as many females as possible while also preventing other males from copulating with his partners by using aggression and other forms of dominance. Alternately, he might adopt a long-term mating strategy in which he mates with a single partner repeatedly over a long period of time, producing multiple offspring with her. In theory, women might also adopt the short-term strategy, although EP has paid little research attention to this possibility.

Within EP, research focused on sexual behavior typically follows this logic, which is known as Sexual Strategies Theory (SST) (Buss & Schmitt, 1993; Schmitt, 2005). SST's proponents, like sociobiology's advocates, rely on and point to several male-female differences in sexual behavior (Buss & Schmitt, 1993; Schmitt, 2005; Symons, 1987), many of which have long been known:

- Many more societies allow polygyny (men having more than one wife or partner) than allow polyandry (women having multiple partners) (Murdock, 1967).
- Men report more *desired* sexual partners than do women, a finding that SST's authors have demonstrated to be applicable worldwide (Schmitt et al., 2003)
- Boys and men report more *actual* sexual partners than girls and women, a finding that has long been documented (Oliver & Hyde, 1993).
- Men agree to sex with a hypothetical partner more quickly than women (Schmitt, 2005).

Whereas sociobiology suggested that all women adopted the long-term mating strategy and all men adopted the short-term mating strategy (Daly & Wilson, 1983), SST posits that both males and females may choose either strategy but that men are more likely to choose the short-term strategy (Buss & Schmitt, 1993; Schmitt, 2005). Reviews conducted outside the SST framework, one examining the role of testosterone (Archer, 2006) and the other examining reported number of sexual partners (Smiler, 2013), indicate that a small number of men routinely engage in short-term mating while the majority choose longer-term partners. Males who choose to have a series of short-term partners tend to have higher levels of testosterone (Archer, 2006).

Violence

Following sociobiologists, evolutionary psychologists have also offered explanations for male aggressiveness, competition, risk taking, and dominance

(Barash & Lipton 1997). Just as rams butt horns to win the right to reproduce with ewes, so do men fight with one another in the competition to inseminate women. According to these theories, a male has to take a chance on being hurt or killed in competition to gain a mate directly or to gain the status which will subsequently give him access to mates. In either case, the benefit of aggressive behavior is an opportunity to pass on his genes. Sociobiologists Daly and Wilson (1983) described the process using an animal example:

> Imagine a bull elephant seal that has no stomach for the dominance battles of the breeding beach. Very well. He can opt out: remain at sea, never endure the debilitating months of fast and battle, outlive his brothers. But mere survival is no criterion of success. Eventually he will die, and his genes will die with him. The bull seals of the future will be the sons of males that found the ordeal of the beach to be worth the price. (p. 92)

Researchers Daniel Kruger and Randy Nesse (2004, 2006a, 2006b) have completed a series of compelling studies that suggest men have long been more violent than women and that this is a worldwide phenomenon. Using mortality data from more than 20 countries, they documented that men age 15 to 34 are approximately three times more likely to die than women of their same age among samples from the United States, Russia, Norway, and Croatia, among others. Where data are available, they suggest this 3:1 ratio has been stable through most of the twentieth century. This is the time in life when males reach the apex of physical development, are most sexually virile, and are attempting to "make their mark" on the world. These researchers and their colleagues find a similar male-female ratio among "teen" and "young adult" chimpanzees. Among humans, homicide and suicide rates drive these disparities. Kruger and Nesse argue that homicide represents an extreme version of male vs. male competition for mates and status, while suicide represents self-identified failure in that same competition. They argue that the historical, cross-national, and cross-species data give credence to the argument that this violence is at least partially the result of evolutionary forces. However, we should remember that the apparent universality of a behavior does not guarantee that it is necessarily "hard-wired" (See Chapter Twelve for an alternate explanation.).

General Critique of Evolutionary Psychology

Darwin himself expressed serious doubts that sexual selection processes are paramount in human behavior, particularly in modern societies (Eagly & Wood, 1999). Evolutionary psychology, like sociobiology before it, has faced serious criticism regarding its underlying propositions as well as some of its research claims.

Many people may find evolutionary psychology theory to be compelling because it provides a simple explanation for a complex phenomenon or because it allows them to maintain current power structures (i.e., patriarchy, masculinities). This theory may be especially appealing for traditional men who may be motivated to dominate, disrespect, and overpower women, and to engage in competitions for dominance with other men. In bookstores, one usually finds sociobiological works in the biology section rather than the social science section despite the fact that these books are almost wholly focused on explaining social behavioral phenomena. It seems that many people view biology as "real" science and view the social sciences with a greater level of skepticism. The relative statuses of the sciences can be used to validate the unequal social statuses of men and women. Although sociobiological propositions based on the theory of evolution are subject to serious criticism, the theory of evolution itself is well accepted, and it may be difficult for an uncritical observer to separate the two. Sociobiologists look for biological correlates of behavior in a quest to prove that sex differences are of "real" nature, not "trivial" nurture (Money, 1987a).

Goldfoot and Neff (1987) argued that sociobiological methods were too simplistic. The typical approach is to hold constant, or to eliminate, social variables that are known to affect the behavior being studied. For example, researchers might study sexual behavior in primates by raising a male and a female primate in a cage together and observing some behavior of interest. Such research ignores the effects of known social influences such as dominance hierarchies and coalition formation within primate troops.

Other critics have pointed to circular or faulty logic. There is often an assumption in biopsychological research that animals (humans included) behave from the "inside out." If there is hormonal variation and change in behavior at the same time, the bias is to see the hormonal change as the cause of the behavioral change. There is evidence to suggest that a hormonal change may sometimes be an effect, rather than a cause, of behavioral change. For instance, although testosterone may be a partial cause of aggression, the attainment of dominance (sometimes through aggressive behavior) results in testosterone surges, both for humans (male and female) and animals, and therefore testosterone can also be seen as an effect of aggression (Archer, 2006; Sapolsky, 1997). This makes it difficult to determine when increases in testosterone cause aggression and when aggression causes an increase in testosterone. We review the link between testosterone and aggression in Chapter Twelve.

Most people can find a good demonstration of the influence of an environmental event on physiology in their experience. Consider the following scenario: you are very attracted to someone. You begin dating this person and become even more attracted to them. At some point, you kiss this person for the first time. You can feel some strong emotional changes (excitement, sexual arousal, happiness), and we could measure concomitant physiological changes in heart rate, respiration, sexual response, and brain waves. Although hormonal and neural fluctuations "caused" your emotional experience, is it not also true that the kiss "caused" the hormonal and neural changes? So, although the brain affects experience, experience also affects the brain. As Lise

Eliot (2009) points out, the more that boys and girls engage in similar activities, the more similar their brains become.

Another logical error is the assumption that a widespread behavior must be genetically based. Anne Fausto-Sterling (1992) cites an example of a primate troop that learned a behavior and passed it down to its next generation. Someone who observed the behavior (which had become universal in the troop) in the second generation, might wrongly assume that this learned behavior was instinctual and genetically-based. In the laboratory, Frans de Waal (2005) has demonstrated several instances of cultural behavior transmission among primates. Fausto-Sterling's criticism is that sociobiologists assume that universal behaviors must be genetic and that genetic behaviors must be universal, a circular logic. Hubbard (1998) makes an eloquent counterargument:

> If a society puts half its children into short skirts and warns them not to move in ways that reveal their panties, while putting the other half into jeans and overalls, and encouraging them to climb trees, play ball, and participate in other vigorous outdoor games; if later, during adolescence, the children who have been wearing trousers are urged to 'eat like growing boys,' while the children in skirts are warned to watch their weight and not get fat; if the half in jeans runs around in sneakers or boots, while the half in skirts totters about on spike heels, then these two groups of people will be biologically as well as socially different. (p. 150)

The largest body of critical attacks on evolutionary psychology comes from counterexamples of human and animal behavior that do not support the theory of differential reproductive strategies, some of which suggest a pattern of selective but "cherry-picked" examples. One challenge is to question the hypothesis that it is natural for all males to lack parental involvement, although providing is a central tenet of masculinity in many countries (see Chapters Two and Nine). In some bird species, such as penguins, the male takes the major responsibility for incubating the eggs, and many birds mate for life. Male primates will protect or adopt orphaned infants, and in the pair-bonding marmoset, the father carries the young more often than the mother after the first few weeks of life (Rosenblum, 1987). Frans de Waal (1997) describes the behavior of the bonobo, a primate that is a close genetic relative of humans. Female bonobos occupy prominent positions in the primate society, which is cooperative and rarely aggressive. On both sides of the argument, the tendency is to choose species-level examples with little attention to biological families or orders.

Franz de Waal (2005) also notes that, contrary to the stereotype that they are aggressive bullies, most primate *alpha males*, defined as the individual at the top of a troop's dominance hierarchy, are more accurately described as peacemakers or "populists" that break up fights and ensure that food is shared within the troop. He also noted that the Darwinian fitness tends to be interpreted as an ability to eliminate the unfit, but that there are many more ways to be fit than to be aggressive, such as having the ability to find food or de-escalate conflicts within the troop (de Waal, 2007).

Critics have pointed out that these types of evolutionary arguments are often used to justify double standards and the status quo. In humans, the greater involvement of females in the care of children can be accounted for largely by cultural factors. In most cultures, girls are encouraged to partake in nurturing behavior from an early age (Whiting & Edwards, 1988). In cultures that encourage boys to take part in caring for children, no sex differences are found in adult parental involvement (Basow, 1992).

Hubbard (1998) notes that some nineteenth-century physicians warned girls that developing their brains through education would sap energy from their reproductive organs and render them unable to bear children. Kimmel and Mosmiller (1992) note how purported biological explanations of women's "fragile" nature were used to argue against allowing women to vote or go to college in the United States. The assumptions about male promiscuity, violence, and competition for mates can be interpreted as justifying destructive masculine behaviors such as rape, violence, and indifference to children.

One could also construct a list of behaviors that are difficult to explain from a sociobiological perspective. Homosexuality and sexual behaviors other than genital intercourse are good examples. So are the large numbers of men who are faithful husbands and good fathers, and men who have never had a physical fight in their lives. Bleier (1984) lists a number of theoretically sound sociobiological hypotheses that are not supported by available data.

Critics have also noted that sociobiologists and evolutionary psychologists often ignore or explain away behaviors that do not fit their models. In the search for the universality of sex-dimorphic behavior across different animal species, one may find that animal behavior is much more diverse than it appears to be at first glance. Human behavior is even more diverse, as almost any social scientist will attest.

Despite many serious criticisms of this theory we should be careful not to "throw the baby out with the bath water." Many researchers who are not identified with sociobiology (e.g., Money, 1987a; Maccoby, 1987) agree that biology probably produces different sensitivities to behavioral influences in males and females. Social influence can exaggerate or modify these sensitivities, and possibly not in a simple, straightforward way. The quest to discover the relative strengths of biological vs. social influences and the nature of the interactions between them is ongoing. It seems certain, however, that biology does not constitute a "whole program" (Money, 1987a, p. 15) for behavior. A man is not "destined" to become violent or promiscuous any more than a tall person is "destined" to become a basketball player.

Gender-Based Critique of Evolutionary Claims

Sociobiologists and evolutionary psychologists temper their claims with the warnings that cultural influences are also important, that no predictions for individuals are possible, and that describing biological influences is different from prescribing how people should act (Barash & Lipton 1997). Nevertheless, a proposed description of a gender-typed "human nature" emerges, and the picture of "male nature" (as well as men's treatment of women) is not a pretty one. Although evolutionary psychologists often propose that learning about sex differences in behavior will allow us to design social interventions that will result in a more gender-egalitarian and less violent world (Thornhill & Palmer, 2000), they rarely say specifically what these interventions should be, and their seeming lack of interest in modifying these destructive behaviors that they see as natural makes their motives suspect in the eyes of many of their critics.

The male is characterized as an aggressive, driven, immoral, impulsive, uncaring, unfaithful, distrustful, jealous, promiscuous, and cruel animal whose core motivation is to fight off other men and impregnate as many women as possible, at almost any cost, even risking his life in the pursuit of his evolutionary goals. This view serves to normalize and excuse many of the most destructive aspects of the masculine gender role: over-competitiveness, attention to task and not relationship, the unimportance of emotions other than sexual and aggressive feelings, and the risking of the body in the compulsive attempt to prove one's masculinity. However, a man can never prove his sociobiological masculinity once and for all, as there are always more men to fight off and more women to impregnate. Until the advent of genetic testing over the last few decades (and in relatively affluent countires), a man could never be 100 percent certain of his own paternity, so he must be on guard against other men at all times. Eventually he will grow old and be supplanted by younger and stronger men. The picture that emerges is one of a roaming, violent, restless creature who can never be satisfied.

From this perspective, the only hope for a civilized society is to tame the barbaric nature of masculinity. Evolutionary psychologists see male nature as antisocial and valueless, and female nature more civilized, positive, and morally superior. They view the two sexes as inherently competitive with each other (Clatterbaugh, 1997). Gilder (1986) argues that a socialized order can only be maintained if male sexual impulses and antisocial tendencies are subordinated to female nature. He assigns the task of civilizing the world to women, who must use their erotic power to keep men in line by demanding monogamy and commitment from them in exchange for sexual access. Gilder's ideal society seems to be one with traditional morals, where women refuse to have sex before marriage, and where monogamy is strictly enforced. Many evolutionary psychologists do not believe that this arrangement will work because of the primacy of biological forces over social ones (Barash, 1982). For these theorists, "boys will be boys" forever, and therefore war, rape, and the adversarial "battle of the sexes" is unavoidable.

This ideal normalizes the sexual double standard, male sexual irresponsibility, violence, noninvolvement with children, and a lack of a human connection with women. If we see these attributes as biologically ordained, then there is little hope in changing the standard of male dominance. Several authors (Fausto-Sterling, 1992; Kimmel & Mosmiller, 1992; Tavris, 1992) have noted that, historically, arguments that appeal to science have been used to justify the exclusion of women from public status equal to that of men and to defend gender inequality as the natural and unchangeable order of things. Gould (1981) noted that the same kind of process has been used to exclude people of color from equal participation in the public sphere. Evolutionary psychologists downplay the effects of social forces, specifically an historical imbalance of power between the sexes (see Chapter Three), that provide plausible alternative explanations to their claims.

Specific Critiques of Evolutionary Claims

Criticism has also focused on the choice to position promiscuous sexuality and acts of violence as the basis for human sex differences because these are relatively infrequent behaviors. Public health studies reveal that no more than five percent of men report having three or more sexual partners for each of three consecutive years (Dariotis et al., 2008; Humblet et al., 2003) and other studies indicate that no more than 15 percent to 20 percent have more than three partners in any given year (Smiler, 2013). Violence, especially at the level of criminal assault or homicide, is committed by a very small percentage of men (Kilmartin, 2010).

Natalie Angier (1999a), challenges the argument of differential reproductive investment, arguing that male promiscuity is not a sound evolutionary strategy:

> Just how good a reproductive strategy is this chronic, random shooting of the gun? A woman is fertile only two or three days a month. Her ovulation is concealed. The man doesn't know when she's fertile. She might be in the early stages of pregnancy when he gets to her; she might still be lactating and thus not ovulating. Moreover, even if our hypothetical Don Juan hits a day on which a woman is ovulating, his sperm only has a 20 percent chance of fertilizing her egg; human reproduction is complicated, and most eggs and sperm are not up to the demands of proper fusion. Even if conception occurs, the resulting embryo has a 25 to 30 percent chance of miscarrying at some point in gestation. In sum, each episode of fleeting sex has a remarkably small probability of yielding a baby… the probability is less than one percent. And because the man is beating and running, he isn't able to prevent any of his one-night stands from turning around and mating with other men…. [If he were] to spend a bit more time with one woman… the odds of his getting the woman during her fertile time would increase and he'd be monopolizing her energy and keeping her from the advances of other sperm-bearers. It takes the average couple four months, or 120 days, of regular sexual intercourse to become pregnant. That number of days is approximately equal to the number of partners our hypothetical libertine needs to sleep with to have one of them result in a 'fertility unit,' that is, a baby. (pp. 336–337)

SST's methods and findings have been critiqued directly. One of the most persistent, and perhaps most concerning challenges comes from the fact that researchers examining the desired number of sexual partners rely almost exclusively on the use of undergraduate students and that the modal, or most common, answer is one partner in the next 30 days. This response is typically produced by approximately three-quarters of the young men who complete surveys. Keep in mind that these are anonymous surveys and the vast majority of survey participants are unmarried 18- to 22-year-old men who live on college campuses alongside thousands of 18- to 22-year-old women. If there were ever a group of young men who could get away with saying they wanted to have a lot of partners in a short time period, this would be the group. Yet the common finding is that approximately 25 percent of men say they want two or more partners in the next 30 days (Hazan & Diamond, 2000; Smiler, 2011). There is a large male-female difference because approximately six percent of women express a desire for multiple partners in that time frame (e.g., Schmitt et al., 2003).

Critics have also pointed out that:

Regardless of whether a society allows polygyny or polygamy, only a small percentage of the population actually has multiple long term partners (Murdock, 1967).

Persistent evidence of a male-female difference in number of actual sexual partners or willingness to have sex with a stranger does not tell us anything about cause. Sexual double standards are also a logical cause.

Overall, Evolutionary Psychology has provided a perspective that explains some widespread—and potentially universal—aspects of male sexuality and male violence. EP is an essentialist theory (see Chapter One) and critics, particularly social constructionists, have pointed to a number of concerns about EP. It is important to note that even the most "hard core" essentialists do not rule out environmental influences; they argue that these are minimal, especially at the macro- and species-level. (The reverse tends to be true for hard core constructionists, who downplay the role of biological factors.)

THE CHILD INSIDE THE MAN: PSYCHOANALYTIC PERSPECTIVES

It is fitting that a discussion of psychoanalysis follows one of biology; the two are somewhat related. Psychoanalysis is based on the interaction of childhood psychological history with purported biological and psychological instincts. The biological perspective is that prenatal events set up propensities for behavior; the analytic perspective attempts to specify the interplay of these propensities and the important events of early childhood.

Psychoanalysis is a psychology of *meaning*. In the area of gender, it addresses questions about the deep, underlying sense of the masculine self in the adult man's life, as understood in the context of the impact of childhood psychological dramas. Many analytic writers view masculine gender behaviors as the result of the typical early experience of being a boy, one that differs markedly from that of being a girl.

There are several different versions of psychoanalytic theories, and so a good starting point is to address the question, "What makes a theory psychoanalytic?" R. J. May (1986) suggests that there are four broad commonalities among these theories. First, analytic theories emphasize the importance of *unconscious processes*. These are the areas of an individual's mind which are outside of awareness, but that nevertheless have effects on behavior and identity. Analytic theorists believe that these deeper regions of the psyche are more important in understanding behavior than the conscious sense of self or the person's thought processes. Psychoanalytic theory is often referred to as an "iceberg theory." Just as most of an iceberg lies beneath the surface of the water, most psychological functioning lies beneath the surface of consciousness. From this perspective, masculinity is a deep process that goes to the core of a man's being and affects a great deal of his behavior, often without his awareness.

Second, analytic theories emphasize a *developmental and historical approach* to understanding behavior. They consider the relevance of early childhood experience to be profound, and they view the adult's behavior as reflecting and reworking childhood psychological issues. The psychoanalytic view of behavior in the gender role arena is that it is mostly a result of the boy's early relationship with his parents.

Third, analytic theories emphasize the importance of *biology and body*. When we combine this emphasis with the relevance of early childhood, we see the importance of the child's awareness of self as separate from mother, the awareness of physical sex differences, and the emergence of sexual feelings in the construction of masculinity.

Finally, analytic theories emphasize the inescapability of *internal conflict*. The person is seen as inevitably caught in the middle of at least two great and irresolvable forces. A man finds himself struggling with the demands of instinct vs. social demands, desire for women vs. fear of women, dependency needs vs. desire for independence, feminine vs. masculine feelings, and the desire for something that he cannot possess. These conflicts are seen as having a never-ending quality; nobody can ever resolve them completely. The best the person can hope for is to develop a workable compromise, such as finding a comfortable way to deal with the need to be connected and the need to be on one's own at the same time.

The Freudian Legacy

Few thinkers have had as much impact on the world as Sigmund Freud (1856-1939). His prolific works, along with those of analytic theorists who followed him, provide interesting and controversial frameworks for the understanding of men and masculinity. Freud's (1925, 1964) perspective on gender can best be understood in the context of his personality theory. Therefore, we now provide a thumbnail sketch of the parts of this theory that are relevant to men's issues.

A major tenet of Freud's biological orientation is the importance of instinct in shaping personality. *Instincts* are innate bodily conditions which give direction to psychological processes (Hall, Lindzey, & Campbell, 1998), such as hunger, thirst, need for oxygen, body temperature regulation, aggression, and reproduction. Freud believed that, in contrast to more basic instincts like hunger and thirst, the complex sexual and aggressive instincts (broadly, love and hate) can be expressed through a wide variety of behaviors, attitudes, and emotions. For instance, one can love a person, conversation, money, learning, or creative pursuits. Likewise, one can express animosity toward a person, an idea, or the self. For Freud (1964), the personality is largely a result of the person's pattern of expressing the sexual and aggressive instincts. And, as mentioned earlier, most of this psychic functioning occurs in the unconscious.

If instinctual gratification were the only problem we ever faced, life might not be easy, but it would be rather uncomplicated. However, as we live with other people, instinctual needs inevitably come into conflict with the social world. One cannot merely act out an aggressive instinct because they might hurt someone else and be punished for it. The person must learn how to gratify needs in a socially acceptable way. The process of maturing is one in which primitive, impulse-driven people become transformed into civilized people who are able to delay gratification until the appropriate time and place. A good deal of what we teach children in kindergarten and elementary school is in the service of learning impulse control and social rules: wait your turn, share, consider others' feelings, and so on.

From the Freudian perspective (1964), newborns are nothing more than instinctually driven bundles of biology with storehouses of psychic energy. Infants are helpless, and parents or caretakers work hard at fulfilling children's instincts. They feed babies, keep them warm enough, and remove irritants from their bodies when they change their diapers. Babies are incapable of doing these things for themselves; they need help to manage their instincts. The part of the personality that is primitive, instinctual, and present at birth is called the *id*. It is a collection of biological needs and undirected psychic energy.

Slowly, children begin to develop another part of personality. They become less and less helpless as they grow. Early in life, people have to feed them, but after a while they begin to grab the food themselves and put it into their mouths. Around age two or three, a new part of personality, the *ego*, begins to form. The ego is more organized than the id and can deal with the real world. In the healthy person, the ego gains more and more strength as the person matures. The ego can plan, and it mediates between the id and the outside world until a suitable object can be found. It becomes the center of the personality, the person's identity. (Note that the Freudian term ego is different from the common social use of the term, which implies self-absorption).

Eventually, parents begin to make social demands on children, and because children are attached to parents, they begin to internalize these demands. In other words, we all carry our parents around with us, for better or worse. The first important imposition of social demand is toilet training, when, for the first time, the child is required to exert physical control over an instinctual process (Hall, Lindzey, & Campbell, 1998).

Robert Bly (1988) is fond of saying, "You came into this world with all kinds of energy, but your parents wanted a 'nice boy' [or a 'nice girl']." In some ways, parents care less about instinctual gratification than they care about your being socialized. They want you to be able to handle your instincts and live in the social world. Freud (1964) called the internalized parent the **superego**, which starts to develop around age five or six and has two parts. The *ego ideal* contains our parents' aspirations for us. It is this part of the superego that makes us feel good when we do something our parents value, like achieving in school. The other part, the **conscience**, causes us to feel guilty or ashamed when we go against parental wishes.

After the formation of the superego, the ego finds itself in a clash between id, which is always pulling for pleasure, and superego, which is always pushing for perfection. Thus, it mediates between these two internal forces as well as the outside world. The healthy person has **ego strength**, which allows him or her to balance these conflicting demands. If the id dominates the personality, the person will be impulsive and antisocial. If the superego dominates, he or she will be tense and uncomfortable due to the unrelieved tension of the instincts (Hall, Lindzey, & Campbell, 1998).

What do id, ego, and superego have to do with masculinity? We can make a number of important connections of both the positive and the negative aspects of masculine gender roles. The analytic ideal is a paragon of positive masculinity: the person who can love and work. Such a man can achieve a satisfactory balance between his biological and his social sides. He is able to be responsible both in his work and his dedication to his partner and family.

Note here that the analytic ideal is quite the social conformist, but note also that there are many men who fit this description: dedicated, principled, hardworking, caring individuals who enjoy life and contribute to the greater good. In psychoanalytic terms, the man described above has high ego strength, which was built by his having learned to deal with problems and assert his will. He is also a person with a strong ego ideal and a reasonable conscience. He can be goal directed and achieving. Socially, society encourages the development of these structures in men. Some men are not so fortunate, however. Destructive masculinity can be conceptualized as being the result of poor superego development, rigid, harsh, or destructive content of the superego, or poor ego strength.

Theoretically, the id is constant. It is biological and innate, so it exerts about the same amount of influence on everybody. Differences among people reflect differences in the way the id is handled and directed. In the case of poor ego and superego development, the id is the most powerful part of the personality, and so it is allowed to run amok. The result is a person who is antisocial and destructive, giving vent to sexual and aggressive impulses without restraint. Sometimes, parents and the society at large teach girls to worry about everyone else except themselves and boys to only worry about themselves. Both of these lessons are problematic because they both lead to a poor balance of id and superego.

We can conceptualize violent criminals as people with poor ego and superego development. Most of these people are men. In fact, males commit more than four of every five violent crimes in the United States (FBI, 2011). The major inhibitor of destructive id impulses is the superego, which makes the boy feel guilty when he is destructive and good when he is prosocial. According to Freud (1964), male superego development depends critically on a boy's identification with his father or "father figure." If the father is absent, emotionally distant, or overly punitive, the identification is weakened. Unfortunately, a lot of fathers fit this description. According to psychoanalytic theory, a lack of ego ideal in the boy leaves him aimless and unable to reward or restrain himself appropriately.

It is also possible for id and superego to be strong but the ego to be weak. In this case, the result is a pattern of behavior in which the person does things which are harmful to someone else, feels guilty about it and expresses regret, but then repeats the same bad behavior later. Baseball great Babe Ruth fit this pattern. He was well known for his public misbehavior. Occasionally, he felt guilty about his negative effects on people, especially on children who looked up to him as a hero and role model, and he would make heartfelt public apologies for his misdeeds. Nevertheless, he would continue to engage in embarrassing incidents, not because he was insincere in his apologies, but because, if one applies Freudian theory, he lacked the ego strength to restrain the id in a society that fails to hold elite athletes accountable for their behavior.

In other cases, the content of the superego may be especially harsh, rigid, and/or destructive. This may happen if the parents' demands on the child are extreme. If the parent inculcates the demands of destructive masculinity into the boy, he will have a punitive superego that can make him feel chronically unworthy and unmasculine. This is the case for many men, for whom the superego demands that he be competitive, wealthy, in control at all times, and dominant over women.

The Oedipus Conflict

We can see another important perspective on masculinity in Freud's (1925, 1964) model of psychosexual development. Freud believed that instinctual energy (called *libido*) courses through stages of psychosexual development that are defined in relation to certain parts of the body (called *erogenous zones*). Each stage entails a crisis which the child must resolve to achieve healthy psychosexual development.

Following the oral and anal stages, in which boys and girls go through similar developmental challenges, children enter the phallic stage, and Freud (1925, 1964) proposed that sex differences emerge at that time. The *phallic period* (roughly, between age three and six) is the first primitive manifestation of what will later become adult sexuality. Children at this age become very aware of and concerned about sex differences. Masturbatory activity and some forms of sexual play among children at this age are not unusual.

Freud (1925, 1964) believed that, for both boys and girls, sexual interest at this stage centers around the penis (hence the term phallic, which refers to the penis, rather than a term that refers to the genitalia of either sex). The child also begins to experience unconscious sexual feelings toward the other-sex parent. It is not unusual for the girl to say she is going to marry her father or a boy, his mother. As a result of the desire for the other-sex parent, the child unconsciously perceives the same-sex parent as a rival for the affection of the other parent. This is a psychologically dangerous and uncomfortable love triangle, and the child must resolve this difficulty. Freud called this crisis the **Oedipus conflict**, after the king of Thebes in Greek mythology who kills his father and marries his mother.

A boy feels desire for his mother, who is affectionate and caring. Strong sexual feelings are centered in his genitals, and he betrays this fact by touching his penis often. Parents often punish this masturbatory activity, and the boy gets the message that he might get punished by having his penis removed. This **castration anxiety** is also fueled by the rivalry with his big, powerful father, who might punish him for having these feelings toward his mother. When the boy first sees female genitalia, he perceives the female as a castrated male and unconsciously perceives that this fate could befall him (Freud, 1925, 1964).

At the height of the Oedipal conflict, the boy senses that gratifying his desire for his mother would mean losing his penis. In the normal resolution of this psychic conflict, he decides it's just not worth it, gives up these sexual feelings for his mother, and displaces them on to a more appropriate object, such as the girl next door. Part of this solution involves the boy's development of a psychological identification with his father. Identification allows the son to feel less threatened by his father and also to experience romantic feelings with the mother vicariously through the father. This is an important step in superego development, as the boy begins to internalize the father's values and characteristics. The sexual love for the mother is converted into feelings of tender affection.

Oedipus and Masculinity

Theoretically, the childhood Oedipal crisis colors the adult man's approach to relationships with women (originally represented by mother) and authority figures (originally represented by father). Fine's (1987) view of the Oedipal situation is that confusion results when parents or other adults punish the boy's sexual expression. He loves his mother, but he cannot approach her sexually, and an early split between sex and affection can result. These are the roots of the so called "Madonna/Whore complex." The man feels that virtuous women, those whom he respects, are not sexual (the Madonna was conceived

> **Box 5.2**
> **Freud, Women, and Femininity**
>
> Freud believed that girls experience themselves as castrated males, and that therefore when they desire their fathers and see their mothers as rivals, their love is mixed with bitter feelings because they want a protruding sex organ like their father's. Thus, according to Freud, girls suffer from *penis envy*. The resolution to girls' conflict is to give up her desire for her father and displace it onto another male. Freud thought that penis envy was converted into the desire to bear a male child. He also thought that, because girls do not experience the powerful motivator of castration threat, they do not give up their father desire as easily and they do not identify with their mothers as fully. As a result, they have less well developed superegos. Freud once stated that women are morally inferior to men for this reason (Freud, 1925, 1964).
>
> Many theorists have roundly criticized Freud for this view of women. The great feminist analyst Karen Horney (1932) countered that women envy men's privileged social positions, not their penises. In support of this hypothesis, Nathan (1981) demonstrated through cross-cultural research that penis envy dreams among women are more common in cultures where women have low social status. Horney's view is that a girl's psychosexual development centers around her own genitalia, and not the male's. Hare-Mustin and Maracek (1990a) noted Freud's sexism in his characterization of "women's bodies as *not having* a penis rather than as *having* the female external genitalia." (p. 32, emphasis original). Freud himself felt unsatisfied with this part of his theory, as he knew many women whose moral development equaled or surpassed that of men. At one point, Freud stated that it was the task of women analysts to describe the female psyche (Freud, 1925, 1964).
>
> Freud's theoretical construction of the Oedipus conflict was partly based on the famous case of "Dora" (Freud, 1905/1963), an 18-year-old patient whom Freud saw for eleven weeks of psychoanalysis in 1900 to treat a number of psychological and psychophysiological symptoms (e.g. migraine headaches and depression) (Freud & Gay, 1989). Dora reported to Freud that, when she was 14 years old, Herr K., a close friend of her father, had embraced and kissed her against her will. Dora was quite disgusted and unnerved by Herr K.'s behavior. She told her parents about it and requested that they break off their friendship with Herr K. and his wife. Dora's father confronted Herr K., who emphatically denied that he had made sexual advances toward Dora, and Dora's father believed his friend rather than his daughter.
>
> Eventually, Freud came to believe that Dora was really in love with Herr K., and he insisted that Dora's disgust was a disguise for her real feelings of sexual arousal. In historical perspective, we now know that it is not unusual for adult men to make such advances upon young girls nor for girls to respond as Dora did. Hare-Mustin and Maracek (1990a) point to the importance of Freud's reframing of Dora's experience in the patriarchal context of privileging men's perspectives over women's. In effect, Freud blamed the victim for her emotional reaction and relegated her perspective to a secondary position to his own, implying that he (and men) knew Dora (and women) better than she knew herself. As psychoanalysis became scientific orthodoxy, its antifeminine character further justified the marginalization of women.

without original sin—absolutely pure), and that sexual women ("whores") are not worthy of respect. Thus, he has a tendency to degrade a woman if she is sexual with him. This sexuality/love contradiction causes extreme problems in the man's relationships with women and perhaps in his sexual functioning. The boy who successfully resolves the Oedipal conflict becomes a man who can love and be sexual with the same woman. The boy who does not may grow up to be misogynist, promiscuous, or sexually dysfunctional as he plays out the unresolved Oedipal drama again and again.

Fathering may have an important effect on the Oedipal situation. If the father is caring and attentive to the boy, he will facilitate his son's positive identification with him and mitigate the son's castration anxiety. If, however, the father is harsh, punitive, and demanding with his son, the identification process will cause the boy to become intropunitive, and castration anxiety may be exaggerated. The boy grows up fearful and without a strong sense of himself as masculine. He may act "macho" to cover up his insecurity. He may be aggressive to defend against the unconscious threat of castration (Tyson, 1986), or he may derogate women to feel better about his masculinity. David Lisak (1991) noted that many sexual assault perpetrators have feelings of bitterness toward their fathers, who caused them to feel inadequate and unmasculine.

Critique of Freud

Many criticisms of Freud are leveled at his assumption that sexual instinct is the primary determinant of personality. Even some of his closest followers abandoned the sexual theory, although most maintained their belief in the importance of the unconscious and early childhood events. If we look at the parent-child attachment as one that is not primarily sexual, very different conclusions about male functioning become possible. And, even if one accepts the premise that sexuality is the basis of human personality, some of Freud's conclusions are open to debate. The description of castration anxiety as being fairly resolvable is highly contested.

Freud's position is that the Oedipal crisis in the boy is touched off by his realization that he could lose something valuable. In the girl, it is stimulated by her imagining that she has already lost it. If you have lost something valuable, it is greatly disappointing at first. After a while, you usually accept that it is gone and move on. If, however, you have a deep-seated fear of losing something, you are obligated to anxiously protect it all of your life. The penis is also in somewhat of a vulnerable place, being outside of the body. It seems that castration anxiety would be more common than penis envy (if the latter exists at all).

In 1932, Karen Horney published a classic essay on male psychology entitled **The Dread of Women** in which she argues that the process of psychosexual development produces in the boy a profound yet unconscious fear of the feminine, and that much stereotypical masculine behavior in adulthood is a reflection of this dread. Horney argued that the vagina, with its ability to engulf, is a psychic threat to the male. The threat of castration by the father does not approach the threat of engulfment from the mother. Horney illustrated this in metaphor: "Sampson, whom no man could conquer, is robbed of his strength by Delilah" (Horney, 1932/1966, p. 84).

If, as Freud believed, the other-sex parent is the love object in this stage, then the size difference between parent and child leads to a difference in how boys and girls experience themselves. Girls, Horney believed, begin to have unconscious desires to take in the penis. If the father is the love object, then her vagina is too small for him, and so she fears that he could hurt her. The boy, with his mother as love object, senses that his penis is much too small for her, and reacts with feelings of inadequacy. He anticipates that his mother will ridicule and deride him, as well as other love objects later in life.

The implications of Horney's theory for masculine psychology are far reaching. Horney proposed that every man has a deep sense of apprehension that a woman can destroy his self-respect, and that his penis (and thus his manhood) is not large enough nor good enough. Masculinity, then, must perpetually be proved. This demand can create or contribute to persistent anxiety regarding masculine (in)adequacy that a man must manage. He has basically two options: he can withdraw from women or compensate for these uncomfortable feelings.

Withdrawal solutions include staying away from women either physically or emotionally. Compensation solutions involve going to extremes to prove one's manhood over and over again. Part of this strategy may involve debasing and controlling women. By doing so, the man can deny that women have the power to hurt him. At the extreme of masculine inadequacy, we see desperate behaviors like rape and domestic violence, which can be seen as aggressive reactions to the extreme dread of the feminine. Horney goes so far as to suggest that patriarchy, men's institutional oppression of women, is a reaction to this inadequacy in the collective male psyche. Horney's theory also provides a possible explanation of the core attitude of antifemininity that characterizes traditional masculinity.

IDENTIFYING WITH MOM:
EGO PSYCHOLOGY AND MASCULINITY

Many of the theorists who followed Freud disagreed with him on one major point. They believed that some aspects of ego functioning were independent of the id. For these theorists, the ego is not something that merely serves to direct and control the instincts, it also drives the person to deal with basic psychological tasks like developing a sense of self, relating to others, learning to work, and developing values. Many of these "neo-analytic" theories center around the person's motivation to develop a sense of identity.

People's behavior varies across different situations and roles, but identity is the part of the person that ties all of this varying behavior together. The formation of this sense of self begins in infancy with the child's realization that he or she is separate from the mother. As the individual progresses through adolescence and adulthood, the expression of identity can be seen through a variety of decisions around relationships, work, sexuality, values, and preferences.

Gender identity is the part of overall identity that defines for the person what it means to be male or female. After children learn that they are not a part of their mothers, boys learn that they are similar to their fathers and different from their mothers in a basic way, and girls learn the converse. Children as young as two to four years of age become very upset if someone says to them "What a nice girl (or boy) you are," using the incorrect sex label, evidence that gender identity is learned very early and that it has a strong emotional component (Lewis, 1987). The strength of the emotion associated with gender identity attests to its central place in overall identity, although the origin of that centrality (biological, social, and/or cultural) is open to question.

Because of sex-differentiated child rearing, the formation of gender identity is thought to proceed very differently for males and females, with important implications for the personalities of adult men and women. Gender identity is formed mainly through the child's interactions with his or her parents, and women are the primary caretakers of infants in most cultures. The amount of time a typical mother spends with the infant far outweighs the typical father's time (Cohen, 1998). Thus, the most striking sex difference in early parent-child interactions is that girls are usually raised mainly by the same-sex parent, boys by the other-sex parent.

Ruth Hartley (1959) first proposed that the impact of this sex difference in early experience is considerable. Before they perceive sex differences in early childhood, children of both sexes feel continuous with their mothers and thus identify with her. In the formation of gender identity, girls learn "I am what mom is." They experience themselves as continuous with their mothers and define themselves through the process of attachment. This process continues in the same direction throughout childhood, since girls are the same sex as their mothers.

Boys, on the other hand, learn "I am what mom is not" more than they learn "I am what dad is." The boy experiences himself as different from the mother and defines himself through the process of separation. "I am what mom is not" defines the content of gender identity in a negative way. Rather that starting out with some sense of masculinity, the boy starts out with a sense of antifemininity.

Boys' gender identity development critically depends on switching tracks. From this view, boys must put rigid boundaries between themselves and their mothers to define themselves as masculine. If we believe that some identification with the mother has already taken place by the time a boy knows that he is different from her, then the separation process entails a repression of the mother identification.

Freud (1925) believed that homosexuality was one possible result. Assuming a gender binary, the logic says that if a boy does too many feminine things, he might end up identifying with women. He would then end up being like a woman in every way, including a sexuality that is oriented toward men (and adherents to this position usually see homosexuality as a decidedly negative developmental outcome, although Freud did not). However, Kurdek (1988) reported that gay men and lesbians are more likely to exhibit a mixture of masculine and feminine characteristics as opposed to a set of characteristics usually seen in the other sex. In other words, they tend to be relatively androgynous in their gender expression, not *inverted*, as Freud thought. It is also worth noting that there is a great deal of variation in gender role behavior within the populations of gays and lesbians, just as there is within the population of heterosexuals.

These dramas get played out again and again, according to analytic theory. The result of this separation process is that the boy's gender identity rests on his putting rigid psychological barriers not just between himself and mother, but between himself and anything feminine. Included are "feminine activities" and, of course, girls and women themselves. Having already identified with the mother, the boy must also repress the feminine parts of himself, usually represented by his emotional experiences and feelings of relatedness to others. Girls are under no such pressure. They do not have to deny the masculine to define themselves as feminine (Chodorow, 1978). This is one possible explanation for the tolerance of "tomboys" but not "sissies." Martin (1995) reported that stereotypes of tomboys resembled stereotypes of traditional boys. However, the stereotype of the sissy did not resemble that of a traditional girl. Instead, it was defined narrowly and related to many negative characteristics.

Alan Johnson (2001) noted that there are derogatory terms for men who are dominated by their wives (e.g., henpecked or "whipped") but no corresponding terms for women who are dominated by their husbands. A psychoanalytic thinker—and Johnson is not one—might theorize that female domination in a relationship is seen as a threat to masculine identity.

The mother-identified parts of the boy are relegated to the unconscious because they pose a threat to the ego. When "feminine" experiences like sentimental feelings or a desire for attachment surface from the unconscious, they generate anxiety, which the boy must then defend against. In a typical scenario, a man may go to a sentimental movie, begin to identify with a character and feel some strong and vulnerable emotions. He may sense that this experience is a threat to his masculinity and detach himself from his feelings by putting his mind on something else. Eventually, he may begin to avoid these types of movies. Traditionally masculine men in mainstream United States culture often avoid movies that have feminine themes, calling them "chick flicks" that hold no interest for them.

The early childhood gender-typed mix of separation and attachment is considered by some to result in an enduring approach to the world. Nancy Chodorow (1978) described women as "selves in communion," meaning that they tend to experience themselves in the context of relationships, and men as "selves in separation," oriented toward independence and task completion.

From this standpoint, a straightforward solution to male antifeminine anxiety is an increase in fathers' involvement in child care. Coltrane (1998) provides some anthropological evidence in support of the hypothesis that antifemininity results from boys' lack of meaningful contact with their fathers. He notes that in cultures in which men participate in child rearing (and in which women have the power to control property), there are "significantly fewer displays of manliness, less wifely deference, less husband dominance, and less ideological female inferiority..." (p. 81). One psychoanalytic interpretation is that, because fathers are more psychologically available to sons, there is less need for compulsive separation from the mother, thus less fear of women and femininity, and thus less of a need to compensate for this fear through hypermasculine posturing and mistreatment of women.

SUMMARY

Some theorists and researchers believe that some aspects of masculinity have deep and strong biological roots. Evolutionary psychologists, following in the intellectual footsteps of sociobiologists, argue that our ancient ancestral past exerted a profound influence through selection processes that contributed to the survival of the fittest. Accordingly, male humans have been shaped to have a predilection for violence as well as for promiscuity because each increases the male's chances of reproducing.

A different approach was taken by Sigmund Freud and his followers. Freud argued that instinctual energy provides an inevitable series of crises that the individual must resolve. For boys, this includes a resolution to the Oedipal Conflict, as well as separation from mother and things feminine. Karen Horney suggested that this separation from mother and the feminine creates a dread of women.

1. There is little doubt among developmental psychologists that biology affects personality and behavior, although there is little consensus about the extent of these effects. Since there are some differences in male and female biology, there is a good deal of speculation and research about the behavioral implications of these differences.

2. Chromosomal and hormonal differences appear to cause differences, at least at the level of comparisons between males and females.

3. The exact mechanisms linking chromosomes and hormones to demonstrated behavior remain unclear and hormone levels do not appear to reliably predict differences within sex-based groups.

4. Evolutionary psychologists argue that biology profoundly affects behavior by establishing predispositions toward certain activities. These predispositions have survival value for the organism and its genes, and thus they were established through the process of evolution.

5. Evolutionary psychologists argue that major behavioral sex differences are thought to reflect different male and female reproductive strategies. Males who impregnate a large number of females are "successful" from an evolutionary standpoint because they insure maximum and varied reproduction of their genes. In contrast to females, males can participate in the reproductive process with a minimum investment of time and resources. Differences in reproductive strategies are thought to underlie important differences in male and female "nature."

6. Social scientists have leveled a number of theoretical and methodological criticisms against evolutionary psychology and its predecessor, sociobiology. Criticism includes concerns about oversimplification, logical errors, highly selected examples, and a failure to consider other explanations. Some critics charge these approaches with being patriarchal ideology disguised as science.

7. Psychoanalytic approaches to the understanding of masculinity emphasize biological, unconscious, and early childhood determinants of behavior.

8. Freud emphasized the role of sexual instinct and its conflict with social forces. If the young boy does not develop a strong social structure (superego), he will become impulsive, destructive, self-absorbed, and antisocial.

9. According to Freudian theory, the most important period for the development of masculine gender identity is the phallic stage (ages three to six), in which the boy experiences strong sexual feelings for his mother and views his father as a rival. He fears that he will be castrated for these desires, and so he transfers his sexual feelings onto a more appropriate object. If the Oedipal crisis is resolved poorly, the boy may later have sexual problems and/or problems relating to women.

10. Karen Horney viewed the Oedipal period as a time when males developed deep-seated feelings of insecurity associated with the feminine. She believed that misogyny and even violence toward women are attempts to compensate for masculine inadequacy.

11. Ego psychology theories emphasize the processes of attachment and separation in early childhood. Because boys are usually raised mainly by their mothers, they must put rigid boundaries between themselves and the feminine to attain a strong sense of masculinity. Males tend to avoid "feminine" behaviors because they are accompanied by anxiety, causing difficulty when situations call for such behavior.

GLOSSARY

Sex chromosomes: The twenty-third pair of human chromosomes, which determine an individual's biological sex.

Disorder of sexual development: A group of genetic disorders in which the individual is neither XX (female) or XY (male). This term is intended to replace "intersex" and "intersexual," at least in professional communities.

Spatial rotation: The ability to rotate an object within "the mind's eye."

Adaptive behavior: Any behavior that would have 1) allowed ancestral humans to survive in a life-threatening environment or 2) provided individuals with an advantage that would have increased the likelihood that those individuals would produce offspring and thus pass their genes on to the next generation.

Exapted behavior (or modules): Behaviors, or the neurological modules that underlie them, that come to be used in a situation other than the situation which shaped their evolution.

Reproductive investment: The amount of time and resources that are expended in producing offspring.

Reproductive strategy: The behavioral pattern employed to ensure that one's genes will be passed on to the succeeding generation.

Instincts: Innate bodily conditions which give direction to psychological processes (according to Freudian theory).

(The) id: A part of the personality that is primitive, instinctual, and present at birth. It is a collection of biological needs and undirected psychic energy.

(The) ego: A part of the personality that can plan, mediates between the id and the superego, and mediates between the individual and the outside world. The ego is the center of the personality and the person's identity.

(The) ego ideal: An individual's learned or internalized version of their parents' aspirations for them. The ego ideal is part of the superego.

(The) conscience: The part of the superego that causes an individual to feel guilty or ashamed when the individual goes against parental wishes. The conscience is part of the superego.

(The) superego: An individual's sense of right and wrong. It consists of the ego ideal and the conscience.

Ego strength: The ego's ability to balance the conflicting demands of id and superego.

Libido: Instinctual energy that drives the id.

Erogenous zones: Specific parts of the body that are connected to Freud's stages of psychosexual development.

Phallic period: The first primitive manifestation of what will later become adult sexuality. The period starts at approximately age three and continues until approximately age six.

Oedipus conflict: The conflict a boy experiences when he realizes that his desire to marry his mother will be opposed by his father, thus putting him in conflict with his father.

Castration anxiety: A boy's fear his father might punish him by having the boy's penis removed.

The Dread of Women: The belief that the process of psychosexual development produces in the boy creates a profound yet unconscious fear of the feminine, and that much stereotypical masculine behavior in adulthood is a reflection of this dread.

Chapter Six

"It's the Way I was Raised": Socially-Based Theoretical Perspectives on Masculinity

Boys and girls are treated differently from each other in nearly all cultures (Gilmore, 1990; Whiting & Edwards, 1988). In this chapter, we explore several approaches that take the social setting as the starting point for explanations of gender. Social approaches position gender-typed behavior as the result of how children are raised, so they focus on the child's experiences and understanding of gender, as well as cultural messages they receive during their formative years and beyond.

Imagine, for a moment, that you are the parent of a newborn, your first child. Two days after birth, and again a week later, you are asked to describe your child and rate him or her on several characteristics. Family and friends often ask you to do something similar in a less formal way. So researchers Katherine Karraker, Dena Vogel, and Margaret Lake (1995) decided to ask it too. In open-ended comments when the child was two days of age, fathers and mothers were equally likely to use gender-typed terms, such as "big" or "strong" to describe sons and "pretty" or "beautiful" to describe daughters. A week later, fathers maintained their gender-typed language but mothers had scaled it back. Parents were also asked to rate their children on a variety of characteristics using a one-to-nine scale. They rated boys as stronger, hardier, more masculine, and less fine-featured than girls. For the record, baby boys and baby girls have the same average size. We don't know if you've spent any time with newborns, but we can assure you they don't do much more than eat, sleep, and poop at that age. And it's not as though the uterus includes weightlifting or Pilates classes.

Or imagine that you are visiting the house of some friends who are the parents of an eight-year-old boy, as John Lynch and Christopher Kilmartin (2013) suggested. The boy tells you that he wants to show you his room and you agree. When he opens the bedroom door, what do you expect to see? When you offer to play with him, do you expect to "horse around," play catch, or have a tea party? When you ask him about being a grown up, do you focus on career or his plans to become a parent?

If you were to look at most middle class children's bedrooms in the United States, you would probably have little difficulty guessing the sex of the child. Girls' bedrooms often contain dolls (Snow, Jacklin, & Maccoby, 1981) and are often decorated with flowers, lace, or other stereotypically feminine designs. Boys' bedrooms often contain sports equipment and transportation toys (Pomerleau, Bolduc, Malcuit, & Cossette, 1990).

In the first half of this chapter, we'll describe some research examining children's early experience with gender, the importance of the environments that children are placed in, and some key milestones in gender development. In the second half, we'll review some theories that help us understand how these factors shape children into gender-typed beings.

The Gendered Child: Early Experience

Developmental psychologists often describe parents as children's first teachers, and that is certainly the case for learning gender. Even before birth, many parents (and their families and friends) often choose gender-based colors, clothing, and toys for the newborn. Can you imagine gifting a baby boy with a pink outfit? (Do boys get "outfits?") Buying him Princess movies at age two or three?

It doesn't stop there. Parents tend to communicate gender stereotypes in children's play and household chores (Lytton & Romney, 1991). Parents in Western cultures, especially fathers, play with boys more roughly, perhaps as a result of the perception that boys are stronger and tougher, although this pattern is not universal (Hewlett, 2005). Children who choose gender-typed toys tend to get more positive responses from their parents than those who do not (Caldera, Huston, & O'Brien, 1989). Researchers have demonstrated that children are very sensitive to parents' expressions of disgust even before those children learn how to talk (Carver & Vaccaro, 2007). Thus, an uncomfortable parent does not have to say anything or even intend to communicate to the child that they are choosing a "gender inappropriate" toy or activity; children nevertheless are influenced by parents' facial expressions of disapproval.

Developmental psychologists often view play and family activity as a rehearsal for later social roles. For instance, putting puzzles together is rehearsal for task completion and problem solving. "Playing house" is a rehearsal for relationships and domestic work. Here again, parents tend to be gender-typed in their treatment of children. Boys are taught to develop structures, to experiment with new approaches to solving problems, to attend to task and performance, and to master the situation. Girls are encouraged to be cooperative and compliant (Block, 1984). In household chores, parents often assign boys activities that take them away from the residence, such as yard work, animal care, or taking out the garbage, whereas girls are assigned more domestic chores such as baby sitting, cooking, or doing dishes (Ferrar, Olds, & Waters, 2012; Rowlands, Pilgrim, & Eston, 2008). Although parents' choices may reflect differences in activity levels (Pellegrini, 2004), this pattern of chores keeps girls physically closer to adults both at home and at school, while boys are given more distance. Reflecting on this longstanding pattern (Inchley, Currie, Todd, Akhtar, & Currie, 2005; Lytton & Romney, 1991), developmental psychologist Jeanne Block (1984) described these practices as giving boys "wings" and girls "roots."

Comparisons of fathers' and mothers' gender typing of children reveal that fathers tend to be more stereotypic in their definitions of gender appropriate activities, especially with their sons (Lytton & Romney, 1991). That finding was also true for descriptions of newborns; stereotypical descriptions and ratings were strongest when fathers described sons (Karraker et al., 1995). Perhaps as a consequence of their less frequent contact with children, fathers embellish a lack of information by the use of stereotypes (Basow, 1992). Overall, the level of a son's gender stereotyping is strongly related to the father's level (Tennenbaum & Leaper, 2002). In some ways, father presence (vs. absence) may be the cause; boys raised by a heterosexual couple are usually more stereotypically masculine than boys raised by their single mothers (Stevenson & Black, 1988).

Another consistent research finding is that boys are punished for cross-gender behavior earlier in life and more harshly than girls (Carver, Egan, & Perry, 2003; Wood et al., 2013). Saying to a boy, "you run like a girl," is a frequent insult. A girl can associate with a male group without fearing a loss of status, yet boys who play with girls or prefer stereotypically feminine activities are often ridiculed by and ostracized from male social groups (Carver et al., 2003; Maccoby, 1998). Because of punishment for "feminine" behaviors, boys may begin to view femininity and females with contempt. The inclusion of antifemininity as part of our cultural definition of masculinity has its developmental origins in this devaluing of attributes and behaviors that are thought to be reserved for females.

The typical family, as well as other cultural forces, encourages boys to control their feelings and conform their behavior to external standards like performance in sports. In sharp contrast, these same forces often encourage girls to "look inside" and think about their feelings (Pollack, 1998; Shields, 2013). The research team of Susan Adams, Janet Kuebli, Patricia Boyle, and Robyn Fivush (1995) found that parents refer to most emotions much more frequently when talking with daughters than they do with sons. At 40 months of age, the researchers found no male–female differences in children's use of words that describe emotions but by 70 months, girls' language contained more emotional terms than boys'.

Behavioral differences are observable as early as 24 months. In a laboratory setting where children played while their mothers sat quietly in a chair in the same room, researchers provoked fear responses by having an unfamiliar member of the research team enter the room (i.e., a stranger) and provoked frustration by encouraging children to play with toys in a clear box that the child could not open. The researcher-stranger "realized" their error after two minutes, apologized to the child, and opened the box. Although both boys and girls showed both fear and anger in response to not being able to open the box, girls were more fearful and boys more angry (Buss, Brooker, & Leuty, 2008). We discuss anger and other emotions in more detail in Chapter Seven.

The net result of these differences in childrearing is that parents tend to teach girls about the salience of feelings in the early stages of language acquisition, and they teach boys to attend to other aspects of experience (Tannen, 1990). It is little wonder that boys' and men's emotional worlds—and their emotional vocabularies—are smaller than girls' and women's. Collectively, this lack of emotional focus and encouragement to move away from the house may contribute to social definitions of masculinity that emphasize the external: job status, money, material possessions, athletic performance, power over others, and even the attractiveness of one's partner. It is important to note that this external focus is not only a remnant of childhood rewards from evaluating externally; the encouragement is ongoing. In adolescence and adulthood, many social and other rewards come to males whose behavior conforms to masculine cultural images.

At the same time, these aspects of male socialization may also be responsible for some of the positive aspects of masculinity (Hammer & Good, 2010). Boys are rewarded from an early age for going out into the world, solving problems, achieving, and competing. Although competition and ambition can get out of hand, this orientation to the world is associated with good occupational functioning and enhanced self-esteem, especially when it is balanced with socioemotional orientations. From an egalitarian perspective, there is no reason to limit an adaptive aspect of socialization to males.

Parents' punishment practices are also important to understanding boys' development. Parents punish boys more often than girls, but they also praise boys more often (Lytton & Romney, 1991). One reason is that parents, as well as other family members, peers, and other actors, often punish boys for being insufficiently masculine and thus hope to encourage more masculine gender role behaviors. At the extreme, parents are much more likely to seek psychological treatment for gender-nonconforming boys than girls. Boys age 11 and younger are brought to treatment for **Gender Identity Disorder (GID)** approximately four times more frequently than girls (and 33:1 among only three year old children); among those age 12 to 20, boys and young men are brought for or seek out treatment approximately 2.5 times more frequently (Wood et al., 2013). According to the fourth edition of the *Diagnostic and Statistical Manual* (DSM-IV-TR; American Psychiatric Association, 2007), boys were approximately four times more likely to be diagnosed with a Gender Identity Disorder. The diagnosis was removed from the fifth edition and replaced with **Gender Dysphoria**, which covers a broader range of conditions and includes the individual's distress due to conforming to gender roles (American Psychiatric Association, 2013).

Another reason to examine punishment is that boys are more likely to be punished physically, while girls are more likely to be punished with social disapproval (Lytton & Romney, 1991). Physical punishment has the effect of actually *increasing* aggression in children over the long run (Patterson, Reid, & Dishion, 1992). There may be somewhat of a vicious cycle for the acting-out boy. He is active and undercontrolled as a result of temperament and socialization. He is physically punished for his behaviors, and these punishments are likely to result in further aggression.

Third, fathers tend to do more punishing than mothers (Block, 1984). The boy's experience of physical pain in the presence of the father may inhibit positive feelings and identification, especially if the father is not around much and/or there is a dearth of positive father-son interactions (Lynch & Kilmartin, 2013). In the worst-case scenario, the mother spends much more time with the son, but the punishment duties are relegated to the father. The son who is told, "Wait until your father gets home," does not learn that he gets punished when he does something inappropriate. Rather, he learns that he gets punished when his father gets home, and he may well develop feelings of fear, anger, and resentment toward his father.

Early Experience at School

This differential socialization can cause problems for boys in elementary school settings that emphasize behaviors like cooperating, sitting still, and listening, which are contradictory to these gendered expectations. Concerns that school is a "girl's world" that rewards feminine-type behavior such as self-control and conformity date back to the creation of mandatory schooling in the early 1900s (Hantover, 1978) and have been voiced throughout the last hundred years (Kagan, 1964; Sax, 2009). These contradictory demands for boys may contribute to their higher incidences of behavior and academic problems (Sax, 2009).

Gender typing, which refers to a culture's pressure to conform to gender roles, of children is greatly accelerated by typical early educational experiences, which Luria and Herzog (cited in Maccoby, 1987) refer to as "gender school." Readers, book- and story-series designed to help children learn grammar and vocabulary become more stereotyped as children move from first to fifth grade (Evans & Davies, 2000). And despite teachers' efforts to treat boys and girls the same, there is ample evidence that they often do not. Boys receive both more positive and more negative attention in the classroom than girls (Sadker & Sadker, 1985). Boys' behavior is more likely to be taken seriously than that of girls, and boys learn that what they do has tangible consequences. One of the reasons for greater frequencies of punishment is that boys get into more mischief than girls, perhaps as a result of a relatively higher average activity level (Pellegrini, 2004).

But it's not just about teachers; during the elementary school years, children often segregate themselves into same-sex play groups. They will mix when adults reward them for doing so or punish them for not doing so, but they frequently re-segregate when adult sanctions are removed (Maccoby, 1998). Social scientists have observed this type of sex segregation in many different cultures (Whiting & Edwards, 1988). In boys' play groups, we see a great deal of reward for aggression, beginning at an early age (Fagot & Hagan, 1985). Boys' groups tend to demand rigid conformity to masculine behavior by harshly punishing cross-gender behavior, or anything they perceive as "girly" or feminine (Pascoe, 2007). In fact, there is a "social dosage effect" — the more time that children spend with same-sex peers, the more stereotypical their behavior is (Martin & Fabes, 2001). Thus, parents, teachers, and same-sex peers all "conspire" to promote gender-typical behavior.

Situational Influence

So far, we have talked about who influences boys, including how and when they encourage or punish gender-typical behavior. We now turn to the effect of the settings, or immediate environments, where boys often spend their time.

A person often finds himself or herself in the company of others, and there is powerful pressure to behave in certain ways in these situations. For example, when you go to a restaurant, you are highly likely to wait to be seated, be polite, ask for the food that you want, and pay the bill when you are finished. You are highly unlikely to push people aside because they are sitting where you want to sit, get your own food from the kitchen, put it on the floor and stir it up with your feet, and leave without paying for your meal. Except for very unusual people, restaurant behavior falls within a rather narrow and predictable range. Children in restaurants often behave in ways that are considered inappropriate for adults, partly because they have not learned the normative adult perception of the situation. Under most circumstances, most (teens and) adults act in ways that situations dictate.

Men (and women) often experience pressure to behave in gender-typical ways that they perceive as appropriate to the social setting. For example, it is not unusual for men to describe women in denigrating terms in some all-male groups. There is tremendous pressure in these situations for individual men to laugh, or at least remain silent in reaction to these comments. In a survey of college males, Kilmartin and his colleagues (2008) discovered that most young men reported feeling uncomfortable with these kinds of comments, yet only a very small minority of men expressed their discomfort or confronted the man who made the offensive comment. Doing so would require a man to resist the group pressure to go along with the attitude being expressed, and this study attests to the considerable power of this group pressure. In the typical male peer group situation where a misogynist (anti-woman) attitude is displayed, it is not necessarily the attitudes of individual men that allow this behavior to go unchallenged, it is the influence of a social context that carries its own momentum.

Of course, groups are made up of individuals who can affect the social atmosphere and its influences. In the above example, it is quite possible for an individual man to recognize his discomfort and confront the man who made the misogynist comment. In doing so, he might be successful in changing the social pressure of the group in the direction of disapproval of these kinds of comments. As we shall see, it is likely that he will find support for his view from others in the group who hold attitudes that are similar to his. Education and training to help college men break out of the passive bystander role in these kinds of situations are a promising development in efforts to decrease violence against women (See Chapter Twelve).

In the 1950s and 1960s, social psychologists began to describe and measure the considerable influence of interpersonal situations, often in quite dramatic fashion. Three landmark studies, all conducted by male researchers using male assistants and mostly male participants, demonstrated how the social context could dominate an individual's personality or preferences.

Solomon Asch (1965) demonstrated that group pressure can cause a person to report incorrect perceptual judgments. Experimenters presented a series of three lines and asked research participants in groups of eight to say which of the lines was closest to the length of a (fourth) standard line. The people in the group consistently gave answers that were obviously wrong, because they were actually accomplices of the experimenter who were hired to pose as volunteers. The study was designed to investigate the frequency with which the actual research participant will go along with the group. Only 20 percent remained independent of the group opinion on every trial, even though one line was unquestionably more similar to the standard than the others. By contrast, when people were asked to make the same judgment without influence from others, they gave the correct answer nearly every time. Asch's experiments demonstrated the power of *conformity*, defined as a change in behavior in response to implicit and unspoken social pressure.

The next key study was conducted by Stanley Milgram, who had studied with Asch. He performed a series of studies in which a "teacher" was asked to help a "learner" learn a series of word pairs by administering an electric shock for every wrong answer. (In reality, the learner was one of Milgram's assistants and was never shocked). The teacher's control panel started at 15 volts and worked up to 450 volts in increments of 15 volts. It was labeled with "mild" to "severe" and finally "XXX." The learner was in a separate room but his scripted reaction to the shocks could easily be heard by the teacher (Milgram, 1963). In this scenario, more than 50 percent of research volunteers were willing to inflict 450-volt shocks to the victim in response to pressure from an authority figure in a white lab coat, even though they expressed concern for the learner's health and well-being. Milgram's experiments demonstrated the power of *compliance*, defined as a change in behavior as the result of direct and explicit social pressure. We note that Milgram completed a series of studies using this format, with a variety of alterations that changed the distance between teacher and learner as well as between teacher and experimenter. The iteration described here was the first reported and reflects the most widely known iteration of this study.

Recently, Jerry Burger (2009) performed a partial replication of this study. Although the teachers had the same 15 to 450 volt range, the researchers stopped them at the 150-volt level because very few of Milgram's participants stopped between 150 and 450 volts. Burger's results were essentially the same as Milgram's, and there were no differences between men's and women's compliance.

The final study that we'll highlight was conducted by Phillip Zimbardo and his colleagues (Haney, Banks, & Zimbardo, 1973), who set up a mock prison in the basement of the Stanford University psychology building. Male students volunteered to be randomly assigned to the roles of prisoners and guards. The prisoners were "arrested," given numbers, dressed in prison garb, and put behind bars. Within a short time, a significant number of guards became abusive toward the prisoners, who responded with a variety of symptoms: panic, physical illness, depression, and apathy. The experiment was terminated earlier than originally scheduled because of the danger to prisoners. Zimbardo's experiment demonstrated the power of **social roles,** the expected behaviors for a person in any given social position.

(We note here that Zimbardo's prison experiment was unethical because researchers placed volunteers in dangerous psychological and physical situations and did not allow them to stop participating. The same concerns have been raised about Milgram's study. Modern safeguards have since been enacted to prevent experiments like these from taking place today, as was the case in Burger's 2009 replication of Milgram.).

These studies point to some of the difficulties a man might experience when he challenges gender norms. Perhaps most notably is the assumption that conformity may be inferred when agreement—and disagreement—is unspoken. Christopher Kilmartin and his students demonstrated that college men overestimate their male peers' acceptance of sexist and rape supportive attitudes (Kilmartin, Smith, Green, Kuchler, Heinzen, & Kolar, 2008). Said differently, young men believed their peers were moderately to highly sexist and held attitudes that generally supported rape but the reality was that most of the men in the group had low levels of sexism and didn't support ideologies that are commonly used to justify rape. Second, the presence of a single ally in the group significantly reduces conformity. Having just one person who voices a dissenting opinion emboldens others. In other words, it is much easier to be one of two against eight than it is to be alone against nine. Therefore, if men speak up when they are offended by sexism, they may well find that there is more support among other men than they might have predicted.

Together, these classic studies and related follow-ups tell us that people do not always behave from the "inside out." It would be foolish to characterize all of Asch's judges as blind, Milgram's teachers as sadistic, or Zimbardo's guards as cruel. Yet a large number of these otherwise normal people responded to the direct or indirect social pressure of the immediate environment.

We discuss these studies here because these social settings influence people's decisions to conform to gender stereotypes. When coupled with consideration of direct consequences such as praise or mocking, as well as implicit consequences such as maintenance or loss of a friendship, understanding the environmental context furthers our understanding of the power of gender norms.

Milestones

When it comes to gender, there are a few things that all children do. They learn about their culture's stereotypical beliefs about gender, they learn that they have a gender identity, and they develop gender constancy. Research on gender stereotypes or gender roles with very young children is difficult due to their limited language and researchers' desire not to ask leading questions. Yet children as young as two years of age can often tell researchers if a toy, piece of clothing, or anything that can be easily illustrated is appropriate for a girl, a boy, both a boy and a girl, or neither a boy nor a girl (Martin & Ruble, 2010).

In a classic experiment, Sandra Bem (1989) presented three and four year old children with pictures of a boy dressed as a boy, as a girl, and fully nude, as well as a girl dressed as a boy, as a girl, and fully nude; the "clothed" pictures were partial nudes that showed the children's genitalia. Although the vast majority of children could accurately list the content of gender stereotypes, slightly fewer than half were able to correctly identify the sex of the child in all the photos they saw. And only about half knew that their own sex would remain unchanged, called *gender constancy*.

This study was inspired by an experience Bem had. Or rather, her four year old son Jeremy had. Sandra and Daryl Bem were trying to raise him without gender schemas and, at his request, allowed him to wear a barrette to nursery school. A schoolmate told him that he must be a girl because he was wearing a barrette. Four year old Jeremy informed his classmate that being male only means "having a penis and testicles" and, somewhat exasperatedly, "finally pulled down his pants as a way of making his point more convincingly" (Bem, 1985, p. 216). The other child remained unconvinced of Jeremy's maleness.

Although we may find Jeremy's experience amusing, it comes from our greater knowledge. As adults, we know that gender differences are related, at least conceptually, to the sexual binary; they're about being XX or XY, having a penis or a vagina. Most children don't know that these biological differences are the basis for our categories of male and female, nor are those differences readily visible. Instead, children rely heavily on superficial cues like clothing and hairstyle to determine the sex of other children (Bem, 1993). By contrast, preschool children use body shape to determine the sex of adults (Johnson, Lurye, & Tassinary, 2010). These age-differentiated patterns are also true for adults. If you saw a five-year-old child with one of its parents while you were at a store, how would you decide if it was a girl or boy?

Bem's findings are important because she helped demonstrate that children's acquisition of gender stereotypes is separate from their development of their own gender identity or the concept of gender constancy. *Gender identity* refers to a child's knowledge that they are male or female (or, theoretically, intersex) and *gender constancy* refers to the knowledge that one's sex is constant or permanent. Approximately half of six-year-olds understand that gender is constant (Zhentao & Fuxi, 2006). In the most theories, a child first learns his or her gender identity and then makes an effort to conform to that gender's stereotypes.

THEORETICAL EXPLANATIONS

Theories help us understand research by telling us how different findings fit together. We're going to review three theories in detail. The first, social cognitive theory, emphasizes the individual and his or her immediate environment. The second, social structural theory, emphasizes the cultural setting. The third, gender script theory, combines both the individual and the culture. Although there are other theories, we focus on these three theories because they illustrate the breadth of factors that can be included in social explanations.

Experience: Social Cognitive Theory

Albert Bandura developed *Social Cognitive Theory (SCT)* to explain how humans and other organisms learn from their environment (Bussey & Bandura, 1999). The emphasis is on the role of experience, including both personal experience and learning vicariously by watching others.

Bandura recognized that we engage in *vicarious learning* by watching both the actions others perform and the consequences they experience, pleasant or unpleasant. Bandura's initial experiment involved children who were in a play room that included a "Bobo doll," a blow up toy with a weighted bottom that stands back up after it is knocked over. You hit Bobo, it falls over, then "stands" back up. The play room had a monitor that showed a pre-recorded (undergraduate) model in the same room who either punched the Bobo doll or ignored it. Almost all children who witnessed the model punching Bobo were themselves aggressive toward Bobo; less than half of children who saw the video in which the model ignored Bobo were violent towards the doll (Bandura, Ross, & Ross, 1961). In follow up studies, the violent video was changed so that the model either got in trouble for attacking Bobo or was joined in the attack by a second (undergraduate) model. Children who saw the model get in trouble had moderate rates of attacking Bobo, whereas nearly all children who saw both models attack Bobo were aggressive towards the doll (Bandura, Ross, & Ross, 1963b). From these results, Bandura demonstrated how children learn by watching others.

Subsequently, researchers have examined the issue further and have revealed that some models are more likely to be imitated than others. One factor is contact: the more time a person spends with the model, the more likely he or she is to imitate this person's behavior (Bandura et al., 1961). This factor may help explain why boys raised with a mother and a father display more gender-typed behavior than boys raised by a single mother (Stevenson & Black, 1988).

Another factor is the child's perception of having characteristics similar to the model. In other words, you are more likely to imitate someone if you think you are like them in important ways. As sex is a basic division among human beings and is often highlighted as important by cultural forces, it is not surprising to find that children imitate same sex models more readily than models of the other sex, and this process begins to occur as early as three years of age (Bandura, Ross, & Ross, 1963a). Boys imitate females less often than girls imitate males (Bussey & Bandura, 1992). This difference may be due to a number of factors, including differential punishment for cross-gender behavior, the antifemininity bias in masculine gender roles, and the higher social status of males in most cultures (which disempowers males who act in feminine ways and empowers females who act in masculine ways).

Drawing from cognitive psychology, Bandura (1989) argued that we develop *scripts*: sequences of behaviors to be enacted in particular settings. For a stereotypical heterosexual family, the "take out the trash" script might specify that the adult male gathers trash from all rooms in the house, takes it out to the trash can, and brings the trash can to the street in front of the house on Tuesday night. Note that this script specifies who does what, as well as the setting or context which triggers that script (Tuesday night). If a child has enough scripts that are male-specific, he or she may then develop an abstract, unarticulated concept of masculine behavior (Perry & Bussey, 1979). If the child is male, he is more likely to imitate these behaviors.

From a social cognitive perspective, gender identity is formed through the abstraction of masculine and feminine categories of behavior together with the understanding of physical sex differences and the imitation of same-sex models (Bussey & Bandura, 1999). As the boy increasingly behaves like his father and other males, his identification as masculine becomes more and more stable (Lips, 2008). Because of this abstraction, however, he is less likely to imitate a male whom he perceives as behaving in a feminine way (Eisenstock, 1984). Within social cognitive theory, behaving in a gender-stereotypical way helps the child develop an identity that includes his or her gender group, male or female.

David Lynn (1959; 1966; 1969) was one of the first modern writers to theorize about the implications of the historical inaccessibility of fathers as role models. When they are young, children tend to spend much more time with mothers than with fathers. This arrangement continues when children move into child care and elementary school; women comprise more than 80 percent of those fields (National Center for Education Statistics, 2010). Therefore, girls get a good deal of exposure to same-sex models. In constructing ideas about how women act and femininity, they have a lot of information on which to base their imitation.

In sharp contrast, boys do not get nearly as much of an opportunity to observe their fathers and other adult males. Therefore, they must extrapolate a good deal in constructing a sense of what masculinity is. Boys must fill in large gaps of information, and they tend to do so by using other, more available male models such as peers, older boys, and males in the media. Herb Goldberg (1977) concluded that girls identify with a real person, whereas boys identify largely with a fantasy.

These other models are sometimes not good sources of realistic, secure, positively defined masculinity. This fantasy may be heavily laden with unrealistic, hypertrophied aspects of stereotypical masculine gender roles. In television and movies, for example, male characters are often rewarded for using violence to solve problems, and the viewing of this "justified" violence may be even more damaging than viewing villainous violence, as boys learn that physical aggression is a part of being one of the "good guys" (Katz & Earp, 2013). This phenomenon may explain why children who spend large amounts of time watching television tend to be more gender-typed than others (Ward & Friedman, 2006). Because their image of adult men is based in fantasy, the transition from boyhood to adult roles may be somewhat discontinuous for many males (Archer, 1984). Sociologist Michael Kimmel (2008) argued that many of today's young men live in an unrealistic "Guyland" that minimizes responsibility while emphasizing promiscuous sexuality, getting drunk and using other drugs, and looking for a relatively quick financial "score."

A sense of emotional invulnerability is an important aspect of many of these unrealistic masculine fantasies (Katz & Earp, 2013). Consider action movies, for example. How often do we see male characters express sadness at the death of a friend or buddy, a romantic or sexual partner? Does that sadness last more than a moment or two? Does the male hero display other common characteristics of grief, such as difficulty focusing, loss of energy, or spontaneous sadness and crying over the next several days? If the boy identifies with a fantasy–or fantastic–version of his father, as many sons do, and if his father does not express vulnerable feelings such as fear or anxiety, then it is easy for the boy to believe his father does not even experience any type of vulnerability.

This model could become his basis for understanding all men. Consider how often you've heard a man say "I'm worried about X" in comparison to how often you've heard a woman say that. Of course, a father experiences fear and anxiety like any other human being, but he may hide his reactions. The son is likely to deduce that worry and fearful feelings do not exist in "real men." Inevitably, the boy experiences fear, as everyone does from time to time, and he may feel unmasculine and inadequate at these times because he compares his inner experience with this appearance of his father and other men (Lynch & Kilmartin, 2013).

Criticism of Social Cognitive Theory

Behavioral models emphasize that humans (and other organisms) are very attentive to the environment (Skinner, 1974). But when applied to the world around us, it is very hard to predict behavior because we can't say exactly what stimulus, or set of stimuli, a person is responding to. Young men tell researchers they behave differently in all-male groups than in mixed-sex groups (Wight, 1994), but we do not know if this is a function of the physical setting (because all male groups also choose different activities), one specific member of the group, the group as a whole, or some combination of these reasons.

Another criticism focuses on models. We do not know how they are selected, if men invoke different models in different settings, or if men create an amalgamated model that blends multiple inputs (Wade, 1998). Imagine the iconic angel and devil on your shoulders. Which one do you listen to and in what settings? Do you have multiple angels and devils?

Society: Social Structural Theory (aka Social Role Theory)

In contrast to Social Cognitive Theory's focus on the individual, Alice Eagly's *Social Structural Theory* attempts to explain why the behavior of males differs from that of females (Eagly, 1987; Eagly, Wood, & Diekman, 2000). The theory focuses on large-scale and cultural factors that create gender-differentiated behavior. It is sometimes also called social role theory (Eagly, 1987).

Social structural theory begins with the recognition that women have long been the primary caretakers of young children. This arrangement is due to the fact that women were (and often still are) young children's primary food source, and thus having multiple children who were relatively close in age required women to "stay home with the children" for multiple years. Taking care of children full-time prevented women from doing (paid) activities that required sustained attention or concentration or uninterrupted time. Men rarely experienced these constraints. Several relevant changes are historically recent: mandatory schooling, women's right to own property, and the marketing of baby formula are approximately 100 years old; modern contraceptives like the birth control pill are about 75 years old. Without these resources, most women had few options but to stay home and raise the kids after they had their first child.

The result, according to Eagly, is that adult women were forced to adopt a caretaking role that kept them with their children, required "common" household skills such as cooking and washing, and prevented them from obtaining or using high wage skills. Men, by contrast, were not limited to the home due to having children and so could engage in any trade or profession and fill almost any societal role. They have greater upper-body strength than women (on average), a fact that makes them better suited to a broad variety of roles and jobs in both agricultural and industrial cultures and settings. Eagly argues that we have effectively blended (or confused) "women" with the caretaking role they have typically and historically filled. Similarly, we have confused men with their roles: producing goods or selling their labor, filling a broad variety of occupations, and able to use their physical strength for pay. Thus, we have come to believe that women's primary focus is on the home and children, that their primary personality attributes are being loving, kind, and caring, and that they are of somewhat limited intelligence. We have come to believe that men are primarily focused on their work, that their primary personality attributes are being active (or doing), solving problems, having a facility for using tools and technology, and capable of learning any skill or knowledge area from medicine to masonry (Eagly et al., 2000).

According to social structural theory, children do not choose gender-typical behavior because they have chosen same sex models as social cognitive theory suggests, but rather they conform to their culture's gender stereotypes because the culture pushes them—and perhaps even requires them—to adhere to the stereotypes. This approach allows societies to vary from highly to minimally gender-typed (Hofstede, 1998; Williams & Best, 1990b) and explains why children come to reflect and possess the gender roles their society endorses (e.g., Gilmore, 1990).

Given its focus on differences between the sexes, social role theory is often positioned as being in opposition with Buss and Schmitt's (1993) sexual strategies theory (described in Chapter Five). Alice Eagly and Wendy Wood (1999) have argued that social structural theory is compatible with the broader evolutionary psychology framework; the challenge is strictly about the explanation of gender differences as biologically- or culturally-based. After David Buss (1989) demonstrated sex differences in desired number of sexual partners in 37 cultures, Eagly and Wood (1999) reanalyzed the data and added measures of gender equality developed by the United Nations. Those equality measures explained much of the difference between men and women. Said differently, the more equal a society was, the smaller the difference in the number of partners desired. Other researchers have demonstrated that these kinds of global measures, as well as women's representation in elected government positions and research jobs, can explain part of the difference in boys' better math performance on international tests (Else-Quest, Hyde, & Linn, 2010). By identifying the factors that cause group differences and statistically demonstrating that they explain some of the difference, social structural theory appears to be a better explanation than sexual strategies theory.

Criticism of Social Structural Theory

The primary criticism of social structural theory is that it does not explain differences among males or among females; it only explains differences between the two groups. (This is also a criticism of sexual strategies theory.) As we discussed in Chapter Four, there is often more variability within these groups than differences between the two groups.

Experience & Society: Gendered Scripts

Sandra Bem (1981; 1985; 1987; 1993) developed her theory of *Gendered Scripts* by combining perspectives on children's cognitive development with cultural factors that emphasize gender. Bem argued that cognitive development and gender role development are parallel in some regards. She also believed that gender-typed information processing is taught to children by a culture that emphasizes sex differences for virtually every domain of behavior. If our culture were not so gender-typed, children would learn to use other categories to organize their experiences.

According to Bem, children categorize events according to gender only because we live in a culture that communicates to people that sex is important in occupation, clothing, hobbies, children's toys, and other areas where it need not be viewed as important. For instance, a high school graduation ceremony made the news when a female graduate was not allowed to participate because she ordered blue graduation robes in defiance of the school tradition in which girls wear white robes and boys blue robes. The excluded graduate stated that a senior class sponsor told her that the school makes this distinction because "white represents purity, while darker colors signify strength" (Krishnamurthy, 1998, p. C1). Bem would say that drawing a distinction between the sexes in such a non-gender dependent activity as graduating from high school encourages children to use sex as a cognitive guide for understanding the world. We wouldn't ask graduating seniors to wear different colors to indicate different races or socioeconomic groups, so why is it appropriate to do so for sex-based groups?

Barrie Thorne (2009) described several elementary school situations in which teachers and other adults needlessly called attention to students' sexes. These included statements like "the girls are ready and the boys aren't" (p. 178), or classroom contests in which a teacher-chosen team of all boys competes against a team of all girls. In these situations, adults highlighted gender and made it more likely that children would also acquire them. Although these examples seem inconsequential, most people in the United States would not consider making such a statement based on racial or ethnic groups. Research indicates that this type of statement may be more powerful than we think, especially when repeated regularly. In a novel experiment, Lacey Hilliard and Lynn Liben (2010) worked with two otherwise similar preschools. In both settings, the teachers tended to be gender neutral; they rarely compared the girls to the boys or otherwise segregated the students based on sex. The research team observed whom each child played with during unstructured times such as "free play" and "playground." At the beginning of the study, students at the two schools were similar in how often they played with familiar same- or other-sex peers and how willing they were to play with an unfamiliar same- or other-sex such as a child from another class. On assessments of their knowledge of gender stereotypes, the students from the two schools were similar.

In one school, the teachers were asked to maintain their gender-neutral behavior. In the other, Hilliard and Liben asked the teachers of three to five year old children to emphasize gender for two weeks by having separate bulletin boards for boys' and girls' work, making the kinds of spontaneous comments Thorne observed, and saying things like "I need a boy [or girl] to do X" instead of "I need a volunteer to do X." Children in both schools were observed and tested at the end of the two week period. In the preschool where teachers didn't do anything differently, the students hadn't changed either. But at the end of two weeks, children in the "gender-salient" preschool showed less interest in playing with familiar other-sex peers, less willingness to play with an unfamiliar child of the other sex, and lower frequency of playing with other-sex peers during observation. The effects were limited to avoidance of other-sex peers; children's preference for same-sex peers did not change in any area assessed by the researchers. And remember, these are the effects for teachers who had been emphasizing gender for less than two weeks.

We see many examples of sex-differentiated terms in the English language. For instance, there are work titles that differ depending on the sex of the person who occupies the role. The linguistic distinctions between waiters and waitresses, policewomen and policemen, actors and actresses, and comedians and comediennes may lead people to believe that the sex of the role occupant is an important distinction for human beings at work. The increased use of nonsexist terms such as firefighter, chairperson, and mail carrier should encourage people to use different, nongendered ways to categorize.

This cultural emphasis on sex distinctions interacts with children's cognitive development. Because humans take in so much information, we must categorize and organize it to avoid a sensory overload (Gelman, 2003). To do so, we develop *schemata* (an alternate plural of *schema*), cognitive structures that allow us to anticipate and understand events. As a child observes males and females in a gender-typed environment, they gather information about gender. The child makes associations among different aspects of masculinity and femininity and uses these resulting associations to organize new information.

Proponents of both gender schema theory and social cognitive theory propose that children learn sequences of behavior (schemata, scripts) and eventually extrapolate larger constructs known as femininity and masculinity. Because social cognitive theory is rooted in behaviorism, the focus is primarily on behavior and memory. Gender schema theory focuses on cognition and adds the ability to anticipate and draw meaning from (or interpret) behavior, reflecting other aspects of thought.

Children are quite good at organizing information, even if they can't always remember it or we adults can't quite understand their organizational system. We have seen that they organize behavior into patterns (schemata, scripts) and ultimately use these patterns to generate concepts such as masculine and feminine. Young children's ability to accurately learn language may provide a useful parallel. They learn to speak reasonably clearly before starting school, and they do so despite the complexity of language and simply by being exposed to adults who use the language (Chomsky, 1957). If you asked a very young child about the rule for past tense, he or she would probably not be able to explain it to you (even if you went to great lengths to explain the question in the child's language). However, you would hear many examples in the child's everyday language, proof that he or she has learned the rule unconsciously. When children have learned a rule but not the exceptions, such as when they say "we go-ed to the store" instead of "we went to the store," researchers call it *over-regularization*. A rigid gender schema would seem to represent the same kind of overregularization. Parents (and others) often correct a child's language errors; they may or may not correct their child's gender "errors."

According to gender schema theory, once children have developed gender constancy, they begin to mold their behavior to fit their understanding of gender. Not only do children learn that certain behaviors are gender-specific and make efforts to conform to their conceptions of gender, they also learn that the same behavior may mean different things for each sex. If you walked into a coffee shop and saw a woman sitting alone, crying quietly, and staring in disbelief at her cell phone, what would you think? If you saw a man doing the same thing, would you think something different? This interpretive step defines what Bem called "the *lenses of gender*."

Bem describes the gendered lens as a "nonconscious ideology" (1987) and a set of "default options" (1993) for behavior. Most people are not aware that they organize their perceptions on the basis of gender, nor are they aware that alternative conceptualizations are possible. As she eloquently stated, "Look through the lens of gender and you perceive the world as falling into the masculine and feminine categories. Put on a different pair of lenses, however, and you perceive the world as falling into different categories." (Bem, 1987, p. 309).

In Bem's view, the only time when it makes sense to be gender schematic is in the realm of biology, and yet the gender schema is extrapolated into many other domains. She suggests that some of the destructive aspects of gender stereotyping could be transformed by providing people with alternative ways of thinking about the world and the self, such as with non-gendered ways to categorize (as described in Box 4.3 on page 91). In this way, gender can be understood as a biological category that is not important in every setting. Bem (1993) clearly emphasizes the role of education in social change, and her theory can be applied to the social change agenda of men's studies.

Criticism of Gender Schema Theory

Gender schema theory has been criticized on several fronts. One such criticism is the claim that young children consistently use schemata to direct their behavior. Bem's description implies a level of conscious control of behavior and activities that likely overestimates children's reality. The theory has also been criticized heavily for its inability to specify the content of scripts, when they are employed, or why two children with similar experiences may develop very different scripts (Martin, Ruble, & Szkyrbalo, 2002).

SUMMARY

There are too many socially-based theories for us to review all of them effectively. Kay Deaux's discussion of how the immediate environment influences gender-typed behavior gives more precedence to the situation than the approaches we've described here (Deaux & LaFrance, 1998). Diane Ruble and Carol Martin's (1998) cognitive developmental theory is more detailed and nuanced than gender schema theory, and these authors have recently developed an approach rooted in dynamic systems theory (formerly known as "chaos theory") that more effectively blends children's cognitive abilities, environmental influences, and biological factors (Martin & Ruble, 2010).

Janet Shibley Hyde (2005) put forth her gender similarities hypothesis. As the name suggests, this is not a theory that explains how boys and girls come to behave differently, but rather a reminder that females and males are more similar than different. Hyde argues that these similarities also need to be explained within a gender-based model. In other words, the gender similarities hypothesis is a reminder to theorists and researchers to avoid the alpha bias.

Socially-based theories identify ways in which gender roles, or at least our understanding of them, develop and can be changed. It is often said that "the fish is unaware of the water" because it has never experienced anything else. Because many aspects of culture have long considered masculinity as a normative referent for experience, many men have not noticed the gender-schematic nature of their approach to the world. Men have often remained unaware of the culture of patriarchy because it benefits them, just as fish benefit from water. Women and other marginalized groups of people are usually more aware of sexism, racism, classism, and other forms of unequal resource allocation because they usually suffer the adverse effects of these arrangements, often on a daily basis. A fish has the luxury to remain unaware of the water. A drowning mammal does not.

To become conscious of one's ideologies would seem to require psychological-mindedness, nondefensiveness, introspection, and a willingness to listen to others' points of view. Males have been socialized away from every one of these activities. As femininity has long been associated with loss of power and status for men, there has been a good deal of reward for men's attending to the world in gender schematic fashion. Men who begin to break out of this stereotyped information processing are finding that they can evaluate themselves with standards that are less punitive and more reasonable. If Bem is correct that gender schematic processing is destructive and unessential to human development, then we ought to support countervailing educational and therapeutic activities such as consciousness raising, gender awareness curricula, women's studies, and men's studies.

1. Parents treat children differently based on the child's sex, starting at birth.

2. Fathers tend to be more stereotypical than mothers, at least with sons. Boys are punished more harshly than girls for violating gender norms.
3. Schools appear to favor feminine-typed behaviors, and teachers respond to boys of different ethnicities in very different manners. Schools continue gender lessons taught at home, both through teachers and through access to peers, which often separate into sex-based groups.
4. Social settings can have substantial and dramatic influence on behavior, including gender-typed behaviors.
5. Gender milestones include the achievement of gender identity (self as male or female) and gender constancy (male and female as permanent and unchanging).
6. Social cognitive theory emphasizes experience, direct and observed, as well as the influence of the environment. Models are particularly important in this theory and boys have direct access to fewer adult male models than girls have to adult female models.
7. Social structural theory emphasizes the power of culture and hypothesizes that our beliefs about men and women have been derived from the social roles they typically inhabit.
8. Gendered script theory emphasizes the interaction between being raised in a culture that highlights gender as a central organizing principle and children's cognitive development.

GLOSSARY

Gender Identity Disorder (GID): A disorder characterized by non-conformity to gender roles. This disorder was first included in DSM-IV and removed when DSM-V was published.

Gender Dysphoria: A disorder characterized by an individual's distress due to conforming to gender roles, as well as the individual's violation of gender roles.

Gender typing: A culture's pressure to conform to gender roles.

Conformity: A change in behavior in response to implicit and unspoken social pressure.

Compliance: A change in behavior as the result of direct and explicit social pressure.

Gender identity: An individual's knowledge of what their gender is.

Gender constancy: The idea that one's gender is constant or permanent.

Social Cognitive Theory (SCT): A theory that explains how humans and other organisms learn from their environment. The theory emphasizes both personal experience and learning vicariously by watching others.

Vicarious learning: Learning from the actions others perform and the consequences they experience.

Scripts: Sequences of behaviors to be enacted in particular settings.

Social Structural Theory: A theory that attempts to explain why the behavior of males differs from that of females. Also known as Social Role Theory.

Gendered Script Theory: A theory that combines perspectives on children's cognitive development with cultural factors that emphasize gender to explain how children learn about and adopt gender roles.

Over-regularization: The application of a rule to a situation where that rule does not apply. The term comes from studies of language development and the errors made with irregular verbs and nouns.

Chapter Seven

It Never Lies, and It Never Lies Still: Emotion and Masculinity

Few human experiences are as basic and ubiquitous as emotion. A person responds to almost any internal or environmental event with some degree of feeling, and the experience of positive emotions is probably one of the most important motivators in life. People seek money, love, knowledge, pleasure, relationships, or human service because they believe that these things will provide some degree of emotional fulfillment. The United States Declaration of Independence holds the "pursuit of happiness," an emotion, as an inalienable human right. Just as the brain structures associated with emotion are at the center of the brain, emotion is at the center of human experience.

But what exactly is emotion? An old psychoanalytic saying states that "emotion never lies, and emotion never lies still," which suggests that emotion is some type of irrepressible force. Some people say that emotion is the opposite of reason. Within this framework, emotion has been characterized as feminine and reason as masculine (Rotundo, 1993), which gives emotion a distinctly gendered flavor. Yet others say that emotion at its most basic level is the manifestation of specific patterns of brain activation and thus no different than any other aspect of human activity.

Even the casual observer will recognize the common belief that men have difficulty understanding, dealing with, and expressing emotions. Restrictive emotionality is one of the most frequently discussed issues in men's studies, and it is related to a number of other problems for men, including relationship difficulties, physical illness, mental health problems, and violence (O'Neil, 2008). Masculine gender roles often encourage men to resist the awareness of affect, avoid emotional vulnerability, and disguise their feelings, especially when those feelings involve hurt, fear, sadness, or any experience that signals weakness or lack of control. Some men believe that tear ducts on men are like nipples—we only have them through a biological accident.

We also note that American linguistic conventions conspire to describe male emotional inexpressiveness in ways that support masculine norms. Men are typically described as "controlling their feelings" consistent with masculine ideals of dominance and surety. We do not typically talk about men "hiding their feelings," which is also an accurate description but makes men sound fearful and thus weak.

In this chapter, we explore the origins and consequences of, and remedies for restrictive emotionality by addressing the following questions such as How is emotion defined? What do sex and gender comparisons in emotional experience, expression and self-disclosure tell us? What typical masculine socialization experiences and social situations lead to restrictive emotionality? What have researchers learned about the effects of emotional constriction on the person? What are the possibilities for helping men and boys improve the quality of their emotional lives?

Defining and Studying Emotionality

Emotion has been studied from several approaches and disciplines, including the fields of emotion science and gender studies. Within emotion science, researchers have examined the rules that govern emotional expression, physiological arousal (e.g., heart rate), neurological events (i.e., brain region activation, such as the amygdala), cognitive appraisals of emotion, subjective experience of emotion, and overt emotional actions (e.g., smiling, crying, hitting) while using a broad range of strategies to measure and observe emotions. By contrast, gender studies researchers have focused almost exclusively on rules governing emotional displays and have relied almost exclusively on surveys where individuals describe themselves (Wester, Heesacker, & Snowden, 2016).

We have previously defined masculine norms as including emotional stoicism (see Chapter One). We note that femininity is often defined in terms of emotional expression (Bem, 1991; Levant et al., 2007; Mahalik et al., 2005), a definition that dates back to at least the middle of the twentieth century (Parsons & Bales, 1955). The close association between femininity and emotion forms the basis for ideologies that masculine directives to not be feminine include injunctions to avoid emotional expression (O'Neil, 1981a, 2008, 2013).

Examination of trait-based measures of gender adherence include emotional expression as a component of femininity (Bem, 1974; Spence & Helmreich, 1978); in Chapter Four, we noted that trait-based measures emphasize positive aspects of gender roles. Undergraduate men's scores on these measures increased from the 1970s through the 1990s and have subsequently leveled out (Twenge, 1997b; Wells & Twenge, 2005). Scores are now relatively high, suggesting that recent generations of young American men see themselves as fairly emotionally expressive. At the same time, measures of masculinity ideology (MI) typically include direct assessment of "restrictive emotionality," "emotional control," and the like (Levant et al., 2007; Mahalik et al., 2003). In Chapter Four, we noted that ideology scales tend to focus on negative aspects of masculinity. Scores on these measures tend to be relatively low (see Smiler,

2014; Thompson & Bennett, 2015). Collectively, these findings suggest that (young) men see themselves as somewhat emotionally expressive.

Reviewing the available literature, Stephen Wester, Martin Heesacker, and Steven Snowden (2016) argued that the gender studies approach has focused almost exclusively on emotional display rules while using a research methodology—self-report surveys—that is highly susceptible to *social desirability*, defined as people's motivation to present themselves in a positive light, even among basically honest people (Kenrick, Neuberg, & Cialdini, 2005). They amplify and expand on concerns about this narrow research focus, as well as the tendency to focus on male–female differences (Shields, 2013; see also Wester, Vogel, Pressly, & Heesacker, 2002). Wester and colleagues describe and summarize the persistent lack of male–female differences in studies examining physiological arousal, neurological activation, and subjective descriptions of emotion, and conclude that the experience of emotion is no different for men-as-a-group than women-as-a-group. They recognize that studies of emotional display rules are consistently different and that studies of overt actions are highly influenced by situational or contextual factors (see also Shields, 2005, 2013; Wester et al., 2002).

Studies on the physiological and subjective experience of pain provide some clarity about these issues. *Physiological assessments of pain* rely on direct assessments of bodily processes such as heart rate and galvanic skin response, both of which typically increase due to pain, anxiety, and other stressors. *Subjective assessments of pain* are individual's ratings of how much pain they experience using, for example, a one-to-ten scale. Researchers find that physiological measures do not typically show male–female differences and that men typically report lower levels of subjective pain. Further, men who describe themselves as more masculine tend to report lower levels of pain (Alabas, Tashani, Tabasam, & Johnson, 2012). Other researchers have found that undergraduate young men report lower levels of pain to female research assistants than to male research assistants, presumably because they want to impress those women (Aslaksen, Myrbakk, Hoifodt, & Flaten, 2007). These findings indicate that men and women have similar physiological responses but display their reactions differently, based on men's beliefs about masculinity and the context men find themselves in.

Male–Female Comparisons in Emotional Expression

We must keep in mind that, although every culture exerts pressure on its members to handle emotion in prescribed ways, these "rules" vary widely from culture to culture. In the United States and many Western cultures, women are expected to express or show emotions and men are not. In many Asian cultures, both men and women hide their emotions. Many Middle Eastern and South American cultures expect both men and women to show their feelings. And in some cultures, men are considered more expressive of certain emotions than women (Tavris & Wade, 2001).

It is also worthwhile to repeat an important consideration from earlier chapters. Although a culture exerts pressure on people to feel, think, and act in certain ways, individual responses to cultural influences are widely variable. Even in cultures that expect women to be highly emotional and men to be less so, individual differences exist and thus there are very expressive men and very inexpressive women.

Leslie Brody and Judith Hall (2010) delineated several important conceptual categories in the study of gender and emotion. First, many researchers have studied gender stereotypes of emotionality. These studies describe people's *beliefs* about men's and women's emotional lives. There is also a body of research on *self-descriptions* of emotionality—people's reports about their experiences. And there is an important distinction between the *experience* and the *expression* of emotion. A person might feel quite strongly but try not to communicate that feeling for any number of reasons.

It is no surprise that, in studies of gender *stereotypes*, most people believe that women are more emotional than men. Fischer and Manstead (2000) noted that this stereotype exists in 30 of the 33 cultures that they observed. People also view women as having more intense emotions than men, although the difference in intensity is smaller than the difference regarding men's and women's experience of emotion in general (Brody & Hall, 2010). Actually, there is little evidence that men-as-a-group experience emotion less often than women-as-a-group (Shields, 2005). Therefore, the prevalent beliefs are that women feel a little bit more than men, but that they display their emotions a great deal more than men.

Self-descriptive studies may be strongly biased by gender stereotypes due to *social desirability*. As gender stereotypes carry with them strong values, males and females are more likely to portray themselves as masculine and feminine, respectively. Thus it is no surprise that women, on average, report greater intensity of emotion than men. We also know that retrospective reports are subject to memory distortion, and that gender ideologies affect memory. Reports asking how one felt in the past day, week, or month tend to reflect gender stereotypes, but when people are asked to chronicle their feelings in real time, their reports often do not match stereotypical expectations (Shields, 2010).

Reviewing the literature, Brody and Hall (2010) found that many researchers have found that women report greater *experiences* of positive emotions (happiness, well-being, joy) than men. At the same time, females also report higher levels of many negative feelings, especially those that are **intropunitive,** or self-punishing, such as shame, guilt, sadness, anxiety, and fear. Although males reported feeling contempt more often, there was no difference between men and women in the intensity of contempt. Studies on sex comparisons in the experience of anger show mixed results, with some finding no differences and others finding differences depending on the target of the anger (Brody & Hall, 2010; Wester et al., 2016).

An important finding is that there is a strong correlation between the reported intensity of positive feelings and the reported intensity of negative feelings (Diener, Larsen, Levine, & Emmons, 1985). According to self-descriptions, it is apparent that high emotionality is a mixed blessing, allowing one to fully experience joy, satisfaction, awe, gratitude, amusement, interest, inspiration, and contentment, but also leaving the person vulnerable to intense negative feelings like sadness, loneliness, embarrassment, and anxiety. The same is true for low emotionality—it allows a person to escape from intense feelings of fear and anxiety, but apparently at the cost of sacrificing positive emotional experiences. Positive and negative emotions are therefore a kind of package deal.

Within the domain of emotional expression, there is little doubt that males tend to display most feelings less frequently and less intensely than females. Interesting data have emerged from developmental studies in this area. Infant boys actually appear to be more expressive than infant girls (Brody & Hall, 2010). Preschool children show no sex differences in expression, but consistent differences begin to emerge by age six and these differences become well established by middle adolescence (Adams, Kuebli, Boyle, & Fivush, 1995). In an older study, Janice Stapely and Jeannette Haviland (1989) found that adolescent boys were much more likely than girls to deny that they *ever* had emotional experiences.

Although females tend to display generally higher levels of emotions than males, the expression of anger, pride, and loneliness are more frequent in males (Brody & Hall, 2010). However, psychological gender is more predictive of level of emotional expression than biological sex. In other words, knowing a person's level of stereotypical masculinity and femininity allows for a better understanding of his or her emotional expressiveness than simply knowing whether the person is male or female. People who believe in the stereotype that men are "naturally" unemotional are more likely to report stereotypical emotionality for themselves (Deaux, 2000). Likewise, men's high levels of adherence to masculine ideology, which includes the belief that men *should be* unemotional, are associated with low expressiveness (Bruch, Berko, & Haase, 1998).

There are also average sex differences in the manner of emotional expression. Among North American adults, women smile and touch others more, use more expressive hand and body movements, and talk about their feelings more (Tavris & Wade, 2008). Males are more likely to act out their feelings (Brody & Hall, 2010; Lynch & Kilmartin, 2013). Females also tend to be better than males at identifying others' feelings from facial, body, and voice cues (Manstead, 1992). These findings indicate that women, on average, see themselves as more sensitive than men to people's emotions, even when those feelings are expressed indirectly. But we need to keep in mind that there are enormous within-group sex variations; some women are not very sensitive to others' emotions, and some men are. After a thorough review of the available research on sex and emotion, one group of scholars concluded that patterns of men's and women's emotionality are much more similar than they are different (Wester, Vogel, Pressly, & Heesacker, 2002).

We should also keep in mind that context is a critical factor in the display of emotion (Brody & Hall, 2010). Because masculinity directs men to be emotionally inexpressive, this may be particularly true for men. Consider the previously mentioned pain study, in which undergraduate men reported less subjective pain to a female experimenter than a male experimenter (Aslaksen et al., 2007). (Female undergraduates' subjective reports did not vary based on the experimenter's sex.) High level athletes, who are often seen as idealized versions of masculinity (Messner, 1992), are allowed to freely show joy or sadness at the end of a playoff or championship game, but not after a regular (season) game. Social forces exert influence on people both in immediate context and the "big picture" of the larger culture (Deaux, 2000). In fact, contextual or situational characteristics often influence emotional expression to a much greater degree than gender factors (LaFrance, Hecht, & Paluck, 2003; Wester et al., 2016).

The Special Case of Anger

Although masculine stereotypes and ideologies include the expectation for men to hide their emotions, the expression of anger is a notable exception. Curiously, in contrast to the vulnerable emotions that are assumed to be in complete control, men's anger is often seen as being completely *out of* control. Moreover, an angry man is expected to express his anger through some sort of action, sometimes in violent ways. Because anger is socially acceptable for men, traditionally gender-typed men tend to convert most other emotions into anger, often resulting in destructive behavior and a lack of awareness of the original, more vulnerable emotions such as jealousy, sadness, and disappointment that gave rise to the anger (Lynch & Kilmartin, 2013). Don Long (1987) referred to anger as the "male emotional funnel system."

One group of researchers noted that men's expressions of anger are associated with their fear of experiencing vulnerable emotional states (Jacupak, Tull, & Roemer, 2005), and men who evidence restrictive emotionality on the gender role strain measure show a greater likelihood to engage in aggressive behavior when their masculinity is threatened (Cohn, Seibert, & Zeichner, 2009). Parents have a tendency to highlight the experiences of anger and the related emotions of contempt and disgust with their sons much more often than with their daughters (Brody & Hall, 2010), and psychological masculinity is associated with aggressive, unacknowledged, and uncontrolled anger (Kopper & Epperson, 1996).

Although emotional expression can have positive health and mental health consequences (Wester et al., 2016), the expression of anger is quite risky from a health perspective. Carol Tavris (1989) noted that giving vent to anger is sometimes dangerous and self-destructive. Many people believe that, when a person is angry, he or she needs to "blow off steam"—to act out the anger in some way. But a conventional belief can be wrong. In many circumstances, the unrestrained expression of anger tends to make a person angrier, and also tends to damage relationships. In extreme situations, the expression of anger can put the person at risk, as in "road rage," in which more than 95 percent of the perpetrators are boys and men (Katz, 2013).

Researchers have identified chronic anger as an important contributor to a number of physical health problems: hypertension, heart attack, and stroke (Williams, et. al., 2002) (See Chapter Nine). The research on anger expression tells us that "counting to ten" is often a much better strategy than "blowing off steam," in both the long and the short term (Lynch & Kilmartin, 2013).

Self-Disclosure

Self-disclosure is the verbal communication of personal information from one person to another (Cozby, 1973). There is ample evidence that self-disclosure is basic to mental health (Pennebaker, 2002). People who are able to reveal their thoughts and feelings to others have the opportunity to express themselves, receive social or emotional support, gain insight into their selves, understand their emotional nuances, and form close relationships. To do so, however, they must tolerate some degree of vulnerability, which requires violating masculine directives to be invulnerable and self-sufficient. In other words, the revelation of the self to important others involves some interpersonal risk, but it also helps people to be understood, connected, and in touch with themselves. Men who place a high value on hegemonic norms of masculinity tend to avoid self-disclosure (Cunningham & Newkirk, 2004; Shepard et al., 2011).

There also appear to be differences in topics about which males and females disclose as well as the sex of the person who more often receives the disclosure. Stapely and Haviland (1989) reported that adolescent boys disclosed more about their activities and achievements than girls, and that boys found performance-based disclosures, with the potential for sub-par performance, to be more emotionally charged than other areas. Girls reported relationships to be more emotionally charged, and they disclosed more in this area. In general, girls tend to reveal personal information and boys tend to reveal what they are doing or thinking (Polce-Lynch, 2002).

The *self-disclosure target* refers to the person to whom the information is given. Here the data are unambiguous. People of both sexes disclose more often to females than to males (Timmers, Fischer, & Manstead, 1998). Gender-typed males tend to reveal very little personal information to other males, although they disclose about the same to females as androgynous men do (Winstead, Derlega, & Wong, 1984). The low levels of male-to-male disclosure may be partly due to difficulty finding other males with whom they are comfortable sharing their feelings (Garfield, 2015; Heasley, 2005; Way, 2011). Males overwhelmingly express more affection toward women than toward men (Brody, 1993). These patterns are consistent with both men's and women's perception that women are more trustworthy than men (Glick, 2005; Steinberg & Diekman, 2016).

Overall, we can make the following conclusions about sex, gender, and emotion: Men and women are overwhelmingly more similar than they are different; emotional restrictiveness varies widely among men and among women; most men are not significantly restrictive, but men who subscribe strongly to stereotypical masculine ideologies tend to display emotion less often. Both sexes tend to disclose more to women than to men. There is little doubt that many cultures discourage males from expressing their emotions, but as with all gender pressures, individual responses to that pressure are widely variable. There is little evidence that males are unemotional or incapable of improving the quality of their emotional lives due to natural, inherent, or biological causes (Wong & Rochlen, 2008).

Learning Restrictive Emotionality

Emotional constriction is one of the hallmarks of traditional masculinity. Males are often socialized to deny and suppress feelings from an early age. The masculine values of toughness, self reliance, task orientation, logic, fearlessness, and confidence are usually perceived to be antithetical to the expression of emotions, especially those associated with vulnerability. Anger would seem to be a potentially empowering emotion, and therefore it is socially allowable for men (Shields, 2010).

There are a number of cultural and social forces that encourage men to restrict their emotionality. James O'Neil (1981a) believes that the antifemininity norm is at the heart of men's fears of emotional expression. He describes the following four commonly held masculine beliefs:

1. Emotions, feelings, and vulnerabilities are signs of femininity and therefore to be avoided;
2. Men seeking help through emotional expressiveness are immature, weak, dependent, and therefore feminine;
3. Interpersonal communication emphasizing emotions, feelings, and intuitions are considered feminine and to be avoided;
4. Emotional expression may expose inner fears and conflicts that could portray the man as unstable, immature, and unmanly. (p. 206)

Some psychoanalytic interpretations of masculine inexpression appeal to the early childhood denial of psychological identification with the mother, as discussed in Chapter Five. Because boys are often raised by their other-sex parent, they must put rigid boundaries between themselves and their mothers to define themselves as masculine. If the boy's mother is emotionally expressive and his father is not (a fairly common case), then emotions are experienced as "feminine" and they threaten masculine identification. When the boy feels something, he becomes anxious about his masculinity and learns to deny and devalue these emotions. Theoretically, girls' gender identity is based on attachment to the mother, whereas that of boys is based on separation from her (Chodorow, 1978). As a result, girls tend to become more relationship-oriented and boys more task-oriented.

If the boy's father is emotionally inexpressive, then this style may become a part of the boy's identification with the father. Sons whose fathers are highly involved parents are more emotionally expressive than other boys, and sons of emotionally expressive fathers display their feelings at similar levels to girls (Brody, 1999). In families where both parents are expressive, boys do not usually view emotional expression as an exclusively feminine trait, and therefore the natural inclination to display feelings will emerge, because it is not associated with threats to masculinity.

We could also easily view the finding that expressive fathers tend to have expressive sons as merely a product of imitation. Fathers tend to use more demanding language than mothers and, especially with sons, use more pejorative language ("you knucklehead!") (Brody & Hall, 2010), hardly a style conducive to the display of vulnerable feeling. If we look at the availability of male role models in mainstream United States culture, it is easy to see how inexpressiveness perpetuates itself generation after generation. Fathers' inexpressiveness is imitated, and male heroes in popular culture are often paragons of traditional masculinity. Movies and television often contain male characters who are task oriented, tough, emotionally inexpressive, and violent (Katz & Earp, 2013; Pecora, 1992).

An interesting research finding is that parents display a wider range of their own emotions to their daughters than to their sons (Brody, 2000). Therefore, girls usually have more opportunities than boys to observe and imitate expressive models. In one longitudinal study (in which a group of children is followed over a number of years), The research team of Susan Adams, Janet Kuebli, Patricia Boyle, and Robyn Fivush (1995) demonstrated that parents' more frequent use of emotional language with girls appeared to create a sex difference in children's use of similar language. They found no sex differences at 40 months of age, but clear differences emerged by 70 months. These 30 months are a time of highly accelerated language acquisition, and parents' reluctance to speak to boys about their emotions may limit boys' emotional vocabulary and also communicate the idea that feelings are not important. Overall, the research literature shows that there is a connection between parents' gender-related schemas and their children's gender-related schemas, with children's schemas tending to be similar to their parents' schemas (Tenebaum & Leaper, 2010).

There is also considerable evidence that interpersonal and behavioral influences within the family lead boys away from the world of emotion, except for anger and disgust. Overall, parents talk about emotion more to daughters than to sons. When children feel badly, mothers are more likely to talk directly about the feeling with daughters and to talk about the causes and consequences of the feeling with sons. The former encourages expression; the latter, control (Brody & Hall, 2010). Children are natural pattern-seekers (Gelman, 2003), so interactions that highlight certain aspects of experience help children determine which aspects of their world deserve their attention. For girls, it is often the emotional world. For boys, it is likely to be the world of task, control, and detached analysis.

Rewards and punishments for self-disclosure may also affect the frequency of this behavior. It is clear that "unmasculine" behaviors such as crying often meet with disapproval from parents and peers (Brody, 2000). Many men have a storehouse of memories of times when their emotional expression was punished. The crying little boy whose father says to him threateningly, "I'll give you something to cry about," learns not to cry anymore, at least not in front of his father. Elementary school-aged boys who violate masculine norms, particularly through emotional expression, tend to have fewer friends and experience more gender-based teasing than more stereotypically masculine boys (Carver, Egan, & Perry, 2004; Pascoe, 2007). There is solid research evidence that the extensive socialization to control emotional expression can lead to an overlearning of this tendency (Barr & Kleck, 1995). In other words, emotional inhibition can become a habit that is applied automatically across a variety of situations.

Male emotional reticence is reflected in "G" rated movies, where males are twice as likely as females to be depicted as emotionally disconnected, and this difference is even more pronounced for characters who are males of color (Kelly & Johnson, 2009). Thus media models also encourage children to think of males in less relationship-oriented terms than females.

Because of the social dominance of men, out-role behavior is viewed as a loss of masculine power and privilege, and not to be tolerated. Hence, pejorative terms like "sissy" or "wimp" are applied to men who exhibit emotionality, submissiveness, or dependence. Masculine privilege not only devalues and restricts women (via sexism), it devalues and restricts the feminine-defined parts of men as well as making it difficult for others to connect with the person. James Nelson (1997) likens emotional constriction to armor: "It seems to protect us, but it also keeps us from leaping, dancing, and being seen."

Again, context matters. The male peer group can be especially brutal in its enforcement of the restrictive emotionality norm (Polce-Lynch, 2002). In extreme groups, such as street gangs, this standard is rigidly enforced with threats of violence. Besides punishing expressiveness, male groups may also reward emotional inexpressiveness. For instance, in some fraternity initiation rites, a group symbol is burned into the arm of the initiate, and he is applauded for remaining unresponsive. Many male initiation rites around the world encourage emotional suppression, which is believed to be an important skill for warriors (Herdt, 1982).

Benefits and Costs of Restrictive Emotional Display Rules

Masculine directives sharply limit males' emotional expression. These display rules are well known and, in the United States, highly gender differentiated. Yet physiological, neurological, and subjective experience studies all show no male–female differences in the experience of emotion. Accordingly, we might ask what benefits and consequences are associated with masculine emotional display rules. For example, men are socialized to view all other men as competitors and one does not exhibit vulnerability to a competitor (Skovholt & Hansen, 1980). Because self-disclosure often involves vulnerability, males tend to avoid it, especially in the company of other males.

Benefits

Many components of masculinity encourage men to solve problems and get things done. Limited emotional display would appear to support these goals in many, but not all, situations. From early childhood, girls are encouraged to look inside of themselves and think about how they feel, and boys are encouraged to look outside of themselves and think about what to do (Brody & Hall, 2010). Strong "feminine" emotions are experienced as threats to masculinity, and these threats are sometimes difficult to ignore. The traditional male deals with these feelings with strategies that allow him to perceive them as nonexistent. In this way, he preserves his masculinity by defending against feminine experience and behavior.

When a girl comes home from school and says, "the kids are picking on me," parents are more likely to engage her in *emotion-focused coping* by addressing her feelings directly and asking how she *feels* about it. When a boy makes the same statement, parents are more likely to talk engage in *task-focused coping* that highlights ways to discharge those feelings, and thus ask what he is going to *do* about it. Thus we sometimes encourage girls to solve problems within themselves and boys outside of themselves (Lynch & Kilmartin, 2013). In the extreme, either style can be maladaptive, as people need to do both to cope effectively.

The context of friendship (and romantic relationship) provides one place in which we can examine the benefits of masculinity's limits on emotional displays. One broad social expectation is for *reciprocity*, the tendency to respond to other people as they behave toward us (Baron & Branscome, 2011). For example, when someone expresses anger toward you, you tend to respond with anger. When haggling over the price of something, a salesperson who reduces an asking price influences a buyer to increase his or her offer. With regard to emotionality, the reciprocity norm influences people to disclose at a level similar to that which they receive. Since males are less often the targets of disclosure than females, then it is not surprising that they tend to disclose less. Males exhibit higher levels of emotional disclosure to females than to other males, perhaps reflecting the influence of the reciprocity norm. Thus, reciprocity helps men maintain low—and thus comfortable—levels of emotionality in their relationships.

Jack Sattel (1998) argued that men are inexpressive simply because they want to maintain power. By being emotionally withholding, men force women to "draw them out" and do the emotional work in the relationship. Sattell notes that some men are quite expressive in the early stages of romantic relationships with women. Later on, they sometimes become inexpressive as a way of asserting control, because masculinity and male privilege demand dominance. He goes so far as to suggest that inexpressiveness is directly related to the power of a person's role. Husbands are more likely than wives to respond to marital conflict by "stonewalling" — minimizing their facial expressions, eye contact, and willingness to listen (Levenson, Carstensen, & Gottman, 1994).

Robin Lakoff (1990) also pointed to power, contending that men's and women's typical communication patterns are better understood in terms of superior and subordinate, noting that similar patterns develop between supervisors and workers, Whites and non-Whites, prisoners and guards. Both women and men in positions of authority use power-assertive language, reveal their feelings less often (except for anger), and display similar nonverbal behaviors (Tavris, 1992). Social status and power are extremely important variables in the study of emotional expression (Deaux, 2000), with gender often operating as a generalized power variable.

Costs

Coping refers to the ability to handle adverse events or feelings. Some psychologists see the main function of masculinity itself as a generic defense against vulnerable feelings (Lynch & Kilmartin, 2013). In other words, masculinity is a form of coping. Psychoanalytic thinkers often talk about coping strategies as *ego defenses* because they are strategies for helping the ego mediate between either the outer and inner worlds or the id and the superego (most ego defenses only address one of these two potential conflicts). If a person develops in a healthy manner, their repertoire of ego defenses becomes broader and more mature.

James Mahalik and his colleagues (1998) found that men with rigid masculine expectations used more immature ego defenses than more gender-flexible men. An example will help to clarify these styles. If you are rejected by a romantic partner, that event can precipitate painful feelings of sadness due to the loss of the valued person, as well as anxiety due to doubts about your adequacy. There are several ways to deal with these feelings. You could talk about them with a close friend and gain support, express the sadness through "having a good cry," convert these feelings into anger and engage in some aggressive behavior, or deal with the feelings as though they were an intellectual problem. The anger and intellectualizing strategies are preferred by masculine men. The expressive approaches (crying, sharing feelings with a friend) are feminine styles which, despite their effectiveness, cannot be accessed by these men, as doing so would constitute a threat to masculinity.

Because everyone feels anxiety, sadness, and grief during their lives, and because these feelings can be experienced frequently and persistently, a more highly gender-typed man might punch a wall, drink heavily, or compulsively and desperately seek new sexual partners. In all of these strategies, solutions come from outside of the self. The man can take out his frustrations on an object or find something (alcohol or another person) that will hopefully soothe him, as he is not good at soothing himself.

There are several negative consequences to this *externalizing*, or outside-the-self, style. First, if the soothing person or object is not available, the man may find it very difficult to deal with his loss. Second, little new learning can take place. He does not have the skills to introspect and think about himself, and thus he has difficulty in learning what caused the troubling situation and how he might (re-)act differently. If he always deals with emotions externally, he can learn little about what is inside. Third, these kinds of behaviors may have a tendency to alienate other people.

Stress can also be mitigated through emotional coping. Poverty is associated with persistent and relatively high levels of stress (Liu, Colbow, & Rice, 2016). Being Black and male in the United States can also be a cause of persistent stress, especially for able-bodied teens and young adults who may be seen as threats (see Chapter Two). Many fear that they will be assaulted and possibly killed by the authorities without reason, as has happened with Rodney King, Michael Brown, and Eric Garner, among others. This stress negatively effects Black men's physical and psychological health (Hammond, Fleming, & Villa-Torres, 2016).

A relationship breakup involves a powerful experience of emotional loss, and one must assimilate that loss into one's sense of self to recover healthy functioning. This course of recovery from loss is known as *grieving*. It is a process by which one expresses, works through, eventually accepts the feelings that have accompanied the loss, and comes to a point of resolution that allows one to move on with one's life. John Lynch and Christopher Kilmartin (2013) describe the problem that traditional masculinity creates for the grieving process:

> Grieving has a life of its own. It is quite natural to feel and behave in certain ways—such as crying, reminiscing, and expressing a wish that one had treated the person better—in response to loss. Every culture has funeral rituals that help people to initiate the grief process following the ultimate loss, death. The grieving process takes time; one cannot spend an hour grieving and be done with it once and for all. Depending on the loss, it can take months or even years. The man who has lost his partner is aware that something is wrong, but many men avoid grieving because it involves the expression of vulnerable feelings, and also involves acknowledging that he feels connected to her. These two behaviors are culturally defined as unmasculine, and so he tends to make efforts to distract himself so that he does not have to deal with his pain. He pays a price for doing so, as he is likely to develop symptoms, which are his body's and his mind's way of telling him that something is wrong. If he does not heed these signals, he will continue to have these symptoms. When there comes a time for him to again become involved in a relationship, he will be predisposed to acting out the psychological issues that arise from an incomplete grieving process. (p. 176)

Alexithymia

Acting like one has no feelings over many years may result in the loss of ability to experience emotion. Sifneos (1972) coined the term *alexithymia* to describe the style of habitual inexpressiveness. It comes from the Greek (*a*=lack, *lexis*=words, as in lexicon, and *thymos*=emotions). Literally, the word alexithymia means "no words for feelings." Alexithymic persons have such an impoverished emotional life that they cannot even identify feelings, much less express them. Nemiah, Fryberger, and Sifneos (1976) described alexithymia as having four features: " a) difficulty identifying and describing feelings; b) difficulty distinguishing feelings from bodily sensations; c) reduction or absence of symbolic thinking (lack of imaginative ability); d) an external, operative cognitive style" (p. 227–228.).

A large body of research provides strong support for the hypothesis that emotion never lies still. People who do not deal with feelings directly do not make them go away. The alexithymic style often becomes destructive to the person either physically, psychologically, or both. Although only a small percentage of men are truly alexithymic, and some women also suffer from this problem, the connections between alexithymia and masculinity can hardly be denied. In a series of studies, Ronald Levant and his colleagues have found a strong relationship between alexithymia and masculinity ideology (e.g., Levant et al., 2003; Levant, Allen, & Lien, 2013; Levant, Hall, Williams, & Hasan, 2009). In a large, four-city, multicultural sample, Ronald Levant and his colleagues (2003) found a strong relationship between alexithymia and masculinity ideology. Using meta-analysis, a statistical technique that combines findings from a group of studies, researchers found small but consistent sex differences across 45 studies, with males more likely to show evidence of alexithymia (Levant, Hall, Williams, & Hasan, 2009).

Other Costs

The hypothesis that "emotion never lies; emotion never lies still" is supported by a number of studies indicating that men are more likely than women to express negative emotions through physiological processes such as heart rate reactivity and elevated blood pressure. When this style of reaction becomes ingrained and habitual, it can have a negative effect on men's physical health (Jansz, 2000) (see Chapter Nine), the quality of their relationships (Wong, Pituch, & Rochlen, 2006), their ability to be effective as parents (Lynch & Kilmartin, 2013), and their willingness to seek medical or psychological help (Addis & Mahalik, 2003).

Restrictive emotionality also has societal consequences. *Empathy* is the emotional awareness of another person's distress and thus an inhibitor of violence. In other words, if you can put yourself in the victim's place in an emotional way, you will be less likely to hurt him or her intentionally. However, it is impossible to understand someone else's feelings if you do not understand your own. David Lisak (1997) coined the term *empathy for the self* in his work with male victims of childhood abuse. Lisak found that those men who were able to acknowledge the emotional and physical pain of their experience as victims showed a strong tendency to not become violent as adults. In contrast, those who denied their pain tended to later act it out in a violent way. For a survivor of childhood abuse, being able to understand his own vulnerable feeling—having empathy for the self—allowed him to have empathy for other people, and thus not harm them. In other words, it appears that a person must have an experiential referent to connect emotionally to others' pain.

Men who have embraced task-oriented and inexpressive gender role characteristics may find it easy to perceive people as if they were things, and subordinate human welfare to a task that they define as more important. When such men are in power, their potential for destruction is great. War, racism, sexism, violence, exploitive business practices, the pollution of the planet, and other forms of victimization are all at least partly the result of a failure of compassion and empathy. Men have not been the exclusive perpetrators of these human wrongs, but because they have dominated governmental, military, economic, and industrial leadership, they have certainly contributed more than their share.

Expanding Men's Emotional Display Rules

We have seen that restrictive emotional display rules often have negative psychological, physical, interpersonal, and societal consequences. The good news is that we are not doomed to live with them. A number of therapeutic, educational, and social interventions have been designed to help men become more comfortable with affect. Because feelings such as satisfaction, love, and emotional connectedness are critical to quality of life, and because restrictive emotionality has negative consequences, it is not surprising that many men desire to become more aware and expressive of their emotional worlds (Chu, 2004; Garfield, 2015; Levant, 1997a; Way, 2011).

We have already seen that inexpressiveness arises, at least in part, from situations in which males are discouraged from being emotional. Therefore, one solution is to create environments that give men permission to break the social norm of non-disclosure, thus allowing the natural human propensity for expression of feeling to emerge. One popular method for creating such settings has been through the establishment of men's support or therapy groups, where men who want to learn expressive skills come together into an unusual all-male situation. Rather than having the common men's group norms of competition, task orientation, and macho rigidity, group members strive to create an atmosphere of cooperation, empathy, and self-disclosure (Garfield, 2010). In summarizing more than 25 years of leading such groups, Frederic Rabinowitz (2010) concluded that, "Men are deep, but they need a place to explore that depth, and they need time to do it."

Therapists and researchers have designed other interventions and accumulated some evidence of their effectiveness. Ronald Levant (2003) developed a five step, skill-based model for individual treatment of men who display "normative male alexithymia." In the first phase, the therapist educates the client about the connection between masculine socialization and inexpressiveness and helps the client develop the ability to tolerate emotions. Step two is the development of an emotional vocabulary. Levant has the client list as many words for feelings that he can generate over the course of several days. The third step is practice in identifying others' emotions by learning to read their facial expressions, vocal tone, and body language. He can do this in conversations and in watching movies and television and attempting to take the perspective of the characters. In the fourth stage, the client keeps a daily log where he tracks his emotional responses, concomitant physical sensations, and the contexts in which the feelings arise. The final step involves practice to reinforce the emotional skills he has learned. Levant (1998) reports that this new emotional awareness is empowering and exciting for many men. One client remarked that "it was as though I had been living in a black-and-white television set that had suddenly gone to color" (p. 48). Robert Garfield (2015) describes similar effects through his use of **emotion wheels** in his clinical work with men. An emotion wheel is a graphic representation of emotions that helps individuals differentiate feelings based on intensity and similarity to other feelings.

Y. Joel Wong and Aaron Rochlen (2008) suggest an approach based on solution-focused therapy (SFT). Although most therapy tends to focus on reducing problem behavior and experience, SFT focuses on "successful exceptions" to the problem. A therapist treating a man for restrictive emotionality would explore instances in which the man made an exception to hiding his feelings and instead was able to express vulnerable feelings such as sadness or gratitude. They would also help identify situations in which he feels more comfortable showing his feelings, people with whom he feels more comfortable with emotional expression, and the types of feelings that he is more (or less) comfortable sharing. This approach helps the client to identify the situational and other factors that affect his emotional expression and to expand his emotional competence to a wider variety of settings.

Increases in male expressiveness can also be realized through societal changes. We are seeing some movement in this direction in the United States in recent years. As women increasingly share the involvement in economic activities, many men are increasing their family involvement, with its emphasis on expressive activities, albeit at a slower pace (Marsiglio & Pleck, 2005). Balswick (1988) first suggested that, in the traditional structure of the family, women are economically dependent on men, while men are emotionally dependent on women. Just as many women are beginning to attain economic independence, many men are beginning to work toward emotional independence. This kind of self-sufficiency does not refer to disconnection, but rather to the man's expressive management of his emotions in the context of relationships, self-awareness, and attainment of his life goals.

SUMMARY

1. Even though emotion is at the center of human experience, masculine gender roles define it as feminine and discourage it in men, with the exception of the expression of anger. However, the display "rules" for emotion vary with changing social contexts.
2. There is some evidence that men, especially gender-typed men, tend to be less expressive and self-disclosing than women.
3. The origins of restrictive male emotionality are in the gender role definitions of vulnerability, inner conflict, dependence, and the definition of feeling as an unmasculine experience. These norms are often enforced by family and peers, as well as by media images of masculinity.
4. Emotional constriction may have a number of negative consequences for men and those around them. Men who are uncomfortable with their feelings are prone to using external defenses and acting out. These methods of coping are often less effective and efficient than self-disclosing and asking for help.
5. The extreme of inexpressiveness is alexithymia, which involves a poor awareness of and ability to describe feeling states. Alexithymia has been associated with a wide variety of physical and mental health problems. The hypothesis that "emotion never lies, and emotion never lies still" is supported by the research in this area. Restrictive emotionality also appears to have negative effects on relationships and parenting skills.
6. There are many men who have expressed a desire to improve their abilities to express and disclose. Interventions for this purpose have met with significant success.
7. Male expressiveness should also increase as a function of more progressive gender roles. Because restrictive emotionality is strongly influenced by the expectations of social settings, the creation of nontraditional settings with alternative expectations holds a great deal of promise for improving the quality of men's emotional lives.

GLOSSARY

Social desirability: People's motivation to present themselves in a positive light.

Physiological assessments (of pain): Direct assessments of bodily processes such as heart rate and galvanic skin response. When in pain, these typically increase.

Subjective assessments (of pain): An individual's rating of their experience using, for example, a one-to-ten scale.

Intropunitive feelings: Feelings that are self-punishing, such as shame, guilt, sadness, anxiety and fear.

Self-disclosure: The verbal communication of personal information from one person to another.

Self-disclosure target: The person to whom the information is given.

Emotion-focused coping: Strategies designed to cope with emotions by addressing them directly, such as asking how the person feels about the situation.

Task-focused coping: Strategies that highlight ways to discharge emotions, such as asking what a person is going to do about their feelings.

Coping: Refers to the ability to handle adverse events or feelings.

Ego defenses: Strategies for helping the ego mediate between either the outer and inner worlds or the id and the superego (most ego defenses only address one of these two potential conflicts). The term ego defenses is a psychoanalytic parallel for the term coping strategies.

Externalizing: Outside of the self or outwardfacing. In the case of coping strategies, it refers to the use of external stimuli (e.g., substances) or other people (e.g., sexual partners) as ways to reduce stress.

Grieving: The assimilation of an interpersonal loss into one's sense of self to recover healthy functioning.

Alexithymia: The style of habitual inexpressiveness.

Empathy: The emotional awareness of another person's distress.

Empathy for the self: The emotional awareness of one's own emotional and physical pain. This is often difficult for men who were victimized.

Emotion wheel: A graphic representation of emotions that helps individuals differentiate feelings based on intensity and similarity to other feelings.

Chapter Eight

No Man is an Island:
Men in Relationships

The stereotypical image of men in the United States is that their relationships with one another focus on doing things together and tend to be emotionally shallow. We might imagine them hanging out in a ***mancave***, a term developed by marketers to refer to spaces that house and facilitate stereotypically male activities such as watching or talking about sports, playing video games and "bar" games (e.g., billiards, darts), and joking around, but not having intimate conversations. We might also imagine them as loners who do not confide in others, drawing on images of gunslingers in old Westerns like *Shane* or current day superheroes like Wolverine or Spiderman (see also Strate, 1992). When we think about all-male groups, American stereotypes tell us they take risks and get into trouble (or barely escape it) as in movies like *American Pie* and *The Hangover*, as well as television shows like *The Suite Life of Zack & Cody* and *Fineas and Ferb*. These stereotypical depictions apply particularly well to White and Black American men, but are less relevant among Latinos due to their cultural emphasis on *simpatía* and *familismo*, which increase the likelihood of emotionally intimate conversations (see Chatper Two).

    But this is not how male-male friendship is seen across cultures. In some parts of the world, same-sex best friends go through a ceremony similar to a marriage to formalize their commitment to each other. When one of the friends dies, people express more sympathy to his best friend than to family members. In Java and parts of Ghana, and in some native North American tribes, the man turns to his best friend for fulfillment of his primary emotional needs, and husband-wife relationships are marked by less emotional intensity. The romantic ideal of mainstream United States culture dictates that a spouse meets all the emotional needs of his or her partner, an ideology that makes deep friendships more difficult (Williams, 1992).

    As is often the case, the stereotypes disguise the reality. Most boys and men value, want, and have close connections with others (Smiler & Heasley, 2016; Vasquez et al. 2014; Way, 2011). When 18-year-old Ethan described his best friend to researcher Judy Chu (2004, p. 96), he said "We're like, very different. But at the same time, I have a very strong bond with him. Every time I see him, it's just the greatest time ever. It's just, he's the best."

As we have seen repeatedly, context matters. The contours of men's relationships can vary dramatically depending on the type of relationship, leading one researcher to describe friendship as "part of a performance of masculinity" that can vary from one setting to the next (Migliaccio, 2009, p. 227). In this chapter, we define some of the most common—and therefore "basic"—aspects of friendship, as well as the aspects of hegemonic masculinity that are most closely related to friendship. Then we shift to particular types of relationships, including friendship (male groups, male-male dyads, male-female dyads) and romantic relationships (male-female, male-male). Throughout this chapter we focus on relationships that occur with similary-aged peers. We address men's family relationships in Chapter Nine.

Relationship Basics

Humans are inherently social animals (Maslow, 1943). Relationships, particularly those in which we choose to invest time, energy, and effort, serve a variety of purposes. Any given relationship may provide:

Practical support, such as a willingness to provide material resources including information, transportation, labor, and money. In practice, these may be thought of and treated as "favors."

Emotional or social support, defined as helping someone when they need help (e.g., when in a bad mood) or sharing pleasure (e.g., when in a good mood).

Emotional intimacy, which refers to a "deep" connection with someone, as indicated by the sharing of highly personal information such as hopes, fears, and "deep secrets."

Status, particularly among one's peers, refers to an individual's position within the social hierarchy. Knowing (or dating) the right—or wrong—person (or people) can enhance or inhibit a person's social mobility and how they're viewed.

Any specific relationship may include any number of these qualities, in any combination. Further, the qualities within that relationship may change over time (Smiler, 2016; Way, 2004, 2011).

Boys and men often use distinct terms to help differentiate their relationships. *Acquaintances* usually describe individuals who may be known by name, tend to appear in only part of a person's life (e.g., at work), and do not fill any of the functions described above. A *buddy* is a person with whom a specific activity is shared; an activity may be considered a form of practical support.

Buddies may or may not share emotional support related to topics outside of the activity. For example, buddies who play together in an athletic league may—or may not—talk to each other about their romantic relationships. The term *friend* is typically used to denote some level of emotional support, with *best friend* designating friends who are emotionally intimate. The quality of any relationship partner is determined, in part, by his *reliability*, indicated by his ability to complete tasks he has agreed to do, while the quality of a friend or best friend is determined by his ability to be *trustworthiness*, determined by his ability to respect and keep secrets (Garfield, 2015; Way, 2011).

There is a wealth of research examining the characteristics desired in a friend, as well as in a romantic partner. Regarding friends, undergraduate participants typically identify warmth-kindness, (emotional) expressiveness-openness, exciting personality, and sense of humor to be most important, with similar demographic characteristics (e.g., racial category) and social class as least important. The importance of appearance varies from moderate to minimal. As a group, participants rate these factors no different for same- and other-sex friends (Sprecher & Regan, 2002; Vigil, 2007).

Although we discuss romantic relationships later in the chapter, we note similarities in the characteristics desired in a friend vs. a romantic partner here. Generally speaking, the characteristics that people want in a friend are also the characteristics they want in a dating partner, although men (and women) tend to rate them as more important for a dating partner than a friend. This is particularly true for characteristics such as physical appearance and earning potential. Sexual passion, but not prior sexual experience, also receives a fairly high score for a dating partner (Sprecher & Regan, 2002).

THE INFLUENCE OF MALENESS AND MASCULINITY

As we have seen throughout the book, even though there is great similarity and within-sex variability, there are also some average differences between the sexes. Those general trends contribute to and are reflected in the interpersonal relationships typical of boys and men. We begin our discussion by focusing on those gendered experiences and then examine how the definition of masculinity connects to relationships.

Male Social Development

Developmental psychologist Eleanor Maccoby (1998) has described distinct, gender-typed interaction patterns that emerge early in life. She contends that these are largely a function of children's preferences for same-sex interaction. By the age of six and a half, children choose to spend the majority of their time with same-sex peers. They will play in sex-integrated groups at times, especially when adults force them to do so, but often default to sex-segregated groups when the setting allows. This segregation is not limited to gender-typed activities such as playing with dolls or trucks. It also occurs in gender-neutral activities such as drawing or playing with clay.

These manners of relating to others begin in childhood. By the second grade, female best friends' conversations begin to center around personally significant events, while boys' conversations focus on activities. By early adolescence, friendships are somewhat less stereotypical (Golombok & Fivush, 1994). Still, many gender-typed communication patterns continue into adulthood (Tannen, 1990). Because interpersonal interactions serve to form and maintain relationships, men's long-established pattern of communication colors the character of their social ties with women, children, and other men.

Martin and Fabes (2001) found that sex-differentiated behavior is a consequence of the frequency of same-sex play. Often finding themselves in the company of male peers, most boys develop a way of relating to others that is distinctly masculine. This style involves an orientation toward dominance, competition, and rough-and-tumble play (Maccoby, 1998). Boys also tend to play in larger (Levant, 1995), less intimate (Maccoby, 1990), and more publicly visible groups (Thorne, 2009).

In these all-male groups, we see boys interrupting each other, bragging, telling stories, ridiculing others, and using commands much more frequently than girls. Their conversations are more like turn-taking monologues, with one boy telling a story, followed by another boy (who often tries to "top" the first boy's story). Girls' conversation rely more on a give-and-take format. The tendency is to request rather than demand, express interest in others' stories, perspective, or feelings, and a variety of other strategies that non-verbally communicate a desire to connect to the other person instead of competing with him or her. Maccoby's (1998) view is that typically masculine conversation tends to be self-assertive and self-promotional whereas typically feminine speech serves the dual purpose of collaboration and self-assertion. These male-female differences in interactional "style" continue throughout life and thus create and maintain a certain amount of separation between men and women. Change is possible, of course, but substantive change requires intent and effort.

Masculinity

When we think about relationships, the things that indicate closeness are sharing feelings, secrets, hopes and fears (Smiler & Heasley, 2016; Way, 2011). In a series of interviews with the same boys throughout their teens, boys repeatedly told Niobe Way (2011) and her research team that the most important attributes of a close or best male friend was knowing that he would be there for you, stand up for you, and that he could be trusted with your deepest secrets (see also Kaplan & Rosemann, 2014). These attributes are also among the most important characteristics of a romantic partner (Buss, Shackelford, Kirkpatrick, & Larsen, 2001). Yet masculinity ideologies dictate that boys not do any of these things because they require being somewhat emotionally open, vulnerable, and non-competitive. Reflecting on these patterns, James Nelson (1988) suggested that, for men who conform to the stereotype of masculinity, "There is a deep tension between intimacy and masculinity. He wants both, and each seems to be purchased at the price of the other" (p. 42).

This strategy works for some men, at least to an extent; many men who buy into hegemonic concepts of masculinity report relatively high levels of relationship satisfaction (Wade & Donis, 2007). Men on athletic teams, in military units, or those who work together often form close bonds (Kaplan & Rosenmann, 2014; Messner, 1992; Migliaccio, 2009). But other researchers have found that men who subscribed to stereotypical masculine ideologies reported fewer close friends, were more likely than other men to experience loneliness, and experienced more conflict around psychological intimacy (Blazina, Eddins, Burridge, & Settle, 2007; Shepard, Nicpon, Haley, Lind, & Liu, 2011). Many men experience relationship dissatisfaction even with their best friends (Elkins & Peterson, 1993).

Research illustrates some of this cost. Boys and men with higher masculinity ideology scores perceive less need to ask for assistance and tend to be less emotionally expressive within their friendships (Cunningham & Newkirk, 2004; Migliaccio, 2009). Moreover, men with greater gender role conflict scores tend to have poorer quality relationships. They report lower levels of intimacy and less self-disclosure, as well as fewer friends (O'Neil, 2008).

Competition is one component of masculinity that seems to contribute to boys' and men's difficulty achieving relational intimacy. Boys and men are taught to be competitive with one another, but the establishment of intimacy rests partly on revealing one's weaknesses and vulnerabilities to another (Kaplan & Rosemann, 2014; Way, 2011). It is not wise to reveal your weaknesses to a perceived competitor who might well exploit them. You probably wouldn't make a $20 bet with a friend that you can win at any Xbox game, tell your friend your weakest one, and then ask which game he would like to play. Men who feel competitive with other men tend to have friendships that are inhibited by an undercurrent of distrust, which may help to explain why adolescent boys trust their same-sex friends less than girls do (Berndt, 1992), and why both men and women tend to trust women more than men (Diekman & Steinberg, 2016).

A boy who fares poorly when competing with his male peers may find himself with low (social) status among this group as a result of his poor skill. In some sense, he may be failing to prove his masculinity. His low status may make it difficult for him to exert any influence on his male peers and thus see himself as powerless. As a result, his interactions with other boys may also become aversive. This emphasis on male-male competition, even among friends, illustrates one way in which masculine norms do not foster egalitarian relationships among boys. The unequal statuses between masculinities (see Chapter Two) is analogous, but on a broader level.

The masculine demand for independence and self-sufficiency also inhibits self-disclosure. Taken to the extreme, a man might come to believe that he should not need others and that he should always be able to get by on his own.

Yet we are members of a variety of social systems and are dependent on others for information, resources, support, and human contact. Imagine what your life would look like if you had to produce your own food, clothing, and electricity, could not use the Internet (because other people maintain it and create webpages), and if you did not have conversations with the same people day after day (in person, by text, through social media, etc). The masculine focus on independence does not exactly discourage relying on others for goods and services, but it does seem to look down on men's needing interpersonal connection. One study with African-American teens found that boys who had higher masculinity scores saw less need to talk to others when they had problems (Cunningham & Newkirk, 2004). More broadly, there is strong evidence that lack of social support has severe negative effects, such as greater levels of major depression (Courtenay 2011; Kendler, Myers, & Prescott, 2005).

Emotional display rules (Chapter Seven) that direct men to avoid emotional expression are also problematic for creating deep friendships. One characteristic of more substantive friendships is the sharing of our deepest hopes and fears, as well as moments of joy and sadness (Migliaccio, 2009; Vasquez et al., 2014; Way, 2011). In fact, men with closer relationships report lower levels of isolation, depression, and violence (Courtenay, 2011; Levant & Richmond, 2007), while men with higher levels of masculine gender role conflict report having more problems achieving and maintaining intimacy (O'Neil, 2008).

Yet masculinity directs men to avoid sharing feelings. Even when they do, their upbringing shortchanges them: on average, their emotional vocabularies tend to be smaller than women's, and thus their understanding of feelings tends to be poorer (Adams et al., 1995; Garfield, 2015). As you might expect, men who do not experience intimacy as children or teens have difficulty demonstrating it as adults (Garfield, 2010).

Homophobia is perhaps the greatest barrier to friendships between men (Reid & Fine, 1992), although generational differences may be reducing its impact (Anderson & McCormack, 2015; Savin-Williams, 2005), as discussed in Chapter Three. Because many heterosexual men believe emotional intimacy is restricted to romantic relationships, many of these men feel uncomfortable when they experience emotional intimacy in a non-sexual relationship and may interpret it as a sign of sexual interest or attraction. Among heterosexual men, particularly those who adhere more strongly to masculine norms, this may cause panic—or at least some anxiety and discomfort—to set in. To avoid these feelings, men often keep other men at arm's length, both physically and psychologically. The friendships of highly homophobic men are significantly less intimate than those of other men (Devlin & Cowan, 1985). Greg Lehne (1998) illustrated the role of homophobia in distancing heterosexual men from one another:

> "I've asked men to describe their relationships with their best male friends. Many offer descriptions that are... filled with positive emotions and satisfaction... However, if I suggest that it sounds as if they are describing a person

whom they love, they become flustered... 'Well, I don't think I would like to call it love, we're just best friends. I can relate to him in ways I can't with anyone else. But, I mean, we're not homosexuals or anything like that.'... The social stigma of homosexual love denies these close relationships the validity of love in our society. This potential loss of love is a pain of homophobia that many men suffer because it delimits their relationships with other men." (p. 246)

According to Thorne and Luria (1986), boys in the United States begin to use homophobic labels such as "queer" or "fag" as insults by the fourth grade. As sociologist C. J. Pascoe (2007) documented, male and female teens use these terms to refer to any behavior they find distasteful, especially those that violate the masculine gender role. In fact, most of the adolescents Pascoe spoke with said they would not use these terms to refer to their openly gay peers (see also Reigeluth & Addis, 2016; Rosenberg, Gates, Richmond, & Sinno, 2017; Slaatten, Andersson, & Hetland, 2014). Thorne and Luria theorized about the impact of homophobic labeling on boys' physical contact:

> As 'fag' talk increases, relaxed and cuddling patterns of touch decrease among boys. Kindergarten and first-grade boys touch one another frequently and with ease, with arms around shoulders, hugs, and holding hands. By fifth grade, touch among boys becomes more constrained, gradually shifting to mock violence and the use of poking, shoving, and ritual gestures like 'giving five' (flat hand slaps) to express bonding. (p. 182)

Thus, males appear to have strong desire to maintain interpersonal contact with other males, but (historically and developmentally) the threat of homophobic labeling increasingly forces this contact to become highly ritualized and sometimes aggressive.

Researcher Eric Anderson and his colleagues (Anderson, McCormack, & Lee, 2012) recently argued that young men are becoming less homophobic, as we discussed in Chapter Three. They observed the initiation rituals of the rugby and (male) field hockey teams over a seven-year span at a single British university, and also interviewed several of the participants. Initiates were often required to drink large quantities of alcohol during this process, and one of the teams was put on probation due to their extreme levels of drinking. During the time frame, the researchers found that young men became less squeamish about being required to wrestle each other while nude or nearly nude, and they were increasingly willing to engage in open-mouthed kissing with one another. One participant said he would rather kiss his friend than be required to drink another beer when already intoxicated. It is unclear how many young men would make the same choice.

Context

Social norms and contextual factors constrain behavior in significant ways, as we discussed regarding men's emotional displays in Chapter Seven. These factors also influence men's enactment of friendship. Both women and men behave in more gender-stereotypical ways in public than they do in private (Burn, 1996; Heasley, 2005) even though many males express a desire to be more disclosing (Chu, 2004; Way, 2011). These findings suggest that masculine and feminine styles of friendship are at least partly a function of the social expectations that women and men tend to bring into interactions with others.

It may not be unusual for two male friends to both have a desire for greater levels of intimacy with each other but continue to keep each other at an emotional arm's length because both overestimate the degree to which the other expects gender-stereotypical behavior (Wade & Donis, 2007; Way et al., 2014). Masculinity inhibits them from talking about their expectations—which would be intimate in itself—and therefore their distorted views of each other's masculinity prevent the friendship from moving in the direction that both would like to go. As we have mentioned repeatedly throughout the text, boys who behave in gender-inconsistent ways are likely to experience disapproval from their friends and lose popularity or see themselves pushed to the margins of the social hierarchy (Carver, Egan, & Perry, 2004). One outcome is that many boys who would like to have more emotionally connected relationships with their male friends are unable to find other boys who share that desire because no one is "allowed" to say so (Way et al., 2014).

FRIENDSHIPS

Friendship is probably the most common form of relationship. From childhood through old age, most people have friends and they typically have more than one friend at any given time. Accordingly, we start our discussion of intimate relationships with friendship.

Male-Only Friendship Groups

The behavior of boys and men in friendship groups can look quite different than the behavior of a male-male friendship dyad or in a male-female friendship dyad (Kaplan & Rosenmann, 2014). The term *homosocial* is used to refer to all male (or all female) groups that come together for reasons related to friendship (but not for employment, for example). In all-male groups, cultural norms regarding masculinity are often more visible and harder to challenge, as we discussed regarding emotional development (Chapter Seven) and conformity (Chapter Six). However, it is not true that every all-male group conforms to these norms or desires to do so; some may adhere to masculine norms at only a minimal level while others may challenge them entirely. The Boy Scouts of America, for example, emphasizes a nineteenth century conception of American masculinity that prioritizes loyalty, honesty, trust, and thrift (Hantover, 1977), as discussed in Chapter One.

In formal male-only settings (e.g., athletic teams, military-type organizations, fraternities, gangs, etc.), groups often have an explicit hierarchy that specifies who holds power and thus controls (or dominates?) the group. This hierarchical pattern is often reflected in all-male friendship groups as well, where the group can be said to coalesce around a single individual. Reflecting masculine norms, male-only groups are often activity based instead of relationship based, and thus their members come together to do a specific thing and not to build or maintain their relationships. This difference in focus had lead some people to describe all-male activities as "side-by-side" (i.e., working together to accomplish a task) and all-female activities as "face-to-face" (i.e., being together to maintain relationships via conversation) (Kilmartin & Lynch, 2013).

Within these settings, the members of a male-only group routinely use insults, silences, and direct questioning as part of their interaction (McDiarmid, Gill, McLachlan, & Ali, 2016). Explicit discussion of emotion, intimacy, or the quality of a relationship tends to be rare (Chu, 2004; Heasley, 2005; Way, 2011). These sets of strategies are parallel to hegemonic masculinity's emotional display rules (Chapter Seven), as well as norms limiting affectionate behavior between men, norms promoting dominance (or hierarchy), and norms promoting homophobia. Note that these interactional strategies can be used to demonstrate acceptance of, or agreement with, a friend's actions, as well as non-acceptance or disagreement; the difference in agreement/non-agreement may be explicit (i.e., word choice) or implicit (e.g., tone, such as sarcasm). Direct questioning, for example, can be used to demonstrate concern by checking on the reasoning behind a decision.

This interactional style can be used to demonstrate closeness, gratefulness, concern, and dominance (McDiarmid, Gill, McLachlan, & Ali, 2016; Way, 2011). Within the context of a homosocial group, competition is often minimized (or limited to specific venues) as a way to maintain group cohesion (Thurnell-Read, 2012); in effect this allows the group to "come together as a team." Explicit competition may be seen as a threat to the group's leadership structure.

Although male-only groups are often supportive of their members, they may be offensive to others. Researchers have repeatedly documented ways in which male-only groups demonstrate higher levels of sexist, homophobic, risk-taking, and violent behaviors than individual males perform alone or when the group has at least one female member. Several researchers have suggested that multiple dynamics are in play, including perception of the group's masculine norms, pressure to conform to those norms, and greater adherence to hegemonic norms of masculinity (Iwamoto & Smiler, 2013; Kilmartin et al., 2008; Lefkowitz, 1999). Michael Flood (2008) found that heterosexual male friends told and retold sexual hookup stories over years to maintain their friendships; their stories often focused on aspects such as risk-taking, competition (e.g., most or least attractive partner), and methods of seduction, while omitting discussion of the women's feelings or the relationship between the man and the woman. Thus, they used sexual hookups for the purpose of male-male bonding, as well as sexual pleasure.

Male-Male Friendship Dyads

Although boys and men may report having more friends than girls and women (Vigil, 2007), they usually report less support and intimacy from their friends (Bank & Handford, 2000; Claes, 1992; Kendler et al., 2005). Generally speaking, women often spend time talking about their experiences and feelings while men share activities (Lips, 2008).

It is sometimes said that men have many "buddies" but few true friends. The formation of emotional support and intimacy between men is many times the result of an indirect process of spending time in a mutual pursuit or interest rather than a more direct process of emotional self-disclosure. The expression of closeness between men often takes the form of continuing to spend time with each other and helping each other with tasks rather than more direct expressions such as touching, or saying "I like you," "I'm glad you're my friend," or "I feel close to you." In one recent study, researchers asked Israeli men, for whom military service is mandatory, to rate the men in their military units and their best male friend. Although scores were higher for best friends than military unit peers, the six highest rated characteristics (of twelve) were identical: enjoying doing things together, comradeship, chemistry and shared language, desire to be together, admiration, and seeking validation. Love was in seventh (unit) and eighth (best male friend) place (Kaplan & Rosenmann, 2014). These findings tell us men see relationships with best male friends and military unit members in very similar ways, including experiencing these relationships as not necessarily loving.

Research has shown that boys and men who offer greater endorsement of masculine norms of emotional control and homophobia tend to report lower levels of intimacy and emotional support from their friendships, but adherence to the competition norm and greater endorsement of a masculine identity were not related to their experiences of intimacy and emotional support (Bank & Hansford, 2000).

Overall, "male bonding" as it occurs in male-only groups may be adequate for fulfilling some of the functions of friendship, but it does not appear to be sufficient for addressing men's need for emotional intimacy. Thus, it may be viewed as a poor substitute for the deeper connections of intimate friendships. Researchers have documented that men tend to experience more loneliness than women (Brody & Hall, 2000), probably because they experience lower levels of social support. For boys and men who have a decades-long pattern of being buddies rather than true friends, shifting to a deeper version of friendship may be very difficult. Box 8.1 describes techniques for doing so.

> **Box 8.1**
> **Guerilla Tactics for Making a Friend**
>
> Letich (1991) makes some excellent, step by step suggestions for working on deeper friendships:
>
> 1. First, you have to want it: Breaking patterns not only causes anxiety, it is hard work. "You have to remind yourself that there's nothing weird or effeminate about wanting a friend" (p. 87).
> 2. Identify a possible friend: Seek someone who seems to want to question the values of traditional masculinity.
> 3. Be sneaky: Get involved in a comfortable, nonpressured activity. Get used to spending time with this man.
> 4. Invite him to stop for a beer or a cup of coffee: Try to make honest, personal conversation at these times.
> 5. Call just to get together.
> 6. Sit down and talk about your friendship.
>
> Letich calls these suggestions "guerilla tactics" because, in a culture that discourages male-male intimacy, they seem extreme and difficult for men who conform to hegemonic masculinity. The last two suggestions are especially antithetical to masculine gender role norms. Men who try these "tactics" will feel awkward, but as with any skills, they improve and become more comfortable with practice.

Male-Female Friendship Dyads

Earlier in the chapter, we described boys' typical interactional style as boisterous and competitive and girls' as quieter and relational. Friendships are based partly on reciprocity, or mutual influence (Youniss & Haynie, 1992). Among boys, especially pre-teens, influence tends to be exerted through direct demands. By contrast, girls of the same age are more likely to use polite suggestions. Although girls' styles work well with adults, they are not very effective with boys. Therefore, girls may find it quite frustrating and unpleasant to interact with boys who will not respond to their influence attempts (Maccoby, 1998).

While boys' interaction style keeps girls away from them, the antifemininity norm keeps boys away from girls. The boy who acts like a girl in any way, including being friends with girls, risks losing his place in the masculine dominance hierarchy (Carver et al., 2004). Boys' interactions are often geared toward competition, they are barraged with messages that they should not act like girls, and they are encouraged to value girls and women only as sexual objects. These patterns do not facilitate the creation of cross-sex friendships.

Yet male-female friendships have become increasingly common among adolescents and adults over the last few decades. In the late 1970s, only about 18 percent of American adults reported having a close friend of the other sex. That figure grew to between 25 and 40 percent by the mid-1980s (Basow, 1992). As late as 1992, one leading childhood friendship researcher speculated that male-female friendships were rare and would continue to be uncommon (Hartup & Overhauser, 1991). Today, cross-sex friendships have become increasingly common and having at least one cross-sex friendship may now be the norm among teens and young adults (Kimmel, 2011; Smiler, 2013).

Both males and females tend to self-disclose more often to female friends, and so a cross-sex friendship frequently offers a man something that may well be lacking in his friendships with other men. Not surprisingly, women have a stronger tendency than men to describe their cross-sex friendships as less satisfactory and less reciprocal than their other friendships (Parker & De Vries, 1993).

ROMANTIC RELATIONSHIPS

We now shift from friendship to romantic relationships because they share many features, including companionship, emotional intimacy, trust, and shared interests (Connolly, Craig, Goldberg, & Pepler, 1999; Sprecher & Regan, 2002). Romantic relationships that include a strong friendship between dating partners tend to last longer (Giordano, Manning, & Longmore, 2010; VanderDrift, Wilson, & Agnew, 2013). We discuss relationships separately from sexual activity even though most males prefer their sexual contact with a known partner (Bradshaw, Kahn, & Saville, 2010; Smiler, 2013; Smiler & Heasley, 2016). See Chapter Ten for a detailed discussion of sexual behavior.

Male-Female Dating Relationships

The average heterosexual United States male has his first "real" or "serious" relationship with a female at age 16 or 17 (Regan, Durvasula, Howell, Ureno, & Rea, 2004; Smiler, Frankel, & Savin-Williams, 2011). Many of these relationships last for relatively long periods of time; almost half of tenth grade boys reported a relationship of 12 weeks or longer and approximately one-sixth of high school seniors reported a relationship of 11 months or longer (Connolly & Johnson, 1996; Fiering, 1999).

Many men, and some women, believe that "nice guys finish last"—that women are only interested in dominant men, and that men who are kind, sympathetic, attentive, or caring are viewed as less desirable. But one group of researchers (Jensen-Campbell, Graziano, & West, 1995) found little support for this belief. In fact, women rated men who were described as being kind, cooperative, and attentive as more desirable—sexually, physically, and socially— than those described as less agreeable or less caring. In fact, the "nice guys" cliche may tell us more about the label than the reality of dating. One research project included the same survey protocol repeatedly from 1939 through 1996; the researchers asked undergraduate women and men to rate the characteristics they most desired in a mate. The top four (of eighteen) characteristics were almost identical in every round of surveying: dependable character, emotional stability/maturity, pleasing disposition, and mutual attraction/love (Buss,

Schackelford, Kirkpatrick, & Larsen, 2001). In other words, women want nice, stable guys.

How do the tough guys, the men who conform to the hegemonic norms fare? Women tend to report lower levels of relationship satisfaction when they judged their partners to be emotionally restricted and highly concerned with success, power, and competition (Rochlen & Mahalik, 2004). More broadly, men with higher masculinity ideology scores tend to be less respectful of women and report lower levels of relationship satisfaction (Levant & Richmond, 2007; Smiler, 2013).

One interesting research finding is that heterosexual males tend to "fall in love" faster than females (Huston & Ashmore, 1986), contrary to the popular belief that women are more emotional and love-hungry. We can make some guesses about the origins of this tendency. First, men tend to place more value than women on a partner's physical attractiveness (Buss et al., 2001). Thus they may be more likely to report being in love largely on the basis of this attraction, which can happen very early in the relationship (or even from across the room). Second, men have not been socialized to understand and manage their emotional lives except through suppression (see Chapter Seven). Feelings that are difficult to squelch may be experienced as a "flood" of emotion. Third, the level of intimacy in a romantic relationship is likely to be very different from that of a male's other relationships, which are often centered on activities. This level of intimacy is likely to be less different from the intimacy level of the female's other relationships, which are often focused on feeling and disclosure. The man's hunger for emotional intimacy is greater because he has few or no other places to get this need met. The heterosexual relationship becomes the only safe haven from the masculine demands for independence and inexpressiveness, the only place where he can show the "softer" side of himself. A man might well experience the (stereo-)typical feminine interactional style of reciprocity and consideration as love.

These tendencies may explain why men often perceive sexual interest from a woman when it is not present. Men are more likely than women to interpret her suggestion of getting together for coffee, and even her agreement to meet for coffee when he asks, as a prelude to sexual activity (Fisher & Walters, 2003), which may explain why it can be difficult to convince other-sex romantic partners that an other-sex friend is only a friend (Swain, 1992). Men's readiness to sexualize behavior may result in men misperceiving friendliness as flirtation, making it difficult to establish nonsexual cross-sex relationships.

Male-Male Dating Relationships

In some ways, the experiences of boys who are romantically attracted to other boys are quite similar to the experiences of boys who are attracted to girls. As Ritch Savin-Williams (1995) pointed out, "The intimacy needs of gay and bisexual youth are common, even normative" (p. 159). Yet their day-to-day experience is one in which homophobic insults like "dude, you're a fag" are common (Pascoe, 2007; Slaatten, Anderssen, & Hetland, 2014), school events are geared towards male-female couples (homecoming court, Sadie Hawkins day), and they may fear rejection by their parents, friends, and others in their community. A boy who has overcome these challenges and publicly acknowledged his same-sex attractions may still have difficulty finding a partner because there might not be very many out gay boys in his school or town, let alone one he is romantically attracted to (Savin-Williams, 1998; Smiler, 2013).

Given this context, it should not be surprising that only a minority of gay youth find romantic partners at school; instead, they are more likely to find partners at gay bars, gay organizations or clubs, or online (DeHaan, Kuper, Magee, Bigelow, & Mustanski, 2013; Savin-Willams, 1998). Many, perhaps most, gay boys do not have their first romantic relationships until age 18 or later. Despite their difficulty finding dating partners, many report having fleeting sexual encounters with other boys and a sizable minority find partners who are more than a decade older (Savin-Williams, 1998, 2005). In studies of 16- and 17-year-old gay boys, these teens often indicate that first sex occurred at age 13 or 14, while in studies with advanced undergraduates and graduate students, reports of the average age of first male-male sexual contact is 16 (Savin-Williams, 1998, 2005; Smiler et al., 2011).

The combination of early sexual experiences outside of a relational context, combined with masculine norms, may contribute to some gay men's difficulties in finding relationship partners. As one teen explained, "I'm looking for someone very special, but it is really hard to meet such a guy. They all just want sex" (Savin-Williams, 2005, p. 137). Adult gay men have echoed this concern (Sanchez, Greenberg, Liu, & Vilain, 2009). They also expressed beliefs that masculine norms adversely affect their relationships by encouraging gay men to prefer "macho" or "butch" men and avoid effeminate ones, as well as by restricting emotional sharing and intimacy. Although most of these masculine norms provide no help to gay male relationships, a minority identified the provider role as a benefit (Sanchez et al., 2009).

Marriage and Long-Term Romantic Relationships

We now turn to the factors associated with long-term relationships. Maccoby (1990) described successful couples, defined as those who are together for a long period of time and report relatively high levels of relationship satisfaction, as ones who have "develop[ed] a relationship that is based on communality rather than exchange bargaining. That is, they have many shared goals and work jointly to achieve them. They do not need to argue over turf because they have the same turf" (p. 518). In short, couples who are not competing with each other or trying to dominate each other tend to be successful.

There is a substantial body of literature that examines long-term relationships among heterosexual couples and a growing number of studies of same-sex couples. Among both groups, several factors have been repeatedly identified as important to maintaining the relationship over the long term: affection, dependability, shared interests, similar religious beliefs, liking, and loving. For men, their partners' physical attractiveness also influences their comfort in the relationship, regardless of whether the partner is male or female. Higher levels of sexual satisfaction, which is closely connected to frequency of sex, is correlated with greater levels of relationship satisfaction. The most frequent topics of disagreement are also unrelated to sexual orientation: money, affection (or lack thereof), sex, criticism (of partner/self), and distribution of household tasks. It is also worth noting that in addition to love for and satisfaction with one's partner, having access to alternative partners and having few barriers to separation (e.g., not needing a legal divorce, not needing to address child support and custody, etc.) also affect a couple's decision to stay together and again, these factors influence both same- and mixed-sex couples (Peplau & Fingerhut, 2007).

Gender norms and socialization patterns also affect long term couples, albeit differently for heterosexual and gay couples. It is important to note that all of the research on gay male couples, including the information above, relies heavily on studies of male-male couples who are often highly educated and highly paid and those in which European-Americans are over-represented (Peplau & Fingerhut, 2007). This is not the case with research on male-female couples.

Male-Female Couples

Perceived equality, or lack thereof, can affect many aspects of a couple's experience. Although men earn more than women on average, there are a growing number of couples in which this is not the case. Not surprisingly, men who adhere to hegemonic norms of masculinity, including the provider role, place greater importance on earning more than their partners, while men who are more flexible place less importance on this disparity. These emphases come with relational costs, as more dogmatic men report lower levels of relationship satisfaction than their more progressive peers (Bradbury, Campbell, & Fincham, 1995; Couglin & Wade, 2012) and men who experience higher levels of gender role conflict report lower levels of marital satisfaction (O'Neil, 2013). At the other extreme, many men who are stay-at-home-fathers report that they chose this role and that they are quite satisfied with their relationships as long as they receive relatively high levels of support from their partners and their families (Rochlen, Suizzo, McKelley, & Scaringi, 2008). We describe stay at home fathers in more detail in Chapter Nine.

Couples who hold more egalitarian ideals tend to be more equal in their division of household labor than more stereotypical couples (Schwartz, 1994). At the same time, women in egalitarian couples still tend to do more housework than their husbands (Hochschild & Machung, 1989). It's important to note that men's subscription to egalitarian ideals has a greater effect on the couple's relationship than that of his partner. Among other things, more egalitarian men report higher levels of sexual satisfaction in their long term relationships; women's perception of their partners' egalitarianism is related to both her relationship satisfaction and sexual satisfaction (Rudman & Phelan, 2007).

Communication is also a key predictor of relationship satisfaction (Perren, Von Wyl, Burgin, Simoni, & Von Klitznig, 2005). This should not be surprising: talking to your partner may be the only activity you undertake together almost every day. Yet men and women demonstrate group-level differences in a number of aspects of communication (McHugh & Hambaugh, 2010). These differences in interactional styles, which date back to childhood patterns of socialization, can create problems. Males are often not responsive to the typical feminine influence style of polite suggestion, are more likely to interrupt, and more likely to use profanity, all of which may lead females to feel somewhat powerless (McHugh & Hambaugh, 2010). By contrast, the masculine preference for direct requests or demands may feel aversive and overpowering to women. At the extreme, masculine expectations of dominance and power over women may encourage some men to ignore even direct influence attempts by their partners.

Men's lower levels of intimacy with their male friends may lead them to rely heavily, and possibly entirely, on their wives for intimacy. Not only do men tend to have less intimate friendships (Bank & Handford, 2000; Kendler et al., 2005), married men tend to be less intimate than single men with their male friends (Tschann, 1988) and they often have difficulty filling their intimacy needs should their long-term relationship end (Nolen-Hoeksema & Girgus, 1994). Ultimately, these interactional patterns may lead to the "masculine dilemma" that John Lynch and Christopher Kilmartin (2013) called "not too close; not too far away," in which the man comes closer when he fears abandonment but then distances his partner when he fears engulfment.

Disparities in income and housework, levels of emotional support directed toward the partner, beliefs about egalitarian gender roles, and styles of communication may ultimately lead the couple to dissolve the relationship. Given that many of these factors are related to aspects of the masculine gender role that dictate how he interacts, it should be little surprise that wives tend to report lower levels of relationship satisfaction when their husbands endorse hegemonic masculine ideologies or that wives are more likely than husbands to file for divorce (Bradbury, Campbell, & Fincham, 1995; Brinig & Allen, 2000).

Male-Male Couples

Masculine ideals affect male-male couples as well. For example, coupled gay men tend to report lower levels of restricted affective behavior between men than single gay men, and also possibly lower levels of restricted emotionality (Wester, Pionke, & Vogel, 2005). Power within the relationship may play out in similar ways to male-female relationships, with greater influence being determined by income, although this pattern may only reflect a minority of gay male couples (Peplau & Fingerhut, 2007).

Masculine norms regarding promiscuity play an important role among male-male couples, who are sometimes more willing to explore and practice non-monogamy than male-female or female-female couples (Parsons, Starks, Gamarel, & Grov, 2012). As we noted earlier, sexual satisfaction within a relationship is often related to relationship satisfaction, and relationships endure longer when partners are more satisfied (Greene & Britton, 2013). On average, gay men's relationship satisfaction was higher among those who were less interested in casual sex (Sanchez, Bocklandt, & Vilain, 2009) and higher in monogamous and "monogam-ish" than in "open" relationships (Parsons et al., 2012). Although it is unclear which comes first—open relationship status or lower levels of relationship satisfaction—it is clear that gay male couples, as well as the mental health professionals who work with them, would do well to discuss the sexual boundaries of their relationships (Houts & Horne, 2008; Sanchez et al., 2009).

SUMMARY

Men engage in various types of relationships as friends and romantic partners. The interactional patterns that are common among all-male groups and men's adherence to masculinity ideologies may affect the quality of these relationships, often in negative ways. In particular, men's ability and willingness to express their intimate thoughts and feelings are often under-developed and meet with disapproval, leading many men to find their intimate relationships to be not-quite-enough. But we should not overemphasize the negative; most men and boys achieve satisfying and healthy relationships despite gendered barriers.

1. Boys' development, particularly in all-boys groups, teaches them an interactional style that is self-promoting and dominant but not responsive or attentive to other's feelings, wants, and needs.
2. Masculine norms of emotional restriction and independence encourage boys and men not to share their inner thoughts and feelings, thus diminishing their opportunities for intimacy.
3. Homophobia exacerbates this dynamic in male-male friendships. It also serves to diminish physical contact between males.
4. These factors combine to leave men with relationships that often are not as intimate as men would like them to be and a framework that gives them little opportunity to deepen their relationships without risking their masculine status.

5. Friendships and romantic relationships share many of the same characteristics: intimacy, trust, sharing of secrets, and loyalty. These attributes are the same for both male-male and male-female dyads.
6. Although male-male friendships are often deep and carry great importance to their participants, they are rarely described as "loving," possibly because shared time is often spent in side-by-side activities where the emphasis is on doing rather than direct interaction.
7. Male-female friendships have become commonplace. They face challenges from masculine directives to dominate women as well as from some men's tendency sexualize intimacy. At the same time, males often place great value in the intimacy and support offered by their female friends.
8. Male-female dating relationships usually begin to appear in mid-adolescence. They too are negatively affected by men's adherence to masculine norms, including the erroneous belief that "nice guys finish last."
9. Male-male dating relationships often do not appear until later adolescence, in part due to lack of available partners. Gay men say that the masculine role is more of an impediment to relationships than it is a support.
10. Long-term romantic relationships, including marriage, often rely on factors such as affection, dependability, shared interests, sexual satisfaction, and a man's appreciation for his partner's appearance. These findings apply to both homosexual and heterosexual men.
11. Long-term heterosexual couples' satisfaction is also related to practices of equality within the relationship, as well as their ability to communicate effectively.
12. Long-term gay male couples' satisfaction is also related to their ability to negotiate (and maintain) sexual boundaries.

GLOSSARY

Mancave: A term developed by marketers to refer to spaces that house and facilitate stereotypically male activities such as watching or talking about sports, playing video games and "bar" games (e.g., billiards, darts), and joking around, but not having intimate conversations.

Practical support: Willingness to provide material resources including information, transportation, labor, and money in a relationship. In practice, these may be thought of and treated as "favors."

Emotional or social support: Helping someone when they need help (e.g., when in a bad mood) or sharing pleasure (e.g., when in a good mood).

Emotional intimacy: The "deep" connection with someone, as indicated by the sharing of highly personal information such as hopes, fears, and "deep secrets."

Status (or social status): An individual's position within the social hierarchy.

Acquaintance: An individual who may be known by name, tends to appear in only part of a person's life (e.g., at work), and does not routinely fill any the functions of friendship.

Buddy: A person with whom a specific activity is shared; an activity may be considered a form of practical support. Buddies may or may not share emotional support related to topics outside of the activity.

Friend: An individual with whom some level of emotional support is shared.

Best friend: Friends who share emotional support and are also emotionally intimate.

Reliability: An individual's ability to complete friendship-related tasks he has agreed to do.

Trustworthiness: An individual's ability to respect and keep secrets (within a friendship).

Chapter Nine

Fathers and Fathering

One of the first questions many adults ask when they encounter a pregnant woman is some version of "what sex is the baby?" or "do you want a boy or a girl?" The fact that this is among the first questions, and often the very first question, provides some indication of how important sex and gender are in many cultures. Anecdotally, we note that complete strangers are easily frustrated when they do not receive an answer to this question. Baby showers have increasingly become mixed-gender parties instead of female-only events, reflecting cultural expectations about both men's and women's roles. A relatively recent and alternate trend is to have a "gender reveal" party in which the expectant parents share the unborn child's gender by, for example, cutting the cake to reveal the interior as either pink or blue (via food coloring).

When we talk about *fathering*, it is important to recognize that the word has two distinct meanings. The first meaning is that a man has impregnated a woman who has carried the pregnancy to term and given birth. The second use of this word refers to the act of being a parent and indicates what he does as a father or the quality of his fathering. This use of fathering is a gender-specific synonym for parenting (Pleck, 2007). For some men, living out the provider role and actively being a father may signify and validate masculinity. For others, impregnating someone may serve this purpose, especially for young men living in poverty and regardless of the man's ethnic or racial background (Lohan, Cruise, O'Halloran, Alderdice, & Hyde, 2010). Historically and cross-culturally, procreation has often been viewed as one way to demonstrate masculinity (Gilmore, 1990).

In this chapter, we discuss several aspects of fathers and fatherhood. We begin with some history, briefly tracking some macro-level cultural changes in what it means to parent a child. We then discuss who becomes a father before addressing the behaviors that men engage in as parents, with particular attention to the factors most consistently related to healthy child development. We end the chapter with discussions of the ways that gender norms influence childrearing, with discussion of similarities and differences between mothers and fathers as well as the development of sons' masculinity.

History of Fathers at Home

You will often hear people speak of the ***traditional family***, which refers to a married heterosexual couple in which the husband works outside of the home and the wife works full-time on child care and other domestic duties. Stephanie Coontz (1997) points out that this conception of the family has only existed for about 150 years. Moreover, a substantial proportion of United States families do not and have never fit this pattern. In the 1950s, when the male-earner-and-female-homemaker model hit its peak in the United States, approximately two-thirds of American families had this structure. This "traditional" arrangement was mostly found among White, heterosexual couples who were middle class (or higher); those living in poverty couldn't afford to have an adult who was capable of earning that did not earn an income. Discriminatory practices in the United States effectively kept non-Whites, especially Black and Latino men, from achieving the "ideal" of a male breadwinner and female homemaker. Thus, this "tradition" became idealized during a specific era (the 1950s) and a specific ethinc and economic class (White and middle-class). Today, approximately one-quarter of families fit this model and the number is expected to fall to approximately one-sixth by 2030 (Clay, 2005).

Stephanie Coontz (1997) dispels the myth that a sex-based labor division is traditional, except in a very narrow historical frame: "One of the most common misconceptions about modern marriage is the notion that coprovider families are a new invention in human history. In fact, today's dual-earner family represents a return to older norms, after a very short interlude that people mistakenly identify as 'traditional'" (p. 54). We detail the shifts in employment, work, and technology that have driven these changes in our discussion of work (Chapter Eleven).

Perhaps the most profound effects of the cultural shifts on masculinity associated with early twentieth century industrialization were that it effectively banished men from their homes (Keen, 1991) and devalued domestic work. It is no surprise that many men who emphasize the breadwinner aspects of masculinity are not very relationship-oriented. In the industrial workplace, emotional expression and connection are seen as having little value. When that industrial worker returns home at the end of the day, he may find it very difficult to "flip the switch" that turns on all of the emotional and relationship attitudes that he has suppressed all day at work. As Robert Bly (1990) put it, "When a father, absent during the day, returns home at six, his children receive only his temperament, and not his teaching." The result is the disconnection of father and child (Keen, 1991) and an intergenerational pattern of masculine alienation. Much of Freud's (1925) discussion of castration anxiety is also related to this separation between father and son (see also Chodorow, 1978).

Although the amount of time that fathers spent with their sons decreased as the United States transitioned from being a rural and agrarian society to a city-based and industrialized society, the ethic of paternal discipline continued unchanged. However, fathers now had to assert this role after coming home from the industrial workplace. This perceived need for control may have involved more physical punishment both as a function of diminished contact with children and work strain on the father (Stearns, 1990, 1991). One result is that many sons now experienced fewer positive contacts with fathers, combined with potentially harsher discipline.

Becoming a Father

Although there is debate as to whether or not there was ever a single, universally agreed upon definition of what it means to be a good or successful father, it is clear that the idea of father as financial provider and disciplinarian is no longer the mainstream United States standard, nor is there currently a single definition of what it means to be a successful father (Cabrera, Tamis-Lemonda, Bradley, Hofferth, & Lamb, 2000). Although some individuals still prefer the father as the sole financial provider formulation, the trend is toward a more emotionally involved father than in the past (Cabrera et al., 2000; Genesoni & Tallandini, 2009; Stewart & Newton, 2010). For many families today, the reality includes two working parents and may include a man as the primary or stay-at-home parent (Department of Labor, 2005; Livingston & Parker, 2011; Rochlen et al., 2008). This definitional variability reflects the fact that while women's roles as mothers are fairly well-defined on a societal level, men's roles as fathers are much more subject to negotiation, the boundaries much more flexible, and their participation often requires less time than mothers (Cabrera et al., 2000; Marsiglio & Pleck, 2005).

For the last few decades, psychological researchers have focused on a range of parenting behaviors that include engagement, accessibility, responsibility, parental warmth, support, control/monitoring, economic support, and aspects of the father's belief system that underlie these behaviors (McKelley & Rochlen, 2016; Pleck, 2007). As one research team summarized, "It now appears that fathers generally perceive that they are expected to assume the twin responsibilities of providing economical and emotional support for their family" (Genesoni & Tallndini, 2009, 315). Ronald Levant and David Wimer (2009) call this image the "good family man."

For heterosexual adult couples, the "transition to parenthood," but not the event of getting married, is typically associated with a shift to more traditional roles in which the man becomes the primary earner and the woman the primary caretaker (Burke & Cast, 1997). Even in couples where both adults work outside the house for at least 20 hours per week and both adults are responsible for solo childcare at least 15 hours per week, working class couples often describe their activities in term of the man "helping" with the kids and the woman providing "extra" income (Deutsch & Saxon, 1998). This shift may be accounted for by the finding that mothers are more likely than fathers to be involved in basic child care activities such as feeding, dressing, washing clothes, and bathing. Fathers spend more time playing with children (Lips, 2008). Men's average higher earnings likely also play into these distinctions.

Who Becomes a Father?

Data from the National Survey of Family Growth (NSFG), a federal effort to understand family composition, collected from 2006 to 2010, indicates that the mean age of first childbirth was approximately 23 for women and 25 for men. Approximately two-thirds of fathers were in their twenties when their first child was born, while approximately twenty percent were 30 or older. Education is a key predictor here, as men with more education are less likely to have their first child prior to age 20 and tend to have fewer children. Approximately ten percent of men with less than a high school diploma had fathered three or more children, compared to approximately three percent of men with a bachelor's degree or higher (Martinez et al., 2012). Because education and income are linked, the greater number of children born to those living in poverty increases the likelihood of those children remaining in poverty, thus continuing the cycle of poverty discussed in Chapter Two. Although only a minority of Black men fail to complete high school, the rate among this ethnic group is notably higher than for other United States ethnic groups, and thus reinforces the higher rates of poverty among Black men and families (see Table 2.1).

According to the NSFG, the majority of men who become fathers do so while married (59 percent) or living with their partner (25 percent). However, nearly half of men who became parents at some point in their lives had fathered a child outside of marriage, with rates notably higher for Black (79 percent) and Hispanic (81 percent) men (Martinez et al., 2012).

Approximately 180,000 teens become fathers each year in the United States, and they account for as many as 20 percent of all births in any given year (Kiselica & Kiselica, 2014; Martinez et al., 2012). The vast majority have been in a romantic relationship with their partners, often exceeding one year in length (Kiselica & Kiselica, 2014). There is no single factor—or set of factors—that predict who will become a teen father. However, several factors increase the likelihood that a boy will become a father as a teen, including (Kiselica & Kiselica, 2014; Martinez et al., 2012):

- growing up in poverty
- doing poorly in school or dropping out entirely
- engaging in delinquent behaviors
- struggling with mental health problems
- being raised in a single parent home
- had a mother who had her first child at a relatively young age
- had at least one parent who was depressed

- had impoverished or non-existent relationships with their fathers
- had multiple large-scale transitions (e.g., residential moves, changes in parental employment, changes in adults in parenting roles).

Teen fathers' lives don't get any better as they age. By the time they reach their mid-30s, they tend to be less educated, earn less money, are more likely to live in poverty, and are more likely to have been in jail than their age-mates who did not become fathers during their teens (Dariotis et al., 2011).

Although half of teen fathers are of European descent, young men of African and Latino heritage are more likely to become teen fathers than their European heritage peers (Kiselica & Kiselica, 2014). Discussions of teen fathers tend to focus on Black and Latino fathers, who are over-represented in this population; each ethnic group accounts for about 12 to 13 percent of the general population and about 25 percent of teen fathers, causing substantial problems in those communities. At the same time, Whites are under-represented in this statistic because they represent about 67 percent of the population but only half of teen fathers (see Table 2.1). If efforts to reduce teen fatherhood focus exclusively on Black and Latino boys, then those efforts will miss half of all teen fathers.

Anticipating Fatherhood

Adult men, for whom pregnancy is often at least somewhat planned or not actively prevented (Kaye, Suellentrop, & Sloup, 2011), tend to say that the experience of having a pregnant partner creates mixed feelings. There is often an excitement about being a parent and being an active partner to the pregnant woman, as well as a sense of unreality before the pregnancy is visible. Ambivalence is furthered by other changes and transitions, including those within the couple's relationship, creation of the new identity as a father, a sense of powerlessness over the pregnancy, difficulty connecting emotionally to a fetus inside their partner's body, and reorganization of social life, including the loss of free time (Genesoni & Tallandini, 2009).

When faced with news of pregnancy and impending fatherhood, most teen and young adult males see this potential change as a negative event that limits their current freedoms as well as their future aspirations and goals. A minority of young men see the event as an opportunity to change their lives for the better. This ambivalence, at both the group level and among individuals, is quite common (Lohan et al., 2010; Kiselica & Kiselica, 2014).

Across studies, males under age 24 who unintentionally impregnate their partners often say they want to keep the child and that they want to be involved in the decision to keep, abort, or adopt the child (Lohan et al., 2010). Both men's involvement in prenatal care (e.g., attending doctor's appointments with their pregnant partners) and their presence in the household at the time the child is born predict involvement in the child's life at five years of age. In one large-scale study, only half of men who were not involved in their children's prenatal care were still involved with their children three months after birth. By contrast, almost two-thirds of men who were involved in prenatal care and were also residing with the child's mother remained involved where their children reached their fifth birthdays (Shannon, Cabrera, Tamis-LeMonda, & Lamb, 2009).

Parenting

The realities of parenting can be quite difficult. Most parents appear to learn their parenting skills "on the job" and women usually spend more time on this job than men (Lamb, 2012). In contrast to most women, many men have no childhood parent-like experience, such as babysitting or playing with dolls, nor with the psychological skills of nurturing or empathy during their upbringing (see Chapter Seven). Despite the general lack of training prior to childbirth, most parents raise children who are relatively well-adjusted (Lamb, 2012; Pleck, 2007).

Fathers' perceptions of what it means to be a good parent are derived from a variety of sources, including their own parents and grandparents, their wives and her parents, their parenting peers, and television (Kuo & Ward, 2016; Masciardelli, Pleck, & Stueve, 2006). A man's beliefs about what constitutes a good father, in terms of both providing and caretaking, are a key determinant of how he acts as a father; those beliefs may reflect his own assessment, his understanding of his wife's expectations, his understanding of other fathers his age, or some combination of these factors (Masciardelli et al., 2006; Maurer & Pleck, 2006). Television portrayals often present men as less effective and less competent than women, which may explain why first-time expectant fathers who watched more hours of television rated their (upcoming) contribution to childrearing as less important than that of their partner (Kuo & Ward, 2016). A man's experience of his own father is also important. Men whose childhood experiences were with highly involved fathers are more likely to be actively involved themselves. Men who perceived their fathers as less-than-positive models, and who display a commitment to doing better, also tend to be highly involved (Hofferth, Pleck, & Vesely, 2012). Those who report having been involved in child care responsibilities as boys or adolescents, and who responded positively to these experiences, were also more involved. There is some cross-cultural evidence that boys who provide early infant care tend to become involved fathers. (Pleck, 1997)

For much of the twentieth entury, researchers and the general public believed that a father needed to be present in the household for a son to become a well-functioning adult male. This approach has subsequently been called the *essential father* theory (Silverstein & Auerbach, 1999). By the end of the century, research on fathers had become more detailed and investigators began to examine what fathers actually do instead of focusing on whether or not they were in the house or how much time they spent with their children, and thus the research on fathers became quite similar to the research on mothers (McKelley & Rochlen, 2016; Pleck, 2007). Across thousands of studies over the last few decades focused on infants, young children, elementary-aged children, and teens, researchers have consistently demonstrated that three parental factors have substantial impact on children's development: the quality of the child's relationship with their parents/parental figures, the quality of the relationship between the parents and other significant adults in the child's life, and the availability of adequate economic, social, and physical resources (Lamb, 2012; Pleck, 2017). We briefly describe each of these, as well as the ways they intersect with masculine norms.

Quality of the Child-Parent Relationship

The *quality of the parent-child relationship* refers to how well the child and parent function together, and thus includes aspects of liking, loving, and respecting each other as demonstrated in their ability to communicate effectively, establish and enforce rules, and demonstrate emotional warmth. *Authoritative parenting*, which consists of relatively high levels of emotional warmth and parental control, is typically associated with positive outcomes in child development, as indicated by relatively better academic performance and lower levels of involvement in delinquent behavior (Lamb, 2012).

From a masculinity perspective, authoritative parenting may be difficult to achieve because emotional warmth, which includes the ability to read and respond to a child's feelings, can be challenging due to the limited emotional vocabulary and framework men typically develop. This is not to say that most men fail to demonstrate warmth to their child or have children who see them as "cold," but rather that warmth may appear different for mothers and fathers, especially when children are able to develop emotional intimacy with their mother but not their father. In fact, men with higher levels of gender role conflict typically report poorer connections with their sons (O'Neil, 2008). But early interaction with very young children may help fathers overcome gendered challenges. When men are allowed to interact with their children shortly after birth, they react similarly to mothers, showing strong emotional reactions and becoming enthralled with the baby (Parke & Tinsley, 1981; Storey, Walsh, Quinton, and Wynne-Edwards, 2000). Meta-analysis has demonstrated that mother-child and father-child warmth produced similar effects on eight of nine outcomes assessed; the one difference being that both maternal and paternal warmth were associated with better academic performance, although the effect was stronger for mothers than fathers (Pinquart, 2016).

Quality of the Adults' Relationships

Parents who get along with each other, regardless of the legal status of their relationship (never married, married, separated/divorced), are more likely to have better adjusted children. Those who have conflict, especially when this conflict is demonstrated in front of the children, tend to have children who have adjustment problems. This is true regardless of the combination of biological/adoptive parents, step-parents, extended family members, and other adults involved in the child's upbringing. Note that some level of conflict is inherent: parents will not agree on every aspect of childrearing. It is parents' ability to resolve disagreements without interfering with the household's day-to-day functioning and with the children having minimal awareness of parental conflict that is central to this component. Summarizing the research, Michael Lamb reports that "researchers have repeatedly shown that factors such as (level of) maternal employment, paternal involvement, and the division of family labor have much less (if any) impact on child development than the parents' satisfaction with the arrangement" (Lamb, 2012, p. 101). By contrast, children in families with higher levels of parental conflict tend to report higher levels of symptoms related to depression and anxiety (Yap, 2014, 2015).

Men who adhere to masculine norms face a range of potential challenges when it comes to maintaining a minimal conflict zone. Heterosexual men who adhere to norms of dominance, power over women, and men as primary (or only) breadwinners, may overrule the child's mother regarding parenting even though she is the primary caretaker, believe that they are "within their rights" to yell at (or "correct") the child's mother in front of the child, and speak disparagingly of the mother (or women in general) in front of their children and thus demonstrate high levels of conflict. Alternately, men who lack confidence in their parenting may respond poorly when corrected by their partner, as reflected in either yelling/arguing or withdrawing from parenting activities, regardless of their masculine beliefs. We address additional aspects of parental conflict in the section on divorce later in the chapter because divorce is a common outcome among couples with high levels of conflict.

Resource Availability

Generally speaking, children who grow up in households with adequate or good access to resources fare better than children who grow up without such access. **Resource availability** includes economic, social, and physical resources. We have addressed poverty throughout the text, and will do so again later in this chapter, and note that *economic resources* also includes factors such as access to health care and access to educational resources such as libraries and the Internet. *Physical resources* refers to a combination of factors, including clean air and water, safety outside the house (as indicated by high levels of neighborhood crime/violence, for example), and recreational spaces (e.g., parks and playgrounds). Social resources include access to both other children and other adults, as well as community-based activities (e.g., scouting, athletic teams). Lamb reports that "there is substantial evidence that children raised in impoverished circumstances are not only at greater risk for abuse, but also at risk of psychological maladjustment in a number of domains" (Lamb, 2012, p. 101).

Resource availability is clearly related to the breadwinning aspects of masculinity. Greater income is typically associated with greater access to physical resources as well, in part because income is linked to residential safety (through property values) and greater access to social resources. We detail men's work in Chapter Eleven.

Despite the importance that many men place on providing for their family by earning money (via work), many men report feeling strong conflicts between work and family roles (O'Neil, 2008). Employers in the United States have been slow to accommodate employed parents who wish to participate more fully in family roles through, for example, "flex time" arrangements that allow them to synchronize the workday and school day schedules (Bem, 1993), with maternal leave being more commonly offered and more commonly utilized than paternal leave. This is unfortunate because the more time a father spends at work, the less involved he tends to be with his children, which is not true for mothers (Hofferth & Anderson, 2003).

Teen fathers have relatively low levels of education compared to other fathers, and their jobs and income opportunities are more limited, increasing the likelihood that they will turn to illegal activities to earn money and thus increasing their chances of becoming incarcerated during their twenties (Dariotis, Pleck, Astone, & Sonenstein, 2011; Kiselica & Kiselica, 2014). Young fathers also face difficulties that prevent them from receiving services. Some barriers are structural, such as programs that are designed for mothers and may or may not allow teen fathers to participate, while other barriers are inaccurate stereotypical beliefs among providers or policymakers, such as the beliefs that men are incompetent or uninterested parents (Bellamy & Banman, 2014; Devault, 2014; Kiselica & Kiselica, 2014). Researchers have consistently demonstrated that parent training programs developed for White populations can be effectively adapted for non-White groups to improve parenting behavior and children's outcomes when the program modifications have a deep sensitivity to the culture to which they are being adapted to (van Mourik, Crone, de Wolff, & Reis, 2017). This would suggest that programs for mothers could be effectively adapted for fathers if masculinity were considered throughout the adaptation, although we are unaware of documentation of such efforts. In effect, their low educational levels leave these young men, especially those from impoverished backgrounds, in "double jeopardy" because they may not have the resources needed to become good fathers and they are often unable to obtain the supports they need (Devault, 2014).

PARENTING, SEX, AND GENDER

Questions about how and from whom children learn about gender roles are longstanding. As noted earlier, the quality of the parent-child relationship, quality of the adults' relationships, and provision of resources are primary predictors of children's development and they are aspects of parenting that can be completed by individuals of any gender. Indeed, most parents are effective and capable at each of these tasks. Yet questions related to gender—the child's and the parent's—are common and have been explored. In this section, we examine ways in which the parent's gender impacts their own childrearing, as well as the specific cases of father absence and stay-at-home-fathers, before turning to boys' development of masculinity.

Similarities and Differences Between Mothers and Fathers

Newborns, infants (less than 12 months old), and children under age five have a narrowly defined set of needs and wants that focuses parents on feeding and protecting the child, as well as providing various sources of stimulation that facilitate language acquisition and other aspects of development. The child's needs and wants expand as they go through the elementary years, and then expand further as when they experience puberty and the teen years. Given the relatively narrow set of needs during childhood, especially prior to age six, it's not surprising that mothers and fathers do many things similarly. The differences between the parents are almost entirely a matter of extent, not of kind (Jeynes, 2016; McKelley & Rochlen, 2016). Yet there are also differences between mothers and fathers based on their personalities and identities, as well as differences that appear to be elicited by whether that adult is raising a son or a daughter.

As we have stated earlier in the chapter, parents' behaviors and beliefs tend to be quite similar on the general level and tend to have similar effects on their children's development regarding development in general, academic performance, children's autonomy, and a range of other behaviors (Lytton & Romney, 1991; Pinquart, 2016; Tenenbaum & Leaper, 2002). Children's and parents' descriptions of parental behavior have similar levels of agreement regardless of the child's gender or the parent's gender (Korelitz & Graber, 2016). However, maternal warmth has a stronger effect on children's academic achievement than paternal warmth (Pinquart, 2016). Although both maternal and paternal anxiety levels predict a child's anxiety levels, children's anxiety

---

Box 9.1
Orphans in Mainstream Culture

Orphans, individuals who are not raised by either biological or adoptive parents during childhood, have a unique place in popular imagination: they are purveyors of great good or great evil. A range of superheroes such as Batman, Superman, Spiderman, and Harry Potter, among others, were orphaned as youngsters (Pecora, 1992). This is also true for some villains, including Voldemort and the title character of the 2009 movie "Orphan." The parents' deaths are often depicted as especially significant events for the superheroes.

levels tend to be more strongly affected by paternal than by maternal anxiety (Möller, Nikolić, Majdandžić, & Bögels, 2016).

Divorce and Father Absence

Marital separation and divorce have become increasingly prevalent in the United States. Although much early research has been done in the context of what John Hill (1987) called "Dick and Jane" families (those with a father who works outside of the home, a housewife mother, and two or more children, none of whom are from the parents' previous relationships), these families constitute less than three percent of United States households (U.S. Department of Labor Statistics, 2005). One in every two or three United States marriages ends in divorce, and the average length of a marriage that ends in divorce is 6.3 years (Coontz, 2005).

The breakup of a marriage is rarely, if ever, easy on any of the people involved. Children of divorce have a higher risk than other children of psychological difficulties for several years, although most children of divorce are mentally healthy (Hetherington, Stanley-Hagen, & Anderson, 1989). Some researchers have discovered that the process and aftermath of **marital dissolution** has an especially negative impact on boys.

Researchers Jeanne and Jack Block began to follow a cohort of young children in the late 1960s in a longitudinal study designed to investigate several developmental hypotheses. **Longitudinal studies** collect data from the same individuals repeatedly over months or years; in this case, the individuals were young children at the beginning of the study. During that time, some of these children's parents divorced, and together with another colleague, the researchers investigated the effects of parental conflict and divorce on children (Block, Block, & Gjerde, 1986). This study is an especially important one because it is a **prospective study**, meaning that the researchers were able to gather data on these children prior to the marital breakup, often for several years. They did not have to rely on children's memories of what happened to them and how they felt.

Comparisons of 60 "intact" families with 41 subsequently divorced or separated families revealed that sons were more vulnerable than daughters to the negative effects of parental conflict. Boys from subsequently divorcing families showed more aggression, more difficulty in controlling impulses, less cooperation, and higher anxiety in novel situations than boys from intact families. These characteristics also stood in contrast to girls from subsequently divorcing families, who showed different and milder symptoms than boys (Block et al., 1986).

Another important finding from this study was that parents were much more likely to engage in marital conflict in the presence of boys than in the presence of girls (Block et al., 1986). If you think about the experience of your parents fighting with each other when you were a child, you might recall (or imagine) it to be very frightening indeed. The sex difference in witnessing parental conflict may be a critical factor in explaining the significantly more negative impact of marital difficulties on sons. It is also important to note that these effects are not simply a result of divorce *per se*, but from the conflict preceding the divorce. The researchers observed these sex differences in symptomatology for years prior to the marital separation.

The fact that parents in conflict are much more comfortable expressing their animosity in front of their sons may reflect the beliefs that boys can "take it" and that boys' emotions are nonexistent or less important than those of girls. One can see that childhood gender role strain in interaction with family stress can have pronounced negative effects on the personality development of the boy. Boys who have internalized dominant masculine norms tend to have more difficulty adjusting to the separation and divorce of their parents (DeFranc & Mahalik, 2002).

However, we should not overstate the problem and neglect the wide range of effects in marriage dissolution. Many children of divorced parents adjust very well with a minimum of symptoms, especially when their mothers and fathers cooperate with each other in parenting tasks. Although divorce doubles the risk of emotional and behavioral problems, it raises that risk from about ten percent to about 20 percent (and part of the difficulty can be attributed to relocating and economic stress). Therefore, about 80 percent of children do well despite the unfavorable environment that parental conflict produces (Hetherington & Stanley-Hagen, 1997). Moreover, these risk differences reduce sharply within two to three years following the divorce. Children of divorce who live with a competent single parent are only one-half at risk for problems compared with children living in two-parent conflicted families (Coontz, 1997). Political movements to require marriage before providing government assistance or to make divorce more difficult tend to ignore the fact that staying married against one's will perpetuates a conflictual environment that may have adverse effects on children. Although divorce has negative effects on children when it results in the dissolution of a low-conflict marriage, divorce benefits children when it removes them from high-conflict situations (Amato & Booth, 2001).

The effects of father absence on boys are difficult to separate from the effects of parental conflict, economic changes, relocation, and other stressors that accompany marital dissolution. Although parental separation is probably the most prevalent cause of father absence, fathers may also be gone from the home because of death, work-related travel, military deployments, shift work (e.g., evenings or overnights), extended illness, or other causes. Additionally, many males have complained about fathers who, although physically present, are psychologically absent because of their emotional unresponsiveness. At the same time, there are physically absent fathers who may be somewhat psychologically present through telephone and email communication, letters, and visits. Father absence may be especially damaging when the father refuses to contribute to his children's economic support, as do an estimated one-quarter of non-custodial fathers (Hetherington & Stanley-Hagen, 1997). Demographic data indicate that 14-year-old sons who lived with both of their birth (or adoptive) parents were less likely to father a child outside of marriage as adults than their peers who lived in some other family arrangement, although a substantial number from each group have children outside the marital context (~40 percent vs. ~63 percent; Martinez et al., 2012).

It is entirely possible that the type of absence (physical, psychological, both), the circumstances that caused the separation, the characteristics of the resident/continuing caretaker, the gender-typing of father and son, and/or other factors combine to determine exactly what effects the child experiences, as well as how severe those effects are. Although there is a widespread societal assumption that father absence is damaging to males, researchers studying the connections between father absence and mental health have demonstrated that it is not necessary for boys to have same-sex role models to develop healthily (Lamb, 2012; Pleck, 2007).

Whatever the effects of father absence on boys are, we can be quite certain that relationships with fathers and feelings about fathers are of profound importance to sons. In an extensive research study of men, one research team found that the quality of the adult son's relationship with his father was significantly associated with the son's level of mental health (Barnett, Marshall, & Pleck, 1992), and a later meta-analysis indicated that both sons and daughters were better adjusted when their fathers remained active as parents after a divorce (DeAngelis, 2005). These conclusions support an earlier finding from an equally extensive study by Kamarovsky (1976) that male college seniors with psychological adjustment problems tended to report low levels of satisfaction in their relationships with their fathers.

Although current research indicates that the absence of a (biological) father does not necessarily harm children's adjustment, a negative impact had been documented for prior generations (Stevenson & Black, 1988), although those studies often conflated father absence and poverty. However, father absence does appear to have a lasting impact on men's understanding of themselves and their lives. This feeling is sometimes referred to as "father hunger" (Bly, 1991) or even as "the wound" (Lee, 1991). One author positioned the death of one's father as a rite of passage in which a "son's reaction may surprise both himself and others... [and] propel a son toward despondency and even self-destruction... [or] inspire in the son a new appreciation for his life and move him with urgency to make the most of his remaining years" (Chethik, 2001, p. 2). The monumental nature of this event may help to explain why men's autobiographies regularly mentioned the loss of a father, but rarely mentioned a father who was (still) alive, wives, or children (Gergen & Gergen, 1993).

In all of these studies, the son's relationship to the father was much more predictive of mental health than his relationship to his mother. This research corroborates a great deal of anecdotal evidence from therapists and men's studies educators that feelings about the father constitute a major psychological issue in men's lives.

Stay-At-Home-Fathers

Some men do the majority of child care in their families and do not work outside the home. There are approximately 2 million stay-at-home-fathers (SAHFs, also known as stay-at-home-dads or SAHDs), representing approximately 16 percent of all stay at home parents (Livingston, 2014). The majority of men become stay at home fathers because they are unable to find work, are ill or disabled, are in school or retired, or for some other reason (Livingston, 2014).

There is little research on SAHFs. Researcher Aaron Rochlen and his team conducted a series of studies to help us better understand the lives of men who chose to be SAHFs. The majority of participants in these studies were European-American, highly educated, and had family incomes equivalent to the upper-middle class (or more) (Rochlen, et al., 2008) and thus the results summarized here may not describe the majority of men who find themselves in this role.

SAHFs gave multiple reasons for choosing to become primary caretakers. The most common of these were that the couple strongly believed one parent should be home to raise the child (i.e., no paid childcare), consideration of the adults' personalities and preferences, and employment or wage earning factors. About half of SAHFs, and three-quarters of their partners, said the fact that the woman earned more was an important consideration (Dunn, Rochlen, & O'Brien, 2013; Rochlen, McKelley, & Whittaker, 2010; Rochlen, Suizzo, McKelley, & Scaringi, 2008).

These fathers also talked about feeling both excited and anxious about being their child(ren)'s primary caretaker, at least initially. By the time they participated in the research, most were very confident of their parenting abilities. Perhaps more importantly, most were highly satisfied with this role. Although there was quite a bit of variability among the men who participated in the research, most were psychologically healthy in general, reported good relationships with their partners, had slightly lower than average masculinity ideology scores, and had chosen to become stay at home parents (Rochlen, McKelley, Suizzo, & Scaringi, 2008; Rochlen, Suizzo, et al,. 2008). At the same time, approximately half reported at least one event in which they had been stigmatized, most commonly because they were violating gender roles (Rochlen et al., 2010).

Sons' Masculinity

Before discussing the ways in which parents influence their children's gender-related beliefs and behaviors, it is important to remember that definitions of masculinity and femininity change over time, and thus one generation's gender beliefs may be the next generation's quaint ideas. Several researchers have documented that men of different age groups endorse masculine norms at different rates (Cournoyer & Mahalik, 1995; Smiler, 2006a; Theodore & Lloyd,

2000). Similar patterns have also been documented regarding gender equality, with teen and adult children tending to be more egalitarian than their parents (Kulik, 2005; Myers & Booth, 2002; Starrels, 1992).

Fathers' perceptions of their sons as masculine begins early. And we mean early. In one study described earlier in Chapter ___, parents of newborns asked to describe their child within 72 hours of birth and prior to leaving the hospital tended to describe their children in gender-based terms, such as talking about sons as strong and active, and the use of gender typed language was more common for fathers, especially fathers of sons (Karraker, Vogel, & Lake, 1995). The importance of masculinity for both parents, especially fathers, may be underscored by the fact that newborns do little other than eat, sleep, and poop.

Parents' emphasis on masculinity is not limited to this study. One review of studies from the 1950s through 1987 found no consistent or persistent differences in parental behavior based on child sex in a range of developmental areas including interaction, achievement, encouragement, discipline, encouragement of aggression, and clarity of communication. They did find differences in gender-typed activities such as playing football or playing with dolls, with parents emphasizing this more strongly for boys and fathers doing so more strongly than mothers (Lytton & Romney, 1991). Newer reviews that have focused specifically on children's gender-related beliefs show that they bear some resemblance to those of their parents. Across studies, girls' gender-related beliefs tend to be closer to both their mothers' and fathers' beliefs than are boys' beliefs (Tenenbaum & Leaper, 2002). The exact mechanisms are not clearly understood and one longitudinal study revealed that while both mothers' and fathers' beliefs about gender equality were related to both sons' and daughters' equality beliefs, fathers' beliefs had a closer relationship to their sons' beliefs in subsequent years than did those of their mothers (Crouter, Whiteman, McHale, & Osgood, 2007).

Although parents' gender-based beliefs seem to have little effect at the general level for most areas of children's lives, some specific effects have been documented. Parents often act in accordance with their own gender beliefs, which can influence the activities that children are exposed to, chores they are assigned, and even the topics of conversation that parents and children share, especially for explicitly gender-typed activities (Lytton & Romney, 1991). In a pair of studies, Harriet Tenenbaum and her colleagues examined differences in how parents interact with their elementary-aged children (ages six to twelve) regarding science and scientific concepts. They found that parents believed that science was more interesting and less difficult for boys, mothers spent more time talking about science with their sons than their daughters, and fathers used more cognitively demanding speech with sons than with daughters in some situations (Tenenbaum & Leaper, 2003; Tenenbaum, Snow, Roach, & Kurland, 2005).

Children, especially boys, do not need to have an adult male in the house, exactly two adults in the house, or heterosexual parents to develop into healthy adults or heterosexual adults, or to endorse gender roles in a similar manner as their peers (Golombok et al., 2014; Lamb, 2012). For example, one recent study of parents' sexual orientation on child development included approximately 150 adoptive two-parent families in England, with nearly equal numbers of gay male, lesbian, and heterosexual couples. On average, their adoptive children were approximately six years old and had been adopted between their second and third birthdays (often younger for heterosexual than for same-sex parents). There were no differences between children in gay male and lesbian households. Comparisons of gay male and heterosexual households indicated that children being raised by gay male couples were less likely to demonstrate conduct problems or show signs of hyperactivity, which are "classic" boy problems. Compared to heterosexual couples, gay male couples reported less parenting stress, reported lower levels of depression, were less likely to use aggressive discipline approaches, showed more warmth toward their children, and were more responsive to their children's needs. Children's endorsement of stereotypical gender roles were similar across households (Golombok et al., 2014). Reviewers have found no differences in children's development based on the parents' sexual orientation, leading at least one reviewer to argue that gay marriage should be legal because it would help solidify family ties and thus prevent disruption via parental separation (Lamb, 2012).

SUMMARY

1. In summary, the research tells us that there is no singular definition of fatherhood that applies equally to all men. Rather, the definition has changed over time, with some groups experiencing substantial challenges in their efforts to achieve the idealized version of masculinity, consistent with our earlier discussions of within-group differences, power dynamics, and masculinities.

2. We also learned that men experience a range of emotions when they discover that they're going to become a father, including both excitement and anxiety. The research on parenting indicates that men and women perform the same tasks (except breastfeeding), although they do them in different amounts (or with different frequencies). Perhaps it is not surprising that the effects of these behaviors on children's development are quite similar. That said, there are some areas that fathers emphasize more strongly or where fathers' behaviors have stronger effects than mothers, especially regarding gender-typed activities.

3. Men's role as parents and wage-earners have shifted over time, particularly as a result of early twentieth century changes related to greater industrialization and fathers' greater time away from their children due to work.

4. The "traditional" family structure of a male breadwinner and female homemaker reflects an ideal that is relatively new in human (and United States) history, and was enacted by a majority of the population for only a short period of time.
5. The age at which men become a father for the first time is influenced by a range of factors, including education, income/socio-economic status, and ethnicity, all of which are linked to one another.
6. Men's reactions to becoming a father for the first time tend to be both positive and negative, at least among adult men who are not actively avoiding pregnancy. Among teen fathers, reactions are more likely to be negative than positive.
7. Three factors have been consistently shown to be associated with more positive aspects of child development across thousands of studies over the last few decades. Those factors are the quality of the child-parent relationship, the quality of the adults' relationships, and resource availability.
8. Most children and parents have fairly good quality relationships, although fathers may find this particularly challenging due to masculine norms against emotional expression.
9. Boys are especially at risk for suffering negative effects from parental conflict and family separation. Sons witness more of their parents' marital conflict than daughters, and this experience is thought to be a critical factor in the development of psychological distress. Although connections between childhood father absence and mental health problems have not been convincingly demonstrated, it is clear that sons usually have powerful psychological issues around their relationships with their fathers.
10. The quality of the parents' relationships may be adversely impacted by masculine norms of dominance, sexism, and the belief that fathers should be the primary (or only) breadwinner.
11. Fathers' abilities to provide for their children may be enhanced by men's emphasis on being the breadwinner, yet this can also lead the father to experience conflict balancing the demands of work and family.
12. Decades of research reveals that fathers' and mothers' childrearing styles and practices are much more similar than different, with the differences being a matter of extent and not a matter of kind.
13. Divorce typically leads to poorer child development, at least for a few years until a new equilibrium is established. It is unclear the extent to which those negatives are the result of the parental conflict that typically precedes the divorce, changes in family income, residential moves, father absence, or other factors.

14. Stay-at-home fathers (SAHFs) choose this role for a range of reasons, and those with relatively higher levels of education and income often describe the experience quite positively.
15. Sons' masculinity is influenced by a range of factors, with fathers' gender-related beliefs (and subsequent actions) often serving as stronger predictors of their sons' gender-related beliefs and activities than mothers.

GLOSSARY

Fathering: The first definition is that a man has impregnated a woman who has carried the pregnancy to term and given birth. The second definition refers to the act of being a parent and indicates what a man does as a father or the quality of his fathering. The second use of fathering is a gender-specific synonym for parenting.

Traditional family: A married heterosexual couple in which the husband works outside of the home and the wife works full-time on child care and other domestic duties. This tradition came to prominence in the mid-twentieth century among White, middle-class, heterosexual culture.

Quality of the parent-child relationship: How well the child and parent function together, and thus includes aspects of liking, loving, and respecting each other.

Authoritative parenting: A parenting style that consists of relatively high levels of emotional warmth and parental control.

Resource availability: The economic, social, and physical resources available to an individual or family.

Longitudinal studies: Research studies in which data are collected from the same individuals repeatedly over months or years.

Prospective study: A longitudinal study in which the researchers gather data on the participants prior to and after the event of interest, without the ability to control (or know) which individuals will experience the event of interest.

Orphans: Individuals who are not raised by either biological or adoptive parents during childhood.

Stay-at-home-Fathers (SAHF) or stay-at-home-dads (SAHD): men who provide the majority of child care in their families and do not work outside the home.

Marital dissolution: The ending period of a marriage, including the time that parents reach the decision to separate through the actual separation (and divorce).

Chapter Ten

Pleasure and Performance: Male Sexuality

Few areas of human behavior are as fraught with emotion as *sexuality*, which includes sexual beliefs and behaviors, as well as sexual orientation and identity. Dealing with oneself as a sexual person can involve a wide array of experiences, including pleasure, mystery, wonder, lust, love, anxiety, guilt, repression, and confusion. During socialization, people receive quite a few messages about sexual feelings and relationships, presumed differences between male and female sexuality, sexual orientation, seduction, intimacy, and sexual communication. Many of these messages are highly value-laden and specify morally correct ways to behave. Some messages, particularly from abstinence-only programs, involve misinformation, half-truths, and highly stereotyped presentations of masculinity and femininity (Guttmacher Institute, 2012; Santelli et al., 2006). These messages influence how biological sexual tendencies are shaped into sexual behaviors and feelings, as well as how the person experiences his or her sexuality within the larger picture of the total self-concept (Marston & King, 2006).

Anthropological evidence indicates that there is wide cross-cultural variation in the social rules for handling sexuality. For example, some cultures value marital fidelity, but some peoples in the Arctic consider it proper etiquette for a man to offer to make his wife sexually available to a male visitor. Kissing is unpopular in some societies. Some cultures encourage sexual experimentation in adolescence while others punish it severely (Rathus, Nevid, & Fichner-Rathus, 2008). And, adolescent boys in some tribes on Papua, New Guinea are expected to perform oral sex on the older men of the tribe as a rite of passage into manhood (Gilmore, 1990).

In the United States, the Victorian era of the early twentieth century was very sexually repressive, in sharp contrast to the sexually permissive values of the late 1960s (Strong, DeVault, Sayad, & Yarber, 2007) and today, including the focus on *hookups*, defined as one-time sexual encounters with someone the individual is not currently dating, does not intend to date, and with whom has no emotional connection (Bogle, 2008; Epstein, Calzo, Smiler & Ward, 2009; Garcia, 2012). One outcome of this shift is a change in the ideal expression of male sexuality from men who were faithful to their wives and fathered several children to men who had multiple short-term sexual partners (Smiler, 2013).

In this chapter, we explore the connections between masculinity and sexuality, as well as men's actual practices of and experiences with sex. We start by discussing comparisons between males and females, then examine direct links between masculinity and sexuality, including risk-taking, competition, and intimacy. We then address changes in sexuality related to different points in the lifespan and the effects of online pornography, and end with a discussion of sexual orientation. Some topics related to sexuality are addressed elsewhere, including romantic relationships (Chapter Eight), sexual harassment in the workplace (Chapter Eleven), and sexual violence (Chapters Twelve and Thirteen).

Male-Female Comparisons

There are several well-documented differences between males and females regarding sexual behavior. In *attitudinal* research, which assesses people's beliefs, males have been more accepting of teen sex, pre-marital sex, and non-relational sex than females since the 1920s, at least among United States samples (Fass, 1977; Oliver & Hyde, 1993). Men are much more likely than women to view sex as a physical activity that is relatively unconnected to relationships (Laumann, Gagnon, Michael, & Michaels, 2001). They also report higher levels of sexual desire (Schmitt, 2005) although the popularly held belief that men have *biologically* stronger sex drives than women is not supported by any available scientific evidence (Rathus et al., 2008). Remember that these are aggregate, average differences between males and females and that there is substantial variability within each of those groups.

Studies of sexual *behavior,* which examine what people do (instead of what they believe), also reveal several differences and again, many of these differences have been documented as far back as the 1950s and earlier. Specifically, men and boys are more likely to report that they masturbate and evidence indicates that among men and women who do masturbate, males do so more frequently (Strong et al., 2007). In fact, the difference in masturbation rates is among the largest and most consistently documented sex differences in sexual behavior (Oliver & Hyde, 1993). Men are more likely to "hook up" or have sex with someone they have recently met (Bogle, 2008; Maticka-Tyndale, Herold, & Mewhinney, 1998) and are more likely to cheat or have an extra-dyadic partner without approval from their primary partner (Humblet, Paul, & Dickson, 2003). Although boys have often had their first sexual intercourse or lose their virginity at a younger average age than girls (Oliver & Hyde, 1993), a small number of recent studies have reported no meaningful difference in *average* age of first sexual experience.

You may have also heard or been taught that girls usually do not enjoy their first heterosexual intercourse but boys typically do. This statement is inaccurate. Both girls and boys evaluate the experience more positively than negatively with scores suggesting that most people describe the experience as "good with little-to-no bad" or "more-good-than-bad." In those same studies, boys rated their experience both more positively and less negatively than girls (Bauserman & Davis, 1996; Smiler, Ward, Caruthers, & Merriwether, 2005).

Sexual Orientation

The narrowest definition of *sexual orientation*, and the definition most typically used by researchers, refers to an individual's preference for sexual partners of a specific sex. This is sometimes differentiated from **sexual orientation identity**, which refers to the way an individual identifies or labels their sexual orientation. Examples include heterosexual, homosexual, bisexual, pansexual, asexual ("not sexual") among other terms.

As we have noted repeatedly, heterosexuality—or rather, being not-homosexual—is an important part of the dominant definition of masculinity. As we discussed in Chapters Two and Three, this idea is rooted in the acceptance of a gender binary, stereotypes of gay men as effeminate (Green & Ashmore, 1998; Madon, 1997), and religious and moral perspectives (DeBlock & Adriaens, 2013). Researchers Michael Parent and Bonnie Moradi (2009) have argued that some masculinity ideology scales measure the importance of presenting oneself as heterosexual more than they measure homophobia *per se*, as their authors claim (e.g., Mahalik et al., 2003). We discuss the romantic relationship experiences of gay men in Chapter Eight.

Origins

Although some people believe homosexuality is a choice and thus can be changed (see Box 10.1), research increasingly points to a significant level of biological causation. Factors linked with sexual orientation include genetics, brain structure, and hormones (Saucier & Ehresman, 2010), although the latter two may be effect, cause, or both. Gay men tend to have more older brothers than heterosexual men and are less likely to be right-handed, although the birth order effect may be limited to right-handed men. There is no effect for number of older sisters (Blanchard, Cantor, Bogaert, Breedlove, & Ellis, 2006). The data are also clear that family structure, such as being raised by a single mother or gay (or lesbian) parents is not predictive of homosexuality (American Association of Pediatrics, 2013; Lamb, 2012).

In some ways, discussions of the causes of homosexuality are somewhat offensive in and of themselves. After all, we do not ask people "What do you think caused your heterosexuality?" or "If you have never slept with a person of the same sex, is it possible that all you need is a good gay lover?" (Rochlin,

> **Box 10.1**
> **Sexual Conversion "Therapies"**
>
> Can sexual orientation be changed? Should it change? A small group of psychologists and psychiatrists answer both questions in the affirmative, but only with regard to homosexual orientation; no one seems to be interested in converting people from heterosexuality to homosexuality. Efforts to reorient people to heterosexuality are viewed as remarkably offensive by most gay and lesbian people and their heterosexual allies.
>
> Jack Drescher (2002) notes that there are three prevalent types of theories on the origins of homosexuality. **Normal variant** theories define homosexuality as a minority but naturally-occurring orientation, analogous to left-handedness (e.g., Money, 1987a). **Pathology** theories define homosexuality as an abnormal condition, and **immaturity** theories regard this orientation as a (perhaps passing) phase. Although the American Psychological Association (APA) once endorsed a pathology theory, it changed to a normal variant theory in 1973. Thus, adherents to either of the other two theories are clearly outside the psychology mainstream in the United States. However, there are many people who continue to believe that homosexuality is a pathology, and in recent years, some have sought to change it in individuals, mainly because of a perceived contradiction with fundamentalist Christian religious beliefs. Moberly (1983) coined the term **reparative therapy** to describe these efforts.
>
> The title obviously implies that something is broken and needs repair, a claim that many find profoundly offensive. A broad collection of professional organizations, including the American Psychological Association, American Psychiatric Association, American Counseling Association, and National Association of Social Workers, have taken the official position that therapy to change an individual's sexual orientation is inappropriate and unethical (Just the Facts, 2008). States such as California and New Jersey have made it explicitly illegal.
>
> The research study that most strongly supported the effectiveness of reparative therapy (RT) was published by Robert Spitzer in 2003. Relying on self-reports from 143 men and 57 women who had experienced RT, he concluded that it helped some people change their sexual orientations, although never from strictly homosexual to strictly heterosexual. No subsequent researcher was able to replicate Spitzer's findings, his research methodology was (rightly) questioned, and in 2012 he published a statement saying that his results were likely erroneous. He apologized to the gay community and "any gay person who wasted time and energy undergoing some form of reparative therapy because they believed that I had proven that reparative therapy works with some 'highly motivated' individuals" (Spitzer, 2012, p. 757).

1982, p. 1). For years, researchers did not include people with other-sex attractions as research participants, so there are relatively little data on how heterosexuals determine that they are "straight." Yet an examination of the available evidence tells us that by age six, some boys are clearly attracted to girls while others are clearly attracted to boys. Some do not report any attractions until their teen years (Eliason, 1995; Savin-Williams, 1998). These similarities and others suggest that we need to understand what causes sexual orientation, not just what causes homosexuality.

Current-day sexuality researchers rarely ask the categorical question "Are you gay, heterosexual, or bisexual?" Instead, many use some version of Alfred Kinsey's seven-point scale, sometimes known as the ***Kinsey Scale***, which is anchored by "completely heterosexual" (score: 0) and "completely homosexual" (score: 6). A score of three indicates someone who is equally heterosexual and homosexual, or in current terms, bisexual (Kinsey et al., 1948). Assessing categories of sexual orientation can be further compounded by the distinction between the partners an individual wants and the ones they have, as well as evidence that some men change categories (Baumeister, 2000; Savin-Williams & Vrangalova, 2013; Smiler et al., 2011).

Rates

Given the different ways to measure sexual orientation, it should not be surprising that there is no accurate count of exactly how many people fall into any particular category. Assessing the presence of homosexual and heterosexual men within the populations becomes even more complicated when we acknowledge that many self-identified gay males have some type of sexual experience with females and that some self-identified heterosexual men have some type of sexual experience with males (Laumann et al., 2001; Savin-Williams, 1998; Savin-Williams & Vrangalova, 2013; Smiler, Frankel, & Savin-Williams, 2011). For example, if a heterosexual man kisses another man because he is dared to do so (Anderson, McCormack, & Lee, 2012), or simply because he wants to "experiment" and see what it's like "the other way," does that one-time behavior say anything about his orientation? The same questions might be asked of a gay man with a female partner. And how should we classify men who identify as heterosexual, have wives, and also have male lovers "on the down low" (King & Hunter, 2004)?

Yet results are somewhat consistent. To demonstrate that *mostly heterosexual* (1 on Kinsey's scale) is a distinct sexual orientation, researchers Ritch Savin-Williams and Zhana Vrangalova (2013) evaluated data from 53 studies of men's and women's sex-of-partner preferences. In 43 of them, at least 90 percent of men said they were strictly heterosexual; for most of the remaining studies, the rate was between 85 percent and 89 percent. Mostly heterosexual was the next largest group of men, consisting of approximately 3.5 to 4.1 percent of the population. In most studies, between one and three percent of men identified as exclusively homosexual.

Sex and Masculinity

Gendered expectations and ideologies pervade virtually every area of experience, and sexuality is no exception. Masculine norms in the United States contain many prescriptions for sexual behavior and experiences, and these are embedded in the larger context of masculine values and ideologies. Being a "real man" has often included expectations for certain ways of being a sexual man.

The primary image of male sexuality in United States culture is that of an attractive heterosexual (white) male who is interested in having sex with a large number of hookup-type partners in relationships where he takes the initiative and there is no emotional connection (Brooks, 1995; Smiler, 2013). He is typically paired with an attractive female who is relatively inexperienced and re-active (or passive).

The television show *The Bachelor* can be seen as a template for this image of male sexuality. In this unscripted show—we find very little "reality" in the on-screen product—he chooses from among a variety of contestants. Throughout the show's American seasons, the bachelor has almost always been White, always had a large income or is rich (including one prince), treated the women to fancy and expensive "dates," always appeared to be in control, routinely commented on the women's appearance, had never been divorced (although one was a widower), did not have children, and had sexual contact with the "contestants" prior to making his selections (Manning, 2011; Palmer-Mehta & Haliliuc, 2009). By contrast, gay male dating shows such as "Boy Meets Boy," have not allowed sexual activity, the "dating pool" included heterosexual confederates, and the producers had partial control over who was eliminated

---

Box 10.2
The Circumcision Debate

Circumcision, the cutting and removal of the penile foreskin (prepuce), is performed on more than half of male infants in the United States, which is the only Western country where this practice is routine (Zak, 2009). Perhaps because of heightened awareness of its risks and/or beliefs that it is unnecessary, circumcision rates have decreased in much of the world. In 1975, 93 percent of newborn boys in the United States were circumcised. That figure fell dramatically to 56 percent by 2006 (Zak, 2009), although there are significant variations among religious affiliations and regions. Globally, the practice is much less common, with an estimated 85 percent of male infants not circumcised (Goldman, 1992). In Australia and Canada, for example, approximately 20 percent of boys undergo the procedure as infants, and the neonatal circumcision rate in Britain is only one percent (Laumann, 1999).

A century ago, circumcised men were also a small minority in the United States. The rise to the high rate of circumcision in the mid-twentieth century was fueled by beliefs about its value for hygiene, disease avoidance, reduction of cancer risks, and other concerns (Hussey, 1989). Circumcision also has ritual meaning within some religions (Allgeier & Allgeier, 2000). However, complications from circumcision such as hemorrhage, infection, or mutilation, occur in as many as four percent of cases (Niku, Stock, & Kaplan, 1995).

In 1989, the American Academy of Pediatrics (AAP) recommended that parents carefully weigh the risks and benefits of circumcision before deciding whether to subject their newborn boys to it (Rathus, Nevid, & Fichner-Rathus, 2008). A decade later, in 1999, the AAP issued a statement saying that the benefits of circumcision do not outweigh its risks, and that therefore the operation should not be carried out routinely (Rathus et al., 2008). In 2004, The Circumcision Resource Center stated that, "no medical organization in the world recommends routine circumcision of male infants." Why, then, does circumcision remain the majority experience in the United States? Milos (1992) cited several persistent myths about the value of circumcision:

Myth: A circumcised penis is cleaner than an uncircumcised penis. Although circumcision may reduce the frequency of urinary tract and other kinds of infections (Wiswell & Geschke, 1989), an uncircumcised penis is easy to care for. Infections can easily be avoided by simple hygiene procedures, which most men around the world use routinely.

> However, there is newly-emerging evidence that circumcision may offer a significant measure of protection from Human Immunodeficiency Virus (HIV) and that therefore it is possibly a valuable tool for fighting the worldwide AIDS pandemic. The World Health Organization and UNAIDS now recommend it (WebMD##, 2009; http://www.who.int/hiv/topics/malecircumcision/en/). Safer sexual practices would have the same effect, however condoms and proper safer sex information are not always available, especially in non-industrialized nations.
>
> *Myth*: Babies don't remember the pain. In a review of the controversy around circumcision, Laumann (1999) stated that, "Even four to six months later, babies circumcised without anesthesia exhibit greater pain reactions to vaccination than uncircumcised boys or babies whose circumcision pain was attenuated by anesthetics." (p. 70). This finding tells us that infants certainly are affected by the experience for at least a period of several months.
>
> *Myth*: A boy needs to look like his father or the other boys in the locker room. This belief did not appear to be a concern when, from 1870–1900, most United States boys were circumcised and their fathers were not not (Hussey, 1989). Milos (1992) suggests that boys readily accept the explanation that "When I was a boy, they thought circumcision was necessary for health, but now we know better." (p. 15). However, for U.S. parents, the circumcision status of the father is strongly related to the decision of whether or not to subject the baby boy to the procedure. Ninety percent of sons of circumcised fathers undergo the operation compared with 23 percent of sons of uncircumcised fathers (Laumann, 1999).

(Manning, 2011). Even more striking is the contrast with "Flavor of Love," featuring Flavor Flav, originally of the rap group NWA, and featuring mostly Black contestants. Here, Flav has a criminal record, has been divorced (more than once), has children from prior relationships, and is not financially stable. Further, the dates are decidedly downscale and cheap, the female contestants are required to do mundane tasks such as cleaning (Manning, 2011; Palmer-Mehta & Haliliuc, 2009). We discuss media portrayals in further detail later in the chapter.

Promiscuous sexuality may be central to current definitions of masculinity because, unlike some other masculine expectations, adolescent boys can achieve it. Manhood rituals have typically revolved around the Three P's: providing, protecting, and procreating (Gilmore, 1990), also known as the Three F's: feeding, fighting, and fornicating. Current-day United States culture does not allow most teen boys to meaningfully protect or provide for their families, but they can procreate—or be promiscuous—and that behavior has become one way to demonstrate masculinity.

Regardless of the rationale(s), the idea that males should be sexually promiscuous is connected to other aspects of gender (David & Brannon, 1976). One link is the close connection between masculinity and being not-homosexual, a theme we've discussed throughout the book. Another is the value that being promiscuous can qualify a boy or man for a high level of status among other males, or at least among others who adhere to the hegemonic definition of masculinity. Today, we might call a promiscuous male a "player." In the past he's also been called a "stud" or a "Don Juan," among other terms (Smiler, 2006a, 2013).

This ideal of heterosexual promiscuity is so central that several masculinity ideology measures such as the Conformity to Masculine Norms Index (CMNI; Mahalik et al., 2003) and the Male Role Norms Index (MRNI; Levant et al., 2007) explicitly include it as a component of masculinity. In fact, promiscuity subscale scores are strongly related to measures of aggression, dominance, and emotional restriction (Levant et al., 2007; Mahalik et al., 2003).

Perhaps, then, it is no surprise that teen boys and undergraduate men with higher scores on these and other scales report having more total sexual partners and having their first sexual experience at a younger age (Pleck, Sonenstein, & Ku, 1993; Smiler, 2008), as well as more partners per year, than other men (Sinn, 1997; Smiler, 2013). In fact, even among young men who entered college with no sexual experience, those with higher masculinity scores had intercourse sooner than their less masculine virginal male peers (Forste & Haas, 2002).

A younger age of first sexual experience and the total number of partners one has had are seen as ways to compete with others. Both of these numbers feed into the masculine emphasis on getting something accomplished rather than on the experience of doing something. Masculine achievements are, by definition, things that have happened in the past that contribute to the sense of gendered identity. They are also quantifiable; masculine success means "putting up numbers." Carrying this ideology over into sexual behaviors has often created problems for hegemonic men and those around them.

This goal-oriented attitude toward sex focuses the man on the good feelings that come from having "conquered" someone and leads to a focus away from enjoying the sexual experience. Some men even want to hurry sex so that they can go and tell their friends about having "scored," and thus gain admiration and status while maintaining and enhancing their friendships with other males (as discussed in Chapter Eight). The sexual partner, however, is often a victim of disrespect. They are dehumanized by being treated as merely an avenue to achievement for the "player." Commenting on this aspect of masculinity, philosopher and men's studies pioneer Harry Brod (2005) stated, "Unless you are as concerned with your partner's free will as you are with your own, you are treating [them] as less than human and therefore you are the only person in the room. We have a name for solitary sex. You are not having sexual intercourse, so don't congratulate yourself."

Risk-Taking

Taking risks is sometimes necessary to achieve the goal of more partners or a younger age of first sex. Farrell (1986) summarized the social message young men receive: "Be prepared to risk rejection about 150 times between eye contact and sexual contact. Start all 150 over again with each girl" (p. 126). Because men are expected to be tough and strong, rejection is not supposed to hurt.

The directive to take sexual risks also harms men in other ways. Generally, those with higher masculinity ideology scores, especially those who endorse stereotypical gender beliefs, tend to underestimate the risks involved in sexual behaviors (Courtenay, McCreary, & Merighi, 2002). Heterosexual boys with higher masculinity scores report lower levels of intentions to use condoms, in part because they believe pregnancy prevention is a woman's responsibility (Pleck, Sonenstein, & Ku, 1993, 1994). Failure to use condoms also puts them at greater risk for contracting sexually transmitted infections (STIs) and research indicates that many men do not defy the odds for long. Men who do not use condoms and are more promiscuous are more likely to have an extra-dyadic sexual interaction without approval from their partners, contract a sexually transmitted infection, and initiate an unintended pregnancy (Dariotis et al., 2008; Humblet et al., 2003). One result of these ideologies is that the United States has notably higher rates of unplanned teen pregnancy and teens with STIs than any other industrialized nation (Weinstock, Berman, & Cates, 2004; World Health Organization, 2004).

Competition

One aspect of the *sexual double standard,* which refers to activities for which a culture maintains different (moral) standards for the same behavior based on a person's gender, is that promiscuous boys and men are rewarded for having a lot of partners while girls and women are shamed for the same behavior (Crawford & Popp, 2003). A promiscuous male is often praised as "The Man," at least among teen boys and young adult men (Brooks, 1995; Kimmel, 2008; Smiler, 2013).

To compete in this "game," men learn to equate sex with physical pleasure and minimize their desire for emotional intimacy with their sexual partner(s) (Levant, 1997b; Smiler, 2013). The result is an approach that positions partnered sex as a physical release or an adventure and may explain why one expert was astonished by men's frequent reports that they do not enjoy sex (Zilbergeld, 1992). This approach makes it easier for men to engage in hookup sex (Bogle, 2008; Bradshaw, Kahn, & Saville, 2010). It likely also explains why men are more likely than women to interpret an ambiguous event, such as an invitation from a woman to have a cup of coffee together, as indicating sexual interest or availability (Fisher & Walters, 2003).

In Chapter Five, we discussed sexual strategies theory (SST) (Buss & Schmitt, 1993; Schmitt, 2005), which positions male promiscuity as evolutionarily derived. Proponents of this theory argue that men who spread their seed widely and eschew long-term commitments with women are more likely to produce children and thus propagate their genes. However, one anthropological review of foraging tribes (i. e., hunter-gatherers) demonstrated that children who were raised by both biological parents were more likely to survive to puberty than children whose fathers were not involved (Quinlan, 2008). If your children fail to reproduce, is that really a "win" in evolutionary terms?

Others have criticized the methodology and interpretation of results. SST research relies on long-documented male-female differences. It also focuses heavily on evidence that men are more likely than women to say they would like two or more sexual partners in the next 30 days (Schmitt, 2005), a gender difference David Schmitt and his colleagues demonstrated in every one of 52 nations (Schmitt et al., 2003). The data, which rely heavily on unmarried undergraduate students age 18 to 22, showed that approximately 25 percent of young men and six percent of young women wanted multiple partners. As critics have pointed out, that is a minority of men who completed anonymous surveys and who have extensive access to unmarried young women without meaningful adult supervision, at least in Western nations. If there were ever a group who could have—or admit to wanting to have—high numbers of partners, this is it (Diamond & Hazan, 2000; Smiler, 2011).

The research regarding actual number of partners is fairly consistent and indicates that most men have few partners. Only an estimated 15 percent to 20 percent of young men have three or more partners per year. When the time frame is expanded to three years or longer, the percentage of men who consistently have three or more partners per year drops to 5 percent or lower (Dariotis et al., 2008; Humblet et al., 2003; Offer, Offer, & Ostrov, 2004).

Researchers exploring the attitudes that support male promiscuity have revealed a set of ideologies that are consistent with mainstream United States definitions of masculinity such as competition with other men, "stealing" a friend's girlfriend (Messner, 1992), endorsement of sexual double standards, a desire for power over women, and the belief that lying to women during seduction is "fair play" (Smiler, 2013). Moreover, endorsement of this approach to masculinity is associated with endorsement of various *rape myths,* a set of assumptions and beliefs that inaccurately position rape as an event that happens to women who have somehow behaved inappropriately and thus are at least partly responsible for being rape (e.g., "Only bad girls are raped") and the use of aggression in sexual scenarios (Murnen, Kaluzny, & Wright, 2002).

Intimacy

According to researchers who examine the subjective understanding of sex, most men do not conform to stereotypical expectations (Smiler, 2013). Men routinely report that their experiences are grounded in love, or at least affection, for their partners (Fiering, 1996; Smiler, 2008; Smiler, Ward, Caruthers, & Merriwether, 2005). An emphasis on physical intimacy combined with emotional intimacy can shift the center of sexual activity away from penetrative sex and on to other forms of sexual activity that emphasize pleasure and may or may not include orgasm. In addition to the focus on a broader array of physical pleasures, men desire and often attain this *sensuality*. We discuss other aspects of romantic relationships, such as emotional support, in Chapter Eight.

Many adult men report making a transformation away from a "selfish," penis-based sexuality to a couples-based approach emphasizing sensuality.

By the time a man reaches his 60s or 70s, his sexual activity may have shifted from being focused on penetrative sex to cuddling and mutual masturbation (Potts, Grace, Vares, & Gavey, 2006; Sandberg, 2013). This approach seems more similar to many women's experiences of sex, which often include caressing, intimate conversation, or other aspects of sensuality. It would also seem to minimize the heterosexual women's oft-expressed frustration with male partners who seem overly focused on the physical aspects of sex.

Overall, we see that male-female differences, combined with a cultural emphasis on male promiscuity, teach both boys and girls how men are expected to behave. Many see this set of sexual behaviors as central to definitions of masculinity, in part because of double standards that prescribe differences in male and female sexual behaviors (Brooks, 1995; Crawford & Popp, 2003).

Sexual Development

The sexual behaviors in which boys and men engage can change over the lifespan. In this section, we describe boys' experiences of puberty, as well as shifts in men's experiences of sexuality in the second half of life.

A boy discovers his penis very early in life. Compared with the girl's vagina and clitoris, the penis is more external and visible. Once he is out of diapers or learns to take them off by himself, his penis is easily accessible to his hands, and he finds that touching it produces very pleasurable sensations. A boy will often learn his culture's beliefs about sex before he learns to seek out sexual information.

Puberty

Puberty is the process of physical and sexual maturation. Some changes are specifically related to reproduction, including growth in genital size and production of semen, called **primary sexual characteristics**. Other changes, such as development of facial hair and deepening of voice, are called **secondary sexual characteristics** and can be understood as signals that the boy is sexually mature (or soon will be).

Puberty includes a series of hormonal changes. Perhaps most relevant here is a dramatic increase in the level of testosterone. We note that girls' level of testosterone also increases, but not as much as boys. Similarly, everyone's levels of estrogen increases, except for individuals with certain disorders of sexual development, and the increases are substantially larger for girls than boys (Dorn & Biro, 2011; Saucier & Ehresman, 2010; Vilain et al., 2007). Changes also occur at the neurological level. The shift in hormones appears to both reorganize neural circuitry and activate those newly reorganized systems, especially those specifically related to sexual behavior. Ultimately, the interaction between pubertal hormones, adolescent brain structure, and a boy's experiences all influence his sexual behavior (Sisk, 2006).

Another change is an increase in penis size. Pre-pubertal boys' penises are smaller than those of adult men's, which average approximately 14 to 15 cm (5.5 to 5.9 inches) when erect (Reece, Herbenick, & Dodge, 2009). Yet men report that they would prefer to have penises between 18.5 cm (7.25 inches) or 20 cm (.80 inches) longer than men actual average. Very few men tell researchers they would prefer shorter penises (Johnston, McLellan, & McKinlay, 2014; Lever, Frederick, & Peplau, 2006). Women consistently provide lower estimates of actual and ideal length than men and the vast majority (approximately 85 percent) are satisfied with the size of their partner's penis (Johnston et al., 2014; Lever et al., 2006). Statements like "it's not the size of the wand, it's the magic in the magician" or "it's not the size of the ship, it's the motion of the ocean" provide little comfort to men who think their penises are too small.

Boys often describe puberty as both exciting and somewhat embarrassing, and in the media, male puberty is almost always depicted as funny (Hust, Brown, & L'Engle, 2008). Although parents know they should talk to their sons about puberty and first ejaculation before these events occur, few do (Frankel, 2002; Stein & Reiser, 1994). Boys say puberty is exciting because they want to be more mature and be seen that way. Yet it is also embarrassing because their bodies behave differently and in ways that remind the boy (and others) that he is not in full physical control (Frankel, 2002; Stein & Reiser, 1994). The most embarrassing moments seem to be the spontaneous erections that occur for no conscious reason. These events are most likely a manifestation of growth and biological "system checks" that have little to do with either conscious or unconscious desire, but that bulge in a boy's pants may be visible all the same. Math class is rarely *that* interesting.

In industrialized nations, and among the middle- and upper-middle classes of non-industrialized ones, recent research reveals that older teens and undergraduates typically report entering puberty at age 12 or 13. There is some evidence that the average age of pubertal onset became younger during the twentieth century (Bhalla, 2003; Ponton & Judice, 2004; Goldstein, 2011).

On average, sexual behaviors start soon after the onset of puberty. Many boys report that their first open-mouthed kisses with girls took place around age 13 or 14. This experience is typically followed by increasingly more intimate sexual behaviors such as manual-genital contact and first intercourse around age 16 (Regan et al., 2004; Smiler, Frankel, & Savin-Williams, 2011). Most boys follow this sequence (Jakobsen, 1997). Or, more precisely, most boys follow this sequence when they have female partners (Smiler et al., 2011). First "serious" relationships with girls typically occur around age 16 or 17 (Smiler et al., 2011). We discuss romantic relationships in Chapter Eight.

For boys with male sexual partners, average age of these firsts and the sequences in which they experience them is much more variable. On average, first sexual penetration (oral or anal) occurs around age 16, alongside manual-genital contact, with first kiss following at age 16 or 17. For these boys, the most common sequence is to have one's first kiss and first sex at the same age. First "serious" relationships often begin around age 18 (Smiler et al., 2011).

Researchers typically find ethnic differences in the ages at which teens achieve some of their sexual "firsts." In one study that did not report male–female differences by ethnic group, White (non-Hispanic) community college students reported the youngest average age of first kiss and first date (both around 14.5 years) and that first intercourse occurred at nearly 17.0 years. Latinos followed a similar but slightly older pattern (kiss: 15.2 years, date: 15.7; intercourse: 17.3). Blacks reported that their first kisses occurred at a similar age to other groups (14.8 years), but their first intercourse occurred at a younger age (16.3) than other groups while their first date occurred at an older age (17.5). Asian youth tended to start later in general, the result of a cultural focus on academics that downplays socializing; their first kiss (17.6), first date (16.1), and first intercourse (18.9) were older than most other groups (Regan, Durvasula, Howell, Urena, & Rea, 2004). The relatively younger age at first intercourse for Black youth is the result of this group's overrepresentation among those in poverty, their poorer education and job outlook, and a lack of easily accessible males who have managed to establish sustainable claims to manhood within a racist system. Many youth of color who grew up in poverty have explained to us that they don't expect to live past 21 or 25 but want to be seen as manly and hope to leave a child as their legacy. This perspective is also adopted by some Latinos, although it may be tempered by cultural values of *familisimo* and their "lesser" experience of systemic racism (see Table 2.1). These patterns of younger sexuality also contribute to the overrepresentation of Black and Latino young men as teen fathers (Martin et al., 2011), a topic we discuss further in Chapter Nine.

Adulthood & Older Age

The typical man in the United States reports having sex between two to three times per week and once every few months. For most, sexual activity becomes less frequent as they enter their 30s and more often occurs with long-term partners (Laumann et al., 2001). Unfortunately, with older age also comes a greater likelihood of experiencing sexual problems such as difficulties with sexual desire, functioning, or enjoyment. Clinicians often use the terms ***sexual dysfunction*** or ***sexual disorder*** to describe these problems. The term dysfunction seems to imply that the "equipment" is not working; disorder implies a pathological condition. Since male sexuality is not only in the penis, and since sexual difficulties do not necessarily mean that there is something fundamentally wrong, the term "problem" seems more appropriate. Generally speaking, problems become more common as men age; men with poorer health and lower levels of happiness also tend to report sexual difficulties at higher rates than their age-mates (Laumann et al., 2001).

The *Diagnostic and Statistical Manual of Mental Disorder* (DSM-V) (American Psychiatric Association, 2013) directs clinicians to consider if sexual problems are lifelong or acquired as well as generalized or situational. Most diagnoses, including those reviewed here, require the problem to be present in at least

75 percent of (attempted) sexual experiences over the course of at least six months. In addition, the problem cannot be the result of an issue related to one's partner, the relationship, other characteristics or mental conditions in the individual (such as high anxiety), cultural or religious practices, or a medical condition (such as high blood pressure), and it must also be associated with distress. These considerations are important with regard to treatment. If a condition is longstanding and global, it usually presents a more serious problem than transient or situational difficulties. A problem that is largely biogenic usually points to different interventions than a problem of psychological origin. And there is no need to treat a condition when it is not associated with distress.

The overall incidence of sexual problems is difficult to estimate because sex is usually such a private matter, but it is probably the case that most people have, at some time in their lives, experienced sexual disinterest, arousal difficulties, and/or sexual performance problems (Laumann et al., 2001). Males are also much more likely than females to develop sexual arousal to atypical or deviant stimuli such as children, inanimate objects or parts of the body not usually associated with sex, pain and suffering of self and/or partner, exhibitionism, and voyeurism (American Psychiatric Association, 2013). The following discussion centers on problems with arousal and performance.

Male Hypoactive Sexual Desire Disorder

Male Hypoactive Sexual Desire Disorder focuses on a lack of interest in sex. It only becomes a problem if it is distressing to the man and/or his partner. The gender prescriptions that a man should always want, need, and be ready for sex may produce negative feelings in the man when he experiences even a normal ebb in his sexual appetite. Fewer than two percent of men report a persistent, lifelong lack of interest in sex (American Psychiatric Association, 2013).

Low levels of sexual desire can stem from physiological causes such as fatigue, drug use, or illness, and/or from psychological/interpersonal causes. Other problems, such as work stress or conflicts in the relationship with the man's sexual partner, might also lead to a decrease in sexual desire. Declines in testosterone levels after midlife, which are a common part of aging (Saucier & Ehresman, 2010), may also play a role. Occasional experiences of low sexual desire appear to affect approximately 15 percent of men age 49 or younger and 22 percent of men in their 50s. It is estimated that approximately six percent of men age 18 to 24 and approximately 40 percent of those age 66 to 74 have severe and persistent enough symptoms to qualify for diagnosis (American Psychiatric Association, 2013).

Erectile Dysfunction

Transient or longstanding difficulties in attaining or maintaining erection are relatively common in men, and these problems often produce significant distress. Historically, the term "impotent" was used to refer to men who experience these difficulties. Literally, this word means "powerless" and parallels the conception of erection as a cultural symbol of man's strength. Clinically, these problems are now referred to as erectile dysfunctions to more specifically describe the problem and to avoid implicit value judgments about the man's personality (just as the term "frigid" is no longer used to describe a woman with orgasmic difficulty).

It is estimated that five to ten percent of men age 49 or younger suffer from occasional erectile problems, with the rate increasing to approximately 20 percent of men in their 50s (Laumann et al., 2001). The DSM-V indicates that erectile problems are severe enough to be diagnosed in approximately two percent of men younger than age 40, with rates rising to between 40 and 50 percent of those beyond age 70. Although the exact contributions of physical and psychological causes is not known, the estimate of physical origin has increased in recent years, and some researchers believe that close to half of erectile problems are based more in biology than psychology (Shabsigh, Fishman, & Scott, 1988), a view that has become more popular since the release of drugs like Viagra and Cialis in the late 1990s (Potts et al., 2006). Physical causes include illness, disease, high blood pressure, use of some types of prescription and nonprescription drugs, injury, hormonal imbalance, fatigue, and vascular problems (Allgeier & Allgeier, 2000; Crooks & Baur, 2007).

Emotional factors can also play a role in erectile difficulty. Anxiety is probably the most common one (Zilbergeld, 1992). Many men feel a good deal of pressure to penetrate their partners with their erect penises (or else it's not "really" sex). Paradoxically, the fear of losing one's erection can result in dysfunction. Men who think of intercourse as the only mode of sexual expression often believe that they must have an erection for sexual pleasure to occur for both self and partner. Something of a vicious cycle may result: he feels self-induced pressure to attain an erection and perform, which leads to anxiety, which leads to erectile difficulty, which results in more pressure, more anxiety, etc. As Nelson (1988) opined "[Erectile dysfunction] is a man's threat, always waiting in the wings while he is on stage" (p. 33).

There are several treatments for erectile problems, including vascular medications such as Viagra, Cialis, and Levitra. One could argue that these drugs, or the advertising around these drugs, has reinforced the concept of male sexuality being all about penetrative sex and not a broader sensuality (Potts et al., 2006). Men with intractable physiological barriers to erection can opt for penile implants, which produce erections by the pumping of liquid into a cylinder that has been surgically implanted in the penis (Wienke, 2005).

Psychological treatments for erectile problems usually involve turning attention away from penis, intercourse, and performance, and toward sensuality, the partner's pleasure, and sexual communication. Among men whose erectile problems are largely psychogenic, most can achieve erections when the pressure to do so is removed. Erectile problems specifically related to (Internet) pornography viewing are addressed elsewhere in this chapter.

Ejaculatory Problems

This category includes both premature and delayed ejaculation. Many experts believe that *premature (early) ejaculation* is the most common sexual complaint for men (Zilbergeld, 1992), with 20 to 30 percent of adult men reporting some concern of this type (American Psychiatric Association, 2013; Laumann et al., 2001). The DSM-V specifies a time frame of less than one minute after penetration and sooner than desired. The two-part definition is important because it is difficult to define the problem in absolute terms. How soon is too soon? A subjective criterion of "sooner than desired" may simply be more practical: if the man and/or his partner are unhappy with the man's level of ejaculatory control, some attention may be warranted.

Although the cause or causes of premature ejaculation are not well understood, sex therapists have developed reliable treatments for this problem. Pharmacological treatments using low doses of antidepressant drugs have been somewhat successful (Forster & King, 1994; Wise, 1994). Behavioral techniques involve the starting, stopping, and restarting of stimulation at various points of arousal, the squeezing of the base or glans of the penis, and a number of other exercises that the man can do alone or with a partner. These treatments are also highly effective. Success rates are estimated at between 80 and 98 percent (Zilbergeld, 1992).

Fewer than one percent of men experience an opposite problem: the inability to ejaculate during a reasonable period of time, or sometimes at all, known as *delayed ejaculation* (American Psychiatric Association, 2013). This problem is thought to be anxiety-based, perhaps related to a fear of impregnating the partner or a discomfort with one's own erotic pleasure. Sex therapists have prescribed a number of techniques for increasing arousal (Zilbergeld, 1992). Alternately, substantially delayed ejaculation can also be the result of masturbating regularly to pornography, as discussed in the next section.

TELEVISION, MOVIES, AND PORNOGRAPHY

Knowledge of sexuality in general, and the dominant image of male sexuality in particular, comes from parents, peers, and media (Sutton et al., 2002) and these sources provide different amounts of input and variant messages. For many boys in the United States, parents provide—or are remembered to provide—the least amount of information and media the most; parents tend to be most negative and media almost exclusively positive (Epstein & Ward, 2008). At the same time, most parents want their children to have healthy sex lives in adulthood (Vernacchio, 2013).

Men as attractive, promiscuous, uninterested in longer-term relationships, and taking the initiative are among the most common and frequently repeated components of male sexuality, according to content analyses of the television programs, movies, and music videos most popular with children and teens

(Cope-Farrar & Kunkel, 2002; Jhally, 2007; Montemurro, 2003; Morrison & Halton, 2009; Turner, 2011; Ward, 1995). Magazines like *Maxim, Rolling Stone, Cosmopolitan,* and even *Golf Digest* (Hatton & Trautner, 2011; Joshi, Peter, & Valkenburg, 2011; Krassas, Blauwkemp, & Wesselink, 2003; Vokey, Tefft, & Tysiaczny, 2013) also reinforce this image, as do romance novels (Clawson, 2005) and pornography (Picker & Sun, 2008). Popular music has provided something of an exception, with a greater focus on romantic men than sexual men, although the stereotypical image has become more prominent in the 1990s through the 2010s, primarily in rap music (Smiler, Shewmaker, & Hearon, 2017). Very few media messages promote a healthy sexuality characterized by mutual respect, good communication, condom use, and explicit consent (Hust, Brown, & L'Engle, 2008).

We focus primarily on the effects of pornography because it has been the subject of both cultural debate and research interest. However, from a media effects perspective, pornography may be understood as a content category that is delivered through the same technologies as other forms of content, and thus may be viewed as one end of a spectrum from not-at-all sexual to highly and explicitly sexual (e.g., Ley, 2016).

Scope

The sale of sexually explicit material worldwide is a $56 billion-per-year industry (Dines, 2005). In the United States, this $13 billion industry brings in more revenue than the National Football League, the National Basketball Association, and Major League Baseball *combined* and more than the three major television networks *combined.* There are 4.2 million pornography websites (12 percent of all websites) containing 420 million pages (89 percent from the United States), and 25 percent of search engine requests are for sexually explicit material (Internet Filter Review, 2009). Robert Jensen (2007) reported that the pornographic film industry released 13,588 new films in 2005, an average of 37 per day, and that pornographic film revenues in the United States are larger than those generated by the Hollywood film industry. Mainstream corporations like General Motors, AT&T, and Time Warner own subsidiary companies that produce pornographic material (Dines, 2005).

Viewing online pornography is a common activity among males. Estimates suggest that one-quarter to one-third of 14-year-old boys have intentionally viewed sexually-explicit media online (Brown & L'Engle, 2009; Sabina, Wolak, & Finkelhor, 2008) and nearly all young men have done so by age 18 (Brown & L'Engle, 2008; Steeves, 2014). At the same time, approximately 70 percent of children's first exposure is accidental (Kaiser Family Foundation, 2012) and the average first exposure for boys is at age 11 (Johnson, 2013). Among younger boys, the primary reason given is to "learn about sex" (Cameron et al., 2005).

While pornography certainly provides the most basic information about how to have sex—insert rod into hole and create friction—those images are provided within a larger visual context. In "mainstream" porn, that context is often violent. Ana Bridges and her research team (2008) randomly selected scenes from the 250 most popular sexually explicit films and coded randomly-selected segments of them for aggressive acts. They found that 82.8 percent of the 304 scenes had physical aggression (such as slapping, hair pulling, or spitting), that 95 percent of the aggression was directed toward women, and that the female performers were almost always depicted as enjoying these acts. Thus, whether or not sexually-explicit films are diverse, the ones that are viewed most often contain elements of violence against women. Pornography researchers and anti-pornography advocates have documented instances of extreme violence against women in sexually explicit films, including rape, violent assault, and death ("snuff films"). Pornography producers defend their industry by saying that films are very diverse and that anti-pornography activists point to only the most extreme examples of violence and degradation. Yet the results of Bridges' study suggests that violence is normal in pornography (see also Picker & Sun, 2008).

Attitudes

Does pornography *cause men to become violent toward women*? Given the increasingly violent nature of pornography, (Bridges et al., 2008; Picker & Sun, 2008), the question seems obvious. Because there is more than 60 years of research on the negative effects of viewing violent media (see Chapter Twelve), it seems reasonable to expect that the effects of viewing violence would extend to the content category of pornography. We note that the violence in porn, where women may be gagged, bound, hit, or otherwise assaulted before or while men enjoy their own sexual pleasure, is consistent with hegemonic norms not only of promiscuous sex, but also violence, dominance, and anti-femininity. Generally speaking, men who endorse these aspects of masculinity offer greater acceptance of rape myths (Murnen et al., 2002), which suggests they may perceive such scenes as quasi-realistic.

Research specifically examining pornography use suggests that although pornography does not directly cause men to become violent toward women, regular pornography viewing multiplies the risk of sexual aggression by about 400 percent among men and boys who have other risk factors such as histories of child maltreatment and association with deviant peers, (Ybarra & Mitchell, 2004). In one study of fraternity men, researchers found that pornography users reported being less likely to intervene as bystanders in dangerous situations, more likely to endorse rape myths, and more likely to report a behavioral intent to rape compared with non-users (Foubert, Brosi, & Brannon, 2011). Other researchers have found a strong relationship between pornography use and objectification of women (Peter & Valkenburg, 2007). Anti-pornography activist Gail Dines (2013) described women in pornography as being viewed as having "no past, future, biography, goals, or aims," and as being disposable (in part because the average length of their careers is about three months because they become injured and/or diseased).

Does pornography *cause rape*? Again, not directly. There are many men who view pornography and are not sexually aggressive and men who are sexually aggressive and do not view pornography. But as Jensen (2007) points out, the important question is does pornography constitute a factor that contributes to rape? Evidence suggests that it does, as it "can perpetuate, reinforce, and be part of a wider system of woman-hating" (p. 103). If other predispositions to rape are present (see Chapter Thirteen), aggressive pornography has the potential of activating or reinforcing these predispositions (Malamuth, Addison, & Koss, 2000). Acknowledging that sexually explicit material is quite compelling but nonetheless harmful if aggressive, Gail Dines (2006) stated, "I don't believe that most boys and men come to pornography because they hate women. But if they stay, they learn to hate women." Dines' summation appears to summarize another finding: teens who start watching pornography at younger ages, do so at relatively high rates, and continue to watch at this level for several years also tend to support more regressive and stereotypical gender role attitudes and report younger ages at first sex (Brown & L'Engle, 2009).

Negative effects of pornography use are not limited to violence toward women or rape. One meta-analysis of nearly 50 published and unpublished studies indicates that men who watch more pornography consistently report lower levels of both relationship satisfaction and sexual satisfaction (Wright, Tokunaga, Klaus, & Klann, 2017). However, effects on men's body image were found to be inconsistent, with some studies finding a negative impact, such as greater self-consciousness regarding their own body and decreased evaluation of their own sexual desirability (e.g., Aubrey, 2007) and others finding no impact. The reviewers ultimately concluded that there is no single large-scale effect that describes most men (Wright et al., 2017).

Men's Sexual Problems

What direct effects does pornography have on the male viewer? "Internet addiction," "online pornography addiction," or even "sexual addiction" have been widely used to describe the problematic use of online pornography that causes many men seek treatment (Cantor et al., 2013; Griffiths, 2012). We note that the DSM-V does not include any of these terms as official diagnoses and professional organizations such as American Association of Sexuality Educators, Counselors and Therapists (AASECT, 2016) have recently taken formal positions stating that such terminology should not be used by professionals for diagnosis or the purpose of providing treatment. Men who seek treatment, whether or not they use these terms, typically report difficulty performing sexually with a live partner due to erectile difficulties or ejaculatory difficulties (premature or delayed), as well as negative effects from spending so much time looking at online sexually-explicit media (e.g., not enough time for other tasks, including work, school, and hobbies) (Cantor et al., 2013; Shaeer, 2013). Thus, the problem does not seem to be caused by viewing pornography *per se*, but rather by repeatedly masturbating while watching pornography.

Assuming there are no physical problems that lead (or contribute) to the erectile and ejaculatory issues, then the problem may be that the individual has effectively "re-wired" his arousal system through watching large quantities of pornography while masturbating. One part of the problem is that he is seeing more naked and sexual bodies in a week than humans evolved to see in a lifetime (Wilson, 2011). Another part of the problem is that more frequent viewers may have trained themselves to become aroused almost exclusively to visual stimuli instead of the combination of tactile and other sensory inputs involved with partnered sex. In many cases, this set of inputs occurs in a single place and physical position (e.g., seated in front of a desktop computer in the bedroom). Depending on whether the man tends to ejaculate quickly or chooses to prolong his arousal (e.g., by increasing and reducing the amount of direct physical stimulation to his penis) helps determine the whether his problem manifests as premature or delayed ejaculation during partnered sex. Effective treatment typically consists of minimizing or avoiding pornography, decreasing the frequency of masturbation, and varying the ways in which the individual masturbates (Perelman, 2016; Shorrock, 2012; Sutton, Stratton, Pytyck, Kolla, & Cantor, 2015).

Clinician and researcher David Ley (2016) draws a parallel between pornography and alcohol, arguing that both have been the subject of public debate and that both are and have been readily available despite legal prohibitions designed to limit their distribution. He notes that over the past several decades, the focus on alcohol has become about responsible drinking, including public campaigns such as "friends don't let friends drive drunk." He suggests that instead of asking whether or not pornography should be legal or illegal, we would be better served by asking how to produce and consume pornography ethically.

SUMMARY

1. In this chapter, we have addressed sex and gender comparisons in sexual attitudes and behaviors, the connections between masculinity and sexuality, sexual development throughout the lifespan, and sexual orientation. As we have seen, there is a strong cultural and individual emphasis on male promiscuity and penetrative sex. This focus obscures the actual experiences of boys and men, which tend to highlight emotional and relational connection, including a more sensual approach to sexuality. As Gary Brooks and Ronald Levant (1997) concluded, "The fundamental problem is the approach to sexuality that we teach to adolescent boys and young men. Until we reconstruct the traditional standards for male sexual conduct, we will continue to be plagued with men behaving badly" (p. 258), or at least in ways that may be less than optimal for men and their partners.

2. The ways people understand, behave, and respond to male sexuality have varied among cultures and historical eras.
3. Many differences between men and women exist regarding both sexual attitudes and behaviors, and several of these differences reflect double standards that praise men and punish women for the same activities.
4. The dominant masculine role encourages (especially young) men to support promiscuous attitudes and engage in sex with multiple partners. Teen boys and young men with higher masculinity ideology scores report younger ages of first sex, more total sexual partners, and more sexual partners per year.
5. Masculine role norms that encourage risk taking appear to encourage boys and men to engage in dangerous sexual practices, especially failing to use condoms, which contributes to high rates of unplanned pregnancies and sexually transmitted infections (STIs) within the United States.
6. Masculine injunctions against emotional expression and intimacy run counter to most men's desire for emotional connection with their sexual partners. Yet as men age and gain sexual experience, they often shift toward a more sensual approach to sexuality that is less dependent on penetrative sex.
7. Puberty involves a series of hormonal and neurological transformations. These two changes interact with a male's experience to shape his behavior.
8. Sexual orientation appears to be a biologically-based phenomenon, akin to handedness. Efforts to change an individual's orientation, known as "reparative therapy," are unethical and ineffective.
9. The majority of males have their first sexual experiences during their teen years. Average ages and specific patterns vary based on an individual's ethnicity and the sex of their partners.
10. At midlife, men report having sex less frequently than during their twenties. In addition, the likelihood of experiencing some type of sexual problem increases.
11. Frequent viewing of online sexually-explicit media contributes to endorsement of more traditional gender roles among teen males. Frequent masturbation while using online pornography can lead to sexual problems such as erectile difficulty and premature ejaculation.
12. Sexual orientation categories are somewhat difficult to define and some individuals change categories during their lifetimes. Despite the challenges of categorization, the proportion of individuals who identify themselves as belonging to any particular category appears to be relatively stable.
13. Regarding media-based images of sexuality, including pornography, the data certainly suggest that unlimited viewing is linked to a set of beliefs

that can lead to harm, and that men who watch more pornography report lower levels of both relationship satisfaction and sexual satisfaction. Men who masturbate with porn at high levels are also more likely to have erectile or ejaculatory problems in their real-world experiences.

GLOSSARY

Sexuality: A general term that includes sexual beliefs and behaviors, as well as sexual orientation and identity.

Hookups (sexual): One-time sexual encounters with someone the individual is not currently dating, does not intend to date, and with whom has no emotional connection.

Sexual double standard: Activities for which a culture maintains different (moral) standards for the same behavior based on a person's gender.

Rape myths: A set of assumptions and beliefs that inaccurately position rape as an event that happens to women who have somehow behaved inappropriately and thus are at least partly responsible for being raped.

Sensuality: An approach to sexuality that highlights pleasure without necessitating sexual penetration or orgasm.

Circumcision: The cutting and removal of the penile foreskin (prepuce).

Puberty: The process of physical and sexual maturation.

(Development of) primary sexual characteristics: Physical changes that begin to occur during puberty that are explicitly related to sexual functioning, such as growth in genital size and production of semen.

(Development of) secondary sexual characteristics: Physical changes that begin to occur during puberty that are not explicitly related to sexual functioning, such as development of facial hair and deepening of voice.

Sexual dysfunction or sexual disorder: Broad terms that refer to the set of sexual problems that an individual can experience.

Male Hypoactive Sexual Desire Disorder: A sexual disorder characterized by a lack of interest in sex that the individual (or their partner) finds distressing.

Erectile Dysfunction: Transient or longstanding difficulties in attaining or maintaining erection. Also known as impotence.

Ejaculatory Problems: A category of sexual dysfunction that includes both premature and delayed ejaculation.

Premature (early) ejaculation: Ejaculation during intercourse that occurs less than one minute after penetration and sooner than desired.

Delayed ejaculation: The inability to ejaculate during a reasonable period of time, or sometimes at all.

Sexual orientation: An individual's preference for sexual partners of a specific sex. This is the definition most typically used by researchers.

Sexual orientation identity: The way an individual identifies or labels their sexual orientation.

Normal variant theories: Theories that define homosexuality as a minority but naturally-occurring orientation, analogous to left-handedness.

Pathological theories: Theories that define homosexuality as an abnormal condition.

Immaturity theories: Theories that regard homosexuality as a (perhaps passing) phase.

Reparative therapy: A psychotherapeutic effort to change an individual from homosexual to heterosexual. The practice of reparative therapy has been found to be ineffective and is considered unethical by all major professional organizations that train therapists.

Kinsey Scale: A scale for assessing sexual orientation anchored by "completely heterosexual" (score: 0) and "completely homosexual" (score: 6).

Chapter Eleven

Men at Work: Jobs, Careers, and Masculinity

If there is anything that men have been about throughout history, it is work. From the assembly line worker to the chief executive officer, most men in the Western world define themselves according to their jobs (e.g., Deutsch & Saxon, 1999). An important part of the masculine socialization process is oriented toward preparing males for the working world. Many scholars (e.g. Basow, 1992; Eagly, Wood, & Diekman, 2000) have argued that gender roles are mainly a result of the historical division of labor between men and women. From this perspective, it is not surprising that the last several decades have witnessed changes in the ways that people think about gender as the working world undergoes significant evolution. Women are entering the paid work force in record numbers and rightfully demanding that they be treated as equals. Some men are having trouble adjusting to increasingly mixed-sex environments, especially those in which women are in positions of authority. More and more labor-saving devices are becoming available, and the competition-oriented, individualistic working culture is giving way to team building and environments where cooperation is valued. As a result, there are fewer and fewer places for the physically powerful working man or the hard-nosed manager, and more and more places for the technician and the executive with "people skills."

Although much of the mainstream masculine value system encourages being a good worker, it may do so at a considerable cost. Additionally, some aspects of masculine gender role socialization are counterproductive to functioning in many modern workplaces. Changing gender roles also create considerable stress for many, as well as providing exciting opportunities for men (and women) in the working world. Despite the centrality of work to men's lives, research examining the interplay between masculine norms, masculinities, and work has been relatively uncommon since the 1970s due to a greater focus on helping women enter high-paying professions.

In this chapter, we investigate the relationships between masculinity and work. To provide a context, we look first at the history of the sex-based division of labor, then shift discussion to sex and race in American employment patterns, including the presence of men in female-dominated vocations. This is followed by discussion of the ways that boys are socialized into the world of work, positively and negatively, before the chapter concludes with discussion of male-female relationships in the workplace and sexual harassment. (We address men who are fulltime homemakers, also known as stay-at-home fathers, in Chapter Nine.)

A History of Work and the Sexes

For the vast majority of human history, labor chiefly consisted of hunting animals and gathering edible vegetation. Societies based on other forms of labor are a relatively recent phenomenon, comprising only about two percent of the time in which people have inhabited the Earth (Collins, 1979). In these hunter-gatherer societies, which still exist in some parts of the world, women nearly always contributed equal or larger amounts of the community food supply compared to men. There is some evidence that gender roles in these societies tended to be more egalitarian and cooperative than in most modern cultures, as men and women worked together as economic partners. As Nancy Bonvillain (2001) notes, "In many foraging bands, women's and men's interdependent contributions to their households were reflected in equality of social relations and social status" (p. 17).

When people learned to plow, plant, and domesticate animals, some 6,000 years ago, the character of gendered labor arrangements changed. Plowing required one to be relatively far from home, thus it became largely the man's job. Producing offspring meant more help in the fields, and thus children became an economic asset. Reproduction became the means of production, and thus it became economically advantageous to control women's sexuality and reproduction (Lerner, 1986).

Another important change characterized agrarian societies. There was no longer a need for people to be nomadic. In hunter-gatherer societies, survival depended on moving to where vegetation and game were available. In agrarian societies, people could stay in one place and produce food with a little cooperation from nature. There was a certain harmony with the earth, and *husbandry*, the cultivation and respect of nature, became a dominant value (Keen, 1991). Sons spent a good deal of time working with and learning from their fathers, which provided a sense of intergenerational continuity (Stearns, 1991). Civilizations and communities took on a relatively permanent, and therefore more elaborate, character.

Land was now useful and valuable for long periods of time, generation after generation. It became something a person owned, dealt, protected, and willed to heirs. Land meant food, and food meant wealth. Institutions were created to deal with land transactions. The most notable of these was ***patriar-***

chy, the system by which males dominated public and private life. ***Primogeniture*** was the patriarchal arrangement by which sons inherited property from their fathers and passed it on to their sons. This system established male social and economic dominance, as well as the control of women's sexuality by men (Lerner, 1986).

This shift to male dominance in concordance with the shift to an agrarian lifestyle has been replicated as recently as the twentieth century. Susan Basow (1992) described changes in the !Kung society of Africa, a foraging society which has moved to the agrarian way of life during the last few decades. She noted that women's mobility became more restricted and that they contribute less to the food supply than before. Children's play groups became more sex-segregated, and aggression increased. Basow argues that agrarian society is historically responsible for gender inequity, and that these types of societies are the bases for every industrialized society in the world.

Property ownership and patriarchy changed masculinity in important ways. Men created institutional laws to protect their land, but physical force also came to be used, hence the transition of man the planter to man the warrior. In hunter-gatherer societies, men bonded together to share resources in the hunt, and the kill was shared by all the community. After property ownership, men's bonds were in the service of killing other men. Therefore, organized violence became a hallmark of masculinity. Sam Keen (1991) speculated that the masculine ethic of cooperation gave way to an ethic of conquest at this time, and that the quest for harmony became a quest for control. He also noted that men from victorious armies routinely raped the women of the conquered territories. Thus, we see in these societies the origins of negative aspects of masculinity: violence, over-competitiveness, dominance over women, and physical risk-taking.

Patriarchy also dictated that men should control their children's (especially their son's) lives. Fathers had to see that their sons learned to act properly, because they would someday control the family wealth. In Western cultures, this need gave rise to an ethic of discipline, which was sometimes administered physically. The punitive nature of their relationship created a tension between affection and resentment for both father and son (Stearns, 1991).

The division of labor in agrarian societies was not nearly as sharp as it has been in the last 150 years in the industrialized world. In agrarian societies, family members worked alongside each other in farming or small businesses. The co-provider family remained the norm, as it has been throughout most of human history (Coontz, 1997). But the turn of the nineteenth century witnessed the dawn of the Industrial Revolution. Hand tools were increasingly replaced by machines, and production became more large-scale and centralized in factories. Industrialization continues to spread throughout the world.

Because patriarchy was firmly established by this time, the vast majority of industrial work was at a distance from the home, and a good deal of this labor required upper body strength, factory work became largely men's work. Women were expected to withdraw from the paid labor force following marriage and to work full-time at domestic duties and child care. Men began to specialize in paid employment outside of the home, and thus away from their sons, and abdicated their traditional child care duties to their wives. In times of male labor shortages, more women worked outside of the home, but their work was devalued, and they were pushed aside by men when jobs became scarce.

In the transition from co-provider to single-earner families, women's contributions to economic life tended to become less direct. Although most families could no longer survive by farming, crafting, and trading, they could not rely solely on ready-to-use goods that they purchased from the husband's earnings. Many families could afford fabric but not clothing, flour but not bread, seeds but not vegetables. Among many other duties, the wife's work was to turn these raw materials into useable goods with her cooking, sewing, gardening, and other skills. Thus, women's work was critical for family functioning, but men's work became increasingly associated with wage earning (Coontz, 1997).

The development of many masculine gender role norms can be laid at the doorstep of industrialization. First and foremost is the establishment of the breadwinner role, which Gould (1974) described as the beginning of "measuring masculinity by the size of a paycheck." Socially, masculine attractiveness is based largely on economic power. Many men attempt to project a masculine image through external success, not internal fulfillment. Gould suggested if a man "flashed a roll of bills, no one would see how little else there was of him." (p. 97).

A second and equally important development of industrialization was a renewal of the antifeminine element of masculinity. The increased polarization of men's and women's work led to a belief that work outside and inside the home are the natural environments for men and women, respectively, an ideology that many writers refer to as the doctrine of separate spheres (discussed in Chapter 1). Doing "women's work" became an increasing threat to men, as did spending too much time in the home and in the company of women. Exclusively male lodges and other social and recreational organizations became popular as avenues for fulfilling a perceived need for safe haven from women's "sphere." Men became increasingly hostile to femininity, and, by extension, to women themselves. Scott Coltrane (1998) and other anthropologists have noted that cultures with higher levels of sex segregation tend to have higher levels of men's violence against women.

The Industrial Revolution ushered in the age of specialization. In agrarian societies, a man plants, reaps, takes care of animals, and is able to see the fruits of his labor. In contrast, the industrial worker may spend the better part of a lifetime putting a single bolt on each of a million machines. Karl Marx (1872) first described the dehumanizing character of such a job. Although agrarian man could take pride in the *process* of planting, growing, and harvesting, industrial man is focused on *outcome*, the amount of money (and goods) produced.

For most men, this was not a lot of money, as the few powerful men exploited the many less powerful men. Most men became (and still are) "work objects" (the term "object" in reference to a person was first coined by Marx). *Objectification* is the denial of the person's humanness. Just as many women have historically been treated as sex objects, men have been exploited as work objects. However, women were, and are, also work objects, as their domestic labor went largely unpaid and viewed as secondary to men's labor (Coontz, 1997).

Men have also been war objects. When the work of the wealthy and powerful involves organized, state-sponsored violence, it often becomes the task of poor young men (Moore, 2004). Most victims of recent wars are young, sometimes even teenaged boys, the least powerful males in the society. A disproportionate number of victims were men of color. More privileged men were (and are) often allowed to opt out of combat, or of military service altogether.

The stereotype of men as socially and economically powerful does not fit the experience of most men. Although men-as-a-group retain much more economic power than women-as-a-group, the vast majority of men have *jobs* (labor done solely for economic survival), not *careers* (reimbursable means of expressing an important part of the self). They sacrifice and labor day after day, under the pressure to be a good provider for their families. Their work is "quietly useful," in the words of World War II photographer Ernie Pyle (Faludi, 1999). Moreover, the necessity of earning a living makes many men vulnerable to exploitive employers.

Far from being a "natural" economic arrangement, the male breadwinner role is a relatively recent development, an historical artifact of the transition from agricultural to industrial society. Although the ideal of male wage earner-female homemaker began to take hold early in the nineteenth century, a majority of families did not have this arrangement until industrialization and urbanization reshaped American society in the 1920s, and, despite many people's nostalgia for the 1950s, only about 60 percent of children in the United States grew up in this kind of family even during that decade. As a result of a decrease in real wages and a sharp increase in the cost of housing, the single-income arrangement is now untenable for most families. Married women who are employed full-time now contribute more than 40 percent to the family income. In historical context, no sooner had the male as sole wage earner family arrived on the scene that it began to disappear (Coontz, 1997). Gender roles are (and will most likely continue to) change in conjunction with changes in the sex-based division (or increasingly, the non-division) of labor. Contrary to popular belief, there is mounting evidence that the majority of two-earner families find considerable satisfaction in both work and domestic life (Barnett & Rivers, 1996).

Historical changes in employment patterns have occurred, and these have been related to the technology available in the workplace (e.g., automation), changes in communication technology (e.g., telephones, the Internet), and economic and political changes (e.g., globalization). The result has been a shift from an agrarian economy dominated by local businesses (pre-1900) to an industrial economy that allowed national and international companies (most of the twentieth century) to an information and service economy (since approximately 1990). These changes have led to a shift away from jobs that required muscular strength and stamina in *blue collar jobs* to jobs that emphasize interpersonal and knowledge skills in *white collar jobs* (Faludi, 1999; Shen-Miller & Smiler, 2015). Taken together, these changes have created a culture in which work outside the home is no longer the exclusive province of men.

Sex and Race in Employment Patterns

Researchers Nadya Fouad, Susan Whiston, and Rachel Feldwisch (2016) report that in the United States, men have always accounted for the majority of employed workers. Their majority has gotten smaller over the last 100 years and by 2010, men represented 53 percent of all workers. These statistics are somewhat misleading, however, because a greater proportion of men work full time than do women (70 percent vs. 57 percent; Proctor, Semega, & Kollar, 2016). They also describe the ways in which the working world is partly segregated by field and job/role. We define a field as *male (or female) dominated* if at least 60 percent of its work force is male (or female), and a field as (relatively) balanced if its work force is 40 to 60 percent male (or female). *Traditional male fields* include the building trades (construction, electrical, plumbing, carpentry) as well as the STEM fields (science, technology, engineering, and mathematical fields). By contrast, *traditionally female fields* and jobs include human services (e.g., childcare, nursing), teaching, and food service, as well as secretarial/reception type jobs (regardless of industry). In part, these differences reflect differences in vocational interests among Americans since the 1950s; men have been likely to express an interest in working with things (e.g., STEM), women have been likely to express an interest in working with people (e.g., teaching, therapy), and the groups have been equally likely to express an interest in working with ideas and data. These differences have been consistent regardless of age of survey participants or when during the last fifty years the survey was conducted (Su, Rounds, & Armstrong, 2009). We note that these general differences obscure changes in the definitions of masculinity and femininity, the influence of gender stereotypes, and the effects of prejudice and discrimination.

In the United States, men earn more than women on average, $51,212 per year in comparison to $40,742 (in 2015; Proctor et al., 2016). There are several factors that contribute to this discrepancy, including a substantial difference in wages between these traditionally male and female jobs. Some professions that could qualify as human services, such as medicine, law, and psychology, have seen substantial numbers of women enter these fields. Psychology has shifted from being a majority male field (in the 1970s) to a majority female field (American Psychological Association, 2013); law school and medical school classes have been female-dominated for most of the last two decades, which has made the fields more gender balanced (American Bar Association, 2014; American Association of Medical Colleges, 2014).

Surveys of teens and undergraduates reflect the gender-differentiated patterns described above (Fouad et al., 2016). In a recent study of American high school students in which they were asked to write in the job/field they'd like to enter when they get older, seven of boys' top ten choices were male-dominated fields, with engineering the most popular of these. Teaching was the only female-dominated job to make the list (fifth place), while the two gender-balanced fields of entrepreneur/business (most popular) and artist/designer (seventh) also made the list (Hardie, 2015).

Men are also more likely to be employed in managerial and administrative roles than women, even in traditionally female fields. Christine Williams (1992, 2013) dubbed this tendency to promote men instead of, or more quickly than, women the *glass escalator*. Evaluations of leaders—managers and administrators—are influenced by both the leader's sex and the gendered character of a field; colleagues, subordinates, and leaders' own evaluations tend to be more positive for those who are in a field that matches their gender than those who are in an other-gender field (Ko, Kotrba, & Roebuck, 2015).

Closer examination of employment patterns reveals that racial factors are associated with macro-level patterns of men's employment. In Chapter Two, we noted that White and Asian men have relatively higher rates of education. As such, men from those groups are more able and likely to pursue STEM fields, most of which require at least a bachelor's degree. It is hardly surprising that those fields have substantial White majorities, with Asians proportionally over-represented but still constituting a minority of those employed in STEM professions. Black and Latino men are much more likely to be found in relatively lower-paying fields and jobs related to food preparation (but not as servers), building maintenance, custodianship/janitorial services, and transportation (Fouad et al., 2016).

Black and Latino men are less likely than their White counterparts to find themselves in managerial and administrative positions. In part, this is the result of their relatively lower levels of education, because large companies often require higher levels of education as a prerequisite for moving into the upper echelons. And in part, this may be a function of subtle aspects of racism, such as implicit bias. Studies suggest that the glass escalator is more readily available to White than ethnic minority men, as well as to men who are fully able in comparison to those who are alternately abled (Woodhams, Lupton, & Cowling, 2015).

The research on career choices that supports fields such as vocational counseling relies on a small number of theories that have dominated the research. Many of these theories, including John Holland's approach, the Theory of Work Adjustment, and social cognitive approaches to vocational choice, include assumptions about individuals' ability to choose jobs and fields that match their interests and personalities (Fouad, et al., 2016). However, this assumption may not be appropriate for men from marginalized groups based on ethnicity, socioeconomic status (SES), health concerns, older age, or ability status.

Men in Female-Dominated Vocations

A number of researchers have examined men who work in female-dominated professions, particularly teaching and nursing. The research often finds that these men redefine their workplaces in ways that are more consistent with dominant masculine norms, particularly their ability to earn good money and their ability to be successful. Men in these fields routinely report that their own masculinity is questioned, with references to femininity or homosexuality (or both). At the same time, many of these men express their own concerns about spending too much time with women and thus becoming more feminine themselves. The research also reveals that many people—women and men—fear that men who want to work with children will sexually abuse them (Fouad et al., 2016). Only a few studies have examined which men choose female-dominated vocations, and thus the population is poorly understood (Williams, 2015).

Nursing provides an intriguing example. From the perspective of masculine norms, nursing is a relatively high paying field with substantial opportunities for employment (and job security), and thus would seem to be a good employment option for men who want to be the primary breadwinner. However, it is a traditionally female field, a field that includes (and may emphasize) emotional care, and is a field that appears to be inherently subordinate to physicians. The field has long attempted to recruit more men, with little consistent or clear success. Some efforts have presented images of stereotypically masculine men or asked if men are "man enough" to be nurses. In one experimental setting, these masculine nurses were rated as less competent and more deviant than a not particularly masculine male nurse. Further, the perception of masculine and less masculine nurses as deviant was higher among male participants who reported higher levels of hostile sexism (Clow, Ricciardelli, & Bartfay, 2015). In a study of employed male nurses, researchers found that men feel less requirement to do emotional work, experience fewer negative effects from doing it, and experience greater job satisfaction from completing some forms of it (Cottingham, Erickson, & Diefendorff, 2015).

NET WORTH EQUALS SELF WORTH: THE SOCIALIZATION TO WORK

Masculine gender socialization is largely oriented toward preparing boys for work. Boys are often asked at a young age, "What do you want to be when you grow up?" They learn that the right answer is not "a husband, father, and friend," but rather a worker of some kind. Boys tend to develop an occupational "dream" in childhood and strive to attain it in adulthood (Levinson, et.

al., 1978). They are taught very early in life that gainful employment is manly. The masculine values of competition, decision making, task completion, and independence serve to provide attitudes conducive to functioning in a wide variety of work settings.

Sports and play are a training ground for the world of work. Sports usually have elaborate sets of rules, score keeping, and clear cut winners and losers (Pasick, 1990). Athletic results are quantifiable in terms of wins and losses, batting averages, and other statistics that invite comparisons among players and teams. The amount of adulation a boy receives for being an athletic success is matched by the amount of adulation a man receives for being a career success. We see connections between sports and work in the language of the business world: "Who are the players?" "They have a good batting average," "Let's see if we can get them to play ball with us." An easy business deal is sometimes referred to as a "slam dunk" or a "home run."

The messages are clear. In the sports world, you are a valued person if you are a winner. Later, being a winner translates into being a *bread*winner — a vocational success. In fact, many men's definition of their masculine value depends on their occupational statuses; the primacy of work also appears in some measures of masculinity ideology (e.g., Mahalik et al., 2003). Although providing for one's family is a long-standing criterion for proving one's manhood (Gilmore, 1990), having real economic power through high earnings qualifies one as "The Man." The important factor is the outcome, not the process. Success for men is often defined in terms of being "better" by getting promotions, having high job status, and making more money. Women tend to be more oriented toward providing a helpful service (Bridges, 1989), although there is a great deal of variability in occupational values both within the population of men and within the population of women.

Positive Aspects of Masculinity and Work

Ruth Hartley's classic (1959) essay on masculine socialization includes the statement that, "On the positive side, men mostly do what they want and are very important." (p. 463). The social status and economic power that men-as-a-group have garnered from work is unmistakable. The fact that men are less often the victims of job discrimination than women has given many men — or at least, many White men — opportunities for self-determination. The glass escalator may also be part of the reason why men continue to hold the majority of industrial and political power. In 2014, there were a record number of women who served as Chief Executive Officer (CEO) of Fortune 500 companies and served as United States Senators. Although women are approximately half of the population, they represented only 4.8 percent of Fortune 500 CEOs and 20 percent of senators (Fairchild, 2014). As of 2005, women made up only 14.7 percent of members of Fortune 500 Boards of Directors, a five percent increase from 1995 (Catalyst, 2006). This gendered workplace advantage is rarely in evidence for minority men (Woodhams et al., 2015), who have been occupationally marginalized throughout United States history.

Work can be quite satisfying. People who are fortunate enough to have careers as opposed to jobs may find the challenge and satisfaction of their work to be one of the most fulfilling aspects of their lives. The historically but reliably higher wages associated with professional employment goes a long way toward making life easier and more enjoyable. Men's orientation toward task completion and self-reliance, together with work opportunity, has made economic and career success a strong possibility for many men, with the greatest benefits available to White men and highly educated Asian men. The "winners" may get some of the best that life has to offer: status, material wealth, and the opportunity to make a difference.

Men who have not been able to enjoy satisfying work have nevertheless been able to take pride in fulfilling the breadwinner role, an expression of masculine love. Historically, many men have felt a deeply emotional investment toward this role, which also has clear social value (Stearns, 1991). Mark Kiselica (2005) describes his feelings about his father's work ethic:

> My father is the most wonderful man I have ever known. He overcame a tragic childhood—including the death of his dear mother when he was only about 8 years old, a neglectful and exploitive alcoholic father, debilitating injuries to his leg and hip, poverty, and a lack of education—to be the most wonderful parent any child could ever wish for. My father worked two jobs—one as a maintenance mechanic in a factory, the other as a painter—always in excruciating pain, and literally had to drag himself out of bed every day in order to limp off to work so that he could earn a living to support our family, consisting of my mom and my four siblings and me. And he did all of this, never once complaining, all out of his love for his family. He is a truly heroic man, and I will always adore him.

Negative Aspects of Masculinity and Work

Although vocational success carries with it great rewards, it can come at a cost to the man's relationships, leisure pursuits, and health. It is also important to note that many, perhaps most, men do not feel successful, and the association of success and masculinity for these men may lead to chronic feelings of inadequacy. There are several potential problems that men—and their partners—may experience.

One problem occurs for men's families: Many men work in frustrating environments, for example the assembly line worker who is bored and unable to find much job satisfaction, the mechanic who faces difficult problems and time pressure, or the middle manager who faces pressure from both his subordinates and his superiors. Some have not learned how to deal with the emotional aspects of work frustration. They have been raised to ignore emotion, especially if it is connected to feelings of weakness or powerlessness. Some of these men deal with these feelings by projecting them outside of the self. As spouses and other family members are most available for these projections, they may bear the brunt of these negative emotions, and this can lead to strained family relationships. A spouse interviewed for Weiss's (1990) study illustrates the effects of "bringing work home":

> He is so proud, telling people that he works things out for himself and he doesn't worry his family.... Well, that really isn't the case. Because what happens is, [if] he has a problem, whatever it is, whether it's a business slowdown or a difficult supplier or whatever, he is just a *bear*... to live with until he has worked it out.... If we say, 'What is the problem?,' he will say, 'What do you mean, what is the problem?' (p. 99)

Men who overemphasize the work role sometimes fall prey to what are commonly referred to as workaholism or work addiction. Current definitions of a *workaholic* define it as a person who invests more time and energy in work than is required; the key being the combination of both time and energy, not simply number of hours (Andreassen, 2014). Men and women are equally likely to be workaholics (Taris, van Beek, & Schaufeli, 2012), and thus put themselves at risk for a number of negative outcomes. Physically, they tend to experience high levels of physical symptoms of stress, such as irritability and high blood pressure, as well as insomnia and chronic fatigue. Psychologically, they often report higher levels of work-family conflict and relatively poorer functioning in non-work settings (Andreassen, 2014). The work-family conflict is likely the result of decreased time with family as well as their irritability and poorer functioning in non-work settings. Workaholism is more common in some fields than others. Men dramatically outnumber women as construction workers, which has some of the highest rates of workaholism. Yet relatively low rates are found among male-dominated law enforcement and the military. Blue-collar or manual labor jobs tend to have higher rates of workaholism than pink-collar (i.e., secretarial) or white-collar (professional) positions (Taris, van Beek, & Schaufeli, 2012). Box 10.1 describes the relationship of a workaholic and his family.

Box 10.1
The Blue Collar Workaholic

A therapist related the story of a woman who "dragged" her husband into marital therapy under threat of divorce. He was an automobile mechanic who worked a 40-hour per week job and had a free-lance business in his home garage on evenings and weekends. His side business provided more than enough work and a good deal of money, but he rarely spent more than a few minutes with his wife or family before the phone would ring or someone would pull into the driveway in need of repairs.

When the therapist asked him why he worked such long hours, the man said, "I don't want to retire at 65 like my father; I'm going to retire at 45." It was clear that this man was chasing a quantifiable and probably mythical definition of success, to the detriment of his family. One has to question the rationality of extreme overwork toward reaching a goal of not working.

A singular striving for success is often incompatible with the formation of relationships. We have already pointed out the negative aspects of the success-masculinity connection on the family. This connection also inhibits the formation of close relationships with other men.

Ochberg (1988) describes an interesting pair of role demands on a group of career men he interviewed. He investigated aspects of these men's relationships with male coworkers and concluded that men are encouraged to present the *illusion* that they are personal with one another while at the same time maintaining limits. Friendliness is expected, but men who get too close to one another are seen as losing control of their situations. According to Ochberg, "Striking this balance between detachment and the appearance of friendliness is actually more of a strain than being either genuinely personal or genuinely indifferent" (p. 11). Although most of the men Ochberg interviewed reported a desire for personal relationships with their colleagues, they work hard to resist it because the man who is a colleague today may be a subordinate tomorrow, and they believe it to be difficult to discipline or give orders to a friend. Ochberg reports studies indicating that "successful executives show that they have an unusual ability to cultivate friendships with those who are ahead of them on the corporate ladder, and disentangle themselves from attachments to people who once were their peers, but whom they have since left behind" (p. 11). Male-male friendships are discussed further in Chapter Eight.

A second concern focuses on men's health. The competitive, pressure-packed nature of masculine occupational striving is associated with a wide variety of physical and mental health problems such as heart disease, back pain, alcoholism, and suicide (Courtenay, 2011). Men are much more likely than women to work in hazardous environments, and an overwhelming proportion of workplace injuries and deaths involve male victims (National Center for Health Statistics, 2008). When they are hurt, men are less likely than women to seek medical help, as described in Chapter Fourteen (Courtenay, 2011).

Third, a man's sense of security may be challenged through perpetual competition and the insecurity it can create. A man who endorses current masculine norms can prove his masculinity by succeeding in work and being "number one." However, a single success, no matter how significant, does not last. There is always another goal to set and accomplish. If a man is fortunate enough to become "number one" at something, he can only remain in this position by continuing to compete with and vanquish his opponents. He must continue to prove and re-prove his position, in effect re-proving his masculinity on a regular basis. Ultimately, feeling satisfied becomes a dangerous feeling, because it may inhibit further competition. In the world of sports (the leading masculine metaphor for work), we hear sportscasters lauding players and coaches who can never be satisfied. We hear athletes talking about next year's season less than an hour after they have won the championship!

Job or career success is often dependent upon factors that are beyond the man's control, and perhaps his understanding. The mainstream cultural belief in the United States that working hard enough always brings success may be a reality for the talented and privileged, but the "average Joe" depends at least partly on opportunity and the vicissitudes of the market. The combination of subscribing to the myth and equating economic success with masculinity leaves the average man feeling powerless and thus emasculated.

Equating masculinity with vocational accomplishment has especially damaging effects on men who encounter significant barriers to meaningful employment. In many poor segments of society, few opportunities for work, education, or training are available, yet the men in these localities still feel pressure to prove their manhood, with money being one way to do so. Is it any wonder that some of these men turn to illegal activities such as drug dealing (Kiselica & Kiselica, 2014; Ogbu, 1994; Majors & Billson, 1992)? They may see such activities as their only opportunity to validate their masculinity through economic success. The high rates of incarceration, violence, and drug use among economically disadvantaged men of color are the result of the oppressive nature of mainstream culture in the United States, which imparts its masculine values to these men while at the same time blocking most avenues for them to participate in the dream of occupational success (Nellis, 2016).

Employed men who lose their jobs through economic downturn, injury, or even retirement face a battle to retain their masculine self esteem. Mirra Kamarovsky (1940/1971) published a classic study of 59 unemployed men and their families. Many of these men were ridiculed, blamed, and rejected by their families for failing to fulfill the provider role. They also tended to blame themselves and to suffer from depressive symptoms. Retirement presents a difficult transition for many men, as they must leave the activity through which they have defined themselves for most of their lives. Box 10.2 depicts the tragic story of an unsuccessful man at retirement.

As we pointed out in Chapter Six, early masculine socialization shapes behavior, but ongoing social contingencies maintain it. Successful men have their masculinity affirmed frequently across many social settings while less than successful men are socially devalued. Men with high levels of wealth and occupational status are defined as the most desirable partners for dating and marriage (Schmitt, 2005). It is not surprising that men learn to connect sexuality with money. A business deal is sometimes referred to as "getting into bed with" the partner. In a classic article on work and masculinity, Gould (1974) discussed the ways in which women have been taught to "catch" the most successful men, an idea that also appears in some evolutionary theories (Buss, 1995).

Fourth, work may lead a man to sacrifice important aspects of himself. A man who wishes to "work his way up" in an organization may have to subordinate his individuality to the wishes of his superiors. Of course, nearly everyone alters their behavior to adapt to social situations, so it is a matter of degree. To what extent are men willing to move against their personalities and values to "fit in" at work?

> **Box 10.2**
> **Death of a Salesman**
>
> Arthur Miller's classic (1949) play, *Death of a Salesman*, is a brilliantly insightful examination of the relationships among masculinity, work, and family. Willy Loman, the lead character, is a salesman in his sixties. His job skills are deteriorating, and thus his value to his employer is decreasing rapidly.
>
> Because Willy is relatively poor, and because his self-esteem is almost wholly invested in his work identity, he is suffering emotionally. He is a traditional man who refuses to admit vulnerability, and so he tries to delude himself into believing that the best is yet to come. He frequently fantasizes about his brother Ben, a financially successful and adventurous man who reminds Willy of the differences between the brothers' wealth: "When I was seventeen I walked into the jungle, and when I was twenty-one I walked out. And by God I was rich."
>
> Willy Loman wholly subscribes to the value that wealth equals masculinity and self-worth. Underneath, he has the painful feeling that he has not been courageous or industrious enough. He says, "The world is an oyster, but you don't crack it open on a mattress." To make matters worse, Willy's two sons, Biff and Happy, are also unsuccessful. Because Willy cannot deal directly with his feeling of failure, he deals with it indirectly through his sons, alternately berating them for their irresponsibility and pumping them up with unrealistic dreams of instant success. Biff occasionally tries to fight through his father's denial, but the effect is to flood Willy with overwhelming pain.
>
> Willy's feelings of emasculation and depression peak in intensity when he loses his job and can no longer deny that his sons are also not on the path to success. He takes the provider role so seriously that he contemplates suicide so that he can bequeath $20,000 (a huge sum of money in the 1940s) in insurance money to his family. In an imaginary conversation with Ben, Willy says, "A man can't go out the way he came in, Ben, a man has got to add up to something." Willy has come to feel that he has only added up to an insurance policy, and thus that he is worth more dead than alive.
>
> Because of his sense of loss and hopelessness, his feelings of failure as a father and worker, and his ardent desire to live up to the masculine ideal of the good provider, Willy finally commits suicide by intentionally crashing his car. Ironically, he does so during the same week that the final payment on the family house is made, a joyous occasion for most families. In some ways, Willy was a success: he provided an acceptable standard of living for years, and purchased a house "free and clear." But traditional standards of masculine success demand much more, and Willy did not feel free or clear. *Death of a Salesman* details the tragedy of a man who would rather die than re-define his masculinity.

Many business organizations expect gender stereotypical behavior from men, and men who do not display such behavior often forfeit the opportunity for advancement. Therefore, the man who refuses to act like "one of the boys" may not succeed, regardless of his level of competence. If he plays the masculine role to gain approval, he may experience a high level of gender role strain. In corporate culture, a large part of this strain is based in the organization's encouragement for men to emphasize the work role over the family role (Bowen & Orthner, 1991).

The extent to which a man will compromise his behavior to fit the work environment involves a decision that each individual must make. Is he willing to engage in derogatory humor, wear ties and white dress shirts, and/or lie to customers? Because men are socialized against introspective skills, they may have difficulty in accessing the emotional responses that might inform their decision-making. Alternately, some men may subordinate their own ethics to fulfill the breadwinner role.

Crites and Fitzgerald (1978) described the constriction of human qualities to meet organizational demand as a "straitjacket of success" that requires the man to "be able to obey rules and follow orders, regardless of how silly and unnecessary they may seem... to control and hide true feelings when faced with an incompetent superior... [to be] intensely loyal to an employer, yet able to transfer that loyalty when you change jobs." These prescriptions produce men who are "expedient, shallow, conforming but competitive, and ultimately ruthless" (p. 44).

According to humanistic theory, extreme conformity to outside demands leaves one feeling alienated and out of touch with the self-actualizing tendency. The man may sacrifice some of his human potential to strive for external success. This conflict is common among working men (Cournoyer & Mahalik, 1995; O'Neil, 1981a, 1981b, 2013).

WORKING IN THE MODERN WORLD

The world of work in the postindustrial world has undergone many changes in recent years. There are increases in women's participation in nearly every segment of the paid labor force, and these increases are accompanied by slight decreases in men's participation. Several men's issues have arisen in response to these changes.

Probably the most important development in the work arena for men is that financial providing can no longer be considered exclusively masculine. In modern societies, most men have not gained much satisfaction from their work. They validated their masculinity through the *results* of their work: money and providing. In some large cities in the United States, unmarried childless women in their twenties earn more than their unmarried childless male peers (Sharockman, 2014). As women continue to make gains in the amount they earn as a group, men who hold antifeminine ideologies will often have to find masculine validation elsewhere, although many do not know where to turn. As Jesse Bernard wrote in 1981, "The good-provider role may be on its way out, but its legitimate successor has not yet appeared on the scene" (p. 12); three decades later, the issue persists. Men who have been marginalized (e.g., men of color and older men) have experienced the greatest difficulty living up to the breadwinner role demand (Wilkie, 1991). There is a small but positive movement toward men's gender-egalitarian beliefs as a result of a decreasing emphasis on the provider role (Zuo, 1997).

Male-Female Relationships in the Workplace

The greater rates of women's employment over the last few decades as well as their greater access to higher education, combined with changes in the workplace that have diminished the importance of physical strength and increased the importance of "people skills," has increased the likelihood that men and women will work together either as peers or with a female manager. The masculine norms of dominance and antifemininity can cause men difficulty when their work peers, superiors, or subordinates are women. Gender-typed men tend to react to a woman in a "man's job" with some mixture of anger, fear, confusion, and anxiety (Astrachan, 1992; Eisler, 1995) and the challenges of having a female supervisor appears in at least one measure of masculine role stress (Eisler & Skidmore, 1987). The greater endorsement of egalitarian gender beliefs by younger generations (Twenge, 1997a) provides some reason to believe this ideology has diminished in recent years. The masculine view of woman as underling and sex object is dysfunctional in a number of increasingly common work situations, a few of which are detailed below:

- When a man and woman are required to work together cooperatively, unreasonable dominance by the man is damaging to employee relationships and the quality of the work.
- When a man and a woman are competing for promotion, he may feel emasculated if she wins and claim that she got the job because she's a woman, not because she's better qualified.
- When organizations engage in hiring, promotion, and pay increase decisions in which they discriminate against women, individuals are victimized and organizations suffer emotional distress, lowered productivity, and sometimes economic hardships brought on by litigation or job action.
- When a man's supervisor is a woman, he may be uncooperative, anxious, resentful, or disrespectful if he endorses current masculine norms (Eisler, 1995). These behaviors and attitudes may result in poorer job performance and thus harm the organization. As a group, men tend to have negative attitudes toward female managers (Schein, 2001), especially when the manager acts in a stereotypically masculine way (Rudman & Glick, 2001).

Sexual harassment in the workplace is pervasive (Holland & Cortina, 2013; Rospenda, Richman, & Shannon, 2009). The man who sexually objectifies women at work and acts on this attitude is engaging in an illegal act, harming other human beings and the organization, and sometimes damaging his potential for vocational success.

Sexual Harassment

In October of 1991, a United States Senate committee held hearings on the confirmation of Judge Clarence Thomas to the Supreme Court. Anita Hill, a University of Oklahoma law professor, testified that Thomas had pressured her for dates and made frequent lewd comments in the workplace while he was her supervisor in the early 1980's. Hill's report of Thomas' behavior and the reactions to them by the all-male Senate Judiciary Committee elevated public awareness of sexual harassment (Jaschik-Herman & Fisk, 1995). In 1992, several women reported similar behaviors by Oregon Senator Bob Packwood (who resigned because of the scandal) (Taylor, 1995), and the allegations of sexual harassment by Paula Jones against President Bill Clinton (along with his "consensual" sexual affair with Monica Lewinsky) cast a pall on his entire presidency (1993–2000). In the 1990s, Mitsubishi Motors lost two harassment lawsuits related to inappropriate behavior at its plant in Normal, Illinois. While the Equal Employment Opportunity Commission (EEOC) was investigating, Mitsubishi officials shut down the plant for a day, rented 59 buses, and transported 2500 employees on a six-hour bus ride to Chicago to protest at the EEOC building. The costs of the plant shutdown and trip were estimated at $21 million (Grimsley & Brown, 1996). Mitsubishi eventually settled two lawsuits for a total of $43.5 million, a record amount for a sexual harassment suit, and undertook a vigorous corporate program to correct sexual harassment in the workplace (Grimsley, 1998; Grimsley & Swoboda, 1997).

Things have changed, at least a little, since the beginning of the twenty first century. In 2007, former New York Knicks executive Anucha Browne Sanders won an $11.6 million judgment against Madison Square Garden because she was fired from her job for refusing the sexual advances of then-coach Isiah Thomas (ESPN, 2007). As we write this edition of the textbook in late 2017, the #MeToo movement and public allegations of sexual harassment and assault have caused a number of men to lose their jobs, some at companies they founded (i.e., Harvey Weinstein, Matt Lauer, Charlie Rose).

The Equal Employment Opportunity Commission (EEOC) (1980) defines sexual harassment as:

> Unwelcome sexual advances, requests for sexual favors and other verbal or physical conduct of a sexual nature when submission to such conduct is made either explicitly or implicitly a term or condition of an individual's employment; submission or rejection of such conduct by an individual is used as the basis for employment decisions affecting the individual; or such conduct has the purpose or effect of unreasonably interfering with an individual's work performance or creating an intimidating, hostile, or offensive working environment. (p. 25024)

For a behavior to be considered sexual harassment, it must meet the following criteria. First, it must be sexual or gender-focused. For example, repeated requests for dates are sexual in nature; frequent derogatory comments about women or men are gender-focused. Second, it must be unwanted. Conduct is sexually harassing if the person who is the target of the sexual behavior feels uncomfortable, attacked, offended, or intimidated. If the person enjoys or is not bothered by sexual comments, flirting, or requests for romantic attention, then there is no sexual harassment in these behaviors (although they may still be viewed as unprofessional). Third, the conduct must occur in the workplace.

In this case, "workplace" is broadly defined. If someone is having a drink at a bar after work and a co-worker approaches him or her with unwanted sexual attention, then we can reasonably assume that the negative impact of this conduct will not just go away when the person returns to work the next day. Although the behavior has not occurred in the physical workplace, it has nonetheless influenced and potentially changed behavior in the workplace.

There are two types of sexual harassment. **Quid pro quo** ("this for that") sexual harassment involves an attempt to gain sexual cooperation through threats of negative job-related consequences and/or promises of positive ones. It is a proposed exchange of influence in return for sex. This category includes *sexual extortion* (e.g., "Have sex with me or I'll fire you") and *sexual bribery* (e.g., "Have sex with me and I'll give you a raise"). Threats can be implicit or explicit. A supervisor can say, "You'll do well in your career if you know how to 'play ball,' if you know what I mean," and this statement can be construed as a kind of offer.

Quid pro quo harassment need happen only once to be **actionable**, defined as a violation of corporate policy or law that can result in a formal response. In fact, sometimes officials can also bring criminal charges under laws that cover bribery, extortion, or sexual assault. This type of harassment is fairly cut-and-dried—when *quid pro quo* harassment results in a formal complaint, the dispute usually centers on whether or not the behavior actually occurred, not whether or not it was harassing.

Hostile environment sexual harassment involves unwelcome and offensive, pervasive and frequent sex-related verbal and/or physical behavior that has the effect of creating discomfort in the working environment. Examples include unwanted touching of a sexual nature, sexually-oriented jokes and conversations, asking about sexual experiences, repeated pressure for dates, staring at a person's body, making derogatory gender-related comments, displaying pornographic pictures in the workplace, and a variety of other behaviors.

In contrast to *quid pro quo* harassment, which needs to happen only once to be actionable, hostile environment harassment must be severe, persistent, and/or pervasive to be actionable. One of the most frequent questions from male employees to sexual harassment prevention trainers is, "What if I slip up and say something inappropriate? Will I lose my job and ruin my career?" They seem to have a fear that the "sexual harassment police" will come around the corner and arrest them if they exhibit even a momentary lapse of discretion. Nothing could be further from the truth. The word "environment" within the phrase "hostile environment" means that behavior must have the effect of coloring a person's entire experience within the workplace to sustain a policy action or legal charge. At the same time, making an inappropriate sexual comment violates the *principle* of workplace respect that underlies sexual harassment policies, and so the person who "slips" would do well to apologize to anyone he or she has offended and make efforts to avoid repeating the behavior.

Legally, sexual harassment law is subsumed under Title VII of the Civil Rights Act of 1964 and the Uniform Code of Military Justice (UCMJ) that forbid discrimination in employment based on sex (and a variety of other characteristics such as race and religion). The United States Supreme Court has upheld the right of individuals to protection from same-sex sexual harassment (Biskupic, 1998). A campus is a student's workplace, and Title IX of the Education Amendments of 1972 entitles all students to a harassment-free environment. This right extends to protection from the unwanted sexual attention from faculty, administrators, staff, other students, vendors, visitors, and any person who might potentially interfere with the student's learning environment. It also extends to travel away from the campus on school-sanctioned business such as athletic teams' games on other campuses, interns' work at off-campus sites, and social media. Schools and employers are legally required to take all reasonable steps to prevent sexual harassment and to provide a swift remedy when given notice of its occurrence. They face legal liability when they knew or should have known that sexual harassment was occurring, yet took inadequate steps to deal with it.

Workplace sexual harassment has been fairly common. In the United States, the Equal Employment Opportunity Commission (EEOC) and Federal Employment Protection Agencies received an average of about 12,000 new complaints per year in the 2010s, approximately 15 percent of which come from men, a decrease from the 15,000 new complaints filed annually in the late 1990s (EEOC, undated). More than 50 percent of women and 40 percent of men reported being harassed at some point in the most recent year, and one sample of women reported a rate of nearly 80 percent (Holland & Cortina, 2013; Rospenda et al., 2009). Women who work in "traditionally male" blue-collar fields (e.g., construction or industrial work) and women in the military are especially likely to experience sexual harassment (Sandler & Shoop, 1997; Saunders & Easteal, 2013; Stockdale & Bhattacharya, 2009; Willness, Steel, & Lee, 2007).

The impact of sexual harassment on victims is enormous and affects both their jobs and mental health. Victims typically report a decrease in job satisfaction, with the focus primarily on co-workers and supervisors and not as much on the work itself. Victims' commitment to their employers, work performance, and productivity also suffer, and they often quit their jobs (e.g., Raver & Gelfand, 2005; review by Willness, Steel, & Lee, 2007). As such, sexual harassment directly affects a company's performance by decreasing workers' effectiveness and productivity while also increasing turnover. It can also have a direct cost; businesses pay approximately $50 million per year in cases settled with the EEOC (EEOC, undated). Cases in which an employee sues their employer are not included in this estimate, and as we noted earlier, Mitsubishi paid approximately $43.5 million to settle two cases, close to the same amount as all cases settled with the EEOC. In the United States federal government alone, sexual harassment is estimated to cost $135 million annually (Foote & Goodman-Delahunty, 2004).

Victims typically report general declines in their mental health, often indicated by greater rates of depression and/or anxiety. They also report somewhat lower levels of life satisfaction (Willness et al., 2007). Masculinity directs men to be invulnerable, not admit weakness, and avoid help seeking, perhaps the reason why male victims may be more likely to drink to the point of intoxication but report no changes in their mental health statuses (Rospenda, Richman, & Shannon, 2009). Compared with women who were frequently sexually harassed, men with similar experiences were more than ten times less likely to seek mental health services (Shannon, Rospenda, & Richman, 2007).

In a large-scale study, researchers found that most harassers are male: 95 percent of female victims and 22 percent of male victims said that they had been harassed exclusively by males (Tangri, Burt, & Johnson, 1982). Men who report high gender role conflict or subscribe to masculine ideologies are more likely than other men to harass (Kearney, Rochlen, & King, 2004; Wade & Brittan-Powell, 2001). This study lends support to Joseph Pleck's (1981a) hypothesis that cultural changes in gender roles, as well as witnessing individuals violate the "old" roles, leads some men to overconform to gender roles. Thus the sex difference in perpetrating harassment is tied to various aspects of masculinity.

Sexual harassment depends on whether or not the target of the behavior experiences the conduct as offensive. This "eye of the beholder" criterion has left many men confused about what they can and cannot do and say in the workplace. It is clear to most people that saying, "Have sex with me or you're fired" to a subordinate constitutes an illegal act, but most sexual harassment is not so blatant. Many men are wondering, at what point does "normal" flirting, sexual discussion, or complimenting cross the line into harassment? Can a man say, "Let's go have a drink after work," "How are things going with your boyfriend?" "You look especially good today," or "I think you have nice legs?"

We see a gender role-related problem in the mere understanding of the behavior. Most men are raised with the sense that rules should be clear and unambiguous. Sports, that basic training ground for masculinity, have clear, rigid rules. "Guidelines" like those established by the EEOC, tend to make conventionally-gendered men uncomfortable.

More importantly, the "eye of the beholder" definition means that men have to make judgments about what another person is feeling. As we have already discussed, many have little experience with this sort of interpersonal orientation. Not surprisingly, although men (especially traditionally masculine ones) are much less likely to perceive sexual harassment than women (Fitzgerald, 1993), it may be possible to use educational interventions to make men more sensitive to the problem (Kearney, Rochlen, & King, 2004). Both men and women who hold traditional gender beliefs often react to sexual harassment policies and training with resistance (Tinkler, 2013).

Other aspects of the masculine gender role contribute to a sexual harassment proclivity. The view of women as subservient sexual objects is a primary one. Men who see women as sexual objects first and human beings (or coworkers) second, are at greater risk for committing harassment. The sense that one has to be dominant to be a man and generally negative attitudes toward women (Pryor, 1987; Robinson & Schwartz, 2004) are associated with higher likelihood of sexual harassment. These behaviors are embedded within an abuse of power, most often perpetrated by people with high status in an organization against subordinates (Basow, 1992). In speaking of verbal harassment on the street (which does not amount to workplace sexual harassment, but has the same kinds of emotional effects), Benard and Schlaffer (1997) described the issue of sexually-based harassing behavior and power: "Whether you wear a slit skirt or are covered from head to foot in black chador (the garb of Muslim and Hindu women who are only allowed to have their eyes uncovered in public), the message is not that you are attractive enough to make a man lose his self-control but that the public realm belongs to him and you are there by his permission as long as you follow his rules and as long as you remember your place" (p. 396).

The traditional roles of man as sexual initiator and woman as sexual gatekeeper also set the stage for sexual harassment. Men who subscribe to the belief that sexual activity is a matter of power and conquest believe that they must persistently pressure women, and the workplace provides opportunities to do so. Men who hold adversarial sexual beliefs—that sexual relationships are a matter of exploitation and manipulation—are more likely than other men to harass. Foote and Goodman-Delahunty (2004) described three types of male harassers:

- *Misperceiving harassers* seek sexual relationships and believe that the workplace is an appropriate location for doing so. They misconstrue women's friendliness or dress as invitations for sexual behavior and also tend to hold the belief that relationships between men and women are adversarial and aggressive.
- *Exploitive harassers* associate sexuality with social power and believe that women enjoy being dominated by men. When in positions of organizational power, they use provocative sexual behavior to intimidate women, and they also tend to subscribe to the beliefs that women invite rape by the way they dress or that women like being raped.
- *Misogynistic harassers* hold hostile attitudes toward women and express these attitudes through displays of pornography, derogatory language in reference to women, denigration of women's abilities, and sometimes direct sexual taunting of women.

These characteristics of sexual harassers are not unlike those of acquaintance rapists. Again we find evidence that underlying masculine inadequacy may be related to damaging others and perhaps the self. Sexual harassment is a men's issue, and it is intertwined with other issues involving men's power, emotionality, sexuality, relationships, antifemininity, and gendered self-definition.

As with all gendered victimizing behaviors, sexual harassment takes place within a context of patriarchal male dominance. One of us (C. K.) was struck by the expectation of male sexual privilege when an older colleague told him that when he had just finished graduate school and arrived on campus as a new assistant professor, the college president invited all new faculty members to his house for a welcoming party, and remarked, "Professor, I see that you are a single man. Many of our male faculty members have found their wives from among our student body—I hope you will be as fortunate." Thus, the president not only condoned sexual relationships between people of vastly different power levels on the campus, but actually encouraged them.

There is good evidence that the risk of sexual harassment is greater for both women and men who violate traditional gender standards than for those who do not (Stockdale & Bhattacharya, 2009). Therefore, sexual harassment is an organizational practice that polices the boundaries of acceptable gendered behavior, and thus ending restrictive gender norms is a key step toward ending the practice. The implementation of organizational policies and procedures that clearly define and prohibit sexual harassment are also a particularly effective way to reduce it (Willness et al., 2007).

Solutions to the problem of sexual harassment include education, prevention programs, legal and government policy changes, and effective efforts to hold perpetrators responsible for their actions. Organizations must make strong statements that they will not tolerate the behavior and then follow through with effective institutional policies and strategies (Willness et al., 2007). Communicating respect for women in the structures and activities of the organization will be helpful in working against the attitudinal undercurrent of the problem. In the big picture, sexual harassment is an agent of social control of women by men (Fitzgerald, 1993), and thus efforts to end it also involve social change in the gender and the structure of patriarchy, as well as in the lives of individual men.

SUMMARY

Work has long been central to definitions of manhood and masculinity. Indeed, many men center their identities on their work and their ability to support their family financially. This arrangement is a relatively recent historical phenomenon, although not all men have equal access to employment, consistent with the ideas of within-group differences, masculinities, and power we have previously discussed.

Masculine norms influence men's experience of work and lives in a range of ways. This can be advantageous to men, especially for men who have access to the cultural resources and patriarchal benefits of masculinity. At the same time, adherence to these norms can cause a range of problems for a man and those to whom he is closely connected. Greater adherence to masculine norms, particularly the combination of dominance and anti-femininity, can also lead to problems in the workplace.

1. Work has defined men's identities throughout history, and the masculine socialization process is strongly oriented toward producing workers. The character of work and the sexual division of labor has changed throughout human history.
2. The man-as-provider, woman-as-homemaker arrangement was a temporary transition from agricultural to industrial societies. It does not characterize most of human history, and it is changing. Similarly to the transition to single-earner families, the return to co-provider families is a result of economic exigencies. Women's participation as full economic partners is associated with gender egalitarian values. Sex segregation is associated with the oppression of women.
3. As a consequence of industrial demands, most men were effectively removed from their homes and often specialized in some small part of the production process. As a result, they were alienated from both their work and their families, and they had to rely on the financial outcome of work for the validation of masculinity. The provider role requires sacrifice and emotional restrictiveness. These aspects of masculinity continue to live on in many men.
4. The masculine values of task orientation, competition, and independence are conducive to a wide variety of work settings. Boys' sports and play, with their emphasis on outcome and quantification, socialize males toward work.
5. The advantages of this socialization for men are social status, opportunity, and work satisfaction, but many men who lose jobs or do not succeed feel emasculated. Even men who do well at work may encounter difficulties in relating to family and coworkers, maintaining physical and mental health, dealing with the pressures of competition, and coping with gender role strain.
6. Sexual harassment is pervasive in the workplace, and most perpetrators are men. This problem is costly in both human and financial terms, and it is tied to masculine issues of power and sexual privilege. Solutions to the problem involve a wide range of social, legal, organizational, and personal changes.
7. Changes in economic and social conditions have led to work changes for families. Men who adhere to gender-typed attitudes may encounter significant problems at work and at home as they find it necessary to adjust to newer, more egalitarian gender roles. Issues around the loss of the masculine breadwinner role, sexual harassment, and the sharing of domestic duties have come to the fore. Although the result is a more complicated life for working men, the benefits may outweigh the costs, as many men are expanding their senses of self beyond their occupational roles.

GLOSSARY

Husbandry: The cultivation of land and livestock, as well as respect for nature.

Primogeniture: The patriarchal arrangement by which the oldest sons inherited property from their fathers and passed it on to their eldest sons.

Objectification: The denial of the person's humanness (and treatment of that person as a thing or object).

Male (or female) dominated field: A field of employment in which at least 60 percent of its work force is male (or female).

Traditionally male fields: The building trades (construction, electrical, plumbing, carpentry) as well as the STEM fields (science, technology, engineering, and mathematical fields).

Traditionally female fields: Human services (e.g., childcare, nursing), teaching, and food service, as well as secretarial/reception type jobs (regardless of industry).

Glass escalator: The tendency to promote men instead of, or more quickly than, women, even in traditionally female fields.

Jobs: Labor done solely for economic survival.

Careers: Reimbursable means of expressing an important part of the self.

Workaholic: A person who invests more time and energy in work than is required.

Quid pro quo ("this for that") sexual harassment: Involves an attempt to gain sexual cooperation through threats of negative job-related consequences and/or promises of positive ones. It is a proposed exchange of influence in return for sex.

Sexual extortion: Threatening someone with adverse consequences (e.g., firing) if they do not engage in sexual activities.

Sexual bribery: Offering a bribe (e.g., money, promotion) in return for sexual activities.

Actionable: A violation of corporate policy or law that can result in a formal response.

Hostile environment sexual harassment: Unwelcome and offensive, pervasive and frequent sex-related verbal and/or physical behavior that has the effect of creating discomfort in the working environment.

Misperceiving harassers: Sexual harassers who seek sexual relationships and believe that the workplace is an appropriate location for doing so.

Exploitive harassers: Sexual harassers who associate sexuality with social power and believe that women enjoy being dominated by men.

Misogynistic harassers: Sexual harassers who hold hostile attitudes toward women.

Chapter Twelve

Boys Will Be Boys: Men and Violence

In the United States, violence is understood to be primarily an activity for men. As discussed in Chapter 1, it is part of the singular, hegemonic definition of masculinity. On screen, *action movies*—a broad term that includes films about superheroes, war, westerns, some crime films, and some science-fiction and fantasy films—the protagonist and antagonist are almost always men. "Contact sports" such as football and ice hockey are sufficiently violent that professional leagues have rules specifically designed to minimize the negative consequences of concussions (and thus, brain damage); professional and amateur women's leagues do not allow the types of contact that are most likely to cause such injuries. Engagement with these films and sporting events, through participation, viewing, and attendance, is also dominated by males. Boys and men play violent video games at higher rates than women, including "first person shooters."

The idea that violence is a male-oriented activity is not limited to entertainment and fiction. The United States armed forces consist primarily of men, and debates about women's ability to be part of armed units, be part of front line combat activities, and gain admission to the most elite training and fighting forces (e.g., Navy Seals, Army Rangers) has been a point of contention for several decades. Crime statistics, which we'll detail later in this chapter, also demonstrate that perpetration of violent crimes, including homicide and rape, are also male-dominated activities. Moreover, men constitute the majority of the victims of such violence, suffering potentially life-changing injuries and death through war and as the victims of some criminal activities, with sports "only" putting boys and men at risk for life-changing injuries (but rarely death).

Throughout the chapter, we focus primarily on *physical aggression*, defined as acts of violence that attempt to or cause physical harm to another person. Physical aggression includes assault (fighting), homicide (murder), and rape. We do not address *relational aggression*, which refers to efforts to harm a person's friendships or reputation, or *violence to property*, which includes theft and graffiti (Pepler & Slaby, 1994; FBI, 2013b; Wiseman, 2002). We make specific comments about interpersonal violence and rape throughout the chapter. ***Interpersonal violence (IPV)*** refers to assault against a romantic relationship or marital partner, and was previously known as "domestic violence." ***Rape*** has long been defined as sexual penetration without consent; in the last decade, it also began to include a male who was "forced to penetrate" someone without the male's consent (FBI, 2016). Rape is one type of ***sexual assault***, a broad term that includes any form of nonconsensual touching of areas of the body that are associated with sexuality (Kilmartin & Allison, 2007).

In this chapter, we examine the connections between men, masculinity, and violence in detail. We begin with discussion of differences based on gender, ethnicity, and race. We then address ways that violence is directly and indirectly embedded within the singular, hegemonic definition of masculinity before discussing individual-level factors that increase or decrease the likelihood that any particular man will be violent as well as describing types of men who are more likely to be violent. This is followed by a brief discussion of biological and social factors that facilitate (but do not necessarily *cause*) violence, as well as a brief review of some interventions that have been designed to reduce men's violence. We note that the research reviewed here comes from two research traditions that have few links between them: a general approach to violence that rarely considers gender roles, and a feminist approach that emphasizes gender roles but has focused primarily on men's violence toward women in the forms of interpersonal violence and rape (Kilmartin & McDermott, 2016; Piquero, 2015). We provide a brief discussion of the effects of war and sexual assault on men in Chapter Thirteen.

Differences Based on Sex and Race

Male-female differences in physical aggression do *not* appear prior to preschool age. Once differences appear, research consistently demonstrates that males demonstrate notably higher levels of physical aggression and females demonstrated notably higher levels of relational aggression (Loeber & Stouthamer-Loeber, 1998; Pepler & Slaby, 1994). Middle- and high-school aged boys in the United States are more than twice as likely as girls to engage in physical fights, three times as likely to carry a weapon to school, and nearly twice as likely to threaten or injure someone with a weapon (Grunbaum, et. al., 2004). Teenagers who associate with delinquent peers are several times more likely to engage in criminal behaviors than those who do not (Huizinga, Weiher, Espiritu, & Esbensen, 2003).

Most of the data in this section come from analyses that rely on data from the U.S. Department of Justice (DOJ), including sources such as the Federal Bureau of Investigation and the Bureau of Justice Statistics. There are a range of sources that come from police departments (complaints, arrest records), the court system, and jails. These tend to show similar trends regarding male-female and ethnic differences, although the number of individuals (or reports) necessarily differs from one source to the next, as well as from year to year. Some analyses are performed on behalf of the DOJ while others have been conducted by researchers outside the DOJ (FBI, 2016). We note that the crime rate in the United States, including the violent crime rate, fell by approximately half from 1980 to 2008, with much of the change occurring in the late 1990s and early 2000s (Catalano, 2012; Cooper & Smith, 2011).

DOJ statistics reveal that males dramatically outnumber females in reports of who has committed a crime (i.e., is an offender), who has been arrested, who is convicted, and who is jailed (FBI, 2013a, 2016). Males are approximately 2.5 times more likely than females to be arrested or be a known offender (FBI, 2016). For more violent crimes, the numbers become more imbalanced; males committed approximately 90 percent of all homicides in 2011, and this 9:1 ratio is typical in homicide perpetration (Cooper & Smith, 2011; FBI, 2013a). Men age 18 to 24 are most likely to commit homicide, with the number varying year to year and a notable spike in the homicide rate in the United States through the early 1990s. Although boys aged 14 to 17 commit fewer homicides than 18 to 24 year olds, increases and decreases in the murder rate tend to be similar for both groups. By contrast, men aged 25 and older tend to commit fewer homicides and do so at a fairly constant rate from year to year.

Males are also the primary victims of male violence, accounting for approximately 70 percent of victims in 2013 (FBI 2013a); the male-female difference in homicide victims has remained relatively stable over the last several decades (Cooper & Smith, 2011). Thus, most homicide is committed by men against other men (67.8%), followed by men killing women (21.0%), women killing men (9.0%), and women killing women (2.2%) (Cooper & Smith, 2011). The causes and types of relationship between killers and their victims vary reliably with sex. When men kill other men, they are usually acquaintances (more than 50%) or strangers (about 25%) and the killing is often related to drugs or gangs. When men kill women, the victim is typically an intimate partner or otherwise sexually connected to the perpetrator (Cooper & Smith, 2011). The majority of men commit homicide using a firearm, a statistic that applies to almost every context in which data are available (Cooper & Smith, 2011; Petrovsky et al., 2017).

The data also reveal substantial racial and ethnic differences in offending and incarceration. We note that DOJ statistics did not reliably assess racial categories other than "White" and "Black" until approximately 2000, so our discussion is biased toward these two groups. Recall from Chapter 2 that non-Hispanic Whites account for approximately 62 percent of the United States population, while non-Hispanic Blacks account for approximately 12.2 percent of it.

Table 12.1 provides the arrest rates for a range of violent and sexual crimes in 2012 (FBI, 2013B). For all offenses listed, the proportion of Blacks arrested is disproportionately high; the rate for Whites is often proportional to their representation in the general population, but notably lower than expected for murder. Arrest rates are also disproportionately low for Asians.

Table 12.1
Arrests for Violent Crimes by Racial Group, 2012

	Total (#)	White (%)	Black (%)	Native American or Alaskan Native	Asian or Pacific Islander
Total Arrests	9,390,473	69.3	28.1	1.4	1.2
Murder[1]	8,506	48.2	49.4	1.2	1.2
Aggrevated Assault	299,943	62.8	34.1	1.4	1.6
Arson[2]	402,470	58.7	38.5	1.3	1.4
Other Assault	924,839	65.5	31.9	1.5	1.1
Forcible Rape	13,886	65.0	32.5	1.3	1.2
Weapons[3]	114,979	58.2	39.9	0.7	1.3
Victims	4,158,264	72.0	20.8	0.6	1.5

[1]Includes non-negligent manslaughter.
[2]Violent arson with injury to humans; excludes property-only arson.
[3]Unlawful possession or carrying of weapons.

Because most crimes, especially felonies, are committed by men, the values in Table 12.1 are primarily about men, not women. After being arrested, the legal system comes into play, including issues related to the ability to pay for a private lawyer of one's choosing, the ability to plea bargain, the outcomes of a trial, and sentencing decisions. Analyses have repeatedly demonstrated that the White-Black differences expand as boys and men move through the juvenile and adult court systems (Nellis, 2016; Piquero, 2015; Rhodes, Kling, Luallen, & Dyous, 2015). In 2014, the United States imprisoned 932 people for every 100,000 members of the population. Rates varied by race and ethnicity, with non-Hispanic Blacks incarcerated nearly 2.5 times more often than Hispanics and more than six times more than non-Hispanic Whites (3023, 1238, and 478 per 100,000 population, respectively; McDaniel et al. 2013). We note that people convicted of felonies almost never have access to the ballot box while imprisoned and most U.S. states do not allow felons to vote after they have been released (McDaniel et al., 2013).

Incarceration rates in the United States are different than in other countries. In England and Wales (together), the incarceration rate is 150 individuals per 100,000 population, approximately one-sixth of the rate in the United States Further, although Blacks are arrested more often than Whites in England and Wales, the racial disparity does not increase as people move through those nations' justice systems (Ministry of Justice, 2015).

Victims' characteristics also vary with race and ethnicity, with Whites and Blacks over-represented and Asians under-represented (FBI, 2016). Analyses have repeatedly demonstrated that crime is more likely to be *intra-racial*, with offenders and victims of the same race, than *inter-racial*, with offenders and victims of different races (Cooper & Smith, 2011; Morgan, 2017). Recent analyses suggests the intraracial crime rate is approximately 75 percent for both Whites and Blacks, and about 50 percent for Hispanics, and these rates are linked to residential locale. Whites are most likely to experience intraracial crime in rural areas, while Blacks and Hispanics are most likely to experience it in urban areas (although the rate is much higher for Blacks than Hispanics) (Morgan, 2017). Across all racial and ethnic groups, victims are most often ages 18 to 24 (like the perpetrators), with smaller numbers in the 25-and-older or 14 to 17 age ranges (Cooper & Smith, 2011).

Regarding interpersonal violence (IPV), male partners or ex-partners assault more than half a million women in the United States every year (Catalano, 2012). The most common type of wife batterer is violent only in his own home and has little or no problem controlling his aggression elsewhere (Holtzworth-Munroe & Stuart, 1994). Some assessments of interpersonal violence indicate that women use physical violence against their partners as much or even more than men (Straus, 2004; Archer, 2000) because the questions are fairly simplistic (e.g., "Have you done _____ to your partner in the last 30 days?"). Without assessment of the context or differences in the ability to cause harm, statistics using these scales may have little practical meaning because men are usually much less fearful of being harmed by their female partners than vice-versa (Kilmartin & Allison, 2007). Therefore, although female domestic physical aggression is common and should not be ignored, it is male aggression that engenders the highest levels of terror and danger. More than 40 percent of female IPV victims sustain injuries (Arias & Ikeda, 2006).

Males were nearly the only perpetrators of rape prior to a recent change in the definition that allowed women to be charged with "forcing a male to penetrate" (FBI, 2016). In a large study of female Navy recruits, approximately 39 percent reported being the victim of an attempted rape, with 13 percent of male recruits admitting to perpetrating sexual violence (Stander, Merrill, Thomsen, Crouch, & Milner, 2008). As noted earlier, women are more likely than men to be killed by an intimate partner, with approximately 11 percent having experienced violence in the 30 days prior to their death. Jealousy and concerns about another partner play a role in approximately 12 percent of all such deaths, with jealousy a precipitating factor in nearly 20 percent of IPV deaths among Native Americans and Alaska Natives, as well as Hispanics (Petrosky et al., 2017). Federal statistics also indicate that IPV-related deaths rarely occur within the context of some other crime (Petrosky et al., 2017), indicating that these women's deaths are primarily the result of his violence and not, for example, the result of her being killed by police while the couple attempts to commit robbery.

Masculinity and Violence

The willingness to be violent became a central part of United States masculinity during the twentieth century (Hebert, 2002; Rotundo, 1993), as described in Chapter One. Adherence to the hegemonic definition of masculinity has been consistently associated with various aspects of aggression, including the acceptance of violence, a willingness to be violent, and having been violent (Cohn & Zeichner, 2006; Cohn, Zeichner, & Seibert, 2008; Moore & Stuart, 2004). American culture includes the stereotype of the *alpha male*, the animal at the top of the troop's dominance hierarchy, as a bully who attains his status by aggression or the threat of it. Primatologist Franz de Waal (2005) debunked this stereotype by demonstrating that although some alphas fit this description, they usually do not maintain their positions for very long, as other animals will form coalitions and overthrow them. The most successful alphas are what de Waal terms "populists" who keep the peace among the troop by, for instance, breaking up fights and helping with food sharing. The Darwinian "survival of the fittest" is often interpreted as an ability to eliminate the unfit, but the successful alpha's fitness is more in the service of helping with the troop's harmony and survival (de Waal, 2005, 2007).

At various points in the text we have discussed the importance of proving one's masculinity. Violence provides one avenue for doing so, particularly as a response to feeling insufficiently masculine or worthless (Toch, 1992). Broadly speaking, committing verbal or physical violence toward others, including groups that are already disempowered or marginalized, can serve to bolster a man's self-esteem, as long as the man receives support from his friends. (We address peer support for violence later in the chapter.) Several measures of masculinity ideology (MI) specifically include violence as a component (Levant et al., 2007; Mahalik et al., 2003). James O'Neil (2008) reports that gender role conflict is linked to self-reports of violent behavior as well as a variety of violence-encouraging characteristics, including sexually aggressive behaviors, dating violence, hostility toward women, rape myth acceptance, and tolerance for sexual harassment. The singular, hegemonic set of masculine norms we have referred to throughout the text may be particularly useful in understanding male violence because each of these norms supports or encourages violence.

Antifemininity

Women are often viewed as caring, nurturing, compassionate, and vulnerable, the very antitheses of aggression. One hallmark of the "sissy" is an unwillingness to fight. Men may engage in physical aggression because they fear being dominated by another male, which is viewed as feminine.

Antifemininity may also contribute to men's willingness to rape women. Men who adhere to hegemonic views of masculinity (and femininity) view men and women as (sexual) adversaries, and believe that a heterosexual date is a competition in which he attempts to obtain sex and she attempts to obtain affection and/or persuade him to spend money on her. For these men, the woman's refusal to be sexual at the end of the date may be viewed as breaking an unspoken contract or as token resistance (Knight & Sims-Knight, 2013). From a psychodynamic perspective, a man who fears being (seen as) feminine or fears recognizing his own feminine traits may attempt to overpower and control a woman as a means of demonstrating control over women and femininity. His efforts may include derogatory nicknames, misogynist jokes, and other behaviors that disrespect women. One group of researchers found that when ranking military officers allowed others to make demeaning comments or gestures in servicewomen's presence, women under their command were at a 600 percent increased risk of rape than when officers did not tolerate these kinds of behaviors (Sadler, Booth, Cook, & Doebbeling, 2003).

Several anthropologists have observed that social separation of the sexes and the lack of gender-egalitarian attitudes are both linked to perpetration of rape (Lepowsky, 1998; Sanday, 1981, 1996), with one group of scholars concluding that "Rape is probably universal across societies, but its frequency varies considerably. Rape is associated with male fraternal interest groups, warfare, gender antagonism, constraints on women's sexuality, and generally low status of women." (Lalumiere, Harris, Quinsey, & Rice, 2005, p.13). One researcher found that rape was virtually nonexistent in 44 nonpatriarchal societies, and that only 18 percent of cultures are "rape prone," including the United States (Sanday, 1981). At the cultural level, rape may be seen as a symptom of economic and political systems in which women have been rendered relatively powerless by men (Kilmartin & Allison, 2007). Mainstream culture in the United States traditionally encourages men to dominate women, and victimizing a woman with something as emotional and intimate as sex is an extreme form of domination.

Status and Achievement

Aggression can facilitate the hegemonic directives to gain status and demonstrate achievement in two ways, and thus move up the masculine hierarchy (Messner, 1995). First, dominance through aggression is one way of raising status in some male social groups (e.g., gangs). Second, the male who does not succeed often suffers from doubts about his masculinity, and violence is both a way of proving to himself that he is a "real man" as well as a way of venting his anger at having to live up to masculine norms. In football, hockey, boxing, mixed martial arts (MMA), and other "contact" sports, athletes who are known for their violence are often "respected"—or feared—by other players and the coaches responsible for those players; this too is a form of status. Men who are systematically oppressed due to their racial or ethnic background, SES, or enactment of a subordinated form of masculinity may have few options to obtain status or demonstrate achievement within the existing power structures and thus turn to aggression or other forms of illicit activity to achieve their goals (Ogbu, 1991). One example is the rise of (American-)Italian organized crime families during the first half of the twentieth century, when Italians were seen as inferior to many other Whites.

Status concerns may also increase the likelihood of rape. Men can achieve status from male peers via sexual activity, as described in Chapter Eight. There are several potential "options," including having (ever) greater numbers of partners or having sex with partners who are particularly attractive (cf. Flood, 2008; Smiler, 2013). Cultural directives for to "go after what he wants" and "don't take no for an answer" can feed into this decision in problematic ways. Again, we note that endorsement of promiscuity is often strongly related to endorsement of other problematic aspects of masculinity as measured by masculinity ideology scales, including violence (Mahalik et al., 2003; Smiler, 2006b; Walker, Tokar, & Fisher, 2000). For men who seek status through sexual activity and endorse hegemonic norms, there may be substantial reason to impair a woman's cognitive abilities through drinking, drug use, or other methods, to ignore her refusals (especially if the setting is not public), or to use physical intimidation to ensure her "willingness" to have sex.

Inexpressiveness and Independence

The interplay between vulnerability and emotional display rules (see Chapter Seven) highlights the role of context for understanding violence. Anger is one of the few emotions that males are allowed to express at any time and many men convert any type of negative emotional experience such as sadness, fear, or jealousy, into a visible display of anger. Thus, anger is rarely present by itself (Lynch & Kilmartin, 2013) and may be a way to overcome those more vulnerable feelings. Because anger is the feeling that is most likely to precede a fight, some period of raising the ire of both parties may be necessary. One research team found that "macho" males responded to a (simulated) crying baby with less compassion and more anger than other males (Gold, Burke, Prisco, & Willett, 1992). In the real-life analog to this scenario, a man who is unable to soothe the baby and make it stop crying, and who doesn't have another adult in the house who is able to intervene, may hit or choke the baby; this can put the baby at risk for grave physical harm and is a form of child abuse.

Feelings of shame, which occur when an individual recognizes that they have done something wrong and feels badly about having done so, can be particularly hazardous and may be part of the "trigger" for episodes of interpersonal violence. Because shame includes a recognition of wrongdoing, it may signify that a man's externalizing defenses have failed and, if he lacks introspective skills or sufficient self-esteem to defend against these feelings of failure, he may lash out violently in that moment (Jennings & Murphy, 2000; Wexler, 1999).

Adventurousness and Aggressiveness

Masculinity is partly defined by aggressiveness. However, the line between acceptable and unacceptable levels of violence are not always clearly defined, as acknowledged by the sports expression "no blood, no foul." Nor is the line clear regarding the use of violence by the "good guys" in action movies, the police (Hall, Hall, & Perry, 2016), and the national case for various wars (Mann, 2014; Nagel, 1998). Violence, in the form of beatings, hangings, and lynchings, were also key components in the repression of Blacks during slavery and the Jim Crow era (Caldwell-Colbert, Henderson-Daniel, & Dudley-Grant, 2003; Hebert, 2002). Today, the vast majority of Americans view slavery as an injustice perpetrated against Blacks, and about half the country does not support capital punishment (Oliphant, 2016). At the same time, some members of the populace do believe that there are times when violence may be an acceptable solution to the problem.

Engaging in IPV and rape can be facilitated by this belief in aggression as an acceptable form of problem-solving. Patriarchal ideas that men are supposed to rule the family home included the allowance of corporal punishment of their children and wives, as well as the idea that wives were not truly allowed to refuse their husbands' sexual advances (Smiler, 2013). Greater endorsement of masculine ideology and masculine gender role strain have repeatedly been connected to sexualized violence and the endorsement of rape myths (Lisak, 1997; Murnen, Kaluzny, & Wright, 2002; O'Neil, 2008).

Factors Specific to Rape

Mainstream culture in the United States provides support for a set of *rape myths*, defined as erroneous beliefs that excuse the rape of women. Rape myths include the ideas that women secretly want to be raped, say "no" when they mean "yes," and "ask for it" by dressing or acting provocatively (Burt, 1980; Johnson, 1997). Male undergraduates who viewed films depicting rape myths were more likely to subscribe to the myths, less likely to identify with victims, and less likely to agree that rapists deserved punishment (Briere & Malamuth, 1983; Koss, Leonard, Beezley, & Oros, 1985). One need not see an actual rape depicted in media to accept rape myths. The sexual domination of the woman, followed by her giving in and becoming aroused, conveys the same message in milder form. A typical scene is a leading man who forcefully kisses an unwilling woman, who then "melts into his arms" and falls in love with him. Many romantic comedies portray erotic love as the outcome of his repeated demonstration of love—or at least, interest—despite her repeated statements of noninterest. On screen, the man's refusal to accept a woman's "no" often leads to romance; in real life, it would be grounds for a restraining order.

Psychosocial Factors Related to Violence

We have documented ways in which hegemonic masculine norms may contribute to violence, with specific attention to the realms of IPV and rape. We turn now to other social and psychological factors related to the perpetration of violence. We also note that the presence of some, or even all, of these factors in a man's life does not definitively predict that he will become violent at any point in his life. Overcoming such odds is sometimes referred to as *(psychological) resilience* (Luthar, Cicchetti, & Bronwyn, 2000). Accordingly, we review factors that are associated with both greater and lower likelihood to perpetrate violence.

Separation and Connection to Others

We have repeatedly addressed ways the current hegemonic definition of masculinity in the United States emphasizes independence, including encouragement to separate from mother (and women) during childhood (Chodorow, 1978). If a person experiences the self as unconnected to others, he or she can (better) tolerate others' being hurt. One detailed analysis of individuals with an *insecure attachment style*, which is characterized by emotionally unstable connections to others, have a higher likelihood to perceive dangers and threats within relationships, which then leads to anger, hostility, and often, violence (Shaver, Segev, & Mikulincer, 2011).

Similarly, if an individual is objectified or otherwise not accorded the status of being a real person, it is easier to aggress against that individual. The psychological processes are well known, and are part of the reason why militaries often allow and encourage the use of impersonal and derogatory names for their enemies (e.g., "Gerries," "Gooks," "Charlie"). Gender-based violence—rape, domestic violence, and gay bashing—are also fueled by this kind of insensitivity, as there is a strong masculine socialization to view women and gay men as less than human. Some rapists are able to view their victims strictly as objects (Lisak, 1997).

Relative to their gender-egalitarian counterparts, both college men and women who endorse hegemonic gender ideologies tend to minimize the impact of rape on a victim who is described as a current life partner or even an ex-partner (Ben-David & Schneider, 2005). Benevolent sexist attitudes are related to lower sympathy for acquaintance rape victims in general and a tendency to assign blame for the attack to the victim rather than the offender (Abrams, Viki, Masser, & Bohner, 2003).

The converse is also true. Greater connection to others, whether it appears as sensitivity to, identification with, or concern about the pain of others, is related to lower levels of aggression. Boys are often discouraged from learning or showing empathy (see Chapter Seven), while girls are often encouraged to do so. Efforts to encourage homosexual men and women to come out appear to have helped change cultural attitudes from homophobic to accepting (McCormack, 2013; Savin-Williams, 2005; Shilts, 1991). The #BlackLivesMatter movement includes an effort to generate empathy for unarmed victims of police shootings. The #MeToo movement's encouragement to have women share their stories of being sexually assaulted appears to have a similar function.

Externalizing Style

Males are not socialized to "look inside" and think about how they feel. Instead, they are taught to deal with what is "out there" in the world. Therefore, when bad feelings about the self arise, men frequently deal with them in an external way. News reports about mass murderers often point to the loss of a job or loss of a partner as the cause, or at least the "trigger" of the event. These losses may cause him to feel unlovable or worthless. Experiencing this vulnerability threatens his masculinity, so he projects all of his bad feelings onto the ex-partner or ex-coworkers (or ex-boss) and deals with these emotions symbolically by being violent toward them. When women move out of the house or threaten to do so following intimate partner violence, the risk of greater violence, including murder, increases significantly (Stith & McMonigle, 2009). Nearly 90 percent of school shootings are preceded by some type of social rejection (Leary, Kowalski, Smith, & Phillips, 2003) and rather than dealing with the pain of being excluded, the killer—almost always a teen boy or young man—responds with violence. Men who have difficulty understanding vulnerable emotional states and regulating these experiences show a tendency to react aggressively in response to strong feelings (Cohn, Jakupcak, Hildenbrandt, & Zeichner, 2010).

Although men are encouraged to deny and control emotions, the expression of two feelings, anger and lust, is socially condoned. Interestingly, cultural ideologies consider these two emotions to be *completely out of the man's control*. Further, American culture encourages men to *act out* emotion rather than deal with it in other ways (Lynch & Kilmartin, 2013). Expressions such as a "man's gotta do what a man's gotta do" when he gets angry, that a "man's gotta have it" sexually, and that an erect penis "has no conscience" reflect these ideas.

With anger and lust being the only two culturally permissible emotions, it is not surprising that they can become combined with each other. Violence is often sexualized in television, movies, and video games. This is also true for pornography, especially when one considers that there are a limited number of ways for humans to have intercourse but an almost infinite number of ways that humans can be violent toward each other (Picker & Sun, 2008). We also note that the term "fuck" is used to refer to both intercourse and being victimized, reflecting another point of overlap between sexuality and violence.

Again, the converse is true. Men who are better able to tolerate, understand, and process the emotional pain of their loss are much less likely to be violent. Therapists have developed a variety of techniques such as anger management and communication skill development to inhibit explosive urges (Kivel, 1992). Some men who have histories of violence within their homes have achieved full recoveries (Acker, 2013). Thus, the ability to look inside and understand one's own emotional experience help reduce violence.

Attention, Praise, and Status

Simply put, behaviors that are rewarded tend to increase in frequency. Classroom aggression by boys often meets with loud reprimands from the teacher during which all of the action in the room stops, and attention (which has a strong social reward quality) focuses on the boy. Girls' aggression is usually reprimanded more quietly (Maccoby, 1988a, 1988b). Political leaders are often willing to engage in war to affirm masculinity and gain the approval of the populace (Miedzian, 1991) and there is a well-entrenched belief that American voters would not vote a sitting president out of office during a war. Support from male peers, which we described earlier, provides attention, praise, and potentially status (Boswell & Spade, 1996; O'Sullivan, 1991).

Again, the converse is true. The loss of attention, via ostracism and other penalties, can also serve to change attitudes and behavior. The 2017 firings of media personalities such as Richard Ailes, Matt Lauer, and Harvey Weinstein, as well as the subsequent #TimesUp campaign, represent efforts to change the culture of the entertainment industry. Publicly changing norms to support equality and end men's violence against women can also help. Canada's White Ribbon Campaign is a good example of one such program (see Box 12.1).

Drug Use

Some drugs have the effect of reducing the inhibition toward violence. The most notable of these is alcohol. Intoxicated people tend to overestimate threats to the self, to choose aggressive solutions when they are frustrated, and to be more sensitive to social pressure to either increase or to decrease aggression (Gustafson, 1986). Drinking is also a cultural symbol of masculinity (Strate, 1992). However, we must be careful not to imply that alcohol causes violence, as most people who use alcohol are not violent. The relationship between alcohol and violence can be compared to throwing gasoline on a fire. If there is no propensity for aggression, there will be no violence. Rather than causing aggression, alcohol has the effect of exaggerating the pre-existing propensity toward violence. Some illicit drugs, such as methamphetamines and cocaine, also increase the likelihood of violence.

Anabolic-Androgenic Steroids (AAS), a class of drugs that mimic testosterone at the biological level, are illegal but used by some people who are trying to build muscle quickly. One of the side effects of these drugs is a high level of anger that may be accompanied by a "short fuse," colloquially known as **'roid rage**.

Access to Weapons

Gun control probably does not reduce the frequency of physical aggression, but there is strong evidence that it reduces the amount and severity of physi-

> **Box 10.1**
> **The White Ribbon Campaign**
>
> For a week in December, 1991, tens of thousands of Canadian men wore small white ribbons pinned to their clothing on the anniversary of the 1990 "Montreal Massacre," when Mark Lepine murdered 14 women at L'ecole Polytechnique in Montreal, Canada before committing suicide. The White Ribbon Campaign was an effort to get men to show their support for ending men's violence against women. It was the first large-scale initiative ever developed by men to speak out on a subject usually considered to be a "women's issue."
>
> Supporters of the campaign distributed white ribbons at schools, churches, shops, and places of employment. The Prime Minister, several celebrities, and some corporate heads were among the men who participated. Canadian men of conscience also raised money for rape crisis centers, domestic violence shelters, batterer treatment programs, and other organizations that deal directly with the consequences of men's violence against women. As the campaign became highly visible, men's violence against women became a subject for publicity, discussion, and debate. Many men across Canada talked seriously about the problem for the first time.
>
> One of the goals of the campaign organizers was to break the silence on the issue. In that regard, the effort was an unqualified success. A larger goal is to build a permanent national men's antiviolence organization. That effort is now well underway.
>
> Christopher Kilmartin (1996) brought the White Ribbon Campaign to his United States university campus in 1994. Detractors voiced the opinion that it was a "feel-good" effort fueled by men's guilt, and that it would have no positive effect. A team of researchers were able to document two effects. First, the campaign raised a significant amount of money for the local rape crisis and domestic violence agencies, a very tangible effect. Second, the researchers documented greater student awareness of the problem of men's violence against women and less tolerant attitudes toward the problem as a direct result of the campaign (Kilmartin, Chirico, & Leemann, 1997).
>
> The White Ribbon Campaign is significant in that it is a grass roots movement by men in the direction of dealing with a central men's social issue, and it has sustained itself for nearly three decades. It provides a stimulus for men to begin to understand the impact of gender socialization and sexist culture on their lives (White Ribbon Campaign, 2017) and continues to be active today.

cal injury and mortality. Firearms are involved in more than half of all homicides in the United States (Cooper & Smith, 2011; Petrovsky et al., 2017). In the United States, someone dies from a gunshot wound (many by accident or suicide) once every 17 minutes (derived from Webster & Vernick, 2013). A criminal murders someone with a firearm about once every 45 minutes in the United States (derived from Miller, Azrael, & Hemenway, 2013), and the risk of homicide or suicide is several times higher if a gun is kept in the home (Miller, Lippmann, Azrael, & Hemenway, 2007). The handgun homicide rate fell by approximately one third following the 1994 enactment of the "Brady Law," which imposed background checks and a waiting period for potential gun purchasers ("Pulling the Trigger," 1998). By 2010, when firearm laws had become significantly more lax, the annual firearm homicide rate "reclaimed" about half of the lives that had been saved in prior years (Miller, Azrael, & Hemenway, 2013) even though the overall violent crime rate had fallen considerably. Compared with children in comparably developed countries, children in the United States are 13 times more likely to be murdered and eight times more likely to commit suicide with a firearm (Miller, Azrael, & Hemenway, 2013). Although we cannot attribute a causal link between gun control laws and the reduction of firearm murders, it is hard to believe that individuals would be just as lethal if their violence did not include firearms.

Which Men Are Most Likely to be Violent?

Research examining which men perpetrate violence has examined a range of factors and various types of violence. In this section, we examine the influence of the male peer group, the beliefs a man holds, and some aspects of his upbringing. We focus primarily on factors that increase the likelihood of perpetrating IPV or rape.

Research indicates that many men who commit violence find peer groups that are aggressive and hold misogynist beliefs (Koss & Dinero, 1988; O'Neil, 2008). They use these groups to protect themselves from their insecurities by identifying with the group and having women as an underclass. The street gang is the most common of these negative male peer cultures, although some fraternities (Sanday, 1996, 2007) and some sports teams, especially those that play contact sports (Crosset, 2000), also serve this function. News stories detailing the use of strippers and prostitutes that were made available to high school athletic recruits by collegiate teams (facilitated by older players, training or coaching staff, or booster clubs) illustrate one way in which teams can reinforce these attitudes. The most extreme example of sexual violence in these sub-cultures of masculinity is gang rape. Fraternities and athletic teams have been disproportionately involved in such crimes (O'Sullivan, 1991).

We want to emphasize that not all fraternities endorse attitudes that support rape, and one study detailed some of the differences between low- and high-risk fraternities (Boswell & Spade, 1996). Parties in low-risk fraternities tended to have a friendly atmosphere and a good deal of social interaction between men and women. Music was not so loud as to make it difficult to have conversation. There was very little cursing, yelling, or jokes and comments that degrade women, and bathrooms provided for women were clean and well-supplied.

In contrast, parties at high-risk fraternity houses were marked by separation of the sexes, heavier drinking, louder music, and fewer conversations between men and women. There was more crude behavior and open hostility toward women, and women's bathrooms were filthy, sometimes with vomit in the sinks and clogged toilets. Men at high-risk houses gathered on porches the morning after parties and shouted derogatory comments to women who were walking home after spending the night there. In contrast to low-risk fraternities, men in high-risk fraternities had few long-term relationships with women, and in fact, the fraternity brothers actively discouraged such relationships. These men often highlighted the power distinction between the sexes, with clear messages that men are in charge, women are subordinate to men, and that respectful relationships with women are a threat to the fraternal brotherhood. Some fraternities went so far as to position sexual coercion as a contest or game rather than a crime, and members of the fraternities colluded to facilitate sexual assault as well as to hide it in case of any legal or official investigation (Boswell & Spade, 1996; Martin & Hummer, 2009).

Men who perpetrate IPV tend to be overconforming to the hegemonic masculine norms and the culture of violence (Gondolf, 1988). They have a high need for power and control and tend to blame their partners for their own violent behavior (Arias & Ikeda, 2006). Thus, they often think that they beat their wives because their wives behaved wrongly or "don't know how to listen," not because the men have trouble controlling their tempers or feel threatened by their partners' independence. The blaming of the victim allows the man to abdicate responsibility for and downplay the impact of his violent behavior. When a man perceives the source of his problems to be outside of himself, he sees no reason to explore his inner world or change his behavior. Male batterers also tend to be insecure and have difficulty regulating negative emotional states. As Donald Dutton (2011) describes it, their anger is born of fear. Nearly half of the time when a man murders his female partner, she is either leaving him or threatening to do so (Dutton & Golant, 1995). These data support the hypothesis that violence, including homicide, is a compensatory measure for feelings of masculine failure.

Being raised in a household led by a physically aggressive father appears to put men at greater risk for perpetrating IPV or committing rape. Many are survivors of some form of childhood abuse, themselves, and usually witnessed violence within their parents' relationship. These "risk factors" appear to be true for men in the United States (Dodge, 2011) and elsewhere (Heilman, Hebert, & Paul-Gera, 2014). One research team explained the connection between childhood experience and its connection to dominance as: "Essentially, the individual not only witnessed his father physically aggress against his mother and be reinforced for this behavior (the individual's mother often gave in to the father's demands), but his own violent behavior goes unpunished and is reinforced by his partner's surrendering to his will" (Sugarman & Hotaling, 1989, p. 1035). Others have noted that a substantial proportion of battering men have antisocial personality tendencies or full blown sociopathic disorders (see Chapter Fifteen) (Holtzworth-Munroe & Stuart, 1994).

Sadly, only a minority of rapists are incarcerated, with one research team estimating the number to be approximately one percent of offenders (Lisak & Miller, 2002). Although we do not know what motivational and personality factors may differentiate incarcerated and unincarcerated rapists, we review Nicholas Groth's (1979) categorization of three types of rape and thus, three types of rapists.

Power rapists are focused on conquering and controlling the victim to possess the person sexually. Sexual penetration serves as evidence of conquest, and the rapist uses whatever force he deems necessary to subdue the victim. Groth argued that the power rapist uses sex as a way of "compensating for underlying feelings of inadequacy and serves to express issues of mastery, strength, control, identity, and capability" (p. 25). In other words, the rapist makes a desperate attempt to demonstrate his masculinity. He is desperate because his underlying feelings are so painful, and because he has no emotional resources to use in dealing with his pain. Groth estimated that 55 percent of convicted offenders were power rapists.

Anger rapists are focused on harming the victim. They typically use more force than needed to overpower the victim and include verbal abuse as part of the attack; his goal is to make the victim feel as badly as possible, both psychologically and physically. Anger rapists believe that they have been (unfairly) wronged and hurt by women. Any woman can serve as the symbolic source of his pain, and thus any woman can serve as the target of his rape. Although he committed a mass shooting instead of rape, the writings and videos of the 2014 Isla Vista shooter fit this description. Groth estimated that approximately 40 percent of imprisoned rapists fit this category.

For both power and anger rapists, the goal is dominance over women and not sexual pleasure. Groth (1979) reported that most of these rapists were not sexually aroused at the time of their attacks, nor did they derive much sexual pleasure from their crime. Many reported masturbating or forcing the victim to stimulate them to obtain an erection prior to penetrating her. Further, many anger rapists reported that they did not have an orgasm during the assault or that they were unable to remember if they had.

Sadistic rapists eroticize power and violence and find sexual gratification in hurting another person. Thus, sex and violence are closely connected and the rapist rarely has difficulty with penetration or climax, unlike power and anger rapists. Sadistic rapists were similar to other rapists regarding their underlying feelings of masculine inadequacy. Groth estimate that approximately five percent of incarcerated rapists fit this category.

THE BIOLOGICAL PERSPECTIVE

Are men naturally predisposed to be violent? Given the extent of the differences between men and women, this seems like a reasonable question. We address potential answers from the perspective of evolution, genetics, and testosterone.

Evolutionary Psychology

Some evolutionary psychologists, like sociobiologists before them, say this is indeed the case. They recognize that in many different animal species, males engage in violent, confrontational, and sometimes mortal competition for breeding access to females (Daly & Wilson, 1985). Dominant males overcome other males through ritualized violence (such as rams butting horns), and these dominant males mate with more females than their submissive counterparts, who sometimes do not mate at all. Given the broad range of animal species in which this occurs, they argue that the same must also be true of humans. Cross-historical and cross-national studies demonstrate that the murder rate is highest among 18- to 29-year-olds, a time at which men are trying to "make their mark," and thus establish their status, in society. Most victims are also males of this age group and thus could be seen as competitors (Kruger & Nesse, 2004, 2006).

Sociobiologists Mary Daly and E. O. Wilson accurately described the population who are most at risk for being involved in violence—young, poor males. Men with higher socioeconomic status, they argued, tend to be less violent because they are higher on the dominance hierarchy and thus able to attract suitable mates. Daly and Wilson were probably also correct in describing much of this violence as taking place for reasons that most people would consider trivial... unless they realized that it was about mating and reproduction.

However, to say that this kind of behavior is a result of breeding competition seems to be quite a leap of logic. In fact, even in other animals, male aggression is not always associated with increased breeding opportunities, nor is it universal (Basow, 1992). Would there be so many angry, aggressive young men if we took better care of their emotional and material needs, ceased to expose them to so many violent models, and stopped holding them to impossible standards of masculinity? As we shall see, other explanations of male violence (and young, poor men's violence) are at least as plausible as the sociobiological one.

Genes

Genetic factors may affect emotional arousal, perception, and neurotransmitter levels, some of which may predispose one to aggression (Huesmann, Dubow, & Boxer, 2011). One study of five generations of violent Dutch men found an apparent genetic marker on the X-chromosome (Richardson, 1993). People with close relatives who have antisocial personality disorder are at increased risk for developing the disorder, even when they have no contact with the antisocial relative (Sue, et. al. 2014). There is also evidence of brain abnormalities in some violent people (Densen, 2011).

Testosterone

Testosterone levels have been identified as a potential explanation of the different violence levels between men and women. In part, the link seems "obvious" given the male-female differences in both the sex hormones (testosterone and estrogen) and violence. There is some evidence in support of this hypothesis. For example, in some animal species, males with high positions in social dominance hierarchies, which are often established by fighting, have higher testosterone levels than lower status males. But there are complicating data.

First, testosterone levels drop when an animal falls in the hierarchy. Therefore, although testosterone level may be a cause of aggression (or lack of it), it may also be an effect. Second, the excretion of high levels of testosterone in the urine of the animal may stimulate other animals to aggress toward him, and he must then fight back to protect himself. This evidence comes from an older study in which male rats were more likely to attack a castrated male rat after it had been coated with the urine of a dominant male (Pleck, 1981a).

The extent to which testosterone is a cause, effect, or simply a marker of aggression is a continuing subject of inquiry. In a classic study, testosterone levels were measured in prison inmates who were labeled as either "fighters" or "nonfighters" on the basis of prison records of aggressive incidents. There were no significant differences in testosterone levels between these two groups of men, casting considerable doubt on the straightforward "testosterone leads to aggression" hypothesis (Kreuz & Rose, 1972). Another study revealed that testosterone replacement therapy actually resulted in an increase in friendliness in men (Angier, 1999b).

Several reviews of the literature examining connections between testosterone and violence have been published over the years (Archer, 2006; Kemper, 1990; Sapolsky, 1997). These reviews indicate that while there appears to be some connection between testosterone and violence, the connection is complex and influenced by both the individual and the situation in which he finds himself. One line of evidence is obvious but bears mentioning: almost all boys experience a dramatic increase in testosterone levels during puberty, but only a small percentage actually engage in violent behaviors or seek dominance during this time period (Archer, 2006). If testosterone levels were very closely related to violence, there would be so much fighting in the hallways that middle and high schools would not be able to operate. Research has repeatedly demonstrated that the most aggressive humans, and the most aggressive animals, are not typically those who possess the highest testosterone levels (Sapolsky, 1997).

Instead of directly causing violence, these reviewers all conclude that testosterone facilitates aggression (Archer, 2006; Sapolsky, 1997). Endocrinologist Robert Sapolsky, for example, drew two conclusions: "testosterone isn't causing aggression, it's *exaggerating* the aggression that's already there" (p. 155, emphasis original), and "the more social experience an individual has [with violence] prior to castration, the more likely that the [violence] behavior persists [after castration]" (p. 156). Psychologist John Archer (2006) concluded that testosterone levels rise in response to specific challenges to dominance, including athletic contests, and these different contexts account for much of the connection between testosterone and violence. He asserts that different baseline levels of testosterone between men do not help us understand why some men are violent and others aren't, nor why men are more violent than women.

Models and Media

Young children discover the basics of violence by without being taught. Pushing, punching, kicking, and even biting are readily observable among toddlers. But being violent in ways that help a man get what he wants is a learned behavior. It requires both teaching and experience (practice).

Albert Bandura, along with his students and colleagues, demonstrated the ways in which humans learn from watching others, including the contextual cues that increase or decrease the likelihood of those behaviors (e.g., Bandura & Walters, 1963). Although Bandura's initial research focused on learning from television (in the 1960s, when television was still relatively new), the underlying principles are relevant for any form of *observational learning,* which refers to learning actions and their consequences by watching (Bussey & Bandura, 1999). The terms *vicarious reinforcement* and *vicarious punishment* specify when the witnessed behavior is encouraged through effectiveness, praise, or other positive rewards (reinforcement) or discouraged through restriction, loss, or other forms of punishment. Bandura's research demonstrated that boys were more likely to imitate a physically aggressive model in the absence of a reward (or prize); when a reward was present, boys and girls imitated the model at similar rates (Bandura, 1973). Imitation is more likely when a character is viewed as being similar to one's self (Bandura & Walter, 1963; Bussey & Bandura, 1999) and males are more violent than females in both fiction and fact.

Paternal Modeling

Males may pattern their behavior after violent male role models, who are not hard to find. Sons of aggressive fathers tend to become aggressive themselves. When they grow up, they tend to produce aggressive sons of their own (Holtzworth-Munroe & Stuart, 1994), and so imitation is a strong factor in this intergenerational pattern of violence. The son of a violent father sees his father re-establish power and control through beating his wife. The boy learns that using violence is effective, and thus the behavior is vicariously reinforced and the boy's likelihood of using this behavior increases.

Media Modeling

Violence is readily available in mainstream media in the United States. Among movies, the action-adventure genre, often produces the year's top-grossing films. One analysis of top-grossing movies in the United States over the course of more than a half century (1950–2006) revealed that 89 percent contained violence and that the proportion of characters engaging in violence increased over time (Bleakley, Jameison, & Romer, 2012). Nearly 80 percent of video games include violence; 28 percent depict women as sex objects, and 21 percent depict violence directly toward women (Dietz, 1998). Violent video games remain among the best-selling titles today.

On screen, male characters are much more likely to perpetrate violence than female ones. By the time an average child in the United States finishes elementary school, they will have witnessed 8,000 murders and 100,000 other acts of violence on television (Gentile, 2003). More often than not, characters show no remorse for their violent actions, and rarely do scripts portray the long-term physical, emotional or financial consequences of violence (Murray, 1998). Although 0.2 percent of crimes in the United States are murders, 50 percent of television crimes are murders. If real life were as violent as television, it would take only 50 days to exterminate the entire United States population (Bartholomew, Dill, Anderson, & Lindsay, 2003).

In an older analysis, "good" characters—attractive role models whom children are likely to imitate—committed 40 percent of violent television acts (Murray, 1998). Simon Moore and Tracey Cockerton (1996) summarized the impact of these types of portrayals: "when the 'bad guys' are punished, the violence used by the 'good guys' to achieve this is often portrayed as justified.... Rather than inhibiting aggression, these programs serve to facilitate it.... The viewer attributes 'good guy' violence as a justified means to an end, and in the same way, their own aggressive actions can be permissible as long as these achieve the same end" (p. 932). Thus, justified violence allows a person to avoid considering the moral dimension of their actions. Media violence that is carried out by attractive heroes provides the "best prescription for encouraging imitation of violent scripts and adoption of pro-violence beliefs and attitudes" (Bartholomew, Dill, Anderson, & Lindsay, 2003, p. 5).

Television programs specifically aimed at child audiences are among the worst offenders. Prime time television shows contain an average of five violent acts per hour, but children's programming contains an average of 20 (Strasburger, Wilson, & Jordan, 2014). Many of these shows not only portray violence as an acceptable way to solve problems, and as having no long-term consequences, but they also portray it as being *fun*! In an experimental study, one set of researchers documented a sevenfold increase in children's violent play immediately after they watched an episode of the *Mighty Morphin Power Rangers* (Boyatzis, Matillo, & Nesbitt, 1995). In general, mass media depicts violence as masculine and fails to communicate the terrifying and painful aspects of violence, thus rarely encouraging viewers to identify with the suffering of victims or to inhibit their aggression.

Males play violent video games at least twice as often as females (Gentile & Anderson, 2003). In contrast to passive forms of entertainment, the aggression in violent video games is participative, to the point of "first person shooter" games where the user can upload a photo of his/her face on to the body of the character wielding the firearm. Frequent use of violent video games among children is associated with increased defiance of teachers, greater risk of being involved in a physical fight or engaging in relational aggression, an increase in aggressive cognitions, and a decrease in positive social behaviors (Gentile, Coyne, & Walsh, 2011).

Adolescents exposed to sexualized media are more likely to view women as sex objects, and thus less than human than their less-exposed peers (Peter & Valkenburg, 2007). This attitude strongly supports heterosexual men's interpersonal violence against their partners as well as rape.

Violent media are not likely to turn an otherwise nonviolent person into a highly aggressive one any more than smoking a single cigarette is going to give someone lung cancer or eating junk food once is going to make someone obese. But as with smoking and unhealthy food, the effects of violent media are indirect and cumulative, and small effects add up in large populations (Gentile & Sesma, 2003). Because violence is a low-frequency behavior that has profound effects, even a small reduction of media violence can have important quality of life implications.

Beyond reducing children's exposure to violence, it is also possible to teach children (and adults) to be critical of the messages they view, called *media literacy*. A team of researchers (L. Rosenkoetter, S. Rosenkoetter, Osretich, & Acock, 2004) engaged third and fourth grade children in brief lessons to help them understand how television contains distorted messages about violence. The children identified low-probability outcomes, such as the bad guys' best troops inability to shoot the good guy as he runs across an open field, as well as alternative methods of conflict resolution. Over time, girls, but not boys, began to watch less violent television. Boys' levels of playground and classroom aggression decreased over time, so that even though they were watching as much violent television as before the intervention, they were less likely to demonstrate those behaviors.

Interventions

Thus far, we have described a broad range of factors that increase men's likelihood of perpetrating violence, including ways that violence is connected to the hegemonic definition of masculinity. We now address strategies to reduce violence. This discussion is primarily informed by efforts to reduce IPV and rape of women, reflecting the differing agendas that underlie research on violence (Kilmartin & McDermott, 2016).

The reduction of rape can involve a variety of strategies, including those that thwart the attempted rapist, prevent the rapist from committing repeated crimes, prevent potential rapists from ever committing the crime, and change the rape-supportive aspects of the culture. These varied interventions can involve legal, educational, economic, family, community, therapeutic, and political systems. To describe all of the possibilities would require several volumes, but we can outline some ideas here. We address programs designed for individuals who commit IPV or rape, then address programs designed to alter the community or larger culture.

Individual-Level Interventions

Many men who commit IPV are treatable, and a number of strategies for intervention have emerged in recent years. Among these are social skills training, therapy groups, and educational programs. The goals of these programs are to sensitize men to the personal and interpersonal consequences of their violence, to help them take responsibility for their violence, and to teach them ways of changing their thinking, emotional responses, and behaviors in conflict situations. In one study, researchers found that the combination of more severe criminal penalties and an emphasis on rehabilitation resulted in a 10 percent increase in arrests and a 50 percent decrease in recidivism (Gover, MacDonald, & Alpert, 2003).

The alarming estimates of the incidence of acquaintance rape at colleges and universities have stimulated a number of programmatic efforts to decrease violence against women. Services designed specifically for men include rape awareness programs (Brod, 2005), experiential workshops (Allison, 2005; Foubert, 2005; Heppner, 2005), peer education and counseling (Allison, 2005), and specialized workshops for fraternity members (Mahlstedt, 1998; Kilmartin & Ring, 1991) or athletes (Katz, 1995; Messner & Stevens, 2002). The most effective efforts include convincing people to challenge the gender-based norms that encourage sexual violence and to build the skills necessary to intervene as bystanders in dangerous situations (Banyard, Plante, & Moynihan, 2004; Gidycz, Orchowski, & Edwards, 2013). Some programs are "one-shot" or annual events, and others are ongoing, comprehensive, institutional efforts (Koss, White, & Lopez, 2017).

Recent efforts in sexual assault prevention have emphasized the role of male peer support (Kilmartin & Berkowitz, 2005; DeKeseredy & Schwartz, 2013, Foubert, 2005), with some positioning violence in the context of toxic masculinity (Kilmartin & Allison, 2007; Kilmartin & Berkowitz, 2005). When men remain silent or "go along with the joke" when their peers make derogatory comments about women, they contribute to a social atmosphere that makes sexual assault possible. When men learn to confront other men's sexist behavior, they can be effective in undermining the peer cultural support of sexual assault. Doing so requires a good deal of courage and a willingness to be independent enough to resist the cultural pressure to express indifference or hatred toward women when in an all-male group. Both courage and independence are traditionally masculine attributes, yet traditionally masculine men show extreme levels of conformity to sexist behavior.

Most men underestimate the degree to which their peers are made uncomfortable by other men's sexism and bragging about sexual conquest (Kilmartin, Conway, Friedberg, McQuoid, Tschan, & Norbet, 1999; Kilmartin, Smith, Green, Kuchler, Heinzen, & Kolar, 2008). Correcting the misconception that men are not bothered by sexist behavior in all-male groups may be useful in helping men to break the silence, as pressure for group conformity is sharply reduced when a group member perceives that he or she has an ally within the group (Asch, 1965) and men show a greater willingness to confront perpetrators when they believe that they share their concerns with other men (Berkowitz, 2010). As many as 75 percent of college men report discomfort with male peers' sexist behavior (Berkowitz, 1994). Therefore, the attitude that rape prevention strategists wish to impart already exists in large part, and so increasing the positive influence of this attitude is a matter of leadership (Berkowitz, 1997), another traditionally masculine attribute. Courageous, independent, risk-taking college men must take the lead by speaking out against their peers' sexist behavior.

In the United States military, where sexual assault is more rampant than in mainstream society, comprehensive solutions are being implemented. At Naval Station Great Lakes, sexual assault decreased by 60 percent over a two year period (Shanker, 2013) and training of the top leaders has proven to be an essential component of the solution (Stern, 2014), as commanders have great power to influence the climate of respect within their units (Sadler, et. al., 2003). Overall, sexual assaults within the United States military decreased by approximately half from 2006 to 2016 (SAPRO, 2018).

John Foubert (2011) and his colleagues deliver a peer education effort called "The Men's Program," which consists of four young male presenters educating college men about the extent of the problem of sexual assault and its effects on victims, and helping audience members to learn how they can help someone who survives an assault (they have also recently introduced a risk reduction program for women). The Mentors in Violence Prevention program (MVP) designed by Jackson Katz employs a similar bystander-to-ally approach. Gail Stern and Christian Murphy's interactive play, *Sex Signals*, has had remarkable success in educating audiences around the world, and the organization Men Can Stop Rape coordinates comprehensive efforts in prevention education. The international organization Promundo is reducing gender-based violence by educating men and getting them more connected with their families.

Community- and Cultural-Level Interventions

As with any violence, the best solutions are in prevention. At the cultural level, lower levels of intimate partner violence result from greater gender equality, lower poverty, less overcrowding, and better education. Public policy changes can influence social norms, and workplaces are good entry points for prevention efforts (Parks, Cohen, & Kravitz-Wirtz, 2007).

Preventing a rapist from committing repeated crimes is a critical component of rape prevention, as perpetrators tend to commit multiple rapes as well as other crimes, and only an estimated one percent are ever incarcerated (Lisak & Miller, 2002). These efforts include vigorous legal enforcement and rehabilitative interventions such as facilitating the rapist's acceptance of responsibility for the crime, building the criminal's empathy for the victim, developing social skills, and decreasing sexual arousal to rape. The term ***rape prevention*** should be used for these interventions, particularly with male audiences, to give the clear message that women are not responsible for preventing rape (Kilmartin & Berkowitz, 2005).

At the community and cultural level, attempts to thwart the potential rapist have historically taken the forms of rendering environments less conducive to rape, and of educating potential victims. Lighting of dark areas, police patrols, and teaching self-defense skills are strategies in this area. On some college campuses, risk reduction strategies such as escort services, danger avoidance education (i.e., don't walk alone at night, make sure windows and doors are locked, learn what kinds of men are likely to assault), alcohol rules, and fraternity policies are fairly common. Carole Corcoran (1992) described these approaches as *victim control strategies* because they subtly place the responsibility for rape prevention on women. Others have called these approaches *(rape) risk reduction* (Kilmartin & Berkowitz, 2005).

Efforts to change the ways that law enforcement and the legal system approach IPV and rape have also been attempted. Police and prosecutor education is critical for rapes that are reported to the legal system. Untrained police investigators sometimes approach complainants with skepticism about their truthfulness, especially when the victim had been drinking, had engaged in consensual behaviors such as kissing, had no physical injuries, and was not threatened with a weapon. They tend to believe that sexual motives are paramount in rape, and that therefore attractive, charming, socially-skilled men would never commit this crime. Educating investigators about rape myths, the psychology of the victim, and more sensitive approaches to questioning can be helpful in improving the quality of police work in this area (Kilmartin, 2007). Prosecutors also need to educate jurors about these issues. Legal advances are also helpful. These include "rape shield" laws that prevent defense attorneys from bringing up irrelevant topics like the victim's past sexual behavior, and "affirmative consent" laws that define consent as the presence of "yes" rather than the absence of "no" (Caringella, 2009).

SUMMARY

Men's violence has historical, economic, social, biological, and cultural roots that interact with the personal histories and ideologies of individual men, and with their decisions to act violently. The cross-cultural variation and striking differences in men's and women's violence lead us to the conclusion that violence is largely centered in the social meanings attached to gender. Solutions to the problems created by men's violence must be broad in scope, encompassing a range of strategies and targets.

Examination of violence statistics illustrates ways in which violence is mostly perpetrated by and against males. The statistics also illustrate the influence of contextual factors, such as the relationship between perpetrator and victim, racial background, age, and nation.

We know that biology and social forces both affect behavior, and so we should do whatever we can to work against the social forces that push a person over the threshold into violent behavior. Just as there are probably biological forces that work against violence and those that work toward it, there are psychosocial forces that both facilitate and inhibit violence. Physical aggression, then, is a behavior that can be either encouraged or inhibited in various ways. We can look at violent men as men who have experienced encouragement to be violent, have likely had violent models, demonstrates little empathy, and have an externalizing attribution style.

Claims about the biological universality of male violence provide a measure of justification for it and leave us with few options for resolving the problem besides punishment and confinement. The view that it is natural and normal to be physically aggressive if you are male is disrespectful to men, most of whom are not violent. But even if there is a biological propensity toward aggression, we should keep in mind that there is also a biological propensity to resist violent impulses—the instincts to protect the self and to empathize with others.

Modeling, from fathers and the media, also plays a role. Because males commit more on-screen violence than females, it should be cause for concern for all of us, especially when one considers that aggressive men who engage in what is perceived as "legitimate" violence obtain the love of women, the admiration of others, and a feeling of self-righteous satisfaction. Teaching media literacy appears to reduce the impact of on-screen violence.

The reduction and elimination of male violence involves the reduction of the needs and the incentives for this kind of behavior, the increase of disincentives, and the provision of alternative ways for dealing with the feelings that precede the aggression (Toch, 1992). Violence is deeply ingrained in our definition of masculinity and in many other cultures. Therefore, efforts toward violence reduction must cover a broad range of settings, including parenting practices, education, the legal system, politics, economics, and therapeutic settings. Because violence is so much a part of the masculine gender role, the very fabric of masculinity must change if violence is to be reduced.

In the big picture, sexual assault against women and girls is a toxic product of societal sexism, which is in turn a product of inequality between the sexes (Kilmartin, 2014). Therefore, it will end when women's status is equal to mens', and in fact, there is evidence that increases in gender equality within a culture are accompanied by decreases in sexual violence (Yodanis, 2004).

In summary, men who commit IPV and rape tend to be angry, hypermasculine, and disenfranchised men who often see violence as natural and normal. They are unable to deal with vulnerable emotions and so they convert these feelings into anger. They also have learned that engaging in violence gets them what they want: dominance, power, and control. And their behavior takes place within a patriarchal socialcultural context that condones and even encourages physical aggression.

1. Men commit the vast majority of violent crimes, and this fact leads researchers to investigate the origins of violence and the connections between aggression and masculinity.
2. Male victimization occurs at alarming levels, especially with regard to murder in the United States.
3. There are substantial differences in perpetration, arrest, and incarceration rates based on race and ethnicity in the United States The White-Black racial disparities tend to increase as individuals move through the system, reflecting the impacts of direct racism as well as subtler effects of growing up in impoverished neighborhoods and having few vocational opportunities.
4. Evolutionary psychologists and sociobiologists view male aggression as an evolutionary strategy for propagating one's genes, yet aggression is not always associated with an increase in breeding access, even in non-human animals.
5. The hormone testosterone is another possible biological link to male violence. Although testosterone may set the stage for aggression, implicating it as the singular cause of male violence ignores the complexity of human behavior and the powerful influence of psychosocial forces. Cross-cultural variations in the character of violence make singular biological explanations untenable.
6. Socioculturally, aggression is a defining feature of masculinity. A number of factors encourage aggression in men, including the privilege of patriarchy, a socialized external defensive style, unmitigated attention to task, violent modeling, and rewards for aggressing. Compared with females, violence-inhibiting factors such as empathy, nonaggressive modeling, and consistent punishment for aggression are less in evidence for males.
7. Men who commit IPV often have exaggerated needs for power and control as well as the externalizing style of blaming their partners for their own negative feelings and behaviors. Domestic violence often follows an intergenerational pattern against the backdrop of a patriarchal system that tolerates violence against women and even children. A number of interventions are focused on legal, therapeutic, and educational systems.
8. Many researchers believe that rape is fueled by aggressive, not sexual motivations. The social construction of masculinity, with its emphasis on misogyny, sexual promiscuity, performance, and homophobia, is both cause and effect of a rape-tolerant social climate.
9. Rape is often perpetrated by men who are attempting to compensate for feelings of masculine inadequacy through hypermasculine displays of dominance, anger, and control. For many acquaintance rapists, low

masculine self-esteem may be related to poor relationships with emotionally and/or physically distant or abusive fathers.
10. Interventions for decreasing rape include more vigorous law enforcement, rehabilitative efforts, safety measures, and the education of potential victims. However, rape is a men's issue, and men need to address it. Recent interventions have included bystander approaches to men, especially in college populations, where acquaintance rape is rampant. Men who can understand, at a deep level, the negative consequences of rape, the origins of male violence, the pain of victims, and the continuum of violence against women, will be less likely to rape or to support violent peers. Education with powerful people within institutions like the military also shows great promise.

GLOSSARY

Action movies: A broad term that includes films about superheroes, war, westerns, some crime films, and some science-fiction and fantasy films
physical aggression: acts of violence that attempt to or do cause physical harm to another person

Relational aggression: Efforts to harm a person's friendships or reputation

Violence to property: Acts that cause damage to property (things), including graffiti and theft

Interpersonal violence (IPV): Assault against a romantic relationship or marital partner, previously known as "domestic violence."

Rape: Defined as sexual penetration without consent; in the last decade, it also began to include events in which a male was "forced to penetrate" someone without the male's consent.

Sexual assault: A broad term that includes any form of nonconsensual touching of areas of the body that are associated with sexuality

Intra-racial crime: Crimes in which the offender and victim are of the same race.

Inter-racial crime: Crimes in which the offender and victim are of different races.

Rape myths: Erroneous beliefs that excuse the rape of women (e.g., women secretly want to be raped).

(Psychological) resilience: Overcoming multiple challenges that predispose an individual to experience a negative outcome, such as perpetrating violence.

Insecure attachment style: A manner of relating to others is characterized by emotionally unstable connections

Anabolic-Androgenic Steroids (AAS): A class of drugs that mimic testosterone at the biological level.

'Roid rage: A high level of anger, possibly accompanied by a "short fuse," that occurs as a side effect of using Anabolic-Androgenic Steroids (AAS).

Observational learning: Learning actions and their consequences by watching.

Vicarious reinforcement: Observational learning that includes encouragement of the behavior through effectiveness, praise, or other positive rewards (reinforcement)

Vicarious punishment: Observational learning that includes discouragement of the behavior through restriction, loss, or other forms of punishment.

Media literacy: Teaching people to be critical of the messages they receive from the media.

Rape prevention: Strategies and programs to reduce rape that target individuals who are likely to commit rape.

Victim control strategies: Efforts to reduce the likelihood of rape by encouraging potential victims to minimize their risk of being raped. Also called (rape) risk reduction strategies.

Chapter Thirteen

The Risk of Masculinity

Adherence to hegemonic masculine norms brings a range of benefits, or so we teach people. In theory, men who enact (most) masculine norms will gain status, power, money, and sexual partners in the process of becoming "The Man." These are substantial and powerful motivators in U.S. culture, and many men choose to pursue them. When we introduced the concept of masculinities in Chapter 2, we noted that many men buy into these norms but are unable to fully enact them, and thus may demonstrate a complicit form of masculinity in which they receive some, but not all, of these benefits. What would you risk to gain status, power, and money? Would you put your physical health on the line and potentially shave twenty years off of your life to become rich and join the top one percent of earners with a salary in excess of $3 million per year for a decade? Would you risk your life in combat to escape a bad neighborhood and bad education while gaining a sense of pride and marketable skills that would allow you to be a breadwinner?

Some men face questions of this sort. In this chapter, we explore some of the trade-offs that American masculine norms present to men. We do so by focusing on four groups of men who are presented with the dilemma of choosing their masculinity and some of the trade-offs they make. Specifically, we address the experience of being in combat, long-term participation in contact sports, male victims of sexual assault and rape, and aging men.

Combat

The United States military has almost always been comprised of volunteers, with the exception of some short periods during times of large-scale war. As a volunteer force, the military must offer some combination of benefits that would entice physically healthy young men to enter the military. In addition to being a noble form of service and demonstration of patriotism, it provides guaranteed employment at a reasonable wage over several years while also potentially offering training that might not otherwise be available. For boys growing up in impoverished areas with inferior skills, this might provide the only viable path for exiting poverty. For boys from families with more financial resources and the academic skills to attend and graduate from college, the ROTC officer track also sets the stage for higher rank (i.e., status). However, there are clear health risks during training and combat.

Combat is, by definition, hazardous to soldiers' health, causing substantial injuries to physical and mental health in addition to death. Over the last 100 years, the United States has been involved in World War I, World War II, the Korean Conflict, the Vietnam War, two Persian Gulf Wars, and the ongoing wars in Afghanistan and Iraq, as well as a number of other military actions. Draft registration, known as **selective service,** has been mandatory for able-bodied American males upon turning 18 since 1917. In U.S. society, dying or being maimed in war is considered an act of heroism, but this does not change the fact that more than one million American men have died in war.

The wars of the twentieth century have been described as "holocausts of young men" in which millions of men were killed and over 100 million were injured. The average age of World War I and II casualties was 18.5 years (Kimbrell, 1991). Thus, the victims of war tend to be the youngest men, who feel (and often are) less powerful, and who feel the strongest need to establish a sense of masculinity. Poor men and men of color who are marginalized by mainstream U.S. culture have also been disproportionately represented among the war dead. Many men who survived the modern, technological war in Vietnam returned with physical and emotional scars of profound proportions. It is perhaps no coincidence that some men began to question the dictates of cultural masculinity at about this time, when it was becoming obvious that soldiers were finding it difficult to "take it like a man." (Recent combat veterans also experience these same scars, but return to a culture that is not challenging gender roles to the extent that occurred in the 1970s.)

For the bulk of human history, combat has been conducted in a face-to-face manner in which one can see his enemy. Facing one's enemy is typically a kill-or-be-killed scenario, and represents one of two situations in which a nation officially sanctions killing (execution of criminals is the other). The fear associated with the possibility of death, including the possibility of sudden unexpected death while in a combat zone, as well as the personal cost of taking another person's life, can cause severe emotional distress. Some men respond negatively immediately upon entering the combat zone, but others are able to suppress these emotional reactions and do the work of soldiering (Marlantes, 2011).

When that emotional reaction finally comes to the surface, men report a variety of symptoms that include feeling depressed, guilt over having killed, guilt over having survived when one's mates have been killed, high anxiety, difficulty falling asleep or maintaining a regular sleep schedule, unwanted and intrusive memories (typically of injuries and death), and flashbacks. The anxiety often takes the form of *hypervigilance,* which refers to being highly alert to one's surroundings (typically from watching for threats). Clincially, these symptoms are characteristics of **Post-Traumatic Stress Disorder (PTSD)** (American Psychiatric Association, 2013).

Our knowledge and awareness of PTSD has changed over the years, and its incidence also appears to have increased. One potential explanation for this increase is technology: at the end of World Wars I and II, American soldiers had to (re-)cross the continent to get to a port, sailed back to the United States, and then often spent some time with their unit after returning to the mainland and before being discharged. The result was a period of two to three months after hostilities ended and before leaving the military during which soldiers could unwind and re-acclimate to a non-combat life while in the company of friends who'd had similar experiences and were having similar emotional reactions. For veterans of Korea and Vietnam, the return home occurred by plane and typically took no more than a week. Since the 1990s, that time has dropped to no more than three days for most veterans (Marlantes, 2011). The decreased time means less time to re-adjust to civilian life and less opportunity to discuss the experience of war with large numbers of people who shared the experience.

In the digital age, the distance between the combat zone and civilian life has become even smaller. Military bases typically have space set aside to allow soldiers to call home using voice and video technology for settings where personal cell phones are not allowed. The challenges that soldiers face due to routinely switching between their private life, including conversations with their partners about mundane activities or their children or their parents, and the realities of living in a war zone, including the maiming and death of squad mates and threats to their own health and well-being, are poorly understood. For some soldiers, the transition may be even more dramatic. Drones, which can be used to kill, may be operated by soldiers based in the United States who return home to their families at the end of their work day (Marlantes, 2011). In essence, these individuals have little meaningful separation between war and peace, the combat zone and home.

Contact Sports

Sports and masculinity are strongly interconnected in United States culture. The almost religious fervor with which many men approach athletics is evidence that sports have more importance to men than mere physical fitness. Indeed, for the lucky few who are able to gain employment as professional athletes, the minimum salary is in excess of $100,000 per year with the possibility of making millions of dollars each year for a decade or so. Some scholars argue that professional athletes represent the pinnacle of hegemonic masculinity in the United States (Messner, 1992). The money, fame, and presumed access to attractive sexual partners are rewards that many boys (and young men) are willing to work toward.

The sports that are most heavily dominated by male participation are those with high risks of injury (Courtenay, 2011), which may explain why males sustain around 70 percent of the sports injuries that result in emergency room visits (Flores, Haileysus, & Greenspan, 2008). An unfortunate minority of men and boys have suffered debilitating injuries and even death as a result of overexertion, physical contact, or accidents in sporting events. The most dangerous sports would seem to be auto racing and professional boxing. The object of the latter is to pummel one's opponent into unconsciousness. Between 1950 and 2007, 339 professional boxers died as a direct result of brain injuries suffered in the ring (Baird, et. al., 2010). Others—such as former heavyweight champion Muhammad Ali, who suffered from Parkinsonian symptoms prior to his death—have suffered irreparable brain damage as the cumulative result of many years of repeated head traumas. For several years prior to his death in 1999, former heavyweight Jerry Quarry needed help putting on his shoes and cutting his food because of neurological impairment. It is estimated that 20 percent of professional boxers suffer some degree of permanent brain damage (Trafford, 1996), resulting in symptoms such as "memory loss, inattention, impaired hearing, paranoid ideas, and a decrease in general cognitive functions" (Newfield, 2001, p. 20).

Football appears to be particularly bad for the health of boys and men. An average of 12 high school and college players die each year from football injuries or heat-related illnesses sustained in football practice or games (*The New York Daily News*, 2013). More than a half-million high school boys and college men are injured playing football every year (Shankar, Fields, Collins, Dick, & Comstock, 2007). The average number of concussions in the National Football League (NFL) is between two and four per game (Fainaru-Wada & Fainaru, 2013). A *concussion* is a traumatic injury that disrupts the functioning of the brain, and is caused when the brain is thrown against the inside of the skull. Having a single concussion renders the victim more susceptible to subsequent concussions, and multiple concussions can result in permanent neurological damage. Former Jets wide receiver Al Toon estimated that he suffered as many as 13 concussions during his eight-year professional career (Alloy, Jacobson, & Acocella, 1999) and reported that his head "has never been clear" since that time (ESPN, 1994).

As many as 50 percent of high school football players report having had symptoms of concussions (Schwarz, 2007) and there are an estimated 250,000 head injuries to football players annually (Mueller, 2001). Many high school and college football players say that they do not report their head injuries to team trainers or coaches because they do not think their symptoms are serious and/or because they do not want to be taken out of the game (Schwarz, 2007). Some football programs test their players' cognitive skills to assess the possibility of unreported concussions and to evaluate injured players' recovery (Williams, 2008).

Dementia is a general term to describe cognitive impairments such as memory failures, language disturbances, and problems in planning and abstract thinking (Sue, et. al., 2014). One survey of retired NFL players showed a dramatic difference in reported dementia between the former players and their same-age peers in the general population. Retired players over 50 years old were over four times more likely to report dementia symptoms than non-players (6.1% to 1.2%). In the relatively rare case of dementia before age 50, retired players showed a 19-fold increased risk (1.9% to 0.1%) (Weir, Jackson, & Sonnega, 2009). In the same study, researchers noted that retired players were more likely to be non-smokers and had higher rates of physical activity than men in the general population, and perhaps as a result, they had better cardiovascular fitness as a group and are less likely to have diabetes. At the same time, they also report more arthritis and pain and greater problems with mobility. Although this research cannot demonstrate a causal link between football playing and later cognitive disturbances, the possibility of such a link appears strong; their cardiovascular health and lower rates of diabetes suggest that their dementia is not the result of a general but premature decline.

Playing football may be the ultimate expression of hypermasculinity in the United States. It involves sacrifice of the body for a task and denial of basic instincts for self-preservation and safety. The average NFL player engages in thousands of impacts per season, the worst of which are the equivalent of a 25 mile per hour head-on automobile accident (Gugliotta, 2003). This may contribute to findings that the median age of death of NFL veterans is in the early-to-mid-50s (Baron, Hein, Lehman, & Gersic, 2013). Today, linemen weighing 300 pounds or more are more the rule than the exception, and it was estimated that the momentum generated by a 340-pound player running at 15 miles per hour (the equivalent of the 40 yard dash in 5.1 seconds, average for these players) is the same as a 17-pound bowling ball shot from a cannon at 30 miles per hour (Mihoces, 2002). Many retired players report chronic headaches and dementia symptoms, but the NFL has been reluctant to provide medical services, saying that the players cannot prove that their symptoms are directly related to football (Leahy, 2008). However, in 2013, the NFL offered to settle a class action lawsuit filed on the behalf of former players for $765 million without admitting responsibility. A federal judge denied approval of the settlement in 2014, assessing it as too small (*Sports Illustrated*, 2014).

Television commentary of sports injuries almost always involves reference to the task: "Will he return to play later in the game?"; "How will his team compensate for his absence?"; "Will the other team exploit the substitute?" Imagine a television commentator reacting to an injury with "That must be painful," "I wonder if he's disappointed to be out of the game," or "Do you think he'll retire to protect his health?"

Male Victims and Survivors of Sexual Assault and Rape

There is a growing awareness that men are also victims of rape in greater numbers than people would have ever believed; the United States Centers for Disease Control and Prevention reports that approximately one in six males will be sexually abused, assaulted, or raped during his lifetime (and one in four females; Black et al., 2011) It is estimated that sexual assault perpetrators victimize as many as one in 8 men at some point during his life (Bolton, Morris, & MacEachron, 1989) and the incidence of prison rape is much higher (Johnson, 2009). Recently, the sexual assault of United States military personnel by others within their ranks has been identified as a major problem. Although men's statistical risk of being victimized (1.2 perent per year) is much lower than that of women (6.1 percent), because men are a large majority (six of every seven) of military personnel (Active Duty Gender Distribution, 2013), in terms of raw numbers they are actually a slight majority (53%) of victims. Military male sexual assault victims are even less likely than female victims to report the assault to military authorities (Scarborough, 2013).

Male rape survivors experience some similar responses to female survivors. They may suffer from posttraumatic stress disorder (PTSD) and experience various psychological symptoms, including depression, anxiety, anger, shame, relationship difficulties, suicidal thoughts, sexual problems, sleep disturbances, increased alcohol use, and psychosomatic symptoms (Gartner 1999, 2017a, b; Lew, 2004; Sue, et. al., 2014). They also experience difficulties that are somewhat unique to male survivors: doubts about their masculinity and sexuality, extreme isolation, and even fewer resources for treatment and support than female victims have available (Isely, Isely, Freiburger & McMackin, 2008). It is estimated that 90 percent of male survivors never report the rape to police or hospitals, and 70 percent never tell anyone at all (VAASA, 1989). Research into the specific effects of sexual assault on men is growing, but this population remains substantially under-studied (Gartner, 2017a, b).

There is one very important way in which male and female survivors' responses to sexual assault and rape are very different: male survivors often report very high levels of shame as a result of having been sexually victimized. This shame results partly from their conception of masculinity, including the idea that only females are penetrated, only females can be victims of sexual assault, and a male should *always* be able to defend himself (even in the case of a boy fighting off an adult man). Because masculinity states that guys should always want sex and never refuse it, he may also have difficulty understanding—and convincing others—that this "sexual experience" was unwanted (Gartner, 2017ab; Lew, 2004). These feelings of shame often contribute to male victims' reluctance to disclose their victimization. Further, many male victims feel that their experience prevents them from living up to the full dictates of masculinity.

Several researchers have made suggestions for dealing with the largely hidden problem of male-on-male rape. Michael Scarce (1997a; 1997b) recommended lobbying for gender-neutral rape laws where they do not currently exist, providing referrals and information tailored specifically to male survivors, training emergency room and rape crisis workers on the reality and unique character of male victimization, and educating the general public about the extent of the problem. The Centers for Disease Control and Prevention (CDCP) found that approximately 1 in 21 men had been "forced to penetrate" someone during their lifetime (Black, 2011). This information appears to have contributed to the FBI's (2016) decision to change its definition of rape to include situations in which a male was "forced to penetrate." Paul Isely and his colleagues (Isely, Busse, & Isely, 1998) suggested that school counselors and health services professionals be trained to recognize symptoms of sexual victimization and learn how to respond appropriately, as untreated symptoms often develop into chronic behavioral and psychological difficulties. In a subsequent article on men who were abused as children by Catholic clergy, Isely and collegues (Isely, Isely, Freiburger & McMackin, 2008), described child sexual victimization as a "developmental insult with a high likelihood of compromising social, relational, and intrapsychic functioning in later life." (p. 209).

Traumatic psychological experience also increases the risk that a male survivor will become a perpetrator if he fails to acknowledge his pain. The refusal to deal directly with vulnerable emotions like fear and shame is central to mainstream cultural masculinity. Lisak (1997) noted that men who have been abused in some way as children *and* have accepted masculinity's traditional values are more likely to become violent adults, in comparison to other child abuse survivors. His contention is that, as children, these men have experienced powerful and painful emotional events. At the same time, they have gotten the social message that expressing vulnerable feelings is taboo for males—the classic "big boys don't cry" dictum. These boys find that they can follow one of two paths: they can reject traditional masculinity and deal with the tragedy of their victimization, or they can accept it and act out their intense rage by becoming abusive to themselves, through risk taking or drug use, or being abusive to others.

The male abuse survivor who seals over his pain cannot feel empathy for his victims because he is so unaware of his own feelings of shame and vulnerability. In other words, it is impossible for a person to feel for others when his own emotional life is impoverished. He has no frame of reference for emotional pain because his defenses against his own pain are so rigid.

David Lisak (1997) suggested that re-humanizing men entails helping them to recover the vulnerable emotionality that accompanied their victimization. He refers to full awareness of one's vulnerable emotions as *empathy for the self* and tells the heart-rending story of a death row inmate who refused to deal with the painful reality of his childhood victimization until, after 10 years in prison, he finally began to acknowledge his pain. One day, during a prison psychotherapy session, he began to cry, perhaps for the first time in his adult life, and sobbed uncontrollably for 45 minutes as he relived the horrors of multiple abuses in his youth. He recovered from this episode and, 15 minutes later, became anguished again as, for the first time, he came to a full emotional awareness of the pain that he had inflicted on his victims. Lisak saw the connection between empathy for the self and empathy for others in this dramatic hour.

AGING MEN

What is the pattern of continuity and change in the gendered behavior of men as they age? If you think about the older men that you know, you may be acquainted with some who have seemed to change and some who have not. Actor Jack Palance, in his seventies, demonstrated his physical fitness by doing one-armed pushups on stage after receiving an Academy Award, a "macho" display that one does not expect to see from an old man. On the other hand, there are many older men who seemed to have shifted from this kind of behavior as they have aged into styles that we might describe as androgynous. And, of course, as we have stated many times, there are many who never really fit the mainstream masculine image in the first place.

There is some evidence of adult developmental changes in gendered behavior that appear to be driven by significant changes in family status, physical changes, social position, career, or health. Middle-aged and elderly men are likely to encounter several psychologically transformative events such as their parents' deaths, retirement, changes in parental status, and adjustments in relationships. These gradual and abrupt life changes have the potential to affect their gender ideologies and behaviors.

A common misunderstanding about adult developmental change is the belief that men encounter a predictable *midlife crisis* during which they make profound changes in the ways that they approach their work, relationships, and leisure pursuits as a result of the psychological pressure produced by reaching this milestone. Two very popular books in the 1970s (D. J. Levinson, Darrow, Klein, M. H. Levinson, & McKee, 1978; Sheehy, 1976) proposed and popularized the idea that this "crisis" is universal and based on chronological age. In other words, one could expect that, around age 40, a man is very likely to do things like change jobs, get divorced, buy a sports car, and find a young woman to date. Subsequently, researchers demonstrated that the so-called male midlife crisis is non-normative. Although some men's behavior at midlife might be characterized in this way, most men experience no such crisis (Kilmartin, 2004a). When there is a crisis during this time of life, the chances are that it is brought on by changes in the man's job situation or relationships, not merely by the fact that he is aging. Even substantial changes in important areas such as these are no guarantee that a full-blown life crisis will ensue. Most psychologically healthy people manage to handle a crisis in one area of their life without causing crises in others.

Psychoanalyst Carl Jung believed that people's gendered sense of self tends to expand during the second half of life (Hall, Lindzey, & Campbell, 1998). Jung's belief came largely from essentialist notions about personality development, but it is also quite possible to assess gender shift (or lack of it) as a result of social environmental forces. For instance, most men encounter several life changes in their forties or fifties that may affect their gender ideologies and behavior. Physical declines are inevitable and may include minor hearing loss, graying hair, decreased muscularity, weight gain, and more frequent aches and pains. Men who are athletes see their abilities diminish and/or have to "retire" from some sports. There may be changes in workplace status, such as big promotions or declines in duties. Men whose work involves physical labor may find themselves having more difficulty keeping up with younger men or avoiding injury on the job. Children grow up and move out of the house. There may be a realization that some of the things they dreamed about as younger men are not going to take place. Bruce Rybarczyk (1994) summarized the impact of these events: "The consequences of these changes can be positive (e.g., new roles, new goals) and negative (e.g., feelings of disappointment). For men whose self-concepts rely heavily on youth-oriented masculine traits, these changes undoubtedly force a redefinition of their gender identities" (p. 114).

We have to be cautious with generalizations about older men from research, because of the inevitable confounding of generation (also known as *cohort*) and age. Comparisons of the current generation of older adults and the current generation of younger adults cannot demonstrate age differences, only age and cohort differences as they occur together. The level to which each factor contributes is a matter of speculation. For example, we could assume that older men are less likely to exercise than younger men because this is currently the case. However, it is quite possible that this generation of younger men might exercise at the same level when they become older. Separating cohort and age effects is difficult, if not impossible (Rybarczyk, 1994).

There is also a lack of research on all but White, middle-class men in the United States. Black and Latino men, as well as lower SES men, may experience aging in very different ways. There is very little examination of the interactions between these statuses and adult psychological development. For example, many working class retirees may not fit the stereotype of the person who spends a lot of time traveling, playing golf, and enjoying other leisure activities, as they may not have the money to do so.

David Gutmann (1987) proposed that gender role differentiation becomes minimal in later life and that this gender shift is a universal, not a culture-specific phenomenon. Based on anthropological studies of several different cultures, he concluded that women tend to become more powerful and assertive as they age and men tend to become more passive and more involved in domestic matters. Like sociobiologists, Gutmann believed that these changes are a result of evolutionary adaptation, however he never considered the possibility that a lack of gender-differentiated roles in older age could produce this universal phenomenon, if in fact it is universal.

A number of researchers disagree with Gutmann's proposed universal midlife gender transformation. Peskin (1992) followed a small sample of college graduates for more than 25 years and found little evidence of such a shift. Huyck (1992) found that these gender changes tended to be confined to relationships between spouses, with men and women becoming more similar in their behaviors as time went on. Feldman, Biringen, and Nash (1981) demonstrated that gender changes were more related to parenting status than to a person's chronological age.

These contradictory findings have led some theorists to conclude that age-related shifts in gendered behavior result largely from the expansion of social role opportunities for older men. For example, most men can spend more time at home after they retire, and thus they are freer to pursue more activities associated with traditional femininity, like cooking and gardening. Social forces that encourage men to be traditionally masculine may not apply as much to older men, and, even if they do, older men may become less invested in maintaining a masculine image (O'Rand, 1987).

Aging men face special challenges in dealing with the influence of masculine social demands. Even those who were once "successful" in traditional masculine realms often find it difficult to live up to dominant gender standards. Traditional masculinity is defined as very physical, work-oriented, and independent, yet older men experience physical decline, retirement, and the increasing need to depend on others and ask for help. It seems that very few older men can hold on to the macho ethic and survive, either physically or psychologically.

Considerable evidence points to the negative effects of certain aspects of hegemonic masculine norms on the lives of older men. They are less likely than women to see a physician or psychotherapist (Addis & Mahalik, 2003), more likely to downplay their symptoms even if they seek help (Komiya, Good, & Sherrod, 2000), and overwhelmingly more likely to commit suicide (Arias, 2004). Men who attempt to deal with old age using the psychological approach of hegemonic masculinity often find themselves lonely, ill, and depressed. We often refer to "macho old men" as *developmentally unsuccessful*, as they have not learned the behaviors they need to negotiate this stage of adult development.

But the picture of elderly men is not usually so bleak, as most adjust well to changes in gender identity. They take on new social roles and often come to appreciate aspects of their lives that were previously "off-limits" because they were defined as feminine (Gutmann, 1987). As a result, they report a wider range of self-expression and less worry about whether or not they are being masculine enough to suit others' wishes.

SUMMARY

There are many ways to adhere to masculine norms and yet still not gain the full range of benefits that are provided through masculine privilege. Some men risk their lives, or at least their full able-bodied functioning, to achieve the highest level of masculinity's benefits. Other men feel disqualified, either through having been victimized or advanced age.

1. Combat has taken the lives of over one million U.S. men and may have injured as many as one hundred million men.
2. Many combat veterans live with Post-Traumatic Stress Disorder (PTSD) as the result of having been in combat. PTSD includes a variety of symptoms, including hypervigilance, high anxiety, and sleep disorders.
3. Contact sports put boys and men at risk for a range of physical injuries. The most severe of these injuries may be repeated concussions, which can cause long term brain damage.
4. Male-on-male rape is much more common than is generally believed, and male rape survivors face a unique set of recovery issues. Males with a history of any kind of victimization are at increased risk for becoming perpetrators if they embrace traditional masculine gender role norms.
5. Male survivors of sexual abuse and rape often suffer from PTSD and other disorders. Many never disclose their victimizations due to shame at not having lived up to masculine norms.
6. Some male survivors repress their pain and in doing so, are unable to be empathic toward themselves or others. These men are at greater risk of hurting themselves or others.
7. Although the idea of a midlife crisis is well-entrenched in American culture, the evidence suggests that only a minority of men have such an experience.
8. The decreases in functioning associated with older age, including decreases in physical abilities, sensory losses, and cognitive slowing and decline, may signify the loss of ability to enact all of masculinity's dictates. Losses of independence, salary, or employment status may also contribute to these feelings.

GLOSSARY

Selective service: The requirement in the United States that men register for the draft when they reach their eighteenth birthday.

Hypervigilance: Being highly alert to one's surroundings

Post-Traumatic Stress Disorder (PTSD): A diagnostic category whose symptoms include feeling depressed, guilt over having killed, guilt over having survived when one's mates have been killed, high anxiety, difficulty falling asleep or maintaining a regular sleep schedule, unwanted and intrusive memories (typically of injuries and death), and flashbacks.

Concussion: A traumatic injury that disrupts the functioning of the brain. Concussions are caused when the brain is thrown against the inside of the skull.

Dementia: A general term to describe cognitive impairments such as memory failures, language disturbances, and problems in planning and abstract thinking.

Midlife crisis: An event that occurs during a person's forties during which they make profound changes in the ways that they approach their work, relationships, and leisure pursuits as a result of the psychological pressure produced by reaching this age milestone. Note that only a minority of men appear to experience such a crisis.

Chapter Fourteen

Surviving and Thriving: Men and Physical Health

In the not-too-distant past, before it was possible to know a baby's sex before birth, it was common to ask expectant parents if they had a preference for either a boy or a girl. One of the most frequent responses to this inquiry was, "We don't care as long as 'it's' healthy." As the data show, "it" has a greater chance to live a long, healthy life if it is a girl, as sex and gender have a significant relationship to physical well-being. As we will see, the reference to females as "the weaker sex" is misleading when it comes to serious health problems and longevity.

A good deal of evidence has led scholars to suggest that certain aspects of traditional masculinity are at least partially responsible for men's problems with disease and longevity (see reviews by Gough & Roberston, 2016; Griffith & Thorpe, 2016; Wong, Liu, & Klann, 2016). Researchers have found that people of both sexes who score high on measures of masculinity were more likely to die at every age than those who scored low (Lippa, Martin, & Friedman, 2000). Thus gender-related beliefs are a significant factor in mortality and the relationship is a strong one. As one research team noted, "The increase in mortality risk in masculine individuals... was comparable to increases in mortality risk associated with physiological factors such as elevated blood pressure." (Lippa et al., 2000, p. 1568). Furthermore, results from a comparative study of 51 countries indicated that higher levels of patriarchy in a society were associated with higher mortality in men (Stanistreet, Bambra, & Scott-Samuel, 2005). At the same time, African and African-American men who endorse nontraditional masculinity ideologies tend to engage in more positive health behaviors than their counterparts who do not (Wade, 2008a, 2008b). Generally speaking, men could be healthier than they are.

In this chapter, we discuss *physical health,* which we define to include bodily health, disease, and mortality issues. We describe some of these problems and review the relevant psychological literature on sex and gender as it relates to physical health. We begin with discussion of male-female differences, then shift our focus to racial and ethnic differences before discussing some intersections between sex and race. We then offer explanations for some of these group differences, pointing specifically to the ways hegemonic masculinity contributes to men's mortality. Although our discussion acknowledges the ways that race and ethnicity impact men's health and thus necessitate an intersectional perspective, a complete discussion of these interconnections is beyond the scope of this chapter (for more discussion, see Gough & Robertson, 2017; Griffith & Thorpe, 2016; Wong et al., 2016).

Sex and Racial Differences in Morality and Disease Rates

There are male-female differences in the *epidemiologies*, defined as the statistical incidences within a population, of many physical problems. We begin our discussion with data reported by the Centers for Disease Control and Prevention (CDC). Although many of the values reported in this table are approximately five to ten years old, the authors of several of these reports note that population-level changes over time tend to be gradual and that shifts from one year to the next tend to be small (MacDormand & Mathews, 2013; Meyer et al., 2013; Zack, 2013).

Sex Differences

On average, men live shorter lives than women; Table 14.1 provides some of the relevant statistics. Longevity is not the whole story; men start to lose their physical abilities at a younger age than women and have more years of life with some type of activity limits (10.1 vs. 7.6). In part, the differential in full life span is the result of greater male mortality due to suicide, homicide, drug use (primarily as accidental overdose), or motor vehicle accidents, all of which claim a greater percentage of younger lives and thus have a relatively larger impact on the mathematics behind *average* lifespan. The higher rate of infant mortality among boys also contributes to a lower average lifespan. Hypertension rates are also provided here because it is a major risk factor for both heart disease, the leading cause of death in the United States, and stroke, the fourth leading cause of death. Although men suffer from hypertension at slightly higher rates than women, they are notably less likely to gain control of their blood pressure, suggesting that men are less likely—or possibly less effective—in treating their hypertension.

Men in the United States have died an average of five to eight years younger than women since the decade of the 1950s (Arias, 2005). This "mortality gap" varies internationally, from a low of 3.3 (Israel) to a high of 13.3 (Russian Federation) (National Center for Health Statistics, 2008).

Table 14.1
Sex Differences in Physical Health Indicators

Mortality	Rate per	Males	Females
Life Expectancy (years)		74.1	79.3
Life Expectancy Years Free of Activity Limits		64.3	67.7
Infant Mortality	1,000	7.22	5.97
Homicide rate	100,000	8..473.0	2.4
Suicide rate	100,000	19.2	5.0
Drug induced deaths	100,000	16.1	13.1
Motor vehicle deaths	100,000	16.8	6.8
Physically unhealthy days	Last 30 days	3.4	4.0
Mentally unhealthy days	Last 30 days	3.0	4.1
Hypertension	population	30.5%	28.6%
Hypertension treatment*	population	42.7%	55.5%

References: Life expectancy from Molla, 2013; Drug induced death rate from Mack, 2013; Homicide rate from Logan et al., 2013), infant mortality from MacDormand & Mathews, 2013; Motor Vehicle deaths from West & Naumann, 2013; Suicide rate from Crosby et al., 2013; Unhealthy days from Zack, 2013; Hypertension rates and treatment from Gillespie & Hurvitz, 2013.

At birth, there is a slight imbalance in the ratio of males to females. Conception favors males because Y-chromosome bearing sperm (androsperm) are more motile than X-chromosome bearing sperm (gynosperm), and thus they are more likely to fertilize the ovum. There are somewhere between 120 and 160 males for every 100 females at conception (Stillion, 1995). However, male fetuses are more likely to have problems *in utero*, leading to higher rates of spontaneous abortion (miscarriage). By birth, the large sex imbalance that was produced at conception has shrunken considerably; there are between 104 and 106 male births for every 100 female births (Stein, 2005). The male:female ratio is further reduced by the higher rates of *infant mortality*, defined as deaths in the first 12 months of life not due to accident. Collectively, the differences in miscarriage and infant mortality point to some amount of fragility among male fetuses that cannot be linked to hegemonic norms of masculinity. We discuss biological (or "biogenic") factors in more detail later in the chapter.

Identifying *all* of the factors that contribute to these male-female differences, as well as the ethnic differences discussed later, requires attention to biological factors (inherited or acquired), individual factors (personality, gender socialization, etc.), environmental factors (e.g., pollutant levels, access to healthcare), and issues within the social and health care systems (e.g., institutional racism) (Meyer et al., 2013). However, greater adherence to the hegemonic norms of masculinity appears to play a role (Courtenay, 2011; Gough & Robertson, 2017; Griffith & Thorpe, 2016). Directives to take risks, for example, contribute to men's greater mortality rates from risky driving, drug use, and dangerous sports. Directives to not show weakness or vulnerability may help explain why men are less likely to treat illness (e.g., hypertension) or reach out to others who might provide emotional support; social support is recognized as a key factor in reducing the mortality rates for suicide, cancer, and a variety of chronic conditions (Courtenay, 2011).

Racial and Ethnic Differences

As can be seen in Table 14.2, men's mortality rates vary substantially across United States ethnic groups, and this variation contributes to differences in longevity and life expectancy (Molla, 2013); Table 10.3 lists the Top 10 causes of death. Two general trends are visible from these data. One is that Asians have the lowest rates for each of these causes of death, except suicide, where their rate of 8.8 completed suicides per 100,000 members of the population places them slightly worse than Latinos at 8.5 completed suicides per 100,000 in population. The other is that Blacks and Native Americans tend to have the two worst rates for most of these causes of death, although rates for suicide and drug induced deaths are highest among Whites. In fact, Whites are overrepresented among completed suicides, where they account for approximately 83.5 percent of all deaths (Crosby, Ortega, & Stevens, 2013).

The adverse effects on Black men's lives are reflected in these tables, but the numbers provide only part of the story. In Chapter Two, we documented the relatively higher rates of incarceration and poverty, as well as the relatively lower rates of access to healthcare among Blacks; these factors also influence health behaviors, as do generational issues and the cultural discourse. Drug induced deaths, most of which are accidental, were highest among Blacks during the 1980s and 1990s, but are now dominated by Whites (Mack, 2013).

Table 14.2
Male Mortality Rates Among U.S. Ethnic Groups

	Rate per	*Hispanic*	*Black*	*White*	*Asian/Pacific Islander*
Life expectancy	—	n/a	71.8	77.3	n/a
Homicide rate	100,000	6.6	19.9	2.6	2.2
Suicide rate	100,000	8.5	8.9	24.4	8.8
Drug induced deaths	100,000	7.6	11.5	20.0	2.7
Motor vehicle deaths	100,000	14.7	18.5	17.3	6.3
Infant mortality rate (male and female)	1,000	5.6	12.7	5.5	4.5

References: Life expectancy from Molla, 2013; Drug induced death rate from Mack, 2013; Homicide rate from Logan et al., 2013), infant mortality from MacDormand & Mathews, 2013; Motor Vehicle deaths from West & Naumann, 2013; Suicide rate from Crosby et al., 2013

During the former period, lawmakers and the media focused on incarceration as the primary response to the drug problem, while current responses to the issue (related to opioids) have increasingly acknowledged the importance of addressing drug dependence. Blacks are also disproportionately affected by the homicide rate, which is at least twice that of the next highest morality rate for every other ethnic group; they are the only racial group for which homicide ranks among the top five causes of death. Sadly, these statistics represent some level of progress: from 1999 to 2009, the homicide rate was approximately half of what it was from 1990 to 1994.

Black men and women also have concerns about the medical system in general and many mistrust the medical system due to a series of racist events over the last 100 years. These events include allowing Black men to experience the worst effects of syphilis despite knowledge that a cure existed (aka the "Tuskeegee Syphilis study"), the use of Henrietta Lacks blood for research without her permission, and a range of other examples. Thus, it should be of little surprise that Black men (and women) are less likely than White men (and women) to seek medical help and less likely to follow doctor's orders and thus die at relatively higher rates for many of these diseases (Hammond et al., 2016).

Asian-Americans are sometimes referred to as the "model minority" because they tend to outperform all racial and ethnic groups, including Whites, on a range of indicators. Their success is typically attributed solely to hard work and excludes any recognition of structural and institutional barriers they may need to overcome. Originally coined in the 1960s, some commentators have suggested that the concept of a "model minority" has risen to the level of myth that implies Asians do not need help of any sort (Ibaraki, Hall, & Sabin, 2014). Endorsement of these beliefs among Asians and Asian-Americans living in the United States was associated with higher rates of physical symptoms, higher rates of mental health symptoms, and a lower likelihood of seeking help (Gupta et al., 2011). In a separate study, Asians and Asian-Americans reported underutilizing physical health services due to cultural barriers as well as a lack of knowledge that culturally appropriate and linguistically accessible services were available. In this community sample, men reported fewer chronic health conditions than women (Tendulkar et al,. 2012).

The data in Tables 14.2 and 14.3 obscure some age-related differences. Homicide rates are highest among 15- to 29-year-olds, followed by 30- to 49-year-olds, and continue to decline with older age (Logan, Hall, McDaniel, & Stevens, 2013). A similar pattern is evident regarding suicide, where rates are highest among 15 to 34 year olds (especially for American Indians and Native Americans) and typically fall through later life, although non-Hispanic Whites show an elevated rate of completed suicide among 40- to 54-year-olds as well as among those age 65 or older (Crosby et al., 2013; National Center for Health Statistics, 2008). The adolescent and young adult period reflects a time when men are supposed to begin their ascent towards power and status (Levinson et al., 1978; O'Neil, 2013), including major life accomplishments such as finding a

Table 14.3
Leading Causes of Male Deaths by Racial Group

Rank	Hispanic	Black	White	Asian/Pacific Islander	Native American/Alaska Native
1	Cancer 20.7%	Heart disease 24.1%	Heart disease 25.1%	Cancer 27.1%	Heart disease 24.1%
2	Heart disease 20.6%	Cancer 23.3%	Cancer 24.6%	Heart disease 23.5%	Cancer 23.3%
3	Unintentional injuries 9.5%	Unintentional injuries 5.5%	Unintentional injuries 6.2%	Stroke 6.6%	Unintentional injuries 9.5%
4	Stroke 4.25	Stroke 4.8%	Chronic lower respiratory diseases 5.7%	Unintentional injuries 5.0%	Diabetes 4.2%
5	Diabetes 4.2%	Homicide 4.6%	Stroke 4.1%	Diabetes 3.5%	Chronic liver disease 3.9%
6	Chronic liver disease 3.9%	Diabetes 3.9%	Diabetes 2.7%	Chronic lower respiratory diseases 3.4%	Chronic lower respiratory diseases 4.1%
7	Homicide 3.1%	Chronic lower respiratory diseases 3.1%	Suicide 2.6%	Influenza & pneumonia 3.1%	Suicide 4.0%
8	Chronic lower respiratory diseases 2.7%	Kidney disease 2.8%	Alzheimer's disease 2.2%	Suicide 2.8%	Stroke 3.0%
9	Suicide 2.7%	HIV disease 2.1%	Influenza & pneumonia 1.9%	Kidney disease 2.0%	Homicide 3.1%
10	Kidney disease 2.1%	Septicemia 1.8%	Kidney disease 1.9%	Alzheimer's disease 1.3%	Influenza & pneumonia 2.0%

*The Black, White, American Indian/Alaska Native, and Asian/Pacific Islander categories include individuals of Hispanic and Non-Hispanic origin. Data from CDC, 2011.

long term partner and starting their career (Arnett, 2000; Erikson, 1968). Being the victim of a homicide may represent an extreme outcome of the competition for power, status, or partners (Kruger & Nesse, 2004, 2006), while suicide may be understood as one response to failing to achieve these goals.

Ethnic differences are also reflected in assessments of disease rates and self-reported quality of life as it pertains to health, as described in Table 14.4. Note that the values in this table reflect incidence among both males and females, although males fare worse than females in each of these categories (CDC, 2017; Gillespie & Hurvits, 2013; Zack, 2013). Again, we see that Asians and Whites tend to fare best while Native Americans and Blacks fare poorly.

These differences partly reflect the impact of social class, poverty, and health insurance coverage, as discussed in Chapter Two. Black and Latino men are less likely to have insurance and, on average, have lower levels of education than either Whites or Asians. Analyses indicate that college graduates tend to have better health than high school graduates and those who did not complete high school, reporting fewer physically and mentally unhealthy days (Zack, 2013) as well as lower rates of hypertension and higher rates of treatment to control hypertension (Gillespie & Hurvitz, 2013). The issue is further compounded by one of the general differences between jobs requiring a college degree and those that require less than a college education: control over one's schedule. College graduates are much more likely to have paid time off, greater schedule flexibility (which minimizes the need to use paid time off), greater ability to work from home, and greater flexibility in their use of paid time off (in hours instead of half days, via shifting work times, etc.). As such, college graduates are less likely to need to choose between a doctor's visit and earning money (or providing childcare), which provides them with greater opportunities to access health care.

Table 14.4
Selected Disease Rates and Quality of Life Issues Across U.S. Ethnic Groups (Men and Women)

	Rate per	Asian	Black	Hispanic	White	Native American
Physically unhealthy days	last 30 days	2.5	4.3	4.4	3.5	6.3
Mentally unhealthy days	last 30 days	2.0	4.0	3.8	3.5	5.7
Hypertension*	population	n/a	41.3	27.7	28.6	n/a
Hypertension treatment	population	n/a	42.5	34.4	34.4	n/a

Note: *Hypertension treatment was assessed as blood pressure control. References: Unhealthy days from Zack, 2013; Hypertension rates and treatment from Gillespie & Hurvitz, 2013

Socio-economic status (SES) also plays a role, as impoverished men are more likely than majority men to live in hazardous, stressful, and/or impoverished environments, as well as to lack access to health care, with Blacks and Latinos overrepresented among those living in poverty (Ro, Casares, Treadwell, & Thomas, 2004). In poor urban areas, two-thirds of African American males fail to reach the age of 65. They also experience ongoing stress from being Black in the United States (Hammond et al., 2016). According to health scholar Arline Geronimus (quoted in Blitstein, 2009), "American minorities face a bevy of chronic obstacles that Whites and the socioeconomically advantaged cope with far less often: environmental pollution, high crime, poor health care, overt racism, concentrated poverty" (p. 51).

Biogenic Explanations for Group Differences

Around the beginning of the twentieth century, men's lives and women's lives, on average, were about the same length. In modern industrial and post-industrial nations such as the United States, there has been a dramatic reduction in the risk of death from pregnancy and childbirth, which were relatively dangerous at the beginning of the twentieth century (Stillion, 1995). The decrease of this risk contributed to the lifespan sex differential. It could be said that both women's and men's lives were shortened 100 years ago, and that we have found ways to prevent many early deaths for women. Hopefully, the same can be done for men. However, it may become apparent to you that this is a complicated process (Gough & Robertson, 2017; Griffith & Thorpe, 2016).

There are two basic types of explanations for the sex difference in average lifespan. The first is a *biogenic* explanation. From this viewpoint, men die earlier because of genetic, hormonal, or other biological differences between the sexes or ethnic groups. The second type of explanation is a *psychogenic* one, in which differences in lifespan are attributed to gender and ethnic differences in psychological and social areas such as behaviors, socialization, and methods of problem solving.

Note that these two types of explanations do not necessarily compete with each other. It is possible for both biogenic and psychogenic factors to contribute to differences in longevity and there is good evidence to suggest that both factors are operating in many cases. The question is one of the relative contribution of each factor. There has been a trend among researchers in recent years to speak of *biopsychosocial* models that take biology, individual psychology, and the effects of other people and social systems into account in constructing comprehensive pictures of behavioral phenomena.

It is also possible for biogenic and psychogenic factors to interact with one another. For instance, a White man who is at high risk for heart disease because of his physiology (biogenic factor) might be less likely than a White woman to see a physician for regular checkups because he sees doing so as an admission of weakness and vulnerability, which he considers unmasculine and therefore undesirable (psychogenic factor). The man in this example might have a shorter life than would be the case if either factor were operating in isolation. At the same time, that hypothetical White man may be more likely than a Black man to receive healthcare due to different levels of access to healthcare and trust in the medical system. These psychogenic factors would also contribute to differences in longevity.

As we mentioned earlier, male fetuses are more vulnerable *in utero* and during infancy (less than one year) than female fetuses; the death rate for males aged one to four also exceeds that of females. These data are ample evidence that biological factors operate in the lifespan sex differential, as it would be difficult to argue that masculine socialization could have an effect on mortality at such early ages. Explanations of biological factors include genetic and hormonal sex differences.

Genetic Differences

The difference in males' and females' genetic makeup is in the 46th pair of chromosomes ("the sex chromosomes"): genetic females have two X-chromosomes and genetic males have one X- and one Y-chromosome. When there are recessive disease genes on the X-chromosome, having a second X-chromosome turns out to be a genetic advantage. The second X-chromosome often contains a dominant corresponding gene that protects the female from contracting the genetic disease. For example, if there is a gene for hemophilia on one X-chromosome, the female will not contract the disease unless there is also a hemophilia gene on the other X-chromosome, an extremely rare occurrence.

Because the form of the Y-chromosome does not correspond exactly with that of the X-chromosome, the male is not always afforded such protection. In fact, the Y-chromosome is far and away the smallest of the 46 chromosomes, containing about 60 genes compared with about 800 on the X chromosome (Eliot, 2009). Genetic abnormalities on the X-chromosome are much more likely to appear in the male because of the absence of a second (corrective) X-chromosome. Some "X-linked" abnormalities like color blindness or baldness are relatively innocuous. Others are more serious. For instance, there is some speculation that dyslexia (a learning disability) and hyperactivity might be X-linked. A few genetic abnormalities, such as hemophilia, can be life threatening.

In the search for explanations of the sex differential in longevity, genetic differences account for a relatively small number of deaths, although they may have a large statistical impact on average lifespan because they are associated with deaths among the youngest segment of the population. As Waldron (quoted in Dolnick, 1991) stated, "Most of the common X-linked diseases aren't fatal, and most of the fatal X-linked diseases aren't common." (p. 12).

Hormonal Differences

A major sex difference in hormones is in males' higher levels of testosterone and females' higher levels of estrogen. These two hormones account for physiological sex differences in average muscle size, body fat percentage, and metabolic speed. There is evidence to suggest that testosterone may render men somewhat more vulnerable to certain diseases, and that estrogen may have some protective effect.

The most demonstrable effect of these two hormones is in the area of heart disease. The effect of cholesterol on heart disease has been the subject of much research and discussion. There are two kinds of cholesterol, high density lipoprotein (HDL), called "good cholesterol" because it protects against heart disease, and low density lipoprotein (LDL), called "bad cholesterol" because of its damaging effects.

In prepubescent males and females, HDL levels are about equal. At puberty, HDL levels drop rapidly in boys, but they hold steady in girls. This change coincides with the large surge of testosterone in boys and estrogen in girls. It is assumed that adolescent testosterone production is responsible for the reduction of HDL cholesterol, while estrogen has little or no effect on HDL levels (Dolnick, 1991).

LDL ("bad") cholesterol begins to rise in both males and females after puberty. However, males show a more rapid increase, leaving them more susceptible to heart disease. After menopause, when women's estrogen level is greatly reduced, LDL levels show this same kind of sharp increase. Therefore, researchers believe that estrogen has a protective effect against LDL cholesterol, while testosterone probably has little effect (Kevorkian & Cepeda, 2007). These hormonal effects are important ones because heart disease is the leading cause of death. However, there is also some evidence that testosterone may shorten men's lives in other ways that are not fully understood.

Psychogenic Explanations for Group Differences

There are at least four ways in which psychological processes can contribute to illness, injury, and/or premature mortality. First, behaviors can be directly self-destructive. Suicide may provide the clearest example of this type of psychogenic factor, but one might also consider the use of tobacco products or the excessive use of alcohol and other drugs in this category. These behaviors involve the person's active harm of his or her body. Second, it is also possible for the person to passively harm his or her health by neglecting to perform behaviors that maintain health. For example, a man with high blood pressure who refuses to take prescribed medication to control it, or someone who does not see a physician even though he has detected a symptom of cancer (when he has medical resources available to him) adversely affects his health through his behavior.

Third, some behaviors involve physical risk of illness, injury, or death. These behaviors include: sharing needles in intravenous drug use, risky and drunk driving, and engaging in dangerous sports. Fourth, some psychological processes seem to have adverse effects on the body. For instance, the effects of stress on physical health are well documented, and there are also certain personality characteristics that are predictive of some physical conditions. We have separated these four categories of psychogenic factors for purposes of discussion.

Self-Destructive Behaviors

Suicide. Suicide is the ultimate self-destructive behavior and the overwhelmingly most common motive for it is to escape from one's pain. Although females in the United States are more likely than males to make suicidal gestures or attempts, Males in the United States complete suicide attempts almost four times more often than females (see Table 10.1; Crobsy et al., 2013). Among older people, the ratio of male to female suicides is striking. U.S. men over 65 commit suicide at more than seven times the rate of women; at age 85, the ratio is more than eleven to one (National Center for Health Statistics, 2008). William Pollack (2000a) pointed out that, although more people die from suicide than from homicide in the United States, homicide prevention accounts for ten times the financial expenditure of suicide prevention.

There is some belief that women are more likely than men to use suicide attempts to "cry for help" rather than as determined efforts to die, which are more common in men (Harrison, Chin, & Ficaratto, 1995). Women are also more likely to use suicide methods that have relatively low potential for death, such as overdose or wrist slashing, whereas men are more likely to use violent and highly lethal methods such as firearms or motor vehicles (Nolen-Hoeksema, 1998). However, it is important to note that males complete more suicides with every method (Canetto, 2000). Firearm suicides accounted for 60 percent of all male suicides, compared to 39 percent of all female suicides (Anderson & Smith, 2005), and among older American men, 80 percent of completed suicides are with firearms (Kaplan, Huguet, McFarland, & Mandle, 2012). White males commit four out of five firearm suicides (National Institute of Mental Health, 2003).

Hegemonic masculinity has several connections to suicidal behavior. Foremost among these is a gender-differentiated socialization for dealing with psychological pain. Whereas women have been taught to think about and express feelings, access social support, and take care of themselves, men are socialized to act on problems, be independent, neglect emotional self-care, and "play through the pain." In general, social support is protective of health (Karren, Smith, Hafen, & Gordon, 2009). Yet the stereotypically masculine man in severe emotional distress is often alone with his pain. He cannot express it, and he cannot ask for help with it. If the pain becomes great enough, it may seem to him that suicide is his only option. The masculine norm of independence may exacerbate these difficulties in expressing emotion because needing and requesting help is antithetical to traditional masculinity. Teenagers who feel connected to their families are much less likely to engage in suicidal behavior (or violence and drug abuse), and the adolescent suicide sex differential may be related to families' demands for independence in boys (Pollack, 1998). Despondent men often feel alone with problems that seem unsolvable and pain that seems intractable. For these men, suicide may seem like the only alternative. It is apparent that, more often than females, males are unwilling to ask for help either before their problems escalate to the point of suicide contemplation, or by giving messages through a suicide gesture rather than a serious attempt.

The success, status, and problem-solving orientation in gender-typical males may also contribute to men's higher rate of completed suicides. The masculine value of "getting the job done" may actually relate to the "job" of taking one's life. The combination of pain and masculine bravado can be a quite volatile one. In a strongly worded statement, Stillion and McDowell (1996) describe this association:

> If we wanted to write a prescription for increasing suicide risk, we could not improve on the traditional male socialization pattern. Take one male child, who has higher levels of aggression and activity than his female peers. Put the child into competitive situations. Tell him he must win at all costs. Teach him that to admit fear or doubt is weakness and that weakness is not masculine. Complete the vicious circle by assuring him that his worth is dependent on winning games, then salary and promotion competitions, and you have the perfect recipe for enhanced suicide risk. (p. 243)

In old age, the impact of this masculine "formula" may also be felt, particularly as some aspects of masculiniity begin to fade away. Men are culturally defined by physical abilities and the work role. The older man must face the facts that his body is declining and, after he retires, that he is no longer a valued contributor in the working world. If his sense of self is overly dependent on these aspects of masculinity, the decline of physical ability and work can seriously undermine his sense of self-worth. Additionally, the man may also be faced with a loss of independence at some point during his physical decline, which is also antithetical to current masculine norms. The transition away from these markers appears to be particularly difficult for White men, as reflected by their higher rate of completed suicides starting at age 50. As the demographic group that benefits the most from patriarchy, masculinities, and competition between male sub-groups, as well as the invisibility of systemic barriers through privilege (see Chapter Two), this group of men have likely experienced either the lowest levels of threat to their sense of (masculine) self or the greatest ability to overcome such threats through individual effort. When faced with the end of their work life, they would seem to have the least experience and flexilbility to adjust their definitions of masculinity, and thus view their impending old age as a perpetual source of inability and failure.

Use of Tobacco. Tobacco products are the only commodities legally sold in the United States that, when used as intended, will ultimately kill the consumer. The most common results of extended tobacco use are bronchitis, emphysema, asthma, and cancers of the respiratory system, mouth, and throat. Male smokers tend to engage in more dangerous smoking habits than women, including smoking more than 25 cigarettes a day, inhaling deeply, using products with high tar and nicotine content and/or cigarettes without filters (Courtenay, 2000a). Racial differences also occur; Black men are more likely than other men to smoke menthol cigarettes, with some evidence suggesting that menthol increases the likelihood of addiction (Griffith & Thorpe, 2016). Will Courtenay (2000b) summarizes the connections between gender and tobacco use:

> Cigarette smoking is considered the single most preventable cause of illness and death in the United States.... Tobacco use accounts for roughly one in five deaths overall, and one in four deaths among those aged 35 to 64 years. *Twice as many male as female deaths are attributed to smoking,* and men's higher lifetime use of tobacco is considered a primary reason for their higher rates of cardiovascular disease and stroke. One quarter of all heart disease deaths are associated with smoking. The risk of heart disease and stroke among smokers is more than double the risk for nonsmokers, and the risk of sudden cardiac death is up to 4 times greater.... Three of four men who get *any* kind of cancer are smokers. The lung cancer death rate for men is 2.5 times higher than the rate for women, and 9 of 10 male lung cancer deaths can be directly attributed to cigarette smoking. Men who smoke double their risk of prostate cancer. Regularly smoking cigars doubles a man's risk of lung cancer and increases his risk of oral cancer between 5 and 10 times. Smokeless tobacco users increase their risk of developing oral cancer by *nearly 50 times*. (pp. 8–9, emphases added)

"Smokeless" tobacco (chewing tobacco and snuff) is used by males almost exclusively. According to 2015 CDC data (2016), one out of six male high school seniors had used these products within the past year. The average first use of smokeless tobacco is at age nine, and one quarter of users had their first taste of chewing tobacco before age five! There are 30,000 new cases of oral cancer each year in the United States, with a mortality rate of one-half of new cases within five years of diagnosis. Males are diagnosed with mouth and throat cancer two and a half times more often than females and account for two thirds of all deaths from this cause (American Cancer Society, 2014).

Socialization of destructive masculine behaviors can certainly be implicated in tobacco use. Advertisers know that they can sell a great deal by playing on people's insecurities and then offering a product that promises to remove their misgivings about their adequacy. When one is asked to live up to vague and impossible standards of masculinity, what man would not feel insecure? Advertisers have long used masculine mystique approaches to sell their products by associating tobacco with desirable images such as the Marlboro Man and Joe Camel, who reflect masculine norms of self-assuredness, independence, and adventurousness. Approximatley six times more males than females smoke on prime time television, and *Sports Illustrated*, the number one magazine read by adolescent males, used to contain more tobacco advertisements than any other magazine (Courtenay, 2000a). Smoking advertisements tend to be more common in neighborhoods with higher numbers of black residents (Griffith & Thorpe, 2016). This advertising is both reflective and encouraging of a theme often directed at men: act now and worry about the consequences later.

Neglectful Behaviors

Men sometimes shorten their lives or become ill because they fail to perform the behaviors necessary to maintain their health. As noted earlier, hypertension is only slightly more common in men than women (30.5 percent vs. 28.6 percent), but women are able to bring their blood pressure under control at notably higher rates than men (55.5 percent vs 42.7 percent) (Gillespie & Hurvitz, 2013). There is no physiological explanation reason why this should be the case.

Men can also create problems by failing to seek help or take time off from work when it is indicated, such as when they are injured, sick, emotionally distraught, or when they have not had a physical examination for a long time. Stereotypically masculine men may see taking necessary medication and seeking help as admissions of weakness, vulnerability, and dependence, which go against the masculine cultural prescriptions to handle problems on one's own, focus outside of the self, be strong and invulnerable, and "take it like a man."

Males are less knowledgeable than females about health in general and about symptoms of specific diseases, less responsive to health information, and less likely to utilize the health care system (Courtenay, 2011). This set of problems may cause embarrassment when talking to a health care provider, and was cited as the major reason for failing to discuss medical problems (Royner, 1992). By contrast, women give more information and ask more questions during doctor visits than men. The average number of questions that a woman asks during a 15-minute visit is six; men average zero (Pleck, 1995)! Furthermore, men who subscribe to hegemonic masculine gender ideologies show a greater willingness than other men to engage in a wide range of risk behaviors (Courtenay, McCreary, & Merighi, 2002).

Prostate cancer effects approximately one in nine men, mostly men over age 65 and men of African American descent. For most men, the disease is not fatal; approximately one in 41 will die from prostate cancer (American Cancer Society, 2018). Half of men do not know the symptoms of prostate and colorectal cancer, nor those of prostate enlargement, which affects half of men over the age of 50 (Fortin, 2007). The Movember Foundation was created to raise awareness of these diseases and their symptoms; they are probably best known for their November mustache campaign ("Movember").

Men are also less likely than women to practice preventive health care such as taking vitamins (Wardle, et. al., 2004), performing self-examinations, having regular physicals (Courtenay, McCreary, & Merighi, 2002), taking prescriptions as directed, and returning to physicians for follow-up visits (Helgeson, 2011). Researchers have documented a range of ways in which men's diets are poorer than women's, including eating fewer fruits and vegetables, eating more red meat, and eating more calories than are appropriate (Gough & Robertson, 2017; Griffith & Thorpe, 2016). Indeed, greater adherence to hegemonic masculine norms is associated with lower levels of approval of a vegetarian diet (Rothgerber, 2013), which may provide insight regarding the audience for the cookbook *Eat What You Want and Die like a Man: The World's Unhealthiest Cookbook* (Graham, 2008).

Risk Behaviors

Men sometimes choose to engage in behaviors that involve the risk of injury, death, or legal sanction. They also tend to underestimate their health risks across every domain of dangerous behavior (Courtenay, McCreary, & Merighi, 2002). For instance, habitual excessive drinking puts one at increased risk for liver disease and accidents, but many men downplay the risks and argue that they can stop or reduce their drinking whenever they want. Yet males are twice as likely to abuse alcohol as females (Nolen-Hoeksema & Hilt, 2006), and are more than 80 percent of those arrested for alcohol and drug abuse violations (Schwartz, 2008). As described in Table 10.2, males die in car accidents more than twice as often as females (West & Naumann, 2013). They drown more than four times as often (National Safety Council, 2010). Males account for 82 percent of spinal cord injuries (National Spinal Cord Injury Association, 2005). United States males are eighteen times more likely than females to die on the job (derived from National Center for Health Statistics, 2008). Risk-taking starts early; among preschool children, gender stereotype conformity is a predictor of injury risk behaviors (Granie, 2010). Among teens and undergraduates, greater endorsement of hegemonic masculine norms is related to higher rates of many of the risk behaviors listed here (Giaccardi, Ward, Seabrook, Manago, & Lippman, 2017; Iwamoto & Smiler, 2013).

Physical Problems with Psychological Inputs

The field of *behavioral medicine* is focused on understanding and treating physical disorders that are thought to be strongly influenced by the person's psychological functioning. Masculine socialization may well contribute to some health problems that are disproportionately experienced by men. We examine three such disorders here: cardiovascular disorders, body image disturbances, and HIV/AIDS.

Cardiovascular Disorders. It has long been suspected that coronary artery disease and hypertension have strong relationships to stressful work settings and certain behavioral patterns of response to those environments. Hypertension is quite common among workers in highly stressful occupations (e.g., air traffic controllers, police officers). It is also common among those described as projecting an image of being easygoing but at the same time suppressing a good deal of anger (Hackett, Rosenbaum & Cassen, 1985).

Several decades ago, cardiologists Meyer Friedman and Ray Rosenhan coined the term *Type A behavior* to describe a personality pattern commonly found in people who had suffered myocardial infarction (heart attack). This pattern described the classic compulsive, hostile, competitive, emotionally inexpressive "workaholic." Friedman (cited in Hackett, et. al., 1985) defined *Type A* as, "a characteristic action-emotion complex which is exhibited by those individuals who are engaged in a relatively chronic struggle to obtain an unlimited number of poorly defined things from their environments in the shortest period of time and, if possible, against the opposing efforts of other things or persons in this same environment" (p. 1154). Research indicates that the hostility component of Type A is more predictive of coronary heart disease than the other characteristics (Benson, 2003), and chronic anger and hostility is estimated to increase the risk of heart attack by a factor of three (Smith, 2003). Hostile personality is associated with four to five times the risk of death from all causes for the age group 25 to 50, thus it also carries risks beyond heart disease, most notably, cerebrovascular accident ("stroke") (Williams et. al., 2002).

Again we see vestiges of the destructive aspects of masculine norms in this pattern: a continual attempt to measure up to vague standards of achievement and competition. Type A individuals tend to be independent; they seize authority and dislike sharing responsibility. Contrary to popular belief, they tend to be less successful than those who are more relaxed and less aggressive (Hackett, et. al., 1985). Type A behaviors are significantly related to masculine gender typing (Grimm & Yarnold, 1985). Negative or extreme masculinity is also related to heart attack severity (Helgeson, 1990). Higher femininity scores in men are predictive of decreased death risk from coronary heart disease after controlling for other risk factors (Hunt, Lewars, Emslie, & Batty, 2007).

Vicki Helgeson (1995) proposed that certain aspects of masculine norms interact with biological factors to produce high levels of coronary risk. Not only is the hegemonic form of masculinity associated with Type A behavior, it is also linked with low levels of social support and poor health care practices, which are both linked to masculine hyperindependence as well as coronary risk.

Body Image Disturbances in Men. The drive for thinness and resultant risk of eating disorders in females is a well-documented phenomenon that is strongly associated with cultural standards of beauty that emphasize body types that are impossible to achieve for most women. The diagnoses most commonly associated with these standards, *anorexia nervosa* and *bulimia ner-*

vosa, are approximately four to eight times more common in women than men according to the DSM-V (American Psychiatric Association, 2013). The same patterns and influences are also working on American men, to the detriment of many, although the focus is on being more muscular.

Several researchers have documented changes in the "ideal" male figure, which consists of well-defined and large muscles, a low level of fat, and a V-shaped upper body (Murnen & Karazsia, 2017; Parent, Schwartz, & Bradstreet, 2016). Researchers Harrison Pope and Roberto Olivardia have conducted much of this research. They have documented that action figures produced when the movie Star Wars was originally released in 1977 were much less muscular than when the action figures were reproduced 20 years later. The change was even more dramatic for G. I. Joe, whose biceps grew from the equivalent of 13 inches (estimated by their proportion to the rest of the body) to 28 inches (Pope, Olivardia, Gruber, & Borowiecki, 1999). For contrast and scale, actor Dwayne "The Rock" Johnson's biceps are approximately 20 inches. Other action figures have undergone similar transformations (Baghurst, Hollander, Nardella, & Haff, 2006), and male characters in action movies have become more muscular in the last few decades (Morrison & Halton, 2009). An analysis of male models in advertisements in women's magazines from 1958 to 1998 revealed that, over time, the men were revealing more of their bodies (Pope, Olivardia, Borowiecki, & Cohane, 2001), with those bodies generally more muscular and better "cut." Pope and Olivardia ultimately described men who demonstrated pursuit of this idealized muscular bodies as suffering from the "Adonis Complex" (Pope, Philips, & Olivardia, 2000). Some commentators believe this cultural change reflects a crisis of masculinity accompanied by high anxiety in men around their desirability and manliness (Katz, 2013). Although there is no formal diagnosis for this particular pattern of body image and eating disturbance, men have relatively higher rates of body dysmorphic disorder, a general diagnosis to catch problematic behavior that does not fit other eating disorder criteria (American Psychiatric Association, 2013). Colloquially, their symptoms are sometimes called "bigorexia."

Most teens and undergraduate men have little difficulty imagining a conversation about their body with another man, expecting it to happen at the gym or while playing sports, and to include discussion of overall muscle amount, abdominals, and chest/pectoral muscles ("pecs"), but not, for example, hips or legs (Engeln, Sladek, & Waldron, 2013; Martin & Govender, 2011). Being more muscular or better defined are typically the focus of male body concerns, and most men pursue these goals via exercise and diet. However, cosmetic or "plastic" surgery may also an option for achieving a more desirable body. To be clear, we are discussing procedures that are strictly voluntary and not due to prior accident or injury. The American Society of Plastic Surgeons (2011) reports that although men account for only 10 percent of such procedures, they continue to do so in greater numbers and thus represent a "growth area." The three most common minimally-invasive procedures are Botox injections, laser hair removal, and microdermabrasion (removal of the top-most layer of dead skin). You may have noticed that current-day male actors and models lack chest or armpit hair compared to, for example, the 1970s, when men showed off and even moussed their chest hair (Smiler, 2016).

Although the muscular ideal is most frequently displayed in mainstream culture in the United States, it is not the body type that all men seek to achieve; some prefer a thinner, toned body. This thinner ideal is more common among sexual minority men than heterosexual men, as well as some types of athletes where greater weight or muscularity would inhibit performance (e.g., marathoners) (Calzo et al., 2012; Parent, Schwartz, & Bradstreet, 2016). Men who seek this thinner body type are at greater risk of developing anorexia nervosa or bulimia nervosa than men who strive for the muscular ideal (Murnen & Karazsia, 2017; Parent et al., 2016).

Being gay appears to bring additional risks, including greater dissatisfaction with one's body. It is unclear if these risks are due to minority stress, the greater presence of objectification within gay male culture (compared to straight male culture), some other factor(s), or some combination of these factors (Murnen & Karazsia, 2017). The minority stress argument is weakened by evidence that Black men appear to be more satisfied with their bodies than White or Latino men (whose scores tend to be quite similar) (as reported by Murnen & Karazsia, 2017).

Generally speaking, being more muscular is one way that men appear to demonstrate their masculinity (Parent & Broadstreet, 2017), although the connections between masculinity and muscularity vary across cultures (Murnen & Karazsia, 2017; Parent et al., 2016). Evidence indicates that men with higher scores on trait-based, positive measures of masculinity tend to be more satisfied with their level of muscularity, while those with higher scores on the negative, ideology type measures are less satisfied (Murnen & Karazsia, 2017). There is no consistent pattern of relationships between muscularity and gender role conflict (O'Neil, 2013). Despite the connections between muscularity and masculinity in empirical research and in common culture, no frequently used measure of masculinity includes muscularity as a component of masculinity (see comment by Parent, Schwartz, & Bradstreet, 2016).

Donald McCreary and Doris Sasse (2000) coined the term *drive for muscularity* to reflect men's desire to have leaner, more muscular bodies, and their Drive for Muscularity Scale (DMS) has been the most widely used measure of the phenomenon (Murnen & Karazsia, 2017). The DMS is particularly noteworthy for being statistically validated with a wide range of ethnic subgroups (Murnen & Karazsia, 2017). Reviewers have noted that men with greater drive for muscularity also tend to have lower self-esteem, feel less confident, and may be more depressed. They are also more likely to eat a poorer quality diet, engage in binge eating, use the oral supplement creatine to build muscle (which may or may not be harmful to humans), use anabolic-androgenic steroids (AAS), and share needles while using AAS (Murnen & Karazsia, 2017; Parent, Schwartz, & Bradstreet, 2016). Some men spend so much time working out that it interferes with other regular activities, such as work, sleep, or socializing outside the gym. However, reviewers also argue that it is important to consider the context of men's drive for muscularity, noting differences between athletes and non-athletes, for example (Murnen & Karazsia, 2017; Parent et al., 2016).

HIV/AIDS. In the United States, HIV (Human Immunodeficiency Virus infection) and AIDS (Acquired Immune Deficiency Syndrome) are primarily thought of as a disease that affects gay men, because when the disease was first identified in the 1980s, it disproportionately affected this population (Shilts, 1997). In the nearly 40 years since, the disease has continued to affect a disproportionately high number of gay men in the United States (CDC 2013), although the majority of men suffering from the disease in Africa and South America ("the global south") are heterosexual (Gough & Robertson, 2017). As researchers clarified the disease's transmission routes, they became aware of a fairly large number of men who identified as heterosexual but were having sex with men. Author J. L. King (2004) brought this pattern of behavior to national attention when he began talking about heterosexually-identified black men, often married, who were having sex with men "on the down low." To more accurately reflect these men, the designation "Men who have Sex with Men" (MSM) has been adopted and become commonplace among researchers and the general public.

As we discussed in Chapter Three, HIV infection was originally known as Gay-Related Immune Deficiency and no additional funding was provided to combat the disease's spread during the Reagan administration, despite it being fatal at the time (Shilts, 1997). After the name was officially changed to AIDS, public funding for research and treatment became available. In the last 30 years, more than 7,000 journal articles, chapters, and books have been published and referenced in the primary psychological database, including at least two journals specifically devoted to the topic (*Journal of HIV/AIDS & Social Services*, *AIDS and Behavior*). Many other journals publish material related to the diseases, as do a broad range of journals examining the disease's biological underpinnings and the medical treatment of those who are HIV-positive or suffering from AIDS. In the United States, the research has primarily focused on MSM because they remain the group most likely to be infected (CDC, 2017). In most other parts of the world, the disease primarily affects heterosexual men and women, and thus non-United States studies tend to focus on these populations (e.g., Howard-Payne & Bowman, 2017).

Although HIV and AIDS are often listed together, they refer to distinct physiological conditions. An individual's *HIV status*, defined as whether or not the virus is present in their bloodstream, is referred to as negative (absent) or positive (present). Individuals who are HIV+ are not necessarily ill or suffering from a disease. Those who are suffering from AIDS, however, have a weakened or impaired immune system and thus have difficulty fighting off other diseases and infections. Individuals suffering from AIDS are also at an increased risk of demonstrating mild to moderate neurocognitive impairment, although these impairments are not typically severe enough to officially qualify as dementia (Saloner & Cysique, 2017). In the mid-1990s, anti-retroviral (ARV) drugs were developed and found to be effective at helping individuals who were HIV+ or had AIDS to slow the virus' progress. In the early 2010s, a newer generation of ARVs were found to be effective in preventing the transmission of HIV when taken using a Pre-Exposure Prophylaxis (PrEP) regimen. As a result of these gains, individuals who are HIV+ and are able to follow an ARV medication regime may treat their HIV status as a chronic health condition that may never lead to AIDS (Koechlin et al., 2017). The ability to follow this prevention regime is related to intersectional factors such as SES, access to healthcare, race and ethnicity.

As we stated earlier, HIV infection in the United States is much more common among men who have sex with men (MSM), which includes men who also have sex with women and may identify as heterosexual (CDC, 2012). Black and Latino men have disproportionately high rates of HIV infection, as well as several other sexually transmitted infections (CDC, 2012, 2017). These ethnic disparities are also present among women, with heterosexual women reporting higher rates of infection that heterosexual men (CDC, 2012). One research team estimated that approximately 17 percent of female sex workers in the United States are HIV-positive (Paz-Bailey, Noble, Salo, & Tragear, 2016). There are no symptoms associated with being HIV+; symptoms are associated with developing AIDS. Accordingly, there have been substantial efforts to encourage people to get tested for HIV. Reviewers have found that approximately 85 percent of MSM reported having been tested at some point in their life, with approximately 58 percent saying they've been tested in the last 12 months. Individuals who are more likely to get tested are more likely to be age 30 or older, have completed college, and identify as gay or homosexual; race/ethnicity has appeared as a factor in some studies but not others (Noble et al., 2017).

Because HIV infection is fatal if not properly controlled with ARVs, and because of the expense of treating those dying from AIDS, there has been extensive research on the factors associated with preventing HIV transmission. Intervention programs have primarily focused on increasing access to condoms or testing (for HIV status), although efforts to change local policies and procedures, decrease stigma, and build capacity are also fairly common (Sipe, Berham, et al., 2017). Programs to reduce the stigma associated with HIV (or being gay) often lead to better knowledge about HIV/AIDS as well as more positive attitudes toward persons living with HIV (Mak, Ho, Ma, & Lam, 2017). Others have noted that peer-led programs tend to be more effective than those led by professionals (Shangani et al., 2017).

Several authors have specifically focused on aspects of masculinity that contribute to a greater risk of HIV transmission. Expectations that males will be sexually promiscuous and adventurous, as discussed in Chapter Ten, are relevant here. Condom use is a primary method of risk reduction because use of condoms reduces the risk of infection, but there is a good deal of resistance to using condoms, perhaps because their use involves an acknowledgment of one's vulnerability, caring for the self and the sexual partner, and explicitly not taking risks.

Among MSM, notions that the male sex drive is uncontrollable, that maintaining an erection and using it skillfully validate masculinity, and that a desire for power over others have all been linked to riskier HIV practices (Fleming, DiClemente, & Barringont, 2016). In separate studies, Gay men and Black men both reported high levels of adherence to hegemonic masculine norms related to promiscuity and risk-taking in efforts to prove their masculinity; we note that as minority groups, men in these groups face substantial barriers to achieving hegemonic masculinity (Fields, Bogart et al., 2015; Zeglin, 2015). A similar but more nuanced pattern was found among Latinos and reminds us of the importance of more positive definitions of masculinity. Latinos who adhered to *machismo*, as defined by power and aggression, were less likely to adhere to their HIV medication regime, while those who adhered to principles of *caballerismo*, as defined by fairness, emphasis on family, and respect for others, demonstrated greater adherence to their HIV medication regime (Galvan, Bogart, et al., 2014).

Research with general samples, as well as samples restricted to men who have sex with women, demonstrate that men with greater adherence to masculine norms of anti-femininity and toughness tend to hold more negative attitudes towards condoms, while those who report greater adherence to status norms tend to hold more positive condom attitudes (Vincent et al., 2016). Research indicates that White and Black teens who endorse hegemonic norms view condoms negatively and report less willingness to use them (Pleck, Sonenstein, & Ku, 1993a), with these patterns continuing into the undergraduate years (Shearer, Hosterman, Gillen, & Lefkowitz, 2005). As might be expected, the associations between masculine norms and condom use are much weaker among couples who are expecting a child (Vincent et al., 2016), reflecting ways that attitudes and behaviors may change due to other decisions (i.e., pregnancy).

Only by educating males about gender and providing alternate models of health can we inoculate boys and men against these negative influences.

SUMMARY

1. There are many health problems that are more common in men than in women. Men's average lifespan in the United States is more than five years shorter than that of women as a result of a number of factors.

2. Biogenic explanations for sex differences in disease and longevity include male chromosomal vulnerability, the damaging effects of testosterone, and the protective effects of estrogen.

3. Psychogenic explanations for sex differences in disease and longevity include the masculine denial of vulnerability, self-destructive behaviors,

eschewal of self-care, risky sexual behaviors, and the cultural expectation to take part in dangerous sports and in war.

4. Stressful work environments and typical masculine responses to them also take their toll on health and longevity. There is a growing awareness that living up to masculine gender demands involves the denial of some basic human needs, and that the results may be illness, injury, and/or premature death.

GLOSSARY

Physical health: A general term that includes issues related to bodily health, disease, and mortality.

Epidemiology(ies): The statistical incidence(s) of a physical condition or illness within a population.

Androsperm: Sperm that carry a Y-chromosome.

Gynosperm: Sperm that carry an X-chromosome.

Infant mortality: As deaths in the first 12 months of life not due to accident.

The sex chromosomes: The 46th pair of human chromosomes. Genetic females have two X-chromosomes and genetic males have one X- and one Y-chromosome.

Behavioral medicine: A sub-field of medicine focused on understanding and treating physical disorders that are thought to be strongly influenced by the person's psychological functioning.

Type A Personality: "A characteristic action-emotion complex which is exhibited by those individuals who are engaged in a relatively chronic struggle to obtain an unlimited number of poorly defined things from their environments in the shortest period of time and, if possible, against the opposing efforts of other things or persons in this same environment" (Friedman & Rosenhan as reported in Hackett et al., 1985).

Body Dysmorphic Disorder: A general diagnostic category used to identify problematic behavior that does not fit criteria for other eating or body image disorders.

Bigorexia: A colloquial term to describe men who are trying to develop a highly muscularized body and have problematic eating habits or a disturbed body image.

HIV status: An indication of whether or not the HIV virus is present in an individual's bloodstream.

Chapter Fifteen

Coping in a Difficult World: Men and Mental Health

A middle-aged man gets so distraught after his wife leaves him that he has to be admitted to a psychiatric hospital. A teenaged boy commits frequent robberies and assaults. A young man cannot resist the urge to expose his genitals to pubescent girls. A senior citizen, despondent from loneliness and the decline of his body, contemplates suicide. An alcoholic experiences significant difficulties with his job, relationships, finances, and the law.

The problems that these men have in dealing with their life problems have become unmanageable. All of them are experiencing a good deal of psychological discomfort, although some might be able to hide it. Many would have trouble admitting to others, or even to themselves, that they need help, or believing that they could benefit from treatment. Even if they come to an awareness that their problems are out of control, they might be very reluctant to ask for assistance from professionals or even their closest friends.

Throughout this book, we have described many of the negative psychological effects of uncritically adhering to rigid and unreasonable gender demands. On the other hand, certain masculine norms may also contribute positively to mental health. In this chapter, we explore in more depth the relationships between gender and psychological well-being for men. The chapter is structured in four parts. First, we look at definitions of mental health and their connections with cultural conceptions of gender. Second is a discussion of mental health problems that boys and/or men experience disproportionately in relation to girls and/or women and the associations of these disorders with gender role characteristics. Third, we examine life experience factors that either protect men from mental illness or put them at increased risk. Finally, we explore the issues specific to men in counseling and psychotherapy.

DEFINING MENTAL HEALTH

Virtually every abnormal psychology textbook begins with a chapter on the definitions of mental health and mental illness. If these were easy concepts to define, it would not take an entire chapter to cover the territory. Setting forth criteria for mental health and illness turns out to be a rather complicated enterprise. Nearly everyone agrees that a person who hallucinates frequently or cannot remember his or her name is suffering from a mental disturbance. On the other hand, when does "normal" sadness become "abnormal" depression? What if a person is satisfied with a lifestyle that others consider "sick?" How about the person who is a member of an oppressed group—if he or she is suspicious of others' motives, is that "paranoia," or is it "accurate reality testing?" (Sue, et. al., 2014).

Some major definitional difficulties lie in the culture-bound character and historical context of definitions of mental health and illness. For instance, suppose that you were visiting the United States without knowing anything about the mainstream culture. You find out that every Saturday and Sunday during autumn, men get together, run as fast as they can, and knock each other down. Some of these men become severely injured and are carried off on stretchers. Others experience a good deal of lingering pain from these frequent violent collisions, and occasionally some even suffer catastrophic spinal cord injuries. Moreover, tens of thousands of people gather to watch these spectacles, and sometimes they even cheer when someone gets hurt.

As an outside observer, you wonder if the term for "war" in the United States is "football," yet you see the players shaking hands afterwards. You might be likely to go back to your native land and describe these "crazy," self-destructive men who engage in these exhibitions and the "sadistic" people who watch and cheer. If you did, you would be making a judgment about the mental health of these people that few inhabitants of the United States would make.

Even the professional community has difficulty agreeing on criteria for mental illness, and in fact these standards change over time. In 1968, the American Psychiatric Association published the second edition of the *Diagnostic and Statistical Manual of Mental Disorders* (DSM-II), a guide for labeling psychological disturbances. In this version of the manual, homosexuality was defined as a mental disorder. When the next revision (DSM-III) (American Psychiatric Association, 1980) was published, the diagnostic category was called "ego-dystonic homosexuality," which meant that if you were gay, you had a mental disorder only if you were dissatisfied with being gay and wanted to become heterosexual.

This development prompted psychiatrist Thomas Szasz to describe himself as having "ego-dystonic chronological disorder" because he was older than he wanted to be! His point was well taken. Everybody has some aspects of themselves with which they are dissatisfied. Why have we chosen only sexual orientation to pathologize? Perhaps as a result of convincing arguments by

Szasz and others, this diagnostic category disappeared in the next three editions (DSM-III-R; DSM-IV, DSM-V, American Psychiatric Association, 1987; 1994; 2013).

Landrine (1988) pointed out the cultural bias in defining mental health and illness:

> Contemporary concepts of normalcy and psychopathology perpetuate the construction of the behavior of minorities and women as pathological along with the view that culture is peripheral to psychopathology.... The term *normal* suggests, among other things, an individual who exhibits abstract and logical thinking, emotional control, independence, delay of gratification, happiness, a concern with developing one's own potential to the fullest, and a sense of self as an autonomous individual who exerts personal control over self and environment... the sense of self described above—from which many other characteristics derive—is not how the poor experience the self... how Blacks experience the self... how Asian Americans experience the self... how women experience the self... or how most people throughout the world experience the self.... This concept of normalcy, held by U.S. public and professionals alike...is largely synonymous with the characteristics of upper income White men in this country... and is firmly rooted in the social meanings shared by middle-class White Americans. (p. 40)

Especially since the publication of DSM-III in 1980, some feminist scholars have argued that the mental health establishment pathologizes women for the way that they have been socialized (e.g., to be interdependent, emotional, and self-sacrificing). Pantony and Caplan (1991) suggested that a diagnostic category of "Delusional Dominating Personality Disorder" be used to describe people who have an "inability to establish and maintain meaningful interpersonal relationships, an inability to identify and express a range of feeling in oneself and others, and difficulty responding empathically to the feelings and needs of close associates and intimates" (p. 120). This proposed diagnosis is, of course, a description of a hypermasculine interpersonal style. Rather than labeling the behavior as emotionally disturbed, it is more often cast in a language of moral failure. As Prior (1999) stated, there is a tendency to see women as "mad" and men as "bad."

These objections to gender bias in the diagnostic criteria focus on the negative social consequences of being labeled as "disordered," and psychiatry has a rather long history of bias against women that constitutes a serious issue. However, we should not overlook the fact that it is not the purpose of diagnosis to stigmatize and blame people for their problems. Stigmatization is an unfortunate byproduct of diagnosis in a society that is prejudiced against the mentally ill.

The real purpose of diagnosis is to identify problems that require attention. In most cases, the willingness of health insurance providers to pay for treatment hinges on the diagnos-ability of the person seeking mental health services. Failing to label the hypermasculine behaviors described above as disturbed therefore has at least two consequences. First, it reinforces masculine privilege by tacitly approving the behavior. In other words, it says to the mental health community that it is all right to be emotionally withholding, aggressive, and unempathic. Second, it says that men who behave in such a way merit no attention. There is a denial that such behavior limits the quality of the man's life to a significant enough extent that we should do something for him.

The concepts of gender role conflict and strain show some promise in the study of gender and men's psychological adjustment. Gender role conflict is a negative psychological state that results from the contradictory and\or unrealistic demands of the gender role. The hypothesis of the gender role conflict and strain model is that men who accept traditional gender ideologies, yet do not feel that they fulfill the prescriptions inherent in the role, will experience the highest levels of psychological conflict and negative health consequences. For example, a man thinks that being unemotional means being manly, but he finds it difficult to suppress his emotions. This man would experience more role conflict than either: a) a man who accepts low emotionality as manly but has no difficulty suppressing his feelings, or b) an emotional man who does not experience much pressure from the masculine prescription for emotional restrictedness. There is a substantial body of evidence linking male gender role conflict with negative psychological states (O'Neil, 2008, 2013).Similarly, there is a substantial body of research demonstrating that greater endorsement of the negative aspects of masculinity ideology is associated with poor mental health and lower likelihood of seeking mental health services (Wong, Ho, Wang, & Miller, 2017).

Men, Masculinity and Mental Disorders

There are significant variations in the proportions of men and women who are diagnosed within several categories of mental illnesses. Researchers believe that a number of factors contribute to these sex differences, including gender socialization, which may strongly affect how a person expresses his or her psychological distress. For instance, a gender-typed woman who experiences psychological pain may often become depressed. A gender-typed man might react to the same kind of pain by abusing alcohol. These tendencies may be at least partly fueled by the woman's socialization to "act in" or internalize—to introspect and think about how she feels—and the man's gender-typed encouragement to deny vulnerability and "act out" or externalize—to look to the environment for solutions to his problems. Some theorists (e.g., Lynch & Kilmartin, 2013; Real, 1997) maintain that a depressive psychological base underlies many common symptoms in men, but that diagnostic criteria reflect a feminine mode of depression (more on this subject later).

A related possibility is that gender socialization sometimes prevents a person from acquiring certain coping skills (O'Neil, 1981b). A highly gender-typed man may not have learned well how to deal with emotions and relationships. A highly gender-typed woman may not have learned well how to deal with independence. Thus, gender socialization can contribute to behavioral deficits as well as to negative patterns of behavior.

People use psychological *defense mechanisms*, defined as mental strategies for protecting one's self from perceived threats to the self (Clark, 1998). Sometimes, their use is very adaptive. For instance, it is quite common for a person who has recently lost a loved one through death to experience some level of initial *denial* about the death. If the person were to come to a full emotional realization of such a profound loss, he or she might be flooded with anxiety and sadness and become completely incapacitated. The defense mechanism allows the person to protect the self and deal with the loss over time. On the other hand, all defenses involve distortion of reality, and so overusing them results in impaired psychological functioning.

Largely because of early gender socialization, males and females tend to develop somewhat distinct defensive styles. When defensiveness becomes problematic, these gendered styles express themselves in a differential vulnerability to several mental disorders. The masculine-feminine externalizing-internalizing dimension leads men to use the defense of *projection*, defined as attributing one's own conflicts to others, more frequently than women (Clark, 1998). Faced with psychological discomfort such as low self-esteem, a man is more likely than a woman to project his negative feelings on to other people or objects instead of his own shortcomings, and thus deal with these feelings in a distorted way. As we discussed in Chapter Twelve, violent behavior is often a projection of unacceptable negative feelings about the self on to another person. Unfortunately, projection leaves the person who is experiencing the conflict with no avenue for dealing with it directly and no process for improving his or her functioning. A person is unlikely to see the need for a change in behavior when that person experiences the problem as external to the self.

As with many areas of investigation, gender is a better predictor of defensive behavior than sex. Men who experience high levels of rigid beliefs around masculinity as it relates to success, power, competition, and emotional expression are significantly more likely than other men to use less developed defenses—those that are common in three- to 15-year olds and people who are personality disordered (Mahalik, Cournoyer, DeFranc, Cherry, & Napolitano, 1998). In other words, high levels of gender role conflict and strain tend to result in grown men acting like children.

There is a tendency to think that individuals are predisposed toward certain types of mental disorders only because of the way they were raised. In addition to the contribution of past socialization to current behavior, we should also remember that, in an important sense, men and women live in different gendered cultural worlds. We saw in Chapter Six that sex-segregated social groups tend to have gender-characteristic interpersonal styles. In the sociocultural context, different behaviors are anticipated, rewarded, and punished on the basis of sex. For example, expressions of sadness and helpless feelings by a woman might be met with sympathy and emotional support. The same behavior in a man might result in social isolation and loss of status.

Researchers have observed the following sex differences in mental illness:

1. Males experience a disproportionate number of most childhood disorders, such as Attention Deficit Hyperactivity Disorder and Conduct Disorder.
2. Women are somewhat more likely to be diagnosed with depression and most anxiety-based disorders, and much more likely than men to have eating disorders. However, there is a growing awareness of body image disturbances in boys and men (see Chapter Fourteen).
3. Males constitute a majority of substance abusers, sexual deviates, and people with behavior control problems such as pyromania, compulsive gambling, and intermittent explosive disorder (a pattern of rageful outbursts) (Sue, et. al., 2014).
4. There are unequal sex proportions for a variety of personality disorders: more men than women are diagnosed as paranoid, schizoid, schizotypal, narcissistic, obsessive-compulsive, and antisocial; more women than men are diagnosed as borderline (Sue, et. al., 2014).
5. Men are much more likely than women to commit suicide (Crosby et al., 2013; Heron, 2013), although women make more incomplete suicide attempts (Stillion & McDowell, 1996) (see Chapter Twelve for a discussion of suicide and masculinity.).

MENTAL HEALTH ISSUES FOR MEN

There has been much speculation about the relationships between some aspects of masculinity and the disorders listed above. The following discussion will focus on a few areas of diagnosis (substance abuse, personality disorder, and depression), as well as the role of marriage in men's mental health.

Substance Abuse

Men are more than twice as likely as women to demonstrate abuse or dependence on alcohol (Grant, et. al., 2004) or other drugs (Sue, et. al., 2014). Alcoholism is one of the most serious mental health problems in the world. In the United States, nearly 14 percent of people have these disorders at some point during their lives (American Psychiatric Association, 2013). Gary Brooks and Louise Silverstein (1995) reported that alcoholics occupy half of all hospital beds at any given time in the United States, that they attempt suicide 75 to 300 percent more often than non-abusers, and that as many as one in ten men become alcoholic (compared with one in 50 women). Alcohol abuse is also strongly related to violence, crime, accidents, work absenteeism, relationship problems, and disease (Lex, 1995).

David Sue and his colleagues (2014) note that there is considerable cultural variation in rates of alcoholism. Although there are possible genetic factors in alcoholism, e.g. many Native Americans and Asians often have highly sensitive physiological reactions to alcohol (Butcher, Hooley, & Mineka, & 2014), the cross-cultural variability in rates of problem drinking suggests that cultural values also play an important role in the prevalence of the disorder.

Gender is one of the central organizing principles of mainstream culture in the United States, and we do not have to look far to find social connections between masculinity and alcohol abuse. Following are a few of these connections:

1. *Externalizing defensive style*: As noted earlier, men are encouraged to look outside of themselves for solutions to problems. Being in any kind of psychological pain is considered unmanly, as it implies emotional vulnerability. Drinking can function as self-medication. Alcohol reduces anxiety and clouds the person's consciousness so that he or she will be both emotionally and physically numb. Men who rely on avoidant forms of coping with negative emotions are more likely to exhibit abusive drinking patterns (Cooper, Russell, Skinner, Frone, & Mudar, 1992).

2. *Toughness and risk-taking*: Some men perceive becoming dead drunk to be a way of demonstrating one's masculinity, since "real men" can hold their liquor (de Visser & Smith, 2007; Peralta, 2007). Binge-drinking men have been known to continue drinking *after* throwing up (a body's signal that it has had enough, if ever there were one). Driving and taking other risks while drunk are ways of demonstrating a masculine disregard for safety. In the United States, men are nearly four times as likely as women to be arrested for drunken driving (Halsey, 2009) and more likely to die in motor vehicle accidents (West & Naumann, 2013). Greater endorsement of the masculine norm of risk-taking is consistently related to higher scores on measures of mental health problems (e.g., depressive symptoms, substance abuse) and lower scores on measures of positive mental health (e.g., life satisfaction, self-esteem) (Wong et al., 2017).

3. *Competition:* Boys and men are socialized into a range of activities where their abilities can be quantified and thus they can be ranked. This includes stereotypically masculine activities such as sports and video games, as well as academic performance. Drinking can also become a competition whereby the man who drinks the most "wins." Drinking games, where players are forced to drink, bring a masculine sport-like structure into the social arena. Greater endorsement of the masculine norm of competition is consistently related to higher scores on measures of mental health problems (e.g., depressive symptoms, substance abuse) and lower likelihood of seeking help for mental health problems (Wong et al., 2017).

4. *Dealing with emotions and relationships indirectly*: It's a cliché that American men need to be drunk to say "I love you, man," although that cliché reflects a reality for most men: they are not allowed to directly express their feelings toward their friends (Garfield, 2015). Alcohol allows men to lower their masculine inhibitions and behave in affectionate ways with each other (Blazina & Watkins, 1996). Many men feel that they can walk down the street with their arms around each other when they are drunk, but not at other times. The next day, they can maintain their interpersonal distance by not mentioning their affectionate behavior or attributing it to their drunkenness. Therefore, alcohol abuse enables men to deal with their feelings of attachment while at the same time maintaining a façade of masculine independence (Capraro, 2000). Greater endorsement of the masculine norm of emotional control is consistently and strongly related to less likelihood of seeking help for mental health problems, as well as lower scores on measures of positive mental health (e.g., life satisfaction, self-esteem) (Wong et al., 2017).

5. *Modeling and social group factors*: Males are more likely than females to have same-sex peers who are heavy drinkers (Brooks & Silverstein, 1995), and some male social groups actively promote binge drinking. Chiefly among these groups on college campuses are fraternities. Nearly 40 percent of fraternity members went from being low level drinkers in high school to being high level drinkers in college (compared with 17 percent of non-members) (Lo & Globetti, 1995). Heavy drinkers tend to seek fraternity membership (Wechsler, Kuh, & Davenport, 1996), and the majority of fraternity members are binge drinkers (Smith & Mathews, 1997).

6. *The cultural association of masculinity with alcohol*: Drinking is interconnected with the social meanings attached to being masculine (Uy, Massoth, & Gottdiener, 2014). Male television actors are portrayed drinking significantly more often than females, and alcohol advertisements are largely oriented toward the associating masculine fantasy with alcohol use. Traditional gender attitudes are associated with alcohol-related problems in adult men (McCreary, Newcomb, & Sadava, 1999) and adolescent males (Iwamoto & Smiler, 2013).

Beer advertisers present images of their products as "related to challenge, risk, and mastery over nature, technology, others, and the self" (Fejes, 1992, p. 14). Men in these commercials are usually portrayed in occupational and leisure pursuits, especially in outdoor settings and sometimes with an element of danger. Beer is often presented as a substitute for the overt communication of affection between men, a rite of passage into manhood, and as a reward for hard work. Men are often shown participating in activities that involve speed and coordination, like race-car driving, skiing, and calf-roping, despite the fact that drinking would severely decrease one's performance in these pursuits and increase the risk of injury. (Strate, 1992). When women are portrayed, they are often presented as an audience for men (Fejes, 1992), or as sexual objects (Strate, 1992). Advertisers often imply that alcohol is a means of sophistication and heterosexual seduction (Barthel, 1992).

In an article titled "Beer Commercials: A Manual on Masculinity," Lance Strate (1992) summed up the impact of this advertising: "No other industry commercials focus so exclusively and exhaustively on images of the man's man... in reflecting the myth, the commercials also reinforce it" (pp. 78–79). Fejes (1992) adds: "Men who are sensitive, thoughtful, scholarly, gay, or complex are not present in beer commercials." (p.14). Beer commercials also portray a sanitized version of drinking—the bars are always clean and well lit, nobody ever pays for a drink, and nobody ever gets drunk (Strate, 1992).

7. *Gender role conflict and strain*: Men use alcohol to deal with the pressures of social masculinity. Researchers have found that men with high levels of gender role conflict also had higher levels of reported alcohol use and alcohol-related problems than men with lower levels of gender role conflict (O'Neil, 2008, 2013).

Williams and Ricardelli (1999) describe two basic gendered dimensions to men's alcohol use. First, alcohol is clearly associated with traditional masculinity. Therefore, drinking is a way to display one's manliness (the *confirmatory* function). Second, drinking can help men to handle the stress and strain of living up to difficult standards of masculinity (the *compensatory* function).

Personality Disorders

Personality is a relatively stable set of behavioral predispositions that characterize a human being's typical functioning (Funder, 2010). In the case of the person who is *personality disordered*, the generalized ways in which he or she approaches the world are marked by an inflexible and self-defeating style that results in poor mental stability (T. Millon, C. F. Millon, Meagher, Grossman, & Ramnath, 2005). The ingrained ways of relating to others that personality disordered individuals use almost always cause them problems in their work and social functioning. They also tend to produce a good deal of personal distress.

The DSM-V (American Psychiatric Association, 2013) lists ten personality disorders. Five affect men more often than women and one affects women more often. The remaining four disorders are distributed fairly equally between the sexes, and the overall sex ratios of personality disorders taken together are fairly equal (Rosenberg & Kosslyn, 2014). A description of the male-dominated diagnoses follows.

Schizoid Personality Disorder is characterized by flat emotionality and interpersonal aloofness. These people seem to lack the capacity to experience emotion and lead dull, joyless, and solitary lives.

Schizotypal Personality Disorder is characterized by peculiarities of thinking and behavior. These oddities of experience and action result in highly impaired interpersonal relationships.

People with *Narcissistic Personality Disorder* display a grandiose sense of self-importance and absorption. They present themselves as exceptionally talented, accomplished, and "special." Narcissists are easily hurt by any kind of criticism and believe that they are entitled to special favors by virtue of being so wonderful. They feel shamed and enraged when others react negatively to them and when they do not receive a steady source of admiration and attention (American Psychiatric Association, 2013). Underneath this grandiose exterior is a fragile sense of self-worth.

Antisocial Personality Disorder is characterized by a long history of behaviors that violate the rights of others, such as lying, stealing, and assaulting. Antisocial people feel little remorse for having mistreated others. They are frequently in legal trouble and fail to sustain any close relationships (American Psychiatric Association, 2013). Many antisocial people are dangerous criminals.

People with *Obsessive-Compulsive Personality Disorder* are stereotypical perfectionists. They often demand that others conform to their unreasonable standards of order and devotion to details, thus they tend to be interpersonal bullies.

One could characterize many of the traits described in these disorders as caricatures of negative masculinity. All of these personality types are marked by some mixture of self-absorption, indifference toward others' feelings, and an overemphasis on independence. Narcissistic and antisocial people are interpersonally exploitive, using others to reach their own goals. All of these styles are characterized by extreme difficulty in relationships, another stereotypically masculine characteristic.

There is also pronounced emotional restrictedness in antisocial, obsessive-compulsive, and schizoid disorders. Schizoids feel nothing or next to nothing. Antisocials and obsessive-compulsives express little emotion except for anger, paralleling our discussion in Chapter Seven. The combination of hostility and hyperindependence in antisocial disorder is an especially volatile one. Lacking a sense of self-compassion, they have no point of reference for empathizing with others, and thus they are prone to violence (See chapter Twelve). Antisocial personality disorder has demonstrated biological heritability, and so the sex difference in this disorder may be a reflection of a differential vulnerability combined with gender socialization and adverse childhood experiences (Rosenberg & Kosslyn, 2014).

Although mental illnesses are caused by multiple factors, dysfunctional interaction styles in the family of origin are strong influences in the development of personality disorders (Millon, et. al., 2005). If we consider hypermasculinity to result from harsh masculine socialization, we could speculate that men who exhibit the above personality disorders may well have received an exaggerated "dose" of overly stern gender socialization in addition to other dysfunctional developmental patterns such as childhood maltreatment and/or neglect.

Depression

Depression involves pervasive feelings of hopelessness, helplessness and worthlessness accompanied by a family of behavioral symptoms like social isolation, sleep problems, and loss of interest or pleasure in activities (American Psychiatric Association, 2013). It has been called the "common cold of mental illness" (Seligman, 1990a), affecting approximately one in five people in the United States at some point during their lives. Rates of depression have risen steeply in the United States during the twentieth century (Nolen-Hoeksema, 1998), prompting psychologist Martin Seligman (1990b), who has spent much of his professional career studying this mental disorder, to label it an epidemic.

Females are diagnosed with clinical depression twice as often as males in the United States. Susan Nolen-Hoeksema (1998) believes that women are more depressed than men because of two basic factors: the patriarchal oppression of women, and the tendency for women to be socialized into a *ruminative coping style*, defined as dwelling on one's distress in passive ways that are not oriented toward problem solving, which tends to make the depression more severe and longer-lasting (Nolen-Hoeksema, 2006). On the other hand, males are more likely to deal with negative emotions by distracting themselves from their feelings.

Several theorists believe that the epidemiology of depression in men as a group approaches that of women, but that men tend to have different, gendered styles of expressing their problem. The reported sex difference in depression may be misleading due to a number of factors. First, women may be more likely than men to seek treatment or to report their depression to others (Sue, et. al., 2014). Males have a tendency to underreport most physical and psychological treatment, as having symptoms implies unmasculine vulnerability (Pollack, 1998). Second, the diagnostic system may be gender-biased. Third, males may manifest depression in different ways from females, leading to different diagnoses. For instance, men are more disposed toward externalizing symptoms such as heavy drinking, angry outbursts, and aggression in response to sad feelings (Real, 1997; Lynch & Kilmartin, 2013, Cochran & Rabinowitz, 2000; Kilmartin, 2005).

In an exhaustive review of the research literature on men and depression, Michael Addis (2008) concluded that acceptance of traditional masculine ideologies puts men at risk for both conventional depression and for externalizing symptoms that co-occur with depression, but that there is significant variability in symptom patterns among men. Mariola Magovcevic and Addis (2008) developed a scale to assess masculine depression. O'Neil (2008) noted that in 24 of 27 studies, researchers have linked men's gender role conflict with depressive symptoms, and a link to low self-esteem is demonstrated in several other studies.

Regardless of the debate around the true prevalence rates of depression for men and women, we should avoid being drawn in to a competition between the sexes to claim the title of "most depressed." All troubled people are in need of help. At the same time, the sex differential in diagnosis may provide important clues to the connections between gender demands and mental illness. It might well be that the roots of the illness are different for the average depressed woman and the average depressed man. In other words, it is possible that rigid gendering is a risk factor for depression, but that the character of that gendering may also produce markedly different modes of expression in the two sexes.

Several pieces of evidence lend credence to the hypothesis that depression is underdiagnosed in males. The strongest is that males commit suicide, the ultimate expression of depression, four times more often than females (Crosby et al., 2013; See Chapter Twelve). There are also very high rates of psychiatric hospitalization in divorced men compared with divorced women, suggesting that female partners may have a strong role in helping men defend from their underlying depressive senses of self (see the discussion below on the protective function of marriage for men.). And, serious psychogenic physical diseases, which are related to psychological conflicts, are more common among men (Lynch & Kilmartin, 2013).

While women are prone toward the aforementioned ruminative coping style for dealing with negative emotions, men's externalizing tendencies lead them to gravitate toward distracting themselves and acting out. Alcohol abuse is a major way to hide one's depression, even from the self, and there is ample evidence linking alcohol problems to underlying depression. As Terrence Real (1997) stated, "While the capacity to externalize pain protects some men from *feeling* depressed, it does not stop them from *being* depressed; it just helps them to disconnect further from their own experience" (p. 82, emphasis original).

Masked depression is also in evidence in a number of other typically masculine problems, including violence, overinvolvement in sports or work, narcissism, criminal behavior, and relationship difficulties. Addressing the underlying depressive dynamics of these problems is a key component of effective treatment (Lynch & Kilmartin, 2013; Kilmartin, 2005; Cochran & Rabinowitz, 2000).

Marriage and Men's Mental Health

Does marriage improve men's mental health? Social scientists have investigated the accuracy of this bias by examining mental illness rates for married men, single men, married women, and single women. If marriage has damaging or beneficial effects for any of these groups, these effects should be reflected by mental illness rates that are at variance with contrasted groups.

In general, the results of this research cast considerable doubt on the accuracy of the cultural myth. An extensive survey of mental hospital patients revealed that single and divorced men were hospitalized at about three times the rate of married men, and also at a higher rate than single or divorced women. Married women were hospitalized at a higher rate than married men. Married people in general were hospitalized less often than single people, but the size of that difference was much greater for men than for women (Rosenstein, Steadman, McAskill, & Manderscheid, 1987).

Although one cannot say from these data that marriage *causes* better mental health in men, there certainly are relationships between being married and staying out of the hospital, avoiding mental illness, reduction in physical risk-taking, and avoiding stress-related physical illnesses. We note that these statistical relationships are much stronger for men that women (Denmark, Rabinowitz, & Sechzer, 2000).

One can make sense of these data by looking at the functions of marriage for men and women. For both partners, marriage would seem to provide opportunities for intimacy and companionship, as well as fulfilling a social obligation—95 percent of people in the United States get married at some time during their lives (Casteneda & Burns-Glover, 2004). We have already discussed in Chapter Seven the gender role prohibitions against emotional intimacy and self-disclosure for men. Yet these are human needs, and failing to attend to them has adverse effects on the person. Although marriage does not necessarily involve psychological intimacy, it certainly sets the stage for it. For many men, then, marriage is an opportunity to fill a void that has been created by harsh masculine socialization.

By contrast, women need intimacy too but they are more likely than men to experience it in relationships with friends (see Chapter Thirteen). In the realm of psychological intimacy, marriage tends to be less novel for women than for men. Men may also tend to be less responsive to women's disclosures. As a result, fewer psychological benefits accrue for women than for men.

Despite their stereotypical resistance to getting married, it appears that considerable benefits are associated with being a husband. The fact that most men eventually marry (despite gender role demands for hyperindependence and promiscuity) is good evidence that men want and need intimacy. Pleck (1995) reported that men usually experience their family roles as more important in their lives than their work roles, and that satisfaction with family roles is strongly associated with psychological well-being.

COUNSELING AND PSYCHOTHERAPY WITH MEN

Everyone will benefit if we can find ways to alleviate the suffering of people who struggle with mental health problems. The processes for doing so include counseling and psychotherapy.

Men as a Special Population

Carl Rogers (1957) first popularized the idea that a counselor's understanding of the client's subjective psychological environment is a critical first step in the therapeutic process. If the therapist is to be helpful, he or she must gain a deep awareness of how the client experiences the self and the world. Rogers was an important early influence in defining the field of *Counseling Psychology*, which is founded on the appreciation and respect of individual differences and perspectives.

One of the important ways in which therapy clients differ is in their identifications with, and memberships in, different sociocultural groups. For example, people of color, physically challenged people, gays, and lesbians have almost always had some different experiences than Caucasians, people without significant physical challenges, and heterosexuals. Some of these experiences have important effects on the person's sense of self and view of the world. When these people see counselors, especially ones who are dissimilar to them, it is important for the counselor to be sensitive to the typical psychological and political issues associated with memberships in various groups.

With this basic assumption in mind, many counselors began to undergo formal and informal training in understanding diversity in the 1960s and 1970s, and this kind of education continues today. One of the basic categories of individual difference is, of course, the sex of the person seeking treatment. In 1979, the American Psychological Association's (APA) Counseling Psychology division published a list entitled "Principles Concerning the Counseling and Therapy of Women." The preamble to these principles begins:

> Although competent counseling/therapy processes are essentially the same for all counselor/therapist interactions, special subgroups require specialized skills, attitudes, and knowledge. Women constitute a special subgroup. (Division 17, 1979, p. 21)

The psychologists who drafted this document believed that it is essential for counselors who treat women to be knowledgeable about biological, psychological, and social issues affecting women, to be aware of their own values and biases about women, and to develop skills that are particularly suited to female clients. At the time, most psychologists were male, an outgrowth of the fact that earlier generations of women were generally not encouraged to seek education beyond high school or admitted to many institutions of higher education. In 2007, the American Psychological Association published a set of *Guidelines for the Psychological Treatment of Girls and Women*. In the 2010s, the fields such as clinical social work, counseling, psychology, and marriage and family therapy are all dominated by women (American Psychological Association, 2013).

Therapists have realized that men also have typical styles and psychological issues that they bring to the therapeutic setting. They have begun to recognize and examine their values and biases about men, and some realized that a gender-aware perspective on masculine socialization would be helpful in their treatment of male clients. William Liu (2005) has subsequently argued that working with men should be considered a cultural competence and a number of authors have reiterated this notion and begun to detail what such competence might look like (Brooks, 2017; Rochlen, 2014; Strokoff, Halford, & Owen, 2016). Guidelines for therapeutic work with boys and men are expected to be published by the American Psychological Association in 2018 or 2019.

A number of excellent books and journal articles have been published in the past two decades on the subject of men as a special population in psychotherapy. Some of these have integrated men's issues with those of special subpopulations of oppressed or unattended-to men such as ethnic, older, divorced, gay, and bisexual men (see Brooks & Good, 2001; Englar-Carlson & Stevens, 2006; Englar-Carlson, Evans & Duffey, 2014, and Rochlen & Rabinowitz, 2014).

Men's Issues in Counseling and Psychotherapy

Counselors are becoming increasingly aware that men constitute a special subgroup of clients. They have identified a number of psychotherapeutic men's issues and developed some specialized treatments for male clients. Traditional individual psychotherapy is a set of methods that were developed by mostly male therapists to treat mostly female clients. If we look closely at the counseling relationship, we see that very little of traditional masculinity is conducive to requesting treatment, sustaining the therapeutic effort, or performing the activities required of clients.

Help Seeking. People who request psychotherapeutic services have often been stereotyped as "crazy," weak, or out of control. This stigma makes it difficult for almost anyone to come to counseling, but it is especially difficult for men, who often place a special value on being rational, self-sufficient, strong, and in control. The act of telephoning or walking into a counseling center and asking for an appointment may feel like the equivalent of a declaration that, "I am weak, afraid, dependent, and vulnerable. I don't know what is going on with me, even though I should, and I can't handle my problems on my own. I need help." Not surprisingly, greater adherence to masculine norms is associated with lower rates of seeking psychological help, with norms of emotional control, self-reliance, and competition among the strongest predictors of not seeking help (Wong et al., 2017).

One would be hard-pressed to find statements that reflect perceived masculine failure more than these. Given the social expectations to work it out for oneself, "take it like a man," and control one's feelings, it is not surprising that men utilize psychological services considerably less often than women (Addis & Mahalik, 2003). Since entering counseling is often perceived as a threat to masculine self-esteem, men frequently resist asking for services until they experience a very deep level of psychological pain and until their problems reach crisis proportions. If they begin treatment, they may drop out when their discomfort reaches a barely manageable level. After dropping out their pain may worsen. At that time, it may be even more difficult for them to return and ask for assistance, because they now must admit two failures by doing so: the one that initially brought them to counseling, and the failure on the first attempt as a therapy client (Kilmartin, 2004b; 2005).

Michael Addis and James Mahalik (2003) called for a contextual analysis of help-seeking in men across several dimensions including the perceptions of normality and ego-centrality. People are more likely to seek help if they think that their problem is shared by others (normality) and does not affect the core of their perceptions of self (ego-centrality). The National Institute of Mental Health (NIMH) developed an extensive public information campaign called *Real Men, Real Depression* in an effort to re-cast this increasingly common mood disorder as normal for males and not reflective of one's level of masculinity (Rochlen, Whilde, & Hoyer, 2005). The slogan, "It takes courage to ask for help" is an attempt to re-define a positive masculine attribute as reflective of a culturally proscribed but useful behavior.

Counseling Activities. Counseling is an activity in which clients are usually expected to perform certain behaviors thought to be helpful in solving emotional problems. These behaviors often include emotional self-disclosure, exploration of feelings, nondefensive introspection ("looking inside" of oneself), and emphasizing interpersonal material, often in ways that run contrary to the emotional display rules discussed in Chapter Seven. Men sometimes have little experience in these areas, which are culturally defined as feminine. Therefore, the counseling setting tends to be a rather poor match of person and environment for many men (Bruch, 1980). In other words, asking a man to do these things may make him feel like a fish out of water, and this discomfort may well be another factor that contributes to the high male dropout rate.

Because many counseling activities are uncomfortable for them, men often ask for masculine kinds of help, such as a logical analysis of the problem, an emphasis on thinking over feeling, or help with defending against rather than experiencing the problem. For instance, typically masculine strategies for dealing with the breakup of a romantic relationship might be to find a substitute lover, to use thoughts to master feelings, or to learn how to not think about the former partner (Kilmartin, 2005).Cognitive-Behavioral Therapy (CBT), with its emphasis on identifying thought patterns and testing the accuracy of one's thoughts, perceptions, and judgements, appears to be particularly well-suited for gender-typical male clients (Brooks, 2017).

In the above scenario, the counselor might think that it is more important for the man to deal with powerful feelings and go through the process of grieving for the lost lover. This would not fit very well with a client who expects directive, analytical, problem solving. Thus, counselors find themselves in quandaries when these kinds of situations arise. They do not want to reinforce a maladaptive strategy, yet they also do not want their client to terminate treatment. In these cases, counselors should address the client's needs and expectations in the context of feelings about control, independence, and vulnerability. They should also discuss the man's ambivalent feelings about the process of counseling itself. To do so requires sensitivity to men's issues.

Men's skill levels in these emotionally-focused activities are another consideration. Many have had their emotional experience systematically removed from their lives. Not only are they uncomfortable with the expression of feeling, they are understandably not very good at it. Asked how he feels, a man might often reply, "about what?" The counselor might then say, "about your girlfriend breaking up with you." The man tells the counselor what he *thinks*, "I feel she shouldn't have done it." He may feel sad, disappointed, angry, etc., but these emotion-descriptive words are not in his working vocabulary.

It is also vitally important for counselors to introduce the topic of gender very early in the therapeutic relationship. Since masculinity is an important context in which the male client experiences his symptoms and expectations for therapeutic process and outcome, counselors should assess the client's level of gender conformity, educate him about masculinity, and help him find alternative, more adaptive ways of framing his experiences (Kilmartin, 2004b; 2005).

For counselors, it is an extraordinary challenge to reach a man in the context of questions like, "How do you feel?" when the man has been socially manipulated to the point that the question does not even make sense. The good news is that men who can learn emotion-focused coping in the therapeutic setting may gain a skill that will be helpful to them in virtually every area of their lives.

One way to approach emotional awareness and expression in the therapeutic setting is to help the client to see them as skills which improve with practice, a framework most men are quite familiar with. Clients may believe that emotional competence is an inborn ability and/or one that is found only in women. Christopher Kilmartin's (2005) approach is to find some skill that the client has mastered and say, "Remember the first time you swung a golf club, played a chord on the guitar, or ran a business meeting? It felt awkward at first, but if you stuck with it, you got better at it, and over time it began to feel like second nature." Generally speaking, people invest time and effort in learning a skill when they value the outcome.

Psychological Services for Men. The specific techniques that a counselor would use with a male client are dependent on the individual's problem and the theoretical orientation of the therapist, among other factors. As all men are different, it is hard to make sweeping generalizations about what techniques work with male clients. At the same time, some writers have identified certain approaches that are helpful in the treatment of many male therapy clients. Although we list a number of approaches here, these suggestions have been offered primarily by therapists who work with men. One team of reviewers identified only 15 studies that assessed the efficacy of therapy for men as a distinct population, although they noted that there are many studies that compare the efficacy of therapy for men in comparison to women (Strokoff et al., 2016).

Because the counseling environment feels threatening for many men, several theorists have suggested that structured and psychoeducational approaches be considered as alternatives to traditional individual psychotherapy. John Robertson and Louise Fitzgerald (1992) found that college men were more likely to say they would utilize workshops or seminars than personal counseling. Psychoeducational programs that offer self-help and problem-solving approaches allow men to do some psychological work in a masculine and structured context. Men in corporate settings may respond more positively to psychological work if it is called "executive coaching" rather than "therapy." In this approach, the executive's job performance is explored in relationship to his psychological well-being and relationship skills (Hills, Carlstrom, & Evanow, 2001).

It is important to help men understand the effects of gender on their lives. In therapy, the client's presenting problem can often be viewed in terms of masculine socialization or gender role strain. For example, a man who is feeling very lonely following a breakup could understand his loneliness in the context of the social demands to be independent, non-disclosing, and task-oriented. The mental health practitioner can help the man identify what he believes about masculinity and the sources of these beliefs during this process. Then, the client can start to understand the ways in which he has been restricted by narrow definitions of masculinity and begin the difficult task of freeing himself from gender conformity. In this way, the counselor lets the man know that his problems are understandable, that he need not feel shamed because he has problems, and that he can work toward feeling better.

In addition to helping male clients learn about the danger of avoiding certain behaviors, therapists can help men understand the value of behaviors that they have not learned. When men become clients, counselors often perform the educative role of helping their clients understand that self-disclosure and other nonsexual intimate behaviors are important for the person's mental health. The therapist communicates to the client that these behaviors are expected of him, but also acknowledges that they are difficult and anxiety provoking.

A major therapeutic task is to reintroduce men to the worlds of emotion and connectedness. At the most elementary level, men often need to incorporate "feeling words" into their working vocabulary. Some men at the most basic level need to start with the most elementary emotions (e.g., mad, sad, glad, afraid), and build their affective vocabulary from there. Men who need structure in recognizing and labeling emotions can keep diaries in which they identify emotional reactions and record the situations in which the feelings occurred. Some men need a checklist of possible emotions because the identification of feeling is such a new task (Levant, 1997a); use of an "emotion wheel" can also be helpful (Garfield, 2013). Importantly, men need to explore the vulnerable emotions underneath their anger (Lynch & Kilmartin, 2013).

Therapists can also facilitate men's emotional education by confronting intellectualized interpretations of events, and by communicating the expectation of emotional reaction. This can be done in a very matter-of-fact fashion, by saying in a nonjudgmental way, "I would think you'd have some feelings about [whatever is being discussed]." Again, because most men need a little structure, the therapist is more successful if he or she talks about feelings in the context of some event, rather than in the abstract (Kilmartin, 2005).

One other strategy for helping men access their feelings is by attending to the physiological sensations that accompany emotions (Rabinowitz & Cochran, 2002). The therapist can ask, "What's going on inside your stomach?" or "Can you feel the tension in your forehead?" A jumpy stomach usually accompanies anxiety; a smile reflects pleasure. When the client is able to understand these connections and become more accepting of his natural emotional life, he may be able to resist the masculine propensity to dissociate the self from feeling. Eventually, he may learn to spontaneously identify his affective responses.

Therapists can also be helpful to their male clients by tapping into masculine modes of experience. For instance, men value independence, and the therapist can help the man view nonconformity to stereotypical masculinity as a kind of independence. Men who value risk taking can learn to take risks with emotional self-disclosure. Men who value assertiveness can see objecting to sexist jokes or telling a male friend that he is valued as assertive communications. Men who are good at goal setting can set goals that are related to family, relationships, or play.

Group therapy is increasingly popular as an approach to men's issues. Men in groups can experience other men in completely new ways, and the process of intimate connection to other men can have strong therapeutic effects (Rabinowitz, 2010). Group approaches for men who share a common problem or experience can deal with the interactions between masculine role demands and those experiences. Therapists and educators have recently developed group techniques for working with men of color (Caldwell & White, 2001; Cervantes, 2006), teenage fathers (Kiselica, 2006), survivors of trauma (Crete & Singh, 2014), older men (Robertson, 2014), sexual minority men (Sanabria, 2014), and sex offenders (Becker, 1996; Lazur, 1996), to name only a few. A number of gender-aware self-help books have also appeared in recent years with focuses on subjects such as depression (Real, 1997; Lynch & Kilmartin, 2013), sexuality (Brooks, 1995), anger (Lynch, 2004), friendship (Garfield, 2013) and grieving for a father who has died (Chethik, 2001).

A gender-aware approach to therapy with men involves giving them permission to be who they are and providing a safe atmosphere in which they can express the socially prohibited parts of the self. The therapy room can become a haven from the harsh demands of masculinity. In his exploration, the male client can discover which of these demands have been internalized and self-imposed, and work toward a less restricted experience of the self. He becomes more prepared to take the changes he has made in counseling and expand them into other parts of his life.

SUMMARY

1. Mental health problems are related to gender from several perspectives. Definitions of mental health are culture bound, and gender stereotypes are a central feature of culture.

2. The proportions of males and females diagnosed in some categories of mental disorder vary significantly. Gender seems to be an important factor in determining how psychological distress finds expression. For adult men, the diagnoses of substance abuse, sexual disorders, behavior control problems, and certain personality disorders are more common than for women.

3. Typically male personality disorders tend to share the masculine characteristics of hyperindependence, emotional restrictedness, self absorption, and interpersonal exploitiveness. Men who exhibit these disorders display the most dysfunctional and destructive aspects of traditional masculinity.

4. Although depression is diagnosed twice as often in women as in men, there is evidence that men's depression is underdiagnosed and misunderstood.

5. Contrary to stereotypical beliefs, marriage seems to have the effect of protecting the mental health of men. The marital relationship may offer the man's only avenue for meeting his intimacy needs. When marriages and other intimate relationships dissolve, men tend to have more psychological difficulties than women.

6. Approaches to treating men in counseling and psychotherapy have recently placed an emphasis on the view of men as a special subgroup of clients. Well-trained therapists recognize that men bring characteristic issues to counseling, examine personal and societal biases about men and masculinity, and are aware of the impact of gender on the therapeutic relationship.

7. Individual psychotherapy does not provide a masculine environment. Vulnerability, emotional self-disclosure, and asking for help are connected with the sense that one is unmanly.

8. Because the counseling environment is uncomfortable for many men, other approaches to doing male psychological work have been developed. Workshops, seminars, and discussion groups provide for a structured examination of men's issues. Mental health practitioners can help

men to understand the effects of gender on their lives through these activities, as well as in the traditional therapy setting.

9. Many men have difficulty in dealing with emotions and relationships. In counseling, a man can begin to reconnect with his feelings and intimacy needs. As a result, he can achieve a fuller experience and expression of the self.

GLOSSARY

Internalization: The process of engaging in introspection and thinking about how one might respond to a problem, sometimes referred to as "acting in."

Externalization: The process of looking to the environment for responses to a problem, sometimes referred as "acting out."

Defense mechanisms: Mental strategies for protecting one's self from perceived threats to the self or self-concept.

Projection: A defense mechanism in which one attributes their own conflicts to others.

Personality: A relatively stable set of behavioral predispositions that characterize a human being's typical functioning.

Personality disordered: An individual whose personality is marked by an inflexible and self-defeating style that results in poor mental stability.

Schizoid Personality Disorder: A personality disorder characterized by flat emotionality and interpersonal aloofness.

Schizotypal Personality Disorder: A personality disorder characterized by peculiarities of thinking and behavior.

Narcissistic Personality Disorder: A personality disorder characterized by a grandiose sense of self-importance and absorption.

Antisocial Personality Disorder: A personality disorder characterized by a long history of behaviors that violate the rights of others.

Obsessive-Compulsive Personality Disorder: A personality disorder characterized by unreasonable standards of order and devotion to details, for self and often for others.

Ruminative coping style: A coping style centered around dwelling on one's distress in passive ways that are not oriented toward problem solving.

Ego-centrality: The core of one's self-perceptions.

Emotion wheel: A visual representation of "families" of emotions.

References

"Eating Champ Downs 44 Lobsters in Win" (2005). *The Washington Post*, B3.

"Pulling the Trigger" (1998, April 4). *The Washington Post*, p. A18.

Abrams, D., Viki, G. T., Masser, B., & Bohner, G. (2003). Perceptions of stranger and acquaintance rape: The role of benevolent and hostile sexism in victim blame and rape proclivity. *Journal of Personality and Social Psychology, 84*, 111–125.

Acker, S. E. (Ed., 2013). Unclenching our fists: Abusive men on the journey to nonviolence. Nashville, TN: Vanderbilt University Press.

Active Duty Gender Distribution (2013). U. S. Military Active Duty Demographic Profile. Retrieved August 26, 2013 from http://www.slideshare.net/pastinson/us-military-active-duty-demographic-profile-presentation.

Adams, H. E., Wright, L. W., & Lohr, B. A. (1996). Is homophobia associated with homosexual arousal? *Journal of Abnormal Psychology, 105*, 440–445.

Adams, S., Kuebli, J., Boyle, P. A., & Fivush, R. (1995). Gender differences in parent-child conversations about past emotions: A longitudinal investigation. *Sex Roles, 33*(5–6), 309–323. doi:10.1007/BF01954572

Addis, M. E. (2008). Gender and depression in men. *Clinical Psychology: Science and Practice, 15*, 153–168.

Addis, M. E., & Mahalik, J. R. (2003). Men, masculinity, and the contexts of help seeking. *American Psychologist, 58*, 5–14.

Addis, M. E., Mansfield, A. K., & Syzdek, M. R. (2010). Is "Masculinity" a problem?: Framing the effects of gendered social learning in males. *Psychology of Men and Masculinity, 11*, 77–90. doi:10.1037/a0018602

Adler, L. L. (Ed.) (1993). *International handbook on gender roles*. Westport, CT: Greenwood.

Adorno, T., Frenkel-Brunswik, E., Levinson, D., & Sanford, R.N. (1950). *The authoritarian personality*. New York: Harper.

Alabas, O. A., Tashani, O. A., Tabasam, G., & Johnson, M. I. (2012). Gender role affects experimental pain responses: A systematic review with meta-analysis. *European Journal of Pain, 16*(9), 1211–1223. doi:10.1002/j.1532-2149.2012.00121.x

Allgeier, E. R., & Allgeier, A. R. (2000). *Sexual interactions*. New York: Houghton Mifflin.

Allison, J. (2005). *Violence response and prevention at Pittsburg State University*. Paper presented in symposium: Sexual assault prevention for men (C. Kilmartin, chair) at the Annual Convention of the American Psychological Association, Washington, DC.

Alloy, L. B. Jacobson, N. S., & Acocella, J. (1999). *Abnormal psychology: Current perspectives* (8th ed.). Boston: McGraw-Hill.

Amato, P. & Booth, A. (2001). The legacy of parents' marital discord: Consequences for children's marital quality. *Journal of Personality and Social Psychology, 81 (4)*, 627–638.

American Association of Medical Colleges. (2014). *Table 1: Medical Students, Selected Years, 1965–2013*. Retrieved from https://www.aamc.org/download/411782/data/2014_table1.pdf

American Association of Pediatrics Committee on Adolescence. (2013). Condom Use by Adolescents. *Pediatrics, 132*(973–981). doi:10.1542/peds.2013–2821

American Association of Pediatrics. (2000). Evaluation of the newborn with developmental anomalies of the external genitalia. American Academy of Pediatrics. Committee on Genetics. *Pediatrics, 106*, 138–142.

American Association of Sexuality Educators, Counselors, and Therapists (2016). AASECT Position on Sex Addiction. Retrieved from https://www.aasect.org/position-sex-addiction

American Bar Association. (2014). *A Current Glance at Women in the Law, 2014*. Retrieved from Chicago, IL:

American Cancer Society (2014*). Estimated number of new cancer cases and deaths by sex, U. S., 2014*. Retrieved May 29, 2014 from http://www.cancer.org/acs/groups/content/@research/documents/document/acspc-041780.pdf.

American Cancer Society. (2018). Key Statistics for Prostate Cancer. Retrieved from https://www.cancer.org/cancer/prostate-cancer/about/key-statistics.html

American Psychiatric Association (1980). *Diagnostic and statistical manual of mental disorders* (3rd ed.) (DSM-III). Washington, DC: American Psychiatric Association.

American Psychiatric Association (1987). *Diagnostic and statistical manual of mental disorders* (3rd ed. - revised) (DSM- III-R). Washington, DC: American Psychiatric Association.

American Psychiatric Association (1994). *Diagnostic and statistical manual of mental disorders* (4th ed.) (DSM-IV). Washington, DC: American Psychiatric Association.

American Psychiatric Association (2000). *Diagnostic and statistical manual of mental disorders* (4th ed., text revision) (DSM-IV-TR). Washington, DC: American Psychiatric Association.

American Psychiatric Association (2013). *Diagnostic and statistical manual of mental disorders* (5th ed.) (DSM-V). Washington, DC: American Psychiatric Association.

American Psychiatric Association. (2002). *Guidelines on Multicultural Education, Training, Research, Practice, and Organizational Change for Psychologists*. Retrieved from Washington DC: https://www.apa.org/pi/oema/resources/policy/multicultural-guideline.pdf

American Psychiatric Association. (2013). *Diagnostic and statistical manual of mental disorders: DSM-5™ (5th ed.)*. Arlington, VA, US: American Psychiatric Publishing, Inc.

American Psychiatric, A. (1994). *Diagnostic and statistical manual of mental disorders* (Vol. 4th). Washington, DC: Author.

American Psychological Association Task Force on Appropriate Therapeutic Responses to Sexual Orientation. (2009). *Report of the American Psychological Association Task Force on Appropriate Therapeutic Responses to Sexual Orientation*. Retrieved from Washington, DC: http://www.apa.org/pi/lgbt/resources/therapeutic-response.pdf

REFERENCES

American Psychological Association Task Force on the Sexualization of, G. (2007). *Report of the APA task force on the sexualization of girls*. Washington, DC: American Psychological Association.

American Psychological Association. (2013). *Member Profiles, 2013*. Retrieved from Washington DC: http://www.apa.org/workforce/publications/13–member/profiles.pdf

American Psychological Association. (2015). Guidelines for Psychological Practice with Transgender and Gender Nonconforming People. *American Psychologist, 70*, 832–864.

American Society of Plastic Surgeons. (2011). *Report of the 2010 Plastic Surgery Statistics*. Retrieved from Arlington Heights, IL: http://www.plasticsurgery.org/News-and-Resources/2010–Statistics.html

Anderson, E., & McCormack, M. (2015). Cuddling and spooning: Heteromasculinity and homosocial tactility among student-athletes. *Men and Masculinities, 18*(2), 214–230. doi:10.1177/1097184X14523433

Anderson, E., Magrath, R., & Bullingham, R. (2016). *Out in Sport: The experiences of openly gay and lesbian athletes in competitive sport*. London: Routledge.

Anderson, E., McCormack, M., & Lee, H. (2012). Male Team Sport Hazing Initiations in a Culture of Decreasing Homohysteria. *Journal of Adolescent Research*, 427–448. doi:10.1177/0743558411412957

Anderson, R. N. & Smith, B. L. (2005). Deaths: Leading causes, 2002. *National Vital Statistics Reports, 53 (17)*, 1–90.

Andreassen, C. S. (2014). Workaholism: An overview and current status of the research. *Journal of Behavioral Addictions, 3*(1), 1–11.

Andreassen, C. S. (2014). Workaholism: An overview and current status of the research. *Journal of Behavioral Addictions, 3*(1), 1–11.

Angier, N. (1999a). *Woman: An intimate geography*. Boston: Houghton-Mifflin.

Angier, N. (1999b). *The beauty of the beastly: New views on the nature of life*. Boston: Houghton-Mifflin.

Archer, J. (1984). Gender roles as developmental pathways. *British Journal of Social Psychology, 23*, 245–256.

Archer, J. (2000). Sex differences in aggression between heterosexual partners: A meta-analytic review. *Psychological Bulletin, 126 (5)*, 651–680.

Archer, J. (2006). Testosterone and human aggression: An evaluation of the challenge hypothesis. *Neuroscience and Biobehavioral Reviews, 30*(3), 319–345.

Arciniega, G. M., Anderson, T. C., Tovar-Blank, Z. G., & Tracey, T. J. G. (2008). Toward a fuller conception of Machismo: Development of a traditional Machismo and Caballerismo Scale. *Journal of Counseling Psychology, 55*(1), 19–33. doi:10.1037/0022–0167.55.1.19

Arias, E. (2005). United States life tables 2002. National Vital Statistics Reports, Center for Disease Control. Retrieved June 10, 2009 from http://www.cdc.gov/nchs/data/nvsr/nvsr53/nvsr53_06.

Arias, I. & Ikeda, R. M. (2006). Etiology and surveillance of intimate partner violence. In J. R. Lutzker (Ed.). *Preventing violence: Research and evidence-based intervention strategies*. Washington, DC: American Psychological Association.

Arnett, J. J. (2000). Emerging adulthood: A theory of development from the late teens through the twenties. *American Psychologist, 55*, 469–480

Aronson, E., with Aronson, J. (2012). *The social animal* (11th ed.). New York: Worth.

Asch, S. E. (1965). Effects of group pressure upon the modification and distortion of judgments. In H. Proshansky & B. Seidenberg (Eds.), *Basic studies in social psychology*. New York: Holt, Rinehart, and Winston.

Ashmore, R. D., Del Boca, F. K., & Beebe, M. (2002). "Alkie," "Frat Brother," and "Jock": Perceived types of college students and stereotypes about drinking. *Journal of Applied Social Psychology, 32*, 885–907.

Aslaksen, P. M., Myrbakk, I. N., Hoifodt, R. S., & Flaten, M. A. (2007). The effect of experimenter gender on autonomic and subjective responses to pain stimuli. *Pain, 129*, 260–268.

Astrachan, A. (1992). Men and the new economy. In M. S. Kimmel & M. A. Messner (Eds.), *Men's lives* (2nd ed., pp. 221–225). New York: Macmillan.

Aubrey, J. S. (2007). The Impact of Sexually Objectifying Media Exposure on Negative Body Emotions and Sexual Self-Perceptions: Investigating the Mediating Role of Body Self-Consciousness. *Sex Roles, 10*, 1–23.

Baghurst, T., Hollander, D. B., Nardella, B., & Haff, G. G. (2006). Change in sociocultural ideal male physique: An examination of past and present action figures. *Body Image, 3*, 87–91.

Baird, L. C., Newman, C. B., Volk, H., Svinth, J. R., Conklin, J., & Levy, M. L. (2010). Mortality resulting from head injury in professional boxing. Neurosurgery, 67, 1444–1450.

Balswick, J. (1988). *The inexpressive male*. Lexington, MA: D.C. Heath.

Bandura, A. (1989). Social cognitive theory. In P. H. Mussen (Ed.), *Annals of child development (Vol. 6)* (pp. 1–60). Greenwich, CT, USA: JAI Press.

Bandura, A., & Walters, R. H. (1963). *Social learning and personality development*. New York: Holt, Rinehart, and Winston.

Bandura, A., Ross, D., & Ross, S. (1961). Transmission of aggression through imitation of aggressive models. *Journal of Abnormal and Social Psychology, 63*, 575–582.

Bandura, A., Ross, D., & Ross, S. A. (1961). Transmission of aggression through imitation of aggressive models. *The Journal of Abnormal and Social Psychology, 63*(3), 575–582.

Bandura, A., Ross, D., & Ross, S. A. (1963a). Imitation of film-mediated aggressive models. *The Journal of Abnormal and Social Psychology, 66*(1), 3–11.

Bandura, A., Ross, D., & Ross, S. A. (1963a). Imitation of film-mediated aggressive models. *The Journal of Abnormal and Social Psychology, 66*(1), 3–11.

Bandura, A., Ross, D., & Ross, S. A. (1963b). Vicarious reinforcement and imitative learning. *The Journal of Abnormal and Social Psychology, 67*(6), 601–607.

Bandura, A., Ross, D., & Ross, S. A. (1963b). Vicarious reinforcement and imitative learning. *The Journal of Abnormal and Social Psychology, 67*(6), 601–607.

Bank, B. J., & Hansford, S. L. (2000). Gender and friendship: Why are men's best same-sex friendships less intimate and supportive? *Personal Relationships, 7*(1), 63–78.

Banyard, V. L., Plante, E. G., & Moynihan, M. M. (2004). Bystander Education: Bringing a Broader Community Perspective to Sexual Violence Prevention. *Journal of Community Psychology, 32*(1), 61–79. doi:10.1002/jcop.10078

Barash, D. P., & Lipton, J. E. (1997). *Making sense of sex: How genes and gender influence our relationships*. Washington, DC: Island.

Barber, B. L., Eccles, J. S., & Stone, M. R. (2001). Whatever happened to the jock, the brain, and the princess? Young adult pathways linked to adolescent activity involvement and social identity. *Journal of Adolescent Research, 16*, 429–455.

Barnett, R. C., & Rivers, C. (1996). *She works/he works: How two-income families are happier, healthier, and better-off*. New York: Harper San Francisco/Harper Collins.

Barnett, R. C., Marshall, N. L., & Pleck, J. H. (1992). Adult son-parent relationships and their associations with sons' psychological distress. *Journal of Family Issues, 13,* 505–525.

Baron, R. A. & Branscome, N. R. (2011). *Social psychology* (13th ed.). Boston: Pearson.

Baron, S. L., Hein, M. J., Lehman, E., & Gersic, C. M. (2013). Body mass index, playing position, race, and the cardiovascular mortality of retired football players. *American Journal of Cardiology, 109,* 889–896.

Barr, C. L., & Kleck, R. E. (1995). Self-other perception of the intensity of facial expressions of emotion: Do we know what we show? *Journal of Personality and Social Psychology, 68,* 604–618.

Barthel, D. (1992). When men put on appearances: Advertising and the social construction of masculinity. In S. Craig (Ed.), *Men, masculinity and the media*. Newbuty Park, CA, USA: Sage.

Bartholomew, B. D., Dill, K. E., Anderson, K. B., & Lindsay, J. J. (2003). The proliferation of media violence and its economic underpinnings. In D. A. Gentile (Ed.), *Media violence and children: A complete guide for parents and professionals*. Westport, CT: Praeger.

Basow, S. (1992). *Gender: Stereotypes and roles* (3rd ed.). Monterey, CA: Brooks/Cole.

Baumeister, R. F. (2000). Gender differences in erotic plasticity: The female sex drive as socially flexible and responsive. *Psychological Bulletin, 126*(3), 347–374.

Baumeister, R. F. (2007). Is there anything good about men?

Bauserman, R., & Davis, C. (1996). Perceptions of early sexual experiences and adult sexual adjustment. *Journal of Psychology and Human Sexuality, 8,* 37–59.

Becker, G. (1996). Bias in the assessment of gender differences. *American Psychologist, 51*(2), 154–155. doi:10.1037/0003–066X.51.2.154

Bellamy, J. L., & Banman, A. (2014). Advancing research on services for adolescent fathers: A commentary on Kiselica and Kiselica. *Psychology of Men & Masculinity, 15*(3), 281–283.

Bem, S. L. (1974). The measurement of psychological androgyny. *Journal of Consulting and Clinical Psychology, 42,* 155–162.

Bem, S. L. (1981). Gender schema theory: A cognitive account of sex typing. *Psychological Review, 88*(4), 354–364.

Bem, S. L. (1989). Genital knowledge and gender constancy in preschool children. *Child Development, 60*(3), 649–662.

Bem, S. L. (1993). *The lenses of gender: Transforming the debate on sexual inequality*. New Haven, CT: Yale University Press.

Bem, S. L. (1993). *The lenses of gender*. New Haven, CT: Yale University press.

Bem, S. L. (1998). Gender schema theory and its implications for child development: Raising gender-aschematic children in a gender-schematic society. In D. L. Anselmi & A. L. Law (Eds.), *Questions of gender: perspectives and paradoxes* (pp. 262–274). Boston: McGraw-Hill.

Benard, C., & Schlaffer, E. (1997). "The man in the street: Why he harasses." In L. Richardson, V. Taylor, & N. Whittier (Eds.), *Feminist frontiers* IV (pp. 395–398). Boston: McGraw-Hill.

Ben-David, S. & Schneider, O. (2005). Rape perceptions, gender-role attitudes, and victim-perpetrator acquaintance. *Sex Roles, 53,* 385–399.

Benson, E. (2003). Hostility is among the best predictors of heart disease in men. *Monitor on Psychology, 34* (1), 15.

Berkowitz, A. D. (1997). Effective sexual assault prevention programming: Meeting the needs of men and women. Paper presented at the Seventh International Conference on Sexual Assault and Harassment on Campus, Orlando, FL.

Berkowitz, A. D. (2010). Fostering healthy norms to prevent violence and abuse: The social norms approach. In K. L. Kaufman (Ed.), *The prevention of sexual violence: A practitioner's sourcebook*. Holyoke, MA: NEARI Press.

Berkowitz, A. D. (Ed.) (1994). *Men and rape: Theory, research, and prevention programs in higher education*. San Francisco: Jossey-Bass.

Bernard, J. (1981). The good-provider role: Its rise and fall. *American Psychologist, 36*, 1–12.

Berndt, T. J. (1992). Friendship and friends' influence in adolescence. *Current Directions in Psychological Science, 1*, 156–159.

Bhalla, A. K. (2003). Sexual maturation in well-off Chandigarh boys: A longitudinal study. *Mankind Quarterly, 44*, 175–184.

Biskupic, J. (1998, March 5). Court says law covers same-sex harassment: Justices unanimous in civil rights case. *The Washington Post*, pp. A1, A8.

Black, M. C., Basile, K. C., Breiding, M. J., Smith, S. G., Walters, M. L., Merrick, M. T., . . . Stevens, M. R. (2011). *The National Intimate Partner and Sexual Violence Survey (NISVS): 2010 Summary Report*. Retrieved from Atlanta GA: https://www.cdc.gov/violenceprevention/pdf/NISVS_Report2010-a.pdf

Blake, M. (2015). Mad Men: Inside the Men's Rights Movement—and the Army of Misogynists and Trolls It Spawned. *Mother Jones*.

Blanchard, R., Cantor, J. M., Bogaert, A. F., Breedlove, S. M., & Ellis, L. (2006). Interaction of fraternal birth order and handedness in the development of male homosexuality. *Hormones and Behavior, 49*(3), 405–414.

Blazina, C., & Watkins, C. E. (1996). Masculine gender role conflict: Effects on college men's psychological well-being, chemical substance usage, and attitudes toward help-seeking. *Journal of Counseling Psychology, 43*, 461–465.

Blazina, C., Eddins, R., Burridge, A., & Settle, A. G. (2007). The relationship between masculine ideology, loneliness, and separation-individuation difficulties. *The Journal of Men's Studies, 15*, 101–109.

Bleakley, A.., Jameison, P., & Romer, D. (2012). Trends of sexual and violenct content by gender in top-grossing U. S. films, 1950–2006. Journal of Adolescent Health, 51, 73–79.

Bleier, R. (1984). *Science and gender: A critique of biology and its theories on women*. New York: Pergamon.

Blitstein, R. (2009). Weathering the storm. *Miller-McCune: Turning Research into Solutions, 2*(4), 48–57.

Block, J. H. (1984). *Sex role identity and ego development*. San Francisco, CA, USA: Jossey-Bass.

Block, J. H., Block, J., & Gjerde, P. F. (1986). The personality of children prior to divorce: A prospective study. *Child Development, 57*, 827–840.

Bly, R. (1990). *Iron John*. Reading, MA: Addison Wesley.

Bly, R. (1990). *Iron John*. Reading, MA, USA: Addison-Wesley.

Bly, R. (1991). Father hunger in men. In K. Thompson (Ed.), *To be a man: In search of the deep masculine* (pp.189–192). Los Angeles: Tarcher.

Bogle, K. A. (2008). *Hooking up: Sex, dating, and relationships on campus*. NY: New York University Press.

Bolton, F. G., Morris, L. A., & MacEachron, A. E. (1989). *Males at risk*. Newbury Park, CA: Sage.Bonvillain, N. (2001). *Women and men: Cultural constructs of gender* (3rd ed.). Upper Saddle River, NJ: Prentice-Hall.

Boswell, A. A., & Spade, J. Z. (1996). Fraternities and collegiate rape culture: Why are some fraternities more dangerous places for women? *Gender and Society, 10(2)*, 133–147.

Bowen, G. L., & Orthner, D. K. (1991). Effects of organizational culture on fatherhood. In F. W. Bozett & S. M. H. Hanson (Eds.), *Fatherhood and families in cultural context* (pp. 187–217). New York: Springer.

Boyatzis, C. J., Matillo, G. M., & Nesbitt, K. M. (1995). Effects of the "Mighty Morphin Power Rangers" on children's aggression with peers. *Child Study Journal, 25*, 45–55.

Bradbury, T. N., Capbell, S. M., & Fincham, F. D. (1995). Longitudinal and behavioral analysis of masculinity and femininity in marriage. *Journal of Personality and Social Psychology, 68*, 328–341.

Bradshaw, C., Kahn, A. S., & Saville, B. K. (2010). To hook up or date: Which gender benefits? *Sex Roles, 62*, 661–669.

Bridges, A. J., Wosnitzer, R., Scharrer, E., Sun, C., & Liberman, R. (2010). Aggression and sexual behavior in best-selling pornography videos: A content analysis update. *Violence Against Women, 16*, 1065–85.

Bridges, J. S. (1989). Sex differences in occupational values. *Sex Roles, 20*, 205–211.

Briere, J., & Malamuth, N. M. (1983). Self-reported likelihood of sexually aggressive behavior: Attitudinal versus sexual explanations. *Journal of Research in Personality, 17*, 315–323.

Brinig, M. F., & Allen, D. W. (2000). "These Boots Are Made for Walking": Why Most Divorce Filers Are Women. *American Law and Economics Review, 2*, 126–169. doi:10.1093/aler/2.1.126

Brod, H. (1987a). A case for men's studies. In M. S. Kimmel (Ed.), *Changing men: New directions in research on men and masculinity* (pp. 263–277). Newbury Park, CA: Sage.

Brod, H. (2005, April 2). Working with men against violence: Strategies for date rape prevention. Annual conference of the Amercian Men's Studies Association, Nashville, TN.

Brod, H. (Ed.) (1987b). *The making of masculinities: The new men's studies*. Boston: Allen and Unwin.

Brody, L. R., & Hall, J. A. (2010). Gender and emotion in context. In M. Lewis, J. M. Haviland, & L. F. Barrett (Eds.), *Handbook of emotions* (3rd. ed.). New York: Guilford.

Brody, L. R. (1999). *Gender, emotion, and the family*. Cambridge, MA: Harvard University Press.

Brody, L. R. (2000). The socialization of gender differences in emotional expression: Display rules, infant temperament, and differentiation. In A. H. Fischer (Ed.), *Gender and emotion: Social psychological perspectives*. Cambridge, UK: Cambridge University Press.

Brody, L. R., & Hall, J. A. (2010). Gender, emotion, and socialization. In J. C. Chrisler & D. R. McCreary (Eds.), *Handbook of gender research in psychology, Vol 1: Gender research in general and experimental psychology*. (pp. 429–454). New York, NY, US: Springer Science + Business Media.

Brooks, G. R. (1995). *The Centerfold Syndrome: How men can overcome objectification and achieve intimacy with women*. San Francisco: Jossey Bass.

Brooks, G. R. (2017). Counseling, psychotherapy, and psychological interventions for boys and men. In R. F. Levant, Y. J. Wong, R. F. Levant, & Y. J. Wong (Eds.), *The *psychology of men and masculinities.* (pp. 317–345). Washington, DC, US: American Psychological Association.

Brooks, G. R., & Elder, W. B. (2016). History and future of the psychology of men and masculinities. In Y. J. Wong & S. R. Wester (Eds.), *APA handbook of men and masculinities.* (pp. 3–21). Washington, DC: American Psychological Association.

Brooks, G. R. & Good, G. E. (2001). *The new handbook of psychotherapy and counseling with men: A comprehensive guide to settings, problems, and treatment approaches.* San Francisco: Jossey-Bass.

Brooks, G. R., & Levant, R. F. (1997). Toward the reconstruction of male sexuality: A prescription for the future. In R. F. Levant & G. R. Brooks (Eds.), *Men and sex* (pp. 257–272). New York: Wiley.

Brooks, G. R., & Silverstein, L. B. (1995). Understanding the dark side of masculinity: An interactive systems model. In R. F. Levant, W. S. Pollack, R. F. Levant, & W. S. Pollack (Eds.), *A new psychology of men.* (pp. 280–333). New York, NY, US: Basic Books.

Brown, J. D., Steele, J. R., & Walsh-Childers, K. (2002). *Sexual teens, sexual media: Investigating media's influence on adolescent sexuality.* Mahwah, NJ: Lawrence Erlbaum.

Brown, J., & L'Engle, K. L. (2009). X-rated: Sexual attitudes and behaviors associated with U.S. early adolescents' exposure to sexually explicit media. *Communication Research, 36,* 129–151. doi:10.1177/0093650208326465

Brown, L. M., Lamb, S., & Tappan, M. (2009). *Packaging boyhood: Saving our sons from superheroes, slackers, and other media stereotypes.* NY: St. Marten's Press.

Bruch, M. A. (1980). Holland's typology applied to client/counselor interactions: Implications for counseling with men. In T. M. Skovholt, P. Schauble, & R. David (Eds.), *Counseling men* (pp.101–119). Monterey, CA: Brooks/Cole.

Bruch, M. A., Berko, E. H., & Haase, R. F. (1998). Shyness, masculine ideology, physical attractiveness, and emotional inexpressiveness: Testing a mediational model of men's interpersonal competence. *Journal of Counseling Psychology, 45,* 84–97.

Bunch, T. & Porter, A. (2003). Ending domestic violence: A call to men. Presentation at Congreso Nacional Sobre Violencia Domestica Agresion Sexual, Acecho y Violencia en Cita, San Juan, Puerto Rico.

Burger, J. M. (2009). Replicating Milgram: Would people still obey today? *American Psychologist, 64,* 1–11.

Burke, P. J., & Cast, A. D. (1997). Stability and change in the gender identities of newly married couples. *Social Psychology Quarterly, 60,* 277–290.

Burn, S. M. (1996). *The Social Psychology of Gender.* New York, NY, USA: McGraw Hill.

Burt, M. R. (1980). Cultural myths and supports for rape. *Journal of Personality and Social Psychology, 38,* 217–230. doi:10.1037/0022-3514.38.2.217

Buss, D. M. (1989). Sex differences in human mate selection: Evolutionary hypotheses tested in 37 cultures. *Behavioral and Brain Sciences, 12,* 1–49. doi:10.1017/S0140525X00023992

Buss, D. M. (1995). Psychological sex differences: Origins through sexual selection. *American Psychologist, 50,* 164–168. doi:10.1037/0003-066X.50.3.164

Buss, D. M., & Schmitt, D. P. (1993). Sexual strategies theory: An evolutionary perspective on human mating. *Psychological Review, 100,* 204–232. doi:10.1037/0033-295X.100.2.204

Buss, D. M., Shackelford, T. K., Kirkpatrick, L. A., & Larsen, R. J. (2001). A half century of mate preferences: The cultural evolution of values. *Journal of Marriage and the Family, 63,* 491–503. doi:10.1111/j.1741-3737.2001.00491.x

Buss, K. A., Brooker, R. J., & Leuty, M. (2008). Girls most of the time, boys some of the time: Gender differences in toddlers' use of maternal proximity and comfort seeking. *Infancy, 13*(1), 1–29.

Bussey, K., & Bandura, A. (1992). Self-regulatory mechanisms governing gender development. *Child Development, 63*, 1236–1250.

Bussey, K., & Bandura, A. (1999). Social cognitive theory of gender development and differentiation. *Psychological Review, 106*, 676–713.

Butcher, J. N., Dahlstrom, W. G., Graham, J. R., Tellegen, A., & Kaemmer, B. (1989). *Minnesota Multiphasic Personality Inventory-2 (MMPI-2): Manual for administration and scoring*. Minneapolis: University of Minnesota Press.

Butcher, J. N., Hooley, J. M., & Mineka, S. (2014). *Abnormal psychology* (16th ed.). Boston: Pearson.

Cabrera, N. J., Tamis-LeMonda, C. S., Bradley, R. H., Hofferth, S., & Lamb, M. E. (2000). Fatherhood in the twenty-first century. *Child Development, 71*(1), 127–136.

Caldera, Y. M., Huston, A. C., & O'Brien, M. (1989). Social interactions and play patterns of parents and toddlers with feminine, masculine, and neutral toys. *Child development, 60*, 70–76.

Caldwell, L. D. & White, J. L. (2001). African-centered therapeutic and counseling interventions for African American males. In G. R. Brooks & G. E. Good (Eds.). *The new handbook of psychotherapy and counseling with men: A comprehensive guide to settings, problems, and treatment approaches*. San Francisco: Jossey-Bass.

Caldwell-Colbert, A. T., Henderson-Daniel, J., & Dudley-Grant, G. R. (2003). The African diaspora. In J. D. Robinson & L. C. James (Eds.), *Diversity in human interactions: The tapestry of America* (pp. 33–62). Oxford: Oxford university press.

Calzo, J. P., Corliss, H. L., Blood, E. A., Field, A. E., & Austin, S. B. (2012). Develoment of muscularity and thinness concerns in heterosexual and sexual minority males. *Health Psychology*.

Cameron, K. A., Salazar, L. F., Bernhardt, J. M., Burgess-Whitman, N., Wingood, G. M., & DiCilemente, R. J. (2005). Adolescents' experience with sex on the web: Results from online focus groups. *Journal of Adolescence, 28*, 535–540.

Canetto, S. (2000). The paradox of male suicidal behavior. Symposium: Boys, men, depression, and suicide: Cutting-edge research and practice (J. Mahalik & M. Addis, chairs). Annual Convention of the American Psychological Association, Washington, DC.

Cantor, J. M., Klein, C., Lykins, A., Rullo, J. E., Thaler, L., & Walling, B. R. (2013). A treatment-oriented typology of self-identified hypersexuality referrals. *Archives of Sexual Behavior, 42*(5), 883–893.

Capraro, R. L. (2000). Why college men drink: Alcohol, adventure, and the paradox of masculinity. *Journal of American College Health, 48*, 307–315.

Caringella, S. (2009). *Addressing rape reform in law and practice*. New York: Columbia University Press.

Carlson, P. (2004). A hunger for victory: Sonya Thomas is competitive eating's next small thing. *The Washington Post*, January 31, pp. A1, A14.

Carroll, H. (2011). *Affirmative reaction: New formations of White Masculinity*. Durham, NC: Duke University Press.

Carver, L. J. & Vaccaro, B. G. (2007). 12 month old infants allocate increased neural resources to stimuli associated with adult negative emotion. *Developmental Psychology, 43*, 54–69.

Carver, P. R., Egan, S. K., & Perry, D. G. (2004). Children who question their heterosexuality. *Developmental Psychology, 40*, 43–53.

Casteneda, D. & Burns-Glover, A. (2004). Gender, sexuality, and intimate relationships. In M. A. Paludi (Ed.), *Praeger guide to the psychology of gender*. Westport, CT: Praeger.

Catalano, S. (2012). Intimate partner violence, 1993–2010. Retrieved June 3, 2014 from http://www.bjs.gov/content/pub/pdf/ipv9310.pdf.

Catalyst (2006). 2005 Catalyst census of women board directors of the fortune 500. New York: Author.

Center for American Women in Politics. (2017). Women in Elective Office 2017. Retrieved from http://www.cawp.rutgers.edu/women-elective-office-2017

Centers for Disease Control and Prevention. (2011). *Leading Causes of Death by Age Group, Race/Ethnicity Males, United States, 2010*. Retrieved from Atlanta, GA: https://www.cdc.gov/healthequity/lcod/men/2010/LCODrace_ethnicityMen2010.pdf

Centers for Disease Control and Prevention. (2012). *New HIV infections in the United States*. Retrieved from Atlanta GA: http://www.cdc.gov/nchhstp/newsroom/docs/2012/HIV-Infections-2007-2010.pdf

Centers for Disease Control and Prevention. (2016). *Tobacco Use*. Retrieved from: https://nccd.cdc.gov/Youthonline/App/Results.aspx?TT=J&OUT=0&SID=HS&QID=QQ&LID=XX&YID=YY&LID2=&YID2=&COL=T&ROW1=N&ROW2=N&HT=C02&LCT=LL&FS=S1&FR=R1&FG=G5&FI=I1&FP=P1&FSL=S1&FRL=R1&FGL=G1&FIL=I1&FPL=P1&PV=&TST=&C1=&C2=&QP=G&DP=1&VA=CI&CS=Y&SYID=&EYID=&SC=DEFAULT&SO=ASC

Centers for Disease Control and Prevention. (2017). *Sexually Transmitted Disease Surveillance 2016*. Retrieved from Atlanta, GA: https://www.cdc.gov/std/stats16/CDC_2016_STDS_Report-for508WebSep21_2017_1644.pdf

Cervantes, J. M. (2006). A new understanding of the macho male image: Explorations of the Mexican American man. In M. Englar-Carlson & M. Stevens (Eds.), *In the room with men: A casebook of therapeutic change*. Washington, DC: American Psychological Association.

Chan, J. (2004). Asian American Men's Studies. In M. Kimmel & A. Aronson (Eds.), *Men and masculinities: A social, cultural, and historical encyclopedia*. Santa Barbara, CA: ABC-Clio.

Chethik, N. (2001). *Fatherloss: How Sons of All Ages Come to Terms with the Deaths of Their Dads*. NY: Hyperion.

Chodorow, N. (1978). *The reproduction of mothering: Psychoanalysis and the sociology of gender*. Berkely, CA: University of California Press.

Chomsky, N. (1957). *Syntactic structures*. The Hague, Netherlands: Mouton.

Chomsky, N. (1959). Review: Verbal Behavior by B. F. Skinner. *Language, 35*, 26–58.

Chu, J. Y. (2004). A relational perspective on adolescent boys' identity development. In N. Way & J. Y. Chu (Eds.), *Adolescent boys: Exploring diverse cultures of boyhood* (pp. 78–105). NY: New York University press.

Chua, P., & Fujino, D. C. (1999). Negotiating new Asian-American masculinities: Attitudes and gender expectations. *The Journal of Men's Studies, 7*(3), 391–413. doi:10.3149/jms.0703.391

Claes, M. E. (1992). Friendship and personal adjustment during adolescence. *Journal of Adolescence, 15*, 39–55.

Clark, A. J. (1998). *Defense mechanisms and the counseling process*. Thousand Oaks, CA: Sage.

Clatterbaugh, K. (1997). *Contemporary perspectives on masculinity: Men, women, and politics in modern society* (2nd ed.). Boulder, CO: Westview.

Clatterbaugh, K. (2000). Review essay: Literature of the U. S. men's movements. *Signs: Journal of Women in Culture and Society, 25 (3)*, 883–894.

Clawson, L. (2005). Cowboys and schoolteachers: Gender in romance novels, secular and Christian. *Sociological Perspectives, 48*, 461–479.

Clawson, L. (2005). Cowboys and schoolteachers: Gender in romance novels, secular and Christian. *Sociological Perspectives, 48*, 461–479. doi:10.1525/sop.2005.48.4.461

Clow, K. A., Ricciardelli, R., & Bartfay, W. J. (2015). Are you man enough to be a nurse? The impact of ambivalent sexism and role congruity on perceptions of men and women in nursing advertisements. *Sex Roles, 72*(7–8), 363–376. doi:10.1007/s11199-014-0418-0

Coad, D. (2008). *The Metrosexual: Gender, sexuality, and sport*. Albany, NY: State University of New York Press.

Cochran, S. V. & Rabinowitz, F. E. (2000). Men and depression: Clinical and empirical perspectives. San Diego: Academic Press.

Cochran, S. V. (2010). Emergence and development of the Psychology of Men and Masculinity. In J. C. Chrisler & D. R. McCreary (Eds.), *Handbook of Gender Research in Psychology* (pp. 43–58). NY: Springer.

Cohen, D., Vandello, J., & Rantilla, A. K. (1998). Gender, shame, and culture: An anthropological perspective. In P. Gilbert & B. Andrews (Eds.), *Shame: Interpersonal behavior, psychopathology, and culture* (pp. 261–282). New York: Oxford University Press.

Cohen, J., & Brooks, R. A. (2014). *Confronting School Bullying: Kids, Culture, and the Making of a Social Problem*. Boulder, CO: Lynne Rienner Publishers, Inc.

Cohen, J., & Suen, Y.-t. (2012). Taking stock: Exploring trends in the field of men's studies through a content analysis of the American Men's Studies Association (AMSA) Annual Conference Programs (1993–2011). *The Journal of Men's Studies, 20*(1), 73–83.

Cohen-Bendahan, C. C. C., van de Beek, C., & Berenbaum, S. A. (2005). Prenatal sex hormone effects on child and adult sex-typed behavior: Methods and findings. *Neuroscience and Biobehavioral Reviews, 29*(2), 353–384. doi:10.1016/j.neubiorev.2004.11.004

Cohn, A. M., Jakupcak, M., Seibert, L. A., Hildebrandt, T. B., & Zeichner, A. (2010). The role of emotion dysregulation in the association between men's restrictive emotionality and use of physical aggression. *Psychology of Men & Masculinity, 11*(1), 53–64. doi:10.1037/a0018090

Cohn, A. M., Seibert, L. A., & Zeichner, A. (2009). The role of restrictive emotionality, trait anger, and masculinity threat in men's perpetration of physical aggression. *Psychology of Men & Masculinity, 10*(3), 218–224. doi:10.1037/a0015151

Cohn, A. M., Zeichner, A., & Seibert, L. A. (2008). Labile affect as a risk factor for aggressive behavior in men. *Psychology of Men & Masculinity, 9*(1), 29–39. doi:10.1037/1524-9220.9.1.29

Cohn, A., & Zeichner, A. (2006). Effects of masculine identity and gender role stress on aggression in men. *Psychology of Men & Masculinity, 7*(4), 179–190. doi:10.1037/1524-9220.7.4.179

Colby, S. L., & Ortman, J. M. (2016). *Projections of the Size and Composition of the U.S. Population: 2014 to 2060*. Retrieved from Washington, DC: https://www.census.gov/content/dam/Census/library/publications/2015/demo/p25-1143.pdf

Collins, G. (1979, June 1). A new look at life with father. *The New York Times Magazine*, pp. 30–31.

Coltrane, S. (1998). Theorizing masculinities in comtemporary social science. In D. L. Anselmi & A. L. Law (Eds.), *Questions of gender: Perspectives and paradoxes* (pp. 76–88). Boston, MA, USA: McGraw Hill.

Comas-Díaz, L. (1993). Hispanic/Latino communities: Psychological implications. In D. R. Atkinson, G. Morten, & D. W. Sue (Eds.), *Counseling American minorities: A cross-cultural perspective* (4th ed., pp. 245–263). Madison, WI: Brown and Benchmark.

Connell, R. W. (1995). *Masculinities*. Berkeley, CA: University of California Press.

Connell, R. W. (1993). The big picture: Masculinities in recent world history. *Theory and Society, 22*, 597–623.

Connolly, J. A., & Johnson, A. M. (1996). Adolescents' romantic relationship and the structure and quality of their close interpersonal ties. *Personal Relationships, 3*, 185–195.

Connolly, J., Craig, W., Goldberg, A., & Pepler, D. (1999). Conceptions of cross-sex friendships and romantic relationships in early adolescence. *Journal of Youth and Adolescence, 28*, 481–494.

Constantinople, A. (1973). Masculinity-femininity: An exception to a famous dictum? *Psychological Bulletin, 80*(5), 389–407.

context (pp. 177–188). Washington, DC: American Psychological

Coontz, S. (1997). *The way we really are: Coming to terms with America's changing families.* New York: Basic Books.

Coontz, S. (2005). *Marriage, a history: From obedience to intimacy, or how love conquered marriage.* New York: Viking.

Cooper, A., & Smith, E. L. (2011). *Homicide Trends in the United States, 1980–2008*. Retrieved from Washington DC: http://www.bjs.gov/content/pub/pdf/htus8008.pdf

Cooper, M. L., Russell, M., Skinner, J. B., Frone, M. R., & Mudar, P. (1992). Stress and alcohol use: Moderating effects of gender, coping, and alcohol expectancies. *Journal of Abnormal Psychology, 101*, 139–152.

Cope-Farrar, K. M., & Kunkel, D. (2002). Sexual messages in teens' favorite prime-time television programs. In J. D. Brown, J. R. Steele, & K. Walsh-Childers (Eds.), *Sexual teens, sexual media: Investigating media's influence on adolescent sexuality* (pp. 59–78). Mahwah, NJ: Lawrence Erlbaum.

Cottingham, M. D., Erickson, R. J., & Diefendorff, J. M. (2015). Examining men's status shield and status bonus: How gender frames the emotional labor and job satisfaction of nurses. *Sex Roles, 72*(7–8), 377–389. doi:10.1007/s11199–014–0419–z

Coughlin, P., & Wade, J. C. (2012). Masculinity ideology, income disparity, and romantic relationship quality among men with higher earning female partners. *Sex Roles, 67*(5–6), 311–322. doi:10.1007/s11199–012–0187–6

Cournoyer, R. J., & Mahalik, J. R. (1995). Cross-sectional study of gender role conflict examining college-aged and middle-aged men. *Journal of Counseling Psychology, 42*, 11–19.

Courtenay, W. H. (2000a). Constructions of masculinity and their influence on men's well-being: A theory of gender and health. *Social Science and Medicine, 50* (10), 1385–1401.

Courtenay, W. H. (2000b). Behavioral factors associated with disease, injury, and death among men: Evidence and implications for prevention. *Journal of Men's Studies, 9* (1), 81–142.

Courtenay, W. H. (2011). *Dying to Be Men: Psychosocial, Environmental, and Biobehavioral Directions in Promoting the Health of Men and Boys*. NY: Routledge.

Courtenay, W. H., McCreary, D. R., & Merighi, J. R. (2011). Gender and ethnic differences in health beliefs and behaviors *Dying to Be Men: Psychosocial, Environmental, and Biobehavioral Directions in Promoting the Health of Men and Boys* (pp. 229–240). NY: Routledge.

Cozby, P. C. (1973). Self-disclosure: A literature review. *Psychological Bulletin, 79,* 73–91.

Crawford, M., & Popp, D. (2003). Sexual double standards: A review and methodological critique of two decades of research. *The Journal of Sex Research, 40,* 13–26. doi:10.1080/00224490309552163

Crete, G. K. & Singh, A. A. (2014). Counseling men with trauma histories: Developing foundational knowledge. In M. Englar-Carlson, M. P. Evans, & T. Duffey (Eds., 2014), *A counselor's guide to working with men.* Alexandria, VA: American Counseling Association.

Crites, J. O., & Fitzgerald, L. F. (1978). The competent male. *The Counseling Psychologist, 7,* 10–14.

Crooks, R. & Baur, K. (2007). *Our sexuality* (10th ed.). Belmont, CA: Wadsworth.

Crosby, A. E., Ortega, L., & Stevens, M. R. (2013). Suicides — United States, 2005–2009. *Mortality and Morbidity Weekly Review, 62 Supplement,* 179–183.

Crosset, T. W. (2000). Athletic affiliations and violence against women: Toward a structural prevention project. In J. McKay, M. A. Messner, & D. F. Sabo (Eds.), *Masculinities, gender relations, and sport.* Thousand Oaks, CA: Sage.

Crouter, A. C., Whiteman, S. D., McHale, S. M., & Osgood, D. W. (2007). Development of gender attitude traditionality across middle childhood and adolescence. *Child Development, 78,* 911–926.

Cunningham, M., & Newkirk Meunier, L. (2004). The influence of peer experiences on bravado attitudes among African American males. In N. Way & J. Y. Chu (Eds.), *Adolescent boys: Exploring diverse cultures of boyhood* (pp. 219–234). NY, NY: New York University press.

Daily News (2013, April 6). Average 12 high school and college football players die each year, study says. Retrieved June 2, 2014 from http://www.nydailynews.com/lifestyle/health/average-12–school-football-players-die-year-study-article-1.1309671.

Daly, M. & Wilson, M. (1983). *Sex, evolution, and behavior* (2nd ed.). Boston: Willard Grant.

Daly, M., & Wilson, M. (1985). Competitiveness, risk taking, and violence: The young male syndrome. *Ethology and Sociobiology, 6,* 59–73.

Daniel, H., & Butkus, R. (2015). Lesbian, Gay, Bisexual, and Transgender Health Disparities: Executive Summary of a Policy Position Paper From the American College of Physicians. *Annals of Internal Medicine, 163,* 135–137. doi:10.7326/M14–2482

Dariotis, J. K., Pleck, J. L., Astone, N. M., & Sonenstein, F. L. (2011). Pathways of early fatherhood, marriage, and employment: A latent class growth analysis. *Demography, 48,* 593–623. doi:10.1007/s13524–011–0022–7

Dariotis, J. K., Sonenstein, F. L., Gates, G. J., Capps, R., Astone, N. M., Pleck, J. L.,...Zeger, S. (2008). Changes in sexual risk behavior as young men transition to adulthood. *Perspectives on Sexual and Reproductive Health, 40,* 218–225. doi:10.1363/4021808

David, D., & Brannon, R. (1976). The male sex role: Our culture's blueprint for manhood and what it's done for us lately. In D. David & R. Brannon (Eds.), *The forty-nine percent majority: The male sex role* (pp. 1–48). Reading, MA: Addison-Wesley.

Davis, F. (1991). *Moving the Mountain: The Women's Movement in America since 1960.* NY: Simon & Schuster.

De Visser, R. O., & Smith, J. A. (2007). Alcohol consumption and masculine identity among young men. *Psychology & Health, 22*(5), 595–614. doi:10.1080/147683206–00941772

de Waal, F. B. M. (1997, June 27). Bonobos are from Venus. *The Chronicle of Higher Education, 43,* B8–B9.

de Waal, F. B. M. (2005). Our inner ape: What primate behavior tells us about human nature. Paper presented at the Annual Convention of the American Psychological Association, Washington, DC.

de Waal, F. B. M. (2007, September 21). Our inner ape: What primate behavior tells us about human nature. Presentation at the University of Mary Washington, Fredericksburg, VA.

DeAngelis, T. (2005). Stepfamily success depends on ingredients. *Monitor on Psychology, 36 (11),* 58–61.

Deaux, K. (1985). Sex and gender. *Annual Review of Psychology, 36,* 49–81.

Deaux, K. (2000). Gender and emotion: Notes from a grateful tourist. In A. H. Fischer (Ed.), *Gender and emotion: Social psychological perspectives.* Cambridge, UK: Cambridge University Press.

Deaux, K., & LaFrance, M. (1998). Gender. In D. T. Gilbert, S. T. Fiske, & G. Lindzey (Eds.), *The handbook of social psychology* (Vol. 4th, pp. 788–827). Boston, MA, USA: McGraw-Hill.

DeBlock, A., & Adriaens, P. R. (2013). Pathologizing sexual deviance: A history. *Journal of Sex Research, 50,* 276–298. doi:10.1080/00224499.2012.738259

Defense.gov (2011, July 22). "Don't ask; don't tell" repeal certified by President Obama. Retrieved July 10, 2014 from www.defense.gov/news/newsarticle.aspx?id=64780.

DeFranc, W., & Mahalik, J. R. (2002). Masculine gender role conflict and stress in relation to parental attachment and separation. *Psychology of Men & Masculinity, 3*(1), 51–60. doi:10.1037/1524-9220.3.1.51

DeHaan, S., Kuper, L. E., Magee, J. C., Bigelow, L., & Mustanski, B. S. (2013). The interplay between online and offline explorations of identity, relationships, and sex: A mixed-methods study with LGBT youth. *Journal of Sex Research, 50*(5), 421–434.

Dekeseredy, W. S., & Schwartz, M. D. (2013). *Male peer support and violence against women: The history and verification of a theory.* Boston: Northeastern University Press.

Denmark, F., Rabinowitz, V., & Sechzer, J. (2000). *Engendering psychology.* Boston: Allyn & Bacon.

Densen, T. F. (2011). A social neuroscience perspective on the neurobiological bases of aggression. In P. R. Shaver & M. Mikulincer (Eds.), *Human aggression and violence: Causes, manifestations, and consequences.* Washington, DC: American Psychological Association.

Deutsch, F. M., & Saxon, S. E. (1998). Traditional ideologies, nontraditional lives. *Sex Roles, 38,* 331–362. doi:10.1023/A:1018749620033

Devault, A. (2014). Commentary on The complicated worlds of adolescent fathers: Implications for clinical practice, public policy, and research. *Psychology of Men & Masculinity, 15*(3), 275–277.

Devlin, P. K., & Cowan, G. A. (1985). Homophobia, perceived fathering, and male intimate relationships. *Journal of Personality Assessment, 49,* 467–473.

Diener, E., Larsen, R. J., Levine, S., & Emmons, R. A. (1985). Intensity and frequency: Dimensions underlying positive and negative affect. *Journal of Personality and Social Psychology, 48,* 1253–1265.

Dietz, T. L. (1998). An examination of violence and gender role portrayals in video games: Implications for gender socialization and aggressive behavior. *Sex Roles, 38*(5–6), 425–442. doi:10.1023/A:1018709905920.

Dines, G. (2005). Unmasking the pornography industry: From fantasy to reality. In E. Buchwald, P. R. Fletcher, & M. Roth (Eds.), *Transforming a rape culture* (revised ed.). Minneapolis: Milkweed.

Dines, G. (2006, May 18). Dirty sexy money. Presentation at the Virginia Colleges Against Sexual Assault Conference, Virginia Beach, VA.

Dines, G. (2013, May 20). Discussion comments at the Blue Ribbon Panel on Hypersexualized Media, Richmond, VA.

Division 17, American Psychological Association (1979). Principles concerning the counseling and therapy of women. *The Counseling Psychologist, 8*, 21.

Dodge, K. A. (2011). Social information processing patterns as mediators of the interaction between genetic factors and life experiences in the development of aggressive behavior. In P. R. Shaver & M. Mikulincer (Eds.), *Human aggression and violence: Causes, manifestations, and consequences.* Washington, DC: American Psychological Association.

Dolnick, E. (1991, August 13). Why do women outlive men? *Washington Post Health,* pp. 10–13.

Donnelly, K., & Twenge, J. M. (2016). Masculine and feminine traits on the bem sex-role inventory, 1993–2012: A cross-temporal meta-analysis. *Sex Roles.* doi:10.1007/s11199-016-0625-y

Dorn, L. D., & Biro, F. M. (2011). Puberty and Its Measurement: A Decade in Review. *Journal of Research on Adolescence (Wiley-Blackwell), 21*(1), 180–195. doi:10.1111/j.1532-7795.2010.00722.x

Doyle, J. A., & Paludi, M. A. (1998). *Sex and gender: The human experience* (4th ed.). Boston: McGraw-Hill.

Doyle, J., & Femiano, S. (1999). The Early History of the American Men's Studies Association and the Evolution of Men's Studies. Retrieved from http://mensstudies.org/?page_id=5

Dunn, M. G., Rochlen, A. B., & O'Brien, K. M. (2013). Employee, mother, and partner: An exploratory investigation of working women with stay-at-home fathers. *Journal of Career Development, 40*(1), 3–22.

Dutton, D. G. (2011). Attachment and violence: An anger born of fear. In P. R. Shaver & M. Mikulincer (Eds.), *Human aggression and violence: Causes, manifestations, and consequences.* Washington, DC: American Psychological Association.

Dutton, D. G., & Golant, S. K. (1995). *The batterer: A psychological profile.* New York: Basic.

Eagly, A. (1987). *Sex differences in social behavior: A social-role interpretation.* Hillsdale, NJ: Lawrence Erlbaum.

Eagly, A. (1995). The science and politics of comparing women and men. *American Psychologist, 50,* 145–158. doi:10.1037/0003-066X.50.3.145

Eagly, A. H., Wood, W., & Diekman, A. B. (2000). Social role theory of sex differences and similarities: A current appraisal. In T. Eckes & H. M. Trautner (Eds.), *The developmental social psychology of gender* (pp. 123–174). Mahwah, NJ: Lawrence Erlbaum.

Eagly, A., & Wood, W. (1999). The origins of sex differences in human behavior: Evolved dispositions versus social roles. *American Psychologist, 54,* 408–423.

Edwards, R. (1996). Can sexual orientation change with therapy? APA ponders its stance on a therapy designed to convert gay men and lesbians into heterosexuals. *APA Monitor, 27*(9), 49.

Ehrenreich, B. (1983). *The hearts of men: American dreams and the flight from commitment.* Garden City, NY: Anchor.

Eisenstock, B. (1984). Sex-role differences in children's identification with counter-stereotypical televised portrayals. *Sex Roles, 10,* 417–430.

Eisler, R. M. (1995). The relationship between masculine gender role stress and men's health risk: The validation of a construct. In R. F. Levant & W. S. Pollack (Eds.), *A new psychology of men* (pp. 207–225). NY: Basic Books.

Eisler, R. M., & Skidmore, J. R. (1987). Masculine gender role stress: Scale development and component factors in the appraisal of stressful situations. *Behavior Modification, 11*, 123–136. doi:10.1177/01454455870112001

Eliason, M. J. (1995). Accounts of sexual identity formation in heterosexual students. *Sex Roles, 32*, 821–834.

Eliot, L. (2009). *Pink brain, blue brain: How small differences grow into troublesome gaps—and what we can do about it*. Boston: Houghton Mifflin Harcourt.

Elkins, L. E., & Peterson, C. (1993). Gender differences in best friendships. *Sex Roles, 29*(7–8), 497–508. doi:10.1007/BF00289323

Else-Quest, N. M., Hyde, J. S., & Linn, M. C. (2010). Cross-national patterns of gender differences in mathematics: A meta-analysis. *Psychological Bulletin, 136*(1), 103–127.

Engeln, R., Sladek, M. R., & Waldron, H. (2013). Body talk among college men: Content, correlates, and effects. *Body Image, 10*(3), 300–308. doi:10.1016/j.bodyim.2013.02.001

Englar-Carlson, M., & Stevens, M. (2006). *In the room with men: A casebook of therapeutic change*. Washington, DC: American Psychological Association.

Englar-Carlson, M., Evans, M. P., & Duffey, T. (Eds., 2014). *A counselor's guide to working with men*. Alexandria, VA: American Counseling Association.

Epstein, M., & Ward, L. M. (2008). "Always use protection": Communication boys receive about sex from parents, peers, and the media. *Journal of Youth and Adolescence, 37*, 113–126. doi:10.1007/s10964-007-9187-1

Epstein, M., Calzo, J. P., Smiler, A. P., & Ward, L. M. (2009). "Anything From Making Out to Having Sex": Men's Negotiations of Hooking Up and Friends with Benefits Scripts. *Journal of Sex Research, 46*, 414–424.

Equal Employment Opportunity Commission (EEOC) (1980). Discrimination because of sex under Title VII of the Civil Rights Act 1964, as amended; adoption of interim interpretive guidelines. *Federal Register, 45*, 25024–25025.

Equal Employment Opportunity Commission. (nd). Sexual Harassment Charges EEOC & FEPAs Combined: FY 1997 - FY 2011. Retrieved from http://www1.eeoc.gov//eeoc/statistics/enforcement/sexual_harassment.cfm?renderforprint=1

Erikson, E. H. (1968). *Identity: Youth and Crisis*. NY: W. W. Norton and Company.

Espiritu, Y. L. (2007). All men are *not* created equal: Asian American men in U.S. history. In M. S. Kimmel & M. A. & Messner (Eds.), *Men's lives* (7th ed). Boston: Allyn and Bacon.

ESPN (1994, October 23). *Outside the Lines* (television documentary).

ESPN (2007). Jury rules Thomas harassed ex-executive; MSG owes her $11.6M. Retrieved June 17, 2009 from sports.espn.go.com/nba/news/story?id=3046010

Evans, L., & Davies, K. (2000). No sissy boys here: A content analysis of the representation of masculinity in elementeray school reading textbooks. *Sex Roles, 42*, 255–270.

Fagot, B. I., & Hagan, R. (1985). Aggression in toddlers: Responses to the assertive acts of boys and girls. *Sex Roles, 12*, 341–351.

Fainaru-Wada, M., & Fainaru, S. (2013). *League of denial: The NFL, concussions, and the battle for truth*. New York: Crown Archetype.

Fairchild, C. (2014, June 3, 2014). Number of Fortune 500 Women CEOs Reaches Historic High. *Fortune*, 5.

Faludi, S. (1999). *Stiffed: The betrayal of the American man*. NY, NY, USA: William Morrow.

Fancher, R. E. (1985). *The intelligence men: Makers of the IQ controversy*. NY: W. W. Norton.

Farrell, W. (1986). *Why men are the way they are: The male-female dynamic*. New York: McGraw-Hill.

Farrell, W. (1993). *The myth of male power*. NY: Berkley Books.

Fass, P. S. (1977). *The Damned and the Beautiful: American Youth in the 1920s*. NY: Oxford University Press.

Fausto-Sterling, A. (2000). *Sexing the body: Gender politics and the construction of sexuality*. NY: Basic Books.

Fazio, R. H. & Olson, M. A. (2003). Implicit measures in social cognition research: Their meaning and use. *Annual Review of Psychology, 54*, 297–327.

Federal Bureau of Investigation (FBI) (2011). Uniform Crime Reports: Crime in the United States, 2011: Ten year arrest trends by sex, 2002–2011. Retrieved June 3, 2014 from http://www.fbi.gov/about-us/cjis/ucr/crime-in-the.u.s/2011/crime-in-the-u.s.-2011/tables/table-33.

Federal Bureau of Investigation. (2013a). *Expanded Homicide Data Table 6*. Retrieved from Washington DC: https://ucr.fbi.gov/crime-in-the-u.s/2013/crime-in-the-u.s.-2013/offenses-known-to-law-enforcement/expanded-homicide/expanded_homicide_data_table_6_murder_race_and_sex_of_vicitm_by_race_and_sex_of_offender_2013.xls

Federal Bureau of Investigation. (2013b). *Table 43: Arrests by Race, 2012*. Retrieved from Washington DC: https://ucr.fbi.gov/crime-in-the-u.s/2012/crime-in-the-u.s.-2012/tables/43tabledatadecoverviewpdf

Federal Bureau of Investigation. (2016). *FBI Releases 2015 Crime Statistics from the National Incident-Based Reporting System, Encourages Transition*. Retrieved from Washington DC: https://ucr.fbi.gov/nibrs/2015/resource-pages/nibrs-2015_summary_final-1.pdf

Feiring, C. (1996). Concepts of romance in 15–year-old adolescents. *Journal of Research on Adolescence, 6*, 181–200.

Feiring, C. (1999). Gender identity and the development of romantic relationships in adolescence. In W. Furman, B. B. Brown, & C. Feiring (Eds.), *The development of romantic relationships in adolescence* (pp. 211–234). Cambridge, UK: Cambridge university press.

Fejes, F. J. (1992). Masculinity as fact: A review of empirical mass communication research on masculinity. In S. Craig (Ed.), *Men, masculinity, and the media* (pp. 9–22). Newbury Park, CA: Sage.

Feldman, S. S., Biringen, Z. C., & Nash, S. C. (1981). Fluctuations of sex-related self-attributions as a function of stage in the family life cycle. *Developmental Psychology, 17*, 24–35.

Ferguson, H., Hearn, J., Holter, O. G., Jalmert, L., Kimmel, M., Lang, J., & Morell, R. (2004). *Ending gender based violence: A call for global action to involve men*. Sweden: SIDA Productions.

Ferrar, K. E., Olds, T. S., & Walters, J. L. (2012). All the stereotypes confirmed: Differences in how Australian boys and girls use their time. *Health Education & Behavior, 39*(5), 589–595.

Fields, E. L., Bogart, L. M., Smith, K. C., Malebranche, D. J., Ellen, J., & Schuster, M. A. (2015). 'I always felt I had to prove my manhood': Homosexuality, masculinity, gender role strain, and HIV risk among young Black men who have sex with men. *American Journal of Public Health, 105*(1), 122–131. doi:10.2105/AJPH.2013.301866

Fine, G. A. (1987). *With the boys: Little League baseball and preadolescent culture*. Chicago: University of Chicago press.

Fischer, A. H., & Manstead, A. S. R. (2000). The relation between gender and emotion in different cultures. In A. H. Fischer (Ed.), *Gender and emotion: Social psychological perspectives*. Cambridge, UK: Cambridge University Press.

Fisher, T. D., & Walters, A. S. (2003). Variables in addition to gender that help to explain differences in perceived sexual interest. *Psychology of Men & Masculinity, 4*(2), 154–162. doi:10.1037/1524–9220.4.2.154

Fitzgerald, L. F. (1992). *Sexual harassment in higher education: Concepts and issues*. Washington, DC: National Education Association.

Fitzgerald, L. F. (1993). Sexual harassment: Violence against women in the workplace. *American Psychologist, 48*, 1070–1076.

Fleming, P. J., DiClemente, R. J., & Barrington, C. (2016). Masculinity and HIV: Dimensions of masculine norms that contribute to men's HIV-related sexual behaviors. *AIDS and Behavior, 20*(4), 788–798. doi:10.1007/s10461-015-1264-y

Flood, M. (2008). Men, sex, and homosociality: How bonds between men shape their sexual relations with women. *Men and Masculinities, 10*(3), 339–359. doi:10.1177/1097184X06287761

Flores, A. H., Haileysus, T., & Greenspan, A. I. (2008). National estimates of outdoor recreational injuries treated in emergency departments, United States, 2004–2005. *Wilderness and Environmental Medicine, 19*, 91–98.

Foote, W. E. & Goodman-Delahunty, J. (2004). *Evaluating sexual harassment*. Washington, DC: American Psychological Association.

Forste, R., & Haas, D. W. (2002). The transition of adolescent males to first sexual intercourse: Anticipated or delayed. *Perspectives on Sexual and Reproductive Health, 34*, 184–190.

Forster, P., & King, J. (1994). Fluoxetine for premature ejaculation. *American Journal of Psychiatry, 151*, 1523.

Fortin, J. (2007). Enlarged prostate common in older men. Retrieved June 17, 2009 from www.cnn.com/2007/HEALTH/10/22/hm.prostate.qa/index.html.

Fouad, N. A., Whiston, S. C., & Feldwisch, R. (2016). Men and men's careers. In Y. J. Wong & S. R. Wester (Eds.), *APA handbook of men and masculinities*. (pp. 503–524). Washington, DC, US: American Psychological Association.

Foubert, J. D. (2007). Pornography: Fighting it with feminist thought and scholarly research. Paper presented at Safe Society Zone Conference; October, 2007.

Foubert, J. D. (2011). *The men's and women's programs: Ending rape through peer education*. New York: Routledge.

Foubert, J. D., Brosi, M. W., & Bannon, R. S. (2011). Pornography viewing among fraternity men: Effects on bystander intervention, rape myth acceptance and behavioral intent to commit sexual assault. *Sexual Addiction & Compulsivity, 18*, 212–231.

Frankel, L. (2002). "I've never thought about it": Contradictions and taboos surrounding American males' experiences of first ejaculation (semenarche). *The Journal of Men's Studies, 11*, 37–54.

Franklin, C. W., II. (1984). *The Changing Definition of Masculinity*. NY, NY, USA: Plenum Press.

Freedomtomarry.org (2013). The Defense of Marriage Act. Retrieved July 14, 2014 from freedomtomarry.org/states/entry/c/doma.

French, K. & Poska, A. (2006). *Women and gender in the Western past*. Boston: Houghton-Mifflin.

Freud, S. (1905/1963). *Dora: An analysis of a case of hysteria*. New York: Collier.

Freud, S. (1925). Some psychological consequences of the anatomical distinction between the sexes. In T. Roberts (Ed.), *The Lanahan Readings in the Psychology of Women* (pp. 521–528). Baltimore, MD: Lanahan Publishers.

Freud, S. (1964). An Outline of Psychoanalysis. In J. Strachey (Ed.), *The Standard Edition of the Complete Psychological Works of Sigmund Freud (Vol. 23).* (pp. 144–207). London, UK: Hogarth Press.

Freud, S. & Gay, P. (1989). *The Freud Reader.* New York: W. W. Norton.

Freund, K., Nagler, E., Langevin, R., Zajac, A., & Steiner, B. (1974). Measuring feminine gender identity in homosexual males. *Archives of Sexual Behavior, 3,* 249–260.

Funder, D. C. (2010). *The personality puzzle* (5th ed.). New York: Norton.

Futrelle, D. (2017). Men's-Rights Activism Is the Gateway Drug for the Alt-Right. *The Cut.* Retrieved from https://www.thecut.com/2017/08/mens-rights-activism-is-the-gateway-drug-for-the-alt-right.html

Galambos, N. L., Petersen, A. C., Richards, M., & Gitelson, I. B. (1985). The Attitudes Toward Women Scale for Adolescents (AWSA): A study of reliability and validity. *Sex Roles, 13,* 343–356.

Galvan, F. H., Bogart, L. M., Wagner, G. J., Klein, D. J., & Chen, Y.-T. (2014). Conceptualisations of masculinity and self-reported medication adherence among HIV-positive Latino men in Los Angeles, California, USA. *Culture, Health & Sexuality, 16*(6), 697–709. doi:10.1080/13691058.2014.902102

Garcia, J. R., Reiber, C., Massey, S. G., & Merriwether, A. M. (2012). Sexual hookup culture: A review. *Review of General Psychology, 16,* 161–176. doi:10.1037/a0027911

Garcia-Preto, N. (2005). Latino families: An overview. In M. McGoldrick, J. Giordano, & N. Garcia-Preto (Eds.), *Ethnicity and family therapy* (3rd ed.). New York: Guilford.

Garfield, R. (2010). Male emotional intimacy: How therapeutic men's groups can enhance couples therapy. *Family Process, 49*(1), 109–122.

Garfield, R. (2015). *Breaking the male code: Unlocking the power of friendship.* NY: Gotham.

Gartner, R. B. (1999). *Betrayed as boys: Psychodynamic treatment of sexually abused men.* New York, NY, US: Guilford Press.

Gartner, R. B. (2017a). *Trauma and countertrauma, resilience and counterresilience: Insights from psychoanalysts and trauma experts.* New York, NY, US: Routledge/Taylor & Francis Group.

Gartner, R. B. (Ed.) (2017b). *Understanding the Sexual Betrayal of Boys and Men: The Trauma of Sexual Abuse*: Routledge.

Gastil, J. (1990). Generic pronouns and sexist language: The oxymoronic character of masculine generics. *Sex Roles, 23,* 629–643.

Gelles, R. J. (1997). *Intimate violence in families* (3rd ed.). Thousand Oaks, CA: Sage.

Gelman, S. A. (2003). *The essential child: Origins of essentialism in everyday thought.* New York, NY, US: Oxford University Press.

Genesoni, L., & Tallandini, M. A. (2009). Men's psychological transition to fatherhood: An analysis of the literature, 1989–2008. *Birth: Issues in Perinatal Care, 36*(4), 305–318.

Gentile, D. A. & Anderson, C. A. (2003). Violent video games: The newest media violence hazard. In D. A. Gentile (Ed.), *Media violence and children: A complete guide for parents and professionals.* Westport, CT: Praeger.

Gentile, D. A. & Sesma, Jr., A. (2003). Developmental approaches to understanding media effects on children. In D. A. Gentile (Ed.), *Media violence and children: A complete guide for parents and professionals.* Westport, CT: Praeger.

Gentile, D. A. (Ed., 2003), *Media violence and children: A complete guide for parents and professionals.* Westport, CT: Praeger.

Gentile, D. A., Coyne, S., & Walsh, D. A. (2011). Media violence, physical aggression, and relational aggression in school-age children: A short-term longitudinal study. *Aggressive Behavior, 37*, 193–206.

Gerbner, G., Gross, L., Morgan, M., & Signorielli, N. (1994). Growing up with television: The cultivation perspective. In J. Bryant & D. Zillmann (Eds.), *Media effects: Advances in theory and research* (pp. 17–42). Hillsdale, NJ: Lawrence Erlbaum.

Gergen, M. M., & Gergen, K. J. (1993). Autobiographies and the shaping of gendered lives. In N. Coupland & J. F. Nussbaum (Eds.), *Discourse and lifespan identity* (pp. 28–54). Newbury Park, CA: Sage.

Ghavami, N., & Peplau, L. A. (2013). An intersectional analysis of gender and ethnic stereotypes: Testing three hypotheses. *Psychology of Women Quarterly, 37*(1), 113–127. doi:10.1177/0361684312464203

Giaccardi, S., Ward, L. M., Seabrook, R. C., Manago, A., & Lippman, J. R. (2017). Media use and men's risk behaviors: Examining the role of masculinity ideology. *Sex Roles, 77*(9–10), 581–592. doi:10.1007/s11199-017-0754-y

Gibbs, J. T. (1994). Anger in young black males: Victims or Victimizers? In R. G. Majors & J. U. Gordon (Eds.), *The American Black male: His present status and his future* (pp. 127–143). Chicago: Nelson-Hall.

Gidycz, C. A., Orchowski, L. M., & Edwards, K. M. (2013). Primary prevention of sexual violence. In M. P. Koss, J. W. White, & A. E. Kazdin (Eds.), *Violence against women and children, Volume 2: Navigating solutions*. Washington, DC: American Psychological Association.

Gilder, G. (1986). *Men and marriage*. London: Pelican.

Gillespie, C. D., & Hurvitz, K. A. (2013). Prevalence of Hypertension and Controlled Hypertension — United States, 2007–2010. *Mortality and Morbidity Weekly Review, 62 Supplement*, 144–148.

Gilmore, D. D. (1990). *Manhood in the making: Cultural concepts of masculinity*. New Haven, CT: Yale University Press.

Giordano, P. C., Manning, W., & Longmore, M. A. (2010). Affairs of the heart: Qualities of adolescent romantic relationships and sexual behavior. *Journal of Research on Adolescence, 20*, 983–1013. doi:10.1111/j.1532-7795.2010.00661.x

Glick, P. & Fiske, S. T. (2001). An ambivalent alliance: Hostile and benevolent sexism as complementary justifications for gender inequality. *American Psychologist. 56*(2), 109–118.

Glick, P. (2005). Ambivalent gender ideologies and perceptions of the legitimacy and stability of gender hierarchy. Paper presented in Symposium: New weave sexism research – Tangled webs of feminism, romance, and inequality (S. T. Fiske, Chair). Annual Convention of the American Psychological Association, Washington, DC.

Glick, P., Lameiras, M., Fiske, S. T., Eckes, T., Masser, B., Volpato, C., Manganelli, A. M., Pek, J., Huang, L., Sakalli-Ugurlu, N., Castro, Y. R., D'Avila Pereira, M. L., Willemsen, T. M., Brunner, A., Six-Materna, I., & Wells, R. (2004). Bad but bold: Ambivalent attitudes toward men predict gender inequality in 16 nations. *Journal of Personality and Social Psychology, 86*, 713–728.

Gold, S. R., Burke, C. H., Prisco, A. G., & Willett, J. A. (1992). Vicarious emotional responses of macho college males. *Journal of Interpersonal Violence, 7*, 165–174.

Goldberg, H. (1977). *The hazards of being male*. New York: New American Library.

Goldfoot, D. A. & Neff, D. A. (1987). Assessment of behavioral sex differences in social contexts: Perspectives from primatology. In J. M. Reinisch, L. A. Rosenbaum, & S. A. Sanders (Eds.), *Masculinity/femininity: Basic perspectives* (pp. 179–195). New York: Oxford University Press.

Goldman, R. F. (1992). Questioning circumcision: A growing movement. *Wingspan, 6* (2), 12–13.

Goldstein, J. R. (2011). A secular trend toward earlier male sexual maturity: Evidence from shifting ages of male young adult mortality. *PLoS ONE, 6*, e14826, 14821–14825. doi:10.1371/journal.pone.0014826

Golombok, S., & Fivush, R. (1994). *Gender development*. New York: Cambridge University Press.

Golombok, S., Mellish, L., Jennings, S., Casey, P., Tasker, F., & Lamb, M. E. (2014). Adoptive gay father families: Parent–child relationships and children's psychological adjustment. *Child Development, 85*(2), 456–468.

Gondolf, E. W. (1988). Who are those guys? Toward a behavioral typology of batterers. *Violence and Victims, 3*, 187–203.

Gough, B., & Robertson, S. (2017). A review of research on men's physical health. In R. F. Levant & Y. J. Wong (Eds.), *The psychology of men and masculinities.* (pp. 197–227). Washington, DC, US: American Psychological Association.

Gough, H. G. (1957). *Manual for the California Psychological Inventory.* Palo Alto, CA: Consulting Psychologists Press.

Gould, R. E. (1974). Measuring masculinity by the size of a paycheck. In J.H. Pleck & J. Sawyer (Eds.), *Men and masculinity* (pp. 96–100). Englewood Cliffs, NJ: Prentice-Hall.

Gould, S. J. (1981). *The mismeasure of man.* New York: W. W. Norton.

Gould, S. J. (1987). *An urchin in the storm.* New York: W. W. Norton.

Gover, A. R., MacDonald, J. M., & Alpert, G. P. (2003). Combating domestic violence: Findings from an evaluation of a local domestic violence court. *Criminology and Public Policy, 3*, 109–132.

Graham, S. (1992). "Most of the subjects were White and middle class": Trends in published research on African Americans in selected APA journals, 1970–1989. *American Psychologist, 47*, 629–639. doi:10.1037/0003–066X.47.5.629

Graham, S. H. (2008). *Eat what you want and die like a man: The world's unhealthiest cookbook.* New York: Citadel.

Granie, M. A. (2010). Gender stereotype conformity and age as determinants of preschoolers' injury risk behaviors. *Accident Analysis and Prevention, 42*, 726–733.

Grant, B. F., Dawson, D. A., Stinson, F. S., Chou, S. P., Dufour, M. C., & Pickering, R. P. (2004). The 12–month prevalence and trends in DSM-IV alcohol abuse and dependence: United States, 1991–1992 and 2001–2002. *Drug and Alcohol Dependence, 74*, 223–234.

Green, R. J., & Ashmore, R. D. (1998). Taking and developing pictures in the head: Assessing the physical stereotypes of eight gender types. *Journal of Applied Social Psychology, 28*, 1609–1636.

Greene, D. C., & Britton, P. J. (2013). Predicting Relationship Commitment in Gay Men: Contributions of Vicarious Shame and Internalized Homophobia to the Investment Model. *Psychology of Men & Masculinity, 16*(1). doi:10.1037/a0034988

Griffith, D. M., & Thorpe, R. J., Jr. (2016). Men's physical health and health behaviors. In Y. J. Wong, S. R. Wester, Y. J. Wong, & S. R. Wester (Eds.), *APA handbook of men and masculinities.* (pp. 709–730). Washington, DC, US: American Psychological Association.

Griffiths, M. D. (2012). Internet sex addiction: A review of empirical research. *Addiction Research & Theory, 20*(2), 111–124. doi:10.3109/16066359.2011.588351

Grimm, L., & Yarnold, P. R. (1985). Sex typing and the coronary-prone behavior pattern. *Sex Roles, 12*, 171–178.

Grimsley, K. D. (1998, June 12). Mitsubishi settles for $34 million: Amount is record in harassment suits. *The Washington Post*, p. A1.

Grimsley, K. D., & Brown, W. (1996, April 23). Mitsubishi workers march on EEOC: UAW alleges, company denies "pressure" to protest suit. *The Washington Post*, p. A1.

Grimsley, K. D., & Swoboda, F. (1997, August 30). Mitsubishi settlement said to total $9.5 million: Company still faces larger suit filed by EEOC. *The Washington Post*, pp. F1, F3.

Groth, A. N. (1979). *Men who rape: The psychology of the offender*. New York: Plenum.

Groth-Marnat, G. (2003). *Handbook of psychological assessment* (4th ed.). New York: Wiley.

Grunbaum, J. A., Kann, L., Kincen, S. A., Hawkins, J., Ross, J. G., Lowry, R., Harris, W. A., McManus, T., Chyen, D., & Collins, A. (2004). Youth risk behavior surveillance: United States, 2003. *Morbidity and Mortality Weekly Report, 53 (2)*, 1–96.

Gugliotta, G. (2003, October 11). Concussions, impact studied by the NFL. *The Washington Post*, p. D3.

Gupta, A., Szymanski, D. M., & Leong, F. T. L. (2011). The 'model minority myth': Internalized racialism of positive stereotypes as correlates of psychological distress, and attitudes toward help-seeking. *Asian American Journal of Psychology, 2*(2), 101–114. doi:10.1037/a0024183

Gurian, M. & Stevens, K. (2005). *The minds of boys: Saving our sons from falling behind in school and life*. San Francisco: Jossey-Bass.

Gurian, M., & Stevens, K. (2005). *The minds of boys: Saving our sons from falling behind in school and life*. San Francisco: Jossey-Bass.

Guthrie, Robert V. (1976). *Even the Rat was White: A history of psychology*. New York: Harper & Row.

Gustafson, R. (1986). Threat as a determinant of alcohol-related aggression. *Psychological Reports, 58*, 287–297.

Gutmann, D. (1987). *Reclaimed powers*. New York: Basic Books.

Guttmacher Institute. (2012). *State policies in brief: Sex and HIV education*. Retrieved from NY: www.guttmacher.org/pubs/spib_SE.pdf

Hackett, T. P.; Rosenbaum, J. F. & Cassen, N. H. (1985). Cardiovascular disorders. In H. I. Kaplan & B. J. Saddock (Eds.), *Comprehensive textbook of psychiatry/IV* (pp. 1148–1159). Baltimore: Williams and Wilkins.

Hall, A. V., Hall, E. V., & Perry, J. L. (2016). Black and blue: Exploring racial bias and law enforcement in the killings of unarmed black male civilians. *American Psychologist, 71*(3), 175–186. doi:10.1037/a0040109

Hall, C. S., Lindzey, G., & Campbell, J. B. (1998). *Theories of personality* (4th ed.). New York: Wiley.

Halsey, III, A. (2009, August 20). Rise in drunken-driving arrests of women deplored. *The Washington Post*, A2.

Hammer, J. H., & Good, G. E. (2010). Positive psychology: An emprical examination of beneficial aspects of endorsement of masculine norms. *Psychology of Men and Masculinity, 11*, 303–318. doi:10.1037/a0019056

Hammond, W. P., & Mattis, J. S. (2005). Being a Man About It: Manhood Meaning Among African American Men. *Psychology of Men & Masculinity, 6*(2), 114–126. doi:10.1037/1524–9220.6.2.114

Hammond, W. P., Fleming, P. J., & Villa-Torres, L. (2016). Everyday racism as a threat to the masculine social self: Framing investigations of African American male health disparities. In Y. J. Wong & S. R. Wester (Eds.), *APA handbook of men and masculinities*. (pp. 259–283). Washington, DC: American Psychological Association.

Haney, C., Banks, C., & Zimbardo, P. (1973). Interpersonal dynamics in a simulated prison. *International Journal of Criminology and Penology, 1*, 69–97.

Hantover, J. (1978). The boy scouts and the validation of masculinity. *Journal of Social Issues, 34*, 184–195.

Hardie, J. H. (2015). Women's work? Predictors of young men's aspirations for entering traditionally female-dominated occupations. *Sex Roles, 72*(7–8), 349–362. doi:10.1007/s11199-015-0449-1

Hare-Mustin, R. T., & Marecek, J. (1990a). Gender and the meaning of difference: Postmodernism and psychology. In R. T. Hare-Mustin & J. Marecek (Eds.), *Making a difference: Psychology and the construction of gender* (pp. 22–64). New Haven, CT, USA: Yale university press.

Hare-Mustin, R. T., & Marecek, J. (1990b). On making a difference. In R. T. Hare-Mustin & J. Marecek (Eds.), *Making a difference: Psychology and the construction of gender* (pp. 1–21). New Haven, CT, USA: Yale University Press.

Harrison, J.; Chin, J., & Ficarotto, T. (1995). Warning: Masculinity may be dangerous to your health. In M. S. Kimmel & M. A. Messner (Eds.), *Men's lives* (3rd ed., pp. 237–249). Boston: Allyn and Bacon.

Hartley, R. E. (1959). Sex role pressures and the socialization of the male child. *Psychological Reports, 5*, 457–468.

Hartup, W. W., & Overhauser, S. (1991). Friendships. In R. M. Lerner, A. C. Petersen, & J. Brooks-Gunn (Eds.), *Encyclopedia of Adolescence* (pp. 378–384). NY: Garland Publishing.

Hathaway, S. R., & McKinley, J. C. (1951). *Manual for the Minnesota multiphasic personality inventory (rev. ed.)*. Minneapolis, MN, USA: University of Minnesota press.

Hatton, E., & Trautner, M. N. (2011). Equal opportunity objectification? The sexualization of men and women on the cover of Rolling Stone. *Sexuality & Culture, 15*, 256–278.

Hazan, C., & Diamond, L. M. (2000). The place of attachment in human mating. *Review of General Psychology, 4*, 186–204. doi:10.1037/1089-2680.4.2.186

Heasley, R. (2005). Queer Masculinities of Straight Men: A Typology. *Men and Masculinities, 7*(3), 310–320. doi:10.1177/1097184X04272118

Hedges, L. V., & Nowell, A. (1995). Sex differences in mental test scores, variability, and numbers of high-scoring individuals. *Science, 269*(5220), 41–45.

Heilman, B., Hebert, L., & Paul-Gera, N. (2014). The making of sexual violence: How does a boy grow up to commit rape? Evidence from five IMAGES countries. Washington, DC: International Center for Research on Women (ICRW), and Promundo.

Helgeson, V. S. (1990). The role of masculinity in a prognostic predictor of heart attack severity. *Sex Roles, 22*, 755–774.

Helgeson, V. S. (1995). Masculinity, men's roles, and coronary heart disease. In D. Sabo & D. F. Gordon (Eds.), *Men's health and illness: Gender, power, and the body* (pp.68–104). Thousand Oaks, CA: Sage.

Helgeson, V. S. (2011). *The psychology of gender* (4th ed.). Boston: Pearson.

Heppner, M. (2005). *Theoretically driven rape prevention programming for men*. Paper presented in symposium: Sexual assault prevention for men (C. Kilmartin, chair) at the Annual Convention of the American Psychological Association, Washington, DC.

Herbert, T. W. (2002). *Sexual Violence and American Manhood*. Cambridge, MA: Harvard University Press.

Herdt, G. (1982). *Rituals of manhood*. Berkeley, CA: University of California Press.

Herdt, G. (1994). *Third sex, third gender: Beyond sexual dimorphism in culture and history*. NY: Zone books.

Herdt, G. (2004). Sexual development, social oppression, and local culture. *Sexuality Research and Social Policy: A Journal of NSRC, 1*, 39–62.

Herdt, G., & Boxer, A. (1991). Introduction: Culture, history, and life course of gay men. In G. Herdt (Ed.), *Gay culture in America: Essays from the field* (pp. 1–28). Boston: Beacon.

Herek, G. M. (1985). On doing, being, and not being: Prejudice and the social construction of sexuality. *Journal of Homosexuality, 12*, 135–151.

Heron, M. P. (2013). Deaths: Leading causes for 2010. *National vital statistics reports, 62 (6)*. Retrieved May 29, 2014 from http://www.cdc.gov/nchs/data/nvsr/nvsr62/nvsr62_06.pdf.

Hetherington, E. M., & Stanley-Hagen, M. M. (1997). The effects of divorce on fathers and their children. In M. Lamb (Ed.), *The role of the father in child development* (3rd ed., pp. 191–211). New York: Wiley.

Hetherington, E. M., Stanley-Hagen, M., & Anderson, E. R. (1989). Marital transitions: A child's perspective. *American Psychologist, 44*, 303–312.

Heyl, B. S. (1996). Homosexuality: A social phenomenon. In K. E. Rosenblum & T. C. Travis (Eds.), *The meaning of difference: American constructions of race, sex and gender, social class, and sexual orientation* (pp. 120–129). New York: McGraw-Hill.

Hilliard, L. J., & Liben, L. S. (2010). Differeing levels of gender salience in preschool classrooms: Effects on children's gender attitudes and intergroup bias. *Child Development, 81*, 1787–1798. doi:10.1111/j.1467–8624.2010.01510.x

Hills, H. I., Carlstrom, A., & Evanow, M. (2001). Consulting with men in business and industry. In G. R. Brooks & G. E. Good (Eds.). *The new handbook of psychotherapy and counseling with men: A comprehensive guide to settings, problems, and treatment approaches*. San Francisco: Jossey-Bass.

Hines, P. M. & Boyd-Franklin, N. (2005). Families of African origin. In M. McGoldrick, J. Giordano, & N. Garcia-Preto (Eds.), *Ethnicity and family therapy* (3rd ed). New York: Guilford.

Hochschild, A., & Machung, A. (1989). *The Second Shift* (Vol. 2nd). New York: Penguin.

Hodapp, C. (2017). *Men's Rights, Gender, and Social Media*. Lanham, MD: Lexington Books.

Hoff Sommers, C. (2000). *The War Against Boys: How Misguided Feminism Is Harming Our Young Men*. NY: Simon & Schuster.

Hofferth, S. L. & Anderson, K. G. (2003). Are all dads equal? Biology versus marriage as a basis for paternal investment. *Journal of Marriage and the Family, 65 (1)*, 213–232.

Hofferth, S. L., Pleck, J. H., & Vesely, C. K. (2012). The transmission of parenting from fathers to sons. *Parenting: Science and Practice, 12(4)*, 282–305.

Hoffman, R. M., & Borders, L. D. (2001). Twenty-five years after the Bem Sex-Role Inventory: A reassessment and new issues regarding classification variability. *Measurement and Evaluation in Counseling and Development, 34*, 39–55.

Hofstede, G. (1998). Comparative studies of sexual behavior: Sex as achievement or as relationship? In G. Hofstede (Ed.), *Masculinity and femininity: Taboo dimensions of national culture* (pp. 153–178). Thousand Oaks, CA: Sage.

Holland, K. J., & Cortina, L. M. (2013). When sexism and feminism collide: The sexual harassment of feminist working women. *Psychology of Women Quarterly, 37(2)*, 192–208.

Holland, K. J., & Cortina, L. M. (2013). When sexism and feminism collide: The sexual harassment of feminist working women. *Psychology of Women Quarterly, 37*(2), 192–208.

Holtzworth-Munroe, A., & Stuart, G. L. (1994). Typologies of male batterers: Three subtypes and the differences among them. *Psychological Bulletin, 116*, 476–497.

Horney, K. (1932). The dread of women: Observations on a specific difference in the dread felt by men and women respectively for the opposite sex. *International Journal of Psychoanalysis, 13*, 348–360.

Houts, C. R., & Horne, S. G. (2008). The role of relationship attributions in relationship satisfaction among cohabiting gay men. *The Family Journal, 16*(3), 240–248.

Howard-Payne, L., & Bowman, B. (2017). 'I am the man': Meanings of masculinity in perceptions of voluntary medical adult male circumcision for HIV prevention in South Africa. *Psychology of Men & Masculinity, 18*(1), 70–77. doi:10.1037/men0000039

Hubbard, R. (1998). The political nature of "human nature." In In D. L. Anselmi & A. L. Law (Eds.), *Questions of gender: perspectives and paradoxes* (pp. 146–153). Boston: McGraw-Hill.

Huesmann, L. R., Dubow, E. F., & Boxer, P. (2011). The transmission of aggressiveness across generations: Biological, contextual, and social learning processes. In P. R. Shaver & M. Mikulincer (Eds.), *Human aggression and violence: Causes, manifestations, and consequences*. Washington, DC: American Psychological Association.

Huizinga, D., Weiher, A. W., Espiritu, R., & Esbensen, F. (2003). Delinquency and crime: Some highlights from the Denver Youth Survey. In T. P. Thornberry & M. D. Krohn (Eds.), *Taking stock of delinquency: An overview of findings from contemporary longitudinal studies*. New York: Kluwer Academic/Plenum.

Humblet, O., Paul, C., & Dickson, N. (2003). Core group evolution over time: High-risk sexual behavior in a birth cohort between sexual debut and age 26. *Sexually Transmitted Diseases, 30*, 818–824. doi:10.1097/01.OLQ.0000097102.42149.11

Hunt, K., Lewars, H., Emslie, C., & Batty, G. D. (2007). Decreased risk of death from coronary heart disease amongst men with higher "femininity" scores: A general population cohort study. *International Journal of Epidemiology, 36*, 612–620.

Hussey, A. (1989). Neonatal circumcision: A uniquely American ritual. *Transitions, 9*(4), 18–22.

Hust, S. J. T., Brown, J. D., & L'Engle, K. L. (2008). Boys will be boys and girls better be prepared: An analysis of the rare sexual health messages in young adolescents' media. *Mass Communication & Society, 11*, 3–23. doi:10.1080/15205430701668139

Huston, T. L., & Ashmore, R. D. (1986). Women and men in personal relationship. In R. D. Ashmore & R. K. Del Boca (Eds.), *The social psychology of female-male relations* (pp. 167–210). New York: Academic Press.

Huyck, M. (1992). Evaluating the parental imperative in Parkville. Paper presented at the Annual Meeting of the American Gerontological Society, Washington, DC.

Hyde, J. S. (1984). Children's understanding of sexist language. *Developmental Psychology, 20*, 697–706.

Hyde, J. S. (2005). The gender similarities hypothesis. *American Psychologist, 60*, 581–592. doi:10.1037/0003-066X.60.6.581

Hyde, J. S., & Plant, E. A. (1995). Magnitude of psychological gender differences: Another side to the story. *American Psychologist, 50*, 159–161.

Ibaraki, A. Y., Hall, G. C. N., & Sabin, J. A. (2014). Asian American cancer disparities: The potential effects of model minority health stereotypes. *Asian American Journal of Psychology, 5*(1), 75–81. doi:10.1037/a0036114

Inchley, J. C., Currie, D. B., Todd, J. M., Akhtar, P. C., & Currie, C. E. (2005). Persistent socio-demographic differences in physical activity among Scottish schoolchildren 1990–2002. *European Journal of Public Health, 15*(4), 386–388.

Internet Filter Review (2009). 2006 and 2005 pornography United States Industry revenue statistics. Retrieved July 16, 2009 from internet-filter-review.toptenreviews.com/internet-pornography-statistics.

Intersex Society of North America. (n.d.). How common is intersex? Retrieved from http://www.isna.org/faq/frequency

Isely, P. J., Busse, W., & Isely, P. (1998). Sexual assault in males in late adolescence: A hidden phenomenon. *Professional School Counseling, 2,* 153–160.

Isely, P. J., Isely, P., Freiburger, J., & McMackin, R. (2008). In their own voices: A qualitative study of men abused as children by Catholic clergy. *Journal of Child Sexual Abuse, 17,* 201–215.

Iwamoto, D. K., & Kaya, A. (2016). Asian American men. In Y. J. Wong, S. R. Wester, Y. J. Wong, & S. R. Wester (Eds.), *APA handbook of men and masculinities.* (pp. 285–297). Washington, DC, US: American Psychological Association.

Iwamoto, D. K., & Smiler, A. P. (2013). Alcohol makes you macho and helps you make friends: The role of masculine norms and peer pressure in adolescent boys' and girls' alcohol use. *Substance Use & Misuse, 48*(5), 371–378. doi:10.3109/10826084.2013.765479

Jacupak, M., Tull, M. T., & Roemer, L. (2005). Masculinity, shame, and fear of emotions as predictors of men's expressions of anger and hostility. *Psychology of Men and Masculinity, 6,* 275–284.

Jakobsen, R. (1997). Stages of progression in noncoital sexual interactions among young adolescents: An application of the Mokken Scale Analysis. *International Journal of Behavioral Development, 21,* 537–553.

Jansz, J. (2000). Masculine identity and restrictive emotionality. In A. H. Fischer (Ed.), *Gender and emotion: Social psychological perspectives.* Cambridge, UK: Cambridge University Press.

Jaschik-Herman, M. L., & Fisk, A. (1995). Women's perceptions and labeling of sexual harassment in academia before and after the Hill-Thomas hearings. *Sex Roles, 33,* 439–446.

Jenkins, S. (2005). The age-old question: How young is too young? *The Washington Post,* July 6, pp. E1, E7.

Jennings, J. L., & Murphy, C. M. (2000). Male–male dimensions of male–female battering: A new look at domestic violence. *Psychology of Men & Masculinity, 1*(1), 21–29. doi:10.1037/1524–9220.1.1.21

Jensen, R. (2007). *Getting off: Pornography and the end of masculinity.* Cambridge, MA: South End.

Jensen-Campbell, L. A., Graziano, W. G., & West, S. G. (1995). Dominance, prosocial orientation, and female preferences: Do nice guys really finish last? *Journal of Personality and Social Psychology, 68,* 427–440.

Jeynes, W. H. (2016). Meta-analysis on the roles of fathers in parenting: Are they unique? *Marriage & Family Review, 52*(7), 665–688. doi:10.1080/01494929.2016.1157121

Jhally, S. (Writer). (2007). Dreamworlds 3: Desire, sex, & power in music video.

Johnson, A. G. (2001). *Privilege, power, and difference.* Mountain View, CA: Mayfield.

Johnson, A. G. (1997). *The gender knot: Unraveling our patriarchal legacy.* Philadelphia: Temple University Press.

Johnson, C. (2009, June 23). Panel sets guidelines for fighting prison rape. *The Washington Post*, A4.

Johnson, J. A. (2013, May 20). The effects of hypersexualized media: A review of empirical evidence. Presentation at the Blue Ribbon Panel on Hypersexualized Media, Richmond, VA.

Johnson, K. L., Lurye, L. E., & Tassinary, L. G. (2010). Sex categorization among preschool children: Increasing utilization of sexually dimorphic cues. *Child Development, 81*(5), 1346–1355.

Johnston, L., McLellan, T., & McKinlay, A. (2014). (Perceived) size really does matter: Male dissatisfaction with penis size. *Psychology of Men & Masculinity, 15*(2), 225–228. doi: 10.1037/a0033264

Joshi, S. P., Peter, J., & Valkenburg, P. M. (2011). Scripts of sexual desire and danger in US and Dutch teen girl magazines: A cross-national content analysis. *Sex Roles, 64*, 463–474.

Joyce, A. (2005, June 6). Workplace improves for gay, transgender employees, rights group says. *The Washington Post*, A5.

Jung, C. G. (1959/1989). Concerning the archetypes with special reference to the anima concept. In C. G. Jung, R. F. C. Hull (Translator) & J. Beebe (Ed.), *Aspects of the masculine* (pp. 115–122). Princeton, NJ: Princeton University Press.

Just the Facts Coalition. (2008). *Just the facts about sexual orientation and youth: A primer for principals, educators, and school personnel*. Retrieved from Washington, DC: http://www.apa.org/pi/lgbt/resources/just-the-facts.pdf

Kagan, J. (2013). Temperamental contributions to inhibited and uninhibited profiles. In P. D. Zelazo & P. D. Zelazo (Eds.), *The Oxford handbook of developmental psychology, Vol. 2: Self and other*. (pp. 142–164). New York, NY, US: Oxford University Press.

Kaiser Family Foundation (2012). Generation RX.com: How young people use the Internet for health information. Accessed December 27, 2012 from kff.org/entmedia/loader.cfm?url=/commonspot/security/getfile.cfm&pageid+13719.

Kaplan, D., & Rosenmann, A. (2014). Toward an empirical model of male homosocial relatedness: An investigation of friendship in uniform and beyond. *Psychology of Men & Masculinity, 15*(1), 12–21. doi:10.1037/a0031289

Kaplan, M. S., Huguet, N., McFarland, B. H., & Mandle, J. A. (2012). Factors associated with suicide by firearm among U.S. older adult men. *Psychology of Men & Masculinity, 13*(1), 65–74. doi:10.1037/a0023173

Karraker, K. H., Vogel, D. A., & Lake, M. A. (1995). Parents' gender-stereotyped perceptions of newborns: The eye of the beholder revisited. *Sex Roles, 33*, 687–701.

Karren, K. J., Smith, L., Hafen, B. Q., & Gordon, K. J. (2009). *Mind body health: The effects of attitudes, emotions, and relationships* (5th ed.). San Francisco: Benjamin Cummings.

Katz, J., & Earp, J. (Writers). (2013). Tough Guise 2: Violence, Manhood & American Culture. In Media Education Foundation (Producer). Northampton, MA.

Kaufman, M. (1994). Men, feminism, and men's contradictory experiences of power. In H. Brod and Michael Kaufman (Eds.), *Theorizing masculinities* (pp. 142–163). Thousand Oaks, CA: Sage.

Kawakami, K., Dovidio, J. F., Moll, J., Hermsen, S., & Russin, A. (2000). Just say no (to stereotyping): Effects of training in the negation of stereotypic associations on stereotype activation. *Journal of Personality and Social Psychology, 78* (5), 871–888.

Kaye, K., Suellentrop, K., & Sloup, C. (2009) The Fog Zone: How misperceptions, magical thinking, and ambivalence put young adults at risk for unplanned pregnancy. Washington DC: The National Campaign to Prevent Teen and Unplanned Pregnancy.

Kearney, L. K., Rochlen, A. B., & King, E. B. (2004). Male Gender Role Conflict, Sexual Harassment Tolerance, and the Efficacy of a Psychoeducative Training Program. *Psychology of Men & Masculinity, 5*(1), 72–82. doi:10.1037/1524–9220.5.1.72

Keen, M. (1984). *Chivalry*. New Haven, CT: Yale University Press.

Keen, S. (1991). *Fire in the belly: On being a man*. New York: Bantam.

Kelly, J. & Johnson, L. A. (2009, January 13). It's hard out here for a pop: Stereotypes, silence, and the socialization of future fathers. Presentation at the Minnesota Fatherhood Summit, St. Cloud, MN.

Kemper, T. D. (1990). *Social structure and testosterone*. New Brunswick, NJ: Rutgers University Press.

Kendler, K. S., Myers, J., & Prescott, C. A. (2005). Sex Differences in the Relationship Between Social Support and Risk for Major Depression: A Longitudinal Study of Opposite-Sex Twin Pairs. *The American Journal of Psychiatry, 162*(2), 250–256.

Kenrick, D. T., Neuberg, S. L., & Cialdini, R. B. (2005). *Social psychology: Unraveling the mystery* (3rd ed.) Boston: Pearson.

Kessler, G. (2009, May 25). Clinton to extend benefits to gay partners: Draft memo outlines new foreign service policies for all unmarried couples. *The Washington Post*, A8.

Kevorkian, R. T. & Cepeda, O. A. (2007). The biologic basis for longevity differences between men and women. In B. Lunenfeld, L. J. Gooren, A. Morales, & J. E. Morley (Eds.), *Textbook of men's health and aging* (2nd ed.). London: Informa.

Kilmartin, C. (2010). Incremental terrorism: Cultural masculinity, conflict, and violence against women. In W. Berger, B. Hipfl, K. Mertlitsch, & V. Ratkovic (Eds.): *Kulturelle Dimensionen von Konflikten (Cultural dimensions of conflicts)*. Baden Baden, Germany: Nomos.

Kilmartin, C. (2014). Counseling men to prevent sexual violence. In M. Englar-Carlson, M. P. Evans, & T. Duffey (Eds.), *A counselor's guide to working with men*. Alexandria, VA: American Counseling Association.

Kilmartin, C. T. (2004a). "Midlife crisis". In M. Kimmel & A. Aronson (Eds.), *Men and masculinities: A social, cultural, and historical encyclopedia*. Santa Barbara, CA: ABC-Clio.

Kilmartin, C. T. (2004b). Masculinity as a cultural variable in psychotherapy. Paper presented in Symposium: Men and mental health: New directions in marketing and treatment (M. E. Addis & J. M. Lane, Chairs). Annual Convention of the American Psychological Association, Honolulu, HI.

Kilmartin, C. T. (2005). Depression in men: communication, diagnosis, and therapy. *Journal of Men's Health and Gender, 2 (1)*, 95–99.

Kilmartin, C. T., & Berkowitz, A .D. (2005). *Sexual assault in context: Teaching men about gender*. Mahwah, NJ: Erlbaum.

Kilmartin, C. T., & Ring, T .E. (1991). Understanding and preventing acquaintance rape on college campuses: Services for men. Paper presented at the annual meeting of the Maryland College Personnel Association, College Park, MD.

Kilmartin, C. T., Chirico, B., & Leemann, M. (1997). *The White Ribbon Campaign: Evidence for Social Change on a College Campus*. Paper presented at the Spring Convention of the Virginia Psychological Association, Roanoke, VA.

Kilmartin, C. T., Conway, A., Friedberg, A., McQuoid, T., Tschan, T., & Norbet, T. (1999, April). Using the social norms model to encourage male college students to challenge rape-supportive attitudes in male peers. Paper presented at the Virginia Psychological Association Spring Conference, Virginia Beach, VA.

Kilmartin, C., & Allison, J. (2007). *Men's Violence Against Women: Theory, Research, and Activism*. Mahwah, NJ: Erlbaum.

Kilmartin, C., & Berkowitz, A. D. (2005). *Sexual assault in context: Teaching college men about gender*. Mahwah, NJ, US: Lawrence Erlbaum Associates Publishers.

Kilmartin, C., & McDermott, R. C. (2016). Violence and masculinities. In Y. J. Wong & S. R. Wester (Eds.), *APA handbook of men and masculinities*. (pp. 615–636). Washington, DC, US: American Psychological Association.

Kilmartin, C., Smith, T., Green, A., Heinzen, H., Kuchler, M., & Kolar, D. (2008). A real time social norms intervention to reduce male sexism. *Sex Roles, 59*, 264–273.

Kimbrell, A. (1991, May/June). A time for men to pull together. *Utne Reader*, pp. 66–74.

Kimmel, M. (1996). *Manhood in America: A cultural history*. NY: The Free Press.

Kimmel, M. (2008). *Guyland: The perilous world where boys become men*. NY: Harper.

Kimmel, M. (2011). Keynote address.

Kimmel, M. S. (1987). Rethinking "masculinity": New directions in research. In M. S. Kimmel (Ed.), *Changing men* (pp. 9–23). Newbury Park, CA, USA: Sage.

Kimmel, M. S. (1994). Masculinity as homophobia: Fear, shame, and silence in the construction of gender identity. In H. Brod and Michael Kaufman (Eds.), *Theorizing masculinities* (pp. 119 -141). Thousand Oaks, CA: Sage.

Kimmel, M. S., & Mosmiller, T. E. (1992). *Against the tide: Pro-feminist men in the United States, 1776–1990*. Boston: Beacon.

King, J. L., & Hunter, K. (2004). *On the down low: A journey into the lives of "straight" black men who sleep with men*. NY: Harlem moon/Broadway books.

Kiselica, M. S., Benton-Wright, S., & Englar-Carlson, M. (2016). Accentuating positive masculinity: A new foundation for the psychology of boys, men, and masculinity. In Y. J. Wong & S. R. Wester (Eds.), *APA handbook of men and masculinities*. (pp. 123–143). Washington, DC, US: American Psychological Association.

Kiselica, A. M., & Kiselica, M. S. (2014). Improving attitudes, services, and policies regarding adolescent fathers: An affirming rejoinder. *Psychology of Men & Masculinity, 15*(3), 284–287. doi:10.1037/a0037359

Kiselica, M. S. (2005, May 14). Personal communication.

Kiselica, M. S. (2006). Helping a boy become a parent: Male-sensitive psychotherapy with a teenage father. In M. Englar-Carlson & M. Stevens (Eds.), *In the room with men: A casebook of therapeutic change*. Washington, DC: American Psychological Association.

Kiselica, M. S., & Kiselica, A. M. (2014). The complicated worlds of adolescent fathers: Implications for clinical practice, public policy, and research. *Psychology of Men & Masculinity, 15*(3), 260–274. doi:http://dx.doi.org/10.1037/a0037043

Kivel, P. (1992). *Men's work: How to stop the violence that tears our lives apart*. Center City, MN: Hazleden.

Kline, K. A. (2016). Cardiovascular, Affective, and Behavioral Responses to Masculinity-Challenging Stressors: Active Versus Passive Coping. *Psychology of Men & Masculinity*. doi:10.1037/men0000070

Knight, R. A. & Sims-Knight, J. (2013). Risk factors for sexual violence. In M. P. Koss, J. W. White, & A. E. Kazdin (Eds.), *Violence against women and children, Volume 1: Mapping the terrain*. Washington, DC: American Psychological Association.

Ko, I., Kotrba, L., & Roebuck, A. (2015). Leaders as males?: The role of industry gender composition. *Sex Roles, 72*(7–8), 294–307. doi:10.1007/s11199–015–0462–4

Koechlin, F. M., Fonner, V. A., Dalglish, S. L., O'Reilly, K. R., Baggaley, R., Grant, R. M., … Kennedy, C. E. (2017). Values and preferences on the use of oral pre-exposure prophylaxis (PrEP) for HIV prevention among multiple populations: A systematic review of the literature. *AIDS and Behavior, 21*(5), 1325–1335. doi:10.1007/s10461-016-1627-z

Komiya, N., Good, G. E., & Sherrod, N. (2000). Emotional openness as a contributing factor to reluctance to seek counseling among college students. *Journal of Counseling Psychology, 47*, 138–143.

Kopper, B. A., & Epperson, D. L. (1996). The experience and expression of anger: Relationships with gender, gender role socialization, depression, and mental health functioning. *Journal of Counseling Psychology, 43*, 158–165.

Korelitz, K. E., & Garber, J. (2016). Congruence of parents' and children's perceptions of parenting: A meta-analysis. *Journal of Youth and Adolescence, 45*(10), 1973–1995. doi:10.1007/s10964-016-0524-0

Korobov, N. (2004). Inoculating Against Prejudice: A Discursive Approach to Homophobia and Sexism in Adolescent Male Talk. *Psychology of Men & Masculinity, 5*(2), 178–189. doi:10.1037/1524-9220.5.2.178

Koss, M. P., & Dinero, T. E. (1988). Predictors of sexual aggression among a national sample of male college students. In R. A. Prentky & V. L. Quinsey (Eds.), *Human sexual aggression: Current perspectives* (pp. 133–147). New York: New York Academy of Sciences.

Koss, M. P., Leonard, K. E., Beezley, D. A., & Oros, C. J. (1985). Nonstranger sexual aggression: A discriminant analysis of the psycholotical characteristics of undetected offenders. *Sex Roles, 12*, 981–992.

Koss, M. P., White, J. W., & Lopez, E. C. (2017). Victim voice in reenvisioning responses to sexual and physical violence nationally and internationally. *American Psychologist, 72*(9), 1019–1030. doi:10.1037/amp0000233

Kranz, D., Pröbstle, K., & Evidis, A. (2017). Are all the nice guys gay? The impact of sociability and competence on the social perception of male sexual orientation. *Psychology of Men & Masculinity, 18*(1), 32–39. doi:10.1037/men0000034

Krassas, N. R., Blauwkamp, J. M., & Wesselink, P. (2003). "Master Your Johnson": Sexual rhetoric in Maxim and Stuff magazines. *Sexuality & Culture, 7*, 98–119.

Kreuz, L. E., & Rose, R. M. (1972). Assessment of aggressive behavior and plasma testosterone in a young criminal population. *Psychosomatic Medicine, 34*, 321–332.

Krishnamurthy, K. (1998, June 17). No pomp, but honor student gets diploma. *The Free-Lance Star*, p. C1.

Kruger, D. J., & Nesse, R. M. (2004). Sexual selection and the Male:Female mortality ratio. *Evolutionary Psychology, 2*, 66–85.

Kruger, D. J., & Nesse, R. M. (2006a). An evolutionary framework for understanding sex differences in Croatian mortality rates. *Psihologijske Teme, 15*(2), 351–364.

Kruger, D. J., & Nesse, R. M. (2006b). An evolutionary life-history framework for understanding sex differences in human mortality rates. *Human Nature, 17*(1), 74–97.

Kulik, L. (2005). intrafamiliar congruence in gender role attitudes and ethnic stereogypes: The Israeli case. *Journal of Comparative Family Studies, 36*, 289–303.

Kuo, P. X., & Ward, L. M. (2016). Contributions of Television Use to Beliefs About Fathers and Gendered Family Roles Among First-Time Expectant Parents. *Psychology of Men & Masculinity*. doi:10.1037/men0000033

Kurdek, L. A. (1988). Correlates of negative attitudes toward homosexuals in heterosexual college students. *Sex Roles, 18*, 727–738.

LaFrance, M., Hecht, M. A., & Paluck, E. L. (2003). The contingent smile: A meta-analysis of sex differences in smiling, *Psychological Bulletin, 129*, 305–334.

Lakoff, R. T. (1990). *Talking power: The politics of language.* New York: Basic Books.

Lalumiere, M. L., Harris, G. T., Quinsey, V. L., & Rice, M. E. (2005). *The causes of rape: Understanding individual differences in male propensity for sexual aggression*. Washington, DC: American Psychological Association.

Lamb, M. E. (2012). Mothers, fathers, families, and circumstances: Factors affecting children's adjustment. *Applied Developmental Science, 16*(2), 98–111.

Landrine, H. (1988). Revising the framework of abnormal psychology. In P. Bronstein and K. Quina (Eds.), *Teaching a psychology of people: Resources for gender and sociocultural awareness* (pp. 37–44). Washington, DC: American Psychological Association.

Laumann, E. O. (1999). The circumcision dilemma: Physicians in the U. S. are at odds over neonatal circumcision. Is it preventive medicine, cosmetic surgery, or inhumane mutilation? *Scientific American Presents, 10* (2), 68–72.

Laumann, E. O., Gagnon, J., Michael, R. T., & Michaels, S. (2nd ed., 2001). *The social organization of sexuality: Sexual practices in the United States*. Chicago: University of Chicago Press.

Lazur, R. F. (1996). Managing boundaries: Group therapy with incarcerated adult male sexual offenders. In M. P. Andronico (Ed.), *Men in groups: Insights, interventions, and psychoeducational work* (pp. 389–410). Washington, DC: American Psychological Association.

Leahy, M. (2008, February 3). The pain game. The Washington Post Magazine, 8–13, 21–26.

Leary, M. R., Kowalski, R. M., Smith, L., & Phillips, S. (2003). Teasing, rejection, and violence: Case studies of the school shootings. *Aggressive Behavior, 29*, 202–214.

Lee, C. C. (1990). Black male development: Counseling the "native son." In D. Moore & F. Leafgren (Eds.), *Men in conflict*. Alexandria, VA: American Association for Counseling and Development.

Lee, J. (1991). *At my father's wedding: Reclaiming our true masculinity*. New York: Bantam.

Lee, R. (2009). Ambivalence, Desire and the Re-Imagining of Asian American Masculinity in Better Luck Tomorrow. In E. Watson (Ed.), *Pimps, Wimps, Studs, Thugs, and Gentlemen: Essays on Media Images of Masculinity* (pp. 51–67). Jefferson, NC: McFarland & Company.

Lefkowitz, B. (1997). *Our guys: The Glen Ridge rape and the secret life of the perfect suburb*. NY: Vintage.

Lehne, G. (1998). Homophobia among men: Supporting and defining the male role. In M. S. Kimmel and M. A. Messner (Eds.), *Men's lives* (4th ed., pp. 237–249). Needham Heights, MA: Allyn and Bacon.

Lemann, N. (1991). *The promised land*. New York: Knopf.

Lemle, R., & Mishkind, M. E. (1989). Alcohol and masculinity. *Journal of Substance Abuse Treatment, 6*, 213–222.

Lepowsky, M. (1998). Women, men, and aggression in an egalitarian society. In D. L. Anselmi & A. L. Law (Eds.), *Questions of gender: perspectives and paradoxes*). Boston: McGraw-Hill.

Lerner, G. (1986). *The creation of patriarchy*. New York: Oxford University Press.

Levant, R. F. (1995). Toward the reconstruction of masculinity. In R. F. Levant, W. S. Pollack, R. F. Levant, & W. S. Pollack (Eds.), *A new psychology of men*. (pp. 229–251). New York, NY, US: Basic Books.

Levant, R. F. (1996). The new psychology of men. *Professional Psychology: Research and Practice, 27*, 259–265. doi:10.1037/0735–7028.27.3.259

Levant, R. F. (1997a). Men and emotions: A psychoeducational approach. New York: Newbridge Professional Programs.

Levant, R. F. (1997b). Nonrelational sex. In R. F. Levant & G. R. Brooks (Eds.), *Men and sex* (pp. 9–27). New York: Wiley.

Levant, R. F. (1998). Desperately seeking language: Understanding, assessing, and treating normative male alexithymia. In W.S. Pollack & R. F. Levant (Eds.), *New psychotherapy for men* (pp. 35–56). New York: Wiley.

Levant, R. F. (2003). Treating male alexithymia.. In L.B. Silverstein &

Levant, R. F., & Richmond, K. (2007). A review of research on masculinity ideologies using the Male Role Norms Inventory. *The Journal of Men's Studies, 15,* 130–146.

Levant, R. F., & Wimer, D. J. (2009). The new fathering movement. In C. Z. Oren & D. C. Oren (Eds.), *Counseling fathers.* (pp. 3–21). New York, NY, US: Routledge/Taylor & Francis Group.

Levant, R. F., Allen, P. A., & Lien, M.-C. (2013). Alexithymia in Men: How and When Do Emotional Processing Deficiencies Occur? *Psychology of Men & Masculinity.* doi:10.1037/a0033860

Levant, R. F., Good, G. E., Cook, S. W., O'Neil, J. M., Smalley, K. B., Owen, K., & Richmond, K. (2007). 'The Normative Male Alexithymia Scale: Measurement of a gender-linked syndrome': Correction to Levant et al. (2006). *Psychology of Men & Masculinity, 8*(3), 199–200. doi:10.1037/1524–9220.8.3.199

Levant, R. F., Hall, R. J., Williams, C. M., & Hasan, N. T. (2009). Gender differences in alexithymia. *Psychology of Men & Masculinity, 10*(3), 190–203. doi:10.1037/a0015652

Levant, R. F., Hirsch, L. S., Celentano, E., Cozza, T. M., Hill, S., MacEachern, M., . . . Schnedeker, J. (1992). The male role: An investigation of contemporary norms. *Journal of Mental Health Counseling, 14,* 325–337.

Levant, R. F., Richmond, K., Cook, S., House, A. T., & Aupont, M. (2007). The femininity ideology scale: Factor structure, reliability, convergent and discriminant validity, and social contextual variation. *Sex Roles, 57,* 373–383.

Levant, R., Cuthbert, A., Richmond, K., Sellers, A., Matveev, A., Mitina, O., . . . Heesacker, M. (2003). Masculinity ideology among Russian and U.S. young men and women and its relationship to unhealthy lifestyle habits among young Russian men. *Psychology of Men and Masculinity, 4,* 26–36.

Levenson, R., Carstensen, L., & Gottman, J. (1994). The influence of age and gender on affect, physiology, and their interrelations: A study of long-term marriages. *Journal of Personality and Social Psychology, 67,* 56–68.

Lever, J., Frederick, D. A., & Peplau, L. A. (2006). Does size matter? Men's and women's views on penis size across the lifespan. *Psychology of Men & Masculinity, 7*(3), 129–143. doi:10.1037/1524–9220.7.3.129

Levine, M. P. (1991). The life and death of the gay clone. In G. Herdt (Ed.), *Gay culture in America: Essays from the field* (pp. 68–86). Boston: Beacon.

Levinson, D. J., Darrow, C. N., Klein, E. B., Levinson, M. H., & McKee, B. (1978). *The seasons of a man's life.* NY: Alfred A. Knopf.

Lew, M. (2004). *Victims No Longer: The Classic Guide for Men Recovering from Sexual Child Abuse* New York: Harper Perennial.

Lewis, R. A. (1986). Men's changing roles in marriage and the family. In R. A. Lewis (Ed.), *Men's changing roles in the family* (pp. 1–10). New York: Haworth.

Lex, B. W. (1995). Alcohol and other psychoactive substance dependence in women and men. In M. V. Seeman (Ed.), *Gender and psychopathology* (pp. 358). Washington, DC: American Psychiatric Press.

Ley, D. J. (2016). *Ethical Porn for Dicks: A Man's Guide to Responsible Viewing Pleasure:* ThreeL Media

REFERENCES

Lindberg, S. M., Hyde, J. S., Petersen, J. L., & Linn, M. C. (2010). New trends in gender and mathematics performance: A meta-analysis. *Psychological Bulletin, 136*(6), 1123–1135. doi:10.1037/a0021276.supp (Supplemental)

Lippa, R. A., Martin, L. R., & Friedman, H. S. (2000). Gender-related individual differences and mortality in the Terman longitudinal study: Is masculinity hazardous to your health? *Personality and Social Psychology Bulletin, 26*(12), 1560–1570. doi:10.1177/01461672002612010

Lips, H. (2008). *Sex and gender: An introduction* (6th ed.). Boston: McGraw-Hill.

Lisak, D. & Miller, P. M. (2002). Repeat rape and multiple offending among undetected rapists. *Violence and Victims, 17 (1)*, 73–84.

Lisak, D. (1991). Sexual aggression, masculinity, and fathers. *Signs, 16*, 238–262.

Lisak, D. (1997). Male gender socialization and the perpetration of sexual abuse. In R. F. Levant & G. R. Brooks (Eds.), *Men and sex* (pp. 156–177). New York: Wiley.

Liu, W. M. (2002). Exploring the lives of Asian American men: Racial identity, male role norms, gender role conflict, and prejudicial attitudes. *Psychology of Men & Masculinity, 3*(2), 107–118. doi:10.1037/1524–9220.3.2.107

Liu, W. M. (2005). The Study of Men and Masculinity as an Important Multicultural Competency Consideration. *Journal of Clinical Psychology, 61*(6), 685–697.

Liu, W. M., Colbow, A. J., & Rice, A. J. (2016). Social class and masculinity. In Y. J. Wong, S. R. Wester, Y. J. Wong, & S. R. Wester (Eds.), *APA handbook of men and masculinities.* (pp. 413–432). Washington, DC, US: American Psychological Association.

Livingston, G. (2014). *Growing Number of Dads Home with the Kids: Biggest Increase Among Those Caring for Family.* Retrieved from Washington DC: http://www.pewsocialtrends.org/files/2014/06/2014–06–05_Stay-at-Home-Dads.pdf

Livingston, G., & Parker, K. (2011). A tale of two fathers: More are active, but more are absent. Washington DC: Pew Research Center.

Lo, C. C., & Globetti, G. (1995). The facilitating and enhancing roles Greek associations play in college drinking. *International Journal of the Addictions, 30*, 1311–1322.

Loeber, R., & Stouthamer-Loeber, M. (1998). Development of juvenile aggression and violence: Some common misconceptions and controversies. *American Psychologist, 53*, 242–249.

Logan, J. E., Hall, J., McDaniel, D., & Stevens, M. R. (2013). Homicides — United States, 2007 and 2009. *Mortality and Morbidity Weekly Review, 62 Supplement*, 164–169.

Lohan, M., Cruise, S., O'Halloran, P., Alderdice, F., & Hyde, A. (2010). Adolescent men's attitudes in relation to pregnancy and pregnancy outcomes: A systematic review of the literature from 1980–2009. *Journal of Adolescent Health, 47*(4), 327–345.

Long, D. (1987). Working with men who batter. In M. Scher, M. Stevens, G. Good, & G. A. Eichenfield (Eds.). Handbook of counseling and psychotherapy with men. Newbury Park, CA: Sage.

Luthar, S., Cicchetti, D., & Bronwyn, B. (2000). The construct of resilience: A critical evaluation and guidelines for future work. *Child Development, 74*, 543–562.

Lynch, J. R., & Kilmartin, C. (2013). *Overcoming masculine depression: The pain behind the mask., 2nd ed.* New York, NY, US: Routledge/Taylor & Francis Group.

Lytton, H., & Romney, D. M. (1991). Parents' differential socialization of boys and girls: A meta-analysis. *Psychological Bulletin, 109*, 267–296. doi:10.1037/0033–2909.109.2.267

Maccoby, E. E. (1987). The varied meanings of "masculine" and "feminine." In J.M. Reinisch, L.A. Rosenblum, & S.A. Sanders (Eds.), *Masculinity/femininity: Basic perspectives* (pp. 227–239). New York: Oxford University Press.

Maccoby, E. E. (1988a). Gender as a social category. *Developmental Psychology, 24*, 755–765.

Maccoby, E. E. (1988b). Gender as a social construct. Paper presented at the Annual Meeting of the Eastern Psychological Association, Buffalo, NY.

Maccoby, E. E. (1990). Gender and relationships: A developmental account. *American Psychologist, 45,* 513–520.

Maccoby, E. E. (1998). *The Two Sexes: Growing Up Apart, Coming Together.* Cambridge, MA, USA: Belknap Press.

MacDormand, M. F., & Matthews, T. J. (2013). Infant Deaths — United States, 2005. *Mortality and Morbidity Weekly Review, 62* Supplement, 171–175.

Mack, K. A. (2013). Drug-Induced Deaths — United States, 1999–2010. *Mortality and Morbidity Weekly Review, 62 Supplement,* 161–162.

Madon, S. (1997). What do people believe about gay males? A study of stereotype content and strength. *Sex Roles, 37,* 663–685.

Maffini, C. S., & Wong, Y. J. (2012). Psychology of Biculturalism. In G. R. Hayes & M. H. Bryant (Eds.), *Psychology of Culture: Psychology of Emotions, Motivations, and Actions* (pp. 87–104). NY: Nove Publishers.

Magovcevic, M., & Addis, M. E. (2008). The Masculine Depression Scale: Development and psychometric evaluation. *Psychology of Men & Masculinity, 9*(3), 117–132. doi:10.1037/1524–9220.9.3.117

Mahalik, J. R., Cournoyer, R. J., DeFranc, W., Cherry, M., & Napolitano, J. M. (1998). Men's gender role conflict and use of psychological defenses. *Journal of Counseling Psychology, 45,* 247–255.

Mahalik, J. R., Locke, B. D., Ludlow, L. H., Diemer, M. A., Scott, R. P. J., Gottfried, M., & Freitas, G. (2003). Development of the Conformity to Masculine Norms Inventory. *Psychology of Men & Masculinity, 4*(1), 3–25. doi:10.1037/1524–9220.4.1.3

Mahlstedt, D. (1998). Getting started: A dating violence peer education program for men. West Chester, PA: self.

Mak, W. W. S., Mo, P. K. H., Ma, G. Y. K., & Lam, M. Y. Y. (2017). Meta-analysis and systematic review of studies on the effectiveness of HIV stigma reduction programs. *Social Science & Medicine, 188,* 30–40. doi:10.1016/j.socscimed.2017.06.045

Majors, R., & Billson, J. M. (1992). *Cool pose: The dilemmas of Black manhood in America.* New York: Lexington publishers.

Malamuth, N. M., Addison, T., & Koss, M. (2000). Pornography and sexual aggression: Are there reliable effects and can we understand them? *Annual review of sex research, 11,* 4–17.

Mann, B. (2014). *Sovereign Masculinity: Gender Lessons from the War on Terror.* New York: Oxford University Press.

Manning, J. (2011). Masculinities in Dating Relationships: Reality and Representation at the Intersection of Race, Class, and Sexual Orientation. In E. Watson & M. E. Shaw (Eds.), *Performing American Masculinities: THe 21st-Century Man in Popular Culture* (pp. 167–191). Bloomington, IN: Indiana University Press.

Manstead, A. S. R. (1992). Gender differences in emotion. In M. A. Gale & M. W. Eysenck (Eds.). *Handbook of individual differences: Biological perspectives.* Chichester, UK: Wiley.

Marie, A. (2009). The Code of a Gentleman. Retrieved from http://catholicism.org/the-code-of-a-gentleman.html

Marlantes, K. (2011). *What It Is Like To Go To War.* NY: Atlantic Monthly Press.

Marsiglio, W. & Pleck, J. H. (2005). Fatherhood and masculinities. In M. S. Kimmel, J. Hearn, & R. W. Connell (Eds.), *Handbook of studies on men and masculinities.* Thousand Oaks, CA: Sage.

Marston, C., & King, E. (2006). Factors that shape young people's sexual behaviour: A systematic review. *Lancet, 368*, 1581–1586.

Martin, C. L. & Fabes, R. A. (2001). The stability and consequences of young children's same-sex peer interactions. *Developmental Psychology, 3*, 431–446.

Martin, C. L. (1995). Stereotypes about children with traditional and nontraditional gender roles. *Sex Roles, 33*, 727–751.

Martin, C. L., & Ruble, D. N. (2010). Patterns of gender development. *Annual Review of Psychology, 61*, 353–381.

Martin, C. L., Ruble, D. N., & Szkrybalo, J. (2002). Cognitive theories of early gender development. *Psychological Bulletin, 128*(6), 903–933.

Martin, E. (1991). The egg and the sperm: How science has constructed a romance based on stereotypical male-female roles. *Signs, 16*, 485–501.

Martin, J., & Govender, K. (2011). 'Making muscle junkies': Investigating traditional masculine ideology, body image discrepancy, and the pursuit of muscularity in adolescent males. *International Journal of Men's Health, 10*(3), 220–239. doi:10.3149/jmh.1003.220

Martin, P. Y., & Hummer, R. A. (2009). Fraternities and rape on campus. In V. Taylor, N. Whittier, & L. J. Rupp (Eds.), *Feminist frontiers* (8th ed., pp. 471–479). Boston: McGraw-Hill.

Martinez, G., Daniels, K., & Chandra, A. (2012). *Fertility of men and women aged 15–44 years in the United States: National Survey of Family Growth, 2006–2010.* Retrieved from Washington DC: http://www.cdc.gov/nchs/data/nhsr/nhsr051.pdf

Marx, K. (1872). *Das Kapital*. Hamburg, Germany: Meissner.

Masciadrelli, B. P., Pleck, J. H., & Stueve, J. L. (2006). Fathers' Role Model Perceptions: Themes and Linkages with Involvement. *Men and Masculinities, 9*(1), 23–34.

Maslow, A. H. (1943). A theory of human motivation. *Psychological Review, 50*, 370–396. doi:10.1037/h0054346

Maticka-Tyndale, E., Herold, E. S., & Mewhinney, D. (1998). Casual sex on spring break: Intentions and behaviors of Canadian students. *Journal of Sex Research, 35*, 254–264. doi:10.1080/00224499809551941

Maurer, T. W., & Pleck, J. H. (2006). Fathers' caregiving and breadwinning: A gender congruence analysis. *Psychology of Men & Masculinity, 7*(2), 101–112.

May, R. (1958). Contributions of existential psychotherapy. In R. May, E. Angel, & H. F. Ellenberger (Eds.), *Existence: A new dimension in psychiatry and psychology*. New York: Basic Books.

May, R. J. (1988). The developmental journey of the male college student. In R. J. May & M. Scher (Eds.), *Changing roles of men on campus* (pp. 5–18). San Francisco: Jossey-Bass.

Mays, V. M. (1988). Even the rat was White and male: Teaching the psychology of Black women. In P. A. Bronstein, K. Quina, P. A. Bronstein, & K. Quina (Eds.), *Teaching a psychology of people: Resources for gender and sociocultural awareness.* (pp. 142–146). Washington, DC, US: American Psychological Association.

McCormack, M. (2013). *The Declining Significance of Homophobia (Sexuality, Identity, and Society)*. Oxford: Oxford University.

McCreary, D. R. (1994). The male role and avoiding femininity. *Sex Roles, 31*, 517–531.

McCreary, D. R., Newcomb, M. D., & Sadava, S. W. (1999). The male role, alcohol use, and alcohol problems: A structural modeling examination in adult women and men. *Journal of Counseling Psychology, 46*, 109–124.

McDaniel, M., Simms, M., Monson, W., & Fortuny, K. (2013). *Imprisonment and Disenfranchisement of Disconnected Low-Income Men* Retrieved from Washington DC: https://aspe.hhs.gov/system/files/pdf/56191/rpt_imprisonment.pdf

McDiarmid, E., Gill, P. R., McLachlan, A., & Ali, L. (2016). 'That Whole Macho Male Persona Thing': The Role of Insults in Young Australian Male Friendships. *Psychology of Men & Masculinity*. doi:10.1037/men0000065

McHugh, M. C., & Hambaugh, J. (2010). She said, he said: Gender, language, and power. In J. C. Chrisler & D. R. McCreary (Eds.), *Handbook of gender research in psychology, Vol 1: Gender research in general and experimental psychology*. (pp. 379–410). New York, NY, US: Springer Science + Business Media.

McIntosh, P. (2009). White privilege: Unpacking the invisible knapsack. In V. Taylor, N. Whittier, & L. J. Rupp (Eds.), *Feminist frontiers* (8th ed., pp. 120–126). Boston: McGraw-Hill.

McKelley, R. A., & Rochlen, A. B. (2016). Furthering fathering: What we know and what we need to know. In Y. J. Wong, S. R. Wester, Y. J. Wong, & S. R. Wester (Eds.), *APA handbook of men and masculinities*. (pp. 525–549). Washington, DC, US: American Psychological Association.

Mead, M. (1935). *Sex and temperament in three primitive societies*. New York: Morrow.

Mead, M. (1949). *Male and female: A study of the sexes in a changing world*. New York: Morrow.

Messner, M. A. (1992). *Power at play: Sports and the problem of masculinity*. Boston, MA, USA: Beacon Press.

Messner, M. A. (1995). Boyhood, organized sports, and the construction of masculinity. In M. A. Kimmel & M. S. Messner (Eds.), *Men's lives* (3rd ed., pp. 102–114). Boston: Allyn and Bacon.

Messner, M. A., & Stevens, M. A. (2002). Scoring without consent: Confronting male athletes' violence against women. In M. Gatz, M. A. Messner, & S. J. Ball-Rokeach (Eds.), *Paradoxes of youth and sport* (pp. 225–239). Albany, NY: State University of New York Press.

Meyer, P. A., Penman-Aguilar, A., Campbell, V. A., Graffunder, C., O'Connor, A. E., & Yoon, P. W. (2013). Conclusion and Future Directions: CDC Health Disparities and Inequalities Report — United States, 2013. *Mortality and Morbidity Weekly Review, 62* Supplement, 184–186.

Miedzian, M. (1991). *Boys will be boys: Breaking the link between masculinity and violence*. New York: Doubleday.

Migliaccio, T. (2009). Men's friendships: Performances of masculinity. *Journal of Men's Studies, 17*, 226–241.

Mihoces, G. (2002, January 18). Two big guys are key to success. *USA Today*, 1A.

Milgram, S. (1963). Behavioral study of obedience. *Journal of Abnormal and Social Psychology, 67*, 371–378.

Miller, A. (1949). *Death of a salesman*. New York: Viking.

Miller, M., Azrael, D., & Hemenway, D. (2013). Firearms and violent death in the United States. In D. W. Webster & J. S. Vernick (Eds.), *Reducing gun violence in America: Informing policy with evidence and analysis*. Baltimore, MD: Johns Hopkins University Press.

Miller, M., Lippmann, S. J., Azrael, D., & Hemenway, D. (2007). Household firearm ownership and rates of suicide across the 50 United States. *Journal of Trauma, Injury, Infection, and Critical Care, 62*, 1029–1034.

Millon, T., Millon, C. F., Meagher, S., Grossman, S., & Ramnath, R. (2005). *Personality disorders in modern life*. New York: Wiley.

Milos, M. F. (1992). Circumcision: Don't be conned by the pros. *Journeymen*, 14–16.

Ministry of Justice. (2015). *Statistics on Race and the Criminal Justice System 2014*. Retrieved from London: https://assets.publishing.service.gov.uk/government/uploads/system/uploads/attachment_data/file/480250/bulletin.pdf

Moberly, E. (1983). *Homosexuality: A new Christian ethic*. Cambridge, UK: Clarke.

Molla, M. T. (2013). Expected Years of Life Free of Chronic Condition–Induced Activity Limitations — United States, 1999–2008. *Mortality and Morbidity Weekly Review, 62 Supplement*, 86–92.

Möller, E. L., Nikolić, M., Majdandžić, M., & Bögels, S. M. (2016). Associations between maternal and paternal parenting behaviors, anxiety and its precursors in early childhood: A meta-analysis. *Clinical Psychology Review, 45*, 17–33. doi:10.1016/j.cpr.2016.03.002

Money, J. (1987). Sin, sickness, or status? Homosexual gender identity and psychological neuroendocrinology. *American Psychologist, 42*, 384–399.

Montemurro, B. (2003). Not a laughing matter: Sexual harassment as "material" on workplace-based situation comedies. *Sex Roles, 48*, 433–445.

Moon, M., & Hoffman, C. D. (2000). References on men and women in psychology (1887–1997): PsycINFO as an archival research tool. *Psychology of Men and Masculinity, 1*, 16–20.

Moore, M. (Writer). (2004). Farenheit 9/11. Hollywood, CA.

Moore, T. M., & Stuart, G. L. (2004). Effects of Masculine Gender Role Stress on Men's Cognitive, Affective, Physiological, and Aggressive Responses to Intimate Conflict Situations. *Psychology of Men & Masculinity, 5*(2), 132–142. doi:10.1037/1524-9220.5.2.132

Morawski, J. G. (1985). The measurement of masculinity and femininity: Engendering categorical realities. *Journal of Personality, 53*, 196–223.

Morgan, R. E. (2017). *Race and Hispanic Origin of Victims and Offenders, 2012–2015*. Retrieved from Washington DC: https://www.bjs.gov/content/pub/pdf/rhovo1215.pdf

Morrison, T. G., & Halton, M. (2009). Buff, tough, and rough: Representations of muscularity in action motion pictures. *Journal of Men's Studies, 17*, 57–74.

Mueller, F. O. (2001). Catastrophic head injuries in high school and collegiate sports. *Journal of Athletic Training, 36*, 312–315.

Murdock, G. P. (1967). *Ethnographic Atlas*. Pittsburgh, PA: University of Pittsburgh.

Murnen, S. K., & Karazsia, B. T. (2017). A review of research on men's body image and drive for muscularity. In R. F. Levant, Y. J. Wong, R. F. Levant, & Y. J. Wong (Eds.), *The psychology of men and masculinities*. (pp. 229–257). Washington, DC, US: American Psychological Association.

Murnen, S. K., Wright, C., & Kaluzny, G. (2002). If "boys will be boys," then girls will be victims? A meta-analytic review of the research that relates masculine ideology to sexual aggression. *Sex Roles, 46*, 359–375.

Murray, B. (1998). Study says TV violence still seen as heroic, glamorous: Psychologists call on television executives to embed antiviolence messages in programming. *APA Monitor, 29 (6)*, p. 16.

Myers, D. G. (2008). *Social psychology* (9th ed.). Boston: McGraw-Hill.

Myers, S. M., & Booth, A. (2002). Forerunners of change in nontraditional gender ideology. *Social Psychology Quarterly, 65*, 18–37.

Nathan, S. (1981). Cross-cultural perspectives on penis envy. *Psychiatry, 44*, 39–44.

National Center for Education Statistics. (2010, 2010). Table 212. Enrollment rates of 17- to 24- year olds in degree-granting institutions, by type of institution and sex and race/ethnicity of student: 1967 through 2009. Retrieved from http://nces.ed.gov/programs/digest/d10/tables/dt10_212.asp?referrer=list

National Center for Education Statistics. (2015a). Table 321.20. Associate's degrees conferred by postsecondary institutions, by race/ethnicity and sex of student: Selected years, 1976–77 through 2013–14. Retrieved from https://nces.ed.gov/programs/digest/d15/tables/dt15_321.20.asp

National Center for Education Statistics. (2015b). Table 322.20. Bachelor's degrees conferred by postsecondary institutions, by race/ethnicity and sex of student: Selected years, 1976–77 through 2013–14. Retrieved from https://nces.ed.gov/programs/digest/d15/tables/dt15_322.20.asp

National Center for Education Statistics. (2015c). Table 323.20. Master's degrees conferred by postsecondary institutions, by race/ethnicity and sex of student: Selected years, 1976–77 through 2013–14. Retrieved from https://nces.ed.gov/programs/digest/d15/tables/dt15_323.20.asp

National Center for Education Statistics. (2015d). Table 324.20. Doctor's degrees conferred by postsecondary institutions, by race/ethnicity and sex of student: Selected years, 1976–77 through 2013–14. Retrieved from https://nces.ed.gov/programs/digest/d15/tables/dt15_324.20.asp

National Center for Health Statistics (2008). Health, United States 2008 with chartbook on trends in the health of Americans. Hyattsville, MD: Center for Disease Control.

National Safety Council (2010). *Injury facts* (2010 ed.). Itasca, IL: self.

National Spinal Cord Injury Association (2005). More about spinal cord injury (fact sheet). Retrieved July 30, 2005 from www.spinalcord.org.

Nellis, A. (2016). *The Color of Justice: Racial and Ethnic Disparity in State Prisons*

Nelson, J. B. (1988). *The intimate connection: Male sexuality, masculine spirituality*. Philadelphia: Westminster.

Nelson, J. B. (1997). Male sexuality, masculine spirituality. Paper presented at the 22nd Conference on Men and Masculinity, Collegeville, MN.

Nemiah, J. C., Fryberger, H., & Sifneos, P. E. (1976). Alexithymia: A view of the psychosomatic process. In O.W. Hill (Ed.), *Modern trends in psychosomatic medicine*, Vol. 3. London: Butterworths, 430–439.

Newfield, J. (2001, November 12). The shame of boxing. The Nation, pp. 13–22.

Ng, C. J., Tan, H. M., & Low, W. Y. (2008). What do Asian men consider as important masculinity attributes? Findings from the Asian Men's Attitudes to Life Events and Sexuality (MALES) Study. *Journal of Men's Health, 5*(4), 350–355. doi:10.1016/j.jomh.2008.10.005

Niku, S. D., Stock, J. A., & Kaplan, G. W. (1995). Neonatal circumcision. *Common Problems in Pediatric Urology, 21,* 57–65.

Noble, M., Jones, A. M., Bowles, K., DiNenno, E. A., & Tregear, S. J. (2017). HIV testing among Internet-using MSM in the United States: Systematic review. *AIDS and Behavior, 21*(2), 561–575. doi:10.1007/s10461-016-1506-7

Nolen-Hoeksema, S. & Girgus, J. S. (1994). The emergence of gender differences in depression during adolescence. *Psychological Bulletin, 115,* 424–443.

Nolen-Hoeksema, S. & Hilt, L. (2006). Possible contributors to the gender differences in alcohol abuse and problems. *Journal of General Psychology, 133,* 357–374.

Nolen-Hoeksema, S. (1998). Gender differences in coping with depression across the lifespan. *Depression, 3,* 81–90.

Nolen-Hoeksema, S. (2006). Thinking too much about trauma: The detrimental effects of rumination. Paper presented at the American Psychological Association Convention, August 10, New Orleans, LA.

NOMAS (National Organization for Men Against Sexism) (2014). NOMAS Statement of Principles. Retrieved July 14, 2014 from www.nomas.org.

NPR (National Public Radio) (2005, February 9). Laura Bush: Putting boys into the spotlight. Radio interview.

Ochberg, R. (1988). Ambition and impersonality in men's careers. *Men's Studies Review, 1,* 10–13.

Oeur, F. (2016). Recognizing Dignity: Young Black Men Growing Up in an Era of Surveillance. *Socius: Sociological Research for a Dynamic World, 2,* 1–15.

Offer, D., Offer, M. K., & Ostrov, E. (2004). *Regular guys: 34 years beyond adolescence.* NY: Kluwer.

Ogbu, J. U. (1994). From cultural differences to differences in cultural frames of reference. In P. M. Greenfield & R. R. Cocking (Eds.), *Cross-Cultural Roots of Minority Child Development* (pp. 365–391). Hillsdale, NJ, USA: Erlbaum.

Ojeda, L., & Organista, K. C. (2016). Latino American men. In Y. J. Wong & S. R. Wester (Eds.), *APA handbook of men and masculinities.* (pp. 299–318). Washington, DC, US: American Psychological Association.

Okun, R. A. (2014). *Voice Male: The Untold Story of the Profeminist Men's Movement.* Northampton, MA: Interlink.

Oliphant, B. (2016). Support for death penalty lowest in more than four decades. Retrieved from http://www.pewresearch.org/fact-tank/2016/09/29/support-for-death-penalty-lowest-in-more-than-four-decades/

Oliver, M. B., & Hyde, J. S. (1993). Gender differences in sexuality: A meta-analysis. *Psychological Bulletin, 114,* 29–51. doi:10.1037/0033–2909.114.1.29

O'Neil, J. M. (1981a). Patterns of gender role conflict and strain: Sexism and fear of femininity in men's lives. *Personnel and Guidance Journal, 60,* 203–210.

O'Neil, J. M. (1981b). Male sex role conflicts, sexism, and masculinity: Psychological implications for men, women, and the counseling psychologist. *Journal of Counseling Psychology, 9,* 61–80.

O'Neil, J. M. (2008). Summarizing 25 years of research on men's gender role conflict using the Gender Role Conflict Scale. *The Counseling Psychologist, 36,* 358–445.

O'Neil, J. M., & Renzulli, S. (2013). Introduction to the special section: Teaching the psychology of men — A call to action. *Psychology of Men & Masculinity, 14*(3), 221–229. doi:10.1037/a0033258

O'Neil, J. M., Helms, B. J., Gable, R. K., David, L., & Wrightsman, L. S. (1986). Gender-role conflict scale: College men's fear of femininity. *Sex Roles, 14,* 335–350.

O'Rand, A. M. (1987). Gender. In G. L. Maddox (Ed.), *The Encyclopedia of Aging* (p. 271). New York: Springer.

O'Sullivan, C. S. (1991). Acquaintance gang rape on campus. In A. Parrot & l. Bechofer (Eds.), *Acquaintance rape: The hidden crime* (pp. 140–156). New York: Wiley.

Packard, G. A. (2014). Gays in the military: Why the all-volunteer force didn't "break" with the repeal of "Don't Ask; Don't Tell." Invited address, University of Mary Washington.

Palmer-Mehta, V., & Haliliuc, A. (2009). Flavor of Love and the Rise of Neo-Minstrelsy on Reality Television. In E. Watson (Ed.), *Pimps, Wimps, Studs, Thugs, and Gentlemen: Essays on Media Images of Masculinity* (pp. 85–104). Jefferson, NC: McFarland & Company.

Pantony, K. L., & Caplan, P. J. (1991). Delusional dominating personality disorder: A modest proposal for identifying some consequences of rigid masculine socialization. *Canadian Psychology, 32,* 120–135.

Parent, M. C., & Bradstreet, T. C. (2017). Gay, bisexual, and transgender masculinities. In R. F. Levant, Y. J. Wong, R. F. Levant, & Y. J. Wong (Eds.), *The psychology of men and masculinities.* (pp. 289–314). Washington, DC, US: American Psychological Association.

Parent, M. C., & Moradi, B. (2009). Confirmatory factor analysis of the Conformity to Masculine Norms Inventory and development of the Conformity to Masculine Norms Inventory-46. *Psychology of Men & Masculinity, 10*(3), 175–189. doi:10.1037/a0015481

Parent, M. C., & Moradi, B. (2011). His biceps become him: A test of objectification theory's applicaton to drive for muscularity and propensity for steroid use in college men. *Journal of Counseling Psychology, 58,* 246–256.

Parent, M. C., Schwartz, E. N., & Bradstreet, T. C. (2016). Men's body image. In Y. J. Wong & S. R. Wester (Eds.), *APA handbook of men and masculinities.* (pp. 591–614). Washington, DC, US: American Psychological Association.

Parke, R. D., & Tinsley, B. R. (1981). The father's role in infancy: Determinants of involvement in caregiving and play. In M. Lamb (Ed.), *The role of the father in child development* (2nd ed., pp. 429–457). New York: Wiley.

Parker, S., & De Vries, B. (1993). Patterns of friendship for women and men in same- and cross-sex relationships. *Journal of Social and Personal Relationships, 10,* 617–626.

Parks, L. F., Cohen, L., & Kravitz-Wirtz, N. (2007). *Poised for prevention: Advancing promising approaches to primary prevention of intimate partner violence.* Princeton, NJ: Prevention Institute.

Parsons, J. T., Starks, T. J., Gamarel, K. E., & Grov, C. (2012). Non-monogamy and sexual relationship quality among same-sex male couples. *Journal of Family Psychology, 26*(5), 669–677.

Parsons, T., & Bales, R. F. (1955). *Family, socialization, and interaction process.* NY: Free press of Glencoe.

Pascoe, C. J. (2007). *Dude, You're a Fag: Masculinity and sexuality in high school.* Berkeley, CA: University of California Press.

Pasick, R. S. (1990). Raised to work. In R. L. Meth & R. S. Pasick, *Men in therapy: The challenge of change* (pp. 35–53). New York: Guilford.

Patterson, G. R., Reid, J., & Dishion, T. (1992). *Antisocial boys.* Eugene, OR: Castalia.

Paz-Bailey, G., Noble, M., Salo, K., & Tregear, S. J. (2016). Prevalence of HIV among US female sex workers: Systematic review and meta-analysis. *AIDS and Behavior, 20*(10), 2318–2331. doi:10.1007/s10461-016-1332-y

Peacock, D., & Barker, G. (2014). Working with men and boys to prevent gender-based violence: Principles, lessons learned, and ways forward. *Men and Masculinities, 17*(5), 578–599. doi:10.1177/1097184X14558240

Pecora, N. (1992). Superman/superboys/supermen: The comic book hero as socializing agent. In S. Craig (Ed.), *Men, masculinity and the media* (pp. 61–77). Newbury Park, CA: Sage.

Pellegrini, A. D. (2004). Sexual segregation in childhood: A review of evidence for two hypotheses. *Animal Behaviour, 68*(3), 435–443.

Pennebaker, J. W. (2002). *Emotion, disclosure, and health.* Washington, DC: American Psychological Association.

Peplau, L. A., & Fingerhut, A. W. (2007). The Close Relationships of Lesbian and Gay Men. *Annual Review of Psychology, 58,* 405–424.

Pepler, D. J., & Slaby, R. G. (1994). Theoretical and developmental perspectives on youth and violence. In L. D. Eron, J. H. Gentry, & P. Schlegel (Eds.), *Reason to hope:*

A psychosocial perspective on violence and youth (pp. 27–58). Washington, DC: American Psychological Association.

Peralta, R. L. (2007). College alcohol use and the embodiment of hegemonic masculinity among European American men. *Sex Roles, 56*, 741–756.

Perelman, M. A. (2016). Psychosexual therapy for delayed ejaculation based on the Sexual Tipping Point model. *Translational Andrology and Urology, 5*, 563–575. doi:10.21037/tau.2016.07.05

Perez, A. D., & Hirschman, C. (2009). The Changing Racial and Ethnic Composition of the US Population: Emerging American Identities. *Population and Development Review, 35*, 1–51. doi:10.1111/j.1728–4457.2009.00260.x

Perren, S., Von Wyl, A., Bürgin, D., Simoni, H., & Von Klitzing, K. (2005). Intergenerational Transmission of Marital Quality Across the Transition to Parenthood. *Family Process, 44*(4), 441–459.

Perry, D. G., & Bussey, K. (1979). The social learning theory of sex differences: Imitation is alive and well. *Journal of Personality and Social Psychology, 37*, 1699–1712.

Peskin, H. (1992). Shifts in uses of the past in the Intergenerational Longitudinal Studies. Paper presented at the Annual Meeting of the Gerontological Society of America, Washington, DC.

Peter, J. & Valkenburg, P. M. (2007). Adolescents' exposure to a sexualized media environment and their notions of women as sex objects. *Sex Roles, 56*, 381–395.

Petrosky, E., Blair, J. M., Betz, C. J., Fowler, K. A., Jack, S. P. D., & Lyons, B. H. (2017). Racial and Ethnic Differences in Homicides of Adult Women and the Role of Intimate Partner Violence — United States, 2003–2014. *Morbidity and Mortality Weekly Report, 66*, 741–746.

Pharr, S. (1997a, July 19). Our search for liberation in the time of the Right. Paper presented at the 22nd National Conference on Men and Masculinity, Collegeville, MN.

Picker, M., & Sun, C. (Writers). (2008). The Price of Pleasure: Pornography, Sexuality, & Relationships. In F. Media Education (Producer).

Pinquart, M. (2016). Associations of parenting styles and dimensions with academic achievement in children and adolescents: A meta-analysis. *Educational Psychology Review, 28*(3), 475–493. doi:10.1007/s10648–015–9338–y

Piquero, A. R. (2015). Understanding Race/Ethnicity Differences in Offending Across the Life Course: Gaps and Opportunities. *Journal of Developmental Life Course Criminology, 1*(21–32). doi:10.1007/s40865–015–0004–3

Pleck, J. H. (1975). Masculinity-femininity: Current and alternative paradigms. *Sex Roles, 1*, 161–178.

Pleck, J. H. (1981). *The myth of masculinity*. Cambridge, MA, USA: MIT Press.

Pleck, J. H. (1995). The gender role strain paradigm: An update. In R. F. Levant & W. S. Pollack (Eds.), *A new psychology of men* (pp. 11–32). NY, NY, USA: Basic Books.

Pleck, J. H. (2007). Why could father involvement benefit children? Theoretical perspectives. *Applied Developmental Science, 11*(4), 196–202.

Pleck, J. H., Sonenstein, F. L., & Ku, L. C. (1993). Masculinity ideology: Its impact on adolescent males' heterosexual relationships. *Journal of Social Issues, 49*, 11–29.

Pleck, J. H., Sonenstein, F. L., & Ku, L. C. (1994). Attitudes toward male roles: A discriminant validity analysis. *Sex Roles, 30*, 481–501. doi:10.1007/BF01420798

Plummer, D. C. (2001). The quest for modern manhood: Masculine stereotypes, peer culture and the social significance of homophobia. *Journal of Adolescence, 24*, 15–23.

Polce-Lynch, M., Myers, B. J., Kliewer, W., & Kilmartin, C. (2001). Adolescent self-esteem and gender: Exploring relations to sexual harassment, body image, media influence, and emotional expression. *Journal of Youth and Adolescence, 30*, 225–244.

Pollack, W. (1998). *Real Boys: Rescuing Our Sons from the Myths of Boyhood*. NY: Holt & Co.

Pollack, W. S. (2001). *Real Boys' Voices: Boys Speak out about Drugs, Sex, Violence, Bullying, Sports, Girls, School, Parents, and So Much More*. NY: Penguin Books.

Pomerleau, A., Bolduc, D., Malcuit, G., & Cossette, L. (1990). Pink or blue: Environmental stereotypes in the first two years of life. *Sex Roles, 22*, 359–367.

Pompper, D. (2010). Masculinities, the metrosexual, and media images: Across dimensions of age and ethnicity. *Sex Roles, 63*, 682–696. doi:10.1007/s11199–010–9870–7

Ponton, L. E., & Judice, S. (2004). Typical adolescent sexual development. *Child and Adolescent Psychiatric Clinics of North America, 13*, 497–511.

Pope, H. G., Olivardia, R., Borowiecki, J. J., & Cohane, G. H. (2001). The growing commercial value of the male body: A longitudinal survey of advertising in women's magazines. *Psychotherapy and psychosomatics, 70*, 189–192.

Pope, H. G., Olivardia, R., Gruber, A., & Borowiecki, J. (1999). Evolving ideals of male body image as seen through action toys. *Eating Disorders, 26*, 65–72.

Pope, H. G., Phillips, K. A., & Olivardia, R. (2000). *The Adonis Complex: The Secret Crisis of Male Body Obsessions*. NY: The Free Press.

Potts, A., Grace, V. M., Vares, T., & Gavey, N. (2006). 'Sex for life'? Men's counter-stories on 'erectile dysfunction', male sexuality and ageing. *Sociology of Health & Illness, 28*(3), 306–329.

Prior, P. M. (1999). *Gender and mental health*. New York: New York University Press.

Proctor, B. D., Semega, J. L., & Kollar, M. A. (2016). *Income and Poverty in the United States: 2015*. Retrieved from Washington DC: https://www.census.gov/content/dam/Census/library/publications/2016/demo/p60-256.pdf

Proquest LLC. (2016). *Proquest Statistical Abstract of the United States, 2016*. (4th ed.). Bethesda, MD: Bernan.

Pryor, J. B. (1987). Sexual harassment proclivities in men. *Sex Roles, 17*, 269–290.

Putnam, R. (2000). *Bowling alone: The collapse and revival of American community*. NY: Touchstone.

Quinlan, R. J. (2008). Human pair-bonds: Evolutionary functions, ecological variation, and adaptive development. *Evolutionary Anthropology, 17*, 227–238.

Rabinowitz, F. E. & Cochran, S. V. (2002). *Deepening psychotherapy with men*. Washington, DC: American Psychological Association.

Rabinowitz, F. E. (2010). Group therapy for men. Paper presented at the Annual Convention of the American Psychological Association, Washington, DC.

Rabinowitz, F. E., & Cochran, S. V. (2002). *Deepening psychotherapy with men*. Washington, DC, US: American Psychological Association.

Raphael, R. (1988). *The men from the boys: Rites of passage in male America*. Lincoln, NB: University of Nebraska Press.

Rathus, S. A., Nevid, J. S., & Fichner-Rathus, L. (2008). *Human sexuality in a world of diversity* (7th ed.). Boston: Pearson/Allyn & Bacon.

Raver, J. L. & Gelfand, M. J. (2005). Beyond the individual victim: Linking sexual harassment, team processes, and team performance. *Academy of Management Journal, 48*, 387–400.

Real, T. (1997). *I don't want to talk about it: Overcoming the secret legacy of male depression*. NY, NY, USA: Scribner.

Reece, M., Herbenick, D., & Dodge, B. (2009). Penile dimensions and men's perceptions of condom fit and feel. *Sexually Transmitted Infections, 85*, 127–131. doi:10.1136/sti.2008.033050

Regan, P. C., Durvasula, R., Howell, L., Ureno, O., & Rea, M. (2004). Gender, ethnicity, and the developmental timing of first sexual and romantic experiences. *Social Behavior and Personality, 32*, 667–676.

Reid, H. M., & Fine, G. A. (1992). Self-disclosure in men's friendships. In P. M. Nardi (Ed.), *Men's friendships* (pp. 132–152). Newbury Park, CA: Sage.

Reigeluth, C. S., & Addis, M. E. (2016). Adolescent boys' experiences with policing of masculinity: Forms, functions, and consequences. *Psychology of Men & Masculinity, 17*(1), 74–83. doi:10.1037/a0039342

Retrieved from Washington, DC: http://www.sentencingproject.org/wp-content/uploads/2016/06/The-Color-of-Justice-Racial-and-Ethnic-Disparity-in-State-Prisons.pdf

Rhodes, W., Kling, R., Luallen, J., & Dyous, C. (2015). *Federal Sentencing Disparity: 2005–2012*. Retrieved from Cambridge, MA: https://www.bjs.gov/content/pub/pdf/fsd0512.pdf

Richardson, L. (2009). Gender stereotyping in the English language. In V. Taylor, N. Whittier, & L. J. Rupp (Eds.), *Feminist frontiers* (8th ed., pp. 120–126). Boston: McGraw-Hill.

Richardson, S. (1993). A violence in the blood: Five generations of aggressive men in a Dutch family have led researchers to a gene that seems to lie at the root of violence. *Discover, 14(10)*, 30–31.

Riger, S. (2016). On becoming a feminist psychologist. *Psychology of Women Quarterly, 40*, 479–487.

Ro, M. J., Casares, C., Treadwell, H. M., & Thomas, S. (2004). *A man's dilemma: Heathcare of men across America: A disparities report*. Atlanta, GA: The National Center for Primary Care at the Morehouse School of Medicine.

Robertson, J. M. (2014). Counseling older men. In M. Englar-Carlson, M. P. Evans, & T. Duffey (Eds., 2014), *A counselor's guide to working with men*. Alexandria, VA: American Counseling Association.

Robinson, D. T., & Schwartz, J. P. (2004). Relationship Between Gender Role Conflict and Attitudes Toward Women and African Americans. *Psychology of Men & Masculinity, 5*(1), 65–71. doi:10.1037/1524–9220.5.1.65

Rochlen, A. B. & Rabinowitz, F. E. (Eds., 2014). *Breaking barriers in counseling men: Insights and innovations*. New York: Routledge.

Rochlen, A. B., & Mahalik, J. R. (2004). Women's Perceptions of Male Partners' Gender Role Conflict as Predictors of Psychological Well-Being and Relationship Satisfaction. *Psychology of Men & Masculinity, 5*(2), 147–157. doi:10.1037/1524–9220.5.2.147

Rochlen, A. B., McKelley, R. A., & Whittaker, T. A. (2010). Stay-at-home fathers' reasons for entering the role and stigma experiences: A preliminary report. *Psychology of Men and Masculinity, 11*, 279–285.

Rochlen, A. B., McKelley, R. A., Suizzo, M.-A., & Scaringi, V. (2008). Predictors of relationship satisfaction, psychological well-being, and life satisfaction among stay-at-home fathers. *Psychology of Men & Masculinity, 9*(1), 17–28.

Rochlen, A. B., Suizzo, M.-A., McKelley, R. A., & Scaringi, V. (2008). "I'm just providing for my family": A qualitative study of stay-at-home fathers. *Psychology of Men and Masculinity, 9*, 193–206.

Rochlen, A. B., Whilde, M. R., & Hoyer, W. D. (2005). The Real Men, Real Depression Campaign: Overview, theoretical implications, and research considerations. *Psychology of Men and Masculinity, 6*, 186–194.

Rochlen, A. B., Whilde, M. R., & Hoyer, W. D. (2005). The Real Men. Real Depression Campaign: Overview, Theoretical Implications, and Research Considerations. *Psychology of Men & Masculinity, 6*(3), 186–194. doi:10.1037/1524–9220.6.3.186

Rochlin, C. (1982). The heterosexual questionnaire. *Changing Men, 13*, 1.

Rogers, B. K., Sperry, H. A., & Levant, R. F. (2015). Masculinities among African American men: An intersectional perspective. *Psychology of Men & Masculinity, 16*(4), 416–425. doi:10.1037/a0039082

Rogers, C. R. (1957). The necessary and sufficient conditions of therapeutic personality change. *Journal of Consulting Psychology, 21*, 95–103.

Rosenberg, A., Gates, A., Richmond, K., & Sinno, S. (2017). It's Not a Joke: Masculinity Ideology and Homophobic Language. *Psychology of Men & Masculinity, 18*, 293–300. doi:10.1037/men0000063

Rosenberg, R. S. & Kosslyn, S. M. (2014). *Abnormal psychology* (2nd ed.). New York: Worth.

Rosenblum, K. E. & Travis, T. C. (2003). Framework essay: experiencing difference. In K. E. Rosenblum, & T. C. Travis (Eds.), *The meaning of difference: American constructions of race, sex and gender, social class, and sexual orientation* (3rd ed., pp. 182–202). Boston: McGraw-Hill.

Rosenblum, L. A. (1987). The study of masculinity/femininity from a comparative developmental perspective. In J. M. Reinisch, L. A. Rosenblum, & S. A. Sanders (Eds.), *Masculinity/femininity: Basic perspectives*. New York: Oxford University Press.

Rosenkoetter, L. I., Rosenkoetter, S. E., Osretich, R. A., & Acock, A. C. (2004). Mitigating the harmful effects of violent television. *Journal of Applied Developmental Psychology, 25*, 25–47.

Rosenstein, M. J., Steadman, H. J., McAskill, R. L., & Manderscheid, R. W. (1987). *Characteristics of admissions to Veterans Administrations medical center psychiatric inpatient services, United States, 1980.* Rockville, MD: Department of Health and Human Services.

Rosin, H., & Edsall, T. B. (1998, July 15). Religious right targets homosexuality: Ad, fund-raising drive coordinated. *The Washington Post*, pp. A1, A13.

Rospenda, K. M., Richman, J. A., & Shannon, C. A. (2009). Prevalence and mental health correlates of harassment and discrimination in the workplace: Results from a national study. *Journal of Interpersonal Violence, 24*(5), 819–843.

Rothgerber, H. (2013). Real men don't eat (vegetable) quiche: Masculinity and the justification of meat consumption. *Psychology of Men & Masculinity, 14*(4), 363–375. doi:10.1037/a0030379

Rotundo, E. A. (1993). *American manhood: Transformations in masculinity from the revolution to the modern era*. NY: Basic Books.

Rowlands, A. V., Pilgrim, E. L., & Eston, R. G. (2008). Patterns of habitual activity across weekdays and weekend days in 9–11-year-old children. *Preventive Medicine: An International Journal Devoted to Practice and Theory, 46*(4), 317–324.

Royner, S. (1992, February 4). What men won't tell. *Washington Post Health*, p. 10.

Ruble, D. N., & Martin, C. L. (1998). Gender Development. In W. Damon & N. Eisenberg (Eds.), *Handbook of Child Psychology* (Vol. 5th, pp. 933–1016). NY: John Wiley & Sons.

Rudman, L. A. & Glick, P. (2001). Prescriptive gender stereotypes and backlash toward agentic women. *Journal of Social Issues, 57* (4), 743–762.

Rudman, L. A., & Phelan, J. E. (2007). The interpersonal power of feminism: Is feminism good for romantic relationships? *Sex Roles, 57*(11–12), 787–799.

Rutherford, A., & Granek, L. (2010). Emergence and development of the psychology of women. In J. C. Chrisler & D. R. McCreary (Eds.), *Handbook of gender research in psychology, Vol 1: Gender research in general and experimental psychology.* (pp. 19–41). New York, NY, US: Springer Science + Business Media.

Ruxton, S. (Ed., 2004). *Gender equality and men: Learning from practice.* Oxford, UK: Oxfam.

Ryan, C. L., & Bauman, K. (2016). *Educational Attainment in the United States: 2015.* Retrieved from Washington, DC: https://www.census.gov/content/dam/Census/library/publications/2016/demo/p20-578.pdf

Rybarczyk, B. (1994). Diversity among American men: The impact of aging, ethnicity and race. In C. T. Kilmartin, *The masculine self.* New York: Macmillan.

Sabina, C., Wolak, J., & Finkelhor, D. (2008). The nature and dynamics of internet pornography exposure for youth. *CyberPsychology and Behavior, 11,* 691–693. doi:10.1089/cpb.2007.0179

Sadker, D. (2000, July 31). Gender games. *The Washington Post,* A19.

Sadker, M., & Sadker, D. (1985). Sexism in the classroom of the '80s. *Psychology Today, 3,* 54–57.

Sadler, A. G., Booth, B. M., Cook, B. L., & Doebbeling, B. N. (2003). Factors associated with women's risk of rape in the military environment. American Journal of Industrial Medicine, 43, 262–273.

Saloner, R., & Cysique, L. A. (2017). HIV-associated neurocognitive disorders: A global perspective. *Journal of the International Neuropsychological Society, 23*(9–10), 860–869.

Sanabria, S. (2014). Affirmative therapy with sexual minority men. In M. Englar-Carlson, M. P. Evans, & T. Duffey (Eds., 2014), *A counselor's guide to working with men.* Alexandria, VA: American Counseling Association.

Sánchez, F. J. (2016). Masculinity issues among gay, bisexual, and transgender men. In Y. J. Wong, S. R. Wester, Y. J. Wong, & S. R. Wester (Eds.), *APA handbook of men and masculinities.* (pp. 339–356). Washington, DC, US: American Psychological Association.

Sánchez, F. J., Bocklandt, S., & Vilain, E. (2009). Gender role conflict, interest in casual sex, and relationship satisfaction among gay men. *Psychology of Men & Masculinity, 10*(3), 237–243. doi:10.1037/a0016325.supp (Supplemental)

Sanchez, F. J., Greenberg, S. T., Liu, W. M., & Vilain, E. (2009). Reported effects of masculine ideals on gay men. *Psychology of Men and Masculinity, 10,* 73–87.

Sand, M. S., Fisher, W., Rosen, R., Heiman, J., & Eardley, I. (2008). Erectile dysfunction and constructs of masculinity and quality of life in the multinational Men's Attitudes to Life Events and Sexuality (MALES) study. *Journal of Sexual Medicine, 5*(3), 583–594. doi:10.1111/j.1743–6109.2007.00720.x

Sanday, P. R. (1981). The socio-cultural context of rape: A cross-cultural study. *Journal of Social Issues, 37,* 5–27.

Sanday, P. R. (1996). *A woman scorned: Acquaintance rape on trial.* New York: Doubleday.

Sanday, P. R. (2007). *Fraternity gang rape: Sex, brotherhood, and privilege on campus.* New York: New York University Press.

Sandberg, L. (2013). Just feeling a naked body close to you: Men, sexuality and intimacy in later life. *Sexualities, 16*(3–4), 261–282. doi:10.1177/1363460713481726

Santelli, J., Ott, M. A., Lyon, M., Rogers, J., Summers, D., & Schleifer, R. (2006). Abstinence and abstinence-only education: A review of US policies and programs. *Journal of Adolescent Health, 38,* 72–81.

Sapolsky, R. M. (1997). The trouble with testosterone: Will boys just be boys? In R. M. Sapolsky, *The trouble with testosterone and other essays on the biology of the human predicament* (pp. 147–159). New York: Touchstone.

SAPRO (2012). Department of Defense annual report on sexual assault in the military, fiscal year 2012: Volume 1. Retrieved June 3, 2014 from http://www.sapr.mil/public/docs/reports/FY12_DoD_SAPRO_Annual_Report_on_Sexual_Assault-VOLUME_ONE.pdf.

Sattel, J. (1998). Men, inexpressiveness, and power. In B. M. Clinchy & J. K. Norem (Eds.), *The gender and psychology reader* (pp. 498–504). New York: New York University Press.

Saucier, D., & Ehresman, C. (2010). The physiology of sex differences. In J. C. Chrisler & D. R. McCreary (Eds.), *Handbook of gender research in psychology, Vol 1: Gender research in general and experimental psychology.* (pp. 215–233). NY: Springer Science + Business Media.

Savin-Williams, R. C. (1998). *"...and then I became gay"*. NY: Routledge.

Savin-Williams, R. C. (2005). *The New Gay Teenager.* Cambridge, MA: Harvard University press.

Savin-Williams, R. C., & Vrangalova, Z. (2013). Mostly heterosexual as a distinct sexual orientation group: A systematic review of the empirical evidence. *Developmental Review, 33*(1), 58–88.

Sax, L. (2009). *Boys Adrift: The Five Factors Driving the Growing Epidemic of Unmotivated Boys and Underachieving Young Men.* New York: Basic Books.

Scarborough, R. (2013). Victims of military sexual assault are mostly men; Women are more likely to speak up. The Washington Times, Retrieved August 26, 2013 from http://www.washingtontimes.com/news/2013/may/20/victims-of-sex-assaults-in-military-are-mostly-sil/.

Scarce, M. (1997a). *Male on male rape: The hidden toll of stigma and shame.* New York: Plenum.

Scarce, M. (1997b). Same-sex rape of male college students. *Jounal of American College Health, 45,* 171–173.

Schein, V. E. (2001). A global look at psychological barriers to women's progress in management. *Journal of Social Issues, 57* (4), 675–688.

Schmitt, D. P. (2005). Fundamentals of human mating strategies. In D. M. Buss (Ed.), *Handbook of Evolutionary Psychology* (pp. 255–291). Hoboken, NJ: Wiley.

Schmitt, D. P. a. m. o. t. I. S. D. P., . (2003). Universal sex differences in the desire for sexual variety: Tests from 52 nations, 6 continents, and 13 Islands. *Journal of Personality and Social Psychology, 85,* 85–104. doi:10.1037/0022-3514.85.1.85

Schwartz, J. (2008). Gender differences in drunk driving prevalence rates and trends: A 20-year assessment using multiple sources of evidence. *Addictive Behaviors, 33,* 1217–1222.

Schwartz, J. P., McDermott, R. C., & Martino-Harms, J. W. (2016). Men's sexism: Causes, correlates, and trends in research. In Y. J. Wong, S. R. Wester, Y. J. Wong, & S. R. Wester (Eds.), *APA handbook of men and masculinities.* (pp. 483–501). Washington, DC, US: American Psychological Association.

Schwartz, P. (1994). *Love between equals: How peer marriage really works.* New York: Free Press.

Schwarz, A. (2007, September 15). Silence on concussions raises risk of injury. Retrieved June 2, 2014 from http://www.nytimes.com/2007/09/15/sports/football/15concussions.html?pagewanted=all&_r=0.

Seligman, M. E. P. (1990a). Attributional style and depression. Paper presented at the annual meeting of the Eastern Psychological Association, Philadelphia, PA.

Seligman, M. E. P. (1990b). *Learned optimism: How to change your mind and your life.* New York: Simon & Schuster.

Serwer, A., & Baker, K. J. M. (2015). How Men's Rights Leader Paul Elam Turned Being A Deadbeat Dad Into A Moneymaking Movement. *Buzzfeed*.

Sexual Assault Prevention and Response Office. (2018). *Fiscal Year 2017 Annual Report on Sexual Assault in the Military.* Retrieved from Washington, D.C.: http://sapr.mil/public/docs/reports/FY17_Annual/FY17_Annual_Report_Fact_Sheet.pdf

Shabsigh, R., Fishman, I, & Scott, F. (1988). Evaluation of erectile impotence. *Urology, 32,* 83–90.

Shaeer, O. (2013). The Global Online Sexuality Survey (GOSS): The United States of America in 2011 Chapter III—Premature ejaculation among English-speaking male internet users. *Journal of Sexual Medicine, 10*(7), 1882–1888.

Shanahan, J., & Morgan, M. (1999). *Television and its viewers: Cultivation theory and research.* Cambridge: Cambridge University Press.

Shangani, S., Escudero, D., Kirwa, K., Harrison, A., Marshall, B., & Operario, D. (2017). Effectiveness of peer-led interventions to increase HIV testing among men who have sex with men: A systematic review and meta-analysis. *AIDS Care, 29*(8), 1003–1013. doi:10.1080/09540121.2017.1282105

Shankar, P. R., Fields, S. K., Collins, C. L., Dick, R. W., & Comstock, D. (2007). Epidemiology of high school and collegiate football injuries in the United States, 2005–2006. *American Journal of Sports Medicine, 35,* 1295–1303.

Shanker, T. (2013, July 8). For Navy recruits, basic training now targets sexual assault. *The New York Times,* A1.

Shannon, C. A., Rospenda, K. M., & Richman, J. A. (2007). Workplace harassment patterning, gender, and utilization of professional services: Findings from a US national study. *Social Science & Medicine, 64*(6), 1178–1191.

Shannon, J. D., Cabrera, N. J., Tamis-LeMonda, C., & Lamb, M. E. (2009). Who stays and who leaves? Father accessibility across children's first 5 years. *Parenting: Science and Practice, 9*(1–2), 78–100.

Sharockman, A. (2014). What pay gap? Young women out-earn men in cities, conservative pundit claims. Retrieved from http://www.politifact.com/punditfact/statements/2014/apr/09/genevieve-wood/what-pay-gap-young-women-out-earn-men-cities-gop-p/

Shaver, P. R., Segev, M., & Mikulincer, M. (2011). A behavioral systems perspective on power and aggression. In P. R. Shaver & M. Mikulincer (Eds.), *Human aggression and violence: Causes, manifestations, and consequences.* Washington, DC: American Psychological Association.

Shearer, C. L., Hosterman, S. J., Gillen, M. M., & Lefkowitz, E. S. (2005). Are traditional gender role attitudes associated with risky sexual behaviors and condom-related beliefs? *Sex Roles, 52,* 311–324.

Sheehy, G. (1976). *Passages.* New York: Dutton.

Shen-Miller, D., & Smiler, A. P. (2015). Men in female-dominated vocations: A rationale for academic study and introduction to the special issue. *Sex Roles, 72*(7–8), 269–276. doi:10.1007/s11199-015-0471-3

Shepard, S. J., Nicpon, M. F., Haley, J. T., Lind, M., & Liu, W. M. (2011). Masculine norms, school attitudes, and psychosocial adjustment among gifted boys. *Psychology of Men & Masculinity, 12*(2), 181–187. doi:10.1037/a0019945

Shields, A. E., Fortun, M., Hammonds, E. M., King, P. A., Lerman, C., Rapp, R., & Sullivan, P. F. (2005). The use of race variables in genetic studies of complex traits and the goal of reducing health disparities: A transdisciplinary perspective. *American Psychologist, 60*, 77–103.

Shields, S. A. (2008). Gender: An intersectionality perspective. *Sex Roles, 59*(5–6), 301–311. doi:10.1007/s11199-008-9501-8

Shields, S. A. (2013). Gender and Emotion What We Think We Know, What We Need to Know, and Why It Matters. *Psychology of Women Quarterly, 37*(4), 423–435. doi:10.1177/0361684313502312

Shields, S. A., & Dicicco, E. C. (2011). The social psychology of sex and gender: From gender differences to doing gender. *Psychology of Women Quarterly, 35*(3), 491–499. doi:10.1177/0361684311414823

Shilts, R. (1987/2007). *And the Band Played On: Politics, People, and the AIDS Epidemic* (20th Anniversary Edition ed.). NY: St. Martin's Press.

Shorrock, M. P. (2012). The pragmatic case study of Ed - a man who struggled with internet addiction. *Counselling Psychology Review, 27*, 23–35.

Sifneos, P. E. (1972). *Short-term psychotherapy and emotional crisis*. Cambridge, MA: Harvard University Press.

Silverstein, L. B., & Auerbach, C. F. (1999). Deconstructing the essential father. *American Psychologist, 54*(6), 397–407.

Singh, A., & dickey, l. m. (2017). *Affirmative counseling and psychological practice with transgender and gender nonconforming clients*. Washington, DC, US: American Psychological Association.

Sinn, J. S. (1997). The predictive and discriminant validity of masculinity ideology. *Journal of Research in Personality, 31*, 117–135.

Sipe, T. A., Barham, T. L., Johnson, W. D., Joseph, H. A., Tungol-Ashmon, M. L., & O'Leary, A. (2017). Structural interventions in hiv prevention: A taxonomy and descriptive systematic review. *AIDS and Behavior*. doi:10.1007/s10461-017-1965-5

Sisk, C. L. (2006). New insights into the neurobiology of sexual maturation. *Sexual and Relationship Therapy, 21*, 5–14.

Skinner, B. F. (1974). *About behaviorism*. New York: Alfred A. Knopf.

Skovholt, T. M., & Hansen, A. (1980). Men's development: A perspective and some themes. In T. M. Skovholt, P. Schauble, & R. David (Eds.), *Counseling men* (pp. 1–39). Monterey, CA: Brooks/Cole.

Slaatten, H., Anderssen, N., & Hetland, J. (2014). Endorsement of male role norms and gay-related name-calling. *Psychology of Men & Masculinity, 15*(3), 335–345.

Sloane, M., Hanna, J., & Ford, D. (2013, September 3). 'Never, ever give up:' Diana Nyad completes historic Cuba-to-Florida swim. Retrieved from http://www.cnn.com/2013/09/02/world/americas/diana-nyad-cuba-florida-swim/

Smiler, A. P. (2004). Thirty years after gender: Concepts and measures of masculinity. *Sex Roles, 50*, 15–26. doi:10.1023/B:SERS.0000011069.02279.4c

Smiler, A. P. (2006a). Conforming to masculine norms: Evidence for validity among adult men and women. *Sex Roles, 54*, 767–775. doi:10.1007/s11199-006-9045-8

Smiler, A. P. (2006b). Living the image: A quantitative approach to masculinities. *Sex Roles, 55*, 621–632.

Smiler, A. P. (2008). A psychological summary of masculinity: Short, clear, and relevant. *Sex Roles, 59*, 602–604.

Smiler, A. P. (2011). Sexual Strategies Theory: Built for the short term or the long term. *Sex Roles, 64*, 603–612. doi:10.1007/s11199-010-9817-z

Smiler, A. P. (2013). *Challenging Casanova: Beyond the Steroetype of Promiscuous Young Male Sexuality*. San Francisco: Jossey-Bass.

Smiler, A. P. (2014). Resistance is futile? Examining boys who actively challenge masculinity. *Psychology of Men & Masculinity, 15*(3), 256–259. doi:10.1037/a0037286

Smiler, A. P. (2016). *Dating and Sex: A Guide for the 21st Century Teen Boy*. Washington, DC: Magination Press.

Smiler, A. P., & Epstein, M. (2010). Measuring gender: Options and issues. In J. C. Chrisler & D. R. McCreary (Eds.), *Handbook of gender research in psychology, Vol 1: Gender research in general and experimental psychology*. (pp. 133–157). New York, NY, US: Springer Science + Business Media.

Smiler, A. P., & Heasley, R. (2016). Boys' and men's intimate relationships: Friendships and romantic relationships. In Y. J. Wong & S. R. Wester (Eds.), *APA handbook of men and masculinities*. (pp. 569–589). Washington, DC, US: American Psychological Association.

Smiler, A. P., Frankel, L., & Savin-Williams, R. C. (2011). From kissing to coitus? Sex-of-partner differences in the sexual milestone achievement of young men. *Journal of Adolescence, 34*, 727–735.

Smiler, A. P., Kay, G., & Harris, B. (2008). Tightening and loosening masculinity's (k)nots: Masculinity in the Hearst press during the interwar period. *Journal of Men's Studies, 16*, 266–279. doi:10.3149/jms.1603.266

Smiler, A. P., Shewmaker, J. W., & Hearon, B. (2017). From "I Wanna Hold Your Hand" to "Promiscuous": Sexuality in Popular Music Lyrics, 1960–2008. *Sexuality & Culture, 21*, 1083–1105. doi:10.1007/s12119-017-9437-7

Smiler, A. P., Ward, L. M., Caruthers, A., & Merriwether, A. (2005). Pleasure, empowerment, and love: Factors associated with a positive first coitus. *Sexual research and social policy: Journal of NSRC, 2*, 41–55. doi:10.1525/srsp.2005.2.3.41

Smith, D. (2003). Angry thoughts, at risk hearts. *Monitor on Psychology, 34* (3), 46–48.

Smith, L., & Mathews, J. (1997, December 7). In Va., a sobering lesson doesn't sink in: Binge drinking remains common on college campuses, despite recent tragedies. *The Washington Post*, pp. B1, B7.

Snow, M. E., Jacklin, C. N., & Maccoby, E. E. (1981). Birth- order differences in peer sociability at thirty-three months. *Child Development, 52*, 589–595.

Sodomylaws.org (2009). Sodomy laws around the world. Retrieved June 10, 2009 from http://www.sodomylaws.org/index.htm.

Spence, J. T., & Helmreich, R. L. (1978). *Masculinity and femininity: Their psychological dimensions, correlates and antecedents*. Austin, TX: University of Texas Press.

Spence, J. T., Helmreich, R. L., & Holahan, C. K. (1979). Negative and positive components of psychological masculinity and feminity and their relationships to self-reports of neurotic and acting out behaviors. *Journal of Personality and Social Psychology, 37*, 1673–1682.

Spitzer, R. L. (2003). Can some gay men and lesbians change their sexual orientation? 200 participants reporting a change from homosexual to heterosexual orientation. *Archives of Sexual Behavior, 32*(5), 403–417.

Spitzer, R. L. (2012). Spitzer reassesses his 2003 study of reparative therapy of homosexuality. *Archives of Sexual Behavior, 41*(4), 757–757.

Sports Illustrated (2014). Judge Anita Brody denies preliminary approval for NFL concussion settlement. Retrieved June 20, 2014 from http://nfl.si.com/2014/01/14/nfl-concussion-lawsuit-settlement-2/.

Sprecher, S., & Regan, P. C. (2002). Liking some things (in some people) more than others: Partner preferences in romantic relationships and friendships. *Journal of Social and Personal Relationships, 19,* 463–481.

Stander, V. A., Merrill, L. L., Thomsen, C. J., Crouch, J. L., & Milner, J. S. (2008). Premilitary adult sexual assault victimization and perpetration in a Navy recruit sample. *Journal of Interpersonal Violence, 23,* 1636–1652.

Stanistreet, D., Bambra, C., & Scott-Samuel, A. (2005). Is patriarchy the source of men's higher mortality? *Journal of Epidemiological Community Health, 59,* 873–876.

Stapely, J. C., & Haviland, J. M. (1989). Beyond depression: Gender differences in normal adolescents' emotional experiences. *Sex Roles, 20,* 295–308.

Starrels, M. E. (1992). Attitude similarity between mothers and children regarding maternal employment. *Journal of Marriage and the Family, 54,* 91–103.

Stearns, P. N. (1990). *Be a man! Males in modern society.* New York: Holmes and Meier.

Stearns, P. N. (1991). Fatherhood in historical perspective: The role of social change. In F. W. Bozett & S. M. H. Hanson (Eds.), *Fatherhood and families in cultural context* (pp. 28–52). New York: Springer.

Stearns, P. N. (1994). *American cool: Constructing a twentieth-century emotional style.* New York, NY, USA: New York University Press.

Steeves, V. (2014). *Young Canadians in a Wired World, Phase III: Sexuality and Romantic Relationships in the Digitial Age.* Retrieved from Ottawa: http://mediasmarts.ca/sites/default/files/pdfs/publication-report/full/YCWWIII_Sexuality_Romantic_Relationships_Digital_Age_FullReport.pdf

Stein, J. H., & Reiser, L. W. (1994). A study of white middle-class adolescent boys' responses to "semenarche" (the first ejaculation). *Journal of Youth and Adolescence, 23,* 373–384.

Stein, R. (2005, June 20). Report shows drop in baby boys. *The Washington Post,* p. A5.

Steinberg, M., & Diekman, A. B. (2016). The double-edged sword of stereotypes of men. In Y. J. Wong, S. R. Wester, Y. J. Wong, & S. R. Wester (Eds.), *APA handbook of men and masculinities.* (pp. 433–456). Washington, DC, US: American Psychological Association.

Stern, G. (2014). Personal communication.

Stevenson, M. R., & Black, K. N. (1988). Paternal absence and sex-role development: A meta-analysis. *Child Development, 59,* 793–814.

Stewart, A. J., & Newton, N. J. (2010). Gender, adult development, and aging. In J. C. Chrisler & D. R. McCreary (Eds.), *Handbook of gender research in psychology, Vol 1: Gender research in general and experimental psychology.* (pp. 559–580). New York, NY, US: Springer Science + Business Media.

Stillion, J. M. (1995). Premature death among males. In D. Sabo & D. F. Gordon (Eds.), *Men's health and illness: Gender, power, and the body* (pp. 46–67). Thousand Oaks, CA: Sage.

Stillion, J. M., & McDowell, E. E. (1996). *Suicide across the life span* (2nd ed.). Washington, DC: Taylor and Francis.

Stith, S. M. & McMonigle, C. L. (2009). Risk factors associated with intimate partner violence. In D.J. Whitaker & J. R. Lutzker (Eds.). *Preventing partner violence: Research and evidence-based strategies.* Washington, DC: American Psychological Association.

Stockdale, M. S. & Bhattacharya, G. (2009). Sexual harassment and the glass ceiling. In M. Barreto, M. K. Ryan, & M. T. Schmitt (Eds.), *The glass ceiling in the 21st Century: Understanding barriers to gender equality* (pp. 171–199). Washington, DC: American Psychological Association.

Storey, A. E., Walsh, C. J., Quinton, R. L., & Wynne-Edwards, K. E. (2000). Hormonal correlates of paternal responsiveness in new and expectant fathers. *Evolution and human behavior, 21 (2)*, 79–95.

Strasburger, V. C., Wilson, B. J., & Jordan, A. B. (2014). *Children, adolescents, and the media* (3rd ed.). Thousand Oaks, CA: Sage.

Strate, L. (1992). Beer commercials: A manual on masculinity. In S. Craig (Ed.), *Men, masculinity and the media.* (pp. 78–92). Newbury Park, CA, USA: Sage.

Straus, M. A. (1990). *Physical violence in American families: Risk factors and adaptations to violence in 8,145 families.* New Brunswick, NJ: Transaction.

Street, S., Kimmel, E. B., & Kromrey, J. D. (1995). Revisiting university student gender role perceptions. *Sex Roles, 33,* 183–201.

Strokoff, J., Halford, T. C., & Owen, J. (2016). Men and psychotherapy. In Y. J. Wong, S. R. Wester, Y. J. Wong, & S. R. Wester (Eds.), *APA handbook of men and masculinities.* (pp. 753–774). Washington, DC, US: American Psychological Association.

Strong, B., DeVault, C., Sayad, B. W., & Yarber, W. L. (2007). *Human sexuality: Diversity in contemporary America* (6th ed.). Boston: McGraw-Hill.

Strong, E. K., Jr. (1943). *Vocational interests of men and women*: Stanford University Press.

Su, R., Rounds, J., & Armstrong, P. I. (2009). Men and things, women and people: A meta-analysis of sex differences in interests. *Psychological Bulletin, 135*(6), 859–884. doi:10.1037/a0017364

Sue, David, Sue, Derald, Sue, Diane, and Sue, S. (2014). *Essentials of Understanding abnormal behavior* (2nd ed.) Belmont, CA: Cengage.

Sugarman, D. B., & Hotaling, G. T. (1989). Violent men in intimate relationships: An analysis of risk markers. *Journal of Applied Social Psychology, 19,* 1034–1048.

Sutton, K. S., Stratton, N., Pytyck, J., Kolla, N. J., & Cantor, J. M. (2015). Patient characteristics by type of hypersexuality referral: A quantitative chart review of 115 consecutive male cases. *Journal of Sex & Marital Therapy, 41*(6), 563–580. doi:10.1080/0092623X.2014.935539

Sutton, M. J., Brown, J. D., Wilson, K. M., & Klein, J. D. (2002). Shaking the tree of knowledge for forbidden fruit: Where adolescents learn about sexuality and contraception. In J. D. Brown, J. R. Steele, & K. Walsh-Childers (Eds.), *Sexual teens, sexual media: Investigating media's influence on adolescent sexuality* (pp. 25–55). Mahwah, NJ: Lawrence Erlbaum.

Swain, S. O. (1992). Men's friendships with women: Intimacy, sexual boundaries, and the informant role. In P. M. Nardi (Ed.), *Men's friendships* (pp. 153–171). Newbury Park, CA: Sage.

Symons, D. (1987). An evolutionary approach. In J. H. Geer & W. T. O'Donahue (Eds.), *Theories of human sexuality* (pp. 91–125). New York: Plenum.

Szymanski, D. M., & Carr, E. R. (2008). The roles of gender role conflict and internalized heterosexism in gay and bisexual men's psychological distress: Testing two mediation models. *Psychology of Men & Masculinity, 9*(1), 40–54. doi:10.1037/1524–9220.9.1.40

Szymanski, D. M., Kashubeck-West, S., & Meyer, J. (2008b). Internalized heterosexism: Measurement, psychosocial correlates, and research directions. *The Counseling Psychologist, 36,* 525–574. doi: 10.1177/0011000007309489.

T. J. Goodrich (Eds). *Feminist family therapy: Empowerment in social*

Tangri, S., Burt, M. R., & Johnson, L. B. (1982). Sexual harassment at work: Three explanatory models. *Journal of Social Issues, 38,* 33–54.

Tannen, D. (1990). *You Just Don't Understand: Women and Men in Conversation.* NY: William Morrow & Co.

Taris, T. W., van Beek, I., & Schaufeli, W. B. (2012). Demographic and occupational correlates of workaholism. *Psychological Reports, 110*(2), 547–554.

Tavris, C. & Aronson, E. (2008). Mistakes were made, but not by me: Why we justify foolish beliefs, bad decisions, and hurtful acts. New York: Houghton Mifflin Harcourt.

Tavris, C. & Wade, C. (2001). Psychology in perspective (3rd ed.). Upper Saddle River, NJ: Prentice-Hall.

Tavris, C. (1989). *Anger: The misunderstood emotion* (rev. ed.). New York: Touchstone.

Tavris, C. (1992). *The mismeasure of woman*. New York: Simon and Schuster.

Tavris, C., & Wade, C. (2008). *Invitation to psychology* (4th ed.). Upper Saddle River, NJ: Pearson Prentice-Hall.

Tendulkar, S. A., Hamilton, R. C., Chu, C., Arsenault, L., Duffy, K., Huynh, V., ... Friedman, E. (2012). Investigating the myth of the 'model minority': A participatory community health assessment of Chinese and Vietnamese adults. *Journal of Immigrant and Minority Health, 14*(5), 850–857. doi:10.1007/s10903–011–9517–y

Tenenbaum, H. R., & Leaper, C. (2002). Are parents' gender schemas related to their children's gender-related cognitions? A meta-analysis. *Child Development, 38,* 615–630. doi:10.1037/0012–1649.38.4.615

Tenenbaum, H. R., & Leaper, C. (2003). Parent-child conversations about science: The socialization of gender inequities? *Developmental Psychology, 39,* 34–47. doi:10.1037/0012–1649.39.1.34

Tenenbaum, H. R., Snow, C. E., Roach, K. A., & Kurland, B. (2005). Talking and reading science: Longitudinal data on sex differences in mother-child conversations in low-income families. *Journal of Applied Developmental Psychology, 26,* 1–19. doi:10.1016/j.appdev.2004.10.004

Terman, L. M., & Miles, C. C. (1936). *Sex and personality: Studies in masculinity and femininity.* NY, NY, USA: McGraw-Hill.

Theodore, H., & Lloyd, B. F. (2000). Age and gender role conflict: A cross-sectional study of Australian men. *Sex Roles, 42,* 1027–1042.

Thomas, A., & Chess, S. (1977). *Temperament and Development.* NY, NY, USA: Brunner/Mazel Publishers.

Thompson, E. H., & Pleck, J. H. (1995). Masculinity ideologies: A review of research instrumentation on men and masculinities. In R. F. Levant & W. S. Pollack (Eds.), *A new psychology of men* (pp. 129–163). NY: Basic Books.

Thompson, E. H., Jr., & Bennett, K. M. (2015). Measurement of masculinity ideologies: A (critical) review. *Psychology of Men & Masculinity, 16*(2), 115–133. doi:10.1037/a0038609

Thorne, B. & Luria, Z. (1986). Sexuality and gender in children's daily worlds. *Social Problems, 33,* 176–190).

Thorne, B. (1993). *Gender play: GIrls and boys in school.* New Brunswick, NJ: Rutgers university press.

Thorne, B. (2009). Girls and boys together ... but mostly apart: Gender arrangements in elementary schools. In V. Taylor, N. Whittier, & L. J. Rupp (Eds.), *Feminist frontiers* (8th ed., pp. 176–186). Boston: McGraw-Hill.

Thornhill, R. & Palmer, C. T. (2000). *A natural history of rape: Biological bases of sexual coercion.* Cambridge, MA: MIT Press.

Thornhill, R., & Palmer, C. T. (2000). *A natural history of rape: biological bases of sexual coercion.* Cambridge, MA, USA: MIT press.

Thurnell-Read, T. (2012). What happens on tour: The premarital stag tour, homosocial bonding, and male friendship. *Men and Masculinities, 15*(3), 249–270. doi:10.1177/1097184X12448465

Timmers, M., Fischer, A., & Manstead, A. S. R. (1998). Gender differences in motives for regulating closeness. *Personality and Social Psychology Bulletin, 24,* 974–985.

Tinkler, J. E. (2013). How do sexual harassment policies shape gender beliefs? An exploration of the moderating effects of norm adherence and gender. *Social Science Research, 42*(5), 1269–1283.

Toby, J. (1966). Violence and the masculine mystique: Some qualitative data. *Annals of the American Academy of Political and Social Science, 36,* 19–27.

Toch, H. (1992). *Violent men: An inquiry into the psychology of violence.* Washington, DC: American Psychological Association.

Tooby, J., & Cosmides, L. (2005). Conceptual foundations of evolutionary psychology. In D. M. Buss (Ed.), *Handbook of Evolutionary Psychology* (pp. 5–67). Hoboken, NJ: Wiley.

Trafford, A. (1996, February 20). Boxing's biggest risk. *Washington Post Health,* p. 14.

Tschann, J. (1988). Self-disclosure in adult friendship: Gender and marital status differences. *Journal of Social and Personal Relationships, 5,* 65–81.

Turner, J. S. (2011). Sex and the spectacle of music videos: An examination of the portrayal of race and sexuality in music videos. *Sex Roles, 64,* 173–191.

Twenge, J. M. (1997a). Attitudes toward women, 1970–1995: A meta-analysis. *Psychology of Women Quarterly, 21*(1), 35–51. doi:10.1111/j.1471–6402.1997.tb00099.x

Twenge, J. M. (1997b). Changes in masculine and feminine traits over time: A meta-analysis. *Sex Roles, 36,* 305–325. doi:10.1007/BF02766650

Tyson, P. (1986). Male gender identity: Early developmental roots. *The Psychoanalytic Review, 73,* 405–426.

Unger, R. (1979). Toward a redefinition of sex and gender. *American Psychologist, 34,* 1085–1094. doi:10.1037/0003–066X.34.11.1085

United States Department of Justice (2008). Criminal victimization in the United States, 2006 statistical tables. Retrieved May 7, 2009, from http://www.ojp.usdoj.gov/bjs.

United States Department of Justice, Office of Justice Programs (OJP) (2008). Most victims and perpetrators of homicides are males. Retrieved July 8, 2009 from ojp.usdoj.gov/bjs/homicide/gender.

United States Department of Labor, Bureau of Labor Statistics (2005). Families with own children: Employment status of parents by age of youngest child and family type, 2003–04 annual averages. www.bls.gov.

United States General Accounting Office (2004). Defense of Marriage Act: Update to prior report [GAO-04-353R]. Retrieved June 10, 2009 from www.gao.gov /new.items/d04353r.pdf.

Uy, P. J., Massoth, N. A., & Gottdiener, W. H. (2014). Rethinking male drinking: Traditional masculine ideologies, gender-role conflict, and drinking motives. *Psychology of Men & Masculinity, 15*(2), 121–128. doi:10.1037/a0032239

Van Evra, J. (1998). *Television and Child Development.* Mahwah, NJ: Lawrence Erlbaum.

van Hertum, A. (1992, January 17). WHO removes homosexuality from its list of disorders. *The Washington Blade,* 23 (3), pp. 1, 12.

van Mourik, K., Crone, M. R., de Wolff, M. S., & Reis, R. (2017). Parent training programs for ethnic minorities: A meta-analysis of adaptations and effect. *Prevention Science, 18*(1), 95–105. doi:10.1007/s11121–016–0733–5

VanderDrift, L. E., Wilson, J. E., & Agnew, C. R. (2013). On the benefits of valuing being friends for nonmarital romantic partners. *Journal of Social and Personal Relationships, 30*(1), 115–131. doi:10.1177/0265407512453009

Vásquez, D. A., Newman, J. L., Frey, L. L., Caze, T. J., Friedman, A. N., & Meek, W. D. (2014). Relational Health and Masculine Gender Role Conflict in the Friendships and Community Relationships of Bisexual, Gay, and Straight Men. *Journal of LGBT Issues in Counseling, 8,* 124–145. doi:10.1080/15538605.2014.895662

Vernacchio, A. (2014). *For Goodness Sex: Changing the Way We Talk to Teens About Sexuality, Values, and Health*. NY: HarperCollins.

Vigil, J. M. (2007). Asymmetries in the friendship preferences and social styles of men and women. *Human Nature, 18,* 143–161. doi:10.1007/s12110–007–9003–3

Vilain, E., Achermann, J. C., Eugster, E. A., Harley, V. R., Morel, Y., Wilson, J. D., & Hiort, O. (2007). We used to call them hermaphrodites. *Genetics in Medicine, 9,* 65–66.

Vincent, W., Gordon, D. M., Campbell, C., Ward, N. L., Albritton, T., & Kershaw, T. (2016). Adherence to traditionally masculine norms and condom-related beliefs: Emphasis on African American and Hispanic men. *Psychology of Men & Masculinity, 17*(1), 42–53. doi:10.1037/a0039455

Vokey, M., Tefft, B., & Tysiaczny, C. (2013). An analysis of hyper-masculinity in magazine advertisements. *Sex Roles, 68,* 562–576. doi:10.1007/s11199–013–0268–1

Voyer, D., & Voyer, S. D. (2014). Gender differences in scholastic achievement: A meta-analysis. *Psychological Bulletin.* doi:10.1037/a0036620

Wade, C. & Tavris, C. (2008). *Invitation to psychology* (4th ed.). Upper Saddle River, NJ: Prentice-Hall.

Wade, J. C. (1998). Male reference group identity dependence: A theory of male identity. *Counseling Psychologist, 26,* 349–383. doi:10.1177/0011000098263001

Wade, J. C. (2008). Masculinity ideology, male reference group identity dependence, and African American men's health-related attitudes and behaviors. *Psychology of Men & Masculinity, 9*(1), 5–16. doi:10.1037/1524–9220.9.1.5

Wade, J. C. (2008a). Masculinity ideology, male reference group identity dependence, and African American men's health related attitudes and behaviors. *Psychology of Men and Masculinity, 9,* 5–16.

Wade, J. C. (2008a). Tradtional masculinity and African American men's health related attitudes and behaviors. *American Journal of Men's Health, 3,* 165–172.

Wade, J. C. (2015). Measurement of masculinity ideologies: A commentary. *Psychology of Men & Masculinity, 16*(2), 137–140. doi:10.1037/a0038988

Wade, J. C., & Brittan-Powell, C. (2001). Men's attitudes toward race and gender equity: The importance of masculinity ideology, gender-related traits, and reference group identity dependence. *Psychology of Men & Masculinity, 2*(1), 42–50. doi:10.1037/1524–9220.2.1.42

Wade, J. C., & Donis, E. (2007). Masculinity ideology, male identity, and romantic relationship quality among heterosexual and gay men. *Sex Roles, 57*(9–10), 775–786. doi:10.1007/s11199–007–9303–4

Wagner, E. J. (1992). *Sexual harassment in the workplace: How to prevent, investigate, and resolve problems in your organization*. New York: AMACOM.

Walker, D. F., Tokar, D. M., & Fischer, A. R. (2000). What are eight popular masculinity related instruments measuring? Underlying dimensions and their relations to psychosexuality. *Psychology of Men and Masculinity, 1,* 98–108. doi:10.1037/1524–9220.1.2.98

Ward, L. M. (1995). Talking about sex: Common themes about sexuality in the prime-time television programs children and adolescents view most. *Journal of Youth and Adolescence, 24*, 595–615.

Ward, L. M., & Friedman, K. (2006). Using TV as a guide: Associations between television viewing and adolescents' sexual attitudes and behavior. *Journal of Research on Adolescence, 16*, 133–156.

Ward, L. M., Seabrook, R., Giaccardi, S., & Zuo, A. (2016). Television uses and effects in emerging adulthood. In J. J. Arnett & J. J. Arnett (Eds.), *The Oxford handbook of emerging adulthood*. (pp. 364–381). New York, NY, US: Oxford University Press.

Wardle, J. Haase, A. M., Steptoe, A., Nillapun, M., Jonwutiwes, K. & Bellisle, F. (2004). Gender differences in food choice: The contribution of healthy beliefs and dieting. *Annals of Behavioral Medicine, 27*, 107–116.

Way, N. (2004). Intimacy, desire, and distrust in the friendships of adolescent boys. In N. Way & J. Y. Chu (Eds.), *Adolescent boys: Exploring diverse cultures of boyhood* (pp. 167–196). NY: New York University press.

Way, N. (2011). *Deep Secrets: Boys' Friendships and the Crisis of Connection*. Cambridge, MA: Harvard University Press.

Way, N., Cressen, J., Bodian, S., Preston, J., Nelson, J., & Hughes, D. (2014). 'It might be nice to be a girl... Then you wouldn't have to be emotionless': Boys' resistance to norms of masculinity during adolescence. *Psychology of Men & Masculinity, 15*(3), 241–252. doi:10.1037/a0037262

Webster, D. W. & Vernick, J. S. (2013). Introduction. In D. W. Webster & J. S. Vernick (Eds.), *Reducing gun violence in America: Informing policy with evidence and analysis*. Baltimore, MD: Johns Hopkins University Press.

Wechsler, H., Kuh, G., & Davenport, A. E. (1996). Fraternities, sororities, and binge drinking: Results from a national study of American colleges. *National Association of Student Personnel Administrators, 33*, 831–847.

Weinberg, N. Z., Rahdert, E., Colliver, J. D., & Glantz, M. D. (1998). Adolescent substance abuse: A review of the past 10 years. *Journal of the American Academy of Child and Adolescent Psychiatry, 37*, 252–261. doi:10.1097/00004583–199803000–00009

Weinstock, H., Berman, S., & Cates, Jr. (2004). Sexually transmitted diseases among American youth: Incidence and prevalence estimates, 2000. *Perspectives on Sexual and Reproductive Health, 36*, 6–10.

Weir, D. R., Jackson, J. S., & Sonnega, A. (2009). National football League Player Care Foundation study of retired NFL players. Retrieved October 27, 2009 from http://umich.edu/news/Releases/2009/Sep09/FinalReport.pdf.

Wells, B. E., & Twenge, J. M. (2005). Changes in young people's sexual behavior and attitudes, 1943–1999: A cross-temporal meta-analysis. *Review of General Psychology, 9*, 249–261. doi:10.1037/1089–2680.9.3.249

West, B. A., & Naumann, R. B. (2013). Motor Vehicle–Related Deaths — United States, 2005 and 2009. *Mortality and Morbidity Weekly Review, 62 Supplement*, 176–178.

Wester, S. R., Heesacker, M., & Snowden, S. J. (2016). An elephant in the room: Men's emotion from sex differences to social neuroscience. In Y. J. Wong & S. R. Wester (Eds.), *APA handbook of men and masculinities*. (pp. 457–482). Washington, DC, US: American Psychological Association.

Wester, S. R., Pionke, D. R., & Vogel, D. L. (2005). Male Gender Role Conflict, Gay Men, and Same-Sex Romantic Relationships. *Psychology of Men & Masculinity, 6*(3), 195–208.

Wester, S. R., Vogel, D. L., Pressly, P. K., & Heesacker, M. (2002). Sex differences in emotion: A critical review of the literature and implications for counseling psychology. *The Counseling Psychologist, 30*(4), 630–652. doi:10.1177/00100002030004008

Wetherell, M., & Edley, N. (2014). A discursive psychological framework for analyzing men and masculinities. *Psychology of Men & Masculinity, 15*(4), 355–364. doi:10.1037/a0037148

Wexler, D. B. (1999). The broken mirror: A self psychological treatment perspectrive for relationship violence. *Journal of Psychotherapy Practice and Research, 8,* 129–141.

White Ribbon Campaign. (2017). *Annual Report.* Retrieved from Toronto: https://www.whiteribbon.ca/uploads/1/1/3/2/113222347/white_ribbon_annual_report_2017.pdf

Whiting, B. B., & Edwards, C. P. (1988). *Children of different worlds: The formation of social behavior.* Cambridge, MA: Harvard University Press.

Whitman, J. S., Glosoff, H. L., Kocet, M. M., & Tarvydas, V. (2013, 2013, January 16). Ethical issues related to conversion or reparative therapy. *American Counseling Association Newsletter.* Retrieved from https://www.counseling.org/news/updates/2013/01/16/ethical-issues-related-to-conversion-or-reparative-therapy

Whorley, M. R., & Addis, M. E. (2006). Ten years of psychological research on men and masculinity in the United States: Dominant methodological trends. *Sex Roles, 55,* 649–658.

Wienke, C. (2005). Male sexuality, medicalization, and the marketing of Cialis and Levitra. *Sexuality & Culture, 9,* 29–57.

Wight, D. (1994). Boys' thoughts and talk about sex in a working class locality of Glasgow. *The Sociological Review, 42,* 703–737. doi:10.1111/1467–954X.ep9411295764

Wilkie, J. R. (1991). The decline in men's labor force participation and income and the changing structure of family economic support. *Journal of Marriage and the Family, 53,* 111–122.

Williams, C. L. (2015). Crossing over: Interdisciplinary research on 'men who do women's work'. *Sex Roles, 72*(7–8), 390–395. doi:10.1007/s11199–015–0477–x

Williams, J. E., & Best, D. L. (1990). *Sex and psyche: Gender and self viewed cross-culturally.* Newbury Park, CA: Sage.

Williams, J. E., & Best, D. L. (1990a). *Measuring sex stereotypes: A multination study.* Newbury Park, CA: Sage.

Williams, J. E., & Best, D. L. (1990b). *Sex and psyche: Gender and self viewed cross-culturally.* Newbury Park, CA: Sage.

Williams, J. E., Nieto, J., Sanford, C. P., Couper, D. J., & Tyroler, H. A. (2002). The association between trait anger and incident stroke risk: The atherosclerosis risk in communities (ARIC) study. *Stroke, 33* (13), 13–20.

Williams, P. (2008, April 17). Ending the guessing game in concussion recovery. *The Washington Post Extra,* 8.

Williams, R. J. & Ricciardelli, L. A. (1999). *Gender congruence in confirmatory and compensatory drinking. Journal of Psychology, 133,* 323–331.

Williams, W. L. (1992). The relationship between male-male friendship and male-female marriage. In P. M. Nardi (Ed.), *Men's friendships* (pp. 186–200). Newbury Park, CA: Sage.

Willness, C. R., Steel, P., & Lee, K. (2007). A meta-analysis of the antecedents and consequences of workplace sexual harassment. *Personnel Psychology, 60*(1), 127–162.

Wilson, E. O. (1979). *On human nature.* New York: Bantam.

Wilson, G. (2011). Your Brain on Porn Series: Porn Addiction. Retrieved from http://yourbrainonporn.com/your-brain-on-porn-series

Wilson, S. (2009, June 18). President wades into gay issues: Order gives some benefits to partners of federal workers. *The Washington Post*, A1.

Wilson, W. J. (1987). *The truly disadvantaged*. Chicago: University of Chicago Press.

Winstead, B. A., Derlega, V. J., & Wong, P. T. P. (1984). Effects of sex-role orientation on behavioral self-disclosure. *Journal of Research in Personality, 38*, 541–553.

Winter, D. G. (2016). Taming power: Generative historical consciousness. *American Psychologist, 71*(3), 160–174. doi:10.1037/a0039312

Wise, T. N. (1994). Sertraline as a treatment for premature ejaculation. *Journal of Clinical Psychiatry, 55*, 417.

Wiseman, R. (2002). *Queen Bees and Wannabes: Helping Your Daughter Survive Cliques, Gossip, Boyfriends, and Other Realities of Adolescence*. NY: Crown Publishers.

Wiswell, T. E., & Geschke, D. W. (1989). Risks from circumcision during the first month of life compared with those for uncircumcised boys. *Pediatrics, 83*, 1001–1005.

Wong, Y. J., & Horn, A. J. (2016). Enhancing and diversifying research methods in the psychology of men and masculinities. In Y. J. Wong & S. R. Wester (Eds.), *APA handbook of men and masculinities*. (pp. 231–255). Washington, DC, US: American Psychological Association.

Wong, Y. J., & Rochlen, A. N. (2008). Re-envisioning men's emotional lives: Stereotypes, struggles, and strengths. In S. J. Lopez (Ed.), *Positive psychology: Exploring the best in people*. Westport, CT: Greenwood.

Wong, Y. J., & Wester, S. R. (2016). *APA handbook of men and masculinities*. Washington, DC, US: American Psychological Association.

Wong, Y. J., Ho, M.-H. R., Wang, S.-Y., & Miller, I. S. K. (2017). Meta-analyses of the relationship between conformity to masculine norms and mental health-related outcomes. *Journal of Counseling Psychology, 64*(1), 80–93. doi:10.1037/cou0000176

Wong, Y. J., Liu, T., & Klann, E. M. (2017). The intersection of race, ethnicity, and masculinities: Progress, problems, and prospects. In R. F. Levant & Y. J. Wong (Eds.), *The psychology of men and masculinities*. (pp. 261–288). Washington, DC: American Psychological Association.

Wong, Y. J., Pituch, K. A., & Rochlen, A. B. (2006). Men's restrictive emotionality: An investigation of associations with other emotion-related constructs, anxiety, and underlying dimensions. *Psychology of Men & Masculinity, 7*(2), 113–126. doi:10.1037/1524–9220.7.2.113

Wong, Y. J., Steinfeldt, J. A., Speight, Q. L., & Hickman, S. J. (2010). Content analysis of Psychology of Men & Masculinity (2000–2008). *Psychology of Men and Masculinity, 11*, 170–181. doi:10.1037/a0019133

Wood, H., Sasaki, S., Bradley, S. J., Singh, D., Fantus, S., Owen-Anderson, A., . . . Zucker, K. J. (2013). Patterns of referral to a gender identity service for children and adolescents (1976–2011): Age, sex ratio, and sexual orientation. *Journal of Sex & Marital Therapy, 39*(1), 1–6.

Woodhams, C., Lupton, B., & Cowling, M. (2015). The presence of ethnic minority and disabled men in feminised work: Intersectionality, vertical segregation and the glass escalator. *Sex Roles, 72*(7–8), 277–293. doi:10.1007/s11199–014–0427–z

World Health Organization. (2004). *Adolescent Pregnancy: Issues in Adolescent Health and Development*. Retrieved from Department of Child and Adolescent Health and Development, . http://whqlibdoc.who.int/publications/2004/9241591455_eng.pdf

World Health Organization. (nd). Male circumcision for HIV prevention. Retrieved from http://www.who.int/hiv/topics/malecircumcision/en/

Wright, P. J., Tokunaga, R. S., Kraus, A., & Klann, E. (2017). Pornography Consumption and Satisfaction: A Meta-Analysis. *Human Communication Research, 43*, 315–343. doi:10.1111/hcre.12108

Yap, M. B. H., & Jorm, A. F. (2015). Parental factors associated with childhood anxiety, depression, and internalizing problems: A systematic review and meta-analysis. *Journal of Affective Disorders, 175*, 424–440. doi:10.1016/j.jad.2015.01.050

Yap, M. B. H., Pilkington, P. D., Ryan, S. M., & Jorm, A. F. (2014). Parental factors associated with depression and anxiety in young people: A systematic review and meta-analysis. *Journal of Affective Disorders, 156*, 8–23. doi:10.1016/j.jad.2013.11.007

Ybarra, M. L., & Mitchell, K. J. (2004). Youth engaging in online harassment: Associations with caregiver-child relationships, internet use, and personal characteristics. *Journal of Adolescence, 27*, 319–336.

Yodanis, C. L. (2004). Gender inequality, violence against women, and fear: A cross-national test of the feminist theory of violence against women. *Journal of Interpersonal Violence, 19*, 655–675.

Youniss, J., & Haynie, D. L. (1992). Friendship in adolescence. *Developmental and Behavioral Pediatrics, 13*, 59–66.

Zack, M. M. (2013). Health-Related Quality of Life—United States, 2006 and 2010. *Mortality and Morbidity Weekly Review, 62 Supplement*, 105–111.

Zak, D. (2009, March 31). Rallying in the name of the unkindest cut? Sharp rhetoric abounds in circumcision debate. *The Washington Post*, C1, C5.

Zeanah, C. H., Boris, N. W., & Larrieu, J. A. (1997). Infant development and developmental risk: A review of the past 10 years. *Journal of the American Academy of Child & Adolescent Psychiatry, 36*(2), 165–178. doi:10.1097/00004583–199702000–00007

Zeglin, R. J. (2015). Assessing the role of masculinity in the transmission of HIV: A systematic review to inform HIV risk reduction counseling interventions for men who have sex with men. *Archives of Sexual Behavior, 44*(7), 1979–1990. doi:10.1007/s10508–015–0501–9

Zhentao, F., & Fuxi, F. (2006). Development of the Concept of Gender Constancy in Preschoolers. *Acta Psychologica Sinica, 38*(1), 63–69.

Zilbergeld, B. (1996). *The new male sexuality*. NY: Bantam books.

Zinn, H. (2015). *A People's History of the United States: 1492 - present*. NY: HarperCollins.

Zuk, M. (2005). Animal models and gender. In C. B. Brettell and C. F. Sargent (Eds.), *Gender in cross-cultural perspective* (4th ed.). Upper Saddle River, NJ: Prentice-Hall.

Zuo, J. (1997). The effect of men's breadwinner status on their changing gender beliefs. *Sex Roles, 37*, 799–816.

Name Index

A
AASECT, 216
Abrams, D., 254
Acker, S. E., 255
Acocella, J., 276
Acock, A. C., 265
Active Duty Gender Distribution, 278
Adams, H. E., 67
Adams, S., 125, 147, 151, 166
Addis, M. E., 6, 61, 92, 156, 167, 282, 317, 321, 322
Addison, T., 216
Adorno, T., 82
Adriaens, P. R., 200
Agnew, C. R., 172
Akhtar, P. C., 125
Alabas, O. A., 145
Alderdice, F., 180
Ali, L., 169
Allen, D. W., 176
Allen, P. A., 156
Allgeier, A. R., 203
Allgeier, E. R., 203
Allison, J., 246, 249, 251, 266
Alloy, L. B., 276
Alpert, G. P., 266
Amato, P., 191
American Association of Medical Colleges, 227
American Association of Pediatrics, 99, 200
American Bar Association, 227
American Cancer Society, 297, 298
American Psychiatric Association, 26, 126, 211, 213, 275, 301, 308, 309, 312, 315, 316, 317
American Psychological Association, 4, 210, 226, 320
American Society of Plastic Surgeons, 301
Anderson, C. A., 264
Anderson, E., 64, 166, 167, 202
Anderson, E. R., 190
Anderson, K. B., 264
Anderson, K. G., 188
Anderson, R. N., 295
Anderson, T. C., 35
Anderssen, N., 167, 174
Andreassen, C. S., 231
Angier, N., 108, 262
Archer, J., 100, 102, 104, 249, 262
Arciniega, G.M., 35
Arias, E., 249, 259, 282, 286
Armstrong, P. I., 226
Arnett, J. J., 291
Aronson, E., 26, 42, 64
Asch, S. E., 129–130, 267
Ashmore, R. D., 24, 173, 200
Aslaksen, P. M., 145, 148
Astone, N. M., 188
Astrachan, A., 236
Aubrey, J. S., 216
Auerbach, C. F., 185
Aupont, M., 55
Azrael, D., 257, 258

B
Baghurst, T., 301
Baird, L. C., 276

Baker, K. J. M., 70
Bales, R. F., 6, 144
Balswick, J., 158
Bambra, C., 285
Bandura, A., 11, 132–133, 263
Bank, B. J., 170, 176
Banks, C., 130
Banman, A., 188
Bannon, R. S., 62
Banyard, V. L., 266
Barash, D. P., 45, 103, 106
Barber, B. L., 24
Barham, T. L., 304
Barker, G., 70
Barnett, R. C., 192, 225
Baron, R. A., 153
Baron, S. L., 277
Barr, C. L., 152
Barrington, C., 305
Bartfay, W. J., 228
Barthel, D., 315
Bartholomew, B. D., 264
Basow, S., 59, 106, 125, 171, 221, 223, 241, 261
Batty, G. D., 300
Bauman, K., 28, 69
Baumeister, R. F., 10, 202
Baur, K., 212
Bauserman, R., 200
Becker, G., 325
Beebe, M., 24
Beezley, D. A., 253
Bellamy, J. L., 188
Bem, S. L., 5, 6, 58, 84, 85, 89, 91, 131–132, 137, 139, 144, 188
Ben-David, S., 254
Benard, C., 241
Bennett, K. M., 90, 93, 145
Benson, E., 300
Benton-Wright, S., 16
Berko, E. H., 147
Berkowitz, A .D., 266, 267, 268
Berman, S., 206
Bernard, J., 235
Berndt, T. J., 165
Best, D. L., 136
Bhalla, A. K., 209

Bhattacharya, G., 239, 242
Bigelow, L., 174
Billson, J. M., 28, 29, 233
Biringen, Z. C., 282
Biro, F. M., 208
Biskupic, J., 239
Black, K. N., 125, 133, 192
Black, M. C., 278, 279
Blake, M., 70
Blanchard, R., 200
Blauwkamp, J. M., 214
Blazina, C., 165, 314
Bleakley, A., 263
Bleier, R., 106
Blitstein, R., 292
Block, J., 190
Block, J. H., 124, 125, 127, 190
Bly, R., 15, 112, 181, 192
Bocklandt, S., 177
Bogaert, A. F., 200
Bogart, L. M., 305
Bögels, S. M., 190
Bogle, K. A., 199, 206
Bohner, G., 254
Bolduc, D., 124
Bolton, F. G., 278
Bonvillain, N., 53, 222
Booth, A., 191, 194
Booth, A. G., 251
Booth, B. M., 251
Borders, L. D., 87
Boris, N. W., 97
Borowiecki, J., 301
Boswell, A. A., 256, 258, 259
Bowen, G. L., 234
Bowman, B., 303
Boxer, A., 39, 62
Boxer, P., 261
Boyatzis, C. J., 264
Boyd-Franklin, N., 30
Boyle, P. A., 125, 147, 151
Bradbury, T. N., 175, 176
Bradley, R. H., 182
Bradshaw, C., 172, 206
Bradstreet, T. C., 38, 301, 302
Brannon, R., 4, 5, 6, 75, 89, 204, 215
Branscome, N. R., 153

Breedlove, S. M., 200
Bridges, A. J., 215
Bridges, J. S., 229
Briere, J., 253
Brinig, M. F., 176
Brittan-Powell, C., 240
Britton, P. J., 177
Brod, H., 13, 205, 266
Brody, L. R., 146, 147, 148, 149, 152, 153, 170
Bronwyn, B., 254
Brooker, R. J., 126
Brooks, G. R., 15, 18, 20, 203, 206, 208, 217, 312, 314, 321, 322, 325
Brooks, R. A., 64
Brosi, M. W., 215
Brown, J., 11, 214
Brown, J. D., 209, 214, 216
Brown, L. M., 11
Brown, W., 237
Bruch, M. A., 147, 322
Bullingham, R., 64
Bunch, T., 53
Burger, J. M., 130
Bürgin, D., 176
Burke, C. H., 252
Burke, P. J., 182
Burn, S. M., 168
Burns-Glover, A., 319
Burridge, A., 165
Burt, M. R., 240, 253
Buss, D. M., 101, 102, 136, 164, 172–173, 206, 233
Buss, K. A., 126
Busse, W., 279
Bussey, K., 132–133, 263
Butcher, J. N., 83, 313
Butkus, R., 65

C

Cabrera, N. J., 182, 185
Caldera, Y. M., 124
Caldwell-Colbert, A. T., 253
Caldwell, L. D., 325
Calzo, J. P., 199, 302
Cameron, K. A., 214
Campbell, J. B., 111, 112, 280

Campbell, S. M., 175, 176
Canetto, S., 295
Cantor, J. M., 200, 216, 217
Caplan, P. J., 309
Capraro, R. L., 314
Caringella, S., 268
Carlson, P., 80
Carlstrom, A., 324
Carroll, H., 10, 36, 68
Carstensen, L., 154
Caruthers, A., 200, 207
Carver, L. J., 7, 124
Carver, P. R., 125, 152, 168, 171
Casares, C., 292
Cassen, N. H., 300
Cast, A. D., 182
Casteneda, D., 319
Catalano, S., 247, 249
Catalyst, 229
Cates, Jr., W., 206
CDC, 290, 291, 303, 304
Center for American Women in Politics, 51
Cepeda, O. A., 294
Cervantes, J. M., 325
Chan, J., 31
Cherry, M., 311
Chess, S., 97
Chethik, N., 192, 325
Chin, J., 295
Chirico, B., 257
Chodorow, N., 6, 119, 151, 181, 254
Chomsky, N., 139
Chu, J. Y., 157, 162, 168, 169
Chua, P., 32, 33
Cialdini, R. B., 145
Cicchetti, D., 254
Claes, M. E., 170
Clark, A. J., 311
Clatterbaugh, K., 107
Clawson, L., 214
Clay, R. A., 181
Clow, K. A., 228
Coad, D., 5, 10
Cochran, S. V., 19, 20, 317, 318, 325
Cockerton, T., 264
Cohane, G. H., 301

Cohen-Bendahan, C. C. C., 100
Cohen, D., 118
Cohen, J., 12
Cohen, J. W., 64
Cohen, L., 267
Cohn, A. M., 148, 250, 255
Colbow, A. J., 155
Colby, S. L., 28, 34
Collins, C. L., 276
Collins, G., 222
Colliver, J. D., 97
Coltrane, S., 119–120, 224
Comas-Díaz, L., 34
Comstock, D., 276
Connell, R. W., 17, 25, 36, 37, 43
Connolly, J., 172
Constantinople, A., 55, 83
Conway, A., 266
Cook, B. L., 55, 251
Coontz, S., 181, 190, 191, 223, 224, 225
Cooper, A., 11, 247, 249, 257
Cooper, M. L., 313
Cope-Farrar, K. M., 214
Corcoran, C., 268
Cortina, L. M., 236, 239
Cosmides, L., 100, 101
Cossette, L., 124
Cottingham, M. D., 228
Coughlin, P., 175
Cournoyer, R. J., 193, 235, 311
Courtenay, W. H., 166, 206, 232, 276, 287, 288, 297, 298, 299
Cowan, G. A., 166
Cowling, M., 227
Coyne, S., 265
Cozby, P. C., 149
Craig, W., 172
Crawford, M., 206, 208
Crete, G. K., 325
Crites, J. O., 235
Crone, M. R., 188
Crooks, R., 212
Crosby, A. E., 31, 287, 288, 289, 295, 312, 318
Crosset, T. W., 258
Crouch, J. L., 249
Crouter, A. C., 194

Cruise, S., 180
Cunningham, M., 149, 165, 166
Currie, C. E., 125
Currie, D. B., 125
Cysique, L. A., 304

D
Dahlstrom, W. G., 83
Daly, M., 102, 103, 260, 261
Daniel, H., 65
Dariotis, J. K., 108, 184, 188, 206, 207
Darrow, C. N., 280
Darwin, C., 100
Davenport, A. E., 314
David, D., 4, 5, 6, 62, 75, 89, 204
Davies, K., 127
Davis, C., 200
Davis, F., 58
De Visser, R. O., 313
De Vries, B., 172
de Waal, F. B. M., 105, 250
de Wolff, M. S., 188
DeAngelis, T., 192
Deaux, K., 51, 81, 140, 147, 148, 154
DeBlock, A., 200
Defense.gov, 65
DeFranc, W., 191, 311
DeHaan, S., 174
Dekeseredy, W. S., 266
Del Boca, F. K., 24
Denmark, F., 319
Densen, T. F., 261
Derlega, V. J., 149
Deutsch, F. M., 182, 221
DeVault, C., 188, 198
Devlin, P. K., 166
Diamond, L. M., 109, 207
Dicicco, E. C., 14, 18
Dick, R. W., 276
dickey, l. m., 25
Dickson, N., 199
DiClemente, R. J., 305
Diefendorff, J. M., 228
Diekman, A. B., 7, 17, 56, 60, 87, 135, 149, 165, 221
Diener, E., 147
Dietz, T. L., 264

Dill, K. E., 264
Dinero, T. E., 258
Dines, G., 214, 215, 216
Dishion, T., 127
Dodge, B., 209, 259
Doebbeling, B. N., 251
Dolnick, E., 293, 294
Donis, E., 165, 168
Donnelly, K., 87
Dorn, L. D., 208
Dovidio, J. F., 57, 88
Doyle, J., 18, 19
Doyle, J. A., 45
Drescher, J., 65, 201
Dubow, E. F., 261
Dudley-Grant, G. R., 253
Duffey, T., 321
Dunn, M. G., 193
Durvasula, R., 172, 210
Dutton, D. G., 259
Dyous, C., 248

E

Eagly, A. H., 51, 103, 135–136, 221
Earp, J., 134, 151
Easteal, P., 239
Eccles, J. S., 24
Eddins, R., 165
Edley, N., 16
Edsall, T. B., 64
Edwards, C. P., 106, 123, 128
Edwards, K. M., 266
Edwards, R., 65
Egan, S. K., 7, 125, 152, 168
Ehrenreich, B., 37
Ehresman, C., 200, 208, 211
Eisler, R. M., 92, 236
Elder, W. B., 20
Eliason, M. J., 201
Eliot, L., 55, 104–105, 293
Elkins, L. E., 165
Ellis, L., 200
Else-Quest, N. M., 136
Emmons, R. A., 147
Emslie, C., 300
Engeln, R., 301
Englar-Carlson, M., 16, 321

Epperson, D. L., 148
Epstein, M., 87, 88, 90, 100, 199, 213
Equal Employment Opportunity
    Commission (EEOC), 237, 239
Erickson, R. J., 228
Erikson, E. H., 291
Esbensen, F., 246
Espiritu, R., 246
Espiritu, Y. L., 33
ESPN, 237, 276
Eston, R. G., 125
Evanow, M., 324
Evans, L., 127
Evans, M. P., 321
Evidis, A., 5

F

Fabes, R. A., 128, 164
Fagot, B. I., 128
Fainaru, S., 276
Fainaru-Wada, M., 276
Fairchild, C., 229
Faludi, S., 225, 226
Fancher, R. E., 9, 77
Farrell, W., 19, 70, 205
Fass, P. S., 199
Fausto-Sterling, A., 98, 105, 107
Fazio, R. H., 56, 88
Federal Bureau of Investigation (FBI),
    113, 246, 247, 248, 249
Feiring, C., 172, 207
Fejes, F. J., 314, 315
Feldman, S. S., 282
Feldwisch, R., 226
Femiano, S., 18, 19
Ferguson, H., 71
Ferrar, K. E., 125
Ficarotto, T., 295
Fichner-Rathus, L., 198, 203
Fields, E. L., 305
Fields, S. K., 276
Fincham, F. D., 175, 176
Fine, G. A., 114, 166
Fingerhut, A. W., 175, 177
Finkelhor, D., 214
Fischer, A. H., 146, 149
Fischer, A. R., 94, 206

Fisher, T. D., 173, 206
Fishman, I., 212
Fisk, A., 237
Fiske, S. T., 56, 87
Fitzgerald, L. F., 235, 240, 242, 324
Fivush, R., 125, 147, 151, 164
Flaten, M. A., 145
Fleming, P. J., 26–27, 155, 305
Flood, M., 169, 252
Flores, A. H., 276
Foote, W. E., 239, 241
Ford, D., 81
Forste, R., 205
Forster, P., 213
Fortin, J., 298
Fouad, N. A., 226, 227, 228
Foubert, J. D., 215, 266, 267
Frankel, L., 172, 202, 209
Franklin, C. W., II, 29
Frederick, D. A., 209
freedomtomarry. org, 65
Freiburger, J., 156, 278, 279
French, K., 56
Frenkel-Brunswik, E., 82
Freud, S., 62, 82, 110–111, 112, 113, 114, 115, 118, 121
Freund, K., 83
Friedberg, A., 266
Friedman, H. S., 285
Friedman, K., 134
Friedman, M., 300
Frone, M. R., 313
Fujino, D. C., 32, 33
Funder, D. C., 315
Futrelle, D., 70
Fuxi, F., 132

G

Gagnon, J., 199
Galambos, N. L., 86
Galvan, F. H., 305
Gamarel, K. E., 177
Garber, J., 189
Garcia, J. R., 199
Garcia-Preto, N., 33
Garfield, R., 149, 157, 158, 163, 166, 314, 325

Gartner, R. B., 278
Gastil, J., 59
Gates, G. J., 6, 167
Gavey, N., 208
Gay, P., 115
gaymarriage. procon.org, 65
Gelfand, M. J., 239
Gelles, R. J., 37
Gelman, S., 138, 151
General Accounting Office, 65
Genesoni, L., 182, 184
Gentile, D. A., 264, 265
Gerbner, G., 11
Gergen, K. J., 192
Gergen, M. M., 192
Geronimus, A., 292
Gersic, C. M., 277
Geschke, D. W., 203
Ghavami, N., 26, 30, 31, 32, 35
Giaccardi, S., 11, 299
Gibbs, J. T., 29
Gidycz, C. A., 266
Gilder, G., 107
Gill, P. R., 169
Gillen, M. M., 305
Gillespie, C. D., 31, 287, 291, 298
Gilmore, D. D., 41, 42, 123, 136, 180, 198, 204, 229
Giordano, P. C., 172
Girgus, J. S., 176
Gitelson, I. B., 86
Gjerde, P. F., 190
Glantz, M. D., 97
Glick, P., 56, 57, 60, 87, 149, 236
Globetti, G., 314
Glosoff, H. L., 65
Golant, S. K., 259
Gold, S. R., 252
Goldberg, A., 172
Goldberg, H., 134
Goldfoot, D. A., 104
Goldman, R. F., 203
Goldstein, J. R., 209
Golombok, S., 164, 195
Gondolf, E. W., 259
Good, G. E., 126, 282, 321
Goodman-Delahunty, J., 239, 241

Gordon, K. J., 295
Gottdiener, W. H., 314
Gottman, J., 154
Gough, B., 285, 286, 287, 292, 299, 303
Gough, H. G., 83
Gould, R. E., 224, 233
Gould, S. J., 16, 108
Govender, K., 301
Gover, A. R., 266
Grace, V. M., 208
Graham, J. R., 83
Graham, S., 83
Graham, S. H., 299
Granek, L., 14, 18
Granie, M. A., 299
Grant, B. F., 312
Graziano, W. G., 172
Green, A., 93, 130, 266
Green, R. J., 200
Greenberg, S. T., 174
Greene, D. C., 177
Greenspan, A. I., 276
Griffith, D. M., 285, 286, 287, 292, 297, 298, 299
Griffiths, M. D., 216
Grimm, L., 300
Grimsley, K. D., 237
Gross, L., 11
Grossman, S., 315
Groth, A. N., 259, 260
Groth-Marnat, G., 83, 84
Grov, C., 177
Gruber, A., 301
Grunbaum, J. A., 246
Guffy, 29
Gugliotta, G., 277
Gupta, A., 289
Gurian, M., 67, 68
Gustafson, R., 256
Guthrie, R. V., 13
Gutmann, D., 281, 282
Guttmacher Institute, 198

H
Haas, D. W., 205
Haase, R. F., 147
Hackett, T. P., 300

Hafen, B. Q., 295
Haff, G. G., 301
Hagan, R., 128
Haileysus, T., 276
Haley, J. T., 165
Halford, T. C., 321
Haliliuc, A., 203, 204
Hall, A. V., 29, 30, 253
Hall, C. S., 111, 112, 280
Hall, E. V., 29, 253
Hall, G. C. N., 289
Hall, J. A., 146, 147, 148, 151, 153, 170, 289
Hall, R. J., 156
Halsey, III, A., 313
Halton, M., 214, 301
Hambaugh, J., 176
Hamilton, M. C., 59
Hammer, J. H., 126
Hammond, W. P., 26–27, 29, 30, 155, 289, 292
Haney, C., 130
Hanna, J., 81
Hansen, A., 153
Hansford, S. L., 170, 176
Hantover, J., 9, 67, 127, 168
Hardie, J. H., 227
Hare-Mustin, R. T., 52, 115
Harris, B., 9
Harris, G. T., 251
Harrison, J., 295
Hartley, R. E., 6, 118, 229
Hartup, W. W., 171
Hasan, N. T., 156
Hathaway, C. R., 83
Hatton, E., 214
Haviland, J. M., 147, 149
Haynie, D. L., 171
Hazan, C., 109, 207
Hearon, B., 214
Heasley, R., 149, 161, 164, 168, 169, 172
Hebert, L., 71, 249, 253, 259
Hecht, M. A., 148
Hedges, L. V., 81
Heesacker, M., 144, 145, 148
Heilman, B., 71, 259
Hein, M. J., 277

Heinzen, H., 93, 130, 266
Helgeson, V. S., 299, 300
Helmreich, R. L., 5, 6, 84, 85, 86, 87, 144
Hemenway, D., 257, 258
Henderson-Daniel, J., 253
Heppner, M., 266
Herbenick, D., 209
Herbert, T. W., 31
Herdt, G., 39, 41–42, 45, 62, 152
Herek, G. M., 38
Hermsen, S., 57, 88
Herold, E. S., 199
Heron, M. P., 312
Hetherington, E. M., 190, 191
Hetland, J., 167, 174
Hewlett, B. S., 124
Heyl, B. S., 38, 61
Hickman, S. J., 12, 76
Hildebrandt, T. B., 255
Hill, J. P., 190
Hilliard, L. J., 55, 137–138
Hills, H. I., 324
Hilt, L., 299
Hines, P. M., 30
Hirschman, C., 31, 33, 34
Ho, M.- H. R., 60, 310
Hochschild, A., 175
Hodapp, C., 70
Hoff Sommers, C., 19, 50
Hoff Sommers, S., 70
Hofferth, S., 182, 185, 188
Hoffman, C. D., 13
Hoffman, R. M., 87
Hofstede, G., 136
Hoifodt, R. S., 145
Holahan, C. K., 87
Holland, J., 227
Holland, K. J., 236, 239
Hollander, D. B., 301
Holtzworth-Munroe, A., 249, 259, 263
Hooley, J. M., 313
Horn, A. J., 76, 92
Horne, S. G., 177
Horney, K., 115, 116, 120, 121
Hosterman, S. J., 305
Hotaling, G. T., 259
House, A. T., 55

Houts, C. R., 177
Howard-Payne, L., 303
Howell, L., 172, 210
Hoyer, W. D., 322
Hubbard, R., 105, 106
Huesmann, L. R., 261
Huguet, N., 295
Huizinga, D., 246
Humblet, O., 108, 199, 206, 207
Hummer, R. A., 259
Hunt, K., 300
Hunter, K., 38, 202
Hurvitz, K. A., 31, 287, 291, 298
Hussey, A., 203, 204
Hust, S. J. T., 209, 214
Huston, A. C., 124
Huston, T. L., 173
Huyck, M., 282
Hyde, A., 180
Hyde, J. S., 59, 81, 102, 136, 140, 199

I
Ibaraki, A. Y., 289
Ikeda, R. M., 249, 259
Inchley, J. C., 125
Internet Filter Review, 214
Intersex Society of North America, 98
Isely, P., 278, 279
Isely, P. J., 278, 279
Iwamoto, D. K., 32, 169, 299, 314

J
Jacklin, C. N., 79, 124
Jackson, J. S., 277
Jacobson, N. S., 276
Jacupak, M., 148
Jakobsen, R., 209
Jakupcak, M., 255
Jameison, P., 263
Jansz, J., 156
Jaschik-Herman, M. L., 237
Jenkins, S., 80
Jennings, J. L., 252
Jensen-Campbell, L. A., 172
Jensen, R., 214, 216
Jeynes, W. H., 189
Jhally, S., 214

Johnson, A. G., 45, 119, 253
Johnson, A. M., 172
Johnson, C., 278
Johnson, J. A., 214
Johnson, K. L., 131
Johnson, L. A., 152
Johnson, L. B., 240
Johnson, M. I., 145
Johnston, L., 209
Jordan, A. B., 264
Joshi, S. P., 214
Joyce, A., 66
Judge, E., 1
Judice, S., 209
Jung, C. G., 15, 280–281
Just the Facts, 201

K
Kaemmer, B., 83
Kagan, J., 127
Kahn, A. S., 172, 206
Kaiser Family Foundation, 214
Kaluzny, G., 60, 94, 207, 253
Kamarovsky, M., 192, 233
Kaplan, D., 164, 165, 168, 170
Kaplan, G. W., 203
Kaplan, M. S., 295
Karazsia, B. T., 301, 302, 303
Karraker, K. H., 123, 125, 194
Karren, K. J., 295
Kashubeck-West, S., 38
Katz, J., 134, 149, 151, 266, 301
Kaufman, M., 50
Kawakami, K., 57, 88
Kay, G., 9
Kaya, A., 32
Kaye, K., 184
Kearney, L. K., 240
Keen, M., 57
Keen, S., 181, 222, 223
Kelly, J., 152
Kemper, T. D., 262
Kendler, K. S., 166, 170, 176
Kenrick, D. T., 145
Kessler, G., 66
Kevorkian, R. T., 294
Kilmartin, C., 67, 93, 108, 123, 127, 128, 130, 134, 147, 148, 149, 153, 154, 155, 156, 169, 176, 241–242, 246, 249, 251, 252, 255, 257, 265, 266, 268, 269, 280, 310, 317, 318, 322, 323, 325
Kimbrell, A., 274
Kimmel, E. B., 93
Kimmel, M., 8, 9, 16, 71, 134, 172, 206
Kimmel, M. S., 13, 45, 106, 107
King, E., 198
King, E. B., 240
King, J., 213
King, J. L., 38, 202, 303
Kinsey, A. C., 202
Kirkpatrick, L. A., 164, 172–173
Kiselica, A. M., 183, 184, 188, 233
Kiselica, M. S., 16, 93, 183, 184, 188, 230, 233, 325
Klann, E., 216
Klann, E. M., 26, 32, 285
Kleck, R. E., 152
Klein, E. B., 280
Kline, K. A., 16
Kling, R., 248
Knight, R. A., 250
Ko, I., 227
Kocet, M. M., 65
Koechlin, F. M., 304
Kolar, D., 93, 130, 266
Kolla, N. J., 217
Kollar, M. A., 28, 226
Komiya, N., 282
Kopper, B. A., 148
Korelitz, K. E., 189
Korobov, N., 66
Koss, M. P., 216, 253, 258, 266
Kosslyn, S. M., 315, 316
Kotrba, L., 227
Kowalski, R. M., 255
Kranz, D., 5
Krassas, N. R., 214
Kraus, A., 216
Kravitz-Wirtz, N., 267
Kreuz, L. E., 262
Krishnamurthy, K., 137
Kromrey, J. D., 93
Krug, E. G., 71
Kruger, D. J., 103, 261, 291

Ku, L. C., 91, 205, 206, 305
Kuchler, M., 93, 130, 266
Kuebli, J., 125, 147, 151
Kuh, G., 314
Kulik, L., 194
Kunkel, D., 214
Kuo, P. X., 185
Kuper, L. E., 174
Kurdek, L. A., 118
Kurland, B., 194

L

LaFrance, M., 140, 148
Lake, M. A., 123, 194
Lakoff, R. T., 154
Lalumiere, M. L., 251
Lamb, M. E., 182, 185, 186, 187, 188, 192, 195
Lamb, S., 11
Landrine, H., 309
Langevin, R., 83
Larrieu, J. A., 97
Larsen, R. J., 147, 164, 172–173
Laumann, E. O., 199, 202, 203, 204, 210, 211, 212, 213
Lazur, R. F., 325
Leahy, M., 277
Leaper, C., 81, 125, 151, 189, 194
Leary, M. R., 255
Lee, C. C., 30
Lee, H., 167, 202
Lee, J., 192
Lee, K., 239
Lee, R., 32
Leemann, M., 257
Lefkowitz, B., 25, 36, 169
Lefkowitz, E. S., 305
Lehman, E., 277
Lehne, G., 166–167
Leicht, K. T., 69
Lemann, N., 30
L'Engle, K. L., 209, 214, 216
Leonard, K. E., 253
Lepowsky, M., 251
Lerner, G., 52, 54, 222, 223
Letich, L., 171
Leuty, M., 126

Levant, R. F., 5, 15, 18, 20, 28, 36, 55, 62, 66, 76, 89, 93, 144, 156, 157, 158, 164, 166, 173, 182, 205, 206, 217, 250, 324
Levenson, R., 154
Lever, J., 209
Levine, M. P., 39, 40
Levine, S., 147
Levinson, D., 82
Levinson, D. J., 228–229, 280, 289
Levinson, M. H., 280
Lew, M., 278
Lewars, H., 300
Lewis, R. A., 118
Lex, B. W., 312
Ley, D., 214, 217
Ley, D. J., 214
Liben, L. S., 55, 137–138
Lien, M.-C., 156
Lind, M., 165
Lindberg, S. M., 81
Lindsay, J. J., 264
Lindzey, G., 111, 112, 280
Linn, M. C., 81, 136
Lippa, R. A., 285
Lippmann, J. R., 299
Lippmann, S. J., 257
Lips, H., 3, 59, 80, 133, 170, 183
Lipton, J. E., 45, 103, 106
Lisak, D., 116, 157, 253, 254, 259, 267, 279–280
Liu, T., 26, 32, 285
Liu, W. M., 31, 36, 37, 155, 165, 174, 321
Livingston, G., 182, 193
Lloyd, B. F., 193
Lo, C. C., 314
Loeber, R., 246
Logan, J. E., 287, 288, 289
Lohan, M., 180, 184
Lohr, B. A., 67
Long, D., 148
Longmore, M. A., 172
Lopez, E. C., 266
Luallen, J., 248
Lupton, B., 227
Luria, Z., 167
Lurye, L. E., 131
Luthar, S., 254

Lynch, J., 123, 134
Lynch, J. R., 67, 127, 147, 148, 149, 153, 154, 155, 156, 169, 176, 252, 255, 310, 317, 318, 325
Lynn, D. B., 133
Lytton, H., 7, 81, 124, 125, 126, 127, 189, 194

M

Maccoby, E. E., 3, 79, 106, 124, 125, 127, 128, 163, 164, 171, 174, 256
MacDonald, J. M., 266
MacDormand, M. F., 286
MacEachron, A. E., 278
Machung, A., 175
Mack, K. A., 287, 288
Madon, S., 5, 38, 200
Maffini, C. S., 26
Magee, J. C., 174
Magovcevic, M., 317
Magrath, R., 64
Mahalik, J. R., 60, 66, 76, 88, 89, 91, 144, 154, 156, 173, 191, 193, 200, 205, 229, 235, 250, 252, 282, 311, 321, 322
Mahlstedt, D., 266
Majdandžic, M., 190
Majors, R., 28, 29, 233
Malamuth, N. M., 216, 253
Malcuit, G., 124
Manago, A., 299
Manderscheid, R. W., 319
Mandle, J. A., 295
Manning, W., 172, 203, 204
Manstead, A. S. R., 146, 147, 149
Maracek, J., 115
Marecek, J., 52
Marlantes, K., 274, 275
Marshall, N. L., 192
Marsiglio, W., 158, 182
Marston, C., 198
Martin, C. L., 119, 128, 131, 139, 140, 164
Martin, E., 60
Martin, J., 210, 301
Martin, L. R., 285
Martin, P. Y., 259
Martinez, G., 183, 192

Martino-Harms, J. W., 5, 55
Marx, K., 224
Masciadrelli, B. P., 185
Maslow, A. H., 162
Masser, B., 254
Massoth, N. A., 314
Mathews, J., 314
Maticka-Tyndale, E., 199
Matillo, G. M., 264
Matthews, T. J., 286
Mattis, J. S., 27
Maurer, T. W., 185
May, R. J., 110
Mays, V. M., 13
McAskill, R. L., 319
McCormack, M., 64, 166, 167, 202, 254
McCreary, D. R., 7, 206, 298, 299, 302, 314
McDaniel, D., 289
McDaniel, M., 248
McDermott, R. C., 5, 55, 246, 265
McDiarmid, E., 169
McDowell, E. E., 296, 312
McFarland, B. H., 295
McHale, S. M., 194
McHugh, M. C., 176
McIntosh, P., 52
McKee, B., 280
McKelley, R. A., 175, 182, 186, 189, 193
McKinlay, A., 209
McKinley, J. C., 83
McLachlan, A., 169
McLellan, T., 209
McMackin, R., 278, 279
McMonigle, C. L., 255
McQuoid, T., 266
Mead, M., 20, 40, 42
Meagher, S., 315
Merighi, J. R., 206, 298, 299
Merrill, L. L., 249
Merriwether, A., 200, 207
Messner, M. A., 148, 165, 207, 251, 266, 276
Mewhinney, D., 199
Meyer, J., 38
Meyer, P. A., 31, 286, 287
Michael, R. T., 199

Michaels, S., 199
Miedzian, M., 256
Migliaccio, T., 162, 165, 166
Mihoces, G., 277
Mikulincer, M., 254
Miles, C. C., 82
Milgram, S., 129–130
Miller, A., 234
Miller, I. S. K., 60, 310
Miller, M., 257, 258
Miller, P. M., 259, 267
Millon, C. F., 315
Millon, T., 315, 316
Milner, J. S., 249
Milos, M. F., 203, 204
Mineka, S., 313
Mitchell, K. J., 215
Moberly, E., 201
Moll, J., 57, 88
Molla, M. T., 12, 287, 288
Möller, E. L., 190
Money, J., 79, 82, 104, 106, 201
Montemurro, B., 214
Moon, M., 13
Moore, M., 225
Moore, S., 264
Moore, T. M., 250
Moradi, B., 62, 66, 200
Morawski, J. G., 75, 83
Morgan, M., 11
Morgan, R. E., 249
Morris, L. A., 278
Morrison, T. G., 214, 301
Mosmiller, T. E., 106, 107
Moynihan, M. M., 266
Mudar, P, 313
Mueller, F. O., 276
Murdock, G. P., 102, 109
Murnen, S. K., 60, 94, 207, 215, 253, 301, 302, 303
Murphy, C. M., 252
Murray, B., 264
Mustanski, B. S., 174
Myers, D. G., 75
Myers, J., 166
Myers, S. M., 194
Myrbakk, I. N., 145

N
Nagler, E., 83
Napolitano, J. M., 311
Nardella, B., 301
Nash, S. C., 282
Nathan, S., 115
National Center for Education Statistics, 69, 133
National Center for Health Statistics, 232, 286, 289, 295, 299
National Institute of Mental Health, 295
National Safety Council, 299
National Spinal Cord Injury Association, 299
National Survey of Family Growth, 183
Naumann, R. B., 287, 288, 299, 313
Neff, D. A., 104
Nellis, A., 26, 29, 233, 248
Nelson, J. B., 61, 152, 164–165, 212
Nemiah, J. C., 156
Nesbitt, K. M., 264
Nesse, R. M., 103, 261, 291
Neuberg, S. L., 145
Nevid, J. S., 198, 203
Newcomb, M. D., 314
Newfield, J., 276
Newkirk Meunier, L., 149, 165, 166
Newton, N. J., 182
Nicpon, M. F., 165
Nikolic, M., 190
Niku, S. D., 203
Noble, N., 304
Nolen-Hoeksema, S., 176, 295, 299, 317
NOMAS, 18
Norbet, T., 266
Nowell, A., 81
NPR (National Public Radio), 67

O
O'Brien, K. M., 193
O'Brien, M., 124
Ochberg, R., 232
Oeur, F., 29
Offer, D., 207
Offer, M. K., 207

NAME INDEX • 399

Ogbu, J. U., 233, 251
O'Halloran, P., 180
Ojeda, L., 35
Okun, R. A., 12, 18, 58, 70
Olds, T. S., 125
Oliphant, B., 253
Olivardia, R., 301
Oliver, M. B., 102, 199
Olson, M. A., 56, 88
O'Neil, J. M., 5, 6, 13, 15, 60, 91, 92, 143, 144, 150, 165, 166, 175, 186, 188, 235, 250, 253, 289, 302, 310, 315, 317
O'Rand, A. M., 282
Orchowski, L. M., 266
Organista, K. C., 35
Oros, C. J., 253
Ortega, L., 31, 288
Orthner, D. K., 234
Ortman, J. M., 28, 34
Osgood, D. W., 194
Osretich, R. A., 265
Ostrov, E., 207
O'Sullivan, C. S., 256, 258
Overhauser, S., 171
Owen, J., 321

P
Packard, G. A., 65
Palmer, C. T., 15, 107
Palmer-Mehta, V., 203, 204
Paluck, E. L., 148
Paludi, M. A., 45
Pantony, K. L., 309
Parent, M. C., 38, 62, 66, 200, 301, 302
Parke, R. D., 186
Parker, K., 182
Parker, S., 172
Parks, L. F., 267
Parsons, J. T., 6, 144, 177
Pascoe, C. J., 6, 61, 128, 152, 167, 174
Pasick, R. S., 229
Patterson, G. R., 127
Paul, C., 199
Paul-Gera, N., 71, 259
Paz-Bailey, G., 304
Peacock, D., 70
Pecora, N., 151, 189

Pellegrini, A. D., 125, 127
Pennebaker, J. W., 149
Peplau, L. A., 26, 30, 31, 32, 35, 175, 177, 209
Pepler, D., 172
Pepler, D. J., 246
Peralta, R. L., 313
Perelman, M. A., 217
Perez, A. D., 31, 33, 34
Perren, S., 176
Perry, D. G., 7, 125, 133, 152, 168
Perry, J. L., 29, 253
Peskin, H., 281
Peter, J., 214, 215, 265
Petersen, A. C., 86
Petersen, J. L., 81
Peterson, C., 165
Petrovsky, E., 247, 249, 257
Pharr, S., 40
Phelan, J. E., 176
Phillips, K. A., 301
Phillips, S., 255
Picker, M., 214, 215, 255
Pilgrim, E. L., 125
Pinquart, M., 186, 189
Pionke, D. R., 176
Piquero, A. R., 246, 248
Pituch, K. A., 156
Plant, E. A., 81
Plante, E. G., 266
Pleck, J. H., 83, 89, 90, 91, 93, 158, 180, 185, 186, 188, 192, 205, 206, 240, 262, 298, 305, 319
Plummer, D. C., 6
Polce-Lynch, M., 67, 149, 152
Pollack, W., 5, 67, 71, 125, 295, 296, 317
Pomerleau, A., 124
Pompper, D., 28
Ponton, L. E., 209
Pope, H. G., 301
Popp, D., 206, 208
Porter, A., 53
Poska, A., 56
Potts, A., 208, 212
Prescott, C. A., 166
Pressly, P. K., 145, 148
Prior, P. M., 309

Prisco, A. G., 252
Pröbstle, K., 5
Proctor, B. D., 28, 31, 32, 36, 226
Proquest, 69
Pryor, J. B., 241
Putnam, R., 10
Pytyck, J., 217

Q
Quinlan, R. J., 206
Quinsey, V. L., 251
Quinton, R. L., 186

R
Rabinowitz, F. E., 157, 317, 318, 321, 325
Rabinowitz, V., 319
Rahdert, E., 97
Ramnath, R., 315
Raphael, R., 42
Rathus, S. A., 198, 199, 203
Raver, J. L., 239
Rea, M., 172, 210
Real, T., 310, 317, 318, 325
Reece, M., 209
Regan, P. C., 163, 172, 209, 210
Reid, H. M., 166
Reid, J., 127
Reigeluth, C. S., 6, 61, 167
Reis, R., 188
Reiser, L. W., 209
Renzulli, S., 13, 15
Rhodes, W., 248
Ricciardelli, L. A., 228, 315
Rice, M. E., 251
Rich, A. J., 155
Richards, M., 86
Richardson, L., 59, 261
Richman, J. A., 236, 240
Richmond, K., 6, 36, 55, 166, 167, 173
Riger, S., 17–18
Ring, T. E., 266
Rivers, C., 225
Ro, M. J., 292
Roach, K. A., 194
Robertson, J., 324
Robertson, J. M., 325
Robertson, S., 285, 286, 287, 292, 299, 303
Robinson, D. T., 241
Rochlen, A. B., 156, 158, 173, 175, 182, 186, 189, 193, 240, 321, 322
Rochlen, A. N., 150
Rochlin, C., 200–201
Roebuck, A., 227
Roemer, L., 148
Rogers, B. K., 28
Rogers, C., 320
Romer, D., 263
Romney, D. M., 7, 81, 124, 125, 126, 127, 189, 194
Rose, R. M., 262
Rosenbaum, J. F., 300
Rosenberg, A., 61, 167
Rosenberg, R. S., 6, 315, 316
Rosenblum, K. E., 53
Rosenblum, L. A., 105
Rosenhan, R., 300
Rosenkoetter, L. I., 265
Rosenkoetter, S. E., 265
Rosenmann, A., 164, 165, 168, 170
Rosenstein, M. J., 319
Rosin, H., 64
Rospenda, K. M., 236, 239, 240
Ross, D., 11, 132, 133
Ross, S. A., 11, 132, 133
Rothgerber, H., 299
Rotundo, E. A., 7, 8, 9, 61, 62, 143, 249
Rounds, J., 226
Rowlands, A. V., 125
Ruble, D. N., 131, 139, 140
Rudman, L. A., 176, 236
Russell, M., 313
Russin, A., 57, 88
Rutherford, A., 14, 18
Ruxton, S., 71
Ryan, C. L., 28, 69
Rybarczyk, B., 281

S
Sabin, J. A., 289
Sabina, C., 214
Sadava, S. W., 314
Sadker, D., 71, 127

NAME INDEX • 401

Sadker, M., 127
Sadler, A. G., 250, 267
Salo, K., 304
Saloner, R., 304
Sanabria, S., 325
Sánchez, F. J., 38, 174, 177
Sanday, P. R., 251, 258
Sandberg, L., 208
Sanders, "Red", 5
Sandler, B. R., 239
Sanford, R. N., 82
Santelli, J., 198
Sapolsky, R. M., 104, 262
SAPRO, 267
Sasse, D., 302
Sattel, J., 153
Saucier, D. M., 200, 208, 211
Saunders, S., 239
Saville, B. K., 172, 206
Savin-Williams, R. C., 38, 40, 64, 166, 172, 173, 174, 201, 202, 209, 254
Sax, L., 127
Saxon, S. E., 182, 221
Sayad, B. W., 198
Scarborough, R., 278
Scarce, M., 278
Scaringi, V., 175, 193
Schaufeli, W. B., 231
Schein, V. E., 236
Schlaffer, E., 241
Schmitt, D. P., 37, 101, 102, 109, 136, 199, 206, 207, 233
Schneider, O., 254
Schwartz, E. N., 301
Schwartz, J., 299, 302
Schwartz, J. P., 5, 55, 57, 241
Schwartz, M. D., 266
Schwartz, P., 175
Schwarz, A., 276
Scott, F., 212
Scott-Samuel, A., 285
Seabrook, R., 11
Seabrook, R. C., 299
Sechzer, J., 319
Segev, M., 254
Seibert, L. A., 148, 250
Seligman, M. E. P., 317

Semega, J. L., 28, 226
The Sentencing Project, 28, 29
Serwer, A., 70
Sesma, Jr., A., 265
Settle, A. G., 165
Shabsigh, R., 212
Shackelford, T. K., 164, 172–173
Shaeer, O., 216
Shanahan, J., 11
Shangani, S., 304
Shankar, P. R., 276
Shanker, T., 267
Shannon, C. A., 236, 240
Shannon, J. D., 185
Sharockman, A., 235
Shaver, P. R., 254
Shearer, C. L., 305
Shen-Miller, D., 226
Shepard, S. J., 149, 165
Sherrod, N., 282
Shewmaker, J. W., 214
Shields, S. A., 14, 18, 26, 125, 145, 146, 150
Shilts, R., 38, 40, 63, 64, 254, 303
Shoop, R. J., 239
Shorrock, M. P., 217
Sifneos, P. E., 156
Signorielli, N., 11
Silverstein, L. B., 185, 312, 314
Simoni, H., 176
Sims-Knight, J., 250
Singh, A., 25
Singh, A. A., 325
Sinn, J. S., 205
Sinno, S., 6, 167
Sipe, T. A., 304
Sisk, C. L., 208
Skidmore, J. R., 92, 236
Skinner, B. F., 135
Skinner, J. B., 313
Skovholt, T. M., 153
Slaatten, H., 167, 174
Slaby, R. G., 246
Sladek, M. R., 301
Sloane, M., 81
Sloup, C., 184
Smiler, A. P., 9, 17, 19, 24, 25, 60, 66,

68, 75, 87, 88, 90, 93, 100, 102, 108, 109, 144–145, 161, 162, 164, 169, 172, 173, 174, 193, 199, 200, 202, 203, 205, 206, 207, 209, 214, 226, 252, 253, 299, 302, 314
Smith, B. L., 295
Smith, D., 300
Smith, E. L., 11, 247, 249, 257
Smith, J. A., 313
Smith, L., 255, 295, 314
Smith, T., 93, 130, 266
Snow, C. E., 194
Snow, M. E., 124
Snowden, S. J., 144, 145
Sommers, C. H., 68
Sonenstein, F. L., 91, 188, 205, 206, 305
Sonnega, A., 277
Spade, J. Z., 256, 258, 259
Speight, Q. L., 12, 76
Spence, J. T., 5, 6, 84, 85, 86, 87, 144
Sperry, H. A., 28
Spitzer, R. L., 201
Sports Illustrated, 277
Sprecher, S., 163, 172
Stander, V. A., 249
Stanistreet, D., 285
Stanley-Hagen, M., 190, 191
Stapely, J. C., 147, 149
Starks, T. J., 177
Starrels, M. E., 194
Steadman, H. J., 319
Stearns, P. N., 10, 68, 182, 222, 223, 230
Steel, P., 239
Steele, J. R., 11
Steeves, V., 214
Stein, R., 209, 287
Steinberg, M., 7, 17, 56, 60, 87, 149, 165
Steiner, B., 83
Steinfeldt, J. A., 12, 76
Stern, G., 267
Stevens, K., 67
Stevens, M., 321
Stevens, M. A., 266
Stevens, M. R., 31, 288, 289
Stevenson, M. R., 125, 133, 192
Stewart, A. J., 182
Stillion, J. M., 287, 292, 296, 312

Stith, S. M., 255
Stock, J. A., 203
Stockdale, M. S., 239, 242
Stone, M. R., 24
Storey, A. E., 186
Stouthamer-Loeber, M., 246
Strasburger, V. C., 264
Strate, L., 161, 256, 315
Stratton, N., 217
Straus, M. A., 249
Street, S., 93
Strokoff, J., 321, 324
Strong, B., 83, 198, 199
Stuart, G. L., 249, 250, 259, 263
Stueve, J. L., 185
Su, R., 226
Sue, D., 261, 277, 278, 308, 312, 313, 317
Suellentrop, K., 184
Suen, Y.-t., 12
Sugarman, D. B., 259
Suizzo, M.-A., 175, 193
Sun, C., 214, 215, 255
Sutton, K. S., 217
Sutton, M. J., 213
Swain, S. O., 173
Swoboda, F., 237
Symons, D., 102
Szasz, T., 308
Szkrybalo, J., 139
Szymanski, D. M., 38
Szymanski, D. M., 38

T
Tabasam, G., 145
Tallandini, M. A., 182, 184
Tamis-LeMonda, C., 185
Tamis-LeMonda, C. S., 182
Tangri, S., 240
Tannen, D., 126, 164
Tappan, M., 11
Taris, T. W., 231
Tarvydas, V., 65
Tashani, O. A., 145
Task Force on Appropriate Therapeutic Responses to Sexual Orientation, 65
Tassinary, L. G., 131
Tavris, C., 41, 42, 107, 145, 147, 148, 154

Taylor, P., 237
Tefft, B., 214
Tellegen, A., 83
Tendulkar, S. A., 289
Tenenbaum, H. R., 81, 151, 189, 194
Tennenbaum, H. R., 125
Terman, L. M., 82
Theodore, H., 193
Thomas, A., 97
Thomas, S., 292
Thompson, E. H., Jr., 90, 93, 145
Thomsen, C. J., 249
Thorne, B., 55, 137, 164, 167
Thornhill, R., 15, 107
Thorpe, R. J., 285, 286, 287, 292, 297, 298, 299
Thurnell-Read, T., 169
Timmers, M., 149
Tinkler, J. E., 240
Tinsley, B. R., 186
Toby, J., 82
Toch, H., 250, 269
Todd, J. M., 125
Tokar, D. M., 94, 252
Tokunaga, R. S., 216
Tooby, J., 100, 101
Tovar-Blank, Z. G., 35
Tracey, T. J. G., 35
Trafford, A., 276
Trautner, M. N., 214
Travis, T. C., 53
Treadwell, H. M., 292
Tregear, S. J., 304
Tschan, T., 266
Tschann, J., 176
Tull, M. T., 148
Turner, J. S., 214
Twenge, J. M., 86, 87, 144, 236
Tysiaczny, C., 214
Tyson, P., 116

U

Unger, R. K., 3
United States Department of Labor, 182, 190
Ureno, O., 172, 210
U.S. Department of Justice, 51

Uy, P. J., 314

V

VAASA, 278
Vaccaro, B. G., 124
Valkenburg, P. M., 214, 215, 265
van Beek, I., 231
Van Evra, J., 11
van Hertum, A., 63
van Mourik, K., 188
VanderDrift, L. E., 172
Vares, T., 208
Vásquez, D. A., 161, 166
Vernacchio, A., 213
Vernick, J. S., 257
Vesely, C. K., 185
Vigil, J. M., 163, 170
Viki, G. T., 254
Vilain, E., 3, 98, 174, 177, 208
Villa-Torres, L., 26–27, 155
Vincent, W., 305
Virginia Military Institute, 4
Vogel, D. A., 123, 194
Vogel, D. L., 145, 148, 176
Vokey, M., 214
Von Klitzing, K., 176
Von Wyl, A., 176
Voyer, D., 81
Voyer, S. D., 81
Vrangalova, Z., 202

W

Wade, J. C., 41, 93, 135, 145, 147, 165, 168, 175, 240, 285
Waldron, H., 301
Walker, D. F., 94, 252
Walsh, C. J., 186
Walsh-Childers, K., 11
Walsh, D. A., 265
Walters, A. S., 173, 206
Walters, J. L., 125
Walters, R. H., 263
Wang, S.-Y., 60, 310
Ward, L. M., 11, 134, 185, 199, 200, 207, 213, 214, 299
Wardle, J., 299
Watkins, C. E., 314

Way, N., 149, 157, 161, 162, 163, 164, 166, 168, 169
Webster, D. W., 257
Wechsler, H., 314
Weiher, A. W., 246
Weinberg, N. Z., 97
Weinstock, H., 206
Weir, D. R., 277
Weiss, R. S., 231
Wells, B. E., 144
Wesselink, P., 214
West, B. A., 287, 288, 299, 313
West, S. G., 172
Wester, S. R., 19, 144, 145, 146, 148, 176
Wetherell, M., 16
Wexler, D. B., 252
Whilde, M. R., 322
Whiston, S. C., 226
White, J. L., 325
White, J. W., 266
White Ribbon Campaign, 257
Whiteman, S. D., 194
Whiting, B. B., 106, 123, 128
Whitman, J. S., 65
Whittaker, T. A., 193
Whorley, M. R., 92
Wienke, C., 212
Wight, D., 135
Wilkie, J. R., 235
Willett, J. A., 252
Williams, C. L., 227, 228
Williams, C. M., 156
Williams, J. E., 45, 136, 149, 161, 300
Williams, P., 277
Williams, R. J., 315
Willness, C. R., 239, 240, 242
Wilson, E.O., 16, 66
Wilson, G., 217
Wilson, J. E., 172
Wilson, M., 102, 103, 260, 261
Wilson, W. J., 30
Wimer, B. J., 264

Wimer, D. J., 182
Winstead, B. A., 149
Winter, D. G., 50
Wise, T. N., 213
Wiseman, R., 246
Wiswell, T. E., 203
Wolak, J., 214
Wong, P. T. P., 149
Wong, Y. J., 12, 19, 26, 32, 60, 66, 76, 92, 150, 156, 158, 285, 286, 310, 313, 314, 321
Wood, H., 125, 126
Wood, W., 103, 135, 136, 221
Woodhams, C., 227, 230
World Health Organization, 206
Wright, C., 60, 94, 207, 253
Wright, L. W., 67
Wright, P. J., 216
Wynne-Edwards, K. E., 186

Y

Yap, M. B. H., 187
Yarber, W. L., 198
Yarnold, P. R., 300
Ybarra, M. L., 215
Yodanis, C. L., 269
Youniss, J., 171

Z

Zack, M. M., 31, 286, 287, 291
Zajac, A., 83
Zak, D., 203
Zeanah, C. H., 97
Zeglin, R. J., 305
Zeichner, A., 148, 250, 255
Zhentao, F., 132
Zilbergeld, B., 206, 212, 213
Zimbardo, P., 130
Zinn, H., 9
Zuk, M., 60
Zuo, A., 11
Zuo, J., 235

Subject Index

In this index, page references followed by an italicized *fig* refer to figures; by an italicized *t*, to tables; and by an italicized *b*, to boxes.

A
A Call to Men, 18
ABC model (Affect, Behavior, and Cognition)
  characteristics of, 75–76
  defined, 95
Academics, activists and, 17–18
Acculturation
  defined, 26, 47
  ethnicity and, 26–27
Achievement, masculinity and, 5
Acquaintances, defined, 162, 179
Action movies
  defined, 271
  male dominance in, 245
Actionable events
  defined, 224
  sexual harassment, 238
Activism
  against sexism, 58–60
  male-female, 18
Adaptive behaviors, defined, 100, 121–122
Adolescence, suicide in, 296
Adventurousness, masculinity and, 6, 252–253
African-American men
  crime rates, 28*t*, 29, 247–249
  demographic trends, 28*t*
  discrimination and masculinity, 29–31
  economic challenges, 28*t*, 29–31
  educational levels, 28*t*, 29–30, 69
  in employment, 227–228
  incarceration rates, 26, 28*t*, 29
  masculinity themes, 27–31
  physical health patterns, 288–292
  sexual first experiences, 210
  sexually-transmitted diseases and, 304
  stereotypes, 30–31
  violence and, 247–249
Aggression
  evolutionary psychology perspective, 102–103
  factors encouraging, 270
  masculinity and, 6, 7–10
  physical. *See* Physical aggression
  pornography and, 215–216
  punishment effects on, 127
  video game violence and, 264–265
Aging men
  gendered behaviors, 280–282
  retirement issues, 233, 234*b*
  sexual problems of, 210–213
  suicide and, 234*b*, 296–297
  traditional masculinity and, 296–297
Agrarian societies
  male domination and, 54
  work and the sexes, 222–224

AIDS. *See* HIV/AIDS
AIDS and Behavior, 303
AIDS buddies, defined, 74
Alcohol use
    abuse results, 312
    gendered aspects of, 313–315
Alexithymia
    defined, 160
    masculine ideology and, 156
    treatment methods, 158
Alpha bias, defined, 52, 72
Alpha males
    in American culture, 250
    animal kingdom behaviors, 105
Ambition, masculinity and, 5
American Academy of Pediatrics, on ambiguous genitalia births, 99*b*
American Men's Studies Association (AMSA)
    conference themes, 12
    history of, 19
American Psychiatric Association, on homosexuality, 63
Anabolic-Androgenic Steroids (AAS)
    defined, 272
    drive for muscularity, 302
    violence and, 256
Androgen Insensitivity Syndrome (AIS), characteristics of, 99, 100
Androgynous persons, defined, 95
Androgyny model
    characteristics and measures, 84–86, 87–88
    defined, 79, 95
    summary, 94*t*
Androsperm
    defined, 306
    in fertilization, 287
Anger
    male expression of, 148–149
    masculinity and, 10
    violence and, 252, 255, 260
Anger rapists, characteristics of, 260
Antifemininity
    emotional constriction and, 150–151
    in gender identity formation, 118–120
    Horney's theory and, 115*b*, 121
    masculinity and, 5, 6, 250–251
    violence and, 250–251
    work and, 224, 235–236
Antisocial Personality Disorder
    characteristics of, 316
    defined, 327
Asia, masculinity definitions, 43–44
Asian-American men
    demographic trends, 28*t*
    educational levels, 28*t*, 32–33, 69
    in employment, 227–228
    masculinity themes, 31–33
    physical health patterns, 288–292
    sexual first experiences, 210
    stereotypes, 32
    violence and crime rates, 28*t*, 247–249
Asian Americans/Pacific Islanders, crime rates, 28*t*, 247–249
Attention, violence and, 256
Attitude Interest Analysis Test, 82
Attitudinal research, on sexuality, 199
Authoritative parenting
    defined, 197
    fathers in, 186

B

The Bachelor, 203
Behavioral medicine
    defined, 306
    disorders and masculinity, 299–305
Belief in a just world, defined, 74
Bem Sex Role Inventory (BSRI)
    characteristics of, 85–86
    criticisms of, 87
Benevolent sexism
    chivalry as, 57–58
    defined, 56, 73
    negative results of, 60
    as research factor, 86–87
Berdache, defined, 45, 49
Best friends, defined, 162–163, 179
Beta bias, defined, 52, 72
Between-group differences

child sex differences, 79–81
defined, 23
in men's studies, 17
social structural theory and, 136
Bias
alpha and beta, 52, 72
implicit bias, 56, 73, 87, 95
Big Wheel principle, 5
Bigorexia
characteristics of, 301
defined, 306
Biogenic explanations, for physical health, 292–293
Biological perspectives, on sex and gender, 97–98
chromosomal and hormonal approaches, 98–100
evolutionary psychology. *See* Evolutionary psychology (EP)
in Freudian perspective, 110–113, 121
psychoanalytic perspectives. *See* Psychoanalytic theories
on violence, 260–262
Black Lives Matter, 29
Blacks. *See* African-American men
Blue collar masculinity
characteristics of, 36
defined, 48
Body Dysmorphic Disorder, defined, 306
Body image, disorders in males, 300–303
Boy Code, defined, 4–7
Boy crises
in United States, 10, 67–71
"war" claim, 50
Boy Scouts, traditional masculinity in, 9, 168
Breadwinner role
history of, 224–225
masculinity and, 229, 233–235
Buddies
defined, 162–163, 179
friends versus, 170
Buddyships, defined, 62, 73

C
Caballerismo, Latino men and, 35
California Psychological Inventory (CPI) "Fe" scale, 83
Cancer, male neglect of, 298–299
Cardiovascular disease, masculinity and, 300
Careers. *See also* Work and the workplace
defined, 224
jobs versus, 225
Castration anxiety
defined, 122
in Freudian perspective, 114
Child care, gender identity formation and, 118–120
Chivalry
defined, 57, 73
as sexism, 57–58
Chromosomal approaches, to sex and gender, 98–100
Cigarette smoking. *See* Tobacco use
Circumcision
debate over, 203b–204b
defined, 203b, 219
Clementi, Tyler, suicide of, 64
Cognitive-Behavioral Therapy (CBT), use of, 322
Cognitive dissonance
defined, 49
initiation rites and, 42
Cold pressor task
defined, 23
masculinity and, 16–17
Colleges
alcohol use at, 314
sexual violence at, 257b, 258–259, 266–267, 268
Combat, risks and consequences, 273–275
Coming out
defined, 48
Stonewall Riot effects, 62–63
United States history, 39–40
Communal masculinity
defined, 22
in United States history, 7–8

Communality
    defined, 22
    masculinity and, 6
Communication skills, relationship satisfaction and, 176
Community-level interventions, for violence, 267–268
Competition
    drinking as, 313
    evolutionary psychology perspective, 102–103
    masculinity and, 8, 9
    relational intimacy and, 165
    sexual behavior as, 205, 206–207, 260–261
    violence and, 260–261
Compliance
    defined, 141
    social pressure and, 129–130
Complicit masculinities
    characteristics of, 25
    defined, 25, 47
Concussion
    contact sports and, 276–277
    defined, 284
Conflict
    gender role stress and, 92–93
    Oedipal, 113–117, 122
    parental, 186–187, 188
Conformity
    defined, 141
    social pressure and, 129–130
Conformity to Male Norms Index
    criticism of, 93
    measures in, 76, 88
Conformity to Masculine Norms Inventory (CMNI), 91, 205
Congenital Adrenal Hyperplasia (CAH), characteristics of, 99–100
Conscience
    defined, 122
    in Freudian perspective, 112–113
Contact sports, men's health and, 275–277
Content analyses
    defined, 22
    in men's studies, 12

Conversion therapy, principles of, 65
Cool pose
    African-American use of, 28
    defined, 27, 28, 47
Coping. *See also* Mental health
    defined, 160
    externalization methods, 154–155, 310–312
    internalization methods, 317, 327
    sex comparisons, 153
Counseling
    help-seeking difficulties, 321–322
    men as special population, 320–321
    men's issues and methods, 321–326
Counseling Psychology, men as special population, 320–321
The Creation of Patriarchy (Lerner), 54
Crime
    firearms crime, 256–258
    as masculinity proof, 233
    race, sex, and violence, 246–249
    by racial/ethnic groups, 28*table*
Crises
    boy crises, 10, 50, 67–71
    masculinity crises, 67–71
    midlife, 280, 284
Cross-gender typing, androgyny model, 85
Cultural influences
    on emotional expression, 145–146
    gender schema theory, 137–139, 141
    interventions for violence, 267–268
    and rape myths, 253
    on rape perpetration, 251
Cultural relativism
    defined, 48
    in emotional expression, 145–146
    male sexuality examples, 198–199
    masculinity definitions and, 45–50
    mental health definitions and, 308–310
    as schema, 58*b*, 91*b*
Cultural variations, of masculinities, 40–45

Culture, defined, 47
Cycle of Poverty
    African American men and, 30, 183–184
    defined, 31b
    early fatherhood and, 183–184

D
Dating relationships
    male-female dating, 172–173, 178
    male-male dating, 173–174
Death of a Salesman (Miller), 234b
Defense mechanisms
    defined, 311, 327
    sex differences, 311–312
Delayed ejaculation
    characteristics of, 213
    defined, 219
Dementia
    defined, 284
    football injuries and, 277
Demographic trends, U.S. racial/ethnic groups, 28t
Depression
    in males, 317–318
    sex differences, 310, 312
Diagnostic and Statistical Manual of Mental Disorder (DSM-V) (APA)
    controversial definitions, 308–309
    Gender Dysphoria, 126
    on sexual problems, 210–213
Discrimination
    homosexuality and, 40, 64–66
    racism and, 29–31, 33
Disorders of sexual development (DSD)
    characteristics of, 98–100
    defined, 121
Divorce and separation, father absence, 190–192
DMS. *See* Drive for Muscularity Scale (DMS)
Doctrine of Separate Spheres
    defined, 22
    in history of work, 224–226
    in United States history, 8, 61
Domestic violence. *See* Interpersonal violence (IPV)
Dominated fields (male/female), defined, 224, 226
Don't Ask, Don't Tell (DADT), 65, 74
The Dread of Women (Horney), 116–117, 122
Drive for muscularity, factors in, 302–303
Drive for Muscularity Scale (DMS), use of, 302–303
Drug use . *See* Substance abuse

E
Eat What You Want and Die like a Man: The World's Unhealthiest Cookbook (Graham), 299
Eating disorders
in males, 301, 302
sex differences, 312
Economic resources, in childhood development, 187–188
Economic success
    African-American men, 28t, 29–30, 31b
    Asian-American men, 28t, 32–33
    Latino men, 28t, 34
    sex differences in, 68–69
Educational levels
    African-American men, 28t, 29–30
    Asian-American men, 28t, 32–33
    Latino men, 28t, 34, 35
    physical health and, 291–292
    sex differences in, 68–69
    teen fatherhood and, 188
Ego
defined, 122
in personality development, 111–113
Ego-centrality, defined, 327
Ego defenses
    coping as, 154
    defined, 160
Ego ideal
defined, 122
in personality development, 112–113
Ego psychology, masculinity and, 117–120
Ego strength

defined, 122
in personality development, 112–113
Ejaculatory problems
characteristics of, 213
defined, 219
pornography and, 217
Emotion
cultural relativism and, 145–146
defining and studying, 144–145
early gender-typing, 125–127, 134–135
male display expansion, 157–159
male-female comparisons, 145–149
male violence and, 252
restrictive. *See* Restrictive emotionality
as studies topic, 11
and successful mental health therapy, 321–326
Emotion-focused coping
defined, 160
sex comparisons, 153
Emotion wheel
defined, 160, 327
use of, 158, 324–325
Emotional intimacy
defined, 179
in male-female relationships, 172, 173, 178
in male relationships, 162–167, 170, 177
masculinity and, 11, 164–167, 170, 176, 319
Emotional/social support
defined, 178
in male relationships, 162–163
Empathy
defined, 160
restrictive emotionality and, 156–157, 279–280
and sexual violence, 254
Empathy for the self, 157, 160
and empathy for others, 279–280
Employment. *See* Work and the workplace

Entitlement, defined, 53, 73
Epidemiology/ies, defined, 306
Equal Employment Opportunity Commission (EEOC), sexual harassment and, 237, 239
Erectile dysfunction (ED)
characteristics of, 211–212
defined, 219
Erogenous zones
defined, 122
in Freudian perspective, 113–114
Essential father theory, 185–186
Essentialism
defined, 15, 22
evolutionary psychology as, 109
gender identity model and, 81
power differences and, 55
social constructionism versus, 15–16
Estrogen
in disorders of sexual development, 98–99
physical health and, 294
in puberty, 208
Ethnicity
defined, 47
in HIV/AIDS, 304–305
as men's health factor, 288–292, 304–305
and White designation, 68
Evolutionary psychology (EP)
critiques of, 103–109
on sex and violence, 101–106, 260–261
tenets of, 100–101, 120–121
Exapted behaviors, defined, 101, 122
Experience, social cognitive theory, 132–135
Exploitive harassers
characteristics of, 241
defined, 224
Externalization
coping and, 154–155, 310–312
defined, 160, 327
substance abuse and, 313
violence and, 255

SUBJECT INDEX

F

Familismo
   defined, 48
   Latino men and, 34–35, 305
Family
   traditional, 181, 197
   work and relationships, 230–231, 233, 234
Fathers and fathering
   absence effects, 190–192
   anticipation of fathering, 184–185
   children's development factors, 185–188
   current trends in roles, 182–183
   defined, 180, 197
   demographic data, 183–184
   divorce and absence, 190–192
   in Freudian perspective, 111–117, 121
   gender-typing by fathers, 133–135
   history of in United States, 181–182
   and industrial workplace, 181–182
   male perceptions of role, 185–186
   patriarchy and, 223–224
   punishment and, 127
   in social cognitive approach, 133–135
   sons' masculinity and, 193–195
   stay-at-home, 175, 193, 197
   as violence models, 263
   work and family conflicts, 188
Females
   as biological referent, 3
   counseling guidelines, 320
   depression in, 317
   emotional expression comparisons, 144–149
   Freudian perspective, 115*b*
   history of work, 222–226
   male-female dating, 172–173, 178
   male-female friendships, 171–172, 178
   male power over. *See* Sexism
   physical health data, 291
   race and violence intersectionality, 246–249
   sex comparison research, 144–145, 199–200
Feminine Gender Identity Scale, 83
Femininity
   emotional expression as, 144
   as gender descriptor, 3
Feminism
   activism, 58
   defined, 22
   origins of, 14–15
Firearms, violence and, 256–258
Flavor of Love, 204
Football, risk and masculinity, 276–277
Fraternities
   alcohol abuse patterns, 314
   as violence facilitators, 258–259
Freudian perspective. *See* Psychoanalytic theories
Friends, defined, 162–163, 179
Friendships
   male-female dyads, 171–172, 178
   male-male dyads, 170–171, 178
   male-only groups, 168–170
   men at work, 232

G

Gay men
   body image issues, 302
   dating relationships, 173–174
   HIV/AIDS concerns, 38, 39–40, 63–64, 303–305
   homophobia and, 61–66
   marriage/long-term relationships, 176–177
   masculinity definitions, 37–40
   media portrayals, 203–204
   stereotypes of, 38
Gay Men's Health Crisis, efforts of, 64
Gay rights movement
   recent advancements, 64–66
   Stonewall Riot effects, 62–63
Gender
   defined, 3–4, 21
   power and, 12–13, 37, 53–54
   and successful mental health

therapy, 323–326
Gender binary model
    characteristics and measures, 77–79
    defined, 95
    gender identity model, 81–83
    limitations and criticisms, 83–84
    summary, 94t
Gender constancy
    defined, 131, 141
    development of, 131–132
Gender differences, in history of work, 222–226
Gender Dysphoria
    defined, 141
    sex differences in diagnosis, 126
Gender equality
    efforts for, 70–71
    inequity and violence, 269
Gender identity
    defined, 132, 141
    ego psychology perspective, 117–120
Gender Identity Disorder . See Gender Dysphoria
Gender identity model, characteristics and measures, 81–83
Gender inversion
    defined, 62, 73
    gender identity and, 82
Gender labels, examples, 84
Gender non-conforming (GNC) individuals
    cultural variations, 44, 45
    gender and, 3–4
    sexual harassment and, 242
Gender Role Conflict Scale (GRCS), characteristics of, 92–93
Gender role strain
    alcohol use and, 315
    approach summary, 94t
    counseling and, 324–326
    defined, 96
    in depression, 317–318
    intimacy and, 165, 319
    mental health consequences, 310, 311–312, 317–318
    sexual harassment and, 240
    theory and consequences, 91–92
    violence and, 253
Gender roles
    aging changes, 280–282
    defined, 89, 96
    emotion expression and. See Emotion
    in gender identity model, 82
    history of work and, 222–226
    in marriage, 175–176
    parental influence on, 193–195
    pornography reinforcement of, 214–216
    in role theory model, 89–90
    social influences on, 128–131
    violation exercises, 7b
Gender schematic processing, reducing, 57–58, 91b
Gender-typing
    androgyny model, 85
    defined, 141
    early family experiences, 123–127, 194–195
    evolutionary psychology and, 106–108
    script theory and, 89, 137–139
    social cognitive theory and, 132–135
    social structural theory and, 135–136
Gendered script theory
    defined, 96, 142
    gender-typing in, 89, 137–139
Genetics
    physical health and, 293
    and violence tendencies, 261
Glass escalator
defined, 224
factors in, 227
Great Recession (2007–2008), masculinity crisis with, 68
Grief
    defined, 160
    traditional male response, 155

Group therapy, for men's issues, 325
Guidelines for the Psychological Treatment of Girls and Women (American Psychological Association), 320
Gymnosperm
    defined, 306
    in fertilization, 287

H

He for She, 18
Health insurance coverage, socioeconomic status and, 291–292
Hegemonic masculinity
    alcohol use and, 314–315
    defined, 25, 47
    depression and, 317–318
    global similarities, 41
    homophobia and, 66
    as men's health factor, 287–288
    pornography and, 215–216
    roles in male-female couples, 175–176
    suicide and, 295–297, 318
    violence in. *See* Violence, male
    in the workplace, 235–236, 240
Help seeking, male difficulty with, 321–322
Heterosexism
    defined, 5, 21
    homophobia and, 66–67
Heterosexuality
    dating relationships, 172–173
    marriage/long-term relationships, 174–176
    parenting and, 194–195
Hispanic peoples
    demographic trends, 28*t*
    demographics, 28*t*, 34
    fatherhood data, 183–184
    Latino/a terminology, 33–34
    violence and crime rates, 28*t*, 248–249
Historical considerations (U.S.), homosexuality and sexism, 61–66
HIV/AIDS
    in gay men, 38, 39–40, 303–305
    HIV differentiated from AIDS, 303–304
    United States history, 63–64, 303
HIV status, defined, 306
Homophobia
    defined, 61, 73
    as friendship barrier, 166–167
    military and, 65
    in United States history, 9, 61–66
Homosexuality. *See also* Gay men
    dating relationships, 173–174
    in early twentieth-century America, 61–62
    Freudian perspective, 118–119
    HIV/AIDS effects, 63–64
    marriage/long-term relationships, 176–177
    origins and measurements, 200–202
    parenting and, 194–195
    in recent U.S. history, 64–66
    sexism in United States, 61–66
    Stonewall Riot era, 62–63
Homosocial groups, characteristics of, 168–170
Hookups (sexual)
    in current masculinity, 198–199
    defined, 198–199, 219
    male-female comparisons, 199
Hormonal approaches, to sex and gender, 98–100
Hormonal differences, physical health and, 294
Hostile environment sexual harassment
    characteristics of, 238
    defined, 224
Hostile sexism
    defined, 56, 73
    as research factor, 86–87
Husbandry
    defined, 224
    as value, 222
Hypermasculinity, characteristics of, 82
Hypervigilance
    defined, 283
    in PTSD, 275

I

Id
  defined, 122
  in personality development, 111–113
Ideological approaches
  defined, 89, 96
  in masculinity models, 89
Immaturity theories
  conversion "therapies" and, 201b
  defined, 220
Implicit bias, defined, 56, 73, 87, 95
Incarceration
  African-Americans, 26, 28t, 29
  Asian-Americans, 28t, 33
  Hispanics, 26, 28t, 248–249
  racial differences, 26, 28t, 248
  White, non-Hispanics, 26, 28t
Independence
  male violence and, 252
  masculinity and, 5–6
  in personality disorders, 316
  relational intimacy and, 165–166, 319
Individual-level interventions, for violence, 266–267
Industrial Revolution, work and the sexes, 223–226
Infant mortality
  defined, 306
  sex differences in, 286–287
Infidelity, male-female comparisons, 199
Initiation rituals, purposes of, 41–42
Insecure attachment style
  defined, 271
  violence and, 254
Instincts
  defined, 122
  Freudian perspective, 111
Institutional racism, defined, 47
Inter-racial crime, defined, 271
Internalization
  coping mechanisms, 317, 327
  defined, 327
Internalized sexism, defined, 56, 73
Interpersonal sexism, defined, 56, 73

Interpersonal violence (IPV)
  crime rates, 247, 249, 255
  defined, 246, 271
  intervention strategies, 265–268
  patriarchy and, 253
  perpetrator characteristics, 259–260, 270
Intersectionality. *See also* Race; Sex comparisons and differences
  defined, 47
  race and gender, 26, 224–226
  race, sex, and violence, 246–249
  race, sex, and work, 226–228
Intersexuality
  biological basis of, 98–100
  gender and, 3–4
Intervention strategies, for violence, 265–268
Intimacy
  emotional. *See* Emotional intimacy
  sexual, 207–208
Intra-racial crime, defined, 271
Intropunitive feelings
  defined, 160
  sex differences, 146–147
IPV. *See* Interpersonal violence (IPV)

J

Jobs. *See also* Work and the workplace
  careers versus, 225
  defined, 224
Journal of HIV/AIDS & Social Services, 303
Journal of Men's Studies, origin of, 19

K

Kinsey Scale
  defined, 74, 220
  use of, 201–202

L

Labor, division of, 222–226
Language
  and emotional expression, 143–144, 151
  gender-specific, 138–139
  sexism and, 58–60

Latino men
  demographic trends, 28*t*
  in employment, 227–228
  incarceration rates, 26, 248–249
  masculinity themes, 33–35
  physical health patterns, 288–292
  sexual first experiences, 210
  sexually-transmitted diseases and, 304
  stereotypes, 35
  violence and crime rates, 28*t*, 248–249
Latinx
  college degrees earned, 69
  defined, 33
Legal aspects, of sexual assault, 238, 267–268
Legal considerations
  of non-heterosexual behaviors, 61–66
  of sexual harassment, 238–239
Libido
  defined, 122
  in Freudian perspective, 113–114
Life expectancy. *See* Longevity
Long-term relationships. *See* Marriage/long-term relationships
Longevity, sex differences and factors, 12
Longitudinal studies
  defined, 197
  on divorce and children, 190–191
Lust, violence and, 255

M

Machismo, Latino men and, 35, 305
Mainstream media. *See* Media influences
Male-female relationships
  dating, 172–173
  emotional intimacy in, 172, 173, 178
  friendships, 171–172, 178
  marriage/long-term, 175–176
  work, 235–236
Male Hypoactive Sexual Desire Disorder
  characteristics of, 211
  defined, 219
Male-on-male rape, support measures, 278–280
Male Role Attitudes Scale, 91
Male Role Norms Index, 76, 205
Male Role Norms Inventory, Revised (MRNI-R), criticism of, 93
Male sexuality. *See* Sexuality
Males
  anger expression, 148–149
  as biological referent, 3
  emotional expression, 145–149
  father absence and, 191–192
  race and violence intersectionality, 246–249
Manbox, defined, 4–7
Mancave
  defined, 178
  stereotyped activities, 161
Manhood in the Making (Gilmore), 1
Marginalized masculinities
  characteristics of, 25
  defined, 25, 47
Marital dissolution
  defined, 197
  gender and effects, 190–192
Marked status, defined, 53, 73
Marking, privilege and, 53, 73
Marriage/long-term relationships
  characteristics of, 174–175
  divorce and fatherhood, 190–192
  male-female couples, 175–176
  male-male couples, 176–177
  mental health and, 318–319
  same-sex, 64–66
Masculine dilemma, 176
Masculine Gender Role Stress Scale (MGRSS), 92–93
Masculine Ideology models
  approach summary, 94*t*
  characteristics and measures, 90–93, 144–145
  limitations and criticisms, 93
  promiscuity in, 205
  sexual harassment and, 240
  violence in, 250, 253

work in, 229
Masculine privilege
  defined, 52, 72
  described, 52–53
Masculinities, multiple
  African-American men, 27–31
  Asian-American men, 31–33
  benefits of perspective, 24–25
  cultural power and, 25–26, 37
  defined, 47
  global definitions, 40–45
  Latino men, 28t, 33–35
  sexual orientation and, 37–40
  social class and, 36–37
Masculinity. See also Masculinities, multiple; Sexuality
  biological theories on. See Biological perspectives, on sex and gender
  crises of, 67–71
  cultural messages of, 1–3, 4
  mental disorders and, 310–312
  parental sexual orientation and, 194–195
  procreation as demonstration, 180
  and restrictive emotionality. See Restrictive emotionality
  sexual harassment and, 240–242
  singular definition of, 4–7
  in United States history, 7–10
  violence as proof of, 249–250, 259–260
  work and, 228–235
Masculinity Ideology models. See Masculine Ideology models
Master statuses, defined, 53, 73
Masturbation
  Freudian perspective, 114
  male-female comparisons, 199
  pornography and, 216–217
Mattachine Society, 39, 48
Matthew Shepard and James Byrd Jr. Hate Crimes Prevention Act (2009), 64
Measures
  in androgyny model, 85–86
  in gender binary model, 77–79
  in gender identity model, 82–83
  in masculinity ideology models, 90–93
  and masculinity singular definition, 75–76
  summary of approaches, 94t
Media influences
  cultural effects of, 10, 11
  fatherhood portrayals, 185
  on homosexuality acceptance, 63–64
  loner images, 161
  on male body image, 301
  masculinity portrayals, 86, 151, 152
  orphans in, 189b
  pornography, 214–217
  racial differences in, 32
  sexuality portrayals, 203–204, 213–214, 265
  and violence, 134, 151, 263–265
Media literacy
  defined, 272
  effects of, 265
Men. See Males; *specific group or category*
Men-as-a-group
  defined, 72
  emotional expression, 146–149
  work and masculinity, 229–235
Men Can Stop Rape, 18, 267
Men who have sex with men (MSM)
  defined, 38, 48
  HIV/AIDS and, 303–305
Men's health. See also Physical health
  aging and, 281–282
  body image disorders, 300–303
  cardiovascular disorders, 300
  combat and, 273–275
  contact sports and, 275–277
  HIV/AIDS, 303–305
  homosexual issues, 38
  masculinity and, 285
  neglect of, 298–299
  organizations for, 18–19
  physical. See Physical health

SUBJECT INDEX • 417

racial differences, 30, 288–292
risk behaviors, 299
sexual harassment and, 239–240
work and, 232
Men's Health Network, 18–19
The Men's Program, 267
Men's Rights Activists (MRAs), 19
efforts of, 70
Men's rights movement, organizations in, 19
Men's studies
academic organizations, 19–20
defined, 21, 22
as discipline, 10–14
goals of, 20–21
key debates in, 15–19
origins of, 14–15
Mental health
counseling and psychotherapy, 321–326
depression, 317–318
difficulty of defining, 308–310
gender role strain and, 91–92
marriage and, 318–319
personality disorders, 315–317
substance abuse, 312–315
Mental illnesses, sex differences, 310–312
Mentors in Violence Program (MVP), 18, 267
Meta-analyses, defined, 79, 95
Metrosexuals, antifemininity and, 5
Mf scale, 83, 84
MF test, 82–83
Midlife crisis
defined, 284
research findings, 280
Mighty Morphin Power Rangers, violent play and, 264
Military
female role debate, 245
risks and consequences associated, 273–275
sexual assault in, 249, 251, 278
sexual assault prevention, 267
sexual harassment in, 239, 267

Minnesota Multiphasic Personality Inventory tests (MMPI), 83
Misogynistic harassers
characteristics of, 241
defined, 224
Misogyny, in peer group contexts, 128–129
Misperceiving harassers
characteristics of, 241
defined, 224
MMPI tests. *See* Minnesota Multiphasic Personality Inventory tests (MMPI)
Model minority
Asian-Americans as, 32–33, 289
defined, 47
Models. *See also* Measures
for aggression and violence, 263–265
androgyny model, 84–88
approach summary, 94t
defined, 75, 95
gender binary. *See* Gender binary model
masculinity ideology, 88–93
measurement and, 75–77
sex comparisons, 79–81
sexism and, 86–88
Mortality rates, male, 288–292
Mothers and mothering
gender-typing by, 194–195
male identification with, 117–120
in Oedipal conflict, 113–117
Movember Foundation, 19, 70–71, 298–299
Murder. *See also* Crime; Violence, male
masculinity and, 259
United States data, 247–249, 264
Mythopoetic movement, and men's studies, 12
Mythopoetic scholars, defined, 22

N
Narcissistic Personality Disorder
characteristics of, 316
defined, 327
Narrative reviews, defined, 79, 95

National Organization of Men Against Sexism (NOMAS), works of, 18, 19
National Survey of Family Growth (NSFG), fatherhood data, 183–184
Native American/Alaskan natives
    crime rates, 247–249
    physical health patterns, 288–292
Nice guys, dating and, 172–173
NOMAS. *See* National Organization of Men Against Sexism (NOMAS)
Non-Hispanic Whites. *See* White, non-Hispanic group
Norm-based approaches, defined, 89, 96
Normal variant theories
    conversion "therapies" and, 201b
    defined, 220

O
Objectification
    defined, 224
    media and, 265
    of men at work and war, 224–225
    sexual harassment and, 240
    violence and, 254
Observational learning
    defined, 272
    violence example, 263
Obsessive-Compulsive Personality Disorder
    characteristics of, 316
    defined, 327
Oedipus conflict
    defined, 122
    masculinity and, 113–117
Organization man, in United States history, 9–10
Orphans
    defined, 197
    in mainstream culture, 189b
Over-regularization
    defined, 142
    in gender typing, 139
Overrepresented groups
    crime rates, 247–249
    defined, 27, 47
    in employment, 227–228
    in teen fathers, 184, 210
Oxfam, 71

P
Pain
    physiological assessments of, 145, 159–160
    subjective assessments of, 145, 160
PAQ (Personality Attributes Questionnaire). *See* Personality Attributes Questionnaire (PAQ)
Parents and parenting. *See also* Fathers and fathering; Mothers and mothering
    factors in success, 185–188
    gender-typing by, 123–127, 194–195
    male perceptions of, 185–186
    sex and gender comparisons, 188–195
    as violence models, 263
Passionate manhood
    defined, 22
    in United States history, 8–9
Pathological theories
    conversion "therapies" and, 201b
    defined, 220
Patriarchy
    defined, 53, 73, 222–223
    power and, 53–54
    as sexism, 55–56
    sexual harassment and, 241–242
    violence as norm, 253
    work, masculinity, and, 223–226
Peer groups
    alcohol abuse and, 314
    early gender-typing in, 127–128
    as norms enforcers, 128–129, 152
    sexual assault prevention efforts, 266–267
    as violence facilitators, 258–259
Penile plethysmograph, 67, 74
Penis
    circumcision of, 203b–204b
    sexual development and, 209
    sexual problems, 210–213
Performance comparisons, sex and,

79–81
Personalismo
    defined, 48
    Latino men and, 35
Personality, defined, 315, 327
Personality Attributes Questionnaire (PAQ)
    characteristics of, 86
    criticisms of, 87
Personality disordered
    characteristics of, 315
    defined, 327
Personality disorders
    male-dominated examples, 315–317
    sex differences, 312, 315
Phallic period
    defined, 122
    in Freudian perspective, 113–114, 121
Physical aggression. *See also* Aggression; Violence, male
    in childhood home, 259
    defined, 245
    as proof of masculinity, 249–253
Physical health
    age-related differences, 289, 291
    anger consequences, 148–149
    biogenic explanations, 292–294
    defined, 306
    gender role strain and, 91–92
    neglectful behaviors, 298–299
    psychogenic explanations, 294–295
    psychological inputs and, 299–305
    risk behaviors, 299
    self-destructive behaviors, 295–298
Physical resources, in childhood development, 187–188
Physiological assessments of pain, defined, 159–160
Plastic surgery, body image and, 301–302
Play, training ground for work, 229
Playing the dozens, purpose of, 28–29
Policing, of masculinity, 6–7, 37–38
Political correctness, sexism and, 58–60
Politics, of HIV/AIDS, 63–64
Pornography
    male sexual problems and, 216–217
    prevalence of, 214–215
    violence and, 215–216
Posttraumatic stress disorder (PTSD)
    characteristics of, 274–275
    defined, 283
    from sexual assault, 278–280
Poverty
    African-American men, 28t, 29–30, 31b, 183, 210
    Cycle of. *See* Cycle of Poverty
    defined, 47
    as factor in violence, 267
    physical health and, 291–292
    social class and, 36–37
    stress and, 155
    work, and crime, 233
Power
    boys' and men's crises, 67–71
    defined, 50, 72
    emotional expression as, 153–154
    gender and, 12–13, 37, 53–54
    homosexuality and. *See* Homosexuality
    power structures, 52–55
    sex differences and, 50–52, 229–230
    sexism and. *See* Sexism; Sexual harassment
Power rapists, characteristics of, 259–260
Power structures, development of, 52–54
Practical support
    defined, 178
    in male relationships, 162–163
Premature (early) ejaculation, defined, 213, 219
Primary sexual characteristics
    defined, 219
    puberty and, 208–209
Primogeniture
    defined, 224
    patriarchy and, 223

Prison. *See* Incarceration
Privilege. *See* Masculine privilege
Profeminism
    concepts of, 58
    and men's studies, 12
Profeminist-oriented scholars, defined, 22
Professional class masculinity
    characteristics of, 36
    defined, 48
Projection
    defined, 311, 327
    use by men, 311
Promiscuity
    male, 108–109, 177, 204–205
    male-female comparisons, 206–207
Promundo, 18, 70, 267
Prospective studies
    defined, 197
    on divorce and children, 190–191
Provider role
    breadwinner role, 224–225, 229, 233–235
    masculinity and, 175, 176–177, 187–188
Psychoanalytic theories
    critiques of, 115b, 116–117
    emotional constriction in, 150–151
    factors considered, 109–110
    Freudian background, 110–113, 121
    Horney's theories, 115b, 116–117, 120, 121
    Oedipus conflict and masculinity, 113–117
Psychoeducational programs, male acceptance of, 324
Psychogenic explanations, for physical health, 294–295
Psychological temperament, biological factors, 97
Psychology of Men and Masculinity
    common topics, 12
    origin of, 20
    singular masculinity studies, 76
Psychosexual development, Freudian perspective, 113–117, 121

PsycInfo database, keyword analysis, 13, 14*fig*
Puberty
    defined, 208, 219
    sexual development and behaviors, 208–210
Punishment
    fathers' work and, 182
    sex and gender differences, 126–127
    for "unmasculine" behavior, 125
    vicarious, 263

Q

Quality (of parent-child relationship)
    defined, 186, 197
    father's importance to, 186
Quid pro quo sexual harassment
    characteristics of, 238
    defined, 224

R

Race
    body image comparison, 302
    incarceration and, 26
    as men's health factor, 288–292
    sex, violence, and, 246–249
    and sexes in work, 227–228
Racism. *See also* Discrimination
    defined, 21, 47
    toward African American men, 29–31
Rape. *See also* Rape myths
    antifemininity and, 250–251
    defined, 246, 249, 271
    intervention and prevention, 265–268, 271
    male victims and survivors, 278–280
    pornography and, 215–217
    as proof of status, 251–252, 270–271
    types of, 259–260
    United States statistics, 248*t*, 259
Rape myths
    cultural support for, 253
    defined, 219, 271

hegemonic masculinity and, 215
  promiscuity and, 207, 215
Rape prevention
  characteristics of, 267–268
  defined, 272
Real Boys: Rescuing Our Sons from the Myths of Boyhood (Pollack), 67
"Real man" description, 1–3, 1*fig*
Real Men, Real Depression (NIMH), 322
Relational aggression, defined, 245, 271
Relationships
  basic concepts, 162–163
  effects of masculine ideologies, 164–168
  friendships, 168–172
  male expressiveness and, 314
  romantic, 172–177
  sex comparisons in, 163–164
  stereotypes and reality, 161–162
Reliability
  defined, 179
  in male relationships, 163
Religion, attitudes to homosexuality, 61, 64
Religious Right, HIV/AIDS crisis and, 64
Reparative therapy
  defined, 74, 220
  issues with, 201*b*, 218
  principles of, 65
Reproductive investment
  defined, 101, 122
  sex differences, 101–102
Reproductive strategies
  defined, 101, 122
  sex comparisons, 101–102
Resilience (psychological), defined, 254, 271
Resource availability
  defined, 197
  fathering and, 187–188
Respeto
  defined, 48
  Latino men and, 35
Restrictive emotionality
  benefits of, 153–154
  costs of, 154–157

counseling and, 321–326
  expansion of male display, 157–159
  origins of, 150–152
  in personality disorders, 316
  related problems of, 143–144
Retirement, masculinity and, 233, 234*b*
Risk behaviors
  evolutionary psychology perspective, 102–103
  men's health and, 273–282, 299, 304–305, 313
  sexual, 205–206, 304–305
Risk reductions, for rape, 268
Rites of passage
  defined, 49
  purposes of, 41–42
'Roid rage
  defined, 272
  violence and, 256
Role theory
  characteristics of, 88–90
  defined, 87, 95
Romantic relationships
  male-female dating, 172–173, 178
  male-male dating, 173–174, 178
  marriage and long-term, 174–177, 178
Ruminative coping style
  defined, 327
  female depression and, 317

S

Sadistic rapists, characteristics of, 260
Schemata. *See also* Gendered script theory
  defined, 138
Schizoid Personality Disorder
  characteristics of, 315
  defined, 327
Schizotypal Personality Disorder, characteristics of, 315
School, early gender-typing in, 127–128
Script theory. *See* Gendered script theory
Scripts

defined, 142
    gender-typing and, 133–135
Secondary sexual characteristics
    defined, 219
    puberty and, 208–209
Selective service, defined, 274, 283
Self-control, self-made manhood and, 8
Self-disclosure
    defined, 149, 160
    sex, gender, and, 149–150
    in therapy settings, 321–322, 325–326
Self-disclosure targets
    defined, 160
    sex, gender, and, 149–150
Self-esteem
    men and work, 232–235
    projection and, 311
    violence and, 250
Self-made manhood
    defined, 22
    in United States history, 8
Self-sufficiency. *See also* Independence
    relational intimacy and, 165–166
Sensuality
    defined, 219
    male experience of, 207–208, 212, 218
Sex. *See also* Sex comparisons and differences
    defined, 3–4, 21
    gender versus, 21
    violence and, 101–106
Sex chromosomes
    defined, 121, 306
    in longevity, 293
    sex determination by, 98–100
Sex comparisons and differences
    defined, 72
    divorce effects, 190–192
    in early family experiences, 124–127
    in education and earnings, 68–69
    in emotional expression, 145–149, 153–154
    in gender identity, 117–120
    in language use, 151
    in media violence portrayals, 263–264
    in mental illnesses, 310–312, 317–318
    in parental behaviors, 189–190
    in performance and sex, 79–81
    in physical health, 286–288
    in power positions, 50–52, 229–230
    in proactive health, 298–299
    in promiscuity, 206–207
    race, violence, and, 246–249
    in relationship interactions, 163–164
    in reproductive investment and strategies, 101–102
    in self-reporting, 145
    in sexuality, 199–200, 206–207, 218
    in substance abuse, 299, 312, 313–315
    in suicide rates, 295, 312
    summary, 94*t*
    in wages earned, 69, 226–227
Sex differences. *See* Sex comparisons and differences
Sex Signals, 267
Sexism
    activism against, 18, 58–60, 266–267
    approach summary, 94*t*
    defined, 5, 21, 55, 73, 86
    of Freud, 115*b*
    homosexuality and. *See* Homosexuality
    male discomfort with, 266–267
    negative masculinity correlations, 60–61
    reducing against women, 88*b*
    systemic and individual, 55–57
    violence tolerated, 254, 266–267
Sexual assault. *See also* Rape
    on campus, 259, 266, 268, 271
    defined, 271
    legal considerations, 238, 267–268
    male victims and survivors, 278–280
    in military, 249, 251, 267, 278
    pornography and, 215–217

prevention efforts, 266–268
Sexual bribery
    defined, 224
    in the workplace, 238
Sexual conversion therapies, 201b
Sexual development, and life stages, 208–211
Sexual disorders
    in adulthood and old age, 210–213
    defined, 219
Sexual double standard
    consequences of, 206–207
    defined, 219
Sexual dysfunction
    in adulthood and old age, 210–213
    defined, 219
Sexual extortion
    defined, 224
    in the workplace, 238
Sexual harassment
    defined, 237
    effects of, 239–242
    legal basis, 238–239
    in the military, 239, 267
    recent history, 236–237
    types of, 224, 238, 241
    in the workplace, 236–242
Sexual orientation
    conversion "therapies", 201b
    defined, 220
    legal rights, 64–66
    masculinities and, 37–40, 200
    origins and measurements, 200–202
Sexual orientation identity, defined, 200, 220
Sexual Strategies Theory (SST). *See also* evolutionary psychology (EP)
    critiques of, 108–109
    promiscuity in, 206–207
    tenets of, 102
Sexuality
    defined, 198, 219
    development and life stages, 208–211
    double standards, 206–207
    evolutionary psychology and, 102, 106–109
    in Freudian perspective, 113–117, 121
    intimacy in, 207–208
    male-female comparisons, 199–200
    masculinity norms and, 202–205
    media and pornography, 213–217
    promiscuity. *See* Promiscuity
    risk behaviors and masculinity, 205–206
    sexual orientation in. *See* Sexual orientation
    sexual problems, 210–213
Shame, male sexual assault victims, 278–280
Shepard, Matthew, murder of, 64
Simpatía
    defined, 48
    Latino men and, 35
Social changes, men's emotionality and, 158–159
Social class
    defined, 36, 48
    masculinities and, 36–37
    physical health and, 291–292
Social cognitive theory (SCT)
    criticism of, 135
    defined, 141
    scripts and gender typing, 132–134
Social constructionism
    defined, 16, 22–23
    essentialism versus, 15–16
Social desirability
    defined, 159
    effects on self-reporting, 145, 146
Social role theory. *See* Social structural theory
Social roles
    defined, 96
    prison experiment, 130
    in role theory, 89
Social status
    defined, 179
    in male relationships, 162–163
    masculinity and, 5
    rape and, 251–252
    violence and, 256

Social Structural Theory
    defined, 142
    gender-typing in, 135–136, 141
Social support, defined, 178
Socialization
    and counseling, 324–326
    in early childhood, 126–127
    and mental disorders, 310–312, 316–317
    to work, 228–235
Socially-based theories, on sex and gender
    early family experiences, 123–127
    early school experiences, 127–128
    gender identity and constancy, 131–132
    gendered scripts theory, 137–139
    situational influences, 128–131, 148
    social cognitive theory (SCT), 132–135
    social structural theory, 135–136
Society for the Psychological Study of Men and Masculinity (SPSMM), history of, 20
Sociobiology, as precursor to EP, 103–105
Socioeconomic status (SES). See Social class
Solution-focused therapy (SFT), for restrictive emotionality, 158
Sons
    absence of father, 190–192
    identification with mother, 117–120
    masculinity and parents, 193–195
Spatial rotation
    defined, 121
    sex differences, 100
Sports
    aggression in, 251
    men's health and, 275–277
    as training ground for work, 229
SPSMM. See Society for the Psychological Study of Men and Masculinity (SPSMM)
Status. See Social status

Stay-at-home fathers (SAHF)
    data and characteristics of, 175, 193
    defined, 197
Stereotypes
    activation of, 88b
    African American men, 30–31
    Asian-American men, 32
    defined, 17, 23
    emotion and gender, 146–148
    of gay men, 38
    Latino men, 35
    male relationships, 161
    sexism and, 56–57
    of United States male, 2–3
Stigmatization, mental illness and, 309, 321–322
Stoicism
    masculinity and, 5–6
    in masculinity definition, 10, 144
Stonewall Riot, 39, 48
Strength, masculinity and, 5–6
Stress
    approach summary, 94t
    coping and, 155
    gender roles and health, 91–93
Strong Vocational Interest Inventory, 83
Subordinated masculinities
    defined, 25, 47
    examples of, 25–26
Substance abuse
    African American men, 29
    gendered aspects of, 299, 313–315
    sex differences, 312
    and violence inhibition, 256
Suicide
    male rates, 288–290, 295
    racial and ethnic differences, 288–291
    sex differences, 295, 312
    traditional masculinity and, 295–297, 318
Superego
    defined, 122
    in personality development, 111–113

Support groups, for emotional expression, 157
Systemic sexism, defined, 73

T

Task-focused coping. *See also* Externalization
  defined, 160
  sex comparisons, 153
Teenage parenthood, fatherhood data, 183–184, 188, 210
Testosterone
  in aggression, 104, 261–262
  in aging, 211
  in disorders of sexual development, 98–100
  physical health and, 294
  in puberty, 208
Therapy options
  for emotional expression, 157–158
  for violent behaviors, 265–268
Third genders, examples of, 45
Tobacco use, men's health and, 297–298
Traditional family
  defined, 181, 197
  myth of, 181
Traditionally female fields
  defined, 224
  patterns in, 226–229
Traditionally male fields
  defined, 224
  patterns in, 226–228
  sexual harassment in, 239
Transgenderism, gender and sex, 3–4
Trustworthiness
  defined, 179
  in male relationships, 163
Type A personality
  defined, 306
  health risks of, 300

U

Underrepresented groups
  crime rates, 248
  defined, 27, 47
  in employment, 227–228
  in teen fathers, 184

Undifferentiation (gender measures), defined, 95
United States
  crime rates, 247–249, 259, 264
  fathering in history, 181–182
  homophobia in, 9, 61–66
  masculinity in history, 7–10, 67–71
  work changes and trends, 225–227
United States Supreme Court
  gay rights and, 62, 65
  on sexual harassment, 239
Unmarked status, defined, 53, 73

V

Vicarious learning
  defined, 142
  imitation and, 132–135
Vicarious punishment
  defined, 272
  violence example, 263
Vicarious reinforcement
  defined, 272
  violence example, 263
Victim control strategies
  characteristics of, 268
  defined, 272
Video games, violence and, 263–265
Violence, male
  African-American history, 29–31
  aggression and, 6, 249–253, 264–265
  in agrarian societies, 223
  biological perspectives, 260–262
  definitions and types, 245–246
  evolutionary psychology perspective, 102–103
  intervention strategies, 256, 257b, 265–268
  Latino history, 35
  as masculinity proof, 249–250
  media influences, 134, 151, 263–265
  men as victims, 247, 248–249, 270
  pornography and, 214–216
  powerlessness as cause, 37
  psychosocial factors, 254–260, 269
  sex, race, and, 246–249

statistics on, 11, 247–249, 248t, 259, 264
Violence to property, defined, 245, 271
VoiceMail, 18

W
Western Europe, masculinity definitions, 43–45
White collar masculinity, defined, 48
White men, American
    condoms and masculinity, 305
    cultural dominance of, 24–25
    in employment, 227–228
    incarceration rates, 26, 28t
    violence and crime rates, 28t, 247–249
White, non-Hispanic group
    college degrees earned, 69
    demographics of, 27, 28t
    incarceration, 26, 28t
    physical health patterns, 288–292
    sexual first experiences, 210
White Ribbon Campaign, 18, 257b
Whites, crime rates, 247–249
Within-group differences
    child sex differences, 79–81
    defined, 23
    in men's studies, 17
    and social structural theory, 136
Women-as-a-group**32**
    defined, 72
    emotional expression, 146–149

Women *See* Females
Work and the workplace
    basic socialization to, 228–229
    fathering and, 181–182
    history and the sexes, 222–226
    male-female relationships, 235–236
    modernization and masculinity, 12, 221–222, 235
    negative socialization aspects, 230–235
    positive socialization aspects, 229–230
    sex and race in, 226–228
    sexual harassment, 236–242
Workaholics
    defined, 224
    and workaholism, 231–232
Working class masculinity
    characteristics of, 36
    defined, 48
World Congress on Men's Health, 19
World Health Organization, on homosexuality, 63

X
XY Magazine, 18

Z
Zero sum game
    defined, 22
    power and gender as, 12–13